OXFORD JUNIOR ENCYCLOPAEDIA

GENERAL EDITORS
LAURA E. SALT & GEOFFREY BOUMPHREY
ILLUSTRATIONS EDITOR: HELEN MARY PETTER

VOLUME I

MANKIND

OXFORD UNIVERSITY PRESS

Oxford University Press, Amen House, London E.C.4

GLASGOW NEW YORK TORONTO MELBOURNE WELLINGTON
BOMBAY CALCUTTA MADRAS KARACHI
CAPE TOWN IBADAN NAIROBI ACCRA SINGAPORE

FIRST PUBLISHED 1948
REPRINTED WITH CORRECTIONS 1949, 1952, 1955, 1957

PRINTED IN GREAT BRITAIN
AT THE UNIVERSITY PRESS, OXFORD
BY CHARLES BATEY, PRINTER TO THE UNIVERSITY

PREFACE

IN authorizing the preparation of this work the Delegates of the Oxford University Press had foremost in mind the need to provide a basic book of reference for school libraries. In form it was to be a genuine encyclopaedia, in treatment and vocabulary suitable for the young reader. To many children (and indeed to many adults) reading is not a natural activity: they do not turn to books for their own sake. But they can be trained to go to books for information which they want for some particular purpose—and thus, very often, to form a habit which will be of lifelong value. Their capacity to read continuously for any length of time being limited, they can absorb knowledge better if they get it in small quantities: therefore they will often read reference books when they may reject the reading of more extended matter. Again, it is probably true to say of such readers that their approach is from the particular to the general, and from the application to the principle, rather than the reverse, that their main interest is in the modern world around them, and that since they are not very good at conceiving things outside their own experience, their capacity for grasping abstract ideas is limited. On the other hand, once their interest is aroused, they will often pursue a subject to remarkable lengths, so long as its development is logical and the treatment avoids dullness.

But such generalizations can easily be overdone: many children using the books will not be of this type. Moreover, it was evident from the first that a project involving so great an amount of work, however exactly it might meet its principal mark, would be fully justified only if it could be of service to a far wider circle of readers. Even for the age-group first in mind, anything like 'writing down to children' must plainly be taboo—but clear exposition and simple language are no bad qualities in writing for any audience. Here, then, it seemed was the opportunity to provide a work of reference suitable for many readers to whom the large, standard encyclopaedias are too heavy and technical, and the popular alternatives for the most part neither sufficiently complete nor authoritative. The fact that the plan allowed for an exceptionally large proportion of illustrations to text (between one-quarter and one-third of the total space) is an advantage to any reader, since pictures may, in many instances, save whole paragraphs of involved explanation. With these secondary aims well in mind, then, the General

Editors have ventured to hope that the encyclopaedia may find usefulness not only among certain younger children, but also among older students in clubs, libraries, and Young People's Colleges, and even to no small extent among their parents and other adults who may wish for a simple approach to some unfamiliar or forgotten subject.

SCOPE AND EMPHASIS. Within certain limits the OXFORD JUNIOR ENCY-CLOPAEDIA purports to be reasonably comprehensive, though (in common with all general encyclopaedias) not exhaustive. Chief among these limits is that matter already easily available in school text-books is included only so far as its presence is necessary for the proper understanding of the subject under discussion. Thus, although an immense field of history is surveyed, it will be found mainly under headings dealing with its effects, or in the biographies of those who lived to make it. Purely technical or scientific subjects, also, are omitted except when they have some general interest. In natural history and kindred studies the immense variety of forms necessarily led at times either to their treatment by groups or to their omission on purely arbitrary decisions as to which species would, in all probability, never be looked for, or because there was nothing particularly interesting to say or them. In point of general balance the stress is laid rather on the modern world, though due space is given to the factors which have shaped it, no less than to those which are changing it.

ARRANGEMENT. The encyclopaedia is planned to consist of twelve volumes. Each is arranged alphabetically within itself, and each deals with a particular range of related subjects. Within its terms of reference, then, each volume is virtually self-contained, and, owing to the great number of single-line cross-references, can well be used alone. This arrangement, which has several incidental advantages (as of production, in difficult times, and of prompt revision later), arose mainly from one consideration. If articles were to be kept really short—and, in fact, few approach and almost none exceeds 2,000 words—many subjects could be dealt with comprehensively only by referring the reader to other relevant articles—itself a desirable thing to do. It was clearly preferable for these to be under his hand, rather than be dispersed through any of the twelve volumes at the caprice of the alphabet. This the present arrangement achieves to a great extent. If it has led to a small amount of overlapping, that again is not without its advantages.

Cross-references, then, play an indispensable part in the make-up of the encyclopaedia. They are of two kinds: references in the text to further articles amplifying the particular point under review, and references at the end of an article to others taking the whole subject farther. Therefore, a reader looking up any wide subject, such as MYTHOLOGY, and following up its cross-references either in the text or at the end of the article, can discover under what main headwords the subject is treated. These, again, will refer him to any subsidiary articles, as also, in many cases, to those of a complementary nature. Thus he may be guided either from the general to the particular or vice versa. It is believed that the titles of the twelve volumes (see p. xii), in conjunction with their sub-titles, will usually lead the reader straight to the volume containing the information he wants. In selecting headwords, the rules generally followed have been to prefer the familiar, or even the colloquial, reserving the technical alternative for a single-line entry, and to group narrow subjects under a headword of wider scope. Thus, for NEOLITHIC MAN, *see* PREHISTORIC MAN; for METAPHYSICS, *see* PHILOSOPHY; for MANCHUS, *see* CHINESE PEOPLES; and for TITANS, *see* MYTHOLOGICAL MONSTERS, section A.

L.E.S., G.M.B.

OXFORD, 1948

LIST OF CONTRIBUTORS

PRINCIPAL CONTRIBUTORS

Prehistory

A. HINGSTON QUIGGIN.

JACQUETTA HAWKES.

PROF. STUART PIGGOTT, Abercromby Professor of Prehistoric Archaeology, Edinburgh University.

Early Civilizations

PROF. S. H. HOOKE, B.D., F.S.A., Professor Emeritus of Old Testament Studies, London University.

H. J. BRAUNHOLTZ, Keeper of the Dept. of Ethnography, British Museum.

JACQUETTA HAWKES.

Religion

PROF. E. O. JAMES, D.Litt., Ph.D., Hon. D.D., F.S.A., Professor of Philosophy of Religion, London University, Fellow of University College, London.

Religion (continued)

REV. A. C. BOUQUET, D.D., Hon. C. F., Lecturer in History and Comparative Study of Religion, Cambridge University.

REV. JOHN FOSTER, D.D., Professor of Ecclesiastical History, Glasgow University.

Mythology and Primitive Beliefs

LORD RAGLAN.

Folk-lore

EDWARD A. ARMSTRONG.

Races and Peoples

A. HINGSTON QUIGGIN (general).

D. P. GAMBLE, International African Institute (Africa).

DR. G. M. FRITERS, L. et D. ès Sc.P., Geneva (Central Asia).

F. J. RICHARDS (India).

G. E. HUBBARD, formerly Far Eastern Research Secretary, Royal Institute of International Affairs.

OTHER CONTRIBUTORS

D. P. BICKMORE.

CRANE BRINTON, D.Phil., McLean Professor of Ancient and Modern History, Harvard University.

REV. G. W. BUTTERWORTH, Litt.D., Bodington Memorial Fellow of Leeds University.

MEYRICK H. CARRÉ, Lecturer, University of Bristol.

A. E. P. COLLINS.

KATHLEEN CONYNGHAM GREENE.

MURIEL CURREY.

H. A. DAVIES, Headmaster of Quakers' Yard Grammar School.

ADRIAN DIGBY, Dept. of Ethnography, British Museum.

THOMAS DUNBABIN, Australian News and Information Bureau, N.Y.

DULCIE J. EDMONDS.

A. C. EDWARDS.

C. C. EDWARDS.

P. M. FITZGERALD.

GRATTAN FREYER, Ph.D.

B. M. Hilton.

J. Hussey, B.Litt., Ph.D., London.

J. H. Hutton, C.I.E., D.Sc.

E. J. E. Jeffes.

Hon. M. Lambert.

Sir Harry Luke, K.C.M.G., D.Litt. (Oxon.).

Audrey M. Malan.

David Marquard, Grey College, Bloemfontein.

R. V. Pennington.

D. Petrie.

Jean Petrie.

Helen Mary Petter.

O. Postgate.

P. Postgate.

Cecil Roth, D.Phil., Reader in Jewish Studies, Oxford University.

John Ruddle.

Frank Savery, C.B.E., H.M. Consul General, Warsaw, 1919–39.

D. Sparrow.

O. H. K. Spate, Ph.D., formerly Lecturer in Geography, Rangoon University.

Brian Vesey-FitzGerald, F.L.S.

D. Walker.

R. A. F. Wallis.

Martin Wight.

Assistant Editor—Nora C. Day.

ACKNOWLEDGEMENTS

THE EDITORS wish to thank all those who have lent photographs for illustration. They are particularly indebted to the following: the Director of the British Museum and the Keeper of the Department of Ethnography, British Museum; the Director of the National Gallery; the Librarian of the Haddon Library, University Museum of Archaeology and Ethnology, Cambridge; the Curator of the Pitt Rivers Museum, Oxford; the Visitors of the Ashmolean Museum, Oxford; and the Director and Secretary of the Royal Geographical Society.

COLOUR PLATES

PLAN OF VOLUMES

HOW TO USE THIS BOOK

THIS VOLUME is one of twelve, each on a separate subject, the whole set forming what is called an encyclopaedia, or work from which you can find out almost anything you want to know. (The word comes originally from the Greek *enkuklios*, circular or complete, and *paideia*, education.) Each of the twelve volumes is arranged alphabetically within itself, as twelve dictionaries would be.

The difference between a dictionary and an encyclopaedia is that while the first gives you no more than the meanings and derivations of words, the second tells you a very great deal more about their subjects. For instance, from a dictionary you could learn that a BUSHMAN is a native of South Africa, and little more; but an encyclopaedia will tell you what Bushmen are like, how they eat grubs and insects, and can find water in deserts where white men would die of thirst—and many other things about them. Then a dictionary contains nearly every word in the language; but an encyclopaedia deals only with words and subjects about which there is something interesting to be said, beyond their bare meanings. So you should not expect to find every word in an encyclopaedia—every subject is there, but not every word.

To find any subject, you have first to decide in which of the twelve volumes it comes. Each of these has a title as well as a number, and also a list of general subjects to make the title clearer. All these are set out in the Plan of Volumes on the opposite page. Very often you will be able to tell from the title alone which volume contains the information you need; but if not, the list of sub-headings on the plan opposite will help to direct you. For example, if you want to find out about an animal or plant, you would look it up in Volume II, Natural History; but if you wanted to know how that animal or plant is used in something like farming, fishing, or trapping, you would find it in Volume VI. If your subject were something in nature that does not have life—such as the sun, or a particular country or river, or a kind of stone—you would find it in Volume III, with tides, earthquakes, the weather, and many other things. Matters connected with communication of any kind—of people, or goods, or even of ideas—are in Volume IV. So you would look there for languages, and printing, and broadcasting, as well as for ships, and trains, and roads. But if it is the engineering side of any of these things that interests you, Volume VIII, Engineering, is the place to try.

Business and trade are in Volume VII; and how we are governed and protected by the State, the law, and the armed forces is in Volume X. All kinds of sport and games, as well as hobbies, pets, and entertainments, are in Volume IX; and Volume XI deals with almost everything connected with our homes, from the building and furnishing of the house to the clothes and health of those who live in it. The titles of Volumes V and XII, Great Lives and The Arts, explain themselves; and a rather fuller account of the volume you are reading now is given on page xv.

To find your subject in the volume, think of its ordinary name, and then look it up just as though you were using a dictionary—the As on the first page and the Zs (if there are any) on the last. If you cannot find it, try a more general word. For instance, if you want to read about Cheops, who built the Great Pyramid, and cannot find him under his name (as you cannot) try either Egypt or Pyramid—either of which will lead you to him. As you read any article, you will probably come across the titles of other articles in some way connected with what you are reading. You will know that they are titles of other articles because they will be printed in capital letters. Either they will be followed by (q.v.) in brackets (this is short for the Latin *quod vide*, and means 'which see'), or else they themselves will be in brackets, with the word *see* in front of them. You can look up these other articles at once if you want to know more about the particular point dealt with, or you can save them up until you have finished the article you are reading. At the end of any article you may find the words 'See also', followed by one or more titles in small capital letters. If you look these titles up, they will tell you still more about the subject that interests you. These last 'cross-references' are very useful if you want to look up a particularly wide subject (such as EVOLUTION or FOLK-LORE), because they show you at once the titles of all the main articles dealing with it. You can then decide for yourself which to read.

WHAT YOU WILL FIND IN THIS VOLUME

THIS VOLUME IS ABOUT MAN, THE WAY HE HAS LIVED AT DIFFERENT TIMES AND IN DIFFERENT PLACES, AND THE THINGS HE HAS BELIEVED.

PREHISTORIC MAN AND ANCIENT CIVILIZATIONS. You can read how man developed by EVOLUTION through many stages until FOSSIL MAN appeared (for his earliest remains are so old that the bones have become fossilized). You can read what ARCHAEOLOGY has discovered about how men lived before history was written, and how the great civilizations rose, flourished, and disappeared.

RACES AND PEOPLES. Man has spread all over the world, sometimes moving in large MIGRATIONS, settling in the places where conditions suited his way of life. You can read about the different races, such as the NEGROES in Africa, the AMERICAN INDIANS in America, or the various kinds of PACIFIC ISLANDERS. You can follow the history of our own civilization from the DARK AGES, through the RENAISSANCE, up to the present day. There is a separate article on the history and customs of each nation, and of many of the primitive peoples of the world.

RELIGION AND PHILOSOPHY. The beliefs of man are as varied as the types of people. You can read how ideas about GOD have developed and have become embodied in the great religions of the world. The growth of CHRISTIANITY is described, and there are articles on the various branches of the CHRISTIAN CHURCH. Other articles show how the peoples of the ancient civilizations expressed their ideas on RELIGION through RITUAL, and how MYTHOLOGY grew up from the ritual.

FOLK-LORE. The belief in MAGIC formed part of primitive belief from earliest times, and can still be seen in the customs of people all over the world. Articles on such things as GIANTS, FAIRIES, SPELLS AND CHARMS, and on BIRTH, DEATH, and MARRIAGE CEREMONIES tell how these beliefs and customs came into being in the dim past and still remain alive, although their original meanings may have been lost.

The words in capitals are the headings of some of the general articles.

ALTERNATIVE NAMES AND SPELLINGS

NAMES of places and foreign words which have come into general use are often spelt in various ways. The list below gives some of the forms which are used in this volume with their alternatives in brackets.

Abyssinia (Ethiopia)
Bagdad (Baghdad)
Bedouin (Beduin, Badawin)
Celt (Kelt)
Constantinople (Istanbul)
Druze (Druse, Druge)
Ecuador (Equador)
Eskimo (Esquimau), Eskimoes (Esquimaux)
Fellahin (Fellaheen)
Freya (Frigg)
Gypsies (Gipsies)
Iraqi (Iraki)
Jenghis Khan (Genghis Khan)
Khalifa (Caliph)
Knossos (Cnossus, Gnossus)
Koran (Qur'an)

Manchuria (Manchukuo)
Mogul (Moghul, Mughal)
Mohammedan (Muhammadan, Musselman)
Moslem (Muslim)
Odin (Woden)
Peking (Peiping)
Persia (Iran)
Pygmy (Pigmy)
Roumania (Romania, Rumania)
Shiva (Siva)
Siam (Thailand)
Sinhalese (Cingalese)
Taboo (Tabu)
Tsar (Czar, Tzar)
Tyr (Tiu)
Yugoslavia (Jugoslavia)

A

ABYSSINIANS. The inhabitants of Abyssinia, or Ethiopia as it is now called, in north-east Africa, live in a country which has always been a land of mystery because of its inaccessibility. It consists for the most part of a high tableland surrounded by deep thickly wooded gorges or by sheer desert cliffs and arid desert land. Even to-day communications are still poor, though the establishment of air-routes is making a great difference.

Ethiopia is one of the most ancient kingdoms still in existence. The early kingdom of Ethiopia was probably closely connected with that of Egypt. There is also an old tradition that the kings of Ethiopia are descended from the Queen of Sheba and the Hebrew King Solomon. The Greek rulers of Egypt, the Ptolemies, established colonies and brought Greek arts to Ethiopia in the 3rd century B.C. Judaism had long influenced the beliefs of the people, and in A.D. 330 Christianity was introduced and the first bishop of the Coptic Church consecrated. The Ethiopians have followed Christianity ever since, though it has often been a very corrupt form. In the 6th century the Ethiopian Empire was at its greatest, extending well into Arabia; but in the 7th century the Ethiopians retreated into their own inaccessible country before the increasing power of the Moslem Arabs, and they remained there, a little-known people, until recent times. Towards the end of the 15th century the Portuguese sent an expedition to discover this reported Christian kingdom, whose monarch was known as PRESTER JOHN (q.v. Vol. V). In 1935 the attention of the world was focused on Abyssinia when the Italians, under Mussolini, attacked and occupied the country; but during the Second World War the British defeated the Italians, and in 1941 the Emperor, or Negus, was reinstated.

In Abyssinia there are many contrasts of race, language, religion, and tribal organization. The ruling people and main landowners are the Amharic people of the central plateau, who speak a language partly semitic (like Arabic and Hebrew) and partly derived from a North-African language. In the south-east, round the old walled city of Harar, the people are Arab Moslem traders, speaking Arabic as well as Amharic. In the south-west are the pagan Gallas, an unenterprising, primitive people, speaking their own Galla dialect and following primitive beliefs. As well as the hundreds of village schools in the country, there are now many government schools teaching Amharic, the official language; some of the higher schools also teach English.

The people of the central plateau are for the most part well built and handsome, with straight, regular features, long, dark hair, bright eyes, and dark olive complexion. In the south, however, and on the Sudan frontier, there is some negro blood. Upon the high plateau the climate is pleasant and cool, and in many places the land is fertile. The people are mostly agriculturists. The landowners, proud people, very conscious of their dignity, expect the hard work to be done by peasants; and the peasants are still treated—and seem to be content to be treated —much like slaves. The fields are tilled with primitive ploughs, but in the happy confidence that God and the Emperor will look after the crops.

On ceremonial occasions, such as weddings, Ethiopians eat raw meat with a hot red-pepper sauce called *wat*. With it they eat a bitter, grey, flat bread and drink a heady honey-drink called *tej*. Their houses in the villages are round mud-and-wattle huts with conical thatched roofs,

A STREET IN ADDIS ABABA, THE CAPITAL OF ABYSSINIA
Paul Popper

looking rather like beehives; but in the towns most houses have roofs of corrugated iron. Men wear white jodhpurs, long shirts to their knees, and *shammas*, or very long white scarves of a fine local cotton weave which they wind round their shoulders and whole body.

The religion, the COPTIC (q.v.) branch of the Christian Church, has much pomp and ceremony, which enhances also the dignity of the Imperial Throne. A procession of priests, with their brilliantly coloured umbrellas and silver or gold ornaments, or a royal procession when the Emperor is coming, is indeed a magnificent sight.

The Ethiopian has always been wild and warlike, thinking more of his particular tribe than of the nation as a whole. The Emperor, until quite recent times, has often had little or no real control over his country. Under the Emperor Haïlé Selassié, however, who is personally very much respected and revered by the majority of his people, some real central control and unity is beginning to grow. Ethiopians are still suspicious of foreign influence and modern methods, which they need to bring them into line with modern

civilization, but the Emperor has nevertheless already introduced many Western innovations into the country.

See also Vol. III: ABYSSINIA.

ACHAEANS, *see* GREEK CIVILIZATION, Section 2 a.

ACHILLES, *see* GREEK HEROES.

AEGEAN CIVILIZATION, *see* MINOAN CIVILIZATION; MYCENEAN CIVILIZATION.

AFGHANS. The ten million people of Afghanistan are made up of various races, including Afghans, Turks, Persians, and Mongols; but one factor unifies fundamentally their outlook and different ways of life—they are all fanatical Moslems (*see* ISLAM).

The Afghans have been famed as fighters since the first we know of them in A.D. 982; and the British have experienced their valour and cunning during three Afghan Wars and in frequent raids across the Indian North-West Frontier. These lithe men with flowing robes, white turbans, nail-studded shoes with turned-up toes, rifles, and cartridge belts, are mainly nomadic people consisting of various tribes.

The east and south-east mountains of Afghanistan, which are their strongholds, are arid and infertile, and the inhabitants have been forced to wander far and wide, with their black tents transported on camels, to find grazing for the great herds of fat-tailed sheep which are their principal wealth. It is seldom now that they raid the Khyber Pass—where their deadly hidden rifle fire used to be the terror of merchant caravans and of travellers making their way from India to Kabul, the Afghan capital; but passage through the Pass is still forbidden after sunset. Reservations for winter grazing have now been allotted to them in the fertile plains of north India, so that they no longer have to take it by force.

The most proud and independent of the Afghan tribes is, perhaps, the Ghilzai, whose centre is Ghazni, where the embroidered sheepskin coats and waistcoats (*pustins*) are made. Tall, slender, bearded, and fair-skinned, with aquiline features and piercing eyes, these men might be Old Testament warriors and prophets, and they have a tradition (considered incorrect) that they are a lost tribe of Israel.

The Turks of Afghanistan live to the north and east of the Hindu Kush range, on the plains divided from the steppes of Russian Turkestan by the Oxus river. Besides the Durranis of Herat, they include the Uzbeks, who came over from Uzbekistan in Soviet Russia and settled in north Afghanistan. They live mainly by breeding horses, camels, and sheep, though latterly they have taken to cultivating cotton and rice. Unlike the Afghans, they have ruddy skins, blue eyes, fair or red hair and beards, and wear gay cretonne quilted coats.

Different from the roving peoples are the village-dwelling Persians, or Tadjiks, the oldest settled inhabitants of the country. Probably they lived in all the fertile regions in their village communities before the Afghans surged westwards from the mountains. The Tadjiks are

A GHILZAI TRIBESMAN
Fox Photos.

still the merchants and artisans in the towns, and have remained as tenants of land which the Afghans took from them (*see* SEMITIC LANGUAGES, Vol. IV).

The Hazaras, a Mongol people, probably came into Afghanistan in the 13th century with the armies of Jenghis Khan and settled in the mountains south of the Hindu Kush. They are industrious farmers, and used to make excellent soldiers in the pioneer regiments of the Indian Army. They belong to a different sect of Islam from the Afghans, who despise and oppress them.

In the wild, almost inaccessible, western provinces of Kafiristan live the Shia-Push ('Wearers of Black Clothes') or Kafirs, who are also divided into tribes; but shut away in their isolated valleys, divided by high mountain ranges, they play little part in Afghan affairs.

Iranian (Persian) is the main language of Afghanistan, though Uzbeks speak Turkish, and the Kafirs an Aryan language more ancient than Iranian. Pushtu, the eastern Iranian language, is now counted the official language of the country (*see* PERSIAN LANGUAGES, Vol. IV).

The history of Afghanistan has been shaped largely by the fact that it lay on the overland route into India, used by a sequence of invaders through the ages. The first of importance was the Persian king, Cyrus, who conquered most of what is now Afghanistan in 600 B.C. The next conquerors were the Greeks under Alexander the Great in 328 B.C. The Greeks continued in Afghanistan for nearly 300 years, and Greek coins and Buddhist sculptures strongly marked by Greek influence have been discovered there. BUDDHISM (q.v.) came into south Afghanistan from India in the 3rd century B.C. The next important invader was Jenghis Khan, the ruthless Mongol conqueror, who, in A.D. 1220, massacred whole populations and laid waste areas, many of which have remained deserts ever since. After this came the Turk, Tamerlane, who invaded Afghanistan on his way to India in A.D. 1398. By 1747 the Turkish Durrani tribe had become the most powerful in the country, and one of its members, Ahmed Khan, was elected the first king of an independent and more or less united Kingdom of Afghanistan.

The First and Second Afghan Wars with Great Britain in 1838 and 1878 were really caused by Britain's fear of an invasion of India through Afghanistan by France or Russia. After a long struggle Britain conquered the Afghans and took control of the country's foreign policy. In 1880 Abdur Rahman became Emir (or King) and with the help of British arms got control over the whole country and brought inter-tribal warfare to an end. His son ended slavery and founded a college run on European lines. The Third Afghan War broke out in 1919 when the Emir demanded complete freedom from Britain. The Afghans were quickly defeated, but were granted their freedom.

The next Emir, Amanulla, determined to modernize Afghanistan, and tried to introduce universal education, European clothing, and the unveiling of women. The conservative and fanatically Moslem tribesmen were outraged and, led by the *mullahs* (priests), drove Amanulla from the country. Fortunately there arose a great leader, Nadir Khan, who in the four years before he was assassinated put Afghanistan on a firm foundation. He set up a constitutional government with an elected parliament. His son, Zahir

AFGHANS DRYING SHEEPSKINS ON A FLAT ROOF
Roy. Geog. Soc.

Shah, the present King, succeeded him, and is most successfully welding together the European-educated Afghans and the conservative tribesmen into something more like a modern nation.

See also Vol. III: AFGHANISTAN.

AFRICANS, *see* NEGRO AFRICANS; SOUTH AFRICANS; RHODESIANS; EAST AFRICANS; SAHARA, PEOPLES OF.

AFRIKANERS, *see* SOUTH AFRICANS.

AGAMEMNON, *see* GREEK HEROES.

AGNOSTIC. Most human beings feel convinced at some time or another that there is something binding together the universe of which they form a part, and that this something exists in its own right and is not dependent upon anything else. One scientist identifies it with the-universe-taken-as-a-whole. Some say that it is a supreme super-personal deity. Others say that it is a collection of personal beings of varied dispositions. Others, again, say that it is an impersonal force. Since about the year 1869 the word agnostic (one who says he does not know) has been used to describe a person who says that the nature of the self-existent something is not only unknown to us but must remain unknowable, so that it is both useless and unwise to believe or even to assume that behind the Universe there is a Power, single, supreme, and personal, who loves man, cares for goodness, and wishes men to be friends with and to know that Power. An agnostic remains in a non-committal attitude.

Whether to suspend judgement in this way is not in itself to display bias against faith must be a matter of opinion. Some think it is; others say that it is a sign of honesty and humility, and point to the fact that some agnostics are at least as virtuous as those who claim to be guided by faith. The problem really turns upon whether or not it is possible to say that knowledge of the Self-existent can be reached by faith, revelation, inspiration, mysticism, or experience of life, as well as by reason; or whether by reason only; or again whether all such knowledge is impossible. This is a matter upon which a great deal of discussion is still proceeding, in which there is perhaps a tendency to give more weight to the testimony of the mystics.

See also RATIONALISM.

AINUS, *see* JAPANESE.

ALBANIANS. The little country of Albania, one of the Balkan countries on the Adriatic, north of Greece, has altogether a population of only a little over a million people. They vary a good deal in appearance, some being dark and some fair. But most of them have strong regular features, long oval faces, long necks, and broad shoulders. They have a very upright carriage and proud air. They are as a whole extremely tough and courageous and very patriotic and proud. They are usually intensely loyal to tribal tradition, but fanatical and violent according to Western ideas. An attitude of neutrality or indifference is hardly known to them, and they delight in plunder.

The Albanians were originally an Aryan people called Illyrians. They resisted the attacks of the Ottoman Turkish Empire with great success under their famous leader, George Castriot (Scanderbeg); but after his death, towards the end of the 15th century, they came under Turkish domination, which lasted, at least nominally, until the establishment of an independent kingdom in 1912. But in fact they have had much independence since the time of Ali Pasha (1741–1822), an enterprising and ruthless Albanian leader who loosened the Turkish hold. On Good Friday of 1939 Albania was attacked by the Italians under Mussolini, and occupied until the end of 1944.

The Albanians are mainly an agricultural people who have retained customs and a way of life now discarded by their neighbours. This is partly due to the mountainous and inaccessible nature of their country, which makes communications with outside peoples difficult. The majority of Albanians are followers of the religion of ISLAM (q.v.). The northern people are tribal—a tribe being a group descended in the male line from one male ancestor. So strong is their sense of tribal solidarity and so great is their feeling of personal dignity that a personal insult—even quite a small one—can only be wiped out by bloodshed, and all members of the tribe are responsible for exacting vengeance. To avoid an accidental blow it is a custom for men to walk a rifle's length apart and women a distaff's length apart. Tribal customs are ruled by the law of Lek, and enforced by tribal elders. This is an unwritten law attributed to Lek Dukagjin who lived about 1387.

NORTH ALBANIAN CHIEFTAINS.   *Roy. Geog. Soc.*

Every district has its characteristic native costume for men and women. A mountaineer wears white trousers braided with black and a gaily coloured sash which he uses as a pocket. His jacket of rich-coloured velvet, often embroidered with gold, is only used on rare occasions. He wears sandals, and on his head a white cap with often a scarf wrapped round it. Over all he wears for protection a rough shaggy mantle and hood made of goat-hair cloth or coarse wool. He makes a spectacular figure on his fine horse, for most Albanians are good horsemen.

See also Vol. III: ALBANIA.

ALLAH, *see* ISLAM; GOD, Section b.

AMAZONS. A legendary nation of women-warriors who are supposed to have lived in ancient times somewhere near the Black Sea. Their name means 'without breast'; for the legend tells that they removed their right breasts in order that they might shoot better with bow and arrows. They came to the help of the TROJANS (q.v.) in their struggle against Greece.

AMAZON WARRIORS
Painting from a Greek Vase *c.* 500 B.C. *British Mus.*

It was said also that at one time they attacked Greece, but were repelled by the King Theseus who captured their queen, Hippolyta. One of the ten labours of Heracles was to secure the girdle of this Queen Hippolyta of the Amazons. Most of the accounts of the Amazons come in the works of the Greek historian HERODOTUS (q.v. Vol. V).

See also Vol. III: AMAZON RIVER.

AMERICAN INDIANS, CENTRAL AND SOUTH. In a great part of Central and South America the Indians are still the people of the land; whereas in North America the Indians are very few, surviving almost entirely in reservations, a picturesque and pathetic reminder of bygone days when the Pale-face settled the country and waged constant warfare with the Redskin.

There are two reasons for this contrast. In the first place, the Indians of North America never rose above a primitive level of culture. They were weakly organized, for the most part in small tribes, and they were few in numbers considering the great expanses of the North American continent. In Central and South America, on the other hand, the Indians had already built up civilizations of their own before the Europeans came—the civilizations of the MAYAS and the AZTECS in Central America, and of the INCAS (qq.v.) and others in the Andean plateau of South America. And these regions were consequently much more thickly peopled with a settled population living by agriculture.

In the second place, North America has been much more fully settled from Europe than South. North America lies mainly in the temperate zone; Central and South America mainly in the tropical zone. European immigrants poured into North America, almost wiping out the weakly organized natives, and they built up the nations of the United States and Canada. They came to Central and South America, too, but in far fewer numbers; and though they destroyed the native Indian civilizations, they did not attempt to wipe out the Indians themselves. In the short run they enslaved them; but in the long run they settled down and mixed with them. Perhaps in the future it will become apparent that, in the end, they have been absorbed by them.

The Spanish word for a person of mixed Indian and European blood is *mestizo*; and we can classify the countries of Central and South America according to whether the population is mainly Indian, mainly *mestizo*, or mainly white. There are four mainly Indian republics: Guatemala in Central America, Ecuador, Peru, and Bolivia in South America. There are nine *mestizo* republics:

PERUVIAN INDIANS
Ferrying across the River Perene on rafts. *Pacific Steam Navigation Co.*

Mexico, most of which really lies in North America, Salvador, Honduras, Nicaragua, and Panama, with Colombia, Venezuela, Paraguay, and Chile in South America. There are only three countries whose population is almost wholly white: Costa Rica in Central America, and Argentina and Uruguay in the temperate zone of South America. Brazil is about half white, but it differs from the rest in having a large negro strain. We can see, then, how very important the Indians are in the populations of Central and South America. It has been said that 'the mestizo is the true American man', and some South Americans like to use the word 'Indo-America' instead of 'Latin-America', because they think that although their culture came from Spain and Portugal, it is the Indian and not the Latin element that in the end will prove most important.

It is generally agreed that the American Indians came from Asia, for in various physical characteristics they resemble the MONGOLS (q.v.) more than any other branch of mankind. Their ancestors probably crossed the Behring Straits, where Asia and America lie less than 60 miles apart, and slowly, through many generations, pushed their way down to the fertile and tropical lands of the south. But it is possible that they were influenced, and perhaps even joined, by other peoples from the Old World. It is probable that North America was 'discovered' by the Norsemen 600 years before Columbus, and it may just possibly have been visited by Irish missionaries before the Norsemen. Some scholars have thought that the Toltec and Aztec god Quetzalcoatl—the haunting majestic figure with a white skin, who, they believe, came across the sea in a sailing-ship, and, having stayed several years teaching a new and humane religion, returned to a holy island beyond the ocean, but said he would one day return—was indeed an Irish monk. It is conceivable that South America was visited, too, across the enormous stretches of ocean to the west, by Polynesians from the Pacific Islands in their canoes.

Since they first came to America the American Indians have developed many differences of physical type among themselves, and also a great variety of languages, none of which has any known connexion with the languages of the Old World. In modern Mexico alone more than fifty different Indian languages are spoken. The languages of South American Indians are still very

INDIAN WOMAN
She carries her baby in her gay hand-woven shawl
Paul Popper

little understood, but seventy-five different groups of languages have been discerned among them.

The Central and South American Indians can be divided into two kinds. First, there are the settled peoples who had reached a high level of civilization before the Europeans discovered America. These are now Christian, but retain many of their old native beliefs and customs. They are for the most part peasants, working on the land for landlords who are usually of Spanish descent, and for long they lived in a state of serfdom like that found in medieval Europe under the feudal system. Secondly, there are the simpler peoples who, like the Indians of North America, have remained in a primitive state, or in many cases have died out.

In the first group we find three different regions, whose inhabitants had a generally similar culture:

(*a*) Mexico and Central America. The Indians of these countries are descended either from the Maya and Aztecs themselves, or from the other tribes most of whom these ruling peoples had conquered. Their languages mostly

INSIDE AN INDIAN HUT IN THE FORESTS OF BRITISH GUIANA. *Paul Popper*

belong to the Nahua (a group of languages of which the Aztecs spoke one) and Maya stocks. Those speaking a Nahua language are sometimes called the Nahua group of peoples.

(*b*) The Central Andean Plateau of Ecuador, Peru, and Bolivia was the region of the Inca Empire, from whose peoples the present inhabitants are descended. The chief language is Quechua, which was the tongue of the Inca nation.

(*c*) The Northern Andes of Colombia, with Panama. The most important Indian people of this region are the Chibchas. When the Spaniards came, the Chibchas were not as advanced as the Aztecs, Maya, and Incas, but they were much more advanced than the wild tribes surrounding them. Probably their customs resembled Inca civilization more closely—like the Incas, they worshipped the sun and were skilled craftsmen in gold; but they had some things in common with the Aztecs, for example the practice of human sacrifice. They were an agricultural people, with a system of irrigation

for watering their fields, and, like the Inca, they made roads and rope suspension bridges. When a new chief of the Chibchas began his reign he was covered with gold dust and then bathed ceremonially in the waters of the sacred lake Guatavita. Rumours of this custom came to the ears of the Spaniards and gave rise to the legend of El Dorado, the Golden Man.

In the second group, the primitive Indians, there are also three broad regions:

(*a*) The Caribbean Area includes the great semicircle of the West Indian islands from Cuba down to the Windward Islands, together with the northern coast of Venezuela. Here there were two peoples: first the Arawaks and later the Caribs, both of whom probably came in canoes from the Amazon region to the south. They were fierce and warlike and sometimes cannibals. They were soon almost wiped out by the cruelty of their Spanish conquerors, who brought over slaves from Africa to replace them—that is why the population of this region to-day is

much more negro than Indian (*see* WEST IN-
DIANS).

(*b*) The Tropical Forests and Grasslands.
This, the greater part of South America, includes
the three great river-basins of the Orinoco, the
Amazon, and the Parana–Paraguay. It is mostly
covered with dense tropical forest, and is very
thinly populated. The rivers are the only roads
open to man, and almost all the tribes depend
upon canoes. The people are widely scattered,
but have many similar customs. They invented
the hammock, a hanging network couch made
from the bark of the hamaca tree. In the dim,
rainy forests, where the sun rarely penetrates,
they live in thatched huts, for the most part
going naked. They live on almost every kind
of animal and insect they can catch, some of
them depending chiefly on monkeys. Many of
them use blow-guns with poisoned darts; some
of them are cannibals; all of them have medicine men who treat the sick with charms and
exorcisms, foretell the future, and mystify the
simple tribes with feats of jugglery. In the
interior of Brazil there are still unexplored areas,
and there are dangerous savages who have never
seen a white man and shoot even at aeroplanes
with their bows and arrows. Far up the Amazon, in the interior of Ecuador, are the head-
hunting Jivaros, who shrink the heads of their
enemies killed in battle in order to preserve them.

The four most important groups of tribes of
this enormous region are the Arawaks and Caribs
in the north, and the Tabuya and Tupi-Guarani
in the south. The Tupi-Guarani were the original inhabitants of the low-lying forested country
north of the Rio de la Plata. They form the
Indian element in the people of Paraguay; and
Paraguay is the only American country in which
an Indian language, Guarani, is officially used,
besides Spanish, in newspapers and public
speeches.

(*c*) The Southern Grasslands and Forests.
The grasslands include the southern wedge of
the continent, the greater part of Uruguay and
Argentina. The pampas of Patagonia are similar
to the prairies and plateaux of North America,
and the Indians here were huntsmen like the
North American Indians. They hunted the
guanaco, a South American cousin of the camel
similar to the llama and the rhea, the South
American ostrich. They used lances or the bola,
a kind of lasso. When the Spaniards came and
introduced horses and cattle into America the

Indians soon learned to steal horses and to prey
upon the cattle instead of on the guanaco. The
white settlers, therefore, shot down the free-
riding Indians of the pampas, and now very
few Indians survive in Argentina. In the forest
lands of south Chile it was different. Here the
brave and warlike Araucanians had maintained
their independence against both the Inca and
the Spanish Empires, and when they were at
last conquered and civilized in the 19th century
they were absorbed into the Chilean nation.
Many CHILEANS (q.v.) to-day are proud of their
Araucanian blood.

See also Vol. III: SOUTH AMERICA; CENTRAL AMERICA.
Vol. IV: AMERICAN-INDIAN LANGUAGES.

AMERICAN INDIANS, NORTH. When
Columbus set sail westward in 1492, he expected
to reach India; so when he discovered new
islands and a new continent, he called the
natives 'Indians'. Later explorers, struck by
the copper colour of their skins and also the red
with which some natives painted themselves,
called them 'Red Indians' or 'Red-skins'—the
natives, in return, called the Europeans 'Pale-
faces'. Since American Indian is a cumbersome
name, it is sometimes shortened to Amerind. It
is estimated that there may have been rather
over a million scattered over North America;
but with the advance of white settlement, the
tribes were dispersed, moving northward towards the forests, westward across the plains, and
into the arid south-west. Less than 400,000 still
survive, many of them in reservations, i.e. areas
of land specially reserved for them, about one-
third in Canada and the rest in the United States
(*see* AMERICAN-INDIAN LANGUAGES, Vol. IV).

They belong to the Mongoloid division of
mankind. It is thought probable that their
ancestors came over from north-east Asia after
the Ice Age many thousands of years ago (*see*
MIGRATION OF PEOPLES). They must gradually
have spread down the continent, so that their
descendants reached most parts of South and
Central America as well (*see* AMERICAN INDIANS,
CENTRAL AND SOUTH). They have straight, lank,
black hair and yellowish-brown skins which often
burn a coppery red. They have prominent
cheekbones, but rarely the flat faces and slanting
eyes of the Asiatic Mongols. They differ a great
deal in appearance and in occupation in different parts of the continent, but can be grouped,
however, according to certain main regions and

A TEPEE OF THE PLAINS INDIANS

It is made of bison skins, stretched on poles and decorated with the totems of the owner. *Canadian National Film Board*

occupations. There are the tribes of the caribou or wild reindeer area in the far northern forests; the peoples of the north-west Pacific coast who live mainly on salmon and other fish; the tribes of the eastern woodlands who live partly by cultivating crops and partly by hunting; the Plains Indians who used to hunt the bison, popularly called the buffalo; and the Pueblo Indians, grouped in villages in the south-west and living on maize and vegetables, wild game, and sheep.

Caribou is an Indian name for the reindeer which roam in herds from feeding-ground to feeding-ground in the forests and on the plains extending to the Arctic coasts of North America; they are hunted by the Eskimoes in the summer and by the Indians farther south in the winter. Before the days of guns the Indians caught them in traps or pitfalls, they drove them over soft snow and pursued them on snow-shoes, or they drove them into the water and speared them from their birch-bark canoes. For a big drive they set up rows of stakes and drove them into ambushes or enclosures or into narrow gorges from which they could not escape. By these means they killed many more caribou than they could eat, so they stored the dried flesh in pits

or caches: no hunter would ever rifle the cache of another. Much of the flesh was pounded into pemmican and packed in fat, in which condition it would keep for months.

These Indians made their shirts, leggings or trousers, and moccasins of skins. Women wore much the same clothes as the men, only of softer materials—often doeskin—and their clothes were more richly decorated with shells, dyed porcupine quills, or feathers. Wealthy men wore robes of beaver, wolf, bear, or coyote fur. But most Indians have now come in contact with trading-posts and have adopted white man's clothing.

Like the Eskimoes (q.v.) to the north and the Plains Indians to the south, the Caribou Indians grow no grain or vegetables, though the women collect roots and berries, mash them, and use them for food and flavouring. They had no pottery in earlier days, so they used to make square cooking pots of birch bark or round ones of fine plaited basketry lined with pitch. As these could not be placed on the fire without getting burnt, they dropped heated stones into the pot full of water, and so brought it to the boil, and in this way they were able to stew meat and berries. Trade has now brought kettles, pots, and pans into the caribou area, with new foods and new methods of cooking.

During the winter many Indians live in solid wooden houses, sometimes partly underground for warmth; and in some parts they build a large 'ceremonial lodge', 40 or 50 feet long, for feasts, dances, and great occasions. In many parts there are no permanent settlements, and the Indians, when they are hunting, live in their bark wigwams which are easily moved from camp to camp.

Each hunting group manages its own affairs, recognizing as its leader or chief the most skilful or wealthy hunter of the group. Girls are often betrothed very young, and the marriages are arranged by the parents. In some parts a boy proposes to a girl by asking, 'Will you pack my beaver snares for me?' If she accepts, he hands over his beaver snares, she sets up the tent, and they are recognized as man and wife. If she refuses, it is in the conventional phrase, 'No, there are plenty of women, ask another.'

The Indians of the northern Pacific coast depend mainly on fish, and especially on salmon. These fish come up the rivers once a year to spawn, crowding in such masses that the Indians can scoop them up in buckets. They also catch

A HOPI INDIAN BASKET-MAKER, ARIZONA

them in nets, harpoon them, or take them in staked enclosures. The fish are dried and smoked, sometimes made into a paste, and stored in finely plaited baskets to keep until the next salmon 'run'. The Indians built large houses of spruce or pine planks from the great forests which run down almost to the coast. The villages generally consisted of thirty or more houses set in a line facing the sea along a sheltered part of the coast. The houses used to be large, solid, and rectangular, 40 to 50 feet long, in which several related families lived together. In early days these houses were built without nails, by fitting and tying the timbers together; and reed mats made partitions inside. In front they set up their 'totem poles', carved with the crests of the animals which were linked in mythical tales with the particular clan and family.

Close-fitting clothing is not needed in this mild coastal region—men often went barefoot, wearing nothing but a loincloth. Cloaks were made of skins, fibre matting, and beautiful blankets woven of wool and hair. Women had long garments of dressed skins, often decorated with beads and shells. Traders, railways, and industries such as fishing, canning, mining, and lumber have, in recent years, invaded the region and altered native life: now European houses and clothes are replacing native styles.

PLAINS INDIANS. Tribes whose names are famous in story—Blackfoot, Crow, Dakota, Assiniboin, Arapaho, and Cheyenne—hunted the bison, called 'buffalo', on the treeless prairies of North America, between the Mississippi and the Rocky Mountains. They were tall, well-built and muscular, proud of their physical fitness and of their ability to bear pain and hardships without complaint. Down to the middle of the last century herds of bison roamed the prairies in great numbers and provided the Indians with plenty of food. They stalked them and surrounded them on horseback, shooting them with bows and arrows; they trapped them in various ways. A common plan was to set up rows of stakes or piles of stones in a V-shape, converging to a point at the edge of a cliff. The younger men would lure or urge the herd towards the trap, and when within the lines they were stampeded over the cliff, to fall, injured into an enclosure below, where they were easily slaughtered. Men, women, and children helped in cutting up the animals and carrying the loads back to camp.

A PLAINS INDIAN IN FULL WAR REGALIA
Dorien Leigh

Bison skins, carefully cured, scraped, and softened, were used to cover tents (*tepees*), for bags, and for men's robes. For shirts, leggings, and moccasins the lighter skins of deer were preferred. A thick piece of bison skin supported on sticks was the cooking pot, and this was heated in the same way as that used by Caribou Indians. The hair of the bison was used for stuffing, its paunch as a water-bucket, its sinews for string, its horns for spoons, and its bones for tools.

In early days the Indians used dogs for transport in moving camp; they tied packages either to the *tepee* poles which were trailed along the ground, or to a light framework called a *travois*. But after the coming of the Spaniards in the 16th century the Indians captured some of their horses and used them for transport and also for hunting and raiding expeditions. After the Indians possessed horses their bison hunting was much easier and more profitable, and except for the difficulty of taking the horses across wide rivers, they could round up the bison from much wider areas. So valuable did the horses prove that the acquisition of horses became the main ambition of all Indians, and they always wanted more. So they started systematically raiding the horses of enemy tribes. This form of raiding warfare, generally with the capture of horses as its object, increased greatly and developed a definite technique. The weapons they used were circular shields of hide, bows and arrows, and heavy wooden lances. There were few pitched battles and not as a rule great loss of life; but there was great rivalry to perform the boldest deeds of daring: a man's reputation and status in his tribe depended much on this, and there grew up elaborate conventions about what could be counted a brave deed. These deeds were recorded in picture-writing on the *tepees* or on the hero's bison robes, and when he took part in social or ritual ceremonies, he started by recounting his deeds.

Every Indian had his guardian spirit. The boys and girls, before they became men and women, had to go through a ceremony of INITIATION (q.v.), during which time their friendly guardian spirit would reveal itself in dreams. This guardian spirit might take the form of some animal or bird, water or thunder, or some inanimate object such as a canoe for a boy— for a girl perhaps a basket. This became the

THUNDER BIRD
The totem of a dead man, placed above his grave. It is made of wood, carved, and painted in bright colours. Kwakiutl Tribe, Vancouver Island, B.C.
Miss B. Blackwood

protector through life and is sometimes called a personal 'totem' (*see* TOTEMISM). The owner would wear or treasure some symbol of the spirit protector. Nowadays, however, most Indians are nominally Christian, their numbers are dwindling, and the old ways are disappearing.

As long as bison were plentiful life was enjoyable, but with the advent of the white man, the introduction of guns, and the coming of the railway, the bison had little chance of survival. White and Indian hunters rounded up and slaughtered more and more bison, reducing their numbers until they were practically exterminated. Now the bison, like its Indian hunters, is preserved only in reservations.

PUEBLO INDIANS. In Arizona and New Mexico in the south-west of the United States there are groups of Indians living in villages which the Spaniards called *pueblos*. The houses in the villages are built of stone or of sun-dried clay bricks, sometimes situated on the steep sides of hills or a cliff face. They are several storeys high; some have no doors and are entered by means of a ladder from the flat roof. The small rooms are bare of furniture, for much of the daily work is done on the roof. Every house has its grinding-stones, protected by boards, for grinding corn.

This is a treeless area, too dry to be favourable for crops; but there are patches of soil, flooded after rain, where the Indians grow maize, beans, pumpkins, melons, and other vegetables. They keep turkeys, not for their flesh or even for their eggs, but for their feathers, used in decorations and in ceremonies. Deer were plentiful in earlier days, but now there is little to be caught save rabbits. Many of the villagers now keep sheep and donkeys.

In earlier days they made their clothes of deerskins, but long ago they learnt the art of weaving, and they make squares of cloth worn in different fashions by men and women. The men grow the crops and weave the cloth. The women also help in the fields, but their main duty is to look after the house, prepare the food, grind the maize, and make the bread. The women also make very fine pottery—a craft which has been highly developed for more than 1,000 years. They collect the fine clay, prepare it by sifting, kneading, and moistening, and roll it out into sausage-like strips which are built up spirally from the base. A coating of thin clay, black, red, yellow, or white, is added, and the surface is burnished before the pot is fired. In some villages pots are painted with yellows and blacks in striking designs, representing mountains, thunder, clouds or rain, and animals. This very fine pottery is made without the aid of the potter's wheel, with no more complex tools than

AN INDIAN PUEBLO IN NEW MEXICO. *Dorien Leigh*

the woman's fingers, bits of a broken pot or a gourd for a scraper, a water-worn pebble for a polisher, and a bit of a stiff leaf or a frayed stalk for a paint-brush. The women also make brightly coloured baskets of dyed strips of leaves and stems decorated with the same type of design.

The daily bread depends on the rain in this dry area—and the priests, since they are believed to be the rain-makers and to be able, by their offerings and intercessions, to control the weather, are of great importance. Each clan in a *pueblo* has its *kiva* or ceremonial chamber, often partly underground. Here are held throughout the year elaborate ceremonies with masked dances, the purpose of which is to obtain good rainfall, good crops, and general good fortune for the village.

AMERICAN NEGROES. There are nearly thirteen million Negroes in the United States of America, almost one-tenth of the total population of the country, and nearly all those now living were born in America. Most of them live in the southern states—in 1940 as many as three-quarters. During the two world wars the demand for Negro labour in the northern factories caused great migrations from the country districts of the south to the industrial north; but the northern Negroes are still not nearly as numerous as those of the south. In the two southern states of Mississippi and South Carolina Negroes are still more than half of the population, and in Florida, Georgia, and Alabama they number roughly 40% of all the residents. In the north they tend to concentrate in certain places such as Philadelphia, Baltimore, and Chicago; in New York about a quarter of a million live in the district of Harlem in Upper Manhattan.

The American Negroes are all of African descent (*see* NEGRO AFRICANS). In 1619 a Dutch sea-captain brought a shipload of Negroes from western Africa to the recently founded colony of Virginia. The planters bought them as 'servants', and so started the slave system which was destined to have a fateful influence on American history. In those days the colonies were British, and the colonists, short of labour on their cotton, rice, and tobacco plantations, were glad to buy African slaves. The trade

STUDENTS OF THE HOWARD UNIVERSITY, WASHINGTON
This famous negro University was founded in 1867. *American Information Service*

remained small at first but between 1680 and 1786, over two million slaves were brought to America and the West Indies. Twenty-two years later their importation into the United States was prohibited; but they still continued to be smuggled in—as many as two million more, it is said. In the northern states all slaves were freed in 1804; but it was not until sixty-one years later, after four years of cruel and devastating civil war between North and South, that Negro slavery was abolished in the southern states.

If President Lincoln's 'malice toward none, charity for all' had been applied after the war; if the defeated southern whites had not been grossly humiliated, deprived of the vote, and even subjected to the legal control of their former slaves, there would probably have been no lawless organizations like the Ku Klux Klan, and perhaps no Negro problem—a problem which still remains so disturbing a feature in American life. There was no ingrained hatred for the Negroes at the end of the Civil War: they had kept out of it when their entry might have brought about the earlier defeat of their

white masters; and even if the South had won, slavery would probably have been abolished. But bitter memories of the days after the Civil War still persist. In consequence, when the southern whites recovered their power the rights of Negroes were severely curtailed over the greater part of the southern states. Negroes have, in practice, been more or less excluded from voting, they have been forced to travel in separate railway carriages, and there have been 'lynchings' of Negroes. Even in the north there has been some discrimination. But the position of coloured men has improved, and is improving in the United States. About a third of them live in states where they can actually use their vote, and where their privileges are the same as those of their white fellow citizens; the numbers of skilled Negro workers and of Negro property owners are steadily increasing; the southern state of Tennessee, by its recent repeal of all laws against Negroes, has set an example which must eventually spread to all the states; and the development of education is a powerful influence towards the sweeping away of remaining inequalities. One of the greatest men who has come from the South since the Civil War, the Negro Booker WASHINGTON (q.v. Vol. V), urged his people to seek redress through education. 'The race', he told them, 'like the individual, that makes itself indispensable, has solved most of its problems.' He himself founded Negro schools at Hampton and Tuskegee, setting an example which has been followed with happy results. There are now about a hundred colleges in the United States devoted entirely to Negro education; thousands of Negroes attend state colleges and universities; there are 300 Negro newspapers and journals; illiteracy among Negroes has declined from 95% in 1865 to 16% in 1930; and Negroes, while retaining their own culture in the rhythm of the blues, in spirituals, and in folk-lore, have also contributed much to the general culture as writers, scientists, artists, and musicians. They have also distinguished themselves greatly as singers and as athletes. The Negro actor and singer, Paul Robeson, is one of the best known of modern Americans.

AMERICANS (U.S.A.). There are at present about 133 million people living in the United States of America, more than half of whom live in big cities. There are now 360,000 North AMERICAN INDIANS (q.v.), most of whom live on 200 'reservations'. Some of their land is owned by individuals, some by the tribe, and some held in trust by the United States Government. Indians are to be found in most of the states, but principally in Arizona, Montana, New Mexico, and South Dakota. Then there are nearly thirteen million AMERICAN NEGROES (q.v.), three-quarters of whom live in the southern states, where they still lack the privileges and rights of the white population. The rest of the people of the States are of very mixed origin —British, French, German, Scandinavian, Russian, Finnish, people from the Balkans, Italians, Dutchmen, Greeks, Poles, Jews, even Chinese and Japanese. There is still plenty of evidence of this mixture of races in American surnames, in towns in the states of Maine and New Hampshire which look like parts of Finland, in various settlements which are wholly foreign in appearance, such as German towns in Texas, Italian communities in California, and Chinese quarters in San Francisco and other large cities. But all these different peoples eventually become Americans, learn to speak English, and in the course

FORT KENT, A SMALL TOWN IN THE EASTERN STATE OF MAINE

Typical of the American small town with its wooden 'frame' houses. The 'buggy' still survives in a land where nearly everyone owns a car. *American Information Service*

of two, or at most three, generations completely lose contact with their countries of origin. During the two world wars of the present century, Americans whose ancestors came from enemy countries were quite as loyal as those of British, French, or Russian descent. The commander-in-chief of the united allied armies in the Second World War, General Eisenhower, is himself of German descent.

The British were not the first Europeans to land in America: they were preceded by CHRISTOPHER COLUMBUS (q.v. Vol. V), an Italian, sailing under the flag of Spain, and by JOHN CABOT (q.v. Vol. V), another Italian who sailed from Bristol in 1497. It is probable also that the Vikings reached America about A.D. 1000. The real founders of the United States were, however, British—people like SIR WALTER RALEIGH (q.v. Vol. V), John Smith, who, following Raleigh, successfully colonized Virginia, the oldest state of the Union, and the Pilgrim Fathers, religious refugees who landed on the bleak New England coast in 1620. Some of the early colonists were Dutchmen who settled in the states now known as New York, New Jersey, and Delaware—states which became English colonies in consequence of a war between England and Holland.

The early settlers were almost all people in search of freedom or opportunity. There were adventurers like the original colonists of Virginia; there were people driven by religious persecution to seek lands where they could worship as they pleased, like the Puritans of New England, the QUAKERS (q.v.) of Pennsylvania, and the Roman Catholics of Maryland and the Carolinas. Many others crossed the ocean in the hope of a freer and happier life than Europe had offered them, as, for example, those who followed General Oglethorpe to Georgia, intending to make it a refuge for debtors and other poor people for whom there was no hope in England.

In 1775 there were thirteen colonies on the eastern seaboard of America, all owing nominal allegiance to the British Crown, very loosely bound together, often at variance, and differing widely in many ways from one another. The southern colonies had large rice, cotton, and tobacco estates worked by Negro slaves imported from Africa, while the people of the north were mainly engaged in farming and shipbuilding. The American War of Independence with Great Britain which lasted from 1775 to 1783 not only gained the colonists their independence; it also taught them the urgent necessity of union, without which their new-won freedom would not have lasted long. Those Americans, such as BENJAMIN FRANKLIN, the scientist, and ALEXANDER HAMILTON and JAMES MADISON who helped to frame the constitution of the United States, have as strong a claim to the grateful regard of their countrymen as GEORGE WASHINGTON, the great leader who became the first President, and THOMAS JEFFERSON (qq.v. Vol. V) who drew up the Declaration of Independence in 1776.

There are forty-eight states in the American Union, Arizona, the forty-eighth state, having been admitted in 1912. The government is a Federal Government, in which the powers of the central government and those of the separate states are clearly defined. Each state has a parliament of its own in which it makes laws relating to local matters and raises taxes for its own special needs; it also sends representatives to a central or national parliament. This makes laws binding on the whole nation, raises taxes for national purposes, and decides matters of the greatest importance such as the declaration of war. The American Parliament is called Congress. It sits in Washington, D.C., the capital, and has two houses, the Senate and the House of Representatives. Senators and Representatives are elected by the people—two senators for each state, and a total of 435 representatives, the numbers being based on the population of each state. The head of the government is the President, who is elected for a period of four years. There is nothing to prevent a president from being re-elected any number of times; but only one, FRANKLIN ROOSEVELT (q.v. Vol. V), who was elected four times, has been elected more than twice, and only nine others have been elected for a second term. Some of the great presidents, like Washington, ABRAHAM LINCOLN (q.v. Vol. V), and the two Roosevelts, have done much to shape the course of American history.

There has been only one serious threat to the Union—the Civil War of 1861 to 1865 between the northern and southern states. The triumph of the North made certain the continuance of the United States and the end of Negro slavery. Even while the war was being fought and afterwards, hardy pioneers were extending the boundaries of the country westward until the Pacific Coast had been reached. The sense of equality which came from common struggles against wild and ruthless Nature had a very great effect

SKY-SCRAPERS NEAR WALL STREET, THE FINANCIAL CENTRE OF NEW YORK. *American Information Service*

upon the development of American character. From these experiences the Americans learnt respect for manual skill, forthrightness of manner, open-handed hospitality, and a progressive habit of mind, all of which remain typically American characteristics. The early frontiersmen were rather scornful of education and the refinements of life; but this was a passing attitude, although it may account for the fact that American education does emphasize the practical rather more than does British. There are in the United States such institutions as beauty-culture colleges, barber colleges, and colleges which train people to be salesmen, advertising agents, and radio mechanics. The American is a great believer in education. More than 90% of the children attend public or state schools. In addition there are private schools of many types, the best of which are state inspected. State schools are co-educational and divided into twelve grades, each grade corresponding to a year in a child's life. The last four years are spent in a High School, culminating in a somewhat elaborate ceremony known as 'Commencement', when the student is presented with a graduation diploma signifying the completion of twelve years' study. After this, he may, if he chooses, enter a university, some of which are state and some privately controlled. Certain of the American universities, such as those at Harvard, Yale, Princeton, and Columbia, although young compared with the ancient universities of Europe, are recognized all over the world for their fine scholarship.

It is natural that in the greatest industrial country in the world there should be many great inventors and scientists. EDISON (q.v. Vol. V), who came from Ohio, was the inventor of the phonograph and, jointly with Eastman, another American, of motion pictures, as well as other inventions in the use of electricity. American scientists, in collaboration with British and Canadian, were the first to discover a means of using atomic energy, a discovery likely to affect civilization as profoundly as the invention of the steam-engine. Americans have played a big part in the conquest of the air: two of them, Wilbur and Orville Wright, were the first to fly in a free heavier-than-air machine. In art, literature, and music they have the vitality and enthusiasm of a young nation. Although their spoken language has many idioms and 'slangy' expressions which we find difficult to understand, they have enriched literature by the works of such writers as Washington Irving, Emerson, LONGFELLOW, Poe, WHITMAN, and MARK TWAIN (qq.v. Vol. V). Their symphony orchestras, opera-houses, theatres, museums, and libraries are all on the grand scale. America has taken the lead in the development of the cinema: more than two-thirds of the world's films are made at Hollywood in California. The Americans are also pre-eminent in outdoor activities: they excel in many forms of sport, particularly baseball, American football, athletics, lawn tennis, and boxing.

The Americans are a people who are mentally very much alive. They have always stood for the great principles of liberty and democracy, although there are among them great variations of wealth and poverty and frequent bitter struggles between capital and labour. The spirit of free enterprise, still paramount in America, though it certainly stimulates initiative, may be leading to the development of an individualism which threatens the common good, and may lead Americans to put too high a value on financial and material success. In his political relations the American sometimes shows intolerance, but in religion there is the widest toleration: everyone has a right to worship as he pleases. There are about 250 religious sects in the country, and about a quarter of a million churches. Protestants, Catholics, and Jews are the most numerous, and there are as well some religions which are of purely American origin, such as the CHRISTIAN SCIENTIST CHURCH and the MORMON religion of Utah (qq.v.). Diversity of religion is greater in the United States than in any country of the world with the exception of India.

See also Vol. III: UNITED STATES OF AMERICA.

ANCESTOR WORSHIP is a very ancient widespread religious practice, perhaps the most ancient of all. It is of many different types, ranging from simple reverence for one's family ancestors to the more elaborate worship of ancestral heroes, chieftains, and kings. Ancient as it is, ancestor worship is still practised to-day, in China and New Guinea for instance. Perhaps the reason for the importance of this form of worship in early religions is that, in a world where men felt insecure against forces which they could not control or understand, it was natural to pay respect to the powers of such outstanding human beings as kings and chief-tains—especially as the life-force in these persons was believed to continue, and become increasingly mysterious and perhaps more powerful, after death and detachment from the body. Ancestors also stand for life as a thing which goes on from age to age; and it may well be that early man, like many people to-day, felt this, believing it possible to ensure life and well-being by paying respect to and relying on those who had gone before. Worshippers of ancestors certainly feel in awe of them and wish to keep them friendly. One other thing is certain: they have no doubt that these ancestors survive. They take this for granted and their ceremonies of ancestor worship are as natural to them as conversation with their own next-door neighbours.

Here is a short account of a ceremony among the Min Chia, who live in the province of Yunnan in western China. It is carried on mainly, though not solely, by men, whereas public worship at the temple festivals of the greater gods is attended chiefly by women and girls. Every family has a domestic altar, usually a long table, placed in the principal room on the ground floor, though sometimes, if people are poor, in the store-room upstairs. On this table stand three ancestral tablets, representing the heads of the family for the last three generations, and these are flanked by vases of flowers and other ornaments, with an incense-burner in front. Sometimes there is also the image of a Buddhist saint. On the wall behind the altar are pasted red paper strips bearing the Chinese characters for Heaven and Earth, these rather shadowy powers being vaguely associated with the departed spirits. Before the morning and evening meals one of the male members of the household, usually the son of the house, comes to the altar, strikes a gong, lights a stick of incense in the burner before the tablets, and bows. He then fetches the bowls containing the morning meal, places them on the altar, again strikes the gong, and waits with downcast eyes for about a minute. Then he bows again, takes the bowls away, and the food is eaten. This simple rite is intended to link the life of the ancestors with the daily life of their descendants, and to ensure their well-being. But sometimes more elaborate ceremonies take place. During the first fortnight in August the departed spirits are supposed to come back to the old home for a short stay. The night before they are due to

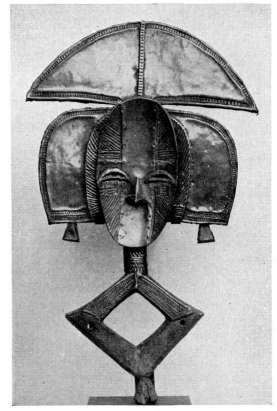

FIGURE USED FOR ANCESTOR WORSHIP IN WEST AFRICA
Wood, overlaid with bronze and copper, about 2 ft. high
British Mus.

depart again an altar is set up in the courtyard of the house, covered with red cloth, and spread with a number of dishes and six cups of rice wine. In the centre of the altar stands an incense-burner, flanked by two candles, and in front is a wood fire in a brazier. The head of the family reads from a pile of cards the names of all the family ancestors, and then hands the cards one by one to one of the children, who burns them in the brazier. When all the names have been read, the head of the family rises and bows three times to the altar, and then all the family, even to the youngest child, pass in front of the altar and bow three times with the head to the ground. The wine is then poured out on the ground and on the fire, and some pinches of the food are scattered on the ground and burned in the brazier. Finally, the family go out to the street gate and let off crackers as a farewell to the departing spirits. Everybody is extremely reverent and solemn.

ANCESTRAL FIGURE FROM NEW GUINEA
Painted wood, about 4 ft. high. *British Mus.*

In certain parts of New Guinea the tribal 'clubhouse' of the men contains curious wooden shield-like objects, each of which symbolizes an ancestor and is the object of certain ceremonies. Among the Nagas, hill-tribes of Assam, large upright stones fulfil the same end. Indeed, if a Naga were to see an English churchyard or cemetery, he would probably think that our tombstones were meant for this purpose. Here, in fact, is an example of a custom which has lasted in two widely separated parts of the world with, however, a big change in its meaning, though human attachment and affection have, no doubt, been alive in it all through the ages.

The worship of the departed is distributed widely in Africa, Asia, and among the East Indians of the Pacific. We find it very elaborately developed in China and Japan, and in the religions of ancient Greece, Egypt, and Rome. There are traces of it among the Hebrews. It is less marked among American, Australian, and Polynesian natives, but more marked among Africans, Indonesians, and Melanesians. Higher types of religion tend to lessen its importance, or to drive it underground; but it has a curious way of reasserting itself, as, for example, in certain forms of modern SPIRITUALISM (q.v.). Ideas about the soul vary and develop, of course, from one age to another, and this may well influence the amount of stress laid upon ancestor-worship and the worship of the dead in general.

See also CHINESE RELIGION.

ANCIENT CIVILIZATIONS. In recent centuries Europeans have been exploring unknown countries and meeting with peoples who were still entirely uncivilized, peoples living on wild animals and plants and with only the simplest possessions. Five thousand years ago the inhabitants of Britain were no more advanced than this, and there seems no reason why Britain should not have remained as backward as Central Africa had it not been changed by invaders and explorers who brought with them civilized ideas which had first grown up in the East, in the lands now known as Egypt and Mesopotamia. It was in the great river valleys of the Nile and the Tigris and Euphrates, valleys which careful farming could make very fertile, that the earliest-known civilizations of the world were made. It was in these valleys that men came to live together in ordered societies where all had their specialized duties, as farmer, builder, metal-worker, merchant, priest, and so forth, forming a community which could be prosperous and secure. This, roughly, is what is meant by civilization, although we also expect a civilized community to develop its arts, to produce poets and musicians, painters, sculptors, and fine craftsmen. Civilization of this sort would not have been possible had not men already taken that earlier great step forward, the development of farming. Farming, which also began in the Middle East, although not in the river valleys, enabled individuals to produce more food than their own families could eat. The extra food could be used to feed specialist workers, craftsmen, and others whose products were wanted by the community. This specialization of duties within the community is an essential part of civilization. As such specialists find it more convenient to live close together for many reasons, civilized societies commonly develop towns and cities. In fact, many of the cities which grew up in Mesopotamia and

Egypt some time before 3000 B.C. stood on the sites of older villages, the homes of simple farming communities.

It is interesting to follow this growth of civilization at a single place. Erech, on the lower Euphrates, is a good example. Had we visited it soon after its foundation we should have seen a village street lined with the small houses of peasant farmers. Returning one or two thousand years later we could have wandered in a large walled city with a population of tens of thousands and with great temple buildings that were the residence of the City Governor, an all-powerful and wealthy ruler. Erech serves well to show how civilization grew in one of its earliest centres, the rich land of the SUMERIANS (q.v.) reclaimed by human labour from the swampy country round the lower Euphrates. But such development could not remain in the hands of the Sumerians alone: it was bound to spread outwards. By 3000 B.C. civilized town life was established also in Egypt (see EGYPTIAN CIVILIZATION), and certainly before 2500 B.C. in the Indus valley of north-west India (see INDIAN CIVILIZATIONS). Civilization is like a spreading fire: from these three most ancient centres it was to extend farther and farther afield. Very largely it was carried by merchants who travelled far to find the raw materials needed by the manufacturers in their cities. These merchants were likely to establish trading posts which then grew into towns, just as we established Hong Kong and many other places in the East. From the trading towns the idea of town life and organized society would be adopted in the new country, which would perhaps in its turn send out its own merchants. It was by these means, and also by direct military conquest, that civilization radiated from Mesopotamia, Egypt, and India. One of the most natural lines for it to follow from the delta lands of Sumer was north-westward up the Tigris and Euphrates valleys. Thus we find Sumerians founding Assur, which long after was to be the capital city of the ASSYRIANS (q.v.), in the plateau country of the northern Tigris basin.

By 2500 B.C. Semitic peoples who were settled in Akkad, the country immediately north of the Delta, under their great leader Sargon conquered the Sumerians. Five hundred years later another great Semitic ruler, Hammurabi, who had his capital in the hitherto modest city of Babylon, welded together Assyria, Akkad, and Sumeria into one—the BABYLONIAN EMPIRE (q.v.), whose capital city became the richest and perhaps the most beautiful in western Asia. But before very long Assyria broke away and again became an independent state—and from that time onward for many centuries there was rivalry and frequent warfare between Assyria and Babylonia. The Assyrians, a hardy people, always more warlike than the highly civilized Babylonians, sacked Babylon at the beginning of the 7th century B.C. Fortune turned rapidly against them, however, and by the end of the same century Assyrian power had been ended by the combined armies of the Babylonians, Scyths, and Medes. It was after this success that the Medes and PERSIANS (q.v.) began their conquests, until, in the 5th century B.C., the Persian Empire included all the ancient centres of civilization from western India to Egypt. It was the Greeks who prevented the Persians from pushing even farther west, into Europe.

To return to earlier times, another region where civilization was destined quite soon to be established was that lying between the two ancient centres of Egypt and Mesopotamia, the lands forming a relatively fertile strip along the eastern margin of the Mediterranean, where in time the HEBREWS, PHOENICIANS, and SYRIANS (qq.v.) were each to have their own important history. This region, through which traffic between Egypt and Mesopotamia passed, was bound always to be a warring ground between these two great countries, sometimes one and sometimes the other gaining control. The Egyptians had early trading-posts on the coast, a famous one being at Byblos in Phoenicia which handled, among other goods, the famous cedar wood of the Lebanon. The Phoenicians themselves became among the greatest trading and seafaring peoples of ancient times. Their adventurous traders pushed as far westward as the Atlantic; they established colonies, including the famous Carthage, and they took with them the first perfected alphabet which was to be adopted by the Greeks and so become the parent of our own. The northern neighbours of the Phoenicians were another Semitic people, the HITTITES (q.v.), whose territory extended from here into the high plateau lands of Asia Minor. At the times of their greatest strength the Hittites pushed southwards, dominated the Phoenicians and other peoples of Syria and Palestine, and even attacked Egypt.

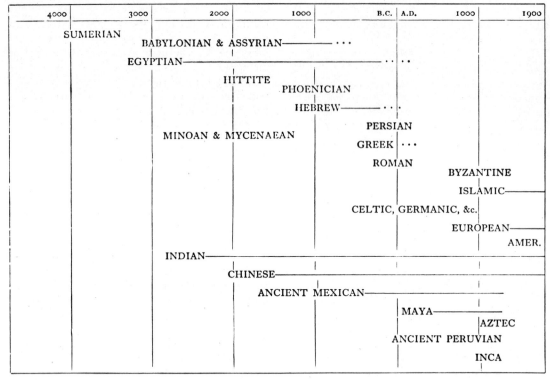

4000	3000	2000	1000	B.C.	A.D.	1000	1900

SUMERIAN

BABYLONIAN & ASSYRIAN———— · · ·

EGYPTIAN————————————————————— · · · ·

HITTITE

PHOENICIAN

HEBREW———— · · ·

MINOAN & MYCENAEAN

PERSIAN

GREEK · · ·

ROMAN

BYZANTINE

ISLAMIC————

CELTIC, GERMANIC, &c.

EUROPEAN————

AMER.

INDIAN————

CHINESE————

ANCIENT MEXICAN————

MAYA————

AZTEC

ANCIENT PERUVIAN

INCA

TIME CHART

This chart shows only approximately when the chief civilizations of the world flourished, for it is often impossible to date the beginning and end of a civilization accurately

So by 2000 B.C. there were civilized peoples living all round the eastern end of the Mediterranean, from Egypt to Asia Minor, all more or less in touch and affecting one another both by warfare and trade. But already, long before this, a first foothold of civilization had been established in Europe, at a time when the western part of the continent, including Britain, was still in the possession of the primitive hunting tribes of the Stone Age. This first centre of European civilization was Crete, a natural stepping-stone between the eastern Mediterranean and Europe. Simple peasant communities were established in Crete, on the neighbouring coasts of Asia Minor, in the islands of the Aegean, and on the mainland of Greece and Macedonia by about 3000 B.C.; but when about that time Upper and Lower Egypt were joined together under the earliest Pharaohs, it seems that refugees from Egypt settled in Crete and helped to develop a high civilization there. This MINOAN CIVILIZATION (q.v.) of Crete was in many ways a very brilliant one, as is well shown by the famous palace of Knossos. The island became the centre of a seafaring civilization which naturally soon spread to the islands and shores of the Aegean. It was carried to the mainland of Greece, where the later civilization is known as MYCENAEAN (q.v.) after the great city of Mycenae, established by Cretan colonists. About 2000 B.C. northern invaders began to enter Greece and the Aegean—uncivilized peoples coming from the heart of the European continent and probably speaking an Indo-European language from which the Greek tongue grew. They spread very gradually through Greece and the Aegean lands, mingling with the old Mycenaean peoples and adopting many of their ideas; it was from this mixture of northern invaders and Mycenaeans that the great GREEK CIVILIZATION (q.v.) was to develop a thousand years later.

At about the time when a high civilization was developing in Crete and Greece, with city life, great palaces, and wealthy kings, the basic ideas on which all civilization rests were beginning to spread towards western and northern Europe, where hunting tribes were still living in the Stone Age. These ideas were, of course,

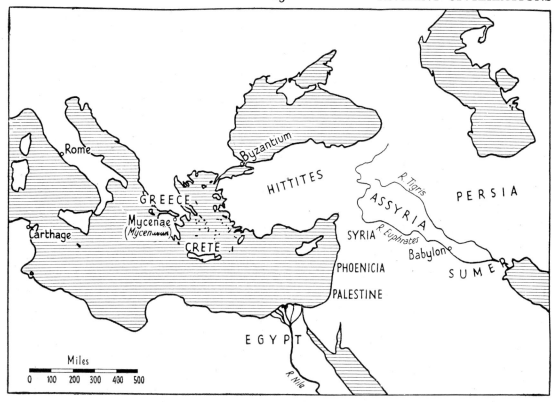

THE ANCIENT CIVILIZATIONS OF EUROPE AND THE NEAR EAST
This map shows the approximate positions of the centres of the chief civilizations, regardless of the periods at which they flourished

those concerned with farming, knowledge of which was gradually carried along the shores of the Mediterranean and Atlantic and along the Danube valley until at last it reached Britain in about 2500 B.C. and Scandinavia a little later.

But although agriculture was now practised all over Europe, it still took an immensely long time for any of the more advanced elements of the Eastern civilizations to follow. Indeed, it was left to the Greeks and Romans to introduce civilized life to western Europe. Greek traders, establishing colonial cities all along the Mediterranean, greatly influenced all the countries with which they made contact. The Etruscans, who were establishing their own unusual civilization in northern Italy, owed much to them, and the Etruscans in turn played an important part in the foundation of the ROMAN state (q.v.) in the 7th and 6th centuries B.C. Greek ideas, too, spreading both from their own trading cities and by way of Italy, helped to develop the still-barbarous but in many ways splendid life of the CELTS (q.v.). Civilization had come slowly to

the West; yet it was from the West, not from the East, that fresh waves of explorers, traders, and colonists were to set out to carry it to America, to Africa, and to the Pacific. So it is that, during recent centuries, ideas and ways of life which originated by the Tigris, Euphrates, and Nile have been spread throughout the entire planet.

When the Spaniards invaded South and Central America in the 16th century they discovered that there already existed well-advanced civilizations which had been developing independently of the civilizations of the Old World. The history of ANCIENT MEXICO (q.v.), though probably not as old as that of Mesopotamia or Egypt, is now thought to date back to many centuries before Christ. That in ANCIENT PERU (q.v.) is not quite so old, but also goes back to before Christ. These were followed up by the great civilizations of the MAYA, the AZTECS, and the INCAS (qq.v.). It is interesting to note that, advanced as these people were in many directions—for instance, in social organization, in mathematical calculations, and in many forms of art—they were, even by the 15th century A.D., without some inventions known in the East for thousands of years. Thus the wheel was not known anywhere in America until the Europeans came; and the Incas had no form of writing.

In the Far East, in China, another independent civilization grew up in another river valley, the Yellow River or Hwang-ho in north China. CHINESE CIVILIZATION (q.v.) is not so old as that of Mesopotamia or Egypt; but it is the oldest civilization still continuing to-day, and it has lasted, with only temporary breaks, for some 4000 years or more.

See also ARCHAEOLOGY.

ANDAMAN ISLANDERS. The earliest account we have of the Negritoes of the Andaman Islands in the Bay of Bengal comes from some Arab travellers about A.D. 870. They reported that the islanders were black, with woolly hair and most terrifying expressions, that they were quite naked, had feet almost a span long, and

NATIVE OF THE ANDAMAN ISLANDS USING A STONE ADZE
British Mus.

that they ate human flesh quite raw. Marco Polo some 400 years later gave an equally bad report, describing them as 'most brutish and savage' with heads, eyes, and teeth resembling dogs. 'Their dispositions are cruel and every person not of their own nation that they can lay hands on they kill and eat.' It is no wonder that the islands were feared and avoided.

Their evil reputation is, however, quite undeserved. They are a pygmy people, the men usually not much over $4\frac{1}{2}$ feet. Their hair is black and frizzy and seldom more than 2 to 3 inches long, and their skin is very black, like a well-polished black-leaded stove. They have slender bodies and small hands and feet. They are not naturally quarrelsome, and their anger soon cools. Husbands and wives show much devotion to each other and to their children, who are generally given whatever they want, however unsuitable.

They live in small bands, spend much of their time in games and sports, and they have a passion for dancing. Dances are held on all ceremonial occasions, such as the beginning of a new season, a marriage, or the end of mourning, as well as at any time of general rejoicing. They dance and sing for hours by moonlight or by the blaze of the camp fires to the accompaniment of beating on a curved piece of wood.

Food is their chief interest in life, and as they have no cultivated crops they depend on hunting, fishing, and collecting forest produce. They collect shell-fish round the coast, they spear turtles and shoot fish with bows and arrows, and they hunt game, especially pigs, in the forest. The men make excellent canoes from hollowed-out tree trunks, some of them up to 30 feet long.

In their hot moist climate, where the thermometer seldom drops below 80° F., there is no need for clothes, but the Andamanese wear such a wealth of circlets, garters, bracelets, waistbands, necklaces and strings of shells and bones that they cannot be called naked. On special occasions they are almost covered with strips of palm-leaves, and they also paint their bodies with elaborate patterns on ceremonial occasions.

Until the coming of Europeans there was no knowledge of iron in the islands, and shell was used instead. The axe or adze had a shell blade, spears and arrows had shell tips, and knives were of sharpened bamboo. The Andamanese had great difficulty in making fire; so they had to keep their fires always burning and, when travelling, they carried a smouldering torch from one camp to another.

Their huts are quickly made from poles and thatched with palm-leaves. They are usually open at the sides, but can keep out the heaviest rains. Several of these huts in a circle round a central dancing-ground form the village. But there is no permanent settlement, as the whole community moves from camping-ground to camping-ground according to the season and the food supplies.

The Andamanese have no chiefs, but as with most hunting groups, whoever has most experience acts as leader. Beyond this all are free and equal, the only restraint being public opinion. They worship the spirits, some good and some bad, of the sun, moon, winds, rocks, and creatures of the forest who, as they believe, were once men and women (*see* ANIMISM). There are no priests, but some men know more about the spirits than ordinary folk, and these are respected and feared, being credited with ability to foretell the future, to cure illnesses, and to control the weather.

See also PYGMIES.
See also Vol. III: ANDAMAN ISLANDS.

THE ARCHANGEL RAPHAEL LEADING TOBIAS ON HIS JOURNEY
Italian Painting, 15th century, School of Verocchio. *National Gal., London*

ANGEL. The word used in the Bible for a divine messenger sent by God to minister to human beings on earth. Some of these messengers may have been originally the old gods and spirits connected with the ancient shrines and sanctuaries of Palestine who had become degraded into the servants of Jehovah, the god of Israel, when He alone was worshipped as the Lord of the land, jealously demanding the sole allegiance of His people. But so high and exalted was the Holy One of Israel that He gathered round Him an increasingly large 'court', like a powerful eastern monarch, composed of the 'cherubim', represented with outspread wings, the 'seraphim' or flying serpents with flaming wings, and the archangels, such as Gabriel, Michael, Raphael, Phanuel, and Uriel, who, as His princes, continually await God's commands. Thus, 'all the host of heaven stood by Him on His right hand and on His left'.

There were also angels who presided over the workings of nature, such as the motions of the stars, the rain, and the hail. Others looked after the different nations, while every human being had his own particular guardian or helper, just as in Persia each individual was assigned a 'double', or *fravashi*, at birth. There were, again, angels who recorded the deeds of men, keeping an account of everything said and done by each individual. Finally, there was the angel of death who sooner or later was destined to visit everybody, good and bad alike, and announce that their last hour had come.

In the New Testament we find much the same beliefs. It was the archangel Gabriel, the 'mighty man of God', who is said to have been sent to Zacharias, the father of John the Baptist, and to Mary the mother of Jesus, to explain to them how God was going to visit and redeem the world. When the long-expected Messiah

THE SEVEN ANGELS OF THE APOCALYPSE

Illumination from a 13th-century Apocalypse. *Bodleian Library*

was born at Bethlehem, the glad tidings were proclaimed to the shepherds by a 'heavenly host'. At the end of the period of temptation in the desert, and after the great struggle in the garden of Gethsemane, an angel ministered to Jesus, and both His resurrection and ascension were declared by angelic messengers. Apart from these special occasions, every child is said to have a guardian helper watching over him, as has every member of the Church. The apostles we are told, were delivered from prison by an angel, and by the same heavenly messengers Philip was shown where to go and St. Paul what to do when he was shipwrecked. Therefore, like the Jews, the Christians thought that they were guided and helped by the ministry of angels and that angels would carry their prayers to God, just as at the last they would bear their souls to Paradise and separate the wheat from the tares (i.e. the righteous from the wicked) when they reaped the harvest of the world on the Day of Judgement.

As the Church spread from Palestine into eastern Europe the angels took the place of the old pagan gods and spirits. Villages, towns, and countries, as well as individuals, were assigned guardians to look after them and protect them from the powers of evil. So numerous, in fact, became the heavenly host that it was divided into ranks and offices on much the same plan as were the officials of the Roman Empire. In all there were nine 'choirs', consisting of Angels, Archangels, Virtues, Powers, Principalities, Dominions, Thrones, Cherubim, and Seraphim. But although prayers sometimes were addressed to them, they were never worshipped as gods. This was strictly forbidden, and some of the early Christian writers thought it unwise to offer prayers to them at all lest they should be confused with the pagan gods they had replaced.

There has been a good deal of discussion about the nature, shape, and characteristics of angels. Some have claimed that they were invisible spirits without any bodily form; others, that they have a thin rather ghost-like or fiery appearance. But all are agreed that they are created beings like man, and since some of them are said to have fallen away from God before the world was made, it has been generally supposed that they are capable of sinning and therefore must have free will. Their life and work consist wholly and solely in serving God in their several ways, but, as John of Damascus very wisely declared in summing up his description of an angel, 'the form and character of its substance God alone knows who created it'. It is perhaps a pity that later writers and thinkers were not content to leave it at that, since there is no way of finding out exactly what an angel is like. But in the Middle Ages much time was spent on speculations which really did not throw any light on the problem. After the Reformation in northern Europe, angels were just taken for granted; but except in the Roman Catholic Church no prayers were made to them or asked from them; so that they have tended to fall into the background, having lost their original purpose as divine messengers. Nevertheless, the doctrine of angels is a reasonable belief if creation is really the work of God Who is spirit, and Who therefore may be expected to employ spiritual agents to do His will and work in the world He has made.

Besides Jews and Christians, the third community who recognize the existence of angels are the Moslems (*see* ISLAM). When the prophet Mohammed in the 8th century A.D. began his movement in Arabia, the Arabs were acquainted with a great company of inferior spirits. These he took over and, borrowing a good many of his ideas from Jewish and Christian sources, he made the good spirits the servants of God (Allah), as angels, and the bad spirits the servants of Satan, as demons. Both, he taught, were formed from one single substance and were given the power of reason, life, and speech. The angels neither eat nor drink and are without sex, their function being to act as the bodyguard of God, and obey His commands fully. Most of their time is spent in repeating the sacred name 'Allah'; but whatever they do is done to His glory. Chief among them are the four throne-bearers, the first of whom prays for all true believers, the second for tame animals, the third for birds, and the fourth for wild beasts. Then come the cherubim who day and night do nothing but repeat the words 'glory to Allah' and live in a particular part of the sky.

Of the four Archangels—Michael, Gabriel, Azra'il, and Israf'il—Michael carried the revelation recorded in the Koran to Mohammed, and has since been responsible for providing food for the body and knowledge for the mind, while his assistants watch over the world for good, and control the forces of nature. His form, however, is so wonderful that it is known only to Allah. Azra'il is the angel of death. So terrible is his appearance that, when the rest of the company first saw him, they fainted and did not recover consciousness for a thousand years. It is he who carries away the souls of men and delivers them either to the 'angels of compassion', or to the 'angels of punishment', according to whether the dying person is a believer or an unbeliever. Israf'il, on the other hand, puts the souls into the body at birth, and he will blow the trumpet at the Last Day and at the general resurrection. At the gate of Paradise an angel called Ridwan is stationed and another terrible being, known as Malik, guards hell.

Every Moslem is protected from evil spirits (jinn) by four angels, two guarding him by day and another two by night. These, it is thought, change places at sunrise and sunset, and keep a record of his doings. The Jinn were created 2,000 years before Adam, but sinned against God and were degraded from their high estate. The greatest among them was Iblis (*see* SATAN),

who was formed of smokeless fire, and has control over the rest of the fallen angels. But although angels play such a prominent part in Mohammedan belief, they are generally thought to be inferior to human believers as they do not share in the delights of Paradise.

See also HEAVEN.

ANGLICAN CHURCH, *see* CHURCH OF ENGLAND.

ANGLO-CATHOLICS, *see* CHURCH OF ENGLAND.

ANGLO-SAXONS, *see* BRITISH PEOPLES.

ANIMISM. This word was originally used to describe the belief that the development of all living things arises from more than merely material causes—that there is, in fact, such a thing as soul or spirit (Latin: *anima*). To this extent, then, all Christians or people of any religion may be called animists; so, too, may anyone who believes in ghosts. But the word has more recently been used in a special sense to describe a primitive form of religion which peoples the world with countless spirits—varying, of course, in size and importance. All sorts of visible objects, and not merely human beings and animals, are thought of as alive: not only is there a great spirit in the sun and in the moon, but there is a smaller one in the tree at your door, and another in the stream that trickles busily beside the road. Not everything is, in practice, believed to be animated by a spirit: many things, such as a bit of flint, a club or spear, are not treated as containing individual spirits in ordinary circumstances. But on occasions when such objects are used in actions beyond man's ordinary power—when, for instance, the spear strikes powerfully from a long distance—then the object is thought of as being animated by a spirit.

One form of animism, known as fetishism or *juju*, is strongly developed in West Africa. In South Nigeria, for example, there are believed to be *jujus* in material objects such as implements, in lakes, rivers, and springs, in the farmland, house, and hearth, and also in specially made objects (fetishes), like the small-pox *juju*, which are worshipped because the spirit is supposed to inhabit them. The *juju* is believed to cause the good or ill fortune connected with the

A WEST AFRICAN FETISH

A nail is stuck into the figure to mark each time a petition is made to the spirit that inhabits it. *British Mus.*

object; and special ceremonies must be used to appeal to its goodwill.

The Greeks believed in little spirits that swarmed like midges or bacteria; and the Japanese have any number of them—indeed, a famous convert to Christianity, Uchimura, exclaimed: 'One God, not ten million, that *is* joyful news.' India knows them by the score as *devatas* or godlings, and a large part of the Hinduism of the village populations has been described as 'spirit scaring and spirit squaring'.

It has been argued that there is another primitive religion older than animism. This has therefore been called pre-animism or animatism. It has also been called dynamism, because it is a belief in a vague force, rather like electricity, which inhabits all sorts of things, and makes them behave as they do. This force is reverenced wherever it occurs. It is certainly the case that in many different parts of the world such a force is believed in, though it is called by a number of different names, *mana* in Polynesia, *orenda* or *wakonda* among some American Indians, in West Africa *orisha*, in Madagascar *andriamanitra*, and perhaps, in Latin, *numen*. But we have no direct evidence as to whether man in the earliest stage of his religious beliefs did in fact develop what we call an 'abstract' idea or use a 'general' term such as a *force*, or *power*, or *principle*. Early man probably thought rather as a child thinks: a child starts with a single 'concrete' thing, like 'my daddy', 'my doll', 'my shoes', and does not as easily grasp the meaning of such words as 'parenthood', or 'mechanism', or 'footgear'. So it may well be that in the beginning man thought of the power or *mana* in his own particular spear-thrower, or in the bull he owned, or in the volcano just above his village, and only came very much later to think of *power-in-general*. The real question is, did he think of the *mana* or power in his spear-thrower as a living person, or simply as a power? If the former, then he was an animist. If the latter, then he was a dynamist.

APE MAN, *see* FOSSIL MAN.

APHRODITE, *see* GODS OF GREECE AND ROME.

APOCRYPHA, *see* BIBLE; SACRED BOOKS, Section 6.

APOLLO, *see* GODS OF GREECE AND ROME.

ARABS. The term 'Arab' is applied firstly to the inhabitants of the Arabian Peninsula, and secondly to people, wherever they live, who speak Arabic and claim descent from the Arab conquerors of North Africa, Syria, and Mesopotamia.

The Arabs are often spoken of as members of the Semitic race; but they are, even those in

Arabia, of mixed origin, and it is better to use the term 'Semitic' only for the group of languages to which Arabic belongs (*see* SEMITIC LANGUAGES, Vol. IV). This group includes Hebrew, Syriac, and Aramaic, the last being the language of Babylonia which was adopted by the Jews in place of Hebrew during the captivity. It is probable that before the time of Mohammed the Arabic language was confined to central and southern Arabia; but as a result of the Moslem conquests in the 7th century A.D. it became the language of Syria (including Palestine), Mesopotamia (now called Iraq), Egypt, and the North African coast as far as Morocco. It spread later to parts of the northern Sudan (Sudan means the country of the blacks).

The great majority of the people of these countries are Moslem (*see* ISLAM); but in Egypt there are many Christian Arabs known as COPTS (q.v.), a branch of the Orthodox Eastern Church, and in the Lebanon there is a large body of Maronites who acknowledge the authority of the Pope, though their clergy are married. The many Jews of these countries also speak Arabic and are very much like the Arabs in dress and customs; they are not, however, usually regarded as Arabs. There are also many sects which, though Moslem in name, are outside orthodox Islam. The best known of these are the Druzes who live in the Lebanon and in part of Syria (*see* SYRIANS).

The great Arab conquests of the 7th century began with the rise of the faith of Islam under the leadership of MOHAMMED (q.v. Vol. V). At this time there was no power in Europe strong enough to withstand the amazing outburst of vitality and energy among the Arab people. The Khalifas (or Caliphs) who followed Mohammed were capable military leaders and rulers, and according to the standards of the day were tolerant as conquerors. The Arabs, in spite of continual fighting, increased enormously in numbers, taking the women of those they had killed, and the children of these captives were reckoned as pure-bred Arabs. They were in this way able to keep in the field large armies. In the west they pushed on to the Straits of Gibraltar and in A.D. 709 crossed into Spain (*see* MOORS). In the east they gradually overran Persia, much of central Asia, and western India.

As well as military conquests the Arabs also carried with them to the lands they overran their religious faith and their culture. At a time

AN ARAB WOMAN CARRYING WATER
Many women still wear veils in public. *Vincent Brennan*

when art and learning were at a low ebb in Europe, the Arabs were directing their great vigour and zeal to science, literature, and art, as well as fighting. They absorbed the culture of Greece and Persia and made it their own, and, when Christian Europe was hardly emerging from the gloom and barbarism of the Dark Ages, the Arab cities of Bagdad (in Iraq), Cairo (in Egypt), and Cordova (in Spain) were centres of a brilliant civilization.

During the 7th and 8th centuries, after periods of civil war, the centre of Arab power was moved first to Damascus and then to Bagdad (of *Arabian Nights* fame). In course of time Persian and Turkish officials began to replace Arabs; and as the Turks became more and more powerful, the Khalifas declined into being little more than their tools, until in 1258, when Mongolian hordes from central Asia invaded Persia and sacked Bagdad, the last of them was murdered. From then until 1918, after the First World War, the eastern Arab countries were either in fact or in name part of the Turkish Empire, although Egypt enjoyed a considerable degree

ARAB TOWNSMEN IN THE BAZAAR AT PORT SAID
Paul Popper

Formerly the tarboosh or fez was the usual head-dress; but since the fall of the Turkish Empire various forms of Arab headgear have become fashionable. It is very rare for a townsman to have more than one wife. One difference between an Arab and a European town is that in the former all the makers and sellers of a particular class of goods live in the same street or quarter, as they used to do in London in the Middle Ages.

The towns of central and southern Arabia are much less Europeanized. It is from the towns of central Arabia, and not from the desert, that the fanatical Wahhabis come. Under the leadership of King Ibn Sa'ud they are now the chief power in Arabia proper. The towns of the Hadramaut in south Arabia are remarkable because they have maintained a thousand-year-old trading connexion with Malaya and the East Indies and have derived much wealth from there.

The great majority of the Arabs, however, are peasants (*fellahin*). They are often confused with the Bedouin, whom they resemble in many ways. They dress very much like the Bedouin, and their women are unveiled. Mostly illiterate, they are organized in tribes and observe tribal law in connexion with blood feuds and so on. But between the peasants and the Bedouin there is a great gulf fixed, each usually regarding the other with hatred and contempt. The peasants live in villages. Their sheikhs are landowners, often employing many ploughmen; but the majority of the peasants are smallholders, who scratch a bare living by toiling from dawn to dusk on their holdings, which average about 25 acres. In Egypt many crops, particularly cotton and sugar-cane, are grown by means of irrigation; but over most of the Arab world the crops depend on the rain. The chief crops grown are wheat and barley; but in many parts there are also olives and vines.

The peasants own many camels which they use entirely for transport, never riding them. They rarely breed these themselves, but buy them from the Bedouin. The sheikhs ride thoroughbred mares, of which they are very proud. The peasants ride donkeys. All ploughing is done with oxen, as it was in England up to about 200 years ago, and the ploughs do not turn the soil over, but merely push through it to break it up. The corn is brought into the villages on camels and piled on the threshing-floors. It is then, in many parts, threshed by means of

of freedom after Mohammed Ali founded the reigning dynasty in 1805.

After 1918 the Arabs were freed from Turkish domination, and a number of separate states were established, either under the protection of, or in alliance with, Britain or France. The Arabs are firmly convinced that the Arab countries are destined to be united once more, and the work of King Ibn Sa'ud of Sa'udi Arabia is directed towards this end. In 1945 the Arab League was founded. It consists of Egypt, Iraq, Sa'udi Arabia, the Yemen, Syria, the Lebanon, and Transjordan. It has its headquarters in Cairo and is intended to enable the Arab states to take common action in matters affecting their interests.

The modern Arabs are divided into three main classes—the townsmen, the peasants, and the BEDOUIN (q.v.). We hear much more of the Bedouin than is warranted by either their numbers or importance. They never intermarry with either the townsmen or the peasants. The townsmen are much the same from Tangier to Basra. They are traders and craftsmen, clerks and government officials. As a rule they can read and write, and wear European clothes.

sledges. These, which are studded with spikes, are drawn by donkeys and driven round and round the threshing-floors by small boys. The corn is then separated from the chaff by winnowing. The peasants also own some cattle and sheep, which, apart from the plough-oxen, are usually put in charge of herdsmen belonging to the smaller and poorer Bedouin tribes.

Unlike the townsmen, the richer peasants often marry up to four wives. These are fully employed in attending to the wants of their large households and the guests whom they often entertain. All rich Arabs keep open house and, though often extremely grasping in money matters, like to have a reputation for hospitality.

See also EGYPTIANS; IRAQI; MOORS; SYRIANS.
See also Vol. III: ARABIA; EGYPT; IRAQ; PALESTINE; SYRIA; and Vol. IV: ARABIC LANGUAGE.

ARCHAEOLOGY. An encyclopaedia published only a little more than a hundred years ago would have contained almost no information about the history of western Europe before the Romans or of any of Europe before the Greeks. Facts about ancient Europe would have been vague, and about other early civilizations of the East even vaguer. At that time little could have been published because little had been discovered. History depended upon written documents and upon documents written in a language which scholars could read: neither Egyptian hieroglyphic writing nor Sumerian and Babylonian cuneiform had as yet been deciphered. As for human history before the beginnings of civilization, nothing at all was understood, and most people still believed in the biblical story of the creation—which was thought to have taken place only a few thousand years before.

To-day it is possible to give in some detail about six thousand years of history in Europe and the East and to write a generally reliable account of human evolution going back some half-million years (see EVOLUTION). This extraordinary increase in the knowledge of our own development is largely due to archaeological discovery. It has been achieved partly by the laborious puzzling-out of ancient scripts and languages, particularly those of Egypt, Sumeria, and Babylonia. Egyptian hieroglyphs were first fully translated about 1820; Sumerian and other languages written in cuneiform began to be read only in 1837 (see WRITING, HISTORY OF, Vol. IV).

This patient deciphering of their writings has, of course, enormously increased our knowledge of the ancient civilizations (see ANCIENT CIVILIZATIONS); but more remarkable still is the amount which archaeologists have learnt about the past without the help of any writing.

Not only have archaeologists found out far more about the old civilizations than their writings have to tell; they have also traced history of which there is no written account at all (see PREHISTORIC MAN). This, the story of man before written records, is usually called prehistory, and it must not be forgotten that this 'before' may mean quite different dates in different areas. For instance, the Britons left no written records before Caesar's expeditions in the middle of the first century B.C.; but in the East writing goes back to 4000 B.C. Beyond that point of time there was no writing anywhere in the world; men had not invented it, and so our knowledge must depend entirely upon archaeology.

How in fact does an archaeologist find out about happenings which have been completely forgotten for thousands or even tens of thousands of years? The simple answer is that he studies the things that men made with their hands— and often such things tell more of the truth about people than anything that could have been written down. Supposing that an observant person were to visit the house of complete strangers at some time when no one was at home. By examining all their possessions he would be able to learn an immense amount about the family, its tastes, habits, and activities. In just the same way, if he examined a whole village which had been abandoned by its inhabitants, he would learn much about the character of the place as a whole, as well as about the different households and all the various ways in which they earned their living. This is what an archaeologist is always doing—exploring places which have been deserted, and finding out all that he can about the people who once lived there. But he usually explores places so long deserted that their remains have become buried in rubbish and soil, and all this must be dug away before he can begin his observations. Often, too, only relics made of hard, durable materials remain for him to uncover, all the other possessions of early men, things of wood or leather or cloth, having long since rotted away. But occasionally even these may be

ARCHAEOLOGISTS AT WORK

The digging must be done with the greatest care so that no evidence of past history shall be overlooked. *Picture Post*

preserved—for instance, in the dry air of Egypt perishable things can survive for thousands of years. A famous example was the tomb of Tutankhamen, where furniture, clothes, and delicate ornaments had lain undecayed since 1350 B.C.

At the other extreme, very damp conditions turn out to be good for preservation—as is shown by waterlogged burials in Schleswig and Jutland, where bodies were found still wearing their woollen clothes, hats, shoes, and even in one instance a hair-net. These people had lived in the Bronze Age, over 3,000 years ago. Britain does not generally offer such favourable conditions, but at the Glastonbury and Mere lake villages in Somerset the excavators found woodwork wonderfully well preserved—palings and hurdles, the foundations of huts, carts, boats, and many utensils, as well as fragments of cloth and the remains of grain and fruits which the villagers had intended to eat (*see* LAKE DWELLINGS).

Even without these exceptional conditions it is possible to find out a great deal about the people of the past by carefully uncovering the places where they lived or buried their dead, and examining their surviving possessions of stone, bone, metal, and pottery. For the very remote past, too, when more primitive human types were in existence, some of the most important discoveries are of the fossilized remains of the men themselves, for they can tell us something of the appearance of most distant ancestors (*see* FOSSIL MAN). But this straightforward study of early men and things which they made is not enough if you want to learn something about the general history of their time, of those great events and changes which took place in prehistoric ages as surely as they do to-day. Here the archaeologist has to deal with time, with the passing of the years, and this he does very largely by the study of stratification. Anyone poking among the rubbish in the cellar of an old house would expect to find the oldest relics at the bottom—perhaps an Elizabethan coin—and the most modern right on top, probably with some Georgian and Victorian oddments in between. The principle of stratification is that in any normal series of deposits the oldest is at the bottom and the most recent on top; and, simple though it is, it has been the most important means by which the archaeologist has been able to piece together our earliest history. It can be applied equally to all kinds of sites. In ancient cities, like Troy, Ur, or Nineveh, as houses crumbled or were destroyed, others were built on top of them, until a raised mound or 'tell' was formed (even in London, the Roman road level is many feet below that of the modern city). In a cave the excavator, digging down through the deposits which have formed on the cave floor, may find on the top the litter of recent picnic parties, and then perhaps a layer with Roman remains before he gets down to several distinct layers or 'strata' belonging to successive periods of the Stone Age. By keeping apart the finds from the different levels the archaeologist can study the types of object or of building which were in use at each period and learn to distinguish between them.

Although there are no recorded names for the different periods, archaeology has invented titles which serve as convenient labels. Once the things characteristic of each period have been identified in this way it becomes possible to recognize them wherever they are found and to know that a particular people have been living there at a particular period. By marking these find-places on a map it may be possible to track the movements of that people. To take an example within historic times, archaeologists have observed that the first Anglo-Saxon invaders to settle in this country wore a certain simple type of brooch; at a later date such brooches were more elaborate in design. By mapping all the finds of simple brooches it has been possible to show just where the earliest Anglo-Saxon settlements were, while the more elaborate type show where they spread later. Exactly the same thing can be done for earlier invasions of Britain by peoples whose names and existence have been forgotten.

While stratification makes it easy to know whether any one people is older or more recent than another, it is difficult in western Europe to fix precise dates to prehistoric events. Sometimes, however, it is possible to find links with

SILVER BOWL FOUND IN THE SUTTON HOO BURIAL SHIP
Diameter 15 in. *British Mus.*

the Mediterranean and the East, where writing was already in use and dates recorded. Thus, certain Egyptian beads known to date from 1500 to 1300 B.C. are found in graves of the English Bronze Age; while, on the other hand, a curious type of gold and amber pendant, very like one known from the earlier Bronze Age in England, has been discovered at Knossos in Crete where it can be dated to about 1600 B.C. Connexions such as these give the archaeologist a few fixed points which help him roughly to estimate the age of the various periods in prehistoric Europe.

So far archaeological discovery has been discussed only as a scientific method, a way of reconstructing the past; for this purpose pieces of broken pot and the like may be of the greatest importance as evidence. But there is also, of course, another more adventurous, treasure-seeking side. Lovely or valuable finds may sometimes be made quite by chance, as, for example, the superb Celtic helmet and shield which were dredged up from the bottom of the Thames, or the British gold coins which a boy found in a hollow flint he was using as a ball. Or sometimes such discoveries may be made unexpectedly during an excavation, as was the case with the riches of the Sutton Hoo Saxon ship burial. Naturally, this treasure-seeking side of archaeology has far greater opportunity in the ancient centres of civilization than it has in western Europe. There almost every day the excavator may hope to find some lovely object, while occasionally really tremendous discoveries are made, such as the tomb of Tutankhamen (*see* EGYPTIAN CIVILIZATION), the royal graves at MYCENAE (q.v.), and the treasures of Ur of the Chaldees (*see* SUMERIAN CIVILIZATION). Finds like these add not only to our knowledge, but also to the priceless artistic possessions of the world. Yet greatly though they add to the enjoyment of archaeology, the first aim of the subject must always be, not to hunt treasures, but to find out more about human history. For this purpose research workers all over the world, studying the remains of the past—often no more than scraps of stone, bone, pottery, or metal, valueless in themselves—are slowly fitting together the whole story of man from his most savage beginnings. The facts of human development, though as mysterious and wonderful as ever, are no longer quite unknown.

See also FOSSIL MAN.

ARGENTINES. The Argentine Republic is the largest and richest of the Spanish American republics, and it rivals Brazil for the leadership of South America. It is the most European in character of all the South American states except Uruguay. Its population is almost entirely of European origin, of which fact the Argentines are particularly proud. The Indians are few in number and are slowly getting fewer.

The great estuary of the Rio de la Plata was discovered by the Spaniards in 1515. In 1536 they built there the city of Buenos Aires, or 'the Port of St. Mary of the Good Airs', which became the capital of the region. But for two hundred years the whole vast expanse of Spanish South America was ruled from Peru, and it was only in the 18th century that the King of Spain appointed a separate viceroy for the Rio de la Plata. In those days Argentine was the least accessible of the Spanish colonies because the main Spanish line of communication ran across the Atlantic to the isthmus of Panama and from there down to the Pacific coast to Peru, instead of round the bulge of Brazil into the South Atlantic. For this reason the Spanish–American War of Independence began later in Argentina than in the more northern countries.

The War of Independence (1807–26) was really an offshoot of the Napoleonic Wars in Europe. When Napoleon conquered Spain in 1808 the Spanish colonies had the chance to gain their freedom and independence, like the United States in North America thirty years before. The Argentine Declaration of Independence was in 1816. The leader in Buenos Aires was San Martin (1778–1850), a Spanish officer and a fine soldier. He became the Liberator of the southern half of the continent, as BOLIVAR (q.v. Vol. V) was the liberator of the northern, and freed all Spanish America up to Peru from Spanish rule. But the Argentines also have a debt of gratitude to the great English minister, Canning, who recognized the independence of the young Spanish-American republics and protected them from being reconquered by Spain. There is a statue of Canning in Buenos Aires in recognition of this.

It was some time after the winning of its independence that the Argentine Republic found peace and stability. For ten years there were disorder and civil war followed by twenty years of dictatorship under Rosas, who destroyed all opposition and united the country by tyranny and force. But in 1853 the Argentines adopted a constitution very similar to that of the United States, and the peaceful development of the Republic began.

The growth and prosperity of Argentina has always depended on the large treeless plains called pampas; but four things were needed to make the pampas fully productive: railways, immigrants, barbed wire, and refrigeration. Railways solved the problem of communications. The pampas are a paradise for railway-makers —the lines can be built there for hundreds of miles with scarcely a curve or a gradient —and a thick railway network grew up, converging on Buenos Aires. Immigrants solved the problem of Argentina's very small population. In the past hundred years great numbers of settlers have flocked from Europe to Argentina as to North America. The most numerous have been Italians, Spaniards, and Poles, but there have been many others—so that Argentina has become a 'melting-pot of nations' no less than the United States. Wire-fencing solved the problem of dividing up the great expanse of the pampas, where there are no natural boundaries, into separate farms and ranches. And the invention of the refrigerator allowed frozen meat to be exported all over the world.

Originally it was sheep-farming that was the chief source of Argentine wealth. This was

GAUCHOS ROUNDING UP HORSES
The horses are caught with lassoes and then tied to a post. *Dorien Leigh*

followed by cattle-raising and beef-production; frozen meat was first exported in 1877. About the beginning of the 20th century, however, wheat became more important than meat. Of recent years Argentina has done much to develop her industries, but she still remains essentially an agricultural country.

The typical Argentino of the pampa used to be the gaucho or cowboy, a wild figure carrying a lasso and a *boleadoras*, an Indian weapon of leather and stones with which he caught horses and other animals by entangling their legs. Argentine music has been much influenced by gaucho folk-songs, haunting and melancholy, expressing the solitude of the wide open spaces; and the gaucho has also played a romantic part in Argentine literature. Perhaps the greatest of Argentine poems is *Martin Fierro*, by José Hernandez, which has a gaucho for its hero, and describes the feelings of the gauchos as their traditional pastoral way of life disappears before the advance of immigration and industrialism. For, like the American cowboy, the gaucho has

almost died out. The herding of cattle to-day is more likely to be done in a motor-car than on horseback.

Ever since the days of Canning, Argentina has had close relations with Britain. (Indeed, the distance by sea from Buenos Aires to Liverpool is very little farther than that from Buenos Aires to New York.) The British, by the loan of their money and their industrial and engineering skill, played a greater part than any other country in the development of Argentina. Most of the railways were British-built, and, until recently, British-owned, though they have now been bought up by the Argentine Government. And Britain has been the greatest customer for Argentine exports of wheat, beef, and mutton.

Buenos Aires, the capital, where more than a quarter of the population now lives, is the largest city of South America, the third largest of the Western hemisphere, and about the ninth largest in the world. With its luxurious shops and brilliant sporting events it rivals the cities of Europe or of the United States, and it possesses two of the world's great newspapers, *La Prensa* and *La Nación*. The language of Argentina is Spanish, but it has developed differently from the Spanish spoken in Spain, just as American has developed differently from English. And though the Argentines are Spanish in their origin and culture, they have long been a distinct nation. They resemble in many ways a blend between Spaniards and Italians, who have been the most numerous settlers; and Buenos Aires has been described as one of the world's greatest Italian cities. The Argentino has the pride and fiery passion of the Spaniard, combined with the Italian's charm and his theatrical and changeful temperament.

See also Vol. III: ARGENTINA; Vol. IV: FRENCH LANGUAGE; ROMANCE LANGUAGES.

ARGUS, *see* MYTHOLOGICAL MONSTERS (a).

ARMENIANS. The country of Armenia lies south of the Caucasus Mountains between the Black Sea and the Caspian Sea. The original

ARMENIAN REFUGEES IN SYRIA
The old woman is spinning wool for carpets. *Roy. Geog. Soc.*

Armenians probably migrated there somewhere about 1200 B.C. They are rather above middle height, with darkish-brown or yellowish skins. They have straight black hair, broad skulls, high foreheads, and large noses. They are as a rule intelligent and quick, and very good at

trade. Armenians to-day are to be found in most commercial cities of the Mediterranean and indeed of Europe. They are often, like the JEWS (q.v.), money-changers, bankers, and merchants, and, like the Jews, have suffered generations of persecution.

The Armenians who have remained in their own country are mostly shepherds and tillers of the soil. They live poorly, generally in low mud cottages or underground dwellings. Their houses are often built round small courtyards, with windows only on the courtyard side, and the cattle often share the house with the family. The flat roof is used in the summer for eating and sleeping upon. Women are generally the craftsmen: in particular they weave carpets and make lace. Generations of oppression have made the people servile and spiritless.

The Armenians call themselves Hai, from Haik, great-grandson of Japheth, son of Noah, from whom they say they are descended. They were conquered successively by the Assyrians, Medes, Persians, and Romans. They became Christians in the early 4th century, and for a time the Armenian Church was the centre of Asiatic Christianity. After a period of independence and prosperity they fell under the Greeks, then the Turks, and then the Mongols. For a long time both Turkey and Persia fought for control of Armenia, and the Armenians looked to Russia for help, especially for protection of their Christianity. The wretched people, especially in Turkish Armenia, suffered continuous persecution and massacres. Between 1894 and 1896 so many were wiped out that Europe was stirred to protest; but the massacres continued at intervals until the Armenian population was reduced from 2,000,000 to about 200,000.

The north-east part of old Armenia is now part of the U.S.S.R., the south-east belongs to Persia, and the south-west, in which practically no Armenians remain, belongs to Turkey.

See also Vol. III: ARMENIA.

ARTEMIS, *see* GODS OF GREECE AND ROME.

ARTHURIAN LEGEND. This takes three forms. In the first Arthur is a fabled leader of the Britons against the Saxons; in the second he is a purely mythical character; in the third he is a hero of romance. The origin of all three was probably a Celtic war-god.

The first known mention of Arthur occurs in the writings of the historian Nennius, who probably lived about the year 900, and describes Arthur as having lived about 400 years earlier. In his *History of the Britons*, which is full of absurdities, Nennius calls Arthur the 'warleader of the kings of Britain', and credits him with twelve glorious victories over the Saxons, in which 'no one overthrew them but he alone'. In one battle he killed 960 men with his own hand. This has obviously no historical value.

Apart from the Welsh Annals, which merely copy and exaggerate Nennius, the only other 'history' which mentions Arthur is Geoffrey of Monmouth's *History of the Kings of Britain*, written in the 12th century. Geoffrey was no doubt born at Monmouth, but he was probably of Breton origin, and he wrote at Oxford. He compiled a fabulous 'history', mixing legends from Brittany with extracts out of Nennius from classical mythology and from the life of CHARLEMAGNE (q.v. Vol. V). In the course of this he makes Arthur conquer not merely England, but a great part of Europe. So much for Arthur as an 'historical' character.

Arthur as a purely mythical character is to be found in a number of Welsh poems and legends of uncertain date. From these it would seem that he was still regarded by laymen as a god, but by the priests as a demon. The former tell of his fights with magic weapons against giants and monsters, but never against the Saxons. The latter tell of his encounters with saints, in which he always gets the worst of it.

It is as a hero of romance that Arthur is now best known. He owes his position as a hero of romance to Chrêtien of Troyes, a French court poet who lived at the end of the 12th century. At this time the ideas of chivalry and courtly love were developing in western Europe, and particularly in France. The origin of these ideas is obscure, but it is very likely that they came mainly from the Arabs. At the same time romances based on corrupt versions of the *Tale of Troy* and of other Greek myths were becoming

KING ARTHUR AND THE KNIGHTS OF THE ROUND TABLE
Illumination from a late 15th-century French MS.
Bib. Nat., Paris

popular. Chrêtien collected material from Celtic legend, from the earlier romances, and from his own readings of the Roman poets, and combined it all into fresh romances so skilfully, and so much in accord with the sentiments of the time, that he not merely gave the highest satisfaction to his patronesses, the court ladies, but set for all time a fashion for chivalrous romance. His King Arthur is a combination of the figures of Celtic myth with Charlemagne and various Greek heroes, particularly Agamemnon. Where the Round Table came from is unknown: it is not mentioned by any writer before Chrêtien, and the so-called traditions which place it at Carlisle, Caerleon, Winchester, and so on are derived from the romances. Many of Chrêtien's heroes bear Celtic names, and some of the incidents are from Celtic sources. But probably more are drawn from the classics: many stories told about Lancelot remind us of Achilles, and many about Guinevere remind us of Helen of Troy. It would be incorrect to say, however, that Chrêtien took Achilles or Helen as models: he merely took these classical stories and put bits of them in where he thought they fitted best.

Chrêtien had many imitators, of whom one of the last was our Sir Thomas Malory, a knight who lived in the middle of the 15th century. His *Morte D'Arthur* was mostly translated from the French; but he was more than a mere translator. He seems to have used English sources as well as French, and he cut out many of the grosser parts of the legend, making it fit more exactly with the ideas and morals of his own day, which had advanced a good deal from those of the 12th century. His book should be read by all who like a good story and at the same time wish to know what the ideas and customs of his times really were. Many later poets have taken the Arthurian Legend as the basis of their own creations, the best known of these being Tennyson's *Idylls of the King*.

See also Vol. XII: ARTHURIAN LITERATURE.

ARYAN (Sanskrit *arya* = noble). The name of a very large group of languages all of which come originally from the same stock. The oldest of these is SANSKRIT (q.v. Vol. IV), an ancient Indian language. Others are Persian, Greek, Latin, Celtic, Teutonic, and Slavonic, and all the languages which have derived from these. The names Indo-European or Indo-Germanic are sometimes used instead of Aryan. From a study of the word-roots found in the different Aryan languages it is thought that the original speakers probably came from the Russian Steppe country. Thence some wandered over north Persia (Iran) and Turkestan. About 1500 B.C. they seem to have split—the majority staying in Turkestan, while the rest went into north India, where they settled and spread their language over a large part of that country (*see* INDIAN CIVILIZATIONS).

Sometime before the Iron Age these Aryan people seem to have spread over Europe, where they were probably responsible for introducing the horse and also the bronze sword. No trace of them remains except in the languages. In spite of this the Germans under Hitler built up a theory of the Aryan origin of the German race in order to develop the idea of its supremacy and to discriminate against the Jews, who belong to the Semitic language group.

See also Vol. IV: INDO-EUROPEAN LANGUAGES.

ASCETICISM. This word has an interesting origin. It comes from a Greek verb, *askein*, which means 'to do athletic exercises' or 'to train the body'. The noun for this is *askēsis* or discipline. In 1 Corinthians ix. 24–7 St. Paul describes this sort of process as being closely akin to what a Christian has to do in order to bring his bodily passions and appetites under control. Christians and Jews especially, but also Easterns, like Hindus and Moslems, have often practised living on a spare diet or going partially or wholly without food for certain periods, in order to keep the body in subjection.

After the Roman government gave up persecuting the Christians, ascetic practices actually increased among Christians, perhaps because they felt the need to replace the hardships of persecution by some other discipline. At about the same time, oriental ideas of the unimportance of this life and of the need for the individual to separate himself from the world were

HINDU ASCETIC. *Indian Railways*

spreading westwards. The citizens of the Roman Empire in the 4th century responded fairly readily to this teaching, partly because life was drab and lacking in zest, and taxes were heavy, and partly because there was a general belief that the world was 'perishing and running down and reaching its last end'. Hence from about A.D. 320 onwards we find a great increase in the number of people of both sexes who left the towns and cities and went to live in out-of-the-way spots, such as the Nubian desert in Egypt. Some of these were solitary hermits, others lived in groups—it is from the latter that the institutions which we call 'monasteries' developed. The first two great organizers of Egyptian groups of ascetics were called Pachomius and

Antony: in their societies each individual lived a solitary life although he was the member of a group. Later, however, other communities came into existence which were more like colleges or schools, and which had a fair degree of social intercourse. These were mainly due to the pioneer work of St. Benedict (q.v. Vol. V) in Italy at Monte Cassino. At the other extreme were the complete hermits, who gave up all contact with other human beings and often went in for the greatest extremes of harsh discipline and self-torture.

Severity to the body is found also among Hindus and Moslems. The Hindu ascetics, who lie on beds of spikes or carry live coals in braziers on their heads are well known; but among the Moslems there are also ascetics who treat their bodies to the same kind of harsh discipline (see Dervish). It seems clear that the object of these grotesque and repulsive practices is partly to keep the animal passions under control, and, as it is said, 'to mortify the flesh', partly to display before the Deity a readiness to give and suffer much for the Divine glory. By far the commonest form of such practices is the beating or scourging of the body, which among Christians is regarded as a mystical sharing in the scourging of Jesus Christ. Both Jesus and the Buddha seem to have discouraged extremes of asceticism, but even they do not deny the need of some discipline; and most probably no high degree of spiritual perfection can be reached without it. It is in fact a simple principle of what has been called 'high religion' of all kinds, that the individual should practise self-denial and aim at doing hard and inconvenient things, and that the more such acts are repeated, the better will be formed habits of self-control, including control of the mind.

There is, however, another reason for asceticism, and this is the main reason which makes men and women become monks and nuns. Those persons who are sure that the Vision of God in His Perfection is the highest aim in life, naturally feel that everything which gets in the way of this Vision is to be avoided, however good or innocent it may seem in itself. Some therefore give up marriage and family life, and even ordinary amusements, treating these as though they were evil, so that they may keep strictly to prayer and meditation: others go so far as to maintain a vow of perpetual silence. Some Protestant Christians, especially those who lay great stress on the sinful and corrupt nature of man, believe that salvation can be won only by avoiding the ordinary pleasures of life, and practising a strict and rather gloomy ascetic self-discipline. They do not, however, believe in separation from the world.

See also Friar, Monk.

ASHANTI (AFRICANS). A negro people of the Gold Coast, fairly typical of the larger negro communities of the West African area. Compared with many other Negro peoples (q.v.) they are progressive and have developed quite an advanced social life, many of them now taking advantage of opportunities offered by European civilization.

At the head of the Ashanti State is a paramount chief; under him there are chiefs of the different tribal divisions of the State, and under them are the village headmen. The chief of each division is always elected from the 'royal family' of the division, and his authority is represented by his 'stool'—a throne which embodies the power and glory of former rulers. A chief docs not speak directly to his subjects or they to him, but through a 'speaker' who is chosen for his ability as an orator. The paramount chief is guided by the advice of a council composed of the most important chiefs, the Queen-Mother, and the chief captains of the Ashanti army. The divisional chiefs also have their own councils. Nowadays, the chiefs with their councils have their own modern law-courts, local treasuries, and prisons, and look after the affairs of their own communities. The Ashanti army was formerly made up of companies provided by the towns or districts, the captains being chosen from special military families. Each company had its own name and flag, and there was great rivalry between the various companies—so that to display the flag of one company in the district of another often led to trouble.

Though there are now large towns, like Kumasi, with electric light, wide streets, and a modern water-supply, most of the people live in villages. Here the houses are usually made of mud and sticks with roofs thatched with palm-leaves; but many of the richer people now have houses of cement. The streets are generally well laid out, with trees planted to give shade from the sun. A typical village consists of two to three hundred compounds—the rooms of the houses being built round central courtyards.

AN ASHANTI VILLAGE MARKET
The women are bartering avocado pears and edible snails. *Dr. Meyer Fortes*

The family group living in a compound is much larger than an English family, for many men have more than one wife. Each wife has a room and a kitchen for herself and her small children.

The Ashanti people are nearly all farmers, and besides growing food crops for themselves, they grow cocoa for sale to the agents of European firms. Much of the world's supply of cocoa comes from the Gold Coast. The farms are often scattered round the village for three or four miles, but they are not easy to see, for there are no hedges or fences. Where you see the undergrowth cut away and food-plants and cocoa-trees growing, it is a farm; where the undergrowth is too thick to walk through, it is 'bush'. The farms of members of one household may be scattered about in different parts of the land round the village. On their farms the men grow cocoa, and in between the trees cocoyams, corn, and ground-nuts; their wives also grow foodstuffs including pepper, okra, and plantains. Their chief food is *fufu*—a mixture of yam and plantain, pounded together in a mortar and dipped in a palm-oil stew. Sometimes they

catch fish in the river or eat dried fish sent up from the coast. They do not get very much meat, for no cattle can live in their country because of the tsetse-fly; but they do keep a few sheep, goats, and fowls. They are very fond of 'bush meat' or antelope, which they hunt in the bush.

The clothing of the Ashanti people consists of a long, gaily-coloured cloth, which the men wear slung over the shoulder. If they wish to pay a mark of respect to a superior, they lower the cloth from the shoulder as an Englishman would touch his cap. The women wear a loose blouse with a cloth wrapped round the waist like a skirt. Small girls wear their cloth wrapped tightly round under the armpits, leaving their shoulders bare, and boys cross the two ends of the cloth round their neck and tie it at the back.

Children are named after the day of the week on which they are born—just as Man Friday was named after the day of the week on which Robinson Crusoe found him—and descent is traced chiefly through the mother, not the father, so that the child belongs to the mother's family. If a woman leaves her husband, she takes her children with her, and the father has no claim over them. An Ashanti mother generally carries her small child on her back wherever she goes, to the farm or to the market.

The most general way of carrying goods is on the head. A porter can carry a load weighing 60–100 lb. and walk 15–20 miles with it in a day. A woman going to market carries a basin on her head in which to carry her produce. Boys and girls going to school can balance a bottle of ink or books in the same way.

Nearly every village has its own small school. Usually there are more boys and girls wanting to go to school than the buildings can hold, and the school-children and their teachers often build new classrooms themselves. The best pupils can go on to the secondary schools in the large towns, and finally to Achimota College, near Accra, where the education reaches university standard.

The Ashanti people have many forms of amusement. Nearly every village now has a football ground; the boys play with bare feet, but they are able to kick the ball very hard. The elder men like to play draughts and *warri*, a game played with beans or beads on a wooden board. On special occasions a big dance is held in which all the villagers can join. But the Ashanti do not dance together in couples like the Europeans: men and women dance in separate groups, each having their own dances.

There are many skilled craftsmen among the Ashantis. There are excellent blacksmiths, as well as goldsmiths and silversmiths who can make rings and ornaments, and wood-carvers who produce articles of fine workmanship. Especially beautiful work is found in the ornamented stools of the chiefs. Nowadays many carpenters are making furniture in European style. Weaving is not practised so much to-day, though formerly many beautiful designs were woven for the Ashanti royal clans. Pottery-making is in the hands of the women; and though they do not use the potter's wheel, they are skilful in shaping round pots entirely by hand.

See also Vol. III: GUINEA LANDS; Vol. IV: AFRICAN LANGUAGES.

ASSYRIAN CIVILIZATION.

It is not easy to make a sharp distinction between the Assyrian and BABYLONIAN (q.v.) civilizations of Mesopotamia. The peoples of both countries belonged to the western Semites, and both borrowed the main elements of their civilization from the SUMERIANS (q.v.), who had settled long before them in the Tigris–Euphrates valley, in what is now Iraq. The history of the two peoples is very closely connected, and their language, laws, religion, and social organization have strong resemblances. Nevertheless, there is a difference between them which is due partly to the different contacts they had with outside peoples, partly to the different geographical and climatic conditions of the two countries, and partly to the different elements of which the populations of the two countries were composed.

ASHUR-NAZIR-PAL II
King of Assyria, 885–860 B.C. *British Mus.*

Assyria sprang, like Rome, from very small beginnings. At the outset of its history the land of Assyria was less than 100 miles from north to south, and about 40 miles at its greatest breadth from east to west. It consisted of a narrow strip of fertile soil on each side of the river Tigris, stretching north to the foot-hills. Archaeologists think that the first inhabitants settled in the country about 3500 B.C.: the fall of Nineveh and the final collapse of the Assyrian Empire took place in 612 B.C.—so that the rise and fall of Assyria covers a period of about 3,000 years.

In the early period of their history the dwellers of Assyria seem to have been completely dominated by the Sumerians, from whom they received their cuneiform, or wedge-shaped writing, their religion, and much else of their material culture. But Sumerian rule in Assyria came to an end about 2500 B.C., and for 250 years Assyria was under the power of a line of Akkadian kings founded by the great warrior, Sargon.

About this time, Assyria was invaded and permanently occupied by a group of Semitic-speaking tribes who were to be known to history as the Assyrians, and whose language and laws clearly marked them out as different from the people of Akkad. After some 250 years the

THE CAPTURE OF A CITY BY TIGLATH PILESER III
Families are evacuated in bullock carts, their flocks are driven away by the captors, and scribes make up the accounts
of the spoil. Relief from the Palace of Tiglath Pileser III (745–727 B.C.). *British Mus.*

Akkadian rulers grew weak, and Assyria came under the rule of the Sumerian kings of Ur for about a hundred years. The prosperity of Ur was largely due to the growth of traffic with north-west Syria and south-east Asia Minor; and because of this traffic the Assyrian city, Assur, became an important industrial and distributing centre for the lands east of the Tigris. This contact with the trading states and with the kings of Ur taught Assyria the art of self-government and prepared her for independence. As the kings of Ur grew weaker, the Assyrians grew more powerful, gaining control of the trade-routes; and the valuable duties on the trade helped to increase their wealth and influence.

While the kings of Assyria were thus laying the foundations of her greatness, the hitherto unknown city of Babylon, under a new line of kings, had risen to the first place among the city-states of Mesopotamia. It is probable that for a period Assyria was under the domination of Babylon; but about 1650 B.C. this first Babylonian Empire came to an end, and Assyria was able to establish her independence. During the following centuries, with various changes of fortune, Assyria built herself up as a military power, holding control of the trade-routes to the south and west and of the principal source of iron in Asia Minor. By 911 B.C. and the accession of King Adad-nirari II, she had become a compact, well-armed, well-organized military state. Until the fall of Nineveh, the chief city in Assyria, in 612 B.C., she pursued her course of expansion and conquest, gaining the undisputed mastery of Elam, Mesopotamia, Syria, Palestine, the Arabian marches, and finally of Egypt.

This period of Assyrian history falls into two parts. The first begins with the successes of King Ashur-nazir-pal II, whose long reign (885–860 B.C.) was spent in unceasing warfare. Assyrian warlike exploits were for the first time vividly set forth on the magnificent bas-relief carvings of the reign of Ashur-nazir-pal, and in consequence this king is credited with the introduction of 'frightfulness' into ancient warfare. But there can be little doubt that the barbarous practices represented on his bas-reliefs and described on his monuments were characteristic of all warfare in those times. Egyptian monuments show similar cruelties and mutilations as practised by the Egyptians in war. Shalmaneser III continued the warlike policy of his father, but directed his attacks specially against the Syrian states. Ahab, King of Israel, is mentioned in Shalmaneser's account of the important battle of Qarqar (854 B.C.), where the advance of the Assyrians clearly received a setback. At the close of his reign in 825 B.C. the fortunes of Assyria were beginning to decline.

The second and final period of Assyrian

ascendancy began with the reign of King Tiglath Pileser III (745–727 B.C.). A series of brilliant conquerors and rulers followed him: Sargon, Sennacherib, Esarhaddon, and Ashur-bani-pal, of whose reigns and achievements we have full historical records, and who raised Assyria to the highest summit of her glory. In 671 B.C. the Assyrian army conquered Egypt; but the conquest brought them no good, and the strain which it threw upon the resources of the state was one of the causes which brought about the sudden and dramatic collapse of the great empire. In 612 a combined army of Babylonians and Medes attacked the great city of Nineveh, and burnt it to the ground.

The civilization of Assyria depended mainly on foreign trade and on military conquest resulting in the control of the great trade-routes and access to the Mediterranean. The three main classes of Sumerian society—the rulers, priests, freemen (merchants, farmers, and craftsmen), and slaves—are found both in Assyria and in Babylonia; but in some ways Assyrian law and customs appear to have developed along independent lines. Assyrian law made special provisions for the dependents of common soldiers in case of death or imprisonment in foreign countries—an important law in a country where military service played so great a part. There was a tendency to make the king supreme in matters of law, and for the administration to become national instead of local. These special

characteristics all helped to build Assyria into a compact centralized military state governed by the king and a body of officials responsible only to him.

In the matter of architecture, stone, which was very hard to obtain in Babylonia, was abundant in Assyria, and, in consequence, Assyrian buildings were generally made of stone. Also, because the climate was much colder, Assyrian houses were built on a different plan from the Babylonian—they had their main entrance at the end of the side-wall instead of in the middle. The Assyrians developed a style of sculpture, the vigour and naturalness of which is excelled only in Crete. Their hunting scenes show a knowledge of anatomy and a power of depicting swift movement which not even the Greeks surpassed. The Assyrians produced no literature of their own. Their myths and sagas were borrowed from Babylonia (*see* BABYLONIAN MYTHS); but their later kings were very active in collecting all the literary material available in Mesopotamia—indeed, our knowledge of Mesopotamian civilization is largely due to the vast collection of tablets which King Ashur-bani-pal brought from every corner of his empire to his great library at Nineveh. But the principal achievement of Assyrian civilization, as of Roman, lay in administration and organization. Sennacherib's great aqueduct, the oldest known in the world, which brought water to the city of Nineveh from the mountains 30 miles away,

A LION HUNT
Relief from the Palace of Ashur-bani-pal (668–626 B.C.). *British Mus.*

is an example of their efficiency. Our idea of the Assyrians has been unduly influenced by the descriptions given in the Old Testament by the prophets. To the Hebrews the Assyrians were the incarnation of mere brute force, just as the Romans seemed to the Jews of a later time; but other evidence goes to show that, while they were ruthlessly efficient as a military power, they organized the trade and commerce of their empire with equal efficiency; they developed artistic skill of very high order, and collected and arranged the literary material of their time in a way which could only have been done by a highly civilized people.

See also ANCIENT CIVILIZATIONS; SUMERIANS; BABYLONIANS.

ASTROLOGY is the mock science which claims to be able to trace a connexion between human affairs and the movements of the stars and planets. It must not be confused with ASTRONOMY (q.v. Vol. III), a science becoming more exact every year, which deals only with the nature and movements of the heavenly bodies. To compare the merits of the two, we need only observe that astronomers are accustomed to predict such events as eclipses centuries ahead with great precision, whereas no modern astrologer foretold so world-shaking an event as the outbreak of the Second Great War even a few weeks in advance. Nevertheless, just as modern chemistry is founded on the painstaking researches of the early alchemists, striving to turn base metals to gold, so modern astronomy owes an immense amount to the observations of astrologers. The movements they noted in the heavens were often astonishingly accurate: it was in their attempts to relate these to human destinies that they failed.

With the background of knowledge and the increasing belief in reason which we possess to-day, it seems absurd to educated people that the position of the stars at the moment of a man's birth should have any influence on his physique, character, or life, or that the destinies even of great nations should be traceable in the heavens. And yet it is easy to see how the superstition arose. The influence of the sun on living things was obvious; that of the moon on the tides at least must soon have been noticed— why should the influence of the heavens end there? Above all, there was man's great and abiding desire to explain things. He did not

like feeling that he was at the mercy of events, that catastrophes such as plagues, famines, wars, and even the death of the individual should come upon him without apparent reason. If he could explain them, it was at least something: if he could foretell them, it would be an immense gain. And so people have always been willing to believe many forms of fortune-telling (*see* DIVINATION). The accidental coincidence of one eclipse with some great event in human affairs would convince him—since he was only too eager to be convinced.

The belief in astrology was widespread among early peoples centuries, if not thousands of years, before Christ. It flourished among the Chinese (whose astrologers were expected to foretell solar eclipses well in advance, so that suitable measures could be taken to prevent 'the dragon swallowing the sun' entirely), among the Babylonians, the Egyptians, the Etruscans, the Greeks, the Hindus, and the Arabs (as the *Arabian Nights* show well). It is still very prevalent in the East. The early Christian fathers differed among themselves as to its truth— though its influence is clearly seen in the charming Bible story of the wise men of the East who were guided by a star which 'moved before them' and led them to the manger at Bethlehem. In western Europe it was at its height in the 14th and 15th centuries, though it flourished until well into the 17th century. Among educated people its death-knell was sounded by the astronomical theories of NEWTON (q.v. Vol. V); and yet, in Britain and America to-day, hundreds of thousands of people read the astrological predictions in certain of the Sunday newspapers each week, with at least a certain measure of belief, and the sales of Almanacks containing prophecies based on astrology still reach a very high figure every year.

It was chiefly the BABYLONIANS (q.v.) who worked out the 'principles' of astrology, although they believed the planets to be actual gods, rather than the mere 'influences' to which they later declined. The basis of the whole system was the subdivision of the celestial sphere (or whole expanse of sky enveloping the earth) into twelve Houses of Heaven, named after the twelve signs of the zodiac. These houses may be thought of as the outer skin of a peeled orange, each 'quarter' or 'pig' of the fruit being a house. According to the system most commonly practised, the top and bottom of the orange lay above the North and below the South poles respectively. To an observer on the Earth here—like a pip at the centre of the orange, six houses would always be visible, the remaining six being below the horizon. Each of the different houses touched upon a special subject covering: (1) life, (2) riches, (3) brethren, (4) parents, (5) children, (6) health, (7) marriage, (8) death, (9) religion, (10) dignities, (11) friends, (12) enemies. Their power varied according to their position at the particular moment of interest, being strongest when they were 'in the ascendant' or just about to rise over the horizon on the astrologer's right as he faced south. Each planet, too, had certain properties, and each the particular house of which it was 'lord'. When it was actually in its own house, its power for good or ill was greatly magnified. On this fantastic framework a vast fabric of superstition was gradually erected until almost everything on earth and every aspect of life was linked in some way with the stars. Animals, metals, colours, stones, drugs, and many other things each had its planet. The zodiac itself was held to parallel the parts of the human body, the first sign Aries, the Ram, being the head, and the Fishes, or 'Pisces', the last, being the feet, while of the remaining signs each claimed its own part of the anatomy.

To cast a horoscope, the astrologer would find out the exact hour and date of his client's birth and then calculate from his tables the position of the heavenly bodies at that time. The particular house in the ascendant would be ascertained and note taken as to whether its influence was strengthened or weakened by the position of its lord. But this was no more than the beginning. Immensely complicated calculations could be made on the relative positions of the houses and planets, those of the sun and moon being by no means omitted. Influences could be estimated to wax or wane in power according to whether planets were in 'conjunction' or 'opposition', or forming the corners of various geometrical figures. The same process was followed in deciding whether a day would be auspicious or inauspicious for joining battle, for starting on a journey, or for beginning any other important enterprise. The opportunities for error in so intricate a series of calculations were great, and were not lessened by the wide variations between the systems used. But beyond all this lies the fact that modern science has been quite

THE ZODIAC MAN

Italian engraving, 1495. The figure shows the parts of the body under the domination of the signs of the Zodiac. Early medicine was greatly influenced by astrology, and doctors would only attempt to cure their patients if the stars were propitious

unable to find any basis in reason for the principles of astrology. Certain astrologers, notably Nostrodamus (1503–66), appear to have made occasional prophecies of almost miraculous accuracy; but against these must be set the many millions of predictions which have proved false. No one, perhaps, did more to kill the superstition than Swift in his feud with Partridge the almanac-maker; but it is astonishing how the superstition lingers on. We may look forward to a day when increasing confidence in the power of reason to mould the future will leave of astrology only those words which we use so frequently, forgetful of their origin—such as 'disastrous', 'ill-starred', 'influence', and 'ascendancy'—and the many picturesque allusions to the subject in literature.

ATHEISM, *see* RATIONALISM; THEISM.

ATHENA, *see* GODS OF GREECE AND ROME.

ATHENIANS, *see* GREEK CIVILIZATION.

AUGURY, *see* DIVINATION.

AUSTRALIAN ABORIGINES. When the first settlers arrived in Australia at the end of the 18th century, they found already inhabiting the country scattered bands of natives, whom they called 'black-fellows'. These peoples had each their own hunting-grounds and lived a very wandering existence, moving from camping-place to camping-place in search of food, never staying long in one spot. The settlers employed many of them, especially on sheep farms; but most of them moved farther and farther away from advancing civilization into the drier and more barren central and northern areas, where crop or cattle raising are impossible. Here they

THROWING A BOOMERANG
It is used in hunting and can be thrown with great speed and accuracy. *Pitt Rivers Coll.*

still survive in dwindling numbers under government supervision and protection, illustrating, in many ways, the life of our own ancestors in prehistoric times.

They were—and many of them still are—

among the most backward people on the earth. They grow no crops, keep no domestic animals but the dingo or native dog, wear no clothes, build no houses, and make no pottery. They hunt the scanty supply of small game without the help of bows and arrows, and depend mainly on birds, fish, lizards, frogs, grubs, moths, roots, and seeds for their daily food, living often on the verge of starvation. In the interior of Australia, where permanent streams are scarce, and droughts of two, three, or more years not uncommon, drink is often a more urgent need than food. The natives have many ingenious methods for getting water, and can journey over dry tracts where a European would die of thirst. They drain moisture from the roots of eucalyptus trees, suck it up from wet sand, collect it from underground tubers, and even on occasion from the bodies of frogs which, after distending themselves with water, have buried themselves to withstand the drought.

The Australian aborigines are generally short, under 5 ft. 6 in. in height, with long, low heads, retreating foreheads, broad noses, and deep-set eyes. Their skins are chocolate-brown (not black) and their hair is wavy, not woolly like that of the Negro. They wear no clothes except skins for warmth when needed; the men grow long hair and beards, while the hair of the women is usually shaved off. Personal decoration is limited to cuts in the skin (cicatrization) and designs in paint and grease over face and body, with tufts of down added on special occasions. Men wear nose-pins of bone, necklaces of shells or teeth, and ornamented plaited headbands to keep their uncombed hair out of their eyes.

They build no houses, and their huts are rarely more than a row of branches set up to keep off the wind, covered with sheets of bark or skins for extra protection. A native folk-tale tells of the wooing of a maiden by a man who describes the wonderful home he has made for her: it was of emu and kangaroo bones, covered with skins—'the most beautiful camp ever made'! Household equipment consists of a few wooden or bark trays, some baskets, stone knives for cutting up food, and grinding-stones to pulverize roots and seeds. They make fire by rubbing together two pieces of wood and cook their food in hot ashes. The men have axes of hard stone, ground and polished with sand and water, spears with points formerly of wood or stone, now of glass or metal, chipped stone knives set in handles

AN AUSTRALIAN NATIVE MAKING A STONE AXE
His simple shelter can be seen in the background. *Australian Information Bureau*

of gum, wooden clubs and shields, and the boomerang. This last is a throwing-stick, of which one variety is so contrived that when thrown at the quarry in hunting, it returns circling to the thrower. The woman's chief tool is the digging-stick, used mainly for digging up roots for food, but also for her defence in quarrels.

In contrast to the simplicity of their daily life, the social rules which regulate the relations between the different members of a tribe are extremely complicated. A tribe is divided into two parts, and these are subdivided again into further groups which have different totems (*see* TOTEMISM). The relations between these groups control marriage and inheritance and religious ceremonies, and are reflected in a complicated system of marriages of relatives belonging to different groups and generations. Thus, in some tribes, a man must select for his wife a woman of another group who is one of his mother's mother's mother's brother's daughter's daughters.

Elaborate ceremonies connected with the totems of the different groups, the purpose of which is to maintain and increase the food supply, all help to keep the various groups in close and friendly relations. The INITIATION CEREMONIES (q.v.) impress on the young, by myths and dramas, the importance of respecting the traditional rules of life. The older men generally have great authority over the younger men and the women; but, as with many primitive peoples, the medicine men are often the most powerful in the group, it being believed that they can cause or cure disease by magical powers (*see* MAGIC).

The ceremonies usually include circumcision of the boys, knocking out of two of their lower front teeth, and decoration with cuts in the skin, which are irritated by rubbing in ashes so that they stand up in patterns. By the end of the ceremonies the boy has given up childish things and become a man. Among some tribes there are similar ceremonies for girls before marriage. Cuts in the skin, leaving raised scars, may be made at any time for ornamental or magical purposes, and the knocking out of two front teeth is a common sign of being grown up.

Children are well treated and never punished; but they have a hard time. Food is often scarce and probably unsuitable for children; so a sick child is a burden, and is often abandoned when the tribe moves camp. Boys and girls begin to hunt for their own food at an early age and soon learn to be independent. The girls are often betrothed at birth, for women are useful as food collectors. They are often married at thirteen or fourteen, and then they become the drudges rather than the companions of their husbands, who may acquire as many of them as they can, provided that they are in the right class of relationship.

Each tribe has its own language, and this is often so different from that of its neighbour that when two tribes meet, signs and gestures have to take the place of words.

See also AUSTRALIANS; RACES AND PEOPLES.

AUSTRALIANS. Nineteen out of every twenty people living in Australia to-day are of British origin—most of them being Australian born and descended from British settlers. The British were by no means, however, the first-comers to Australia. As far as we know, the remote ancestors of the dark, primitive AUSTRALIAN ABORIGINES (q.v.) whom the Europeans found occupying the whole country were the earliest inhabitants, or perhaps the even more remote ancestors of the now-extinct people whom the Dutch discovered in Tasmania in 1642 had originally also inhabited Australia.

It is perhaps strange that none of the Asiatic navigators seems to have visited Australia before the coming of the first Europeans. The great migrations of the POLYNESIAN peoples (q.v.) which reached, among other places, New Zealand, never appear to have touched Australia. From old maps it seems likely that the Portuguese had seen a good deal of the Australian coast more than 400 years ago. The Dutch had reached the country in 1606, and by 1644 they had roughly charted much of the northern, western, and southern coasts of what they called New Holland. The first British visitors were shipwrecked on the coast in 1622. In 1688 and again in 1699 WILLIAM DAMPIER (q.v. Vol. V) landed. He collected Australian flowers, still preserved in Oxford, and formed a very unfavourable opinion of the country and people. The country he described as barren and miserable, and of the natives he wrote: 'The Hodmadods (i.e. Hottentots) of Monomotapa (South Africa), though a nasty people, yet for wealth are gentlemen to these.' JAMES COOK (q.v. Vol. V) visited Botany Bay in 1770 and charted the east coast.

With him came Joseph Banks, who made the first great collection of Australia's curious plants. It was he who suggested the policy which had so great an effect on Australia's development—the use of Botany Bay for a prison colony. Soon after, the 'First Fleet' carried to Australia 717 convicts and their guards. Captain Arthur Phillip founded Sydney, and the colonizing of the country began. The Australian people, now an independent nation of growing importance in the world, have therefore a national history of considerably less than 200 years—whereas most European peoples date back well over 1,000 years, and the Chinese people some 5,000 or 6,000 years.

At first the new colony lived on the ragged edge of hunger, sometimes coming very near starvation. Expansion inland was very slow—it was twenty-five years before any explorers found their way over the Blue Mountains which rise 50 miles inland from Sydney. The early settlements in Australia and Tasmania were mostly of sealers, whalers, sea-elephant hunters, pearlers, and sandal-wood seekers. Until 1833 whale oil and whale-bone made up more than half Sydney's exports. Then began the development of the wool industry. John Macarthur, son of an Argyll Scot, was among those who began to prove that Australia could grow the fine wool that Britain needed. Tasmanian sheepmen crossed Bass Straits and began to develop the pasture lands of what is now Victoria. Pioneers with bullock-carts loaded with supplies drove sheep and cattle overland into South Australia and Queensland to make new settlements. Oxen-teams, usually of eight, guided by a 'bullock-whip' like that used by the Dutch settlers in South Africa, ploughed the land and hauled timber out of the forests. As the sheep began to flourish, the invaluable oxen drew the wool-wagons to the ports, distances of up to 500 miles, from where the wool was carried to London by the fast sailing clippers. The first fleet of convicts had taken eight months to reach Australia; the clipper cut down the time of the passage until the *Thermopylae* ran from London to Melbourne in sixty-one days seventeen hours. The journey can now be made by air in under three days.

By 1850 Australia's European population had reached 405,000, mainly sheep-farmers. Most of the labour was convict—that is to say, made up of persons convicted of some crime (often quite trivial) and transported from the British Isles to Australia. Between 1788 and 1867,

AUSTRALIAN FARMERS DIPPING SHEEP
The sheep are driven through a trough of disinfectant wash to cure sheep scab and to kill parasites
Australian Information Bureau

160,000 convicts were sent to Australia. They became shepherds, shearers, and bullock-drivers; they grew grain, built churches, houses, and government buildings; they made roads and bridges, and in course of time even taught children and acted as police. Most of the bush-rangers, the outlaws and robbers of Australia's history, were runaway convicts.

In 1823 a surveyor, Mr. Brien, had found signs of gold in Australia. Other finds followed; but not much was done until in 1851, when Edward Hargreaves, returning from the Californian goldfields, found traces of gold over a wide area in New South Wales. Then a native black-man, employed as a shepherd, chipped open a quartz boulder and found, mixed with the quartz, a hundred pounds of gold. The gold rush developed at enormous speed: gold-seekers poured in from the British Isles, Europe, America, China, and other countries; and the fame of Ophir, Sofala, Bendigo, Ballarat, and other gold-fields went round the world. The eighteen-fifties were Australia's golden age. By 1860 the European population had increased to 1,145,000.

From this time on Australia went ahead fast. In 1853 the first railway was opened, and in 1854 voyages under steam began. Until 1901 the country consisted of six separate colonies, and very little united planning—for instance, the railways in the different colonies had different gauges, varying from 5 ft. 3 in. to 3 ft. 6 in., a mistake which it will yet cost millions of pounds to put right. In that year, however, the six states formed a federal union with one Commonwealth Government. This Government took over Papua in 1906 and the mandate over German New Guinea after the First World War. In 1930 it annexed 2,274,000 square miles of Antarctica, where Australia has now a common frontier, 1,200 miles long, with the Norwegian antarctic territories. No one lives in Antarctica, but the seas just to the north of it are the world's chief whaling ground. Australia, like Canada, South Africa, and New Zealand, is an independent nation, united to Britain by the link of the Crown and co-operating closely with Britain and the other Dominions. She played an important part in the two World Wars, especially in the Second where the entry of Japan brought the fighting into her part of the world.

Modern Australia is the world's sheep farm, producing one-fourth of the world's finest wool. She has also about fourteen million head of cattle, a fourth of which are dairy cows, and she exports large quantities of meat, butter and cheese, wheat, fruit, and other foodstuffs. Yet most Australians do not now live in the country since, owing to the use of machinery, about 500,000 men are able to do all the work of the land. Half the population live in the seven chief cities; and as their industries grow, the cities and towns claim more and more people. Half of the country—the arid regions of the centre and west—is almost uninhabited.

Australians of European origin tend to be tall and lean, of the type that earned for the people of New South Wales the name of 'Corn-stalks'. On the whole they are taller than the British and more slender in build than New Zealanders. They are capable of great activity when they wish; and the country people, especially in the remoter areas, are amazingly versatile. A man may be a farmer, a carpenter, a wheelwright and wagon-builder, a blacksmith, a bullock-driver, and a sheep-shearer all rolled into one. They are, as a whole, orderly and law-abiding, and serious crime is rare. The lawlessness of earlier days, when Australia produced some notorious law-breakers, such as Ned Kelly and his bushranging gang, seems to have worked itself out. However, as compared to Englishmen, they are rather impatient of restraint and inclined only to obey orders for which they see the reason. This has its advantages; but in a large and complex community it is not always satisfactory for each individual to do what he has decided is best.

Life in the cities and in the more favoured regions, where most of the people live, is pleasant enough. The seven chief cities are on or near the sea. They have warmth and sunshine with surfing and swimming near at hand. Cricket is the national game, and tennis is nearly as popular. In winter they play four forms of football, one being a special Australian form of the game. Horse-racing is also tremendously popular.

Nearly all Australians, except a few in the more remote 'bush' (the back country) can read and write; but they read less than their neighbours in New Zealand. Australian literature, like its art and music, is not yet grown up, though it is showing signs of maturity. In science it has a good deal to show, especially in agricultural science, radio research, and aviation.

During the short period of their occupation of the sprawling, arid country, the Australians have done great things. But there has been a good deal of waste—a squandering of natural resources and a tendency to gamble and exploit with little regard to the future. This may be in part a legacy of the gold-digging days, and most Australians are now seeing the need for care and conservation. It is no doubt the effect of their environment which makes them tougher, more restless, less prudent, more given to movement and change than the British: they are slowly adjusting themselves to an environment so utterly different from that from which their ancestors came. Yet, in essence, the Australians are still British in their way of life, their ideas, and their ideals.

See also TASMANIANS.
See also Vol. III: AUSTRALIA.

AUSTRIANS. Austria to-day is but a very small part of the original Austro-Hungarian Empire, which was split up after the war of 1914–18. This Empire has its beginning in a province founded by CHARLEMAGNE (q.v. Vol. V) in the 8th century, in the eastern part of his great empire, from which comes its name of Österreich, or eastern country—in English, Austria.

Various families, the most prominent of whom were the Babenbergs, governed it until it was taken over in 1268 by Rudolf of Hapsburg, who became HOLY ROMAN EMPEROR (q.v.) five years later. The Hapsburgs, the most powerful rulers in eastern Europe, were the cause of the growth of Austria, and the fact that a Hapsburg was usually elected Holy Roman Emperor until the title was discontinued in Napoleon's time, added greatly to their prestige.

By conquest, marriage, and clever diplomacy, the Hapsburgs acquired a mighty Empire, which has included a large part of Europe at one time or another. Before its fall in 1918, it included present Czechoslovakia, Hungary, and parts of Yugoslavia, Roumania, and Poland, as well as Austria proper. With the revolution of 1918 came the fall of the Hapsburg dynasty, and all the non-German provinces broke away from Austria to form states of their own.

Present-day Austrians, although they speak German and are originally descended from Germanic stock, have such a different background of history from the Germans that their national character has formed quite differently. German as spoken by Austrians is full of foreign words and phrases gathered from the many different nationalities that formed part of the Empire. Racially, too, the Austrians are very mixed and, like the English, rather proud of it. In character they are easy-going, good-humoured, and inclined to like muddling through; as a rule they lack the qualities of efficiency, industry, and discipline which we associate with Germans, especially North Germans. They are very gifted artistically, particularly in music, and their national temperament comes out in their most successful style of architecture, the baroque, which is full of gaiety and exuberance. Austrians are traditionally tolerant of other peoples—for instance, the large Czech colony living in Vienna was provided, at Austrian expense, with its own schools. Indeed, Austrians are probably unique amongst Central Europeans in having no very strong nationalist feeling: they are more conscious of belonging to their own Provinces, each of which has its own parliament and marked individual characteristics. This lack of national feeling explains why, at one time, many Austrians advocated a union with Germany as the best way out of their economic distress. Hitler's occupation, however, by arousing violent anti-German feeling, has made Austrians much more nationally conscious than ever before.

There are few big estates, and about half the population are peasant farmers with a long tradition of independence. In the mountainous regions they are dairy and cattle farmers—the so-called 'Horn' peasants—whilst on the flatter lands of the east the 'Corn' peasants grow cereal crops. Each province has its own traditional and very picturesque peasant costumes as well as local customs. Vineyards thrive in various regions, and sampling the new wine is a special Austrian entertainment (*Heurigen*). Most of the peasants are Roman Catholics.

The other big group of Austrians are the industrial workers, who are extremely well organized in the Austrian Socialist party, not only politically but socially, for welfare, recreation,

OLD HOUSES IN HALL, A TOWN IN SOUTH-WEST AUSTRIA
Roy. Geog. Soc.

and indeed almost every human activity. The Austrian Socialists are strongly democratic and reformist. In their special stronghold, the municipality of Vienna, they have successfully put many of their projects for social welfare into effect. The division between peasants and industrial workers is, in many ways, a reflection of the clash of interests between town and country. Of the other social groups members of the lower middle class of artisans and small tradespeople have played a great part in Austrian town life, especially in Vienna, and, as a result of the good educational facilities in Austria, have often risen to the highest positions. The aristocracy, dependent on the Hapsburgs, lost its importance when the Empire disappeared. The professional classes are perhaps some of the most cultured people in Europe. There was a considerable Jewish community in Austria, especially in Vienna, where they formed over a tenth of the population. They used to be unpopular, on account of commercial jealousy. They have been terribly decimated by Nazi massacres.

All classes in Austria suffered severely from

the economic dislocation and distress which followed the First World War. This in turn led to discontent which Hitler and Mussolini stirred up for their own purposes. The Second World War and its aftermath have also inflicted severe suffering, but the experiences of Nazi occupation have given Austrians a greater sense of national unity and of the value of democratic institutions.

See also Vol. III: AUSTRIA; VIENNA.
See also Vol. V: HAPSBURGS.

village is enclosed within it. First there is an encircling bank no less than 1,200 feet across and with a ditch on the inner side. Inside this again, standing along the lip of the ditch, is a ring of enormous stones, once about a hundred in number. This large stone circle encloses a pair of smaller ones, standing side by side, and each originally made up of twenty-five to thirty stones. At their centres there were, originally, other large upright stones. This sacred area of

AVEBURY FROM THE AIR
The village has grown up along the road which cuts through the prehistoric site. The circular bank can be clearly seen, and within it some of the standing stones. *Ashmolean Mus.*

AVEBURY is one of the most impressive and interesting prehistoric monuments in the whole of Europe. It stands on the north Wiltshire Downs a few miles west of Marlborough, and is a sacred enclosure which may be likened to STONEHENGE (q.v.) and to many other circles built in Britain during the Bronze Age. In the past this great monument has been damaged by builders who wished to split up its stones, and by farmers who found that they got in the way of the plough; but excavation, helped by old records, has rediscovered the original plan. It has even been possible to set up again many stones which had been buried and forgotten.

Avebury, in the final form in which its makers left it, was a very complicated affair indeed and so large that a great part of the present-day

the stone circles could be approached by four entrances through the bank and ditch; and from the southern one an imposing 'avenue', a double line of standing stones, led away for over a mile to Overton Hill where there was another much smaller stone circle. The Overton circle had quite disappeared, but it has been found by excavation and marked out with concrete blocks; many stones of the avenue, on the other hand, are preserved and make a fine sight running by the roadside towards the great enclosure itself. There may have been another avenue leading from the west entrance; but there is no trace of it to-day, and only excavation can show if it ever existed. Excavation has shown the way in which the stones were originally set up. A small hole was dug to receive the base of the stone, which was then slid into it with the help of a sloping ramp. The stone had then to be levered and heaved upright, and to prevent it from tipping right over while this was being done, a line of stakes was driven in along the farther side of the hole.

Careful digging over a number of years has proved that Avebury was built by the Beaker-using people of the Early Bronze Age in about 1800 B.C. Bodies of some of these Beaker people, together with their pots and other possessions, had been buried at the foot of several of the standing stones (see CELTIC CIVILIZATION).

Very many of the Avebury stones are immensely heavy, and the outer bank must have stood 50 feet above the bottom of its ditch—a height as great as a five- or six-storey building. The making of such a place, all carried out with the simplest stone and bone tools, must have taken a very great deal of labour. It suggests that it must have served quite a large number of people living over a wide area, and we can imagine how, on days when special religious ceremonies were being held, tribesmen came to Avebury from all parts of the downs.

See also PREHISTORIC MAN.

AZTEC CIVILIZATION (Mexico).

When the Spaniards, under the leadership of CORTEZ (q.v. Vol. V) conquered Mexico in the beginning of the 16th century, they found established there the remarkable civilization of the Aztec Indians, which was at the height of its political and cultural development. Even a small band of Europeans was able to conquer these people because of the possession of fire-arms and horses, utterly undreamed of by the Aztecs; but the Spaniards were amazed at what they found. Contemporary accounts give us a very vivid picture of the life and achievements of the Aztecs at that time, who, like the INCAS of Peru (q.v.), are thus far better known to us than their predecessors. These descriptions of the wonders of Mexican civilization, which were once regarded as picturesque exaggerations, have now been to a great extent confirmed by the work of archaeologists.

The Aztecs were the last in a series of civilizations in Mexico (see MEXICAN, ANCIENT CIVILIZATION). Until the 13th century they were a tribe of wandering hunters, simple but hardy, who finally reached the shores of the lake on whose dried-up bed the city of Mexico now stands.

STONE MASK OF XIPE, GOD OF SOWING AND PLANTING
Victims were sacrificed to him by flaying and he is usually clad in a human skin. *British Mus.*

There they settled down on a small island and gradually absorbed the culture and way of life of their more civilized neighbours. Traditionally in A.D. 1325 (but actually, perhaps, considerably earlier) they founded their great capital, Tenochtitlan, enlarging their island artificially as the city increased in size. They were an extremely warlike people, and, first by alliances and then by warfare, they gradually extended their power all over Mexico and as far south as Guatemala. The full and final stage of their greatness had lasted barely fifty years when it was completely destroyed by the invasion of the Spaniards.

Underneath the foundations of the modern city of Mexico lie the ruined remains of Tenochtitlan. The old town, dominated by its temples and white buildings, must have been a splendid sight. It was crossed by many canals, along which boats came with merchandise. Three stone causeways, with defensive drawbridges at intervals, ran across the lake to the shores. The sacred enclosure, which occupied the site of the present Spanish cathedral and central square, contained twenty-five temples. The principal temple—only completed in 1485—was dedicated to the gods of war and rain. This, like other temples, was built on a lofty pyramidal platform with steep stairways in several flights leading to the flat top on which stood the sacrificial

The Aztecs derived most of their religious ideas from their predecessors, the Toltecs; but they added some new gods, particularly the god of war. Every month dramatic festivals were held in honour of one of the gods. On these occasions human victims, usually prisoners of war, were sacrificed in a terrible way—by tearing out the living heart, which was believed to be a quite essential food of the gods. Before the sacrifice pageants were staged with gorgeous costumes, and the victims were specially fêted so that they might accept their fate more cheerfully. At some of these festivals thousands of victims were required, and wars had to be waged specially to provide enough of them. Religion was closely bound up with the calendar, which had a recurring ritual period of 260 days as well as the solar year of 365 days.

The Aztecs used an elaborate kind of picture-writing in colours, which they had probably learnt from the people of southern Mexico and the MAYA (q.v.) in Central America. Many of their books or codices have been preserved, one of the best being in the British Museum. The Aztecs, like the Mayas, counted by twenties; dots stood for units and other symbols were used for 20, 400, and 8,000. Names of places were indicated by picture symbols. For instance, the town Caltepec would be shown by drawing a house symbol (*calli*) on a mountain symbol (*tepetl*). Some of the books were written soon after the Spanish conquest, and the meaning of the pictures and symbols is explained by Spanish translations written alongside. Many of the books were sacred almanacs and were used for divining lucky and unlucky days; others were chronicles telling of early wanderings and conquests. Others tell of more personal matters, such as the diet and education of children, who were carefully and severely brought up.

Nearly all the young men, except those destined for the priesthood, were trained as soldiers, and for this purpose they were grouped into different wards, each under its own military chief. Warfare was their greatest glory—warriors killed in battle were believed to go to heaven. They fought with bows, lances, and clubs or swords edged with sharp flakes of obsidian, a kind of volcanic glass. They carried skin-covered wickerwork shields and wore wooden helmets with feather plumes.

They carried on trade mainly by barter, though as a substitute for money they used

THE FIRE GOD XIUHTECUTLI
Stone figure 3 ft. 10 in. high. *National Mus., Mexico*

altar and the shrine containing the images of the gods. These temples were periodically enlarged, the older building being completely covered in a fresh casing of stone and provided with new stairways and shrines. In some cases this was done at least seven times, probably at the end of each period of fifty-two years (the calendar cycle) when the sun was thought to need reviving by special sacrifices and the kindling of 'new fire' (*see* SACRIFICE).

THE GREAT CALENDAR STONE

It represents the disk of the sun. In the centre is the face of the sun-god, surrounded by the names of the 4 previous suns in square panels. In the next band are the 20-day signs of the Aztec calendar. The outermost circle is formed by 2 serpents, each with a human head in its jaws. Diameter 12 ft. *National Mus., Mexico*

cacao beans and quills containing gold dust which had a fixed standard of value. They cultivated maize and many crops long known to the Mexicans. They made chocolate from cacao beans and a fermented drink from the juice of the Mexican aloe, called *pulque*, which is still popular. They were fond of flowers which were grown in the water-gardens of Xochimilco (as they are to-day) and used them at ceremonies or served them up at banquets to provide sweet scents between the courses of food. They caught fish in the lakes or brought them up from the sea-coast by relays of fast runners. There was no other form of transport except boats, as the wheel was unknown in America until the arrival of the Europeans nor were there any draught animals. Dogs and turkeys were bred for food. We owe our turkeys to the American Indians, as well as tomatoes and chocolate.

In their arts and crafts the Aztecs produced some wonderful work. Their architecture was simple and massive with admirable proportions.

MASK OF TURQUOISE AND SHELL MOSAIC ON WOODEN BASE
It probably represents Tonatiuh, the sun-god
British Mus.

They sculptured stone both in relief and in the round: the style was sometimes severely formal or even grotesque, but was often realistic and expressive. Large figures of gods, snakes and jaguars, huge altars, and sacrificial bowls were carved from single blocks of hard stone. One of the most famous of these—the 'Calendar Stone'—in its present incomplete state measures 12 feet in diameter and weighs 20 tons. Its surface is carved all over with pictures in relief of the sun-god, the calendar, and the creation of the world. The Spaniards buried it as being an evil thing, but it has now been dug up and put in the National Museum of Mexico.

Many extremely beautiful miniature figures and heads of men and animals were cut out of jade or crystal. Mirrors were made out of highly polished obsidian and pyrites. No stone was too hard for them to fashion in the shape they desired. Among the most remarkable objects were the sacred masks encrusted with mosaics of turquoise and other precious stones or pearls. The Aztec King, Montezuma, presented some of these to Cortez, the Spanish leader, for the Emperor, Charles V. They are now in the British Museum. The Aztecs were skilful in casting small ornaments of gold and copper.

Copper was also hammered cold into axes and chisels. But otherwise, as elsewhere in ancient America, metals were little used and iron was quite unknown. Most of their building, sculpture, and engraving were done with tools made of stone.

The potter's wheel was not known in ancient America; but the Aztecs made large quantities of attractive hand-modelled pottery which was painted in brilliant colours, or with black designs on an orange background. Cloth was woven of cotton, and the designs of their clothes indicated particular social and military ranks. Bright feathers were worked into patterns to decorate robes and capes. Some of their ceremonial robes were extremely gorgeous and had head-dresses imitating jaguars and eagles. At the festivals poetry was recited or sung, and was accompanied by a rather primitive kind of music. Drums, trumpets, whistles, flutes, rattles, and bells were used, but, strangely enough, no stringed instruments were known in any part of ancient America.

The Maya of Central America and the Aztec of Mexico have sometimes been compared to the Greeks and the Romans in the development of their civilizations. The comparison cannot be pressed too far; but it is true that the early Maya (like the Athenians of Greece) had a special genius for art and mathematical science, while the Aztecs who borrowed these intellectual and artistic accomplishments from the Maya, resembled the Romans in their military skill and capacity for political organization.

See also Vol. III: MEXICO.

PAINTED POTTERY VASE FROM CHOLULA
It is decorated in red on orange and cream. Height 4½ in.
British Mus.

B

BABYLONIAN CIVILIZATION. In the early period of its history Babylon, whose name Babili means 'Gate of God', was an unimportant city situated on the left bank of the Euphrates, just below the point where the rivers Tigris and Euphrates are only about 35 miles distant from each other, 50 miles south of Bagdad. Babylon owed her greatness to the fact that she lay at the meeting-point of two important trading routes, the one connecting her with northern Syria, the Mediterranean, and Egypt, and the other leading northward to Asia Minor and the Black Sea. She also controlled a third route leading into Persia.

Babylon first became leader of the city-states of Mesopotamia in 1894 B.C., when the kings of what is called the First Amorite Dynasty rose to power. This period lasted until the fall of the Amorite Dynasty in 1660 B.C. The most famous king of this dynasty was the great Hammurabi, who is best known for his collection of the ancient laws and customs of the country, now called the Hammurabi Code. The Code was engraved on a pillar of black basalt rock, at the head of which was carved a picture of Hammurabi receiving the laws from the hand of the Sun-god, Shamash. A copy of this pillar is in the British Museum.

The second stage of Babylonian history lasts from 1660 B.C. up to the fall of Nineveh in 612 B.C. During this period Babylon was conquered by a barbaric highland people called Kassites and then fell under the power of ASSYRIA (q.v.). When the Assyrians were conquered by the Medes and Chaldeans and their capital Nineveh was captured, Babylon rose again under Nebuchadnezzar II to an even greater height of power and splendour than she had yet enjoyed—a period known as the Neo-Babylonian Empire. It did not, however, last long: in 539 B.C. the Persian King, Cyrus the Great, entered Babylon in triumph, and the power of Babylon came to a shameful end.

But through all the changes of fortune which Babylon experienced, she remained the chief centre of civilization in Mesopotamia, much as the imperial city of Rome remained the centre of European civilization even after the Roman Empire had lost its power. The civilization of Babylon, like that of her great rival and conqueror, Assyria, rested upon the foundation of the ancient SUMERIAN CIVILIZATION (q.v.) which they followed. The three classes into which Babylonian society was divided were taken over from the Sumerian pattern of social life. They consisted of the *amelu*—the King and the nobles, together with the warrior class and state officials; the *mushkenu*—people who might be called the

THE LAWS OF HAMMURABI
British Mus.

'commoners', that is, merchants, craftsmen, farmers, fishermen, and so forth; and lastly, the *wardu*—the slaves, the foundation upon which the whole social structure rested, as it did in Greek and Roman society. There was an old Babylonian proverb which ran: 'The man is the shadow of the god; the slave is the shadow of the man; but the king is the equal of the god.' The King occupied a very special place as the representative of the god, and in the early period of kingship the King was generally made into a god, either after death, or in some cases during his lifetime. The ritual for making King Lipitishtar into a god has been preserved. As the representative of the god, the King was regarded as the owner of the land, or as the god's tenant-in-chief. All holders of land paid rent to the temple in the form of cattle, grain, fish, wine, and other products of the land. The earliest written records found in the excavation of the temple of Ishtar at Erech consist of the temple accounts, which give details of dues paid in kind to the priests for the goddess. The King also played a very important part in the central event of the Babylonian religious year, the great New Year Festival in the spring. This lasted for eleven days and was a most elaborate and splendid ceremony. Each day had its special prayers and RITUALS (q.v.). Some of the rituals were carried out in secret by the priests; but most of them were performed in the great court of the temple of the god Marduk, in the presence of the whole population of Babylon. The central acts of the Festival were a dramatic representation of the death and resurrection of the god; a sacred combat in which the god vanquished a figure representing the primeval chaos-dragon, Tiamat; a triumphal procession through the city along the Sacred Way; and, as the climax of the ceremonies, a sacred marriage, in which the god, represented by the King, was married to the goddess, represented by a royal princess or a priestess. In all these proceedings the King played a central part, representing the god in his various acts. This festival continued to be celebrated as late as the 2nd century B.C., long

DEMON OF DISEASE
Babylonian terra cotta amulet,
c. 9th century B.C. *British Mus.*

after Babylon had ceased to have any political importance. Even when Babylon had come under Assyrian rule the Assyrian kings did not consider themselves properly enthroned until they had performed the ceremony of 'taking the hand of the god' at the New Year Festival in Babylon, although the same festival was performed in their own capital in Ashur or Nineveh.

The gods of the Babylonian religion, like so much of the civilization, had been taken over from the Sumerians, and many of the Sumerian names were kept. The high god was Anu, the sky-god, corresponding to the Greek Zeus; next to him came Enlil, originally a wind-god, but later regarded as the earth-god; he was gradually replaced by the chief god of Babylon, Marduk; the third of the three principal gods was Ea, the god of the watery deep and the inventor of magic. Although there was an ancient mother-goddess, worshipped under various names, the goddess most widely worshipped in Mesopotamia was Ishtar, who had temples in most of the great cities of Assyria and Babylonia. In addition to these great gods, every city had its own special god. All these gods had wives and large families, and many lesser gods as servants and messengers. So the Babylonian pantheon, or assembly of gods, was a vast affair, running into thousands. Moreover, besides the gods great and small, there were hosts of evil spirits, many of them with special names, such as Lamashtu, a female demon who was particularly dangerous to pregnant women. Several classes of priests had as their main business the task of performing the spells and incantations intended to protect people from the attacks of these hostile demons. Babylonian tablets give us pictures of these horrible creatures, half-beast, half-human; and many of the magical spells and rituals used against these dreaded enemies have been preserved in cuneiform script on clay tablets.

The BABYLONIAN MYTHS (q.v.) were an important part of the religion. One aspect of Babylonian religion which had a close connexion with the mythology was the attention which the

Babylonian priests gave to the study of the stars and planets and their movements. The science of astronomy rests upon the basis of the Babylonian study of the heavens, and much of the modern belief in horoscopes and lucky days and months springs from the Babylonian belief that events on earth were determined by the movements of the heavenly bodies. It was the Babylonians who invented the system of the twelve signs of the zodiac—still used by believers in ASTROLOGY (q.v.) to-day. Each of the three high gods had his own 'way' or section of the heavens over which he ruled, and nearly all the more important gods had their own special stars —for example, Marduk, the high god of Babylon, was identified with the planet Jupiter.

The conditions of social and economic life among the Babylonians are abundantly illustrated by the great collection of laws known as the Hammurabi Code—and from it we may learn how much Hebrew law was like early Mesopotamian law. The Code contained 282 provisions, covering every department of social life. The penalties varied according to the class of the person against whom the crime or offence had been committed. A theft from a noble had to be paid back thirtyfold, but a theft from a member of the second class had only to be paid back tenfold. A feature of Babylonian justice was the ordeal of the river: a man who was accused of sorcery had to throw himself into the river, and if the river 'overcame him', that is, if he was drowned, his accuser took his property; but if he came safely through the ordeal, his accuser was put to death. The right of property in slaves was jealously guarded: anyone who helped a slave to escape was put to death. A burglar who broke into a house was killed and his body thrust into the hole he had made. Looting from a burning house was punished with the utmost severity—the looter was thrown into the fire. If judges were proved to be unjust or corrupt, they were deprived of their offices. Great importance was attached to written contracts: no marriage, sale, or transfer of property was legal without a written contract, and a very large proportion of the tablets discovered in the course of excavations of Mesopotamian cities consist of such contracts, duly signed, witnessed, and sealed. The position of women was honourable: they might hold property, and married women retained the right to their dowry in case of divorce. A man was allowed to take a

BOUNDARY STONE

The sides are carved with reliefs of astronomical and religious emblems and an inscription recording the restoration of rights and privileges to Ritti Marduk by Nebuchadnezzar I, king of Babylon, c. 1120 B.C. The inscription tells how a great victory was won through the prowess of Ritti Marduk and in reward for his bravery Nebuchadnezzar restored to him land which had formerly belonged to his family and gave him and his people certain privileges.
British Mus.

MODEL OF THE ISHTAR GATE

The gateway to Babylon built by Nebuchadnezzar II (604–561 B.C.). The towers were 40 ft. high and were decorated with 575 reliefs of animals. *Berlin Mus.*

maidservant as a concubine in addition to his legal wife, and the children might inherit equally with the children of the legal wife. Marriage between members of different social classes was legal. The unfortunate doctor whose patient died under an operation would have his fingers cut off. If a house collapsed and caused the death of the owner, the builder was put to death. These examples will give some idea of the social conditions of early Babylonian life.

In the arts and handicrafts the Babylonians reached a very high level of achievement, although in the early stages, as with their religious and social ideas, they borrowed from their Sumerian predecessors. The technique of writing on clay tablets, the use of clay bricks and cones for building, the architectural style of the temples, and the great staged towers which they called *ziqqurats*, were all taken over from the Sumerians. But what the Babylonians borrowed they developed to the highest pitch of excellence. In the great period of Nebuchadnezzar II the buildings, fortifications, and the terraced gardens of Babylon were accounted one of the seven wonders of the world. In the art of sculpture the Babylonians never reached the same degree of skill as their neighbours the Assyrians; but the

splendid proportions and the magnificent decorations in enamelled bricks which have been found on the great Ishtar gate of Babylon show that they were no mean artists.

The study of Astronomy, in which they surpassed all the peoples of the ancient world, also involved a high development of mathematics; and the mathematical tablets which have been discovered show that they had mastered some of the most difficult problems of applied mathematics. They had inherited from the Sumerians a remarkable double system of numbers: they not only used the decimal system, but combined with it a sexagesimal mode of reckoning—that is, they used the number six and its multiples in combination with the number ten and its multiples, a fact which shows a degree of mathematical skill unknown elsewhere until the Greeks went beyond them in the science of mathematics.

Our knowledge about the literature of the Babylonians is largely due to the activities of a great Assyrian king, Ashur-bani-pal. For many years Ashur-bani-pal employed special officials to collect and arrange for his great library in Nineveh tablets from every part of his empire relating to all kinds of subjects, especially religious. Hence we now can read not only the diplomatic correspondence of the Assyrian kings, but also thousands of business documents, magical tablets, liturgies, omen-tablets, the great myths of Babylon, chronicles, and so forth. History, however, in the modern sense is hardly represented in what has come down to us of Babylonian literature

See also ANCIENT CIVILIZATIONS; SUMERIANS; ASSYRIAN CIVILIZATION.

BABYLONIAN MYTHS. Among the vast number of clay tablets which have been found on the sites of ancient Babylonian cities, there are some which contain curious and interesting stories commonly called myths (*see* MYTHO-LOGY). Most of these stories are connected with Babylonian religious beliefs and practices, and were taken over from the SUMERIANS (q.v.) who lived in Mesopotamia before the Babylonians and Assyrians came into the country. Many of these myths were borrowed by other peoples and adapted to their own religious ideas, so that even to-day we can find traces of them in the legends and folk-stories of peoples in different parts of the world. For example, there is an old English mumming-play, in which St. George slays the Turkish Knight, the main features of which have come down from the myth which was acted like a play at the great Babylonian

New Year Festival. The most important of the Babylonian myths formed part of certain RITUALS (q.v.) which were carried out on various special occasions or for special purposes. They are too numerous to describe in detail, but four of the most popular will serve as examples of the general character of Babylonian myths.

The first, called the Epic of Creation, played an important part in the New Year Festival, which was celebrated at Babylon in the spring. It was a poem or chant sung by the priests at a central point in the Festival. It told the story of the birth of Marduk, the chief god of Babylon, and how the gods in the Babylonian heaven were threatened by the attacks of a she-monster, the dragon Tiamat, and her brood of evil and monstrous creatures. None of the gods had the courage to withstand her, until Marduk arose in the council of the gods and offered to fight with Tiamat if the gods would promise to make him the chief of the gods. The council of the gods agreed to this, and Marduk armed himself with his bow, spear, and thunderbolts. His father, the god Ea, gave him powerful magic spells, and the goddess Ishtar came as his armour-bearer. He also provided himself with a net in which to catch the monster, and he was followed by the seven winds. In the fight, which the poem describes, Marduk overcame the dragon by catching her in his net, making the winds enter

A SUMERIAN MYTH

The sun-god rises from the underworld between the mountains of the horizon, assisted by the water-god and Ea the magician, and awaited by Ishtar, the morning and evening star. Seal of Adda the scribe, 2300–2150 B.C.
British Mus.

into her open jaws, and shooting an arrow into her inward parts. Then he split her body into two halves, out of which he made the heavens and the earth. He then made the heavenly bodies and arranged their courses, and finished his work of creation by making man out of the blood of a god mixed with clay. This poem was written on seven clay tablets, now generally known as the Seven Tablets of Creation; and after it was found in 1873 in Ashur-bani-pal's library at Nineveh, it was immediately compared with the Hebrew story of the Seven Days of Creation in the first chapter of Genesis. The two stories were seen to be alike in certain points: for example, the Hebrew word for the watery chaos out of which God brought order and life is another form of the Babylonian name for the dragon vanquished by Marduk; the creation of man is the last act in both stories, and in both man is made out of clay mingled with the divine principle of life—blood in the Babylonian story, and breath in the Hebrew story. We now know that the Babylonians had made their form of the Creation Myth of the New Year Festival by weaving together several earlier Sumerian myths, and that the Hebrew stories of Creation and the Flood were not taken direct from the Babylonians, but also went back to the earlier Sumerian forms of these myths (*see* HEBREW MYTHS).

The second great Babylonian myth is perhaps the most widely spread of all myths, the myth of the Flood. The Hebrew story of the Flood is very much like the Babylonian story, and is quite clearly dependent on it. In the Babylonian form of the myth the account of the god's determination to destroy mankind by a flood is part of what is known as the Epic of Gilgamesh, a long and exciting story of the fabulous adventures of the hero Gilgamesh, a semi-divine person who was the fifth king of Erech. The story tells how Gilgamesh set out in search of his ancestor Ut-napishtim, the only survivor of the Flood, who had been granted the gift of immortality by the gods. After a long and hard journey filled with many adventures, Gilgamesh reached his ancestor, Ut-napishtim, and learnt from him the story of the Flood. He heard how the god Enlil, who hated mankind, persuaded the high god, Anu, to destroy them by a flood. But Ea, who was friendly to man, let out to the pious Ut-napishtim the secret of what was going to happen, and told him how to build a great boat

and take on board animals of every kind to preserve 'seed of life' on the earth. Then followed a vivid account of the great storm which raged for seven days until 'all mankind were turned into mud'; the boat grounded on Mt. Nisir, and Ut-napishtim sent out in succession a dove which returned, a swallow which also returned, and finally a raven which did not return because it had found dry land. Then Ut-napishtim brought out everything that was in the boat and offered sacrifice on the top of the mountain. He told how the gods gathered like flies to the sacrifice, attracted by the sweet savour. The god Enlil discovered that someone had escaped the Flood and was full of rage, threatening to destroy the survivor; but Ea succeeded in pacifying Enlil, who then blessed Ut-napishtim and his wife and gave them the gift of immortality like the gods.

This is the Babylonian form of the myth, but the earlier Sumerian form has no connexion with the story of Gilgamesh, being a part of the Sumerian myth of Creation. Two things should be noticed here. First, both myths are part of a ritual; the Creation myth is a central part of the great New Year ritual which was intended to secure the yearly fertility of crops and cattle upon which the well-being of the people depended; and there is evidence that originally the myth of the Flood was also part of a ritual intended to protect the dwellers in the river-valley from the anger of the gods, who might cause another such disastrous flood as the myth describes. The second thing is that both myths grew out of something that really happened. The conquest of the monster, which comes before the act of creation, is a picture of the struggle of the early settlers in the river-valley to overcome the floods and marshes caused by the Tigris and Euphrates and to create a civilization there. In the same way the Flood myth was a reminder of various very bad floods which, from time to time, threatened the existence of the hard-won civilization which the first settlers in the river-valley had built up. The excavations at Ur and Kish have shown that such floods had happened, and that they caused great destruction. It is worth noting that the ship described in the Babylonian and Sumerian Flood stories is not at all like the Noah's ark beloved of the nursery. It was a gigantic round boat like the *quffah*, which is still used on the Euphrates by peasants for carrying grain and cattle.

. THE GOD MARDUK IN CONFLICT WITH A MONSTER
Marduk is attacking a winged lion, one of the monsters in the train of Tiamat. The figure on the left is
King Ashur-nazir-pal

The third myth to be described is the myth of the Adapa. Our knowledge of it came about in an interesting way. The tablet on which the myth was written was found among the famous collection of letters belonging to the Egyptian King, Akhenaten, at Tell el-Amarna. It appears to have served as a Babylonian lesson-book for young Egyptian priests, and shows that Babylonian culture had spread throughout the ancient Near East. Adapa, whose name may be a Babylonian or Sumerian variation of the Hebrew name Adam, was the son of the god Ea, and had a title which means 'the first man'. He served as a priest in the temple at Eridu, and provided the table of the gods with food, among which was fish. One day, as he was fishing, the south wind blew and overturned his boat; in his rage the hero broke the wings of the south wind so that it ceased to blow. The high god, Anu, observed this and sent his messenger to summon Adapa before him. To prepare him for the interview, his father Ea told him how to win the favour of the gods who guarded the gates of Anu's heaven, and further warned him not to take any of the food or drink which Anu would offer him. As Ea had foretold, he was offered food and drink; but he refused them—and when Anu, in surprise, asked why he refused them, he said that his father Ea had so ordered

him. Anu then told him that the food and drink which he had refused were the food and drink of the gods and would have given to him and mankind immortality. Anu then sent him back to earth and gave him dominion over the earth, but declared that mankind's lot should be sickness and death. This interesting myth, like the Hebrew story of the Fall of Adam, which it in some ways resembles, is apparently intended to explain man's failure to attain immortality. It may also have a connexion with some ritual intended to secure the favour of the underworld gods.

The last myth to be described is that of Etana and the Eagle. This is part of a long story about the beginning of the feud between the Eagle and the Serpent. Etana came to the help of the Eagle when it had been wounded by the Serpent; and, in return, the Eagle promised to carry Etana to heaven in search of a magical herb which ensured safety in childbirth. Etana needed the herb because his wife was about to give birth to a child—possibly thought of as the first childbirth that had happened on earth. The story gives a vivid description of the ascent, hour by hour, and how the features of the Babylonian landscape gradually dwindled and disappeared. The tablet breaks off at the point where Etana is overcome by fear, and, together with the Eagle, falls into the sea. The myth may have formed part of a ritual intended to give safety in childbirth. The scene of Etana's ascent on the eagle is depicted on an ancient Sumerian seal.

There are very many more Babylonian myths, the greater part of which were taken over from the Sumerians, together with the rituals with which they were connected and the religious ideas which they embody; but these will serve to give some idea of the general character of the Babylonian myths and their purpose. They will also show how far the Hebrew stories of the Creation, the Fall, and the Flood have been influenced by the far older Babylonian and Sumerian stories.

See also BABYLONIAN CIVILIZATION.

BACCHUS, *see* GODS OF GREECE AND ROME (DIONYSUS).

BANTU, *see* NEGRO AFRICANS.

BAPTISM, *see* SACRAMENTS.

BAPTIST. A member of one of the Nonconformist churches. The services and churches (or chapels) of Baptists are little different from those of other Protestant Christian denominations where there is no set service and the sermon is of chief importance. They usually have the Lord's Supper once a month, with no set form except the words spoken by Jesus. The chief difference is with regard to the other sacrament—Baptism. They do not baptize infants, but only those who are old enough to make a personal profession of faith in Jesus Christ. This they call 'Believers' Baptism'. They baptize by immersion, claiming that this, too, was the custom in the early Church.

In organization Baptists are like CONGREGATIONALISTS (q.v.). Among English Congregationalists who fled to Holland about the year 1600 to escape religious persecution, there were some who added to their 'Independent' ideas these Baptist principles. On the Continent at the very beginning of the REFORMATION (q.v.) almost 100 years before, there had been some extreme sects called Ana-Baptists. This name meant 'people who baptized again' because they believed infant baptism to be meaningless. It is possible that such people influenced these English refugees. In 1611 some of them returned from Holland to resume an uneasy and insecure **existence as a Baptist congregation in London.**

Notable among these early Baptists were John Smyth, formerly vicar of Gainsborough, and Thomas Helwys, a Nottinghamshire gentleman.

Their position in 17th-century England was much the same as that of Congregationalists, with whom they often had close relations. JOHN BUNYAN (q.v. Vol. V), for example, the tinker of Bedford—who, while in prison for unlicensed preaching, wrote his immortal *Pilgrim's Progress* —looked after a company of people which was composed of both Baptists and Congregationalists.

The number of Baptists in Great Britain to-day is about 382,000. Their influence has been much bigger than may be judged from these figures. William Carey (1761–1834), minister of a small Baptist church in Leicester, was prime mover in the modern MISSIONARY MOVEMENT (q.v.). Through him in 1792 was founded the first of the new Missionary Societies, that of the Baptists. He became its pioneer in India. Others of its famous missionaries have been George Grenfell (1849–1906) of the Congo in Africa, and Timothy Richard (1845–1919) of China.

Baptists have long been noted for their outstanding preachers, one of the most famous being Charles H. Spurgeon (1834–92). This great preacher, who came to London in 1854, held huge audiences enthralled, and his sermons, published at the rate of one a week, were far-famed. Baptists have also contributed to biblical scholarship, with an especial wealth of Old Testament specialists in recent years.

The strong missionary spirit among Baptists shows notable results abroad. There were Baptists among the colonists going to America from the middle of the 17th century. During the 19th century, when settlers were driving their ox-wagons to the undeveloped West, the Baptists could do more than most for the religious needs of this shifting population. Their preachers were often farmers themselves, and were therefore self-supporting. Their services were hearty and simple, their message practical and direct. The result is that Baptists are, with Methodists, one of the two largest Protestant denominations in the United States of America to-day, with ten million members. They are to be found, too, in all the British Dominions. Scattered and small Baptist groups are in many countries of Europe. Missionary work, chiefly of American and British Baptists, has led to the planting of churches in India, China, Japan,

Africa, South America, and the West Indies. In Britain the majority of Baptist churches belong to the Baptist Union, founded in the year 1813. This federation of Churches holds an annual Assembly at which it elects its President. This Union is itself a member of the Baptist World Alliance formed in 1905. The estimated total of Baptist Communicants throughout the world is over twelve millions.

See also CHRISTIAN CHURCH.

BARROWS AND CAIRNS. Heaps of earth (barrows) or stones (cairns) covering ancient

legends that had already been recited for hundreds of years. After singing of the death of Hector, he describes how the body was cremated on a great funeral pyre. A day later, when the embers had been quenched with wine—

His brothers then, and friends, the snowy bones
Gather'd into an urn of gold, still pouring out their
    moans.
Then wrapped they in soft purple veils the rich urn,
    digg'd a pit,
Grav'd it, built up the grave with stones, and quickly
    piled on it
A barrow.

NEW STONE AGE LONG BARROW AND BRONZE ROUND BARROWS AT WINTERBOURNE STOKE, WILTS.
Ashmolean Mus.

burials are to be seen almost all over Britain, especially on open country such as the chalk downs of Sussex and Wessex, and the moorland regions of the north and west. The custom of piling up a large burial mound over the dead (Latin *tumulus*, as on the ordnance maps: the word 'barrow' is from a Saxon word with the same meaning) was followed from New Stone Age times up to the coming of Christianity, probably only chiefs and other people of importance being thus honoured. We can read a description of the actual making of a barrow in the *Iliad* of Homer, the Greek poet, whose writings are probably collections of prehistoric

Without excavation it is usually not possible to say what date a simple circular mound might be. In north and west Britain large cairns, which may be long or round, often cover stone-built chambers which were used in New Stone Age times for collective burial—family vaults in which bodies of a local ruling clan were placed for generations. The stones from these chambers, when they are exposed, are often called MEGALITHS (q.v.). In southern England, long barrows are of the same date as these chambered cairns (say, about 2400–1800 B.C.) and also were used for collective burials. No metal objects have ever been found in them. The majority of round barrows or cairns one is likely to see were built during the long period of the Early and Middle Bronze Age, from about 1900 to 900 B.C., and cover individual burials—one person, one barrow. Early in the Bronze Age the corpse was buried in a grave, usually with some tools or weapons or ornaments to accompany it to the next world; but later, religious custom changed, and bodies were cremated and often buried in a pottery vessel. In the Late Bronze Age (about 900 to 700 B.C.) new-comers to England from the Continent brought in the custom of making regular cemeteries. They placed the ashes of their dead in holes in the ground without a barrow over them—but they sometimes used barrows of an earlier time for these cemeteries, since these had a tradition of sanctity. The individual graves under their conspicuous mounds on the hill-crests suggest that the people lived a pastoral and possibly a wandering life under the leadership of great chieftains who were given splendid burials; the more democratic cemeteries of the Late Bronze Age imply a permanent settlement in one place, and something approaching a village community.

Barrows and cairns were built in Roman times, perhaps for romanized British nobles who had a lingering tradition of this ancient barbarian form of burial; and they continued to be made for the pagan Saxons. The famous treasure and ship found at Sutton Hoo near Ipswich were buried under a large barrow in the 7th century A.D.

BASQUES, *see* SPANIARDS; FRENCH.

BASUTOS, a Bantu people of South Africa. *See* NEGRO AFRICANS.

BAVARIANS, *see* GERMANS.

BEDOUIN. Their name comes from the Arabic *bedawi*, a desert-dweller, and is applied by the Arabs only to those who live permanently in tents and have no cultivation, and are therefore nomads or wanderers. There are many ARABS (q.v.) who live permanently in tents near their corn-lands, and many others who live in tents for part of the year; but these are not regarded as Bedouin. It is commonly believed that most Arabs are, and always have been, Bedouin; but this is certainly not the case now, and probably never was. It is more likely that Arabia was once better watered than it is now,

and that many of its inhabitants were settled until parts of the land began to dry up, and the inhabitants had to take to a nomadic life. The vast majority of the Arabs are now either townsmen or settled cultivators, and this applies to central and southern Arabia as well as to the 'Fertile Crescent', that is to say, Palestine, Syria, and Mesopotamia.

The Bedouin usually depend upon the camel, that is to say, upon the one-humped camel or dromedary. Unlike the two-humped camel, which is still found wild in central Asia, the one-humped camel does not exist in a wild state, and no one knows where it originally came from. Breeding camels is the chief industry of the Bedouin: they sell them to the settled Arabs, whose principal means of transport they are. Camels are used not only for long journeys, but for such work as bringing in the harvest and, in Egypt, for drawing carts.

The Bedouin do not just wander about: each tribe has its special grazing areas. Many of the chief tribes spend the winter, when it is cooler and damper, in central Arabia, and the summer on the edges of the Fertile Crescent, moving slowly in spring and autumn from one to the other. Much of their life is spent in raiding one another's herds. In these raids there is generally little fighting, as it is against Bedouin practice to fight against odds. In the summer the Bedouin come into contact with the settled Arabs. They are dependent on the latter to supply them with grain and to buy their cattle and camels; but they also raid their flocks and crops whenever they get the opportunity.

The Bedouin are much less romantic than is commonly supposed. They are brave after their fashion and extremely hardy, but are as a rule poor specimens of humanity, small, wizened, and unwashed. Cheerful and hospitable, full of songs and stories, they are at the same time excitable, unreliable, and easily offended. Though nominally Moslems, they appear to take little account of their religion, and seldom pray, or fast in *Ramadân* (the month of fasting), or go on the pilgrimage to Mecca (*see* ISLAM).

The sheikhs are often fine-looking men, with considerable dignity and charm of manner; but they are usually given to intrigue and treachery.

The usual costume of the Bedouin is a long, dirty white shirt, a brown cloak made of camel-hair, and a checked red-and-white head-cloth held in place by a piece of twisted rope. The

A GROUP OF BEDOUIN
When they travel from one grazing ground to another the Bedouin carry all their belongings on the backs of their camels. *Haddon Lib., Cambridge*

women wear long blue cotton dresses and black head-cloths held in place by turbans of the same material. The women are often not veiled, and enjoy a good deal of freedom. Very few of the men, except the sheikhs, have more than one wife, but divorce is frequent.

Their dwellings are tents made of cloth of black goat's hair. One long strip forms the roof and another goes along the windward side. The lee side is open, and the tents are pitched in lines, all facing the same way. An ordinary man's tent consists only of two small compartments, but some of the sheikhs' tents are very large, with an end compartment which may hold twenty guests.

With the introduction of modern means of transport the demand for camels is falling off, and as it continues to do so the Bedouin will have either to settle down or die out.

See also SAHARA, PEOPLES OF; Vol. IV: ARABIC LANGUAGE.

BEELZEBUB, an ancient god of flies. *See* SATAN.

BELGIANS. In Roman times Belgium was that part of Gaul known as Gallia Belgica and was inhabited mainly by Celtic tribes. However, by the 5th century, when the FRANKS (q.v.) became rulers, immigrations from the north had changed its populations largely to Germanic. Both the Celtic and Germanic elements are to be found in Belgium of to-day: the Walloons, a people of Celtic origin, live in the south-east of the country and speak Walloon, a dialect of the ancient French; while in the north are the Flemish, a Germanic people speaking their own Flemish language. The official and business language of the Belgians is French. Most of the people belong to the Roman Catholic Church (*see* FRENCH AND GERMAN LANGUAGES, Vol. IV).

After several centuries of rule by the Franks the country split into independent duchies, counties, and free cities. In Flanders especially, free merchant cities developed, and played an important part in medieval life. There was a flourishing trade between the Flemish cloth merchants and England in the Middle Ages. Bruges was

RIVERSIDE AT GHENT

Much of the city's merchandise is carried by barge along the River Scheldt to Antwerp. *Roy. Geog. Soc.*

the chief wool market of northern Europe. Bruges, Ghent, and Ypres were famed for their prosperity and civic pride, and the wealth of the merchants is reflected in the magnificent 15th century buildings and in the brilliant painting of the time. By a series of conquests and alliances the Netherlands or Low Countries, as Belgium and Holland (*see* DUTCH) were then called, became part of the Empire of Maximilian of Austria in 1477. Later they became part of the Spanish Empire; but in 1598 Belgium became for a short time an independent kingdom. Between 1621, when it fell again under Spanish rule, and 1815, when it became one state with Holland, Belgium was governed by a succession of countries. In 1831 it separated from Holland, and set up an independent kingdom.

To-day Belgium is the most densely peopled country in Europe; it has great manufacturing industries and is very intensively cultivated. About half the population live by farming, agriculture, and horticulture. The flower market of Brussels is world famous. Belgium is distinguished by having very few large land-owners and a comparatively small number of peasant labourers: most of the land is worked by small landowners.

Flemings and Walloons still differ in more than language. Flemings are fair-complexioned and hard-working. The Walloons are darker-skinned and smaller in height. Intermarriage has resulted in a people who have great vitality and are very enterprising and industrious.

See also Vol. III: BELGIUM.

BENEDICTINE, *see* MONK.

BENGALIS, *see* INDIAN PEOPLES.

BERBERS, *see* MOORS; SAHARA, PEOPLES OF.

BHILS, *see* INDIAN HILL TRIBES, Section 5.

BIBLE. 1. One of the materials on which men wrote in the ancient world was made from a kind of reed called Papyrus or Byblus (*see* WRITING, HISTORY OF, Vol. IV). From the first name comes our word 'paper', from the second 'Bible'. meaning 'books'. When Greek Christians spoke of Tὰ Βιβλία (*ta Biblia*), 'The Books', they meant the sacred books of their religion. It is well to remember that the Greek word was plural. The Bible is not a book, but two collections of books. One collection is the Old Testament, the sacred books of JUDAISM (q.v.). The other is the New Testament.

2. THE OLD TESTAMENT. Its language is Hebrew. It consists of thirty-nine books which the Jews divided into three groups:

The Law—Genesis to Deuteronomy, also called Pentateuch, or five books.

The Prophets—Joshua to 2 Kings, and Isaiah to Malachi (omitting Daniel and Lamentations).

The Writings—the rest of the books, including Daniel and Lamentations.

It may help more to make our own division, according to what the books are about.

History—God and His People. This is set out, not just as a record of events, but as the mighty acts of God, who is preparing a People for Himself, whose work is still going on, to lead to even greater things in the future.

It is God who makes all things in the beginning (Genesis). It is against Him that men do evil. From among all mankind He chooses the family of Abraham. When this family, now grown to a tribe, is in slavery in Egypt, God raises up Moses as leader and makes a Way Out (Exodus). Thus they come to Palestine, under

Moses' successor (Joshua). They believe that God gave them the Law, to shape the life of their tribe (Leviticus, Numbers, Deuteronomy).

Under various tribal leaders (Judges) they try to get a firmer footing in their new country. The greatest of these leaders (Samuel) answers their demand for a King. The greatest King is David. Others succeed to the throne (Kings). About 933 B.C. the kingdom divides into Israel, the Northern part, and Judah, the Southern.

social wrongs of their time, as well as the false idolatry. God is righteous, and His People should show they are His by their conduct. Judgement is about to come for all their evil. The Assyrians will invade Palestine. But this sinful and suffering nation is still God's people.

About 586 B.C. Jeremiah in Jerusalem sees still more certain doom coming from Babylon. He is equally sure of the future, that the nation, after a period of misfortune, will make a fresh start.

TWO PAGES FROM THE CODEX SINAITICUS (Luke xix. 13–xx. 34)
An early MS. of the Bible written in Greek probably in the first half of the 4th century. It was found in a convent on Mount Sinai in the 19th century and given to the Tsar of Russia. It is now in the British Museum. *British Mus.*

Israel falls before the Assyrians in 722 B.C. and Judah before the Babylonians in 586 B.C. Parts of this same story are told from a different point of view in Chronicles.

Some of the Hebrews deported to Babylon return late in the 6th century B.C. and more the following century (Ezra and Nehemiah).

Prophecy—God's Will for His People. Many people think of prophesying as *fore*telling what is going to happen. More often it is *forth*-telling, proclaiming what God wants men to do now. The PROPHET (q.v.) is someone who feels that he has a message from God for the times. The earliest Hebrew prophets to leave their message in writing in our Old Testament belong to the 8th century B.C. The 8th-century prophets, Amos, Hosea, Isaiah, and Micah, speak of the

In Ezekiel's time the doom has come; he is one of the exiles, looking to the reformed and holy nation of the future. The author of Isaiah, Chapters xl–lv, belongs to this time, with his message of comfort and hope. Here is the mysterious figure of the Suffering Servant. It seems likely that the prophet meant God's people who had to suffer because the world was so full of sin. Jesus used these chapters to explain why He must suffer and die.

Haggai and Zechariah, about 520 B.C., stimulate and strengthen both the returning exiles from Babylon and the remnant who had been left in Palestine under enemy occupation in their task of rebuilding God's Temple. Malachi and Obadiah belong to the middle of the next century.

Poetry—the Songbook of the People. The Book of Psalms is by far the most important part. It is a collection of hymns. Lamentations is five bitter laments connected with the Fall of Jerusalem, 586 B.C. The Song of Songs is a cluster of marriage lyrics.

Other Literature—Problems of the People. Job is poetic drama about the problem of innocent suffering. Jonah is a parable showing that God's people ought to preach to heathen nations. Ruth also shows God's care for the foreigner. Proverbs is a collection of wise sayings about conduct. Ecclesiastes is the musings of a man who is tempted to doubt if life is worth living.

Daniel belongs to a late type of Jewish writing which seems as though the writer is telling of strange things seen in a dream. The purpose is to show that God's will does in the end triumph over the evils of the world.

The first Christians continued to read in their services and in their homes these Old Testament Scriptures of the Jews, but they saw new meanings in many of these books. The People whom God had been preparing for Himself, they saw fulfilled in the Christian Church, and boldly claimed themselves to be the True Israel. God's will for His people they found to point to Jesus and His followers—for many prophets had spoken of the Chosen People as having a duty as well as a privilege, the duty of enlightening other nations. Some prophets had spoken in times of suffering of a deliverance, some of a Deliverer whom God would send—the Messiah (Anointed One) in Hebrew, the Christ in Greek. They saw all these prophecies fulfilled in Jesus, and the mysterious words about the Suffering Servant fulfilled in His sufferings, death, and resurrection. The poetry of the Old Testament, especially the Psalms, became the Christians' first hymn-book. The Christians' own literature, the New Testament, is only to be understood against the background of the Old.

3. New Testament. These additional twenty-seven books, most of them letters, were written over the greater part of a hundred years and were not at first thought of as forming a new holy book. The writers use the colloquial Greek of their day. They all have one great subject, Jesus Christ. The first part of the New Testament, the four Gospels, sets out His birth, life, teaching, death, and resurrection. But this is, in the words of St. Luke, only 'what Jesus *began* to do'. The rest of the books go on to show how,

although now unseen, He is still with His People, and still enables men to live triumphantly.

The earliest of the writings are the two letters to the Thessalonians—though some think that the letter to the Galatians may have been even earlier. Paul, the missionary, wrote about A.D. 53, because the young Church had misunderstood some points of Christian teaching, especially about the coming again of the Lord Jesus. During the next few years St. Paul wrote to Christians in Corinth, Galatia (part of Asia Minor), and Rome. The letters to Corinth and Galatia were written because false teachers were leadings his converts astray; that to Rome is the most weighty of all the epistles—perhaps the most important letter ever written. It was to the Church already founded in the capital of the Western World—and it set out the central doctrines of the Christian faith concerning Salvation. A few years later St. Paul wrote the letters to the Colossians, Ephesians, Philippians, and Philemon, in Asia Minor. He wrote from prison in Rome, and he wrote of the universal Church, through which Christ acts, and through which He will triumph. He called the Church Christ's Body.

Both Peter and Paul had nearly reached the end of their lives when the first Gospel appeared. It was written about A.D. 63 by Mark, who had often been interpreter for Peter, who could speak no Greek, and remembered his word-pictures of Jesus. At this time there was also a written collection of 'sayings of Jesus', such as the first Christians had been in the habit of learning by heart and reciting. A little later two people independently decided to combine this early collection and Mark's book into a fuller Gospel. Matthew's Gospel comes from one who was a Jew, and who emphasized that Jesus fulfils all the Old Testament promises; Luke is the only New Testament writer who was a Gentile. He wrote of Jesus as the Saviour of the world.

At the end of the 1st century St. John's Gospel was written by an old man of great spiritual wisdom. His life of Jesus is different from the others, and has been compared to a great artist's painting, which is different from the best of photographs. Finally, apart from ten books of shorter letters, we can mention three other books. The Epistle to the Hebrews represents among the letters what Matthew's Gospel does among the Gospels—Jesus as the crown of Jewish religion. The Acts of the Apostles is a second volume by

idea was that they joined the fairies. In China, to make sure that the baby will not be spirited away, an open lock is moved over its body and closed when it reaches the ground, so anchoring the child to this world. A new-born baby is often presented before the gods, and communion established between it and the ancestors.

One of the most widespread practices is some form of baptism: such rites are found in Central America, Papua, Tibet, and many other parts of the world. Water, especially running water, since it is life-giving and also purifying, is considered specially suitable for birth ceremonies.

There is sometimes a ceremony of readmission of the mother into the tribe after her time of seclusion. A Hopi Indian mother cannot go out until five days have elapsed after the birth. On the twentieth day the child is presented to the sun, and the mother becomes again a full member of the community. In England the custom is often observed that a mother does not go out until she has been 'churched'. A birth is, of course, the occasion for such expressions of joy and goodwill as feasting and the giving of presents.

See also FOLK-LORE.

BLACK FELLOWS, *see* AUSTRALIAN ABORIGINES.

BOERS, *see* SOUTH AFRICANS.

BOHEMIANS, *see* CZECHOSLOVAKS.

BOLIVIANS. The population of Bolivia, a country twice the size of Great Britain, is only about 3 millions—about one-sixteenth of the population of Britain. Three-quarters of the people live on the highland plateau to the east of the Andes Mountains, and most of the rest of Bolivia, particularly the low, hot forest lands to the north, is very thinly peopled. In spite of some immigration, including about 3,000 Germans, the country is under-populated. If Bolivia is to take its place among the South American Republics it needs more people, for much of the wealth of the country has not yet been exploited, and the eastern valleys in particular are very fertile and rich.

The Indian population of Bolivia is descended from the great pre-Spanish Indian civilizations (*see* INCA). They now form the great majority of the people, but they are sadly degenerated. Most of them are illiterate, apathetic,

BOLIVIAN PEASANTS
They still use a primitive hand plough with a stone blade
Haddon Lib., Cambridge

physically poor, and make little effort to rise from their very low standard of living and the state of peonage (a polite word for slavery) under which they exist. The country is governed by a small white or half-caste privileged minority whose reputation for progressive statesmanship has not been very great.

Like most of South America, Bolivia became part of the Spanish Empire in the 16th century. In the early 19th century came the great wars of liberation under the leadership of the Venezuelan soldier-statesman, BOLIVAR (q.v. Vol. V); and in 1825 the state, called Bolivia in honour of Bolivar, was separated from Peru and established as an independent republic. Since then her history has been largely of anarchy and war. In a war with Chile (1879–83) she lost her stretch of Pacific coastline and became a completely land-locked country. In 1932, in an attempt to force an outlet to the Atlantic south-east, she engaged in a disastrous war of much blood and horror with Paraguay. But she gained no outlet to the sea.

Bolivia's social and political backwardness is to some extent the result of her geographical isolation and consequent economic stagnation. There is extremely little sense of national unity; the Indians and whites have no common outlook or purpose; and the late dictator, President

Busch, governed his country on principles little different from Nazism.

See also Vol. III: BOLIVIA.

BRAHMINS, *see* CASTE.

BRAZILIANS. Although the South American state of Brazil has an area more than forty times the size of England, its total population is not as great—and most of this population lives along the coasts and in the eastern highlands. In the tropical forest regions of the Amazon there are large areas where the population is as low as one man per square mile.

The people of Brazil are very mixed in origin. First there are the aboriginal Indians, many of whom were killed by the early settlers or died under forced labour in the gold-mines. There are still many tribes of Indians in the forests of the interior who have had little or no contact with the white man, and continue their tribal life of hunting and fishing. Many an expedition has come to an untimely end through meeting parties of these Indians with their poisoned

AMAZON INDIAN IN A DUG-OUT CANOE
Roy. Geog. Soc.

arrows, and it is still considered dangerous to travel through some parts of the Amazon head-waters because of these tribal raids (*see* AMERICAN INDIANS, CENTRAL AND SOUTH).

The white population are, for the most part, descendants of the early Portuguese settlers, though they have been added to by big European immigrations of fortune-seekers, especially during the 19th century. There are about thirty-two million Europeans, a large proportion being of Italian and German descent. Most of these,

tanned by the tropical sun, are rather the colour of the coffee they grow than white; they are slightly under average height, and the tropical heat has made them a slow-moving people, in a land where no one works between the hours of 11 a.m. and 3 p.m. Brazil is the only South American republic where Portuguese, rather than Spanish, is the official language.

The third element in the Brazilian population is the negro, the descendants of the slaves brought over from West Africa in the 17th century to replace the Indians, first in the sugar plantations and then in the gold- and diamond-mines. Some of these were a good type of educated Moslem negro, and these intermarried with the Brazilians, producing a large class of Mulattos (i.e. half-negro, half-European). The negroes still do a large proportion of the manual work; but they are equal citizens of the Republic with the Portuguese, and there is no colour bar.

The Portuguese first came to Brazil in 1500. They found there the brazilwood tree, which produced a much-prized red dye called brazil, and from this came the name of the country. The early settlers fought with the Indians and enslaved them ruthlessly, making them work too hard in miserable conditions. The only people to consider the welfare of the Indians were the Jesuit missionaries, who made expeditions into the interior of the country, risking hardship and death to bring a better way of life to the Indian tribes. They fought against the slave-gatherers, and did what they could to protect the Indians against the slave-trade. Among them was a priest called Bartoleme de Las Casas who, stirred by the sight of so many Indians dying of forced labour, started an agitation which resulted in substituting negro slaves for Indian.

In 1807 Napoleon attacked Portugal; and the King of Portugal, with many of the best families of nobles, fled from Europe to Brazil, settling in Rio de Janeiro. They brought with them works of art, books, and customs which had a considerable effect on the culture of the Brazilians. When Napoleon was defeated the King returned to Portugal, but his son, Pedro, remained behind. Shortly afterwards Brazil separated from Portugal, and Pedro became the first emperor. His son, Pedro II, who reigned from 1831 to 1889, was the real maker of modern Brazil. He was a progressive, liberal-minded ruler, and built up Brazil on something like democratic lines. By 1888 most of the slave

A BRAZILIAN COFFEE ESTATE

The men are sweeping up the coffee beans which have been spread out on concrete to dry in the sun. *Roy. Geog. Soc.*

owners had freed their slaves, and in that year slavery was officially abolished. When, in 1889, the country decided on a republic, Pedro abdicated, and the revolution was carried through without a struggle. Much money has since been spent in developing modern ports, railways, industries, and other facilities of a modern state, and in improving sanitation, so doing away with the plagues of yellow fever. As the result of the efforts of Santos-Dumont, the aviation engineer, a modern airway system is now growing up; and this will have a great effect upon a country where means of communication are so difficult.

Throughout its history Brazil has been through a series of booms and depressions resulting in sudden changes and the making and losing of great fortunes. These have been caused by the exploitation and collapse of one major product after another. The first settlers put all their efforts into sugar plantations. Then followed the great gold and diamond rush. In 1900 the possibilities of rubber were discovered, and a great rubber boom followed. Then rubber seeds were smuggled out of the country, and new rubber plantations in the East Indies stole the market. In 1754 a Franciscan monk planted some coffee seeds in his monastery; and from this grew the great coffee industry, now the major source of Brazil's wealth—and providing 70% of the world's coffee. There are other sources of great wealth in Brazil waiting to be exploited: the richness of the Amazon forests, in which almost every known tree flourishes; the great iron-ore mountain, containing approximately a quarter of the total world supply; the possibilities of stock-breeding in the Brazilian highlands—all these offer possibilities of a more stable national economy.

See also Vol. III: BRAZIL.

BRETONS, a Celtic people of Brittany. *See* CELTIC CIVILIZATION; FRENCH.

BRITISH ISRAELITE. In 1649 a certain John Sadler wrote a book called *The Rights of the Kingdom,* in which he suggested that the name of Britain was derived from two Syrian words *berat anak*—the land of tin and lead; and he drew attention to resemblances between Hebrew and English law and custom—though, in fact, these are due to the influence of the Bible, and not to any racial connexions. Then between 1757 and 1824 a retired naval officer, Richard Brothers, wrote fifteen volumes on the descent of the British from the Hebrews, claiming himself to be descended from King David. He died insane. From 1840 onwards a number of writers, including C. P. Smyth, Astronomer Royal for Scotland, have developed the idea that the

British are the descendants of the so-called lost ten tribes. In recent years an organized movement called the British-Israel World Federation has attracted a considerable number of adherents, estimated at two million in all, including those on both sides of the Atlantic. It has set up a publishing house which issues a considerable amount of literature. It obtains, however, no support either from competent biblical scholars or from ethnologists, and its teachings cannot be shown to have any assured basis in fact. None of its leaders shows any real learning, much sense of history, or judgement in distinguishing between fact and fable. Though very earnest people, they are inclined to ignore the thought and labour given to the study of the Bible during the past half-century, as well as the work of the new science of anthropology.

The most serious objection to the British-Israel theory is the now well-established fact that the ten tribes never were 'lost'. Even supposing that the British taken as a whole were a Semitic people (and ethnology establishes that they certainly are not) they could not be the descendants of the 'lost ten tribes' because no such body ever existed. When Northern Israel was conquered by the Assyrians, only a very small proportion of its total population was deported by the king of Assyria: the rest remained in the neighbourhood of Samaria, as the evidence of several Bible passages shows. Right to the end of the Bible the Twelve Tribes are spoken of as still existing, and some of them are mentioned by name, such as Benjamin and Asher. The verse in the apocryphal book 2 Esdras xiii. 40, which is used by the British Israelites to suggest that they crossed the Danube into Europe, is a mistranslation, and means nothing of the kind. There is no justification for identifying the Scythians with these 'lost' Hebrews, or the Kimmerians either, and the Anglo-Saxons, Jutes, and Danes were certainly in no sense Hebrews. Josephus in his History (A.D. 93) knows nothing of these 'lost' tribes, and he describes the Babylonian Jews as being still in Mesopotamia, east of the Euphrates, and as being a fusion of Northern and Southern Israelites. It is officially denied by the College of Arms that the present King of England is descended from David, as the British Israelites declare.

It would seem, then, that this sect is a typical example of a mistaken belief being acceptable in spite of its falsity, because it satisfies a human emotion. Like the Nazi *Herrenvolk* theory, it encourages national pride of a rather unwise sort.

A word must be added about the superstition connected with the supposed measurements of the Great Pyramid in Egypt. The Scottish astronomer, C. P. Smyth, began this theory, and it was renewed in 1932 by a series of articles in the British Israelites' magazine, *The National Message*. Archaeologists tell us that this pyramid was erected as a royal tomb, and also as a symbol of the Sun-God. The 'inch' of British measurements was not used in its construction, but apparently some sort of decimal system was known. In spite of these established facts, the British Israelites have filled whole books with calculations of the proportions of the pyramid in inches, upon which are based alleged revelations by Almighty God regarding the future history of the world. It has been said that one might just as well have tried to discover divine prophecies by searching for them in the number of square feet in the roof of the Crystal Palace. The methods used by British Israelites in measuring the Great Pyramid are undoubtedly mistaken, and it is difficult to take very seriously the conclusions which they draw from them.

BRITISH PEOPLES. What are now the British Isles were, perhaps as late as 6000 B.C., part of the continent of Europe with no dividing sea. But even after the formation of the English Channel until the Norman conquest of 1066, the last successful invasion of Britain, these islands lay open to successive waves of wandering peoples. By the 16th and 17th centuries A.D. a really efficient navy had been built up, and the peoples of Great Britain were able to keep other people out. But at all times British culture has been closely connected with the culture of Europe.

Little is known about the earliest human inhabitants of these islands. Scientific study of prehistoric times has taught us something about the tools, the burial habits, and the domestic architecture of these peoples, and has made clear that Britain provided for thousands of generations a suitable environment for human life (*see* PREHISTORIC MAN). About 3000 B.C. a people appeared who probably came by sea from what is now Spain. These short, dark people, called by us Iberians, still survive as a physical type, notably in the Rhondda valley in Wales. We know much more about the latest of prehistoric peoples to come to Britain, the Celts. They certainly came over from north-west Europe in successive waves, perhaps centuries apart. They numbered many fair, tall, long-headed people, but were already a very mixed race even before they came to Britain. They imposed their language, in one form or another, on all inhabitants of the islands; and from one of their tribes or peoples, the Brythons, has come the name Britain (*see* CELTIC CIVILIZATION.)

Subsequent waves of invasion are part of written history, and are much better known. Early in the Christian era the Romans conquered Britain with their legions, and organized part of the island as a province of their great Empire. Relatively little new human stock was added to Britain in the three centuries of Roman rule, for the Romans did not come to settle; but politically and culturally their invasion was of major consequence, for it brought the island for the first time directly in touch with civilization. It brought Roman law and business, and, later, Roman Christianity. In the 5th and 6th centuries, after Roman rule had ended, Britain was subjected to mass invasion by pagan Germanic tribes. Until quite recently it was believed that these invading Germans, the Anglo-Saxons, killed off all the earlier inhabitants, except in Cornwall, Wales, and the Highlands of Scotland, and set up over what now was called England (Angle-land) a new country with a new human stock. In fact, though many of the Britons were driven westwards and many killed, and though some purely Germanic villages were formed in England, especially in Kent and in East Anglia, over the whole country there still survived a considerable element of British stock, which was eventually assimilated with that of the invaders.

In the 9th and 10th centuries came the extraordinary raids of the Vikings from the Scandinavian peninsulas. Some of these sea-raiders

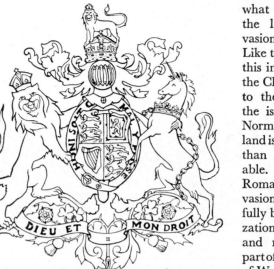

THE ROYAL COAT OF ARMS

stayed in the east of England, in Ireland, and in the north of Scotland, to form important Danish and Norwegian elements in the British nation. Then in 1066 William the Conqueror of Normandy headed what was destined to be the last successful invasion of Great Britain. Like that of the Romans, this invasion from across the Channel added little to the human stock of the islands, and to-day Norman blood in England is more talked about than actually identifiable. But, again like the Roman, the Norman invasion brought England fully back into the civilization of western Europe, and made her history part of the broader history of Western civilization.

Since the Norman Conquest there have been a few small additions to the peoples of these islands—Flemish weavers in the late Middle Ages, refugee French HUGUENOTS (q.v.) in the late 17th century, an irregular trickle of political refugees which grew between 1930 and 1940 to fair size, and a few immigrants attracted by economic or cultural opportunity. With the discovery of new worlds in America and the Pacific, people began to move out from the British Isles, and, though the total population at home has also vastly increased, these islands have added millions of persons to the countries of the new world. Awareness of their mixed racial origins has combined with other factors to make the British peoples as a whole unwilling to base their patriotism and national pride on anything as abstract as race. The British have a very strong sense of pride and superiority, but it is pride as a nation, as a group moulded by a long history, not as a 'pure' race endowed by nature from the start with a mystic superiority.

The British peoples—English, WELSH, SCOTS, IRISH (qq.v.)—were, one after another, brought together in political unity under the English Crown. In general, it may be said that over the four centuries, from the 13th to the 17th, when England was the conscious rival of Scotland and

THE ENGLISH COUNTRY-SIDE: HAYMAKING IN SUFFOLK. *The Times*

Ireland, Englishmen and Scotsmen came to respect one another; Englishmen and Irishmen did not. Union with Scotland has been a success; union with Ireland at least a partial failure. Nevertheless, the British peoples, despite their past quarrels, despite the still incomplete reconciliation with Eire, do possess the unity of a team, the unity of peoples under a common law.

The English became a united nation a long time ago—within a few centuries after the Norman Conquest. The Anglo-Saxons were a loose collection of tribes, and early England was divided into seven independent and warring kingdoms. These had begun to come together under Wessex kings, such as ALFRED THE GREAT (q.v. Vol. V), even before the Norman Conquest. The Normans set up a strong central monarchy with the necessary legal and financial institutions, so making certain that England would not develop, as Germany at the time was developing, into a collection of small rival states. When the French-speaking aristocracy and the Anglo-Saxon-speaking common people had grown together into an English-speaking nation by the later Middle Ages, the unity of the country was complete, though there was, of course, much local diversity of dialect, of customs, of ways of life. Even to-day, in spite of modern communications and education, Dorset is very different from Lancashire. This new unity was tried out against France in the Hundred Years War; it was further tested and forged in the struggle initiated by HENRY VIII (q.v. Vol. V) against the Roman papacy, and in the foundation of the CHURCH OF ENGLAND (q.v.). After the defeat of the Spanish Armada, English patriotism took on the deep assurance it has ever since maintained.

The national character of the English has been very differently described, but most commentators agree over one quality, which they describe as fatuous self-satisfaction, serene sense of superiority, or insular pride, according to the feelings of the individual writer. English patriotism is based on a deep sense of security. Englishmen as individuals may have been insecure, threatened with loss of job, unsure of themselves, or unhappy in many ways; but as a nation they

THE ENGLISH COUNTRY-SIDE: A VILLAGE CRICKET MATCH. *The Times*

have been for centuries secure, serene in their national successes. No other nation has in these centuries taken anything from the English by force. They have not lived in a state of impotent hatred of their neighbours as Frenchmen or Germans have often lived. This national sense of security, hardly threatened by the Spaniards at the time of the Armada, or by the armies of Napoleon, or by the Germans in the First World War, has been greatly weakened by the Second World War and by the invention of the atomic bomb. But the British peoples have still a sturdy psychological heritage of serenity born of security. That security they owe, not merely to the geographical accident of being islanders, but to the fact that they have been able to organize themselves for the defence of the island. Foreigners have long been impressed with the Englishman's ability to organize, to co-operate, to get things done, to reconcile the contrasting demands of liberty and authority, of individual initiative and group conformity.

Many books have been written—even more, perhaps, by Frenchmen, Americans, Germans,

and other foreigners than by Englishmen—on English traits, English ways of life, and the English character. Their authors are by no means always in agreement, but they do tend to point out what seem to them puzzles, contrasts, in the way the English behave. A few of these contrasts may serve to sum up how the world looks at the English.

First, there is the contrast between the unity the English display in a crisis, their strong sense for public order, indeed for conformity, and their extraordinary toleration of individual eccentricities, their love of diversity, their determined individualism—'every Englishman's home is his castle'. Germans are usually astounded by what they regard as the Englishman's lack of respect for authority and discipline. Frenchmen are often puzzled by the vehemence of English political debates, by the Hyde Park public orator, and similar phases of English life, which in their own country would seem signs of grave political disturbance. This sort of contrast has led to the common belief held by foreigners, and indeed by Englishmen themselves, that they are a most illogical people, always preferring practical compromises to theoretical exactness and correctness.

Second, there is the contrast between English democracy, English sense of the dignity and importance of the individual, and the very great social and economic inequalities that have hitherto characterized English life. There has

reputation of the English as hard-headed practical men—the 'nation of shopkeepers'—and as men of poetry and imagination—the countrymen of SHAKESPEARE, KEATS, and SHELLEY (qq.v. Vol. V). The English, indeed the British, tradition in philosophy has always been realistic and hostile to mysticism; yet the English look

INDUSTRIAL ENGLAND: THE POTTERY DISTRICT OF STAFFORDSHIRE. *The Times*

been in very recent times some tendency toward greater economic and social equality. But Victorian and Edwardian England—which foreigners still think of as the typical England—did display extremes of riches and poverty, and, even more, draw an almost caste line between ladies and gentlemen and those not ladies and gentlemen; yet it functioned successfully under popular suffrage with extremely little sense of class conflict. One clue to this puzzle may be in the richness of English group-life: the Englishman finds in his school, church, club, team, and other voluntary associations—including even his 'pub'—the social satisfaction and sense of communal security which he needs.

Third, there is the contrast between the

down on the French as narrow rationalists, and English literature sounds the depths of human nature as profoundly as does that of the mystical Germans. The English appear to reserve their mystic flights for poetry, and keep them out of such matters as politics and morals.

Commentators have also noticed less paradoxical characteristics among the English. One of these is a fondness for understatement, a trait sometimes carried to extremes among the upper classes, but clearly evident as a genuine national habit among all classes. The expression 'not bad' is a typical example. Americans, brought up in a national love of overstatement, exaggeration, and tall tales, find this English trait most conspicuous, and put it down to false modesty. It is not surprising that this often leads to misunderstandings, based though these are on nothing more than a difference in the use of words. The apparent coldness of Englishmen and their reserve has been almost universally noted by foreigners; but foreigners also

historical process of adjustment among many competing temperaments, institutions, and ideas. For the British Isles have been not only a melting-pot of racial stocks: they have been also a melting-pot of ideas. Both mixtures have made for variety, change, enterprise; and yet they have

THE HEART OF THE EMPIRE: TRAFALGAR SQUARE, LONDON. *Keystone*

confess that they find English reserve not unpleasant, and that once one gets to know an Englishman he turns out to be a very companionable fellow. England is also known abroad for what often appears as a willingness to combine expressions of high moral idealism with a very realistic ability to hold on to territory and business. The famous 'White Man's Burden' as a slogan of empire has, for instance, always appeared to Britain's competitors as a piece of hypocrisy.

Finally, however debatable and uncertain is the character of the British peoples, it is clear that they represent the working-out of a long

on the whole been astonishingly stable. Perhaps only in an island security could they have developed this happy equilibrium.

See also Vol. III: ENGLAND; SCOTLAND; WALES; IRELAND. Vol. IV: ENGLISH LANGUAGE.

BRONZE AGE, *see* PREHISTORIC MAN, Section 5.

BUDDHISM. Out of a total world population of nearly 2,000 millions there are on a rough estimate about 138 million Buddhists. The name Buddhist comes from a Sanskrit adjective *buddha*, which means the enlightened one—'a person who has waked up to seeing some great truth'.

It was the name given to GAUTAMA (q.v. Vol. V), the founder of the Buddhist faith. Siddharta Gautama was born in about 560 B.C. on the borders of what is now the State of Nepal on the northern frontier of India. His people were local

A COLOSSAL STATUE OF THE BUDDHA NEAR YOKOHAMA, JAPAN. *G. F. Bacon*

princes, and he was of the *Kshatriya* or soldier caste (*see* CASTE). He grew up as a Hindu (*see* HINDUISM) at a time when the rather simpler polytheism (belief in many gods) of long centuries standing was beginning to dissatisfy the cultured and educated classes of Indians—just as, about the same time, it was beginning to dissatisfy the same set of people in Greece on the one hand and in China on the other. Gautama was not the first to experiment with a better way—there had been philosophers in north India for generations, living in the forests and jungles and training disciples. There was also already in existence another sect of Indians called Jains (*see* JAINISM) who had broken away from orthodox Indian religion, and who may well have influenced Gautama. At this time the more profound teachers were convinced that the ordinary religion of sacrifice to many gods and many lords was futile. There was, they felt, only one Self in the whole universe, and the object of life ought to be to discover one's relation to that Self within one's own little self, and then go on to improve it. But so far the teachers of India had only suggested that this should be done by bludgeoning the body into obedience (*see* ASCETICISM) and by tricks of technique (Yoga). Gautama did not entirely reject these,

but he thought that they were inadequate and that, in particular, the self-torture went too far. So he proceeded to plan a new movement which could be shared by everybody—and not simply by priests, monks, and nuns—in which there should not be too much fasting and body punishment, and in which moral conduct, especially kindness to others, including animals, should play a leading part. The end aimed at was a completely happy state in which the individual ceased to bother about himself and his future, and aimed only at being absorbed into the life of the Great Self, the nature of which he left undefined—though we might call it The Whole, or The Universe.

Gautama died at the age of eighty, after a ministry of about forty-five years, during which he founded many groups of disciples to whom he preached regularly. Even during his lifetime it became clear that a real follower of the Buddha had to live very much as monks and nuns do, and that anyone living in the everyday world could not be a complete Buddhist, though he might minister to the full Buddhists (or *bhikkhus* as they are called; the word means 'one who has withdrawn'). And so it has been ever since.

At first Buddhism remained a reforming sect of Hinduism; but later on, exactly how we do not know, it began to spread outside the country of its origin and gradually extended north, south, and east—till to-day there are large numbers of Buddhists in Japan, Burma, and Siam, a good many in Ceylon and Indo-China, and a great many in China and Tibet. There are, however, hardly any in India proper.

The Buddhist movement has split into two divisions. The larger one we call Northern Buddhism, but it calls itself Mahayana (the Great Way). The adherents of Mahayana contemptuously call the smaller or southern community Hinayana (the Lesser Way); but the latter think themselves more faithful to the original teaching of Gautama. Actually, both are developments, and neither exactly represents what was probably the original message of the Buddha. This was exceedingly practical and kept clear of speculation and theology. What the Buddha certainly taught was that most of life was full of unhappiness and tension; that this was caused by people's thirst for all sorts of unsatisfying things; that to get rid of the unhappiness you must get rid of the thirst; and that to do this the best way was to follow out his own particular system of meditation and disciplined conduct. This teaching is known as the Four Noble Truths. Northern Buddhists believe that Gautama was one of a series of incarnations of the Supreme Being or Buddha-Spirit. These incarnate individuals, who are rather like the Christian saints, are known as *Bodhisattvas*, and are held to have deliberately stopped short of attaining final happiness in order to help and teach other human beings. There are a great many of them—and some are by no means real historical characters, since whenever Mahayana Buddhism has been established in a country it has tended to turn the gods of that country into Buddhist saints, so that people can keep on reverencing them. Southern Buddhism is stricter than this and does not recognize these Bodhisattvas or saints.

Japanese Buddhism has, in addition, some very distinctive sects, one of which teaches that salvation can be obtained and Paradise (called the Pure Land) reached by trusting in the merits and reciting the name of a particular Bodhisattva called Amidha.

For missionary purposes Buddhist teaching has been summarized in the Four Noble Truths, mentioned above, and in the scheme of practice known as the Noble Eightfold Path, comprising 'correct' views, aspiration, speech, behaviour, livelihood, effort, mindfulness, and concentration. But these are rather meaningless, unless you know what Gautama meant by 'correct'. For example, he said that nobody might earn his living by taking life, which would stop one from being a soldier or a gamekeeper. Right behaviour means keeping the equivalent of the sixth, seventh, eighth, and ninth commandments in the Bible, as well as being a total abstainer from alcohol. None of the teaching attributed to Gautama was committed to writing till two or three centuries after his death, so that it is difficult to say how much of the Buddhist scriptures—the *Tripitaka* or *Three Baskets of Tradition*—are really his teaching (*see* SACRED BOOKS). The same kind of comment might be made about Christianity, except that the teaching and life of Jesus were recorded in writing about forty years after he had left this earth.

Here is a description of a Buddhist meeting in Siam, where Buddhism is very much alive. The wat or temple has at one end an altar with statues of the Buddha and saints and with lights and flowers. About one-third of the way

A BUDDHIST MONK BESIDE AN ALTAR IN A CHINESE MONASTERY. *Paul Popper*

to the door is the preacher's throne or pulpit. On the occasion described there were about twenty monks in front of the pulpit and a congregation of about forty-five behind it, all seated on mats. Behind the pulpit was a candle-rack for offerings of candles to the Buddha. While waiting for the service to begin the congregation were chatting, chewing betel-nut, drinking tea, and some even smoking. A few were praying. The service began with chanting in unison by the monks for about ten minutes, followed by reading of a lesson for about twenty minutes, first in Pali, a dialect of north India, then in a Siamese translation. When the preacher left the pulpit there was more chanting, and finally everybody bowed low till their heads touched the ground. Then the monks rose and filed out, the congregation drank more tea and, after a little conversation, dispersed, each member putting a coin in the alms box at the door as he went out. The readings are generally from the records of the discourses of the Buddha and are listened to with great reverence and attention. Buddhist prayer is, for the most part, what we should call meditation. There is no asking; but sometimes the meditation, or the saying of a series of texts from the sacred books of Buddhism, is undertaken with the idea that credit is earned this way. Since to the Buddhist the Universe is strictly ruled by cause and effect, credit gained by prayer may be applied to the benefit of the worshipper himself or of anyone he particularly wishes to help—for example, a sick father.

The goal to be aimed at in all Buddhism is a state of mind called *nirvana*, which was described by one Buddhist monk as 'bliss unspeakable'. There seems to be a difference of opinion as to whether one is conscious or unconscious when sinking in to the condition of *nirvana*. Literally the word means 'waning out' or 'not blowing', i.e. 'the cessation of fanning a fire so as to let it die out'. This fire is the fire of human 'anger, passion, delusion or defect' which the Buddhist feels comes between him and *samadhi*—the 'putting together' or union with the Great Self. The main point on which all Buddhists seem to be agreed is that the sense of being an individual is an illusion to be got rid of, chiefly by meditation. How far Gautama himself was really interested in this we shall probably never know. His disciples may have carried this side of his thought farther than he did himself. The main experience sought after is the feeling of 'release' from illusion into the fullness and freedom of understanding the Truth.

In spite of Gautama's insistence upon the virtue of kindliness, Buddhists are often so concerned with the uprooting of all desire that they seem to be rather indifferent to the needs and sufferings of others and therefore uninterested in social service and social co-operation. But Buddhism, like other faiths, is still in process of change and development, and it is very sensitive to criticism. There are those who say that it has rendered Asia somewhat the same service that Christianity has rendered Europe. Buddhism has been in the past a good deal like those types of Christianity which give up the world as a bad job; but it is not much like those which seek to reform or improve the world.

BULGARIANS. The Bulgars were one of the conquering nomad tribes which came into Europe from the east during the early centuries A.D. They came from the lower regions of the river Volga in Russia and were first heard of as early as the 6th century. By the 8th century they had settled in their present home and mixed with the Slavonic-speaking peoples into whose land they had come, adopting their language,

BULGARIAN PEASANTS. *Roy. Geog. Soc.*

but retaining their own traditions—even to-day they differ in many ways from the peoples of neighbouring countries. They fell under the domination of the Ottoman Empire (*see* TURKS) in 1396 and remained under Turkey until they gained a semi-independence in 1878 and complete independence in 1908. There is still a considerable Turkish minority of Moslems in the country. The Bulgarians belong to the ORTHODOX EASTERN CHURCH (q.v.).

The Bulgarians are a race of dour peasant farmers. Bulgaria is a land of village communities in which there are but ten cities of more than 25,000 people. About 85% of the population are peasant farmers: this has had a marked effect on the national character. Bulgarians have the peasant virtues of being very industrious, hard-working, and prudent—their industry is so well known that there is a Balkan saying 'to work like a Bulgarian'. It has been necessary for them to work hard because much of their country is so mountainous and barren that a living can only be wrested from it by great toil.

In the mountain districts the peasants wear sheepskin hats and coats. National costumes are still worn: the village elders have theirs embroidered in white wool round the cuffs and collars and on the pockets to show their authority. Village elders have dominated the life of the majority of Bulgarian peasants: they are inclined to be rather stern and puritanical and very much against all change. Their permission is necessary before young people can marry; and they arrange how the harvest is sold. The head of a family decrees where the members shall work in the fields.

This puritanical tradition is reflected in city life, too: silk stockings were a rarity in Bulgaria in 1940, and cosmetics were frowned on: the cities of Bulgaria lack the gaiety and night life of many European cities.

Communal ownership is well developed in Bulgaria: even the main banks are communally owned. There are common grounds for grazing and common woods.

As a large proportion of Bulgarians grow their own food they have, as a rule, enough to eat; but they are very frugal, and wages are very low. Their capacity for hard work and frugal living is accompanied by a rather unexpected characteristic of fanaticism which has shown itself many times in the history of Bulgaria. In the 10th century thousands of them were martyred for their fanatical devotion to Bogomilism, a very primitive type of Protestantism; and recently thousands of Bulgarian communists died for their beliefs.

See also Vol. III: BULGARIA; Vol. IV: RUSSIAN LANGUAGES.

BURMESE. Two-thirds of Burma's sixteen million people are the real Burmese; the rest are

A PADAUNG GIRL
Haddon Lib., Cambridge

split up into many tribes in the jungly mountains around the Irrawaddy valley. These jungle people for the most part still live primitive lives and have primitive ideas. A few people, such as the Was on the Chinese border, are still headhunters—not so much because they are ferocious by nature, but because sacrifices are thought necessary to ensure good crops; there are strict rules as to how and whom and when to head-hunt.

One often hears of the scores of languages of India and Burma; but it must be remembered that most are spoken by very few people—for instance, the Padaungs, whose women wear brass rings on their necks, number only a few thousands.

In the north and west are the Nagas and Kachins, who helped us a good deal in the Second World War, both as guerrilla fighters and by rescuing allied airmen who were forced down in the jungle. On the open grassy plateau in the east are the Shans, one of the largest groups: they practise BUDD-

A SHAN GIRL

HISM (q.v.); they are more civilized than the jungle folk but less so than the plains Burmese. The Shans are a very likeable people and great gamblers. They are divided into many small tribes, some of which consist of only a few hundred people occupying tiny patches of land. Farther south, in the wild Salween country, are the hill Karens. Like most of the hill people, they follow ANIMISM (q.v.) or spirit-worship, but the plains Karens, simple and stolid peasants, are now largely Christians.

The ruling classes of the Burmese came from southern China about 1,000 years ago. Their first great king Anawrahta (about A.D. 1066) founded the beautiful city of Pagan, which was sacked by Kublai Khan's Mongols. There followed long wars with the Siamese and other peoples. Sometimes a great leader would unite the country for a while. One of the greatest, Alaungpaya, was a simple village headman (rather like a combination of William Wallace and Robert Bruce) who rallied his people and, when he died in 1760, had built a strong kingdom again. After him there was one really good and wise ruler, Mindon Min; but most of the kings were weak or tyrannical. As a result of three wars with the British (in which there was much injustice on both sides) Burma became a province of India. In 1937 it was separated, and in 1948 became completely independent.

Most people in Burma are farmers, living in small villages of thatched houses. The house-walls are often woven like patterned basket

A BULLOCK CART IN SOUTH BURMA. *Paul Popper*

work in strips of bamboo: bamboo, indeed, is used for all sorts of things from beds to smiths' bellows. The houses are raised off the ground on posts, and the space beneath is used as a shed for bullocks, carts, or even boats, as a workroom where the girls do hand-loom weaving, and not least as a playground for the children. Most houses are half-veranda and, even in the towns, are gay with flowers and creepers. Nearly every village has a white pagoda or Buddhist shrine, while large ones have a monastery or two, generally big wooden buildings with elaborately carved gables and corrugated iron roofs, guarded by gaudily painted statues of beasts like sphinxes sitting up, of elephant-headed geese, and other queer legendary beasts. The monks or *pongyis* wear bright orange or yellow robes and in the morning go through the villages in single file collecting gifts of food in beautiful polished black bowls. On the outskirts of the village is usually a big shady banyan tree, with a little wooden shrine, in which there **are** candles, fruit, and flowers offered to the local

nat or spirit; and often there are big jars of water and a bamboo shelter for weary travellers.

To Europeans Burma is one of the pleasantest countries in the East. One important reason is that ideas of family life and the position of women are much more like our own than among most Eastern peoples—Burmese women run much of the business of the country. The Burmese are very agreeable people on the whole, loving flowers and bright colours and children; though they are rather hot-tempered and, as every farmer has to have a big chopper-like knife or *dah*, murders are quite common. Both men and women wear gaily-coloured skirts or *lungy*, and the women wear white muslin jackets. A Burmese holiday crowd is a mass of vivid, but never clashing, colour. No Burman is happy without a bath in the cool of the evening, and it is very amusing to watch the golden-brown children splashing about in the river or riding on huge water-buffaloes.

Although they are very good at their own work of farming and village crafts, the Burmese do seem to lack 'business sense', and most of the trade is done by Europeans, Indians, or Chinese: town labour is largely carried out by Indian coolies, who will work for less wages than the Burmese and yet manage to send money home to India. The Burmese resent this; and Indian immigration is a major problem of modern BURMA (q.v. Vol. III).

See also Vol. IV: CHINESE LANGUAGES.

BURYATS, *see* SIBERIAN PEOPLES, Section 3.

BUSHMEN. A hunting people who live in south-west Africa, in the Kalahari desert area, the north-west corner of the Union of South Africa. They keep no domestic animals and cultivate no crops, but live solely by hunting and food gathering. They are different from the negro, being small in stature with yellowish-brown skins which wrinkle early. Their hair is extremely tightly curled, their faces flat with broad noses, bulging foreheads, and narrow slanting eyes.

The Bushmen probably came originally from east Africa and in former days were found over the whole of south Africa; but they were caught between the southern movement of the Bantu peoples and the northward advance of the European settlers, and were gradually driven back into the barren desert regions, so that to-day they are found in only a very small area.

They live in small bands, varying from 20 to 100 people, which intermarry with one another. Each band is composed of a number of distinct families. Generally the men have only one wife, and the children belong to the father. Each band has its own particular territory where it hunts.

The Bushmen are expert hunters and use bows and poisoned arrows. When an animal is hit by an arrow they follow it until the poison takes effect; then they cut off the flesh round the wound and eat the rest. The hunters are skilled in stalking and have very keen sight. Sometimes they dress up in animal skins to approach the animal they are stalking; sometimes they imitate the cries of animals to attract their prey closer. Other hunters make traps and set nooses to snare small game. Generally the men hunt alone or with their sons, but sometimes the whole group combines in a hunting drive. Fences are built across a valley, and openings are left in front of which deep pits are dug. The beaters then drive the large animals into the

valley so that they fall into the pits beside which are the hunters waiting to kill them. In the wet season the men drive the animals into swampy ground, where they are caught in the mud and can be easily killed. While the men get food by hunting, the women collect roots, berries, and insects for food, using digging-sticks—long sticks pointed at the end. They are especially fond of termites (white ants) and their eggs, called 'Bushman rice'. Vegetable food is scarce in this barren district, and the Bushmen have to make use of anything edible. They hardly make any attempt to store food, but eat plentifully when

A BUSHMAN ARCHER. *Paul Popper*

they are lucky and go hungry when there is no food.

When the young people grow up they have to pass through INITIATION CEREMONIES (q.v.). The boys are kept apart for a month and are instructed in tribal knowledge and in hunting. Girls have to remain in their huts and observe certain food taboos (*see* TABOO). The Bushmen have no chiefs, but their older and more experienced men act as leaders in hunting. Medicine men play an important part, for they are supposed to be able to bring rain; they look after the boys' initiation ceremonies and act as doctors for the community.

The people have very little clothing. The men wear a three-cornered piece of skin tied round the waist and drawn between the legs, and a kaross, a patchwork cloak made of skins scraped and stretched till they are soft, which is worn over the shoulder by day and as a blanket by night. The women wear small aprons of skin. They make their implements for hunting from wood and bone, their arrows from reeds, bowstrings from the sinews, and bowshafts

from the leg bones of animals. Their houses are
semicircular in shape and are made of branches
stuck in the ground and tied at the top.

During the dry season water is often a more
pressing need than food. The Bushman can
find a drink when a white man would die of
thirst. He can locate underground water and

A BUSHMAN FAMILY. *Haddon Lib., Cambridge*

can suck it up from a patch of wet sand through
a reed. He uses ostrich egg-shells for carrying
and storing water.

The Bushmen are very fond of dancing and
have dances in which they imitate animals, and
for which they decorate themselves elaborately.
They have musical instruments, such as pipes,
drums, and the musical bow—a gourd rind with
strings stretched across. Their ancestors used to
paint drawings on the walls of caves and rock
shelters, but the present-day Bushmen have lost
the art. They have an abundance of folk-tales,
chiefly animal stories, hunting adventures, and
myths of sun, moon, and stars.

The Bushmen are nowadays dying out. They
have not been able to adopt European ways of
living or to take to cultivation or herding, and
only a few thousand of them remain.

See also NEGRO AFRICANS.

BYZANTINE EMPIRE. When the western
half of the ROMAN EMPIRE (q.v.) went to pieces
before the barbarian invaders in the 4th and 5th
centuries A.D., the eastern half kept up the traditions of Rome, and its citizens liked to call themselves 'Romans'. Its capital was Constantinople,
'the Second Rome', which CONSTANTINE (q.v.
Vol. V), the first Christian Roman Emperor,
founded in A.D. 330 on a first-class site commanding the crossroads of Europe and Asia
where the old Greek city of Byzantium used
to be. This eastern half of the Roman Empire,
which is called the Eastern Roman or Byzantine
Empire, lasted throughout the Middle Ages. It
was constantly protecting the rest of the Christian world from various attacks. The Slavs, who
crossed the Danube from the north and settled
in the Balkans, never succeeded in conquering
Constantinople, but finally became Christians
and members of the ORTHODOX EASTERN CHURCH
(q.v.) and learnt a great deal from Byzantine
civilization. There were threats also from wandering Mongolian tribes such as the HUNS (q.v.)
and the Bulgars, who were always making raids
across the Danube. In the east, first the Persians and then the Arabs tried to eat up the
Byzantine provinces and master 'the great city'.
By the 8th century the Byzantines had lost
Egypt, Syria, North Africa, and a good deal of
Italy. But they kept parts of Italy, Sicily, Greece,
parts of the Balkans, and, most important of
all to them, Asia Minor with its prosperous
cities round the coast and its great highlands,
which provided the Empire with men and
supplies. This smaller empire was in some
ways a more workable unit; and from the 9th
to the 12th centuries the Byzantine Empire
was at its greatest. But during the 11th century
a new enemy, the Seljuk Turks, appeared
and began to attack the provinces of Asia
Minor. The emperors, already hard-pressed
elsewhere, asked western Europe to help drive
back the Turks. The answer came in the
form of the First Crusade. Vast hordes of pilgrims and soldiers from all parts of the West
thronged eastwards; but they were not so much
interested in saving Asia Minor for the Byzantine Empire as in reaching Jerusalem or establishing kingdoms for themselves in Syria and
Palestine. The Byzantines never regained complete control of Asia Minor, and this was the
first great blow to their power. The second was
the capture of Constantinople in 1204 by the
Fourth Crusade, another expedition from the
west that was supposed to be going to protect
the Holy Land. The reason for this scandalous
attack of Christian on Christian was partly that
the Western countries were jealous of the political and commercial power of the Byzantine

THE EMPEROR JUSTINIAN AND HIS COURT
The magnificence of the brilliantly coloured mosaic and the impressive dignity of the figures express the idea of the Emperor as Christ's representative on earth. Mosaic from S. Vitale, Ravenna, 6th century. *Anderson*

Empire, and partly a desire to end the split between the Roman Catholic Church and the Orthodox Eastern Church—though this was not a likely way to bring about a union (*see* CRUSADES). From 1204 to 1261 there was a Latin Emperor in Constantinople, and small Latin states were set up in such of the Byzantine provinces as the crusaders could seize—mostly in Greece and the Greek islands. The Byzantine Emperor retreated to Nicaea in Asia Minor. In 1261 he managed to regain Constantinople and some of the lost territory in the Balkans and Greece; but the Byzantines were so weakened by the attacks of Western Christendom as well as by revolts among the Balkan principalities that they were unable to deal with a new danger which threatened them—the rise of the Ottoman Turks. From the end of the 13th century the Turks were establishing themselves in Asia Minor, and by the mid-14th century had got a foothold in Europe. Neither the Byzantines nor the other Christian rulers in the Balkans could drive them back. Constantinople was captured in 1453 and the Eastern Roman Empire fell.

The secret of Byzantine success throughout the thousand years and more of its existence lay in the strength of its imperial tradition and in its undying belief in the validity of the Christian religion. The Christian Emperor at Constantinople was the mainspring of Byzantine life, and although there were many other factors to be taken into account—the army, the senate, heads of government departments, the people of Constantinople—all real authority, in both administration and foreign policy, lay with the Emperor. He was regarded as being Christ's regent on earth, and he had a very special place in court ceremonies and church services. He usually worked very closely with the head of the Byzantine Church, the Patriarch of Constantinople. Together with the church councils at which he presided, he was responsible for seeing that right doctrine was taught and good order kept in the Church. This close relation between Church and State, which is so marked a feature of Byzantine life, is best described as one of interdependence.

In educational matters the Byzantine Empire preserved the fine Greek traditions of learning, and so there was no need to rebuild a system of

ST. JOHN THE EVANGELIST DICTATING TO A SCRIBE
Illumination from a Byzantine MS. on the Lives of the
Saints for September, 11th–12th century. B.M. Add.
MS. 11870. *British Mus.*

education with the help of the Church, as in the
West. The Empire had schools in its provinces
and a state-subsidized university founded at
Constantinople as early as A.D. 425. At first
both the Greek and Latin languages were used,
as in the old Roman Empire, but gradually
Latin fell out, and Greek became the tongue of
the Byzantines. There was a lively interest in
learning and education. In better class families
girls often got as good an education as their
brothers.

It used to be thought that the Byzantine
Empire preserved rather than created, but this
is not true, for it did both. It preserved, because
it admired the works of ancient Greek historians
and dramatists, poets and orators, and made
copies of their writings; but the Byzantines

themselves produced original works of value.
For instance, they wrote first-class histories and
memoirs, and they also wrote many lives of
saints—often vivid, pithy, racy accounts which
are almost the equivalent of our novels. They
had a strong legal sense: they not only codified
earlier Roman law, but from time to time modified the codes in use to meet the need of a new
generation. But their greatest achievements
were in art and religion, and in both these
they were outstandingly original and creative.
They were great architects, and built churches,
palaces, aqueducts, public buildings, and private
houses; and they produced beautiful decoration
for everything they made, from the mosaics and
paintings in their cathedrals and parish churches
to the designs of their dress materials. Their
passionate devotion to Christianity is reflected
in the achievements of their Church. The
Church services, for instance, became gradually
enriched during the early Middle Ages, and in
the later period there were great developments
in the Church music. Many men entered
monasteries or lived as hermits, and some of the
writings of these 'friends of God' are still widely
read to-day in the Orthodox Church and elsewhere. One can get some idea of what Christian
worship meant to the Byzantines by going to
present-day services in an Orthodox Eastern
Church, which are to be found in most large
English cities having a number of Greek residents.

Apart from its major contributions to civilization, the Byzantine Empire must have been
interesting to live in. It was a cosmopolitan
world full of vitality, a great trading-centre, a
half-way house between East and West, where
one could visit the City and enjoy a good ballet
or a learned argument, or watch the magnificent imperial processions or the races in the
Hippodrome. One could go into the country-
side and take part in May-day revels or harvest
celebrations, and find old customs lingering on
in vineyards and fishing-villages. Byzantium,
through its allegiance to Christianity, thought
a good deal about the next world, but it also
knew how to live to the full in this world, and
its relish for life was a reminder of its pagan past

See also CHRISTIAN CHURCH.

C

CALVINIST. A member of the group of Protestant Churches which look back to JOHN CALVIN of Geneva (1509–64) (q.v. Vol. V) as their Reformation leader. These churches are known in the British Isles as 'Presbyterian' and on the mainland of Europe as 'Reformed'. In North America both are to be found, because there are denominations of both British and of continental origin.

Calvin was a Frenchman. His Protestantism caused him to have to flee from Paris University. His book, *Institutes of the Christian Religion*, issued in 1536, made people recognize him, at the early age of twenty-six, as the most important scholar of the Reformation. He would have preferred to continue serving the Protestant cause as a scholar, but as he was travelling through Geneva, in Switzerland, where he intended to stay just one night, he became persuaded that it was his duty to rebuild Christianity there— and there he stayed almost all the rest of his life. The Reformation had already begun there, but only in a negative way. The former bishop had fled; the link with the Church had been broken; the Mass had been abolished, and images of the saints destroyed. Construction was needed. As Calvin rebuilt it, the Church in Geneva became a model for many other reformers. One enthusiast of those times described it as 'the most perfect school of Christ that ever was on the earth since the days of the Apostles'. Six thousand refugees (including Englishmen who fled from Mary's persecution) were to be found there. These spread Calvinism far and wide. One of the most heroic and bitter struggles which followers of Calvin put up against the power of the Roman Catholic Church was fought out in the Netherlands in the 16th century (*see* DUTCH), and was led by the great Dutch patriot WILLIAM THE SILENT (q.v. Vol. V). The Reformed Church of Holland is one of the strongest Calvinist Reformed Churches of to-day.

'Calvinism', as a system of Christian teaching, has as its basic belief the sovereignty of God. God is King. God's will is the cause, and God's glory the end, of all things. So Calvin taught that God had fixed beforehand who was to be saved and who was to be damned, a doctrine that is called 'Pre-destination'; but few even among Calvinists hold so extreme a view nowadays. Some Christians, thinking only of God's love, might have forgotten His majesty and His claim for utmost obedience, had it not been for Calvin's stern reminder.

Calvinism had a very wide influence on all branches of Protestantism: Congregationalists, Baptists, and some of the more Protestant members of the Church of England may almost be called Calvinists.

PRESBYTERIANISM. In the British Isles the state church of Scotland takes the lead among Presbyterian Churches. JOHN KNOX (q.v. Vol. V) had been a disciple of Calvin in Geneva. On his return to Scotland in 1559 he became leader of the Scottish Reformation. English Presbyterianism began with the Puritans of the 16th century. The Presbyterian Church in Ireland dates from 1642; and that in Wales springs from a religious revival in the 18th century.

Presbyterians emphasize the authority of the Bible as the Word of God. The minister in his black gown and bands is first and foremost a preacher of the Word, and therefore the sermon takes a prominent part in the Sunday Service. The ministers are well trained in biblical study and are theologically among the best educated of the Protestant clergy. Holy Communion, also, is accompanied by a sermon. It is held infrequently because the Communion is a great occasion, only to be approached after due preparation.

There are no bishops in the Presbyterian Church. The Ministry is of one order only, that of Presbyter. Elders (laymen) representing the congregation share with the minister in the work and government of the church or kirk (Scotland). A Synod rules an area of many Presbyteries, and a General Assembly rules the whole nation. At the head of the General Assembly is the Moderator who is appointed for one year only. In 1843 a large section of Scottish Presbyterians protested against State intervention in Church appointments. They resigned their livings and organized the Free Church of Scotland. In 1929, however, the divisions were healed, and the reunited Church of Scotland has become a truly national Church, but enjoying so large a measure of spiritual independence that it is not cramped by its State connexion.

Calvinist Churches (Presbyterian and Reformed) are to be found in most countries of Europe, in the Dominions, and the U.S.A., and, through missionary work in the last hundred and fifty years, in many parts of Asia and Africa. In Scotland, Holland, Hungary, and the Protestant parts of Switzerland the State Church is Calvinist.

See also REFORMATION.

CAMPS, PREHISTORIC, *see* EARTHWORKS AND HILL-FORTS.

CANAANITES. Semitic peoples living in the land of Canaan, 'the land flowing with milk and honey', in south Palestine before the arrival of the Hebrews (Num. xiii). When the Hebrews began to migrate into Palestine, between 1400 and 1200 B.C., they found a people much more advanced than the rough Hebrew shepherds. For some 1,000 years they had lived in houses in walled towns, had an organized government and religion, and learnt the art of writing. Jerusalem was originally a Canaanite stronghold. The Hebrews soon mingled with the Canaanites and were so much influenced by their civilization that it became difficult to distinguish them.

The Canaanites worshipped local town gods called Baals, and the Hebrews on occasions showed a tendency to turn to these gods. This brought down upon them the wrath of the prophet Elijah, whose followers on one occasion slew many of the priests of the Canaanite Gods (1 Kings xviii).

See also HEBREW CIVILIZATION.

CANADIANS. Canada was first discovered by the Italian JOHN CABOT (q.v. Vol. V), who sailed from Bristol in an English ship in 1497 in order to find a new route to India. He believed, however, that he had reached China. In the following year he crossed the Atlantic again, and made landings in Newfoundland, Labrador, and Nova Scotia. Nearly forty years later Frenchmen, led by the Breton sailor JACQUES CARTIER (q.v. Vol. V), reached the mouth of the St. Lawrence under the impression that they had found an inlet which led to the Far East. Cartier, like Cabot, made no attempt to colonize the country, and was disappointed because he failed to discover gold and precious stones.

The first real colonizer was Samuel de Champlain: under his leadership the French occupied Quebec, and began to farm and to make permanent homes for themselves in the New World. Later on the Jesuits endured unspeakable tortures and privations in their attempts to convert the native Indians to Christianity. In the meantime English traders began to arrive in Canada, and in 1670 the famous Hudson's Bay Company, which still has trading-posts all over the country, was formed. There followed many years of bitter rivalry between the British and the French, both of whom made use of Indian allies, until in 1759 Wolfe's victory at Quebec brought French authority to an end (*see* WOLFE, Vol. V). The British treated the French-Canadians well, allowing them to retain their religion, language, and schools: in fact, something like one-fourth of the people of Canada to-day speak French.

After the American War of Independence 40,000 Loyalists, who had supported Britain in the struggle, left the United States and made new homes for themselves in Nova Scotia, Ontario, and New Brunswick. They did not mix very well with the French-Canadians, and so the difficulty was solved by dividing Canada into two provinces: Upper Canada for the English, and Lower Canada for the French. But troubles continued until, in 1867, the British North America Act brought the Dominion of Canada into being. The Dominion consisted originally only of the provinces of Ontario, Quebec, New Brunswick, and Nova Scotia. It has since been joined by Manitoba, British Columbia, Alberta, Saskatchewan, Prince Edward Island, and Newfoundland. In 1931 Canada became a sovereign state, voluntarily acknowledging, as a member of the British Commonwealth of Nations, allegiance to the King of England. The King's representative is known as the Governor-General, and he is chosen by the Canadian Government after consultation with the King. The Governor-General is assisted by a Privy Council, and by a Parliament which sits in Ottawa and consists of two houses: the Senate and the House of Commons.

Canada, in spite of its vast size, has only about fourteen million inhabitants. The northern part of the Dominion lies within the Arctic Circle, where the ground is always covered with snow,

LOGGING IN THE FORESTS OF BRITISH COLUMBIA
The forests of British Columbia and Eastern Canada provide much timber for building, paper-making, and other industries. *Canadian National Film Board*

and where even the sea is frozen for the greater part of the year; another large area is 'tundra', cold treeless plain, often marshy, with scant vegetation and almost useless to man. In these regions ESKIMOES (q.v.) manage to exist by hunting and by fishing in the rivers. There are other parts, too, where poor soil or thick forests make difficult living conditions. But Canada is capable of enormous development and of maintaining many times its present population. This is mainly concentrated in the St. Lawrence Lowlands and in the coastal and prairie provinces. The people are predominantly British and French: nearly six million British, and about three and a half million French. But, as in the United States, there are representatives of most of the nations of Europe, notably Germans, Scandinavians, and Ukrainians. There are small numbers of Chinese and Japanese, an Indian population of over 120,000 (*see* AMERICAN INDIANS, NORTH), and over 7,000 Eskimoes.

Among such a mixed population it is natural to find a variety of religions. The largest group is Roman Catholic, followed by the United Church of Canada and the Anglicans. There are some Nonconformists, particularly Presbyterians, and groups of Jews and members of the Greek Church. Immigrants have generally settled down easily. Those from Scandinavia and the Russian Ukraine have not found conditions very different from those in their own countries. They are used to intense cold and to felling trees in forests in order to get wood to build houses for themselves; and the long winters are like the winters of their native countries. Many of the immigrants have introduced their own artistic ideas and songs into Canadian life, and so have added to the culture of their adopted country.

The Canadians are fully alive to the benefits of education. They have numerous colleges and schools, and eighteen universities. Each province makes its own educational arrangements, and levies taxes to cover costs. Even in the remote parts of the country education is not neglected: thus at Aklavik, which is only eighty

distances to patrol, ranging from the industrial cities to the islands guarding the North Pole. They are few in number for so great a task—just under 4,500, but they are so efficient that the crime-rate is lower in the areas which they cover than anywhere else in North America. In the Yukon and the North-west Territories they are the sole judicial authority. They are not well paid, their duties are often dangerous and nerve-racking, especially in the frozen wastes

HARVESTING ON THE PRAIRIES
Wheat-fields stretch to the horizon. The wheat is cut and threshed by the combined harvester.
High Commissioner for Canada

miles from the Arctic, there are two mission schools where Indian and Eskimo children are boarded and taught—one of them run by the Roman Catholics and the other by the Anglican Church. Canada is still a young country as far as music and the arts are concerned. Her writers have produced some good history, biography, and books of exploration; and the humorist and writer Stephen Leacock is a Canadian. Canadian scientists have been prominent in atomic research; their engineers have many great feats to their credit; and Frederick Banting, the discoverer of insulin (*see* Vol. XI: DIABETES), is one of the great benefactors of the human race.

The most prominent part in the maintenance of law and order throughout Canada is taken by forces of the Royal Canadian Mounted Police, popularly known as 'The Mounties', and probably the most famous police force in the world—certainly the force with the longest

of the Arctic; but there is always a long waiting-list of applicants to their ranks. Their traditional dress—rarely seen in Canada to-day except on formal occasions, such as when they are on duty in National Parks or giving evidence in court—is a broad flat hat, red tunic, Sam Browne belt, navy blue breeches with a yellow stripe at the side, and glistening boots and spurs. Much of the force is now mechanized: they have only 144 horses, less than half as many as the New York Police, but they have 800 cars, a fleet of aeroplanes, power boats, and thirty-one sea-going vessels. In the Yukon and the north-west they still, however, use dog teams, and one constable recently travelled 1,400 miles on snow-shoes to bring the murderer of an Eskimo to justice.

Canada has only four cities of over 200,000 people: Montreal, Toronto, Winnipeg, and Vancouver; and only four others with over 100,000 inhabitants. The majority of the people live in small towns or villages, and some in lonely shacks or outposts in the midst of vast distances. In so big a country it is impossible to generalize on how Canadians live, or what a typical Canadian is like. There are too many types both of race and of occupation for such a thing to be possible. The wood-choppers of Quebec live differently from the gold-miners of Ontario; the lumbermen of British Columbia, the steel-workers of Nova Scotia, the prairie farmers of Alberta, and the trappers and fur-traders of the north-west, represent varying types; but they are all Canadians bound by the same loyalties, and all contributing to the wealth and greatness of Canada. There are French communities of Quebec, and English and Scottish communities of Ontario and the Maritime Provinces; there are also many much smaller groups of other European immigrants, particularly in the prairies. Immigration declined after the First World War, but in the 1930's many people came to Canada to escape Nazi tyranny. There is likely to be much more immigration in the future, since Canada can do with a larger population to exploit her potential riches.

The maintenance of friendly relations with Great Britain and the United States is essential to Canada's prosperity. Relations with the United States are very good—old enmities are forgotten, there are frequent consultations on matters of mutual interest, and the frontier between the two countries is undefended. Winston Churchill has declared: 'The long unguarded frontier, the habits and intercourse of daily life, the fruitful and profitable connexions of business, the sympathies and even the antipathies of honest neighbourliness, make Canada a binder together of the English-speaking peoples. She is a magnet exercising a double attraction, drawing both Great Britain and the United States towards herself, and thus drawing them closer to each other.'

See also Vol. III: CANADA.

CANNIBALISM. The eating of human flesh has usually been a religious rite. Many cases have been reported of people being driven to cannibalism by extreme hunger, but hardly any in which human flesh was an ordinary article of diet. Those eaten have almost always been sacrificial victims, enemies killed in war, or, in the case of those who have died a natural death, near relatives. It has been very widely believed that by eating part of a dead man you can acquire part of his strength, courage, and even soul-substance of life.

The AZTECS of Mexico (q.v.) had an elaborate system of human sacrifice in which they ate the bodies of their victims. Cannibalism is reported from tribes of South America, British Columbia, and also the Caribs of the West Indies (of whose name 'cannibal' is probably a corruption). In all these cases cannibalism is said to be ritual. The same applies to the South Sea Islands, in which cannibalism was widespread. Much of their warfare was for the object of obtaining victims for the feasts which took place at the death of a chief, the building of a temple, or the launching of a canoe. Only chiefs, old men, or other qualified persons partook of the human flesh. There, as elsewhere, it seems to have been the general rule that it was forbidden to women.

In Australia among some tribes the bodies of those who die are eaten by special classes of their relatives.

In Africa cannibalism is rare; but some Bantu tribes eat the bodies of their relatives, others those whose souls would otherwise be dangerous, such as witches. Some of the Congo tribes are said to dig up corpses and eat them for enjoyment.

In Asia there are many traditions of cannibalism, but apparently no authentic evidence of its recent practice.

Unpleasant as cannibalism seems to us, there is nothing peculiarly unnatural about it—animals have no objection to eating their own species. The feeling against it probably developed as part of the same set of beliefs which made it compulsory to partake of the flesh of the sacrificed victim (i.e. of the human god); in which case, of course, unauthorized cannibalism had to be frowned on as sacrilege.

CARIBS, *see* WEST INDIANS; AMERICAN INDIANS, CENTRAL AND SOUTH.

CARTHAGINIANS, *see* PHOENICIANS.

CASTE. The English word and its two Indian equivalents, *vărna*, and *jăti*, are now used to describe a most complicated system of sections (we are specially told not to call them classes) into which Indian Hindu society is split up. It has been suggested that the caste system is rather as if the inhabitants of London were classified into families of Norman descent, clergy, noblemen, agnostics, ironmongers, vegetarians,

A BRAHMIN PRIEST.   *Margot Lubinski*

communists, and Scotsmen! Though a good many castes are quite modern, most of them are very ancient and have gone on from generation to generation—for children are bound to be members of the same caste as their parents. Since *vărna* is connected in meaning with colour, perhaps the first caste division was between some fair-skinned invaders and the darker people whom they conquered. The old divisions (*vărna*) were five: Brahmins or priests, Kshatriyas or soldiers, Vaisyas or merchants, Sudras or husbandmen and artisans, and Pariahs or outcastes; but these have little practical meaning in India to-day—the divisions may be there, but they do not fix the occupations of the people. There can be a Brahmin doctor, or a clerk who is really a member of the goldsmiths' caste, and there are many Kshatriyas who are not soldiers. What is seldom to be found is anyone who has changed from one caste to another. There are curious freaks, such as a servant of high caste working for a master or mistress of low caste. For the servant in this case to marry the mistress would discredit him much more than if he were a duke marrying his kitchen-maid.

Worldly position is no index to caste position, and a ruling prince in India might be of quite a low caste. Each caste has all sorts of customs which members must observe—how they must dress, what sort of food they may eat, what work they may do, and even what kind of funeral they may have. It is unusual, though not impossible, to marry outside one's caste, and one should not eat with anyone of a different caste. There are many hundreds of castes (*jăti*), some of them quite recent, for if outsiders wish to become Hindus they cannot join an existing caste, but the group to which they belong has to be formed into a new caste. Other castes, though ancient, are peculiar because they seem to recognize as legitimate occupations which in this country would land a man in jail. Thus there is actually a criminal caste (very low indeed, but just as much tolerated as the castes of barbers and street-sweepers). Caste is not only a great obstacle to the general spread of Christianity (since the latter teaches that all persons are equal in the sight of God): it is also an obstacle to political unity, since it divides citizens from one another and makes a full democratic system unworkable. This is why the followers of GANDHI (q.v. Vol. V) though they wish to remain Hindus, are anxious to modify caste if they can do it without setting too many people against them. There are thousands of Pariahs or outcastes whose presence is supposed to be defiling to any caste person, so that they are sometimes called 'untouchable'. A great deal of successful Christian work has been done in elevating and giving self-respect and hope to these depressed peoples, and Hindus have for some time been conscious that they ought to do something themselves to help and encourage their hitherto-despised fellow citizens.

See also HINDUISM.

CATHOLIC CHURCH, *see* CHRISTIAN CHURCH; ROMAN CATHOLIC CHURCH.

CAVE MAN. This expression is a legacy from the old days of archaeology and is now rather meaningless and misleading. When in the last century many spectacular remains of Old Stone Age man were found in caves in France and England, it was assumed that caves were the constant and permanent dwellings of these peoples, and the term 'Cave Man' was invented. As we now realize, caves (at least the front parts, where it was reasonably light) were used by ancient man as temporary or semi-permanent shelters at all times (in England, as a matter of fact, there is more archaeological evidence of the use of caves in the Roman period than at any other time!); and the recent discoveries in south Russia and Siberia have brought to light well-built houses half-dug into the ground, obviously the winter dwellings of late Old Stone Age man. Like many modern primitive peoples, Old Stone Age man lived a seasonal life varying according to the time of year. There are drawings on cave walls of summer huts made of light brushwood or skins on a frame; in the winter caves would be used by those groups of people who lived in a region where suitable holes in rocks occur, and who did not dig and build winter houses of the Russian kind. Sometimes burials were made in caves by digging a grave in the accumulated litter of earlier occupants.

Caves are, of course, a very permanent form of dwelling, remaining intact for thousands of years; and so we have been able to excavate the accumulated rubbish of countless centuries of occupation from their floors, often separated one from another by the stalactite that forms from the water dripping in limestone caverns. Moreover, the walls of caves in south and west France and in Spain were used by late Old Stone Age man as the surface for his drawings, paintings, and engravings, and these pictures have remained there since they were first painted many thousands of years ago. They show animals of all kinds and are probably connected with hunting magic—if you draw an animal, a primitive

man might say, you catch something of his spirit and so make it easier to hunt him down next day. Human beings are very rarely shown, perhaps because it was feared that some sort of magic might affect a man if he were drawn; but some figures are shown dressed up as animals, and these may be the local magicians themselves.

See also PREHISTORIC MAN.

CELTIC CIVILIZATION. It is very difficult to define exactly what is meant by Celtic civilization or to limit it either in time or place. For the Celtic peoples, whom we know of in western Europe as the Gauls and Britons, and whose language is still spoken in various forms in Wales, Ireland, and Scotland, grew gradually out of the mixture of prehistoric peoples who had settled in western and central Europe during the New Stone and Bronze Ages (*see* PREHISTORIC MAN). The centres of their later civilization were north-east France, south-west Germany, and Bohemia. It was here that the La Tène culture first developed—and La Tène is the name given to the civilization of the Celts during the centuries when they were most powerful and important, roughly from 400 B.C. until the Roman conquest of Britain in the middle of the 1st century after Christ. The whole history of the Celts of this time was shaped by the fact that their homeland lay between the Germans to the north and the various Mediterranean peoples, including the Romans, to the south.

After 1000 B.C. the Germans were almost continuously trying to push southward from their own homelands in the extreme north of Europe, which meant, of course, that they were pushing against their Celtic neighbours in an attempt to occupy their land.

It was partly this pressure from the Germans that made the Celts in their turn start a series of warlike migrations which carried them over much of Europe and brought them into conflict with the Greeks and Romans. In about 400 B.C. Celtic tribes crossed the Alps into

CAVE PAINTING OF A BOAR
Old Stone Age, from the caves at Altamira, Spain. *After Breuil*

CELTIC SHIELD

Found in the Thames at Battersea. Bronze, decorated with coloured enamel. *British Mus.*

earlier part of the European Iron Age the Celtic peoples between north-east France and Bohemia began to receive new ideas brought by traders from the Mediterranean. In this way Celtic artists were able to see things that came from Greece and other countries—painted wine cups, for instance, and fine bronze vessels—and to make use of what they saw in the development of their own work. But they did not copy the Greek forms and designs: they changed them into something that was Celtic, something entirely different from any other art in the world before or since. Unlike the Greeks and Romans, the Celts were interested not in representing nature, but in making curious patterns, abstract forms. They used these designs to ornament their most treasured possessions, incising or embossing them, or picking them out in coloured enamels. When, occasionally, they represented living things, a horse, bird, boar, or human face, they did not make them look realistic, but exaggerated certain features until they appeared altogether strange and haunting.

It is interesting to notice what types of object were decorated in this way, for this will suggest which of their possessions the Celts thought to be the most important, and hence what sort of people they were and the kind of life they led. Much of the art is found on personal ornaments —on necklets, armlets, brooches, and many other things in bronze or gold—and it is clear therefore that this was a people who loved to dress up and make a splendid display. But most often the Celtic artists were employed to decorate fighting equipment—helmets and shields, swords, spears, horse-trappings, and battle-chariots. Evidently, then, the Celts were a most warlike people. Having no central government and very little idea of being a nation, their many different tribes were for ever fighting.

The tribes were led by chiefs or kings, and sometimes one of these might succeed in defeating his neighbours and so building up quite a large kingdom. This was done, for example, by the British King Cunobelin (Shakespeare's Cymbeline), who at the beginning of the first century A.D. was ruling over the whole of south-eastern England. But such conquests seldom lasted: other rulers, growing jealous, tried to destroy them.

As well as in their arms and armour, the Celtic love of fighting is shown in their fortifications. The strongholds which they built, most often on hill-tops, are indeed much the most conspicuous

northern Italy, settled there, and made savage raids against the Romans. Meanwhile other groups of Celts had pushed into Spain, westward into Britain, and eastward along the Danube, making settlements as far east as Asia Minor. In the 3rd century they were raiding also in Greece. Thus at the time of their greatest extent, the Celts held vast territories all the way from Ireland to Galatia (Asia Minor). After 200 B.C., however, their power was gradually destroyed: they were pressed by the Germans in the north, and from the south by the Romans, who took one Celtic land after another, adding them to their expanding empire. The last territory to be conquered in this way was Britain—so that Ireland and Scotland were then left as the only countries where Celts could maintain their independence and something of their civilization.

We must now consider this civilization, the La Tène culture, which the migrating Celts took with them wherever they went. During the

MAIDEN CASTLE, DORSET
One of the largest Celtic fortifications belonging to the early Iron Age. It was built on the site of an earlier New Stone Age fortification, which the Celts enlarged and improved. The Castle was also used later by the Romans.
Ashmolean Mus.

of the remains which they have left behind for us to see to-day. In Britain alone there are hundreds of them. Sometimes the ramparts were made from piled-up chalk or other softer soils; but in rocky country the walls were usually built with stone blocks. These forts might be put up against a foreign enemy such as the Germans, or against other Celts, either hostile neighbouring tribes or migrating bands. Some of these strongholds became more than mere places of refuge; they were also tribal centres with permanent settlements inside their walls. Indeed by the 1st century B.C. actual towns were beginning to grow up among the Celts, although they never became anything like such an important part of their civilization as they were for Mediterranean peoples like the Greeks and Romans.

The Celts could be good farmers—in Britain, for instance, they grew enough corn to export some to the Continent—but cattle were even more important to them, particularly to migrating tribes, since these must have depended almost entirely on the great herds which they could drive with them as they moved about Europe.

The Celtic priests, or Druids, are famous, yet very few facts are known about them (*see* RELIGION, PREHISTORIC). They seem to have been a curious mixture, for while they practised philosophy and poetry, they also engaged in savage and cruel rites, including human sacrifice. Such a contrast is, indeed, characteristic of the Celts. Their love of display, their reckless bravery and lack of discipline in war, their uncouth homes where they ate and drank far too much, as well as the brutality of some of their customs, justified the Romans in regarding them as barbarians. Yet we are right to speak of Celtic civilization, for they had a great and distinctive achievement of their own. The great works of fortification, still so impressive after 2,000 years, prove their energy and skill in military architecture; they were sensitive to poetry and other literature; above all they produced brilliantly gifted artists and craftsmen. It was a tradition, too, which did not come to an end with prehistoric times, but survived to make the largest contribution to the rich and important civilization of Ireland in the early Christian period.

See also ANCIENT CIVILIZATIONS; Vol. IV: CELTIC LANGUAGES.

CENTAURS, see MYTHOLOGICAL MONSTERS (*b*).

CENTRAL AMERICANS. There are six Central American countries: Guatemala, Salvador, Honduras, Nicaragua, Costa Rica, and Panama.

CENTRAL AMERICA

Each of them stretches across Central America from the Caribbean Sea to the Pacific, except Salvador, which is entirely on the Pacific side. These are independent republics. But Central America also includes the British colony of British Honduras, on the Caribbean coast, which is bordered inland by Mexico and Guatemala.

On his first voyage in 1492 Columbus discovered the Caribbean islands of Hispaniola and Cuba (*see* WEST INDIANS). On his fourth voyage ten years later he crossed the Caribbean as well as the Atlantic and discovered the mainland of Central America. Thus Central America became the middle section of the vast Spanish Empire, between 'New Spain' (Mexico) in the north and 'New Granada' (Colombia) in the south. All the Central American states, except Panama, formed the Spanish captaincy-general of Guatemala. The captaincy-general declared its independence of Spain in 1821, along with the rest of Spanish America; but it was some years before its five provinces became five distinct republics. At first they tried to combine in a Central American Union, and this idea is still not altogether dead; but the communications between them are very bad—it was only Spanish rule that had held them together; and in due course they split apart into separate nations.

The republic of Panama came into existence much later. Originally it was part of the South American republic of Colombia. But in 1903 the United States encouraged Panama to declare its independence, because the Americans wanted to build a canal through the Panama isthmus. The new government of Panama allowed them to do so; and the Canal was opened in 1914. The building of this Canal through the fever-infested tropical jungles and mountains is one of the greatest engineering feats in history. It cuts across the narrowest part of the isthmus in the middle of the Panama Republic. The Canal and a strip of land on either side of it are together called the Canal Zone, and belong to the United States (*see* PANAMA CANAL, Vol. IV).

Central America is very thinly populated: all the six republics together have not as many inhabitants as London. They are mainly Indian countries, like Mexico. In Salvador, Honduras, Nicaragua, and Panama, the people are mostly of mixed Indian and European blood, and in Guatemala the majority are pure Indian. Remains of the ancient Indian civilization of the MAYA people (q.v.), much of which has only recently been discovered, are to be found in Central America, especially in Guatemala and Yucatan. For most of their history these countries have been ruled by dictators. Their peoples are very poor, and sometimes the peasants are little better than slaves on the large estates. The official language is Spanish, but the Indians still speak their own dialects, of which there are an astonishing variety. The official religion is Roman Catholic, but it only veils much of the ancient pagan customs and beliefs. From all over Central America the Indians go on pilgrimage to the famous image of the Black Christ of Esquipulas, in Guatemala. In the towns there are splendid churches and houses built by the Spaniards during colonial times; but in the country-side, among the neat villages of the Indians, and on the mountain-slopes where every scrap of level soil has been tilled for centuries, there has been little change since before the Spaniards came.

MARKET-PLACE OF PANAJACHEL, GUATEMALA. *Roy. Geog. Soc.*

But one of the Central American countries is a contrast to the rest. This is Costa Rica. Its population is mainly white, with very few Indians. The land is divided up among many farmers instead of being collected in great estates; and the country is one of the most progressive in Latin America. It has been called 'a small oasis of democracy amidst a desert of Central American dictators'.

See also Vol. III: CENTRAL AMERICA.

CERBERUS, *see* MYTHOLOGICAL MONSTERS, Section (*c*).

CERES, *see* GODS OF GREECE AND ROME (Demeter).

CEYLONESE. The people who live in Ceylon. As in Britain there used to be big differences between English, Welsh, and Scots, so in Ceylon to-day there are big differences between the main groups—the Sinhalese, the Tamils, and the European colonists.

As far as is known, the original inhabitants of Ceylon were a people called the VEDDA (q.v.); but in 543 B.C. (the early days of ancient Greece) the Sinhalese, moving from north India to the more fertile south, drove the Vedda from the best parts of the island into the jungle and hills where they still remain. The Sinhalese flourished in this beautiful and fertile island and built cities with magnificent Buddhist temples which, in course of time, fell into decay and got overgrown with jungle. Recently, archaeologists have discovered the 'Buried Cities', Anaradapura, Polonaruwa, and the rock city of Sigiriya, and have uncovered fine carvings and mural paintings whose colours remain unfaded to-day.

Later the Tamils also overflowed into Ceylon from south India. They were not welcomed by the more numerous Sinhalese and, until European 'invaders' appeared in 1505, the history of Ceylon was of conflict between the Sinhalese and the Tamil minority; nor is the conflict dead to-day though neither side fights about it. The Sinhalese fought between themselves too, and for a long time there was as much difference between the Low Country Sinhalese and the Kandyans of the hill country in the south centre of the island as between the Tamils and Sinhalese: this distinction also persists in a small way to-day.

The first Europeans to come to Ceylon were the Portuguese, in 1505. The Dutch occupied the island from 1656 to 1796 when the British administration started. It was some time before Europeans occupied more than the coastal fringe, for the forests inland were unhealthy—thousands of British soldiers, for instance, died of malaria when, early in the 19th century, the British tried to build roads inland from Colombo to occupy Kandy and the centre of the island.

For the last 150 years the whole island has flourished and developed as a British colony. After the Second World War the Sinhalese, in particular, urged for Dominion status, and a form of Dominion status was granted in 1947.

Nowadays Sinhalese, Tamils, British, and 'Burghers' (as the descendants of the Dutch are called) are fairly well mixed up all over the island. You do, however, find more Tamils in the north and east of the island, and on the

THE TEMPLE OF THE HOLY TOOTH, KANDY
The entrance to the Temple. *Roy. Geog. Soc.*

British tea estates on the highlands of the south-centre. For every one British there are roughly 400 Sinhalese, 125 Tamils, 4 Burghers, and about 31 Moors or Malays. The British live mostly in the capital, Colombo, and on the highlands where the climate is not unlike the English summer (including the rain). The six million of the population are fairly well distributed all over the island—there are few areas where you can go for more than a few miles without seeing a native village, generally of small single-storey houses scattered haphazardly under coco-nut palms. Colombo is the only big town.

The Sinhalese are mostly farmers, each household having its own rice-field somewhere nearby, and at least a few coco-nut-palms. They are Buddhists by religion (*see* BUDDHISM), and every village has its own temple, usually ornately carved and brilliantly painted inside. The Temple of the Tooth at Kandy is one of the most sacred and important of Buddhist temples, and is visited by Buddhist pilgrims from all over the world. This temple is said to contain one of Buddha's teeth. Every August a great festival, called the *Perahera* takes place in Kandy, when every night for a week the tooth is taken round the town on the back of the temple sacred elephant, preceded by the Kandy male dancers and drummers, and followed by a retinue of up to seventy elephants and magnificently clothed priests. Like most Buddhist festivals, the Perahera takes place when the moon is full, and along the route the procession is further lit up by hundreds of flaming torches. The Buddhist priests move round the country from place to place, generally carrying nothing but a stick, their heads shorn, without shoes and almost muffled in the yards of bright yellow material, precariously fastened, which is their only dress. They can often be seen holding services at night by candlelight under a sacred Bo tree, praying, perhaps, either for more rain or for less rain.

The Sinhalese love bright colours—they wear bright clothes and will often decorate their lorries with flowers. The standard dress for men and women is a long cotton skirt or *sarong* which comes right down to their ankles: when working they shorten it by lifting the hem and tucking it in round the waist. Above this the men wear either nothing or a shirt, generally with the shirt-tails outside; the women wear a small blouse. Few wear any shoes at all. Both Sinhalese and Tamils place high value on decency and keep themselves covered even when washing themselves or their elephants or oxen

FISHERMEN LAUNCHING THEIR BOATS NEAR NEGOMBO, CEYLON. *Kingdom Overseas*

in the river, or when ploughing their rice-fields in 3 feet of mud and water. Most of the men are rather handsome and the women rather plain; their features are not unlike our own, and the colour of their skin is often no darker than a very deep sun tan. The men used to wear their hair long, down over their shoulders or rolled up in a bun; but this custom is dying out. In a country where the climate is so kind and the soil so fertile, there is little incentive to energy, and most of the Sinhalese are happily lazy.

The Tamils are Hindus (*see* HINDUISM); fortunately this religion tolerates and is tolerated by Buddhism. For three reasons, it is said, the Sinhalese think the Tamils stupid: first because the Tamil women bore their noses and wear gold rings (as we wear ear-rings), secondly because the Tamils have a rigid CASTE system (q.v.), and thirdly because the Tamils are hard working. In consequence Tamils are employed, rather than Sinhalese, on the British tea estates and rubber plantations and by government departments. Generally they do not mix much with the Sinhalese and have their own language and their own schools.

The British settlers in Ceylon are nearly all civil servants, or managers and owners of tea estates, rubber or coco-nut plantations. They regard, not Ceylon, but England as their permanent home. The Burghers, the Dutch settlers, often with strains of Sinhalese blood, have far less influence in the island than the British, though they are four times more numerous. The more powerful or wealthy Sinhalese— lawyers, doctors, politicians, owners or managers of estates—have been inclined to adopt British speech and ways of living.

There are many schools throughout the island, and half the people can read and write their own language (in India only one in ten can do this). Knowledge of English is spreading fast, but it is now being urged that Sinhalese, as well as English, shall be accepted as an 'official' language. The excellent civil services throughout the island are staffed principally by Sinhalese and Tamils, very many of whom have taken degrees either at the University of Colombo or at Indian Universities: some come to English Universities. Everyone in the country can vote for his Member of Parliament, but many of the people do not, in fact, vote.

See also Vol. III: CEYLON; Vol. IV: INDIAN LANGUAGES.

CHALDEANS, *see* SUMERIANS.

CHILEANS. The people of Chile are, next to the Uruguayans, about the most progressive and democratic of the Latin-American countries. The population is relatively small, about five millions, and it is unlikely that the country could ever carry a much greater number. About 90% live in the fertile central valley.

The country was first colonized in the 16th century by Spaniards from Peru. The journey was a severe one, since the invading expedition had to cross the arid northern desert; and the first expedition in 1535 failed. In 1541 Pedro de Valdivia made a successful invasion and founded the city of Santiago. The hard climatic conditions of heat and cold, and the continuous attacks of the many independent tribes of Indians, made the lot of the earlier settlers no easy one, and resulted in the growth of a hardy, virile people, able to work hard and always on the alert.

Before the arrival of the Spaniards the interior parts of the country were inhabited by scattered Indian tribes, who lived by hunting and fishing, and who have now almost disappeared. Towards the south, however, in the district now called Araucania, lived more hardy and intelligent Indian tribes who practised agriculture. These tribes had learnt many useful arts and indus-

CHILEAN INDIAN MAKING A BASKET. *Roy. Geog. Soc.*

tries, including the working of silver, from the INCAS of Peru (q.v.). They put up a valiant struggle against the Spaniards for some 250 years until, in 1882, a final peace treaty was signed. During this time the Spaniards had learnt to respect the bravery of the Indians: in fact the old Indian leaders, Lautaro and Caupolican, rank among the most famous of Chile's heroes. The Spanish poet, Alonso de Ercilla, wrote a long epic poem, *La Araucana*, about their exploits. The Indians took part in Chile's war of independence, and to-day they are an integral part of the Republic, owning their own lands and ranking as citizens equal with the Spaniards. They are a simple-minded people, many of whom still continue their old heathen superstitions and belief in witchcraft. They are hard-working and orderly, except when they have drunk too much of the cheap wines of the country on the many feast days in the calendar.

Chile owed her independence from Spain largely to the efforts of Bernardo O'Higgins, the son of an Irish immigrant and a Spanish lady. The elder O'Higgins had come from Peru and won the respect of whites and Indians alike by his useful public services, mainly in engineering works. His son, Bernardo, put himself at the head of the independence movement in Chile and, with the help of San Martin, the liberator of the Argentinas, outmanœuvred and outfought the much larger Spanish forces. Bernardo was elected the first president of the Chile Republic.

The modern Chilean has benefited from the fact that the early colonists had to work hard and did not depend on slavery. In consequence there was little aristocracy and a democratic outlook from the beginning. The colonists and the Indians intermarried a good deal, building up a class of *mestizos* (half Spanish, half Indian). Many immigrants came in, especially during the 19th century, and these included thousands of Germans—practical, hard-working, farming people, who own the neat, efficient farms in the south of the country. Most of the agriculture is carried on in enormous estates, called *fundos*, which are run with up-to-date motor-tractors and farm machinery. In the country districts there are still to be seen the heavy wagons drawn by teams of oxen, the farmers' high two-wheeled carts, and strings of horses and mules with barrels of local wine slung on either side of the saddle. The overseer rides round the farm in his broad-brimmed hat, long riding-boots, and brilliantly coloured *poncho* or small woollen blanket, worn over the shoulders, with a slit for the head.

See also AMERICAN INDIANS, CENTRAL AND SOUTH.
See also Vol. III: CHILE.

CHIMAERA, *see* MYTHOLOGICAL MONSTERS, Section (c).

CHINESE CIVILIZATION. China boasts the oldest surviving civilization in the world—older than Abraham and well-advanced when Greece was beginning. It has weathered wars, revolutions, and many barbarian invasions, and not only kept alive, but taken hold on every neighbouring country. Japan, Korea, Tibet, Annam, have all patterned themselves on it, and—mingled in this case with the civilization of India—it colours the life of Burma, Siam, Malaya, and the Indonesian archipelago. All the 'outer barbarians' who have conquered and ruled China have surrendered to its spell and become in due course as Chinese as the Chinese.

The reason for this persistence lies first and foremost in the character of the Chinese themselves, who are extremely pertinacious and conservative. But there are other things which have helped. The first is the Chinese written language. Being a language of 'characters', each a picture, or symbol, of a thing or an idea, it could not change with the passing of time as our written language (which is based upon sound) has done; so that whereas we now find it not easy to read even the English of Chaucer, and really difficult to read the language of Alfred, the modern educated Chinese can easily get the sense of something written thousands of years ago. Then ANCESTOR WORSHIP (q.v.), which is an important aspect of CHINESE RELIGION (q.v.), has the effect of wedding men to the past and to the 'faith of their forefathers'. Thirdly, Chinese civilization was crystallized for all time, four or five centuries before the Christian Era, by the work of the 'Sages', of whom we will speak later.

The story of China begins in the Old Stone Age, when a collection of tribes or clans, held together by common magical beliefs and religious ritual, settled in the valley of the Yellow River. 'China's Sorrow', as the river is often called, has always had a wicked habit of breaking its banks and flooding huge tracts of country. Therefore the people had to work hard at building dykes and cutting canals. (Yü, one of the best known of the early, semi-mythical emperors, was called the 'Harnesser of Floods'.) This could only be done by men working together in gangs, and in consequence the early Chinese developed the organized communal life without which it is hardly possible for a civilization to grow. The same thing happened, of course, in other parts of the world—civilizations have generally risen and prospered in the valley or delta of some great river, such as the Tigris, the Nile, or the Ganges.

The milestones on China's road to civilization are found in the state records, which the Chinese emperors were already having compiled before 1000 B.C. First comes the invention of ploughs, then of wheels—making possible the use of horse-drawn carts and war-chariots—then of the spinning of silk from the cocoon of the silkworm. Silk, by the way, had a very important place in the earlier history of China. She alone had the secret of spinning, so the whole civilized world had to go to her for their silks at a time when cottons were unknown, at least in Europe. The Romans called China *Serica*, the 'silk country'. As early as 2000 B.C. Chinese astronomers are said to have worked out a lunar and solar calendar. This made it possible to calculate each year the right times for farming activities, such as the sowing of the various crops. Incidentally, they fixed the date for clearing their houses of fleas—a rite which is still observed in the early spring of each year.

As in other parts of the globe, for instance the civilization of ancient PERU (q.v.), the Chinese arrived at the discovery of writing through an earlier primitive method of recording things by tying knots in pieces of cord. They appear to have evolved a regular script some 3,000 years ago (*see* WRITING, HISTORY OF, Vol. IV). Excavations in Honan Province not long ago brought to light the earliest known specimens of Chinese characters, dating from the Shang Dynasty (1766–1122 B.C.), which are a rudimentary version of the characters used to-day. They were incised on bones or tortoises' shells. These were used in those days as a means of consulting oracles, magicians 'interpreting' the cracks which appeared on the shells when roasted in the fire. The Chinese were also the first people to invent printing, and they were using a kind of movable type as early as the 7th century A.D. (*see* PRINTING, HISTORY OF, Vol. IV).

Although the Chinese have the name of a peace-loving people, their history is warlike, and war-chariots appear early in it. The Chinese army was 'mechanized', in fact, at a very remote date; and it was only later, when they had learned an object lesson from their old enemies, the Mongols and Huns of the north, that they took to the use of cavalry. To keep out the hordes of barbarian horsemen, they erected one of the chief wonders of the world, the 2,000-mile-long GREAT WALL OF CHINA (q.v. Vol. III). They had also a system of military Feudalism complete with a 'code of chivalry'; but whereas our feudal age began with William the Conqueror and lasted down to about the time of Henry VIII, China's period of feudalism was flourishing before the foundation of Rome and had died out before the Christian era. Gunpowder was first used in China—though only for fireworks, not for purposes of war.

It is, however, in the arts and in the things of the mind that Chinese civilization reached its highest levels. The Chinese love poetry and have great poets living to-day; but their great lyric-writers of the 8th and 9th centuries A.D. (one of the greatest of whom is Li-Tai-Po) are as popular as ever. In developing craftsmanship the early Chinese passed through the customary stages. They began with stone, went on to wood, then learnt to weave baskets, and later invented the potter's wheel. Then came the big jump to the use of metals—first bronze (the period of which lasted unusually long in China) and finally iron. Chinese love of jade and the uses they made of it deserve special mention. From very early times they made sacred and ceremonial objects, including instruments of music, from this beautiful hard stone; and the most exquisite jade carvings are found among the objects buried with dead noblemen for their use in the next world. A visit to any good collection of Chinese bronzes, paintings, and ceramics (pottery and porcelain) will probably leave an impression of the special 'flavour' of Chinese art as a whole—its dignity, restraint, purity of line and colour, and a certain essential 'bigness', leaving no room for the petty and 'pernicketty'.

The keynote of the teaching of China's great thinkers is harmony: Man must strive to live in perfect accord, both with his fellow-man and with everything else in nature. This is the lesson taught by CONFUCIUS (q.v. Vol. V) and the other 'Sages', in whose philosophy the Chinese have found their spiritual anchor all down the centuries to such an extent that the 'Sages' teaching is, as an emperor of the T'ang Dynasty (A.D. 618–907) said, 'like air to birds and water to fishes'. The other main rules of life taught by China's ancient philosophers are these: Do not to others as you would not have them do to you (the 'golden rule' as we call it, turned the other way about); be moderate in everything; cultivate good manners; strive after learning, and—most important—practise 'filial piety' or veneration for parents and ancestors, and respect and obedience towards teachers and those in authority. The Chinese idea of the duty of the government was that it should set a good example to the common people, rather than control them by laws and penalties. This ideal of government has never been entirely lost sight of: even to-day the President of the Chinese Republic often quotes from the 'Sages' when he delivers paternal broadcasts to his people.

FIGURE FROM A CHINESE TOMB
Painted pottery models of figures, animals, and houses were buried with the dead. T'ang Dynasty. *British Mus.*

Over a thousand years ago the Chinese started a system of a civil service recruited by open competitive examination. The candidates were examined in their knowledge of the Chinese 'Classics', the old books of history, poetry, and philosophy—in particular the writings of Confucius, the greatest of the Chinese Sages. The examinations were very stiff and were conducted in most trying conditions, the candidates being locked into cubicles and kept in solitary confinement during their nine days' duration. The effect of this system was that the magistrates and government officials were men of high culture, thoroughly steeped in the ancient ethical codes and rules of behaviour. It is doubtful whether this method secured the most efficient or progressive rulers; but undoubtedly this permanent body of scholar-officials carried on without break, whether dynasties rose or fell, the ancient culture and philosophy of China.

The history of China has shown a tendency to follow a recurring pattern—a gradual building up of political and cultural greatness under a powerful dynasty to a peak period of glory, which is followed by a period of decadence and political weakness and an invasion from without. The new foreign dynasty, instead of crushing Chinese civilization, is gradually absorbed by it; then a new period of building up begins, culminating in another glorious age, followed by another period of decadence and another foreign invasion.

The periods of Chinese history are generally called by the names of the reigning emperors —as we speak in England of the Tudor period or dynasty. The earliest period, 2850–2205 B.C., as reckoned by the Chinese, is a more or less mythical era, including the 'Three Emperors', Fu Hsi, Shen Nung, and Huang-Ti, and their successors. Then, still in the twilight region between legend and history, comes the Hsia Dynasty, 2205–1766 B.C., about which we know little more than that it almost certainly existed. This was followed from 1766 to 1122 B.C. by the Shang Dynasty emperors, who were hardly more than leaders among the clan chieftains. Something is known of them, because the earliest Chinese writing dates from this time. Some magnificent ancient bronzes also belong to this period.

From 1122 to 255 B.C. comes one of the great periods, the Chou Dynasty—the age of Confucius and the 'Sages' and the epoch of Chinese

3000	
2500	THREE EMPERORS AND FIVE RULERS 2850–2205 B.C.
2000	HSIA 2205–1766 B.C.
1500	SHANG 1766–1122 B.C.
1000	
500	CHOU 1122–255 B.C.
	CH'IN 221–206 B.C.
	HAN 206 B.C.–A.D. 220
	THREE KINGDOMS A.D. 220–80
500	SIX DYNASTIES A.D. 220–589
	SUI – A.D. 589–618
	T'ANG A.D. 618–906
1000	FIVE DYNASTIES A.D. 906–60
	SUNG A.D. 960–1280
	YÜAN A.D. 1280–1368
1500	MING A.D. 1368–1644
1900	MANCHU (CH'ING) A.D. 1644–1912
	REPUBLIC 1912—

THE CHINESE DYNASTIES

feudalism. This ended with a general break-up into civil warfare; but in course of time Huang-Ti consolidated China into a cohesive empire. He built the Great Wall as the northern boundary of his empire. But in cultural matters this period was barbarian—Huang-Ti was responsible for the 'Burning of the Books', as a result of which much of the works of the Great Sages was destroyed. After a period of peace, power, and prosperity under the Han Dynasty (206 B.C. to A.D. 220), during which the great silk road across Asia was opened and BUDDHISM (q.v.) came to China, there followed an age of invasions by nomad tribes from the north.

A COURTYARD IN THE FORBIDDEN CITY, PEKING

The Forbidden City, the innermost of the three cities of Peking, was formerly the residence of the Chinese Emperors and was therefore sacred. Inside its walls are many palaces and temples of the Ming and Manchu Dynasties. *C. P. R.*

In 589 the Chinese, under the Sui Dynasty, recovered control; and in 618 began one of the greatest periods of Chinese civilization, the T'ang Dynasty. During this period China was again a great empire, and its capital, like Rome, was the meeting-place of the nations. Painting and poetry approached their highest level; pottery developed into porcelain—the T'ang pottery horses are particularly famous. There followed, however, the inevitable decay and another break-up period with fresh Tartar invasions in the north. In the south, however, the Sung Dynasty carried on for about 450 years. This dynasty was famous for exquisite porcelain and delicate landscape painting; but in practical matters it was ineffective. In 1206 the whole country was swamped by terrible Mongol invasions led by GENGHIS KHAN (q.v. Vol. V). As the Mongol invaders settled down and absorbed the Chinese genius, the Yüan Dynasty established a mighty empire; and its capital, Peking, became famous under Kublai Khan as a centre of

magnificence and culture all over the world. Visitors, including the Venetian, MARCO POLO (q.v. Vol. V), came to visit it and wrote of what they saw. In 1368 a Chinese dynasty, the Ming, returned to power and began to cut China off from the rest of the world—a policy of isolationism which lasted until quite recent times. The Ming period was a great age in cultural matters: among other things the Emperor Yung Lo rebuilt Peking much as it is to-day, and also ordered the compiling of the Great Encyclopaedia, a work of over a million pages.

In 1644 this dynasty again was overthrown by foreign rulers, the Manchus. These conquerors gave China two of her greatest emperors —Kang hsi and Chien hung (each reigning sixty years). The empire again expanded, embracing central Asia and Tibet. But during the 19th century came decay as well as pressure from the Western nations, and China fell upon an evil period, leading to the great revolution under SUN YAT SEN (q.v. Vol. V) and the establishment of the Chinese Republic (*see* CHINESE PEOPLES). If Chinese fortunes follow their usual cycle, perhaps another period of greatness will follow in the near future.

See also ANCIENT CIVILIZATIONS; Vol. IV: CHINESE LANGUAGE.

CHINESE PEOPLES. With their 400–500 million people the Chinese are by far the biggest single group of human beings in the world—a group in the sense of a people united politically as well as by ancestry, language, traditions, and everyday habits of life. (For comparison India has about 350 millions, Russia 150 millions, and the U.S.A. 140 millions.) The Chinese belong to the Mongolian division of humanity (*see* RACES AND PEOPLES), that is to say, they have straight dark hair, a yellowish skin, round heads, flat noses, and narrow slanting eyes. They are as a whole, especially those in the north, of a very sturdy build.

Some of the very earliest traces of man are to be found near Peking (*see* FOSSIL MAN). The Chinese first enter history as a collection of clans settled in the valley of the Yellow River in North China. Later they spread down the Yangtze, where the majority now live, and later still to southern China, absorbing as they went the groups of aboriginal people, except where these have survived in remote places in the south and west. In more recent times they have spread out into other parts of the world—there are now some twenty million 'Overseas Chinese', mostly in Malaya, Siam, and Burma. In some parts of America the Chinese are the most useful manual labourers.

There are pockets of other races inside China's frontiers to-day, the most important being the tribes of Mongol–Turk origin who inhabit the regions of Outer China to the north-west. There are also groups of Moslems of Arab descent whose ancestors may have come in trading dhows, via the Indian Ocean, many centuries ago. And there are comparatively small groups of Europeans in some of the coastal cities. But apart from these minorities, the people of China have all, broadly speaking, the same characteristic outlook and physical features. From the cold, barren north to the tropical south there are, however, considerable differences of physical stature and habits. Perhaps the main differences are

WATER-GATE TO THE TARTAR CITY, PEKING
The name of this part of Peking dates from the Tartar conquests beginning in the 10th century. *Canadian Pacific Railway*

brought about by climate and environment: the northerner is of burlier build and more stolid temperament, the southerner less stalwart, but more agile in mind and body and of a much more excitable nature.

It is not possible to understand the modern Chinaman without knowing something of his history and ancient traditions, for his way of life and mental outlook is rooted in the past and has been very greatly shaped by the teachings of the great sages (see CONFUCIUS), which have formed the main framework of Chinese education for over 2,000 years (see CHINESE CIVILIZATION). The Chinese are essentially a peaceful people—peasant farmers with their lives closely connected with 'the good earth'; but their history has been far from peaceful. They suffered a series of great invasions and conquests from outside, the most important of these being the Mongol invasion under JENGHIS KHAN (q.v. Vol. V) in the 12th century and the Manchu invasion in the 17th century. But these outside peoples, although politically conquerors, soon absorbed the culture and civilization of the Chinese. During the final stages of Manchu rule China went through a difficult and unfortunate period. She resented the attempts of the Western Powers to trade with her, and her corrupt and decadent government tried to keep up a state of isolation. This resulted in a series of inglorious wars both with European Powers and with Japan.

In 1911 the Manchu Dynasty was overthrown and, under the leadership of SUN YAT SEN, 'the Father of the Revolution' (q.v. Vol. V), the Chinese abandoned a monarchy and began to work for a central republican government. Sun Yat Sen realized that, after centuries of rule by an autocratic monarchy, China was not ready for what we should call a fully democratic government. He aimed at a one-party government, the *Kuomintang* or 'National Party', which was to control and guide the people until more education and experience had made them able to work a parliamentary system successfully. Nearly twenty years of disruption and civil war passed before the new Republic was properly established. Sun Yat Sen had invited the Russian communists to help with the revolution, and in consequence a communist left-wing party was formed which clashed with the more moderate anti-communist party. A great deal of fighting followed, and even when the right-wing party under General Chiang Kai Shek got control, the communists still set up a rival state in the north-west and were a constant danger to the central government.

Just before Japan's attack on China in 1936 the communist leaders and Chiang Kai Shek came to an agreement to form a common front, and this lasted through the ten years' stubborn and bitter struggle with Japan. When peace came in 1945 the old differences flared up and civil war again broke out, with the communists demanding a share in the government. President Chiang Kai Shek has declared that the totalitarian character of the Kuomintang should now come to an end, and that a national assembly should be called together to form a new constitution for China based on democratic lines. On this basis it should be possible for the two parties to reach agreement, and the twenty-year-old conflict to be brought to an end.

Modern China is, as it always has been, a nation of peasant farmers. Cut off from the west by great mountain ranges, its most densely populated areas are towards the Pacific coast, in the alluvial valleys of the great rivers and along the coastal plains. During the Japanese war the backward provinces of the west have been much developed, and communications with the outside world have been opened up by the famous BURMA ROAD (q.v. Vol. IV), the 2,000-mile motor-way connecting China with India and from thence to the Western world. During recent years great cities have grown up on the Pacific coast—Shanghai, more than half the size of London, Canton, Tientsin, and the big cities of the Yangtze. But it still remains true that more than three-quarters of the whole immense population find their livelihood in agriculture—some of the most intensive land cultivation in the world. Therefore it is to the villages we must look for a typical picture of modern Chinese life.

Let us take a village in the great northern plain through which runs the Yellow River. The landscape is brown and featureless except when the crops such as millet, wheat, beans, and kaoling are above ground. There is little to catch the eye except the thickly strewn villages themselves, the larger ones walled against bandits, dykes for protection against floods, and, maybe, a few solitary clumps of pines to mark the site of an aristocratic family burial-ground. The fields are dotted with thousands of conical mounds which are the graves of the ordinary

THE YANGTZE AT CHUNGKING
Women are washing clothes and vegetables in the river. In the background a market is being held. *Dorien Leigh*

peasant, for each man is buried on his own little plot of land, using up a substantial part of the precious soil. Unless the village is on one of the new motor highways, the roads are just dirt tracks and the traffic along them mainly mules, donkeys, and wheelbarrows. Wheelbarrows are so much the ordinary means of conveyance in this part of China that an Anglican bishop, making a round of his diocese, will not think it undignified to ride in a wheelbarrow. Sails are often fitted to them to make use of a following wind.

The family strip of land is so small, taxes so heavy, and floods and droughts so prevalent, that the farmer can scrape but the barest existence from the soil. The Chinese peasant puts up with a standard of living extremely low according to our Western ideas. All the same, when times are not too bad, he manages, to be a person of great cheerfulness and good humour, and his life is by no means completely drab. Chinese village life is thoroughly patriarchal: everything centres round the family which is ruled by the head of the household, the father, whose powers are almost of life and death.

Everyone lives on a truly communal basis, sharing almost everything—even the family pipe.

The chief colour and excitement of life are connected with festivals such as weddings, funerals (which are naturally big events among an ancestor-worshipping people), and the great annual holiday of the New Year. At this last the walls of the village temple, the door-posts of every house, and even the donkeys' pack-saddles are decorated with scrolls and streamers of red and gold paper; crackers are let off by the children all through the day and night; and incense is burnt to the tablets which are the shrines of the ancestor-spirits. The kitchen god, which every house possesses, is given special food and drink, for this is the time when he returns to Heaven and he must therefore be propitiated before he goes. The New Year Festival is a time when the whole village feasts, visits, and makes merry.

The belief of the Chinese peasants in the power of spirits, both friendly and malicious, puts them at the mercy of soothsayers and sorcerers, and 'devil-dodging' plays a big part in their lives. But the grip of harmful superstitions is nowadays being loosened by the spread of modern education. Boys and girls are now being given a primary education comparable to our own. Older people, also, who had never learnt to read or write, are getting a working knowledge of written Chinese by the so-called 'thousand-character courses'. This means that the 50,000 and more characters which the Chinese dictionary contains are reduced to a sort of basic Chinese of essential characters. Another organization which is doing valuable work in Chinese rural life is the Chinese Industrial Co-operatives—the C.I.C. Their job is to revive the old village handicrafts, which machine production was killing, and to set up rural industries. This not only helps the country folk to make a reasonable living, but also acts as an influence against the development of huge overcrowded industrial cities.

This rural picture of peasant life is naturally somewhat different in central and south China. There millet and wheat give way to rice and tea, and there is more farming of silkworms. The mule and the donkey are largely replaced by the ill-tempered water-buffalo in the paddy-fields, and by legions of porter coolies tramping

TRANSPLANTING RICE SEEDLINGS
The seedlings are planted out thinly in the flooded fields.
Paul Popper

the flagstone hill paths. In the deltas of the great rivers, canals (some 25,000 miles of them in the Yangtze delta alone) take the place of roads. In these parts also there are thousands of families whose only homes are their barges on the water.

This picture of a very simple peasant life, characteristic of the vast majority of China's people, must not mislead us into thinking that China is without culture and love of scholarship: this is far from the case, as was proved by the thousands of scholars who, during the recent Japanese invasion, rescued their beloved books and carried them hundreds of miles to places of safety. In particular the Chinese of all ages have had a special love for history. In A.D. 1408 the Chinese historians produced the most stupendous work ever attempted—the Great Encyclopaedia of Yung Lo (a Ming emperor). The *Yung Lo Ta Tien* filled 11,100 large-sized volumes bound in yellow silk, containing altogether 366,992,000 characters, roughly equivalent to 500 million words. Three handwritten copies were made, but unfortunately all have been lost or destroyed, except for some 160-odd volumes scattered in various museums.

See also CHINESE CIVILIZATION; also Vol. III: CHINA; Vol. IV: CHINESE AND ALLIED LANGUAGES.

CHINESE RELIGION. We are told that there are over 400 million people in China, so it is only natural to expect that they will show a good many varieties of religion. This is certainly the case. Moreover, if we were to travel through China to-day, we should find that the life of the people was changing very rapidly, and that it was difficult to say exactly how many people belonged to the old religions, how many were Christians, and how many had no faith at all, or were perhaps Marxists, with a kind of substitute-religion. But we should still find a good many holding to the old customs and beliefs. The Chinese used to say that before Christianity they really had three religions: Confucianism for everyday life, Taoism for unusual occasions such as fortune-telling, casting out demons, and working magic, and Buddhism for death-beds and funerals. This may seem to us rather peculiar, but the Chinese never seem to have found any difficulty about it.

Ancient Chinese religion was apparently not very different from that of other nations in antiquity (*see* RELIGION). Even to-day it is not

THE EMPEROR CH'EN HOU-CHOU SEEKING INSPIRATION FOR A POEM

Chinese painting of the Ming Dynasty

unusual to see in country districts in China small shrines containing two little images—a man and a woman, who represent the spirits presiding over the fields, and are called the *t'uti p'oosa*. The farmers make offerings to them for a good harvest—indeed, they are really very much the same as the local godlings of India or of the ancient Romans. Then there is ANCESTOR WORSHIP (q.v.), which fosters that strong sense of duty to parents characteristic of the Chinese. As far back as we can find any records there seems to have been a belief in a number of gods and spirits connected with nature and the different departments of life. But over them all was a sort of celestial emperor, a great sky-god sometimes called Shang-ti, sometimes Ti'en, and he had a special sacrifice offered to him once a year at a great open-air altar at Peking, at which the chief officiant was the Chinese Emperor himself. Religious life to the ancient Chinese was largely made up of ceremonies intended to keep the various supernatural beings friendly, and it was considered most important that all these ceremonies should be accurately, reverently, and punctually performed.

Then, in the 5th century before Christ, at the same time that important changes were coming in India and Greece, a gradual change passed also over Chinese thought and ways of living. China was then in a very disorderly and lawless condition, disunited and full of strife between a number of rival war-lords. As a kind of protest against this unworthy sort of public life there arose what were called 'the Hundred Schools of Philosophy'. Of course, there were not exactly this number, but the teachers and their respective schools were certainly plentiful. The earliest of them to leave any record of himself was CONFUCIUS (q.v. Vol. V), and he had a great many disciples. After him came a number of other teachers, not all of whom by any means agreed with him, but all of whom sought to persuade their countrymen that the most important thing in religious life was conduct. In this respect they were not unlike the Hebrew prophets, though they spoke less about God and more about men's relations with one another. Confucius mainly taught the virtue of right actions, saying that the Supreme God (whom he called Ti'en, or Heaven, rather as we say Providence) had sent him to do so. Another school of teachers, the Taoists, declared that the best thing in life was to forsake the world of action

CONFUCIAN TEMPLE AT CHÜFOO, SHANTUNG PROVINCE
One of the oldest temples still standing, dating from the Yüan Dynasty (1280-1368). *London Missionary Soc.*

and to live quietly and passively in harmony with the great and just Principle of Nature, which they called the Great Tao (pronounced Dao). This way of living they called *wu-wei*, which means literally 'do nothing'. In politics it meant that the ruler was not to interfere with his subjects too much, because it was said that people, being the children of Nature or the Tao, would, if left to themselves, incline to what was good, and anything that was evil would destroy itself by its own impetus. These Taoists said that their standard book, the *Tao-Teh-King*, had been composed by a sage called Lao-Tzu who, they said, had lived a little earlier than Confucius. It cannot be proved that any such person as Lao-Tzu ever really existed, and the *Tao-Teh-King* is certainly a good deal later than the time of the first Taoists. Another teacher, Mo Ti, taught that the remedy for all the ills of society was the practice of all-embracing love. Confucius and a great follower of his called Mencius taught that man was by nature inclined to be good, and only needed to be shown what was right in order to do it: in this respect they agreed with the Taoists. But other thinkers in China taught just the opposite, and said that the nature

TEMPLE OF HEAVEN, PEKING

A ceremony was held in this temple every year at which the Emperor offered sacrifices to the Heavenly Spirits. Built in the 15th–16th century. *Canadian Pacific Railway*

of man was evil and not good, so that strong rule and discipline were the best things for him. They do not seem to have been clear as to how the rulers, being themselves human, and therefore of evil nature, were to govern justly.

The period of disunion and civil war in China was followed by the rise of a dictator, Huang-Ti, who determined to make China into one state under a strong central authority. Huang-Ti gave orders that all the philosophical books of Confucius and others, except those of the Taoists, should be burnt. In some ways Confucius and some of the other philosophers were conservative in their ideas of government, and the new dictator wanted to make the people begin all over again with new ideas. (This is very much what happened at one stage in the setting up of Hitler's new order in Germany.) Fortunately for China, some of the writings of the Confucian school were preserved in secret. When, therefore, after several generations, China secured a better central government, the new emperors, the famous Han Dynasty, thought the teaching of Confucius so good that they determined to revive it, and so they paid the great master special honours. Temples were erected in his

memory, and in these, besides acts of reverence to his statue, many of the old Chinese religious ceremonies of which he approved (such as the spring festival with its proper sacrifices) were revived. These have been carried on, as a kind of established State religion, up to recent times.

But this official State Confucianism did not approve of many of the lesser spirits and godlings worshipped by the Chinese people. The priests of these minor gods, therefore, joined forces with the Taoist teachers; and Taoism, as a result, became less a philosophy of living and more a form of very superstitious religion, including such curious practices as trying to turn other substances into gold, or to invent a medicine which would confer immortality.

Finally, about sixty-five years after the birth of Christ BUDDHISM (q.v.) entered China. At first it was only a small movement, but in the 4th and 5th centuries A.D. it expanded immensely, and in time spread all over China. It supplied what Confucianism had lacked, a persuasive doctrine of the future life. It also had a great influence upon art, especially the art of painting. The Chinese still revered Confucius, and practised Confucian and Taoist rites, but nearly all of them became Buddhists, at least in name.

Another 500 years passed, and then a great and new Confucian school arose, led by six teachers. The last of these, Chu Hsi, aimed at reviving and giving a fresh interpretation to the old teachings of his master. He cut away most of the old ceremonies, and laid stress mainly on the moral teaching itself. It is hardly right to say that Chu Hsi was not religious, but his religious views were so philosophical that they seemed to leave out the ordinary beliefs about Deity. He was so anxious to avoid anything like the old Chinese idea of Deity as a man-in-the-sky that he said Heaven is Law, and Law became the First Cause of the Universe. Chu Hsi was, of course, not the first to comment upon the writings and proverbs attributed to Confucius. From the beginning there were people who did this, and some of their works, such as 'The Doctrine of the Mean' and 'The Great Learning' became the school books of the young Chinese for centuries.

These various elements in Chinese life—(1) among the educated, the various schools of religious philosophy, (2) among the ignorant, Taoism, and (3) everywhere, Buddhism—continued until the 16th century A.D. with comparatively little change, and without any large additions. At a much later date a considerable Moslem population grew up in the western provinces towards inner Mongolia. These Moslems were mostly the families and descendants of mercenary soldiers employed by the Chinese Empire (*see* ISLAM). NESTORIAN Christianity (q.v.) filtered across from Persia about A.D. 635, but did not take any serious hold, and eventually died out, leaving only a rather famous stone monument and various manuscripts, which have been almost accidentally preserved in Buddhist monasteries. There was a further attempt at missionary work by the Franciscan friars in the 13th and 14th centuries, but this also came to little. Then in the 17th century there came the Jesuits, who made much more impression; and the Roman Catholic Church has had a considerable body of followers in China ever since, including many Chinese bishops, one of whom in 1945 was made a cardinal. Other Christian bodies have made large conversions during the past 150 years, and their work has been generally accepted by the Chinese as beneficial.

Since the republican revolution of 1911 the life of the Chinese has been changing rapidly, and their outlook has widened. Nothing, however, can shake the fact that the Chinese still very largely look back with pride to the teachings which the ancient sages set forth, and even if they become Christians, as many of them are doing, they still want to feel that they are building upon foundations which Confucius himself laid. Many others are trying to reconstruct Confucianism and apply it to modern conditions. Buddhism on the whole has declined in China, and many of the Buddhist temples are deserted. The old days are past in which China seemed self-sufficient, whether in politics, culture, or religion. But the Chinese are such a great people that it is almost certain that they will continue to make their own distinctive contribution to the common life and thought of humanity.

See also CHINESE PEOPLES.

CHRIST, *see* JESUS OF NAZARETH.

CHRISTIAN CHURCH. The word Church comes from the Greek *curiacon* (Anglo-Saxon *circe*) and originally meant 'The Lord's (house)', i.e. the building where Christians gather for worship. The first church in Jerusalem in the year A.D. 29 was a house—perhaps the same in which the Last Supper was eaten (Acts i. 13). House-churches continued for 200 years and more before special churches were built. The word Church came to be used also for the community of people who gathered in the church, or all these local churches together—'the whole estate of Christ's Church'. Sometimes the word is used also for all who have belonged, the dead as well as the living.

The first congregation in Jerusalem numbered only about 120 members, the immediate followers of JESUS OF NAZARETH (q.v.). The leaders were the Apostles—twelve, as there were twelve tribes of Israel. They believed that Jesus had called them to build His Church—a new Israel in which all God's promises to His chosen people would be fulfilled. To enter this community a man must be reborn by repentance and baptism—baptism being the INITIATION CEREMONY (q.v.) of the Christian Church. The members joined with each other in repeating the action of Jesus when 'He took bread and brake it' (Acts ii. 26), the sacrament of thanksgiving or Eucharist (*see* SACRAMENT). And this was the central service of the Church.

The first problem which faced the Church was its attitude to the Jewish law. The first

Christians were Jews and were bound by the Law. But was it necessary for non-Jewish Christians also to keep the Jewish Law? ST. PAUL (q.v. Vol. V) declared that the Church must be independent of JUDAISM (q.v.) in order that it might fulfil its destiny as a world-religion. About 100 years later when many of its members wanted to break all Jewish connexions and even throw over the authority of the Old Testament, the opposite danger faced the Church—pagan and magical beliefs began to creep in. The leaders of the Church therefore chose out the most trusted Christian writings and declared these to be 'the faith as we received it from the apostles'. In this way, about A.D. 200 the books which we call the New Testament began to be recognized as the standard writings or 'canon' (see BIBLE). The early Church made several short and simple creeds or statements of its belief, which are similar to the later version called the Apostles' Creed, now used in the Church of England at morning and evening prayer. By the beginning of the 4th century many false doctrines were springing up. The leaders of the Church gathered in a great council at Nicaea and agreed together upon an official creed, which is known as the Creed of Nicaea. This is practically the same as the creed used in the Service of Holy Communion.

During the first 500 years of its life the Christian Church increased in numbers and spread widely, both East and West, in spite of persecution. By A.D. 200 it had reached Armenia, and by A.D. 250 there was an Armenian State Church. By A.D. 200 the Church was also strong in parts of Egypt (see COPT), and in the 3rd century it spread from Syria into Persia (see NESTORIAN). A spirit of local independence later caused Christians in these lands to claim independence of the Church of the Roman Empire, and this resulted in the Coptic, Nestorian, and Jacobite divisions. The Church reached south down the Red Sea to the tip of Arabia and down both shores of the Persian Gulf. Sometime in the 3rd century it had reached India. In 313, during the reign of the Roman Emperor CONSTANTINE (q.v. Vol. V), Christians in the Roman Empire were freed from persecution, and Christianity soon became recognized as the official religion. There was a vast increase in Church membership, and many churches were built, including the Church of the Nativity at Bethlehem, the oldest church building in the world.

The bishops of the four greatest cities—Rome, Constantinople, Antioch, and Alexandria—became important and powerful. They were later called Patriarchs, and to their number was added the Bishop of Jerusalem. Of these five, four belonged to the East and only one, the Patriarch of Rome (the Pope), belonged to the West. He, therefore, became particularly important: Rome was the city associated with St. Peter and St. Paul, the centre of Western Christendom and the one capital of the Roman Empire before Constantinople was made capital of the Eastern Empire. This great worldly power which had come to the Church brought with it the temptation of worldliness and a lowering of standards—a temptation to put temporal power and glory before spiritual glory. But some people still felt that the Christian life should be one of poverty and hardship (see ASCETICISM). As early as the 3rd century in Egypt men had begun to go into the desert as hermits. Later, some hermits joined together in communities and adopted a strict rule of life, and so there grew up the monasteries. The standard rule of life for the MONKS (q.v.) in the West was the Rule of St. Benedict, established in 529.

There followed in Europe a period called the DARK AGES (q.v.), during which hordes of barbarians swept over from the east and north and bit by bit broke down the Western Roman Empire and threw much of Europe back into barbarism. When most things Roman were destroyed, the Church remained. When all other life was becoming local and tribal, the Church stood for a larger unity. Unfortunately the Church herself suffered the ill effects of this break-up of civilization and, though it won over great numbers of the barbarians to Christianity and continued its missionary work far and wide, in an insecure world it often sought for power and security rather than truth and progress. In the 7th century there arose in Arabia the religion which was to prove Christianity's chief rival—ISLAM (q.v.), the religion founded by Mohammed. Within a century this new religion, carried by the armies of Moslem Arabs, swept over the lands of Christianity's origin and early advance—Syria, Palestine, Egypt, North Africa, and as far as Spain. During the following two or three centuries progress in art and learning belonged more to the Moslem than the Christian world. Islam has always remained the greatest rival to Christianity all over the world.

CHURCH OF THE NATIVITY, BETHLEHEM
Built in the 4th century on the site of the stable where Jesus was born. *Matson Photo. Service*

When the Western Roman Empire was crumbling before the attacks of Goths and Huns, the Eastern or BYZANTINE EMPIRE (q.v.), centred at Constantinople, remained intact. The breach between the Church of the West and the Eastern Church became wider, especially because the East would not recognize the supremacy of the Pope over their own Patriarchs. When the Byzantine Empire was faced with attacks from the Turks and appealed to the West for help, the tremendous enthusiasm which brought about the CRUSADES (1096–1291) (q.v.) was stirred, not only by the desire to rescue the Holy Land from the infidel Moslem, but also by a desire to bring the Eastern Church under the authority of Rome.

From the 11th and 12th centuries onwards, as Europe became more settled, a new spirit began to grow within the Church—on the one side encouraging learning, on the other bringing religion more in touch with the needs of the people. The orders of FRIARS (q.v.) were founded —the two great orders being the Franciscans (1209) and the Dominicans (1216). Both these orders provided the Church with zealous evangelists at home and abroad, in Moslem Spain,

Africa, and Persia, and before the end of the century even as far as China. Then in the 15th century came the RENAISSANCE (q.v.) in Italy, and in the 16th, the REFORMATION (q.v.) in the north. The breakdown of the old feudal system, the growing sense of nationality which was awakening in Europe, and the beginnings of democratic government, all constituted threats to the old autocratic absolute monarchy of the Pope as head of the Church. About 1200 Pope Innocent III declared that the Pope was head of a feudal world and that kings held their kingdoms as fiefs from the Pope. But the modern world would no longer accept this: it looked for a Church, no less than a State, managed on a constitutional basis, where national interests would have a chance to be represented. At the same time the earnest, inquiring spirit of the age led men to question things which they had merely accepted before, and to condemn abuses. These two sides to the Reformation, the political and the religious, got a good deal mixed up, and there were both sides to most of the main movements.

The first break came in the early 15th century with John Huss of Bohemia who, influenced by the teaching of WYCLIFFE (q.v. Vol. V), started the MORAVIAN CHURCH (q.v.). In 1517 Luther started the break from the Church in Germany. This produced the LUTHERAN CHURCH (q.v.) to which most people in north Germany, Denmark, Norway, and Sweden belong. In 1536 Calvin started the movement which resulted in the CALVINIST CHURCH (q.v.). This spread from Switzerland over western Germany and the Netherlands, and also to Scotland. The English reformation left medieval church order less disturbed (except for the dissolution of the monasteries), and most of the old forms of service (*see* PRAYER BOOK) were kept in the CHURCH OF ENGLAND (q.v.). The English bishops are in the direct line of succession, bishops appointing bishops from the earliest times by the laying on of hands. This is called 'Apostolic Succession' because behind the original appointments stand the Apostles to whom Christ gave power and authority for their work. The bishops in the Roman Catholic, Orthodox Eastern, Anglican, and other ancient churches always receive their ordination from the hands of other bishops, and so the apostolic succession is kept intact. The Roman Catholic Church, however, denies that the bishops of the English Church have been consecrated in the true Apostolic Succession. The non-episcopal communions emphasize the handing on of the faith, rather than of the office and authority.

In the 16th to 18th centuries groups of English people, dissatisfied with the reformation of the Anglican Church, broke away and formed separate denominations. The Independents or CONGREGATIONALISTS (q.v.) and the BAPTISTS (q.v.) formed separate Nonconformist churches. Bands of Puritans and QUAKERS (q.v.) sought freedom of worship in America. In the 18th century the METHODIST CHURCH (q.v.) was founded by JOHN and CHARLES WESLEY (q.v. Vol. V). In North America, which was largely colonized by Protestant countries, many different divisions of Protestant Christianity have sprung up in the last two centuries. The chart below shows how the Church has branched out through the centuries, and how all the branches have come from the same root and are part of the one religion.

The Roman Catholic Church met the Reformation with a Counter-Reformation in which it stiffened its own discipline, removing many abuses, and launched a bitter attack against the Protestants (*see* INQUISITION). This attack, carried on with violence of feeling, resulted in cruelty and bloodshed on both sides. At the same time, largely through the Jesuits, the Roman Catholics Church started on a great Christian expansion which carried Christianity to the New World (America), to south and central Africa, India and Ceylon, Burma, Malaya, the East Indies, Japan, and China. Protestant missions came into being in the 19th century, and from 1790 to 1840 most of the great missionary societies were founded. During the last century missionaries followed explorers and traders into all parts of the world, so that the Church became at last 'world wide'.

Christians say in their Creed 'I believe in one, holy, catholick and apostolick Church'. The

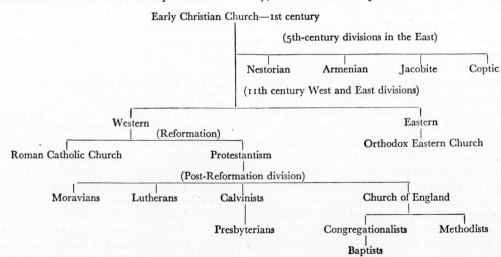

Early Christian Church—1st century

(5th-century divisions in the East)

Nestorian   Armenian   Jacobite   Coptic

(11th century West and East divisions)

Western   Eastern
        (Reformation)   Orthodox Eastern Church

Roman Catholic Church   Protestantism

(Post-Reformation division)

Moravians   Lutherans   Calvinists   Church of England

                    Presbyterians   Congregationalists   Methodists

                                    Baptists

Church is not yet altogether one, holy, or catholic (universal). There is, however, more concern about unity to-day than there has been since the Reformation: the World Council of Churches, to which all the main Churches except the Roman Catholic belong, is a step towards that goal. The Church is more nearly Catholic than ever before. In its human weakness the Church often fails to reach great holiness. It has been accused of opposing new ways of human progress, and of persecuting those who sought after truth. Indeed, like most established institutions, the Church has generally been conservative and slow to accept new ideas. But in this conservatism there is a security against the risk of falling victim to false doctrines, though its immediate effect may be unprogressive. And the Church has always accepted those ideas which were proved by experience to be true.

See also CHRISTIANITY; CHRISTIAN YEAR.

CHRISTIANITY is the most universal religion. Of the world's population nearly one-third are nominal Christians. While these to-day are to be found in almost every land under the sun, they are not evenly spread. In Europe, America, and Australasia, two people out of three would call themselves Christians. In Africa it is less than one in ten. Elsewhere the average is little more than one person in a hundred. Yet this religion began not in Europe but in Asia. It just happened that its earliest great triumphs were in the lands around the Mediterranean, and later, particularly in western Europe. There Christianity radically affected the civilization which was developed.

Christianity is hard to describe because there are so many ideas as to what it is. 'A Christian' may mean a person who has a deep personal religious faith. Or it may mean someone connected with one branch of the CHRISTIAN CHURCH (q.v.). Or it may mean someone brought up to a way of life which was more or less affected by the Christian tradition. Then again in most lands 'Christian' is not a sufficient description; one must say of what kind. And the denominations are bewilderingly many. There are differences of belief, still more differences of organization, and even different standards of 'Christian' conduct. It will be best for us to see what lies behind it all, what it meant to begin with, adding a few remarks as to how it works out in terms of modern life.

ALLEGORICAL FIGURE OF THE CHURCH
Medieval figure, holding the Cross and Chalice, symbols of the Christian Faith. Her crown proclaims the triumph of the Church. 13th-century statue on the porch of Strasbourg Cathedral

'Christians' was not their first name. Followers of this religion used to call each other 'believers', 'disciples', 'saints': believers because they believed certain things about JESUS OF NAZARETH (q.v.), their founder; disciples because they added themselves to the small company which Jesus himself had called together; saints because they began to live a holy life according to the standard Jesus had set up. 'The disciples were called Christians first in Antioch' (Acts xi. 26), a name given them scornfully by the heathen.

Christianity took over from JUDAISM (q.v.) its scriptures (the Old Testament), and much of its teaching about God: that He is One, Creator of all that is; that His Purposes are to be fulfilled in and through His People, who have come into a special relationship with Him; that He is holy, to be satisfied only by those who do good. The Old Testament was reinterpreted by Christians according to what they had come to believe about Jesus.

The Jews had for hundreds of years believed themselves to be God's chosen people. They were always waiting for the Messiah, the Prophet, Priest and King, who was to bring God's message and deliver them from the hands of their oppressors—for they had been for a long time under the domination of overlords, the Babylonians, the Persians, the Greeks, and finally the Romans. And so the idea had grown up that this Messiah was to be a political leader, a King in the material sense. In A.D. 29 Jesus began his ministry by proclaiming 'The time is fulfilled. The Kingdom of God is at hand.' Later the Apostles assured their hearers that the King had come—even though most of His chosen people had not recognized Him.

The Messiah who came was different from the Messiah whom the Jews had expected. They looked for a prophet. The Apostles declared that Jesus was more than a prophet, hearing and declaring the word of God—that He was the Son of God, or as one Apostle described it, 'The Word became flesh and dwelt among us'. Through Jesus, God was revealed in a human life. This is called the doctrine of the Incarnation (*carnis* = flesh) and is the central teaching of Christianity.

Then Jesus did not save His people in the way the Jews expected. Instead of leading His people in triumph, He was rejected, He suffered, and He died on the cross. The Apostles explained this by reminding the Jews of the prophecies in the Old Testament of the Suffering Servant (Isaiah liii) which the Jews had not thought could refer to the Messiah. The Jews expected a priest. The Apostles declared that Jesus was not only Priest but also Sacrifice, given in atonement for the sins of mankind. In the sacrifice of Jesus is shown the love of God which seeks out and saves sinful man. This is the doctrine of Atonement (at-one-ment) and is the meaning of the simple ceremony of the Last Supper which Jesus told men to repeat in remembrance of His sacrifice and of man's salvation. The Apostles also declared that Jesus had risen from the dead and had returned to be with God, leaving his disciples to witness His resurrection to all the world.

The Jews expected a King. The Apostles declared that there was now a new meaning to the chosen people of God. The Kingdom belonged to all who believed. Entry to the Kingdom was not by being born a Jew but by being reborn by repentance and baptism. Therefore the message the Apostles had for the world was for the Gentile as much as for Jew—everyone had an equal right. It is not surprising that most Jews found this new conception of the Messiah and of their own place in God's Kingdom hard to accept.

Jesus summarized His teaching about life in this new society in various ways: in the two Great Commandments 'Thou shalt love the Lord thy God with all thy heart, soul, strength, and mind, and thy neighbour as thyself'; in the eight beatitudes (blessings) (Matt. v) which reverse so many worldly values; most strikingly in that command 'Be ye perfect as your Father in Heaven is perfect'. It all sounded an impossible standard. But the Apostles taught that the Christian life was not a matter of striving to keep a new and higher law, but of a new relationship with God and a new power because of that relationship. Jesus promised a sense of power, a spiritual presence to make up for the lack of His bodily presence. The Apostles claimed that this promise was fulfilled in the coming of the Holy Spirit, and that God's Spirit was in His Church.

Christianity, differently expressed in different ages and in different lands, will be found everywhere to have these ideas behind it. Different branches of Christianity may have stressed one or other of these tenets of belief more than the rest, but all Christians believe in one God,

Creator and Father; in Jesus Christ as God Incarnate (become man) who sacrificed Himself in atonement for man's sin, rose from the dead and returned to God; and in God's Holy Spirit who gives man a new quality of life. This is expressed in Christianity's classical summary, the Apostles' Creed.

The history of Christianity is a record of splendid achievement mixed with recurring unfaithfulness and failure. Western civilization has been built up in the main on Christian standards and way of life. Even those who belong to no part of the Christian Church are indebted to Christianity for their outlook upon life and for the attitude to moral questions which is revealed in the laws and customs of their country. But although Christianity has influenced Western civilization, a real 'Christian civilization' has never yet been seen. A civilization built up on the two Great Commandments and all that they imply would be something very different from anything humanity has yet achieved.

CHRISTIAN SCIENCE. This entirely modern interpretation of Christianity has nothing to do with any of the natural sciences. It was the peculiar work of an American woman, Mary Baker (Mrs. Eddy), who was born in 1821. Her father was a prosperous farmer, a strong and devout Calvinist, and she was his seventh child. She is said to have been very highly strung, if not hysterical, and of a studious disposition. At the age of seventeen she reacted strongly against her father's belief in predestination, and the tension between father and daughter reduced the girl to a state of nervous ill-health, which her mother relieved by telling her to lean upon the love of God. The effect of this crisis remained with her throughout her life. She continued for the time a Congregationalist, and at the age of twenty-two married a Mr. Glover, a building contractor, who owned negro slaves. She disliked slavery, and disagreed with her husband about it; but the marriage did not last long, for Mr. Glover died suddenly of yellow fever, shortly before his son was born. After a brief widowhood, spent in ill-health due to spinal trouble, Mrs. Glover married again, an unqualified medical practitioner called Patterson. He was taken prisoner during the American Civil War, during which time she became interested in spiritualism. She went into trances, saw visions, and practised thought-reading (though later she

MRS. EDDY

Copyright 1910. The Christian Science Publishing Society. Renewed 1938. Used by permission

broke completely with all this). All the time she was trying to cure her nervous ailments.

Finally, in 1862, she went to a man called Phineas Quimby, who claimed to effect faith-cures by sending people into hypnotic sleep and by massaging their heads. After her visit to him, Mrs. Patterson's special trouble disappeared. She explained what had happened by saying that it was due to an act of Divine healing, an explanation about which Quimby himself was not at all enthusiastic. In 1866 Mrs. Patterson found herself deserted by her second husband. She at once began to teach publicly what she maintained to have been the character of her cure; and she supported it further by claiming that she had been divinely healed of an injury caused by falling on some ice. A doctor who attended her on that occasion has recorded that he treated her for concussion with the usual remedies; but she said her cure was due to her special reading of Matt. ix. 2–8.

She continued for some ten years to develop her teaching. In 1877 she married a Mr. Eddy who, until his death in 1882, acted as her business manager, and controlled the sales of her publication, *Science and Health, with a Key to the*

Scriptures—a book, which was intended to be treated with as much reverence as the Bible itself. She herself lived until 1910, when she died of pneumonia at the advanced age of eighty-nine. She had certainly made a wonderful recovery from her earlier ailments, and seems to have secured the secret of a long and successful life. She ended her career at the head of a community which in America alone numbered 668 separate congregations. A year before her death she founded *The Christian Science Monitor*, which is one of the best-informed periodicals of the day. She was a capable business woman, and in later life an imperious personality, though often gentle and spiritually-minded.

She herself summed up her teaching in three lines:

God is all in all;
God is good, good is Mind:
God Spirit being all, nothing is matter.

She did not argue about this. She merely said it over and over again in different ways, and drew the conclusion from it that evil, which is the opposite of God, is unreal, and that therefore all pain and sickness and disease, being evil, are also unreal. It follows therefore that anyone who thinks himself to be ill is seeing things wrongly, and needs to be cured, not of his illness, but of his mistake. Once he sees things as they are—'in science', as Mrs. Eddy says—he will recover his health. Mrs. Eddy's use of the Bible is quite literal; and she had no first-hand knowledge of the natural sciences. The name of her movement seems to be somewhat misleading. It is beyond dispute that faith in God as Love and Righteousness can bring about the cure of nervous diseases, and even increase people's general vitality, so as to enable them to throw off other ailments. In so far as Mrs. Eddy encouraged such a belief, there is no difficulty in accounting for the real success of her movement in restoring many people to health of body and peace of mind. It is more difficult to be sure about the value and consistency of her teaching with regard to the world of matter and the unreality of evil. In any case her complete rejection of the whole of medical and surgical science, as not only worthless but positively harmful, must seem to many thoughtful people extremely rash and hard to justify. With the boldness of an amateur, she made up for herself a system of thought which accounted for her experiences, and so satisfied her; but of its

correctness she was not competent to judge. As so often happens in such cases, Mrs. Eddy believed she could find warrant for her actions in the Bible. She interpreted the woman in Revelation xii 'arrayed with the sun, with the moon under her feet, and crowned with twelve stars', as being a prophecy of herself, and the 'little book' (Rev. x. 2) as her text-book.

Many of the doctrines of Christian Science are very difficult for thinking people to accept. It is, however, worth remembering that a belief may be mistaken in some points and yet have reached the truth in others. For instance, the early Christians believed in the immediate 'Second Coming' of Christ on earth, and this in the literal sense has proved incorrect, so that later generations have believed differently. Mrs. Eddy sought to organize a Christian Church, which should reinstate primitive Christianity and its lost element of healing; and she repeatedly charged her disciples: 'Follow your leader only so far as she follows Christ.'

CHRISTIAN YEAR. Christianity, like all religions, keeps certain days in the year as holy-days and FESTIVALS (q.v.). Some of these are very old in the history of the Church, others have been added at later times. Some have not been observed by the Church of England since the time of the Reformation but are still kept by the Church of Rome.

The Jews, from very early times, kept the seventh day in the week as a sacred day—the Sabbath, the day of rest. The Early Church, however, kept sacred the first day in the week which they called 'The Lord's Day', because it was the day of Christ's Resurrection. It was an early custom to keep a day of fast as preparation before a feast, and the Early Church kept Friday, the day of Christ's Crucifixion, as a partial fast each week.

The Church Year begins, not on 1 January, but on Advent Sunday, four Sundays before Christmas. Advent (coming) is the period in the Christian Year when the Church prepares for the coming of the Lord at Christmas. Christmas, 25 December, the festival of the Nativity or birth of Christ, was not instituted until the 4th century A.D. In the East 6 January was the day kept to mark both the birth and baptism of Jesus. The keeping of 25 December as Christ's birthday arose in this way: the Spring Festival held on 25 March, the festival of Creation, when the year springs to life again, had been widely kept long before Christian times. The Christians took over the ancient festival and used it for celebrating the feast of the Annunciation, when the Angel announced to Mary that she should conceive God's Son. If Jesus were conceived on 25 March, he would be born nine months later, which is 25 December. 6 January, Epiphany (showing forth) is still kept, but in the West it is thought of as celebrating the visit of the Magi (Wise Men) and the showing forth of Jesus to the Gentiles (non-Jews).

The oldest and greatest festival in the Christian Year is Easter, the festival of the Resurrection. The word Easter comes from an Old English word *eastre*, the name of a dawn-goddess worshipped in the Spring. The festival corresponds to the Jewish Passover Feast and is kept on the first Sunday after the full moon on or after 21 March. It is the festival of the beginning of new life which is the reason for celebrating it with Easter eggs. Before Easter comes the period of fast called Lent (Old English, Spring), which has varied in length from three to eight weeks but is now fixed in the West at forty days. Lent begins with Ash Wednesday (ashes being a sign of penitence) and ends with Holy Week. Palm Sunday, the Sunday before Easter, is kept in remembrance of Jesus' triumphal entry into Jerusalem. Good Friday in Holy Week, the day of the Crucifixion, is the most important fast in the year, the only day when the Holy Communion is not celebrated.

The Jews held a harvest festival called Pentecost (Greek 'fifty days'), fifty days after Passover. This became from very early times the Christian Whit Sunday (White-Sunday because the newly-baptized wore white robes)—the festival to celebrate the coming of the Holy Ghost as described in Acts ii. Forty days after Easter is the Feast of Christ's Ascension, which has been kept everywhere since the 4th century. Trinity Sunday, one week after Whit Sunday, was not generally kept till the 14th century, and Corpus Christi (Body of Christ)—the festival in honour of the Holy Eucharist, held on the Thursday after Trinity Sunday—began in the West in 1264. These are the main feast days of the Christian Year.

The days when notable Christians suffered martyrdom were often kept in remembrance of them in early days, and some of these came to be recognized by the Church everywhere. In the 4th century days were allotted to each of the

PAGE FROM A MEDIEVAL CALENDAR

Books of Hours, which contained the forms for the various Church services, usually had a calendar giving all the Feasts and Saints' Days in the Christian Year. This page is for 1–15 July. Every day is a Saint's Day, the most important being written in red. Round the margin are scenes of the occupations of the month. Sobieski Book of Hours. French, 15th century. *By gracious permission of H.M. the King*

Apostles and other SAINTS (q.v.) so that almost every day in the Calendar commemorates some Christian figure. From about 610, 1 November has been kept as All Saints' Day; and from the year 998 the following day has been kept as a day of prayer for the souls of all the departed, All Souls' Day. Other special days are kept to commemorate important events in the life of Christ, such as the Feast of the Circumcision (1 January), or the Transfiguration (6 August). Some branches of the CHRISTIAN CHURCH (q.v.) pay more attention to these minor feast days, others less; but all branches of the Church celebrate the major festivals such as Easter, Christmas, and Whit Sunday.

CHURCH, CHRISTIAN, *see* CHRISTIAN CHURCH.

CHURCH OF ENGLAND

CHURCH OF ENGLAND. The earliest mention of CHRISTIANITY (q.v.) in this country is made by Tertullian about A.D. 200. He wrote about 'places of the Britons, unreached by the Romans, but subject to the law of Christ'. In 314 three bishops, a priest, and a deacon from Britain were present at a Church synod at Arles. In the 5th century the heathen Angles and Saxons invaded Britain and drove the Christian Britons into Wales and Cornwall. England, the land of the Angles, was a heathen country.

In 597 Pope Gregory I sent Saint Augustine and forty monks from Rome to Kent. In 635 a Celtic mission, led by Aidan, came from St. Columba's island of Iona to evangelize Northumbria. Between the two missions the nominal conversion of the whole country was soon secured. That was what Pope Gregory had hoped for. He had planned two archbishoprics, at London and at York, with twelve bishops under each. In fact it was nine centuries before England was divided into so many dioceses, and the southern see always remained at Canterbury, where Augustine first settled. The Roman missionaries, making the typically Roman contribution of organization, drew English Christianity into touch with the Continent and saved it from insularity. The Celtic missionaries contributed a spirit of independence and missionary zeal, both of which have remained features of the English Church. The first 100 years are marked by the rise of outstanding native leaders: CAEDMON (q.v. Vol. V), cowherd at Whitby Abbey, became one of the fathers of English poetry; Cuthbert was the Apostle of the Lowlands; Wilfrid in 664 became first English Bishop of York; BEDE (q.v. Vol. V) was father of English history and a scholar of European reputation; Willibrord went from Ripon as missionary to the Netherlands about 690; Boniface of Crediton joined him in 719 to become Apostle of Germany; Englishmen evangelized Scandinavia in the 11th century.

From the Synod of Whitby 664, which acknowledged the Roman connexion, to the REFORMATION (q.v.) and Henry VIII's break with Rome in 1534, the Church in England was a part of the Church of the West (see CHRISTIAN CHURCH). The Supremacy Act of 1534 declared the King to be 'the only supreme head in earth of the Church of England, called *Ecclesia Anglicana*'. This did not mean that the King claimed any spiritual powers, but that the Church came within the sphere of his rule and not under any outside authority such as the Pope in Rome. Under Elizabeth the term 'head' was changed to 'governor'. The Royal Supremacy, i.e. the State connexion, is not unlike the authority exercised by the Board of Governors of a school—oversight as to general well-being, leaving the actual running to those who, by calling and training, are capable of doing it.

In 1536–9 the monasteries were dissolved—the excuse being reform, the real reason greed for their wealth. In 1538 the English Church was told to use the English Bible (see BIBLE, TRANSLATION OF, Vol. IV). Under Edward VI in 1549 there was issued the first PRAYER BOOK (q.v.), in English instead of Latin, and with many minor alterations of the medieval services. In 1552 this was revised and made more definitely Protestant, and Forty-Two Articles (later revised to Thirty-Nine), statements as to Protestant belief, were made binding on the clergy. In Elizabeth's reign the third Prayer Book was

THE ROYAL COAT OF ARMS

All churches had to display the Royal Arms to show that the King was head of the Church. 17th-century Chancel Screen at Abbeydore, Herefordshire

National Buildings Record

ENTHRONEMENT OF THE ARCHBISHOP OF CANTERBURY
The ceremony at the Chancel steps, Canterbury Cathedral. *The Times*

issued, and permanent independence from Rome was secured.

The English Reformation was different in character from that on the Continent. It was an attempt to purify tradition rather than to change it radically. There was no break with medieval ways of worship, with the succession of bishops, nor with church order as a whole. The Church of England was designed to include a wide variety, 'low-churchmen' and 'high', and this its twofold nature has enabled it to do. It is at once Protestant in the sense of being truly reformed, and Catholic in the sense of holding an unbroken tradition. But its reforms were not thorough-going enough for many people; and consequently, during the 16th and 17th centuries came the break off of some sections (*see* CONGREGATIONALIST *and* BAPTIST).

In the 18th century a revival of religious zeal, led by JOHN WESLEY (q.v. Vol. V), resulted in the formation of the 'Methodist Societies', at first as a part of the Church of England, later as a separate denomination (*see* METHODIST). This movement influenced one section of the Church of England which became known as Evangelical. The marks of an Evangelical were to treat religion as a deeply personal matter, the experience of conversion opening a religious life which was strict, fervent, full of good works and directed towards bringing others to the same way. Prominent among the Evangelicals were William WILBERFORCE (q.v. Vol. V), who did so much to abolish the slave trade (1807), Robert Raikes (1735–1811), who was one of the pioneers of popular education about 1780, and Charles Simeon, a Cambridge vicar, the inspiration behind missionary work which prepared the way for the Church Missionary Society, founded in 1799.

In 1833 began a revival of a different kind, the Oxford Movement. This was a protest against the Church's dependence on the State, and a reassertion that the Church in England was a true part of the Catholic Church—hence came the name Anglo-Catholic. The leaders, nearly all Oxford men, of whom NEWMAN (q.v. Vol. V) is the best known, spread their ideas by writing tracts, so they were sometimes called

Tractarians. This movement too brought revived zeal. A few religious communities were begun; doing what the old monastic orders had done up to 1536. Holy Communion was brought in to greater prominence and frequency, and worship enriched. Enthusiasm in missionary work also began to revive, expressing itself mainly through the increased work of the Church of England's oldest missionary society, the S.P.G., the Society for the Propagation of the Gospel in Foreign Parts (1701).

Until 1784 there was no Anglican bishop overseas, and big overseas churches were attached to English dioceses. The Church in America, for instance, was under the care of the Bishop of London. American Independence made this obviously absurd, and Bishop Seabury was consecrated the first bishop for the Protestant Episcopal Church of America. This marked a notable change. The Church of England, at first purely a national Church, was to become, as the result of the world-wide missionary expansion in the following century and a half, not national but universal—as indeed the Church should always be. After the U.S.A. came Nova Scotia, a bishopric in 1787, then Quebec, 1793. In 1814 the first Anglican bishopric in Asia was founded at Calcutta. Now there is even an Anglican Bishop of the Arctic. The Anglican Church literally stretches across the world. Except where the work is in its early stages, or where population is too scattered to make it possible, these extensions of the Anglican Church have developed into separate Provinces, in full communion with Canterbury and York, but administered by their own Church courts and, increasingly, with native bishops and clergy. When nowadays bishops are summoned for consultation at Lambeth once in ten years, the 320 bishops include representatives of many colours and races.

See also CLERGY.

CINGALESE, see CEYLONESE.

CLERGY. 1. This is the name for those who are separated by ordination for the service (ministry) of the Church, in contrast to the laity, who are the Church's ordinary members. Practically every religion has its PRIESTS (q.v.). This article is concerned only with the clergy of the CHURCH OF ENGLAND (q.v.).

2. ARCHBISHOP. The Church of England is divided into two provinces—Canterbury and York. Canterbury was the first missionary centre in England, and so is always placed first. The Archbishop of Canterbury is (1) Bishop of the diocese of Canterbury (Kent); (2) Archbishop (chief bishop) or Metropolitan of the Southern Province of twenty-nine dioceses, presiding over its Convocation (i.e. 'calling-together' of these twenty-nine bishops and representative clergy); (3) Primate of all England. As Primate it is his duty to crown the King, to be his chief adviser in Church affairs, to preside over the Church Assembly (which, since 1920, has been the Parliament of the Church, with about 300 clergy and 300 laity from every diocese in England) and over other gatherings which represent the Church of the whole nation. The Archbishop of Canterbury is recognized as head of the Anglican Communion, which includes the Episcopal Church in the U.S.A., the Dominions, and many other overseas dioceses; and he presides over the Lambeth Conference of Bishops, which since 1867 has aimed at meeting about every ten years. In this widest of his responsibilities he is what other ancient Churches would call Patriarch.

The Archbishop of York is Bishop of York diocese, Archbishop of the Northern Province of fourteen dioceses, and vice-chairman of the Church Assembly.

3. BISHOP. As Father-in-God of his diocese, he has to secure the right clergy, ordain and institute them, and supervise their work (by visitation at least every three years). He also confirms those who, having been baptized, are ready to become full members of the Church. Bishops were once chosen by the clergy and people of the diocese, and this now happens in overseas dioceses where the Church has no State connexion. In the Middle Ages, when the Bishops became important and powerful, the King generally tried to have a hand in the appointment. Since the Reformation, Bishops in England have been appointed by the Crown, which means that the Prime Minister selects a candidate for

BISHOP IN VESTMENTS WITH HIS STAFF AND MITRE

THE CHAPTER HOUSE, SALISBURY CATHEDRAL
13th-century Chapter Houses were often octagonal. The Canons sat on the stone bench running round
the walls. *Herbert Felton*

the King, and the Dean and Chapter confirm the choice. Of the forty-three English bishops twenty-six have seats in the House of Lords. In big dioceses, where there is too much work for one bishop, a suffragan or assistant bishop is appointed.

4. DEAN AND CHAPTER. The Dean is responsible for the cathedral, chief church of a diocese, and for its services. In ancient cathedrals he, too, is appointed by the Crown. In newer ones the name of Provost is used, and the appointment is made by the Bishop. The Dean presides over the Cathedral Chapter, a meeting so called because in the Middle Ages they used to read a chapter of the Monastic Rule (*see* MONK). The Chapter consists of Canons (Greek for 'rule', because they used to live together like monks), who are the resident cathedral staff. Sometimes canons are given special responsibility for particular work in the diocese, such as religious education or missionary work. An Honorary Canon is non-resident and has no stipend from the cathedral. A few cathedrals have 'Prebendaries', who, though the word means stipend, are now in fact honorary only.

5. ARCHDEACON. Most dioceses are divided into two or more parts called archdeaconries. As the name implies, the Archdeacon was once a chief deacon, but now he is always in priest's orders. He has always been responsible for the business side of his part of the diocese, but now he informs, advises, and assists the Bishop in its spiritual care as well.

6. RURAL DEAN. The diocese also has smaller divisions, called rural deaneries, of perhaps as many as forty parishes. The Rural Dean is appointed by the Bishop to keep him informed concerning this group of parishes and to act for him there, for instance, in inducting new vicars.

7. PARISH PRIEST (Parson, Rector, Vicar). In feudal times the lord of the manor would provide a free-holding to support a priest for the people of his domain. The owners of land in the manor paid a tithe (tenth) to support the 'living' (i.e. the income which goes with a church appointment). Patronage is a relic of feudal society. The patron of the living is the person (or in some cases a body such as a monastery) who has the right to choose a priest for appointment by the Bishop. Livings varied and still vary considerably in the income they produce. The priest who has spiritual charge of the parish and the worship of its church, is called a Rector (ruler) or Vicar (representative)—a term used if the priest represented, for instance, a monastery to which the living belonged. If the parish is large, the Rector or Vicar has an assistant, called a Curate. In the PRAYER BOOK (q.v.), curate, like the French *curé*, means 'one who has a spiritual charge', i.e. the Rector or Vicar himself. Later it came to mean a substitute, and now it means an assistant.

8. DEACON. Of the three orders of clergy—bishop, priest, deacon—this is the lowest. The deacon was an assistant to the priest with especial care for visiting the sick and needy. Now a deacon is generally on the way to becoming a priest. The Deaconess represents the only ordained ministry of women. There were women recognized in the service of the Church in Apostolic times. The Deaconess Order of the Church of England was founded in 1923.

COLOMBIA, PEOPLES OF. This country in the north of South America is the only country

PRIEST IN CHASUBLE

to be named after the discoverer of America, COLUMBUS (q.v. Vol. V), although he himself never reached it. Under Spanish rule Colombia formed part of the viceroyalty of New Granada, together with Venezuela and Ecuador. It was a vitally important part of the Spanish Empire, since it controlled the line of communication between the Atlantic and the Pacific across the isthmus of Panama. At the beginning of the 19th century Colombia, like Venezuela, was liberated from Spanish rule by SIMON BOLIVAR (q.v. Vol. V); and for some years after independence was won, there was a republic of Great Colombia, including Colombia, Venezuela, and Ecuador, which afterwards split up into separate nations. Through most of the 19th century Colombia was in a state of civil war; and at last in 1903 the province of Panama revolted and declared its independence with the help of the United States. Since that time the country has had a period of peaceful progress. It has proved itself one of the more truly democratic of the Latin American states, and has not suffered from dictators.

The majority of the people are of mixed

COLOMBIAN WOMAN WEAVING. *Dorien Leigh*

European and Indian blood, but there are a great many whites of Spanish descent, and smaller numbers of pure Indians and negroes. Most of the people live by farming and cattle herding, and the main crop is coffee. Life is still very primitive in the more remote places, where such modern luxuries as sanitation or good schools are unknown. Spanish, which is spoken in a very pure form, is the language of the country, but some of the Indians in the Andean highlands still only speak their own native dialect. Bogota, the capital city, was one of the intellectual centres of the Spanish Empire, and is often called the Athens of South America, because of its interest in literature and art, and the scholars, scientists, and poets it has produced. With its beautiful cathedral and its fine Spanish buildings and paintings it preserves the atmosphere of a city in Spain.

See also AMERICAN INDIANS, CENTRAL AND SOUTH.
See also Vol. III: COLOMBIA.

CONFUCIANISM, *see* CHINESE RELIGION.

CONGREGATIONALIST. A member of one of the Nonconformist group of churches. Sunday worship in a Congregational Church is usually non-liturgical, that is, without a set form, with the sermon as a main item. The Lord's Supper is celebrated monthly as an after-meeting, and with little set form apart from repeating the words which Jesus used. The local church members form the 'congregation', and it is the congregation which chooses and invites the minister (pastor), appoints lay officials (deacons), and then, under their leadership, governs the life of the church. As the name implies, this denomination believes that the true Church is to be found there in the local congregation, not in any great national institution, and that each local unit should be self-governing. Congregationalists, because of this, have had a great part in the growth of democracy both here and in the United States of America.

They began in this way. When Queen Mary came to the throne in 1553, the English Reformation seemed doomed. Small groups of Protestants, kept together by their own simple leaders, continued their worship in secret, in warehouses, shops, woods, on a ship in the Thames. Queen Elizabeth (1558) broke with Rome again; but many more thorough-going Protestants felt this to be but a half-hearted Reformation. Some such, the Puritans, were content to urge the

Government to go further in reforming the Church, and to wait, though somewhat impatiently, until this was done. Others were more extreme. They urged 'Reformation without tarrying for any'. They opposed the idea of a national Church—at a time when too many people just took the Church for granted as the religious side of national life. 'The Kingdom of God is not to be begun by whole parishes, but rather of the worthiest, be they never so few.' Sometimes this idea is spoken of as 'the *gathered* Church'. These people were given various names: Brownists, after a certain Robert Browne who was a leader from 1571 to 1591; Separatists, because they were not content to wait inside, but felt that they had to come out of the national Church; Independents, because of their principle of local self-government. They were persecuted as Nonconformists, i.e. people who would not accept the one-style religion which the State laid down. A few were hanged on a charge of libel—according to the barbarous law of those days. Many more were imprisoned. Some fled to the Continent.

Among these last was a congregation from Scrooby in Lincolnshire, under their minister John Robinson. They settled at Leyden in Holland in 1609. Later they petitioned King James I and received permission to found the New England of their dreams in his dominions in America. One hundred and two of them— the Pilgrim Fathers—set sail for America in the *Mayflower* in 1620.

A little later in England Congregationalists, essentially democratic, were to be found on the side of the Parliament in the Civil War. CROMWELL (q.v. Vol. V) was a Congregationalist.

After this brief triumph the reaction in the Restoration of Charles II in 1660 is perhaps not to be wondered at. Many who had hitherto been Puritans (i.e. content to wait within the Church of England hoping for a further measure of reform) were now driven into separation. Congregationalists were subject to all manner of restrictions under the Clarendon Code, three laws which aimed at the abolition of Nonconformity. In 1689, however, the Toleration Act brought the beginning of better times.

The attempt to force everybody in England to religion of one pattern, in one inclusive national Church, broke down. Whether this is to our gain or loss, there may be differences of opinion. There is little room to doubt two good things which Congregationalists had done. In politics, under Cromwell they helped to secure once and for all our English liberties. In religion, they opposed the idea (and it was a wrong one) that the Church was only the nation in its Sunday clothes. The Church to them was something higher, holier, and more select than that.

In 1795 the London Missionary Society was founded, and this Society, while inter-denominational, is, as a matter of fact, mainly Congregationalist in its support. Famous pioneer missionaries who worked under this Society have been, Robert Morrison in China (1782–1834), John Williams in the South Seas (1796–1839), David Livingstone in Africa (1813–73), and to-day there are 250 of its missionaries in China, India, Africa, Madagascar, and the South Seas. In 1831 the Congregational Union of England and Wales was formed, a loose federation of Congregational Churches, which elects its Chairman annually.

In the United States of America the position of Congregationalists is unique because, though not in numbers one of the larger American denominations, they are the Church to whom the original Pilgrim Fathers belonged. Congregationalism has influenced the American Constitution: for instance, over clauses against religious tests and against an established Church. The national festival called Thanksgiving, which was the Pilgrim Fathers' gratitude to God for the first harvest, is one of the greatest festivals in American national life.

Being a reaction against uniformity, Congregationalism has always tended to greater freedom with regard to creed, traditions of worship, and even sometimes the observance of the SACRAMENTS (q.v.), than most other bodies.

Congregationalists throughout the world number some two and a half million communicant members in 26,000 churches.

See also CHRISTIAN CHURCH; REFORMATION.

COPTIC CHURCH. The word Copt means Egyptian. Its origin from the Greek may be represented in English by shortening 'Egyptian' to 'Gypt' and then softening it to 'Copt'.

The word is used to denote Christians in Egypt. Their tradition is that St. Mark, who wrote the Gospel, was their first missionary. By A.D. 200 Christianity was strong, especially in Alexandria, which became a great centre of (Greek) Christian learning. A century later it

had spread to the Egyptian population. The Church became separated from the main body of Christians in the Eastern Roman Empire, about 451, largely because of the spirit of local independence. They suffered much after the Arab invasion (about 640), when ISLAM (q.v.) became the official religion. Soon the majority of the population became Moslems. To-day the Church numbers 880,000 members under its Patriarch, the (Coptic) Bishop of Alexandria. Its people speak Arabic, though the liturgy contains some Coptic, i.e. ancient Egyptian. In the 4th century Christianity spread to Abyssinia, entering from the Red Sea coast. There the King was converted, and Christianity remains to this day the official religion. The Abyssinian Church counts itself the daughter of the Coptic. Its liturgy is in its own ancient language, called Amharic (see ABYSSINIANS).

See also CHRISTIAN CHURCH.

CORSICANS, see Vol. III: CORSICA.

COSSACKS. A Turkish people who settled on the banks of the rivers Don and Dnieper, north and east of the Black Sea. They were a very warlike and independent people, determined to resist the domination of either the RUSSIANS (q.v.) or the Mongols (see TARTARS). They were magnificent horsemen, as have been most of the peoples living in the southern steppes of Russia. They lived across the early trade-routes from the eastern Mediterranean countries to the Far East, and often attacked and robbed the caravan parties.

The Cossacks were lovers of freedom, and they organized a remarkably democratic society in times when their neighbours were living under the absolute rule of autocratic princes. Until the 17th century they allowed no class distinctions. All the land belonged to the 'Host' of the community, and was only lent to individual Cossacks. The community was governed by a popular council called the Circle which had absolute power over the lives and possessions of the population. Its methods were crude, and offenders were punished by being drowned in the river. The leader, the Ataman, was elected by the whole community, and had absolute power only in time of war.

By the 17th century the Cossacks had come under the authority of the Russian Czars or the Poles. The Poles formed a Cossack contingent of light infantry, which later became a very important part of the Russian Army. They revolted against the Russians in the time of Catherine the Great, but were severely crushed.

A COSSACK OF THE CAUCASUS
The fur hat and long coat are typical of the Cossack costume. *S.C.R.*

It is strange that these early lovers of democracy should have become, in later Russian history, a very reactionary influence.

The Cossacks, their way of life, their grand horsemanship, and fame as soldiers, have been the subject of much Russian literature. Tolstoy's famous story, *The Cossacks*, gives a vivid description of their way of life in 1852. Pushkin in his story, *The Captain's Daughter*, describes their rebellion against Catherine the Great.

See also RUSSIANS.

CREATION MYTHS, *see* BABYLONIAN MYTHS; HEBREW MYTHS.

CREOLE, descendents of European or Negro settlers in the West Indies (*see* WEST INDIES).

CRETANS, *see* MINOAN CIVILIZATION.

CROATS, *see* YUGOSLAVS.

CRUSADES. In 1095 Alexius, Emperor of the BYZANTINE EMPIRE (q.v.), appealed to western Europe for help to defend the Eastern Christian Empire against the invasions of the Moslem Turks, and especially to win back Jerusalem and the Holy Places which had been taken by the Turks in 1076. Stories had been coming to Europe of the ill-treatment at the hands of the infidel Turks of pilgrims to the birthplace and sepulchre of our Lord, and Europe was ready to respond to the Emperor's appeal.

The idea of a Holy War had been in people's minds long before 1095. The great Arab expansion in the 7th and 8th centuries had resulted in war to defend Christianity from ISLAM (q.v.). There had been expeditions against the infidel saracens. Pope Gregory VII had for some time been planning a crusade to secure the safety of those who wished to perform that very popular act of Christian devotion—a PILGRIMAGE (q.v.). Europe was just emerging from the confusion and weakness of the DARK AGES (q.v.) and was ready to meet this challenge from the East. Gregory's successor, Pope Urban II, saw an opportunity of bringing the Orthodox Eastern Church with its centre at Constantinople to recognize the supremacy of the Roman Pope, and in response to Alexius's appeal, preached the First Crusade. Returning pilgrims, especially PETER THE HERMIT (q.v. Vol. V), preached the Holy War far and wide, and recruits flocked to take the Crusaders' vow, and receive the badge of the Cross.

To rescue the Holy Land from the infidel appealed to the imaginations of devoted and pious Christians. People readily believed that to 'take the cross' and go upon a holy war made them certain of absolution from sin and salvation after death. To those who loved fighting and adventure the Crusades gave a grand opportunity of indulging in the joys and excitement of warfare under cover of a religious duty. Many saw also the chance of getting for themselves not only adventure but riches and land. So from this variety of motives, pious and self-seeking, men sold their possessions and lands to get enough money to equip themselves and their followers, and set forth for Constantinople—a gathering of individual adventurers, rather than the well-organized and disciplined army the Emperor Alexius had hoped for.

The first army to set forth consisted mostly of peasants roused by the zeal of Peter the Hermit. Three successive hordes rushed off from France and Germany by the land route through Hungary and Bulgaria. Only a small fraction ever reached Constantinople. Those that were not killed by the indignant Hungarians and Bulgarians were wiped out in the first battle with the Turks. In 1096, however, a rather more efficient force under various knights and barons,

A KNIGHT OF THE TIME OF THE CRUSADERS
Early 13th-century figure on the West Front of Wells
Cathedral. *Philips, Wells, Som.*

including the great Crusader, Godfrey of Bouillon, made their way by different routes to Constantinople, and from there—an army some 300,000 strong—they started their attack on the Holy Land. Many stories and legends of this First Crusade found their way back to Europe —of the army of saints in white armour on white steeds which came to the assistance of the sore beset crusading armies; of the discovery of the Holy Lance; and of the appearance of St. George himself on Mt. Olivet, waving his shield to stimulate the Crusaders to victory.

The First Crusade did achieve something, though not all that the Byzantine Emperor had hoped. The course of the war was stained by fearful carnage both of Turks and Jews, and by pillaging and treachery horrifying to our modern idea of how an army, fighting under a Christian banner, should conduct itself. But they conquered Jerusalem and drove the Turks out of Palestine. A Kingdom of Jerusalem was set up with Godfrey of Bouillon as King; and others of the leaders seized lands in Palestine for themselves.

The Second Crusade, preached by St. Bernard (q.v. Vol. V), was a complete catastrophe. Then the Moslem world, led by their great Sultan, Saladin, united in a counter religious war in the name of Mohammed, and in 1187 drove the Christians from Jerusalem. This gave rise to the Third Crusade, led by the three great kings of Europe, the German Emperor Frederick Barbarossa, Philip Augustus of France, and Richard Coeur de Lion of England. The Emperor, however, was drowned, and the French and English Kings quarrelled so bitterly that they achieved very little. It was on this occasion that King Richard on his way home was captured and imprisoned in a German castle. The story of how he was discovered by his faithful minstrel, Blondel, is well known.

The Fourth Crusade was planned by Pope Innocent III, and the Crusaders gathered at Venice in 1201. But instead of continuing the war against the Turks, the Crusaders turned against the Byzantine Empire, drove out the Emperor and sacked Constantinople. For fifty years they held Constantinople, choosing an Emperor from among themselves. In 1212 there followed, after this act of treachery of Christian against Christian, the tragic story of the Children's Crusade. The idea arose that the Holy Land could only be freed by the hands of the

THE CASTLE OF MARĜAB, SYRIA
One of the castles built by the Crusaders. *E. K. Waterhouse*

innocent. About 30,000 children from France, led by a shepherd boy, Stephen, and 20,000 German boys and girls led by Nicholas, set forth to rescue our Lord's sepulchre. They disappeared: they perished in sea or land or were kidnapped by slave-dealers, and nothing remained of them except the German legend of the Pied Piper, which has its origin in this tragic event.

Further crusades followed, among them those led by the saintly French King, Louis IX; but none of them achieved anything, and by the end of the 13th century the crusading spirit was dying out in Europe.

Although by the end of the 13th century nothing except the island of Cyprus remained of the conquests of the Crusaders, in less tangible ways the Crusades had an important effect upon the growth of European civilization during the Middle Ages. They stemmed the tide of Moslem invasion, which in the 11th century was a grave threat to Europe and Christendom, and thereby allowed medieval culture to develop in comparative peace. This was also helped by the fact that the knights and barons were able to indulge their love of fighting at the expense of the infidel and not as before amongst themselves. Trade with the East had been growing before the Crusades; but the Crusades opened up the Middle East and allowed a greatly increased traffic. Along with the spices, silks, and metalwork which the Italian traders brought to Europe from the East came books and ideas, especially in the realms of science and mathematics. Knowledge of geography increased as the Crusaders, followed by Christian missionaries and traders, penetrated farther into Asia. The Crusaders also learnt much about fortifications and methods of warfare from their enemies, and a new style of castle was developed. The Welsh castles, such as Harlech and Caernarvon, built in the time of Edward I, are of this new type.

See also KNIGHTS, ORDERS OF.

CRYSTAL GAZING, *see* DIVINATION.

CUBA, PEOPLES OF, *see* WEST INDIANS.

CUPID, *see* GODS OF GREECE AND ROME (EROS).

OUTSIDE THE MARKET IN PEDOULAS, CYPRUS. *Vincent Brennan*

CYCLOPES, *see* MYTHOLOGICAL MONSTERS, Section (*a.*)

CYPRIOTS. The people of the island of Cyprus, at the eastern end of the Mediterranean, can claim the longest continuous political and artistic history of any part of the British Colonial Empire. Traces of their civilization are to be found as early as the 15th century B.C. The Old Testament name Kittium applied both to Cyprus and to the town Kition (Citium), the modern Larnaca, which was a centre of Phoenician civilization as well as the birth-place of the Greek philosopher, Zeno, founder of the Stoic School of philosophy. The island was already artistically prominent in the early Bronze Age and its mythology goes back into some of the earliest beliefs of the human race.

Its position in the centre of eastern Mediterranean civilization caused Cyprus to be the meeting-place and often the battlefield of races, languages, faiths, and civilizations at the very dawn of history. As mythology merged into history, there flourished in Cyprus side by side the cultures, arts, and languages of the three great civilizations of the GREEKS, the PHOENICIANS, and the EGYPTIANS (qq.v.). For centuries the great Temple of Aphrodite in Paphos in the south-west part of the island was the most celebrated shrine of that goddess in the ancient world.

In A.D. 45 St. Paul and St. Barnabas brought Christianity to Cyprus and converted the Roman ruler, Sergius Paulus, so that the island became the first country in the world to be governed by a Christian ruler. When the Roman Empire split, Cyprus belonged to the eastern half, the BYZANTINE EMPIRE (q.v.). For a few years from 1184 the island was independent, and then it was occupied for one year by Richard I of England on his way to take part in the Third Crusade. Then for some 300 years Cyprus was ruled by the kings and queens of the brilliant French dynasty of Lusignan. At this time—perhaps the greatest in the island's history—the port of Famagusta was the busiest in art in the eastern Mediterranean, and vied with Venice in the wealth and luxury of its merchant princes.

In 1489 the Venetian Republic took control of the island in order to fortify it against the advance of the Ottoman TURKS (q.v.). In 1571, however, the Turks captured Cyprus and held it till 1878. During the short period of Venetian rule there held office a certain Christoforo Moro, who was the original of Shakespeare's 'Moor of Venice'. The 'Seaport in Cyprus'—the scene of *Othello*—is the Cyprus port of Famagusta.

During the period of Ottoman rule the history of Cyprus was uneventful. In 1878, however, Britain and Turkey agreed that Britain should occupy Cyprus in order that she might assist Turkey in defending herself against Russia. After the First World War, in which Turkey was on the losing side, Cyprus became a British Crown Colony.

The Cypriot people—except for small groups of Maronites in the north-west and Armenians in the capital, Nicosia—fall into two main divisions: four-fifths are Greek-speaking members of the ORTHODOX EASTERN CHURCH (q.v.), while the remaining one-fifth are Turkish-speaking followers of ISLAM (q.v.) who came over with the Turkish conquerors in the 16th century. The official languages are English, Turkish, and Greek. The Greek and Turkish communities have their own separate schools and a separate social existence. For the most part the people are occupied in cultivating the fertile valleys— the hills are barren and unfertile—and in fishing, which includes fishing for sponges.

See also Vol. III: CYPRUS.

CZECHOSLOVAKS.

The Czechs and the Slovaks are a Slav people belonging to the same language group as the Russians and Poles (*see* RUSSIAN LANGUAGES: Vol. IV). They inhabit a new country, Czechoslovakia, which was formed after the First World War in 1918; but they are a people with a very old and romantic history.

The kingdom of Bohemia, which now forms a part of modern Czechoslovakia, was an important country of the Middle Ages. Prague, the chief city of Bohemia and capital of Czechoslovakia, has the oldest University of central Europe, 600 years old. One of our own English queens, Anne, the wife of Richard II, came from Bohemia. The country is rich with fairy tales and traditional stories, one of which, the story of good King Wenceslas, is known to everybody. This famous Christian King, who ruled Bohemia in the 9th century and was beloved by his people for his good and just rule, was murdered as he was coming out of church by his pagan brother

who was jealous of him. His tomb is still a place of pilgrimage for the Czechoslovak people.

The Czechs and Slovaks first came to Bohemia

100 CROWN NOTE (WORTH ABOUT TEN SHILLINGS, 1947)
It bears a portrait of the famous President Masaryk

and the surrounding country in the 6th century, during the course of a general migration of Slav people from the East. About 300 years later, Christianity was brought to them by St. Cyril and other missionaries from Thessalonica. St. Cyril also invented for the Slav people an alphabet which is still called Cyrillic after him, and which was used in Bohemia until they adopted the Latin alphabet. The Cyrillic alphabet is still used in Serbia, Bulgaria, and Russia. In the 15th century the religious teaching of John Wycliffe spread to Bohemia, and was taken up by the great Czech scholar, John Huss. The followers of Huss, called Hussites or MORAVIANS (q.v.), were bitterly opposed by the Roman Catholics; the people were divided among themselves, and the country was weakened and unable to defend itself against greedy and powerful neighbours. In the 17th century Bohemia was absorbed into the Austro-Hungarian Empire, under whose rule it remained until after the First World War. The Hussites suffered terrible persecution, and in the 17th century 30,000 of them were driven from their country and wandered homeless across Europe. They lived so much like GYPSIES (q.v.), that they were often confused with them, especially in France, where the gypsies were called Bohemians. In England the word 'Bohemian' came to be used to describe people of an artistic temperament and an unsettled and unconventional way of living.

During the time of their subjection to Austria, the Czechs never lost their sense of nationality or their longing for independence; and their national leaders did all they could to foster unity and patriotism. Political organizations were not allowed, but their rulers could hardly object to

PEASANTS OF EASTERN CZECHOSLOVAKIA.   *Fox Photos*

was built up, and great progress was made towards unity and prosperity.

Unfortunately, a discontented minority of German origin, living in a part of Czechoslovakia, gave the German dictator, Hitler, an excuse for attacking. Masaryk's successor, Dr. Benes, led his people to resist the Germans in the Second World War as stoutly as they had resisted the Austrians before. The Mafia societies were revived, and the Government, no longer able to stay in Prague, continued the fight from London till the Germans were defeated and their country once more free.

The Czechoslovaks are an industrious people and, in the period between the two great wars, were greatly developing the natural riches of their country. About half the people are engaged in some form of agriculture, but the rest take part in the ever-increasing industries of the country. Before the Second World War the English shops were becoming full of cheap, but usually well-designed, Czechoslovakian goods. The glass in particular showed how attractive cheap glass could be made. The boots and shoes of the famous Bata brothers are as well known in England and America as in their own country. The Bren gun was a Czech invention, which probably took its name from the town Brno or Brunn. The Skoda armament works were among the largest in central Europe.

Much of the country is mountainous, and covered with great forests which are broken by fertile valleys and clearings. In the more remote districts in the south-east, the forests are still the haunts of fierce wild animals. Bears (like the one that killed Antigonus in Shakespeare's *Winter's Tale*) are still a danger to the lonely shepherd, and packs of wolves and wild boars, driven by hunger in the long cold winters, will make ravages on the flocks and even come to the outskirts of the villages. In the plains of Slovakia, bordering the river Danube, huge flocks of geese are to be seen, often in charge of a small boy. Roast goose is the usual dish for any festive occasion. It is picturesque to watch the village people coming out of church on a Sunday morning, dressed in their national costumes with their elaborate head-dresses.

See also Vol. III: CZECHOSLOVAKIA.

societies formed for physical culture. These societies, called Sokols, were a means of banding the young people together and giving them a sense of unity and purpose. The word *Sokol* means falcon, and the members endeavoured to become as swift and strong and fearless as falcons. The Sokols continued to develop after the Czechs gained their independence: great festivals were held at Prague, where as many as 10,000 young men and women would give their gymnastic displays to enormous audiences.

When the First World War broke out in 1914, the Czechs and Slovaks saw their chance. They had the great good fortune to possess a leader of outstanding wisdom and courage in THOMAS MASARYK (q.v. Vol. V). Through a secret society called the Mafia, they gave help to the Allies against the Austrians and Germans, and in return were given their independence at the treaty of Versailles. Under the leadership of the wise Masaryk, a strong democratic republic

D

DALMATIANS, *see* YUGOSLAVS.

DANES. These are a Scandinavian people, as are their neighbours the SWEDES (q.v.) and NORWEGIANS (q.v.). The ancestors of all three were the Norsemen or Vikings, a great seafaring people who, during the 9th and 10th centuries, sent pirate expeditions to attack their European neighbours. Though the English king Alfred the Great defeated the Danes on land and sea, England was, for a short period—under the Danish King Canute—part of a kingdom that included Denmark and Norway.

The history of Denmark is closely interlocked with the histories of Sweden and Norway. Sometimes they were friends, sometimes enemies. For a time, in the 14th century, all three were united under a Danish queen, Margaret. For many years now they have been at peace with each other, the friendship of the people being strengthened by the fact that the very popular Royal Families of the three countries are closely related.

The King governs through the two Houses of Parliament. He and members of his family live very simply, walking about the streets unattended and mixing with crowds at entertainments. Denmark's position among nations was much strengthened by the great marriages made by Danish princesses at the end of the last century—Princess Alexandra of Denmark became Queen of England and Princess Dagmar (Marie) Empress of Russia, while their brother George was elected King of Greece. The Royal Family gatherings held at Copenhagen before the First World War were important political events.

The life of well-to-do Danes is very much like that of well-to-do English people. They spend the summer in their country houses, some of which have been in the same family for generations. In winter they go to Copenhagen. As in most European countries there are now fewer rich people, and most of the old town 'palaces' have been converted into flats with the descendants of the original owner living on one floor.

The Danish State religion has been a form of Lutheranism since the early 16th century. There is free education in the primary schools, and there are several public schools on British lines. They have had a system of adult education— the People's High Schools—for a hundred years, and there are universities in Copenhagen and Aarhus. People working on the land often come into the towns for further education in the winter, when work on the farms is slack.

The Danes are a tall, broad-chested, fair, blue-eyed people, fond of music, gymnastics, and outdoor games and sports. On a holiday most of the young people are to be seen making their way from the town to the country on bicycling or hiking expeditions. As is natural in the sons of the Vikings, they are fine seamen. The Danish merchant navy is small, but it can be met all over the world. Their long coastline makes fishing an important industry.

THE FISHMARKET AT COPENHAGEN
Fox Photos

TETHERED COWS GRAZING ON A DANISH FARM. *E.N.A.*

The Danes are a nation of farmers, a third of the population being engaged in dairy and pig farming and fruit and vegetable growing. Most of the farms are small holdings, but a system of co-operative production and marketing enables the small farmer to get the advantage of large-scale business. Co-operative creameries, meat-packing plants, butter and cheese factories are run by experts for the benefit of producer and consumer. The co-operatives insure a high quality of goods and a good price in foreign markets.

Their long tradition of independent nationhood has given the Danes a strong and deep sense of national unity. This showed itself very much during the German occupation in the Second World War, when, though powerless to fight, they put up a most effective passive resistance. They are excellent linguists, German and English being the languages most commonly spoken. They are good mixers. The foreigner quickly feels at home in Denmark, and the Dane as quickly feels at home in other countries. Danish immigrants to the United States and Canada are a valuable part of the population.

See also Vol. III: DENMARK; Vol. IV: SCANDINAVIAN LANGUAGES.

DARK AGES. The period in European history, from the decline and fall of the great Roman Empire in the 5th and 6th centuries to the beginnings of the medieval revival in the 11th and 12th centuries, is called 'dark', partly because comparatively little is known about it, and partly because it was a time when civilization in Europe was at a low ebb—very dark compared with the brilliant civilizations of GREECE and ROME (qq.v.) which had gone before, and the great period of the RENAISSANCE (q.v.) which was to follow.

During the 4th and 5th centuries invading hordes of HUNS, GOTHS, and VANDALS (qq.v.) swept across Europe, spreading destruction as they went. They established kingdoms in Europe and were constantly at war with each other and with the Roman Empire, whose power they finally broke. During this period the kings were rarely strong enough to enforce law and order, and the local lords, from the great barons down to every petty knight, had their strongholds from which they attacked their neighbours and laid waste their lands.

During the end of the 8th and beginning of the 9th centuries CHARLEMAGNE (q.v. Vol. V) extended the kingdom of the Franks into a great empire, and in A.D. 800 he was crowned Holy Roman Emperor. He conceived of the HOLY ROMAN EMPIRE (q.v.) as a great civilizing influence in Europe; but, unfortunately, when he died there was no great leader to take his place, and Europe fell back again into anarchy.

The CHRISTIAN CHURCH (q.v.) preserved a little of Roman civilization and learning, and the records of churchmen provide us with almost all the knowledge we have of these centuries. The monks wrote chronicles for their monasteries, and some of these have survived. But the Church also was unenlightened in many of its actions, and often its bishops and abbots were worldly men, more concerned with preserving their power in an insecure world than in fostering truth and progress. The influence of Greek civilization, preserved and fostered in the BYZANTINE EMPIRE (q.v.), spread very little into the West during these centuries because of the difficulty of communication, especially after Arab ships got control of the Mediterranean. The civilization of the ARABS (q.v.) was resisted in the West because it was accompanied by the Moslem religion (*see* ISLAM), and Europe had little knowledge of the arts and sciences of the Moslem world except in so far as they spread along North Africa into Spain with the MOORS (q.v.).

DEATH CEREMONIES. Among many primitive peoples, death is believed to be unnatural and to have come into the world because men displeased a supernatural being or disobeyed his command. The Bataks of the Philippine Islands say that their god punished them by sending death because they once deceived him with a shark wrapped up to look like a corpse; and some Australian natives believe that death came when a woman attacked a forbidden tree with a stone axe and disturbed the bat which lived in it. The book of Genesis tells how mankind became subject to death because Adam and Eve ate the fruit of a forbidden tree.

Most people believe in some kind of life after death. This belief was held by Stone Age men (*see* RELIGION, PREHISTORIC), by the peoples of most ancient civilizations, by the greatest Greek philosophers (*see* PLATO; ARISTOTLE; Vol. V), and gives additional meaning and purpose to life for most people to-day. Ideas differ widely as to what the spirits of the dead are like, but frequently they are thought of as shadowy ghosts. A common idea is that they are born again as other people, animals, or even as stars.

The part of the person which is believed to leave the body at death is imagined in various ways. Some North American Indians think it is a little manikin living in the person's head. There are widespread beliefs that the 'soul' is the breath or the person's shadow and that at death it flies away from the body in the shape of a bird. People open windows after someone has died to let the soul out. The Egyptians combined several of these ideas, believing that a dead man had a spark of intelligence which went back to the gods, a bird-like soul which fluttered round the tomb, a shadow, and a 'double' which rejoined the mummy after 3,000 years when the whole man rose from the dead.

Primitive peoples often take precautions when the corpse is brought out of the house to prevent the spirit's return. All over the world they avoid using the door of the house, hut, or tent. In Holland special 'corpse doors' were even made. Some Siberian tribespeople carry the body out through a corner of the tent; and Pacific Islanders (Melanesians) break down the side of the hut although the door is wide enough. Usually the body is carried out feet foremost, so that the dead man may not see the way, and his ghost be thus prevented from returning; and sometimes the corpse is turned round to confuse the spirit. In parts of Ireland the funeral goes to the cemetery by the longest way; in the Solomon Islands the mourners return by a different route from that by which they went; and in Siberia the order of the returning procession is reversed. To prevent the dead haunting them people bury the body face downwards, stroke the grave with a branch (Melanesia), break the bones (Australia), or tie a clog to it (Ancient India). On one occasion, when a man was murdered in the island of Arran, the police buried his boots below high-water mark to prevent his 'walking'. Sometimes seeds or imitation money are strewn on the road or near the grave, as it is thought that wandering spirits will be delayed counting them. Funerals are sometimes held at night, as it is believed that then the spirits will find it more difficult to capture souls.

It has been very widely believed that the dead have need in the other world of the food, implements, servants, &c., that they have used in this world, and that these things must be provided

MODEL OF A BOAT FOUND IN AN EGYPTIAN TOMB
The sailors are hoisting the sail and a mummy lies beneath the canopy in the stern. 12th Dynasty (*c.* 2000 B.C.).
Ashmolean Mus.

for them at their burial. As long ago as the Old Stone Age, flint implements and marrow bones were buried with the dead; and still, in many parts of the world, provision is made at the time of the burial or afterwards for the needs of the departed person's spirit. Our knowledge of how the ancient Egyptians lived is largely due to the fact that they placed in the tombs of their kings and other important people for their use after death the things they used in everyday life. The ancient practice in Babylonia, Egypt, and China of sacrificing people to minister to the mighty dead in the Otherworld gave place to the custom of burying models instead. In fact, the idea that models would do instead of real things spread

A FUNERAL PROCESSION IN PEKING
The mourners wear gowns of white, the Chinese mourning colour, and carry
embroidered umbrellas. *E. A. Armstrong*

the Ancestral Spirits they carry roast pigs to the tombs of their forefathers as a token offering; then they carry them home and feast on them! In north China, on a certain day in autumn, rolls of paper representing bundles of winter clothing are placed on a bed and the spirit invited to take them. In Babylonia food and drink as well as clothes were left for the use of the dead. Their repose was believed to depend on the sacred breaking of bread by the relatives in a communion SACRIFICE (q.v.) performed monthly. Life-giving charms, such as shells and objects made of gold, were often buried with

widely. In museums you may see the models of people, ships, and houses found in Egyptian tombs, and still to-day paper models of people and houses are carried in Chinese funeral processions and burnt afterwards so that the dead may benefit by them. Amongst Egyptians, Babylonians, Greeks, Celts, Australian natives, and other peoples, there was a belief in Islands of the Dead, and so oars or a miniature boat were buried with the dead to be used on the journey. The Lapps killed a reindeer to help on the journey, which was believed to take as long as three years.

The ritual eating and drinking, which take place after a death, are connected with the custom of providing for the needs of the dead man's soul. During 'wakes', which used to be held in England and are still observed in Ireland and other European countries, the relatives and friends sit up all night by the coffin, eating, drinking, playing games, asking riddles, and telling stories. They are afraid to sleep in the house with a corpse lest they meet its spirit in their dreams and fall ill in consequence: therefore the mourners eat and talk to keep themselves awake, and the dead are often believed also to partake of the meal. In parts of the world as far apart as Ireland and China food is left in the house in case the spirit returns. The Chinese serve regular meals beside the coffin each day until the funeral. On the Festival of

the dead, and it is probable that the games played and dances performed after a death—often by masked or disguised people—were originally intended to represent gods or spirits and believed to help the dead person in some way.

Amongst many peoples mourners 'rend their garments' or even tear their hair or cut themselves to show their grief, and loud wailing cries are uttered by the relatives, friends, and paid mourners. Often those closely connected with the dead person have to bathe or undergo other rites of purification. The custom of wearing mourning probably arose as a way of distinguishing such people (see TABOO). Primitive people in mourning commonly reverse their usual customs; for instance, if they usually wear their hair long they cut it short, or the other way round. The Arapaho Indians unbraid their hair as a sign of mourning, and in Guiana mourners go naked. At our own military funerals rifles are carried reversed. We wear black, but the Chinese wear white. Some Pacific islanders (Melanesia) blacken their bodies, while the Dakota Indians whiten theirs. The Ainu of Japan wear their coats inside out.

Many and varied are the rites and ceremonies connected with death. When someone dies, strong emotions are aroused—grief, fear, and awe—and it is on such occasions that people express their feelings in RITUAL (q.v.). The form the ritual takes depends on the ancestral customs

THE FUNERAL OF KING GEORGE V, 28 JANUARY 1936
The procession is entering Windsor Castle. The gun-carriage bearing the coffin is drawn by sailors. Beside them march the Grenadier Guards carrying their rifles reversed. *The Times*

and magical and religious ideas of the particular people, but we can understand most of these rites if we bear in mind two beliefs which are very widespread. First, the dead person's spirit is liable to prowl about and harm the living; and secondly, the spirit has to make a journey to the land of the dead and has to be provided with what is needful on the way and at its destination.

The mode of disposing of the body is usually connected with the religious ideas of the people concerned. Stone Age man buried the corpse, many peoples cremate or burn it, the PARSEES (q.v.) of India expose it to the vultures on a tower; the Tibetans allow animals or birds to eat it, and some Siberian tribes place the coffin in a tree.

Strange as are many of the beliefs and customs

connected with death, there is always the belief underlying them that death is not the end. The purpose of many death ceremonies is to enable the dead person to graduate to another stage of the community life. As there were ceremonies to receive him at his BIRTH (q.v.) and to give him full membership at his INITIATION (q.v.), so funeral rites usher him into the presence of the ancestral spirits with whom the lives of the members of the tribe are so closely bound up (*see* ANCESTOR WORSHIP). The faith in another life beyond the grave is shown, as we have seen, in the ancient customs of providing for the needs of the spirits and in the more modern folk-tales of how Death was tricked and kept a prisoner, being fettered (Greece), put into a bag or bottle or pouch (Italy), or kept up a tree (Germany). In many ways men have asserted their belief that Death, the great Enemy of Mankind, can be overcome. The highest form of this belief is the Christian 'blessed hope of everlasting life'.

DELPHIC ORACLE, *see* DIVINATION; TEMPLE.

DEMETER, *see* GODS OF GREECE AND ROME (CERES).

DERVISHES. These are groups of friars belonging to the Moslem faith. ISLAM (q.v.) did not at first encourage monastic orders; but after some centuries there arose groups of mystical ascetics (*see* ASCETICISM) called *Sufis* (probably from *suf*, white wool, because of their costume which may have been copied from that of monks). These formed themselves into orders which were called Dervishes (Persian *darwish*, meaning poor). The number of them in recent years has greatly diminished. Some of them have rather curious self-torturing practices, others work themselves up to a state of religious ecstasy by rhythmical dances. These dancing dervishes undergo a severe training, which includes long fasts and the memorizing of the Koran (the Moslem Sacred Book). After their dances, which are circular and accompanied by flute-playing, the dervishes used to heal sick persons by first blowing on them and making passes over them, and then, after the sick had been wrapped in blankets, by walking on them. Faith-cures appeared to be effected in this way. One sect of dancing dervishes chant as they go round in a circle, at first slowly, and then faster, till they reach such a pitch of frenzy that they are said to be able to touch hot iron without feeling pain.

DEVIL, *see* SATAN.

DIANA, *see* GODS OF GREECE AND ROME (ARTEMIS).

DIONYSUS, *see* GODS OF GREECE AND ROME.

DISSENTER, *see* BAPTIST; CONGREGATIONALIST; METHODIST.

DIVINATION. People everywhere are curious about the future—for example, whether they are likely to succeed in such future enterprises as their love affairs or business ventures. If we could look into the future and discover what was going to happen, we could plan our lives much more wisely. So strongly have people wanted to safeguard the future that they have concocted a great variety of ways of divining their best course of action. Also, when people are much afraid or in great anxiety, they clutch at any chance of finding a solution to their difficulties. Nearly everywhere it has been accepted as a fact that certain people, because of their special gifts, are able to read fortunes and foretell events. Such soothsayers, fortune-tellers, oracles, augurs, and diviners used to be consulted by rulers to discover how and when they would be successful in war, and on many occasions they altered history by their good or bad advice. Often, both amongst primitive people and more civilized nations, such as the Greeks, people considered to have these gifts received special training in order to develop them.

In ancient Rome there was a college of augury whose business it was to find whether the gods were in favour of, or against, proposed plans of action. The augur pitched his tent on a hill, asked the gods for a sign, and with head covered waited for the answer, which might consist of the appearance of birds or signs in the heavens, such as lightning flashes. Somewhat similar methods of augury are used by the natives of Borneo to-day. They sit in a shelter made of leaves and watch the sky. If they should see three hawks, one flying to the right, another to the left, and a third circling, this is a good omen. The magpie rhyme—

One for sorrow, two for mirth,
Three for a wedding, and four for a birth.

—comes from ancient augury. Beasts as well as birds are used in divination. Queen Boadicea once released a hare from amongst her clothes and drew a favourable omen from the way it ran away.

A very ancient means of divination was by inspecting the intestines of animals. The Babylonians examined the liver of a sacrificed sheep and drew conclusions from the markings on it. This custom was adopted by the Etruscans and Romans and is carried on nowadays in Uganda, Borneo, and Burma, where the liver of a fowl or pig is used. Divination was also practised in Rome and elsewhere by examining the shoulder-blade of animals. In Europe the breast-bone of a fowl was inspected. Our practice of breaking the wish-bone of a chicken after we have dined off it is derived from this kind of divination.

People who buy fortune-telling almanacs are supporters of ASTROLOGY (q.v.), which is a form

BANTU MEDICINE-MAN READING BONES

He shakes them in his hands and then flings them on the ground. He claims to be able to discover secret information from the way they fall. *Pitt Rivers Coll.*

of divination at least 5,000 years old. It supposes a close connexion between the movements of the stars and the fortunes of people. The false idea still survives that by 'reading the stars' we may tell what is going to happen amongst the nations, or that by noting the planets in the sky when a child is born we may discover his or her future. There is a widespread belief that the spirits of the dead may be conjured up to give information to the living (*see* SPIRITUALISM). We have a famous example in the visit of Saul to the woman at Endor who called up for him the spirit of Samuel (1 Sam. xxviii). Zulu witch-doctors pretend to call up the spirits of their dead ancestors and ask them questions.

The simplest types of divination, such as drawing lots, throwing objects, or shooting arrows depend on the belief that more than mere chance is involved. In parts of Africa pebbles or nuts are shaken out of a horn, an answer being found according to whether the number is odd or even. Wizards in Lapland used to put a ring on a drum which had pictures painted on it, and then beat the drum so that the ring moved about, thinking that secret things could be discovered by noting upon which pictures the ring danced. Some of our games of chance probably arose from such methods of divination.

Although divination by most of these means is entirely a matter of chance, this is not often realized by the inquirers or even by the diviners themselves. The very fact that the interpretation of the omens is sometimes complicated makes people the more convinced that there must be something in it. Where people act as oracles the matter is not quite so simple. Such persons may use their own gifts of intuition or secret means of information to guide them in answering those who consult them. The most famous of all was the Delphic Oracle in Greece.

LAPP WIZARD'S DRUM
It is made of reindeer skin stretched on a wooden frame.
The painted patterns have magical meanings. *British Mus.*

At Delphi throughout many centuries a succession of prophetesses uttered oracles supposed to come from the god Apollo. They were consulted on all matters of importance and often gave very sound advice. The prophetess chewed laurel leaves and drank from a sacred stream, then seated herself on a tripod or stool and uttered prophecies during a kind of fit. Probably her mutterings were made to form sense by the priests and then announced to the inquirer. Often the answer to an awkward question was of the kind which can have two meanings, so that whatever happened the prophecy could be said to have come true.

There are a certain number of people who claim to have the power of 'second sight'—to to able to see into the future or to know what is happening at a distance. We know of such 'seers' amongst the Mongolians, American Indians, Scots, and Gypsies, for example. It is not very uncommon for persons to become conscious of calamities befalling relatives many miles away. Some people develop in their minds images of distant or future things by gazing into a glass ball—crystal-gazing as it is called. These powers are by no means fully understood. Thought-transference between people definitely does occur, and may explain some instances of

people being aware of events happening at a distance from them. Some people claim to be able to dream the future, and from ancient times dreams have been regarded as a means of knowing what is going to happen. Joseph interpreted the dreams of Pharaoh's butler and baker as well as those of Pharaoh himself (Gen. lx; lix), and Daniel was called on to interpret Nebuchadnezzar's dream (Dan. ii).

A special kind of divination was practised in the Middle Ages to discover evil-doers. The suspected person was made to undergo an ordeal in the belief that the result would show whether or not he was innocent. In Britain itself, for instance, women were ducked to find out if they were witches. If they sank they were regarded as innocent, but if they floated this was supposed to be certain evidence that they had been carrying on WITCHCRAFT (q.v.).

The motive inspiring many forms of divination was to get a decision about some important matter when, by ordinary reasoning on the facts available, a person could not be certain what to do. Religious and scientific ideas got mixed up with divination, but it is always most closely connected with MAGIC (q.v.). The desire to know about the future soon leads people to try to alter it, and so those who use divination often employ magic to gain their ends. There have always been, and still are, a great many people who, for payment, are ready to deceive others by pretending to be able to tell their fortunes or unfold the future.

DOMINICAN, *see* FRIAR.

DORIANS, *see* GREEK CIVILIZATION, Section 2*b*.

DRAGON. Of all the queer creatures which appear in MYTHOLOGY (q.v.) there is none more important and few more ancient than the dragon. Very many centuries ago this fabulous monster crawled and wriggled and flew its way all over Europe and Asia. Kings, emperors, and princes have proudly worn the dragon badge, and Roman soldiers followed the dragon standard into battle. Before the Norman Conquest the dragon was the chief English royal ensign in war. One legend relates how King Arthur's father, Uther Pendragon, saw a flaming dragon in the sky which foretold that he would become king. When the prediction was fulfilled and he came to the throne, he ordered two dragon standards to be made, one to be dedicated in Winchester

A CHINESE DRAGON
Detail of the 'Nine Dragon Scroll', Sung Dynasty, 13th century A.D. *Mus. of Fine Arts, Boston*

Cathedral, the other to be borne into battle before him. During the reign of King Edward VII the dragon was included in the armorial bearings of the Prince of Wales. Not in England only, but all over Europe and beyond, the dragon has appeared on military standards. In China the dragon was the symbol of the Emperor, and in Japan there is a national dragon myth.

What is the dragon like? One detailed description by the Chinese writer, Wang Fu, who lived in the Han Dynasty (206 B.C.–A.D. 220), runs: 'His horns resemble those of a stag, his head that of a camel, his eyes those of a demon, his neck that of a snake, his belly that of a clam, his scales those of a carp, his claws those of an eagle, his soles those of a tiger, his ears those of a cow.' The mixture of creatures in the dragon's make-up suggests that the monster was created by adding together bits of various animals. This is, indeed, what happened. One of the earliest pictures of a dragon appears on a Babylonian seal; it shows a serpent-like beast with horns and paws. This dragon is the goddess Tiamat, who is also depicted with wings (*see* BABYLONIAN MYTHS). She had the power to create monsters to help her in her fight against the god Marduk. But she was defeated, for he represented the life-giving spring sun, and she stood for dark confusion and chaos as well as for the ocean which the Babylonians thought of as existing in the beginning of things. The dragon also

appears in the EGYPTIAN MYTHS (q.v.) of the battle between the gods Osiris and Set. Ever since those ancient days the dragon has been thought of as representing evil in the struggle which goes on in the world between the powers of good and evil. Thus in the book of Revelation (xii. 7) we read: 'There was war in heaven: Michael and his angels fought against the dragon.'

Many legends tell how a wicked dragon was challenged by various heroes—Siegmund, Beowulf, Sigurd, Arthur, Tristram, and Lancelot—and, of course, St. George. The French Bishop Arculf, who lived in the 7th century, heard the story of St. George in the Middle East. When he was returning to France his ship was blown off its course and driven to our coasts; so he landed in Britain, came to Iona and met Bishop Adamnan. He seems to have been the person who brought the story of St. George and the Dragon to our shores. At Beirut in Syria people still point out the well into which St. George threw the carcass of the monster. St. George became the patron saint of England. When we had golden sovereigns, he was represented on one side, astride his horse and transfixing the dragon with his spear.

In Japan there are similar dragon legends. One of them describes how an eight-headed dragon came every year to eat a child, until of a family of eight there was only one left. The hero slays him, but not quite in fair fight, for

ST. GEORGE AND THE DRAGON
Painting by Vittore Carpaccio (c. 1450–1522). *Alinari*

he first makes the dragon drunk. The dragon of the book of Revelation (xii. 3–4) has one head less than this Japanese monster, and in the Bible story his tail knocks the stars out of heaven.

According to the mythology of the Greeks and Romans there were, however, some good dragons in Europe. But they became increasingly regarded as bad beasts, and the devil himself was depicted with claws, horns, and wings like a dragon. In China, on the other hand, though there are ancient records of horrible dragon monsters lurking in the rivers which had to be appeased by human sacrifices, the dragon has long been thought of mainly as the bringer of prosperity and good fortune. The mythological beast is always connected in some way with water, either in the rivers, sea, or clouds. The Chinese dragon is believed to be 'the heavenly bringer of the fertilizing rain' without which the crops would fail and people would starve. When the Chinese want rain they perform a dragon dance. These contrary notions about the dragon probably arose from its connexion with the thunderstorm. People thought of the thunderstorm as the source of prosperity, as with it comes the fertilizing rain which matters so much to the inhabitants of parched countries; but they also feared the thunderbolt and noticed how the lightning could shatter trees or strike people dead. Thus the dragon of the rain and thunder-cloud came to be considered in some places and at some times as the bringer of good and at other places and times as an evil power. The dragon is a mythical creature but it stands for something of which

everyone of us has experience—the conflict between good and evil. This is one of the reasons why beliefs about it have been popular over a great part of the world.

See also FABULOUS CREATURES; FOLK-LORE.

DRUIDS, *see* RELIGION, PREHISTORIC.

DRUZES (DRUSES), *see* SYRIANS.

DUTCH. The Netherlanders, as they officially call themselves, are a Germanic people, closely related in race and language to the people of north Germany. They are inhabitants of a country for which they have had to struggle and suffer more than most peoples of the world. This struggle has developed in them some very strong qualities of patriotism, self-reliance, and industry, and made them a frugal, thrifty, practical-minded people with a great capacity for attention to detail. The Netherlands in early times included most of what we now call Belgium. At the beginning of the 16th century they became part of the Great Hapsburg Empire, and there followed through the 16th and 17th centuries one of the most heroic struggles for liberty known in history. The great hero WILLIAM THE SILENT, Prince of Orange (q.v. Vol. V), from the time he was twenty-two led the Dutch in their fight for freedom—not only political freedom but also freedom to follow the Protestant teaching of CALVINISM (q.v.). In spite of continual disasters and very cruel persecutions under the dreaded INQUISITION (q.v.) and the ruthless Spanish Governor, the Duke of Alva, the Dutch people kept up the fight for some eighty years until, in 1648, their independence from Spain was finally established. When they were no longer able to fight on land, they kept up the struggle by sea, and the exploits of the famous 'Water Beggars' will never be forgotten in Dutch history.

The Dutch were such good seamen, in fact, that by the beginning of the 17th century they had become masters of the sea and the chief traders of the world. The Dutch East India Company opened up a vast trade with the East. The trading towns (the most important being Amsterdam) became wealthy and powerful, and the burghers or chief citizens of each town set up their own local governments. This too was the period which produced the famous Dutch School of painters of whom the best known is REMBRANDT (q.v. Vol. V). It was also, however, a time of great rivalry with the English over trade and sea power, resulting in many naval battles between the two countries. During the 18th century the Dutch were involved in a succession of wars with France and England which ended in the setting up of a Dutch republic in close alliance with France. Napoleon for a short time made the Netherlands part of the French Empire; but on his overthrow, in which the Dutch played their part, the head of the House of Orange, another William, was made King of both Belgium and Holland. These two countries, however, with their differences of race, culture, and religion, did not unite well together, and in 1831 they split into the two kingdoms we know to-day.

The Dutch and the English have always had much in common. Both have been pre-eminently a sea-faring people and a people of great enterprise in trade and colonial pioneering, which has led to rivalry in establishing colonies in many parts of the world. The Dutch Empire in the East Indies and Dutch Guiana has been a source of great wealth and employment: indeed, there is hardly a family in Holland which has not some relation who has been out to the Indies, or does not possess curios or ornaments of oriental art brought back from the East.

As a result of the comparative poverty of their own land and the difficulties of reclaiming land from the sea, together with their history of continuous struggle, the Dutch have become skilful at improvising and inventing. Shortage of stone

DUTCH GIRLS IN MIDDELBURG
M. W. Neale

TULIPS ON A BULB FARM NEAR HAARLEM
Paul Popper

has led to a great brick industry: much of the English brickwork of the 17th century was designed by Dutchmen, and their own towns have beautiful brickwork. The land is cultivated intensively, and dairy farming and horticulture, especially the growing of bulbs, are flourishing industries. Before the devastation of the Second World War they had achieved a generally high standard of living.

They have a passion for orderliness which is shown in their gardens with their geometrically shaped flower-beds, high clipped hedges of yew and box-trees trimmed into beasts and ships and birds. Their love of precision was early evident in their achievements as printers and engravers and as mapmakers. Mercator and Ortelius, the first scientific mapmakers, were Dutch (*see* MAPS, Vol. IV), as were also the first hydrographic chartmakers, Wagenaer and Blaev. Dutch maps of their own country and of their East Indian Colonies are still excellent. They put a high value on education and scholarship: indeed ERASMUS and GROTIUS (qq.v. Vol. V) rank among the world's greatest scholars. Their passion for detail is shown in the work of Dutch artists, in the carved gables and fine brickwork of their architecture, in Delft tiles, and in the rich marquetry and patterned veneers which decorated their furniture. All these qualities

combine to form a national character which rates practical achievements very high, which is thorough and painstaking, and if at times it is inclined to be dull and unimaginative, is none the less individualistic and reliable. The Dutch are essentially a democratic race; at the same time they show great enthusiasm for their Royal Family.

See also Vol. III: HOLLAND; Vol. IV: GERMANIC LANGUAGES.

DWARFS. From very early times people have been interested in men and women so far below the normal height as to be considered dwarfs. Homer, in the Greek epic, the *Iliad*, tells of a race of PYGMIES (q.v.), living in the distant southern land to which the cranes fly in autumn, and other Greek writers mention battles which take place between the little men and the birds.

According to one of these writers, when Hercules had defeated a giant called Antaeus, he fell asleep somewhere in Africa and woke up to find an army of pygmies shooting tiny arrows into his arms and legs. The story reminds us of Gulliver's adventures in Lilliput, described centuries later by Dean Swift. The historian, Herodotus, heard of five men who were taken prisoner by dwarfs in the African desert and led to a town beside a great crocodile-infested river. This may have been the Niger, and the dwarfs members of one of the African pygmy tribes.

Amongst people of normal height dwarfs occasionally occur, usually owing to defects in the pituitary or thyroid gland. Because of their quaintness they used to be kept at kings' courts and in wealthy families. Of the Greek poet, Philetas of Cos, who was the teacher of one of the Egyptian kings, the story was told that he was so tiny that he had to wear shoes of lead to prevent his being blown away. The niece of the Roman Emperor Augustus had two dwarfs, each of them 2 feet 4 inches in height. One of the most famous of English dwarfs was Jeffery Hudson (1619–82) who had an adventurous life. He claimed that between the ages of eight and thirty years he was only 18 inches in height, but he then started to grow and stopped at 3 feet 9 inches. When the Duke of Buckingham gave a dinner to Charles I and his queen, the dwarf, Hudson, stepped out of a cold pie to everyone's surprise, and was given as a present by the duke to the queen. He fought and won two duels, one with a turkey-cock and the other with a man. On one occasion he was taken prisoner by the Turks, but was ransomed and brought back to England. Queen Henrietta Maria had two other dwarfs, Richard Gibson and his wife Anne. Their combined height was 7 feet 2 inches, but they had nine children, five of whom grew up and were of normal height. 'General Tom Thumb', another famous dwarf of the 19th century, was 31 inches high. He married an American lady, Lavinia Warren, who was 2 inches taller. The dwarf Richebourg was only 23 inches and lived to the age of ninety. In the siege of Paris a nurse carried him through the enemy lines, dressed as a baby, with important dispatches concealed in his clothes.

Giants are usually dull-witted and die young, but dwarfs are frequently quite bright mentally, strong, active, and long-lived. The bodies of some are well proportioned, but others have rather large heads. Dwarfs are commoner than giants.

Some people think that the belief in Elves and Fairies (qq.v.) arose from glimpses of pygmy people, but this is not very likely, for elves are believed in where no dwarf races ever lived.

See also Folk-lore.

A DWARF AT THE COURT OF PHILIP IV OF SPAIN
Painting by Diego Velasquez (1599–1660) in the Prado, Madrid. *Vernacci*

TOM THUMB

see a modern version of the same idea in the tank-traps and slit-trenches of warfare to-day.

2. EARTHWORK ENCLOSURES, usually called 'camps' and marked as such on the ordnance maps, are known to have been used for enclosing settlements and cattle-yards as early as the New Stone Age (about 2400 B.C.) in Sussex and Wessex. Small squarish enclosures for agricultural purposes were built in the late Bronze Age (about 800 B.C.) in the same regions, and a number of small miscellaneous earthworks with not very large ditches and banks surrounded farms and homesteads in the Iron Age (from about 300 B.C.). In a stony country these early agricultural settlements took the form of hut-circles and 'pounds' built of stone walling.

The most impressive 'camps' are the hill-forts which sometimes have enormous banks and ditches, often forming several lines of defence. One of the very largest of these is Maiden Castle in Dorset. Small hill-forts with single lines of earthworks were being built as early as about 350 B.C. in southern Britain; and in the following centuries most of the earthworks which are so

E

EARTHWORKS AND HILL-FORTS. 1. Prehistoric man in Britain made earthworks for a great number of purposes: for defences; as boundaries between agricultural or political units of land; for surrounding a farm-yard or a burial-ground; or for making the walls of a fort. They were usually ditches dug in the ground with the soil piled up as banks alongside. In regions where the subsoil is rocky, stones were piled up into walls for the same purposes, and both earthwork and wall-making of this kind continued into the Middle Ages. We can still

THE WHITE HORSE AT UFFINGTON, BERKS., WITH THE CASTLE BEHIND
Early Iron Age. *Ashmolean Mus.*

noticeable on our hills to-day were being built or enlarged and re-fortified. They continued to be used, either as semi-permanent settlements or strong places of refuge, down to the Roman invasion of A.D. 43, when many of them are known to have become centres of military resistance. In Wales and Scotland forts built of earthwork or stone were used by the native tribesmen during the Roman occupation.

The banks of these hill-forts were more often than not strengthened and interlaced by timber-work so that they made solid walls. At the entrances there were elaborate gateways which

OFFA'S DYKE NEAR CRIGGION

Built by Offa, the King of Mercia, about A.D. 800 to keep back the Welsh. It stretched from the mouth of the river Dee to the mouth of the river Severn. *G. M. Boumphrey*

could be closed in time of danger. The only traces of gates now remaining, which can be detected by the excavator, however, are the post-sockets and stains indicating rotted timber. When the timber-work in stone-built forts was burnt, as often happened in a siege, the stones might melt together in slaggy lumps. Such fused ramparts are frequently found in Scotland where they are now called 'vitrified forts'. In Scotland and Northumberland there are tiny enclosures which could have served only a chieftain and his immediate dependents: these are really 'castles'.

3. BOUNDARY EARTHWORKS range from huge cross-country dykes, like that built in the late 8th century A.D. by Offa between England and Wales, to small local dykes marking out individual property or forming part of a defence system. The Roman Walls in north Britain are examples of cross-country defences, and indeed these walls may have suggested to the Britons the building of large-scale dykes against the Saxon invaders later on. Early dykes are as old as the late Bronze Age (about 800 B.C.) and mark out cattle-ranches or farms; others, such as those near Colchester and Chichester, belong to the defence system round the capital towns of the British princes in the half-century or so before the Roman Conquest.

There are other earthworks such as those built by the Romans—military camps of the early part of the Roman occupation have been found in many areas but they are usually inconspicuous. Earthworks were built also in the Civil Wars—for example, those for the defence of Oxford; but little now remains of most of these temporary defences. From the Middle Ages onwards banks and ditches were often used to enclose deer-parks and for similar purposes.

A distinctive type of earthwork is the castle of the early Norman period—a high circular mound, known as a *motte*, on which originally stood a timber castle, and a large earthwork enclosure of bank and ditch attached to this (the *bailey*) in which wooden buildings for the retainers and horses, &c., of the owner of the castle were set up.

See also PREHISTORIC MAN; CELTIC CIVILIZATION.

EAST AFRICANS. 'East Africa' is a geographical expression only and includes Portuguese East Africa (or Mozambique), two British Protectorates—Nyasaland and Uganda, a British Mandate—Tanganyika, and a British Colony—Kenya. These territories all have highlands and lowlands, and in all of them European settlement is for the most part found in the highlands, since tropical diseases such as malaria (the most common), blackwater fever, sleeping sickness, and others make the lowlands very unhealthy for Europeans.

The chief inhabitants of East Africa are the

Bantu-speaking people (*see* NEGRO AFRICANS): they number about nineteen million as compared with only about 50,000 Europeans. The Europeans are either government officials, traders, or farmers—usually called settlers. They provide the money for and the management of the estates where cotton, sisal, coffee, and many other tropical products are grown; but all the

EAST AFRICA

manual labour, and in most cases the skilled labour as well, is done by the natives, and done very cheaply.

The great majority of these settlers still talk —and think—of their mother country as being their home. Whereas a RHODESIAN (q.v.), regards Rhodesia as his home, though he will visit England as often as he can afford and keeps in close contact with England, a settler in Nyasaland only thinks of that country as his temporary home where he is making his living, and almost always returns to England when he retires. This is true for all the East African territories, except partly for Kenya, where many settlers have made permanent homes.

The whole of this territory is especially unhealthy for children, except for the real highlands of Kenya and Tanganyika, and most white children have to go to Europe or South Africa for their schooling and university education.

European exploration of these territories naturally started from the coast and was carried out by missionaries, traders, hunters, and explorers. DAVID LIVINGSTONE (q.v. Vol. V), for instance, was a missionary who started from South Africa and was the first European to travel in Nyasaland; STANLEY (q.v. Vol. V), du Plessis, Burton, and Speke were explorers whose travels and books helped to make Africa no longer a 'Dark Continent'. The Dutch Churches in South Africa and many British and other Churches to-day finance mission stations in almost all these areas and have been mainly responsible for what little education the native inhabitants have. They have also been largely responsible for turning the spoken languages of the natives into written languages by making translations of the Bible into the native language.

The first non-native inhabitants were Arabs, who developed a large and profitable slave-trade in the 17th, 18th, and 19th centuries; they are still fairly numerous in the ports but not inland. There has been some Indian immigration, especially into Kenya and Tanganyika: in the latter colony the Indians, who are mostly traders, have been elected members of the Legislative Council. Kenya is the only one of these colonies which has a parliament, some of its members being elected and some appointed by the Governor. The other territories are governed as Crown Colonies—that is, the home government appoints a governor and other officials, these being under the control of the home government and not of a local parliament.

Modern science has in two ways made a big difference to the lives of Europeans in these areas. In the first place medical science has developed new methods of preventing and treating tropical diseases. During the recent wars many allied soldiers had to fight in tropical conditions all over the world. Medical research in all countries tried to make their job easier by working on new types of injections and drugs against malaria and other tropical fevers. The use of these injections and drugs and of insecticides like D.D.T. may make more intensive European settlement in these tropical areas possible. Then air travel has made it very much easier to reach these territories from Europe. Where it used to take some weeks to get from Nairobi to Mombasa by rail and then to England by sea, the air journey now takes a day or so. The coming of air transport will help to speed up the development of East Africa.

See also Vol. III: EAST AFRICA.

KIKUYU WOMEN

The Kikuyu are a Bantu people who live in the Mt. Kenya district. They are skilful farmers and are much employed by the white settlers. Although they are more advanced in agriculture than other native peoples in East Africa, they are still primitive in many ways, such as their method of grinding corn. They wear skins and decorate themselves with rings of brass wire and strings of beads. *Roy. Geog. Soc.*

ECUADOR, PEOPLE OF. This South American equatorial country is an Indian republic like Peru and Bolivia to the south: that is to say, it has more Indians than whites or people of mixed blood. It formed the northern part of the INCA Empire (q.v.) before the Spaniards came, and its capital, Quito, is one of the oldest towns of South America. Most of the people live high up in the Andes valleys where the climate, although on the Equator, is cool all the year round. In their primitive and picturesque villages in the mountain valleys the Indians still speak their own native dialects and lead a life that has changed little since pre-Spanish times. Wrapped in their bright-coloured ponchos or blankets, they drive their llamas into market once a week to sell their goods and buy the

INDIANS OF ECUADOR WEARING BRIGHTLY COLOURED PONCHOS. *Paul Popper*

necessities of life. But the three centuries of Spanish rule have left a deep mark on the country, and it is so cut off from the rest of the world by its mountains that many Spanish colonial ideas and customs still survive.

Ecuador was freed from Spain in 1822 by one of the lieutenants of SIMON BOLIVAR (q.v. Vol. V), the great liberator of Spanish America. It declared its independence of Colombia in 1830. Since then it has had many presidents who have been almost dictators, and a perpetual struggle has gone on between the supporters and opponents of the power of the Roman Catholic Church.

See also Vol. III: ECUADOR.

EGYPTIAN CIVILIZATION. It is possible to trace the beginnings of Egyptian civilization in the Nile valley right back to the Old Stone Age. By the end of the Ice Age an immense change had taken place in the climate of northern Africa. Great areas of forests and grass-lands, over which had roamed vast herds of game, had become stretches of desert, such as the Sahara, incapable of supporting much life. Therefore the great cleft of the Nile valley, where vegetation never failed, became a refuge for men and animals. Excavation at various points along the Nile valley has shown the existence of very early settlements and the beginnings of that river valley civilization which grew into the brilliant civilization of Egypt.

The history of Egypt has been divided into four periods—the pre-dynastic period, the Old Kingdom, the Middle Kingdom, and the New Kingdom. The beginning of the pre-dynastic period reaches back into the Neolithic, or New Stone Age period, somewhere between 10000 and 5000 B.C. The Old Kingdom period began about 3300 B.C. and ended about 2200 B.C. After an intermediate period of disorder of 200 years the Middle Kingdom, the most brilliant period of Egyptian civilization, began about 2000 B.C. and was brought to an end by foreign invasion in 1700 B.C. The foreign conquerors were driven out of Egypt in 1580 B.C., when the New Kingdom began. This lasted until Egypt became a province of the Persian Empire in 525 B.C. After this Egypt was dominated successively by the Greeks (*see* PTOLEMIES, Vol. V) and the Romans, but the influence of ancient Egyptian civilization remained throughout. Only after the fall of the Roman Empire, when Egypt was conquered by the Arabs, did the ancient culture die out. The civilization of modern Egypt is mainly Arab (*see* EGYPTIANS).

The two great factors which have dominated the shape and development of Egyptian civilization are, first, the river Nile, and second, the intense interest of the Egyptians in everything connected with death. The whole of Egyptian life revolves about the NILE (q.v. Vol. IV); it depends upon the Nile for its very existence. The old Greek historian, Herodotus, tells us that the priests of Egypt called their country 'the gift of the river', a description which is literally true, for the soil of Egypt consists of the fertile black mud which the Nile has brought down from the Abyssinian plateau and deposited on the rocky subsoil and the desert sand. The great characteristic of the Nile, which gave shape to so much of Egyptian religion and mythology, is the regularity of its floods. For the Egyptians this was the annual miracle of their river, and its cause was a mystery to them. We know now that the annual flooding of the Nile is caused by the winter rains in the regions of the great African lakes and by the melting snows on the high Abyssinian plateau. The flood, laden with rich earth, reaches the lower valley about 15 June, at a time when the whole land has been burnt black by the sun. It brings what the Egyptian Hymn to the Nile called 'water of renewal' and 'water of life'. From June to September the Nile rises and submerges the whole valley; then in the beginning of October it begins to fall, until by the end of November it returns to its normal level, leaving the land saturated with water and covered with a deep layer of rich black earth, ready for the plough-man and the sower. In the course of centuries the Egyptians learnt how to control and distribute the flow of water by dams and irrigation ditches; and it was the need for having the machinery for controlling the flood under one central authority which brought about the union of Egypt into one kingdom. This was why Egypt became a united kingdom long before the states in the other great river-valley of the Tigris and Euphrates. Another peculiarity of the Egyptian political system was due to the Nile: the Nile had created two Egypts, Upper and Lower Egypt, each of a very different nature and history. Upper Egypt, a long, narrow strip of fertile land stretching for some 500 miles on each bank of the river, and shut in by high limestone cliffs, was cut off from intercourse with the outside world, and this gave rise to that deep-rooted conservatism so characteristic of ancient Egyptian civilization. Lower Egypt, the land of the Delta with its 400 miles of Mediterranean coast was open to all the influences which streamed in from the Mediterranean and Asia, and these gave rise to the inventiveness and resourcefulness which made Egypt the pioneer in so many arts and crafts. This dual character of the kingdom of Egypt is shown in many ways: the king wore

COLOSSAL STATUE OF RAMESES II IN THE TEMPLE OF LUXOR

a double crown—the two crowns of Upper and Lower Egypt combined into one; he was crowned in each of the capitals; most of the officials were duplicated, and all the great royal religious ceremonies were performed twice. In these ways we can see how profoundly the Nile influenced the character of Egyptian civilization.

But the second factor—the Egyptian's intense interest in death—had an even deeper influence upon the character and development of Egyptian civilization. It is not easy to say how this arose. It has been suggested that the discovery of the power of the dry desert sand to preserve from corruption the bodies buried in it gave the early inhabitants of Egypt the idea that by

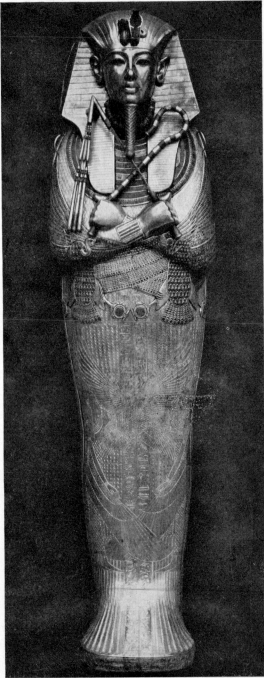

TUTANKHAMEN'S GOLDEN COFFIN
The mummy lies within three coffins in the Burial
Chamber of the rock-cut tomb at Thebes. The outer two
coffins are made of painted wood, the first rectangular and
the next shaped like a figure. The third, which contains
the mummy, is of solid gold and is decorated with symbols
and hieroglyphics. The King holds the crook and flail,
the insignia of Osiris, to show his divine origin. Middle of
14th century B.C. *Ashmolean Mus.*

preserving the body from decay, life could be
made to last for ever. But however the idea
started, it is clear that the original purpose of
embalming the body (mummification) was to
preserve the life of the one person whose continued existence was essential to the well-being of
the community, namely, the king, the Pharaoh.
The myth of Osiris (*see* EGYPTIAN MYTHS)
embodies this belief that the dead Pharaoh
became Osiris; it gives the pattern of the funeral
ritual for the dead king by which his body undergoes all the processes of mummification, is
magically brought to life again and becomes the
god Osiris, united with the sun-god, Re, in the
Egyptian heaven, the land of the Blessed.

From this central belief and the practices connected with it all the main elements of Egyptian
civilization developed. First, the desire to build
splendid tombs for the kings led to the development of the extraordinary skill in masonry and
architecture which the Egyptians had attained
before the end of the Old Kingdom period. The
pyramids, the greatest witness to the skill of
the Egyptian builders, were built in the time of
the 4th Dynasty dating from about 3000 B.C. The
pyramids were royal tombs, and developed from
the simpler stone-built, flat-topped tombs of the
3rd Dynasty. The Great Pyramid, the most
magnificent tomb in the world, was built by the
4th Dynasty Pharaoh Khufu, better known as
Cheops, for his own last resting-place. It is 450
feet high and contains 85 million cubic feet of
masonry. Herodotus says that it took ten years to
quarry the stone and ten more years to build, and
that 300,000 men were employed in the work.

Then the desire to make the mummy resemble
the dead person, and to make portrait-statues
of the deceased to stand in the outer chamber
of the tomb, led to the development of the arts,
particularly of painting and sculpture. In the
same way the need to provide the dead with
adornment led to the employment of all the
skill of the jewellers and goldsmiths which produced such exquisite jewellery as that discovered
in the tomb of Tutankhamen. The requirements
of the funeral rituals stimulated the making of
various musical instruments and the development of the art of music with its sister art of
dancing. The need for fine linen wrappings for
the mummies developed the art of weaving to
such a pitch that 'the fine linen of Egypt' was
famous throughout western Asia and the seaports of the Mediterranean.

Another important element of Egyptian civilization, the art of writing, also grew from the same kind of religious activities. In Egypt writing was probably first used for inscribing on papyrus and on parchment magical formulae for use in funeral rituals. Like the Sumerian writing, the earliest writing in Egypt, of the pre-dynastic period, is 'pictographic', that is, picture-writing.

cumbrous system by a list of between twenty and thirty signs, and it is one of the most curious examples of the extreme conservatism of the Egyptians that they should have made this important discovery and yet made so little use of it (see WRITING, HISTORY OF, Vol. IV).

This is enough to show how much of Egyptian civilization had its origin in and was shaped by

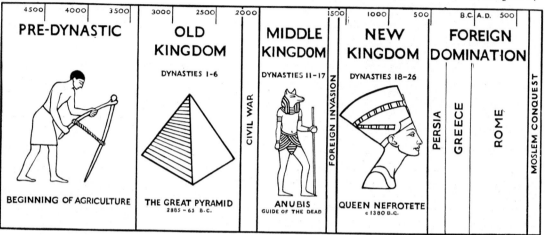

THE EGYPTIAN DYNASTIES

The history of writing in Egypt followed more than one line of development. The picture-writing, known as HIEROGLYPHIC (q.v. Vol. IV), remained, with very little change, the type of writing used for sacred purposes and for inscriptions on monuments. But in the course of time the hieroglyphic writing was found too slow for ordinary use, so the scribes evolved a shortened form of it which was called 'hieratic', and by about the 3rd century B.C. a still simpler form called 'demotic' or 'the people's writing'. Long before these developments had taken place, however, the Egyptians had discovered the principle of the alphabet—the representation of each sound in the language by a single sign or letter. All the early forms of writing, like many oriental forms of writing to-day, were syllabic, that is, each sign represented a syllable. As the number of syllables in a language is very great, anyone who wished to write had to learn a great number of signs. The Egyptian sign-list as we now know it contains between 700 and 800 signs (at an early period of the development of Sumerian writing the sign-list contained more than 2,000 signs). So it is not surprising that writing remained largely in the hands of professional scribes. But the alphabet replaces this

these two central facts, their remarkable river, and their unusual interest in death and the after life. But our picture of Egyptian civilization would be incomplete without some account of the way in which the country was governed, and of Egyptian literature.

The political development of ancient Egypt may be divided roughly into four stages. First, there was the pre-dynastic period, when the country was divided into a number of small city-states, as they might be called, each with its own capital and without any central government. Then by a series of events of which we know very little, the states of Upper and Lower Egypt were united under the absolute rule of the Pharaoh. During the Old Kingdom period the king was regarded as a god, who possessed the power of life and death over the whole of Egypt: his will was the only law. But in the early part of the Middle Kingdom a change took place, and the feudal lords, the chiefs of the states, reduced the power of the king to a shadow, somewhat as the English barons did in the time of King John. Then, in the middle of the 12th Dynasty, about 2000 B.C., the king was able to throw off the power of the feudal lords, and set up a government by a local system of

COLLAR FOUND ON THE MUMMY OF TUTANKHAMEN
It represents the vulture Nekhbet, the emblem of Upper
Egypt, holding the symbol of eternal life. Gold inlaid
with 250 plaques of coloured glass. *Ashmolean Mus.*

sheriffs and royal officers throughout the land. This system lasted for over 300 years, and was gradually transformed into the bureaucratic system of the New Kingdom, whereby Egypt was ruled by a kind of civil service, a network of viziers, mayors, scribes, and priests. The priesthood always had a very powerful hold on the people because it possessed the keys of the after life, the magical secrets of mummification.

Lastly, a word must be said about Egyptian literature and science. Besides the great collections of magical and ritual texts contained in the Pyramid Texts and the *Book of the Dead*, the Egyptians produced a large body of other literature dating from the period of the Old Kingdom. There are several collections of moral precepts and wise sayings, like the Hebrew book of Proverbs. Egypt, from very early times, was famous for its wisdom. A popular book, known as *The Admonitions of an Egyptian Sage*, was a kind of prophetic book, containing warnings to the king and a prophecy of better times. There is a great deal of love-poetry of a high order, and of religious hymns, of which the best known is King Akhnaten's great hymn of praise to Aten, the sun's disk. The earliest romantic literature comes from Egypt: the well-known *Tale of the Two Brothers* is the best example of this kind of literature. The Egyptians were a seafaring

people, and some of their literature consists of works of travel: the *Travels of an Egyptian*, belonging to the 19th Dynasty, and the *Journey of Unamon*, from the 20th Dynasty, are valuable accounts of travel and adventure in Canaan. Finally, we have a number of medical papyri coming down from the Old Kingdom, showing that the Egyptians had a good knowledge of anatomy and of the nature and cause of various diseases, though the treatment was largely magical.

This is only a brief picture of one of the greatest civilizations that the world has ever known.

See also ANCIENT CIVILIZATIONS.

EGYPTIAN MYTHS. In the ancient religion of Egypt, and throughout all the stages of its growth, the great myths played a very important part. As in the case of the BABYLONIAN MYTHS (q.v.), so in the case of the Egyptian myths, it is impossible to separate myth from religious ritual, or to understand the myth apart from the ritual of which it is the spoken part (*see* MYTHOLOGY). The Egyptians were the most conservative people that history has ever known, and so they retained all the religious ideas and customs which they had taken from the various peoples who formed the Egyptian kingdom. In consequence, the religion and mythology of Egypt are extremely complicated. It will make it easier to understand the nature of Egyptian religion and its mythology if we bear in mind the four main strands out of which it grew.

First, in its very early history, the Nile valley was inhabited by a number of separate clans or tribes, each of which had its own gods and form of worship. These gods were mostly animals, such as the crocodile, the jackal, the ibis, and so forth; this explains why so many of the gods represented on Egyptian tombs and monuments have human forms with animal heads. When the tribes were united into a single kingdom, their local gods and the myths connected with them became part of the state religion.

Secondly, Egypt was from the first mainly an agricultural country, and its agriculture depended wholly on the Nile. Hence some of its most important rituals and the myths connected with them are concerned with the fertility of the crops and with the regular flooding of the Nile, upon which the whole agricultural life of Egypt depended.

Thirdly, a very early form of religion in Egypt was the worship of the sun. The great city of Heliopolis was the headquarters of the sun-worship, and of the priests of Re, the sun-god. Quite early in the history of Egypt Heliopolis became the political centre of the country

SYMBOL OF THE GOD RE

under a line of kings who came from the 'hawk' tribe in the north-western Delta. Their god was the hawk-god Horus, who therefore became associated with the sun-worship of Heliopolis and with the elaborate system of myth and ritual which had grown up at Heliopolis round Re, the sun-god.

Lastly, one of the most curious and interesting things about the Egyptians was their intense preoccupation with and fear of death and everything connected with death. Therefore they built up a whole complicated system of myth and ritual together with the practice of mummification and funeral rites, the purpose of which was to preserve the physical body of the dead person for future life. The most important and elaborate of the Egyptian myths, the myth of Osiris, is specially concerned with mummification and funeral rites, but, as will be seen later, it has become interwoven with every aspect of Egyptian religious life.

This shows why we find in the Egyptian myths a strange mixture of sun-worship, of ritual connected with the fertility of the soil on which all life depended, of the god-king, and of funeral rites to preserve the conditions of human life in a future existence. We will now describe some of the chief Egyptian myths.

Our knowledge of the myth of Osiris and his wife Isis in its earliest form comes from very ancient magical papyri known as the Pyramid Texts, written between 4000 and 3000 B.C. The myth of Osiris, pieced together from the Pyramid Texts, contains four main parts: the life, death, and resurrection of Osiris, and the victory of Horus, his son, over Set, his brother and enemy. According to the myth, Osiris was the son of Geb, the earth-god, and was descended from Re, the sun-god. He was a great king, perhaps the first king of Egypt, who taught the Egyptians agriculture—how to grow the vine,

wheat, barley, and other useful plants—and how to make bread, wine, and beer. With the help of his queen, Isis, and the god Thoth, the scribe of the kingdom, he gave Egypt laws and the knowledge of writing, together with the various arts and crafts upon which the civilization of Egypt rested. This figure, the hero who brings the beginnings of civilization to his people, is to be found in the myths of nearly all primitive peoples; for instance Prometheus in early GREEK MYTHS (q.v.) is the same type of hero.

The death of Osiris was brought about by the hatred of his brother Set. By a trick Set persuaded Osiris to get into a chest which was then fastened and cast into the Nile. The chest floated out to sea and finally came to land at Byblos in Syria. There a sycamore tree grew up and enclosed the chest. The king of Byblos, struck by the size of the tree, had it cut down and made into a pillar for his palace.

In the next part of the myth Isis set out to search for the body of her lost husband. She found the chest at Byblos and brought the body of Osiris back to Egypt in a coffin. There Set again found it and cut the body up into pieces which he scattered through all the tribes of Egypt. Isis succeeded in collecting all the scattered parts save one, and by a magical ritual, in which she was helped by her sister Nephthys and the gods Thoth and Anubis, the severed parts were brought together and restored to eternal life. Osiris had become the risen god.

OSIRIS

The final stage of the myth tells how Horus avenged his father Osiris and defeated Set. According to the myth, Horus was born after Set had murdered his father. He was brought up in secret to protect him from the hatred of Set. On coming to manhood he took up the task of avenging his father, and the myth describes his personal victory over Set, and how he was declared by the tribunal of the gods to be the rightful heir of Osiris.

This is the outline of the Osiris myth. In this story some of the main features of Egyptian history were represented. The history of the struggle between the two kingdoms of Egypt is represented by the conflict between Set, the ruler of Upper Egypt, and Osiris, the ruler of Lower Egypt. The victory of Horus over Set after a long struggle, represented the union of the two kingdoms. Then the death and resurrection of Osiris represented the sinking of the Nile waters and its highest point of flood respectively. As part of the ritual, figures of Osiris made of Nile mud were sown with various seeds and at a certain point were thrown into the Nile with lamentations to represent the 'drowning'

HORUS

of Osiris; and when the seeds began to sprout, the moment of his resurrection was similarly hailed with cries of joy. This part of the myth is clearly a magic fertility ritual, such as are to be found in Babylonian myths. The curious connexion with Byblos in Syria, from where, according to the myth, Isis brought back the body of Osiris, may perhaps represent an old tradition of a hero who came from Asia to Egypt bringing some important elements of civilization. It is well known, for instance, that the cultivation of wheat and barley did not originate in Egypt and they were probably brought from Asia. Further, that part of the myth which tells of Osiris in the chest, and of the magical ceremonies by which Isis and Nephthys restored the body of Osiris to life, was directly connected with mummification ritual. Then the myth, which makes Osiris the son of Geb, the earth-god, and so descended from Re, the sun-god, was invented by the priests to connect Osiris with the ancient sun-worship of the Egyptians. Thus the myth of Osiris gathered up into itself all the main features of Egyptian life and thought.

It is strange that there is no Deluge (or Flood) myth in Egypt, as there is in the mythology of the Babylonians and Hebrews. This is perhaps because the seasonal flooding of the Nile brought fertility and prosperity to Egypt, whereas the destructive river floods in the Tigris–Euphrates valley brought disaster and death. Nevertheless, there is a very early Egyptian myth concerning the destruction of mankind, but not by a flood. The myth tells how Re, the sun-god, grew old, and men began to mock him and complain of his neglect. Re summoned a council of the gods, and they agreed upon the destruction of mankind. Man's destruction was entrusted to the daughter of Re, the goddess Hathor. The myth describes the slaughter of mankind by Hathor and gives a gruesome picture of the goddess wading in blood. The killing is brought to an end because Hathor is made drunk with blood mixed with the narcotic mandrake and 7,000 vessels of beer, so that she becomes stupefied and ceases to slay. This myth suggests a primitive African origin, and is connected with the ancient ritual beer-drinking at the Festival of Hathor and Re. There is also nothing in Egypt corresponding to the Babylonian myth of Creation or the Hebrew Genesis story. Instead we find various scattered and unconnected myths intended to account for the existence of man and animals. Some are very gross and come from a very primitive stage of society: one relates how men were made from the tears of Re, while another represents Ptah, the potter-god, as making man out of clay on the potter's wheel. But it is clear that the work of creation never occupied such an important place in Egyptian

HATHOR

religious thought as it did in the mythology of the Babylonians and Hebrews.

See also EGYPTIAN CIVILIZATION.

EGYPTIANS. As well as taking her place among the nations of to-day, Egypt had an ancient civilization which is thousands of years old (*see* EGYPTIAN CIVILIZATION). The Step Pyramid of King Zoser was built in 2815 B.C.; the wonderful treasures of Tutankhamen's Tomb are 3,300 years old. Those Pharaohs, of whom we read in the Old Testament, were followed by a time of change, until Alexander the Great came to Egypt in 329 B.C. He was followed by the rule of the Greek PTOLEMIES (q.v. Vol. V); and they in their turn yielded to the Romans who retained Egypt as their corn-growing colony. In the 7th century the country was invaded

FOWLING IN THE MARSHES

Egyptian painting, 1420–1375 B.C.

AN EGYPTIAN VILLAGE. *Paul Popper*

by the ARABS (q.v.), and became part of the great Moslem empire of the followers of Mohammed (*see* ISLAM). Egypt remained part of the Moslem empire until in 1517 she was conquered by the Ottoman Turks under SULEIMAN (q.v. Vol. V). Mohammed Ali, an Albanian soldier, led a successful revolt against the Turks in the early 19th century; and in 1882 the British went into Egypt to restore order, especially in the nation's finances, and also to ensure the safety of the SUEZ CANAL (q.v. Vol. IV). In 1922 Egypt, under King Fuad, gained her independence, although British troops still remained stationed in the country. After the Second World War agreements were made between Britain and Egypt for removing British troops to the canal zone.

The Egyptian people of to-day are a mixture —partly descended from the Ancient Egyptian, partly from Arab stock, with some contributions from Hebrew, Turkish, and other peoples. Their language is ARABIC (q.v. Vol. IV), a Semitic language akin to Hebrew, dialects of which are

spoken in all the Arab lands from Syria to Morocco. The majority of the people are Moslems, but there is also an active Christian minority, members of the COPTIC CHURCH (q.v.), who believe that their Church was founded by St. Mark himself.

Life in the country depends upon the river NILE (q.v. Vol. III). From the river the *fellah* (Arabic for peasant) gets the water for his fields, for his beasts, and for himself. Several simple wooden devices, all of them ancient, are used for drawing up the water; some are worked by hand, others by a bullock or donkey turning a wheel, with its eyes bandaged to stop it from becoming dizzy. The fellah washes his cattle, and his wife washes her clothes in the river or canal, and all rubbish is tipped there. From this source come the diseases which are the scourge of his life—typhoid, bilharzia, hookworm, and other water-borne plagues. The donkey carries his loads and often the fellah himself, but never his wife, who has to walk. The bullocks draw the plough, with perhaps a scraggy horse, or occasionally a little help from a superior-looking camel.

The fellah and his family feed simply but on a healthy diet: the round, flat, tough 'breads', with onions or tomatoes, some white cheese, a few black olives, a handful of dates or a piece of water-melon, and a cup of strong, sweet coffee or tea flavoured with herbs. Meat is reserved for special occasions. They live in mud huts not far from the canal or river, believe in Allah, and distrust the men from the city and all modern scientific progress. They still believe in a number of spirits, some of them evil, against whom they bar their doors at night. The fellah is poorly paid, but he is a good worker, strong and blest with a sense of humour.

Life in the city is very different: the *effendi* (Arabic for educated man) is dressed in European clothes, though he wears the *tarboosh*, the red hat with a black tassel. Unlike the fellah, he is not fond of hard work. The city Egyptian is, however, an enthusiast for education. In Cairo there is the Royal Egyptian University, with a branch at Alexandria. There is a network of schools all through the country, including many foreign schools, mostly French. French is much spoken in the towns, and English is on the increase. Many Egyptian students now come to Europe to finish their education.

Egyptian cities are very noisy places with a strange mixture of ancient and modern. Cairo is said to be one of the most cosmopolitan cities in the world. The modern part of the city is provided with trams from Belgium, buses from Britain, ancient Fiat taxis from Italy, and private cars from America. Mixed with these are the street vendors in their long, dirty white robes, called *galibiyehs* crying their wares at the top of their voices. Not far away is the native quarter, and the bazaars where many old hand-crafts are still carried on. Into the noise and hurry of the modern town the life of Ancient Egypt sometimes breaks, when a string of leisurely camels, laden with dark-green melons, pads across the main street, holding up the traffic, noiseless except for the deep note of the camel-bells; or when a stout, bearded sheikh mounted on his donkey threads his way through buses and cars *en route* for the market.

See also Vol. III: EGYPT.

EIREANS, *see* IRISH.

EL DORADO, *see* INCA CIVILIZATION.

ELVES. A general name for imaginary small beings with partly human characteristics, which are supposed to inhabit mountains, old earthworks, and mines. The mountain dwarfs of Europe are little men, rather ugly and misshapen: some of them are metal-workers, but not iron-workers, because, like most supernatural beings, they do not like iron. Other elves are thought of as being of the goblin type, sometimes definitely harmful (such as the boggart and pooka), and often mischievous and capricious in their ways. Some are helpful, such as the brownie and kobbold which tidy up the house and look after the animals on the farm, but even these are easily offended, sometimes disappearing when food has been offered to them in a tactless way or a suit of clothes has been provided.

See also DWARFS; FAIRIES; FOLK-LORE.

ELYSIUM, *see* HEAVEN.

ENGLISH, *see* BRITISH PEOPLES.

EPICUREAN, *see* Vol. V: EPICURUS.

EROS, *see* GODS OF GREECE AND ROME.

ESKIMOES. A small people, with yellow skins, straight black hair, and Mongolian features, living along the northern shores of North America and round the coasts of Greenland. In their country the temperature rarely rises above

AN ARROW STRAIGHTENER
It is made of bone with animal heads carved at either end and reindeer on the sides. The wooden arrow is placed in the hole and bent straight near a flame. *British Mus.*

freezing-point, save in the few summer weeks, and snow may fall in any month of the year. Few edible plants can grow in such a climate, so the Eskimoes' food must be mainly fish and flesh—reindeer (called caribou in Canada), seals, walrus, polar bears, and smaller game such as foxes, hares, rabbits, lemmings, and birds.

Most of the country is treeless, so the Eskimoes build semi-underground houses of earth and stones, and roof them with whale bones and turf. When they move out on to the ice-floes in winter, they make snow-houses (*igloos*). These are low, domed houses built of blocks of frozen snow, with transparent ice for windows. A skilled Eskimo can build a perfect snow-house in less than three hours. Skins line the inner walls, and a bank of packed snow forms the bed, with skins for bed-clothes. The one essential piece of furniture is the lamp. This is usually of soap-stone, with a wick of dried moss. It is filled with the blubber of whale, walrus, or seal, and gives light and heat. Over it is slung a kettle or cooking-pot carved out of soft stone. In the summer months they leave the coasts and go inland on hunting expeditions. Then they live in skin tents carried from hunting-ground to hunting-ground. Tools in pre-trading days were all made of stone, bone, or, in some areas, of copper. They are very well made and often beautifully carved and decorated. The daily work of the Eskimoes is hunting, fishing, and trapping, according to the season and locality. All demand physical fitness, skill, experience, and infinite patience—a seal hunter may have to wait for hours at a blow-hole, at a temperature well below freezing, watching, with his harpoon ready in his hand, for the seal to come up to breathe. Dogs help in the hunting, especially in smelling out the seal's blow-holes; but their main use is to drag the sledges over the snow and ice. These sledges are made of wood, when trees or driftwood can be found; but sometimes they are of bone—often the jawbones of a whale. The Eskimoes travel by water in boats of skin, stretched over a wooden framework. The *kayak* or hunting-boat is a light, skin-covered canoe. The deck is covered in, leaving a hole just large enough for him to squeeze into. When he has tied the edges of the skins round his waist, he and his craft are waterproof and almost unsinkable. The Eskimo canoer is extraordinarily clever at managing his craft and, if accidentally

AN ESKIMO FAMILY IN ITS SNOW HOUSE

The flat shelf of ice is used to sit on by day and as a bed at night. On the left is the soap-stone lamp with a pot cooking over it. *National Mus., Copenhagen*

capsized, can quickly right himself with his paddle—or even deliberately roll himself and his canoe over and over sideways.

Men, women, and children wear fur coats, with hoods, trousers, and boots—all of sealskin for summer and of heavier caribou skins in winter. Most garments are made double with the fur both outside and in. Caribou hair is stuffed between an inner and outer pair of boots to keep out frostbite.

The Eskimoes are very independent. They live in small hunting groups, each group managing its own affairs. The most experienced hunter probably acts as leader, but only by common consent, because he knows best. In religious affairs, also, they refer to the man who knows best, the *shaman*. They believe that, with the help of guardian spirits, he can discover the cause of sickness and cure it, can visit the world of spirits and see what is invisible to ordinary folk, can advise about what to do and especially what not to do, and can ensure protection against evil influences by means of charms and magic words. There are no gods, goddesses, or 'Great Spirit' in Eskimo beliefs; but the world is full of the spirits of animals, birds and fishes, trees, stones, rivers, and clouds—and these can be controlled by MAGIC (q.v.) for good or evil.

AN ESKIMO DRUMMER
He is sitting outside his tent which is made of skins
National Mus., Copenhagen

Christianity has been widely spread by missions, and, on the mainland of America, it is only in remoter districts that the shaman is still all-important. Greenland was converted to Christianity as early as A.D. 1000. It has its own educational system and its own newspapers; but there are still parts of the central mainland which have been very little explored. Where the Eskimoes have come into contact with traders their customs have been altered to some extent. The traders wanted skins and brought trade goods in exchange. They brought guns and knives of steel which replaced native tools of stone and bone. They brought brandy and whisky, which were all the more tempting because the Eskimo had no native fermented drink. They also brought manufactured clothing and manufactured foods which, in general, are

despised. During the last century there have been many changes, and, except in the central districts, there has been a great mixture with whites: it is now estimated that some half of the total population of about 30,000 have more or less white blood.

The language of the Eskimoes is extraordinarily complicated. They use prefixes and suffixes where we should use separate words, and a single word where we should use a sentence. For instance, 'He wants to find someone to build him a large house' is 'Igdlorssualiortugssarsiumavoq'. Still, in spite of local variations, the Eskimoes seem to understand each other all along their 5,000 miles of coastline (*see* AMERICAN-INDIAN LANGUAGES: Vol. IV).

Notwithstanding their harsh surroundings, the perpetual ice and snow, rain and fog, and the long winters when the sun scarcely rises above the horizon, the Eskimoes are a cheerful merry folk, contented, good-humoured, and peaceful. Although there is no authority but public opinion, and each man is a law to himself, quarrelling is rare, and there are no specialized weapons of war. Children are petted and spoilt, seldom rebuked (there is a belief that scolding a child will make its ears grow too big) and never punished—but they are usually docile and affectionate. They gain independence early, the girls helping their mothers to run the home and the boys going off hunting with their fathers.

The Eskimoes are quite satisfied with their hard life, and seldom wish to change it. Unlike the Indians, they rarely wear white men's clothing. Indeed, it is the other way round, for white men, living in their area, adopt native dress. The Eskimoes think that their country, their climate, their houses, food, and clothes are the best in the world, and have little wish to travel in search of anything better.

See also Vol. III: GREENLAND.

ESTONIANS. Estonia became an independent republic, as did Latvia and Lithuania, in 1918 after the First World War; but in 1940 these republics were annexed by the U.S.S.R. Before this the Estonians had suffered six centuries of subjection, mainly under the Germans or Russians. In spite of this the people have retained strong national characteristics: they have preserved their language, customs, and way of dress, and they have a flourishing literature. Most of them are LUTHERANS (q.v.) but a minority belong to the ORTHODOX EASTERN CHURCH (q.v.). The peasants are mainly Estonians, a people akin to the FINNS (q.v.), but the rest of the population, once known as Baltic Germans, are a mixed people. The largest minority is Russian.

See also Vol. III: ESTONIA.

ETHICS, *see* PHILOSOPHY.

ETHIOPIANS, *see* ABYSSINIANS.

ETRUSCANS, *see* ROMAN CIVILIZATION.

EUCHARIST, *see* SACRAMENTS; SACRIFICE.

EVOLUTION OF MAN. The theory of evolution, which is based on the careful study of the actual history of many forms of life, asserts that all living forms, plants, and animals, including Man, have developed from earlier and simpler forms by processes of change and selection, so far only partly understood. Up to the middle of the last century most people believed that plants, animals, and men were all created at the beginning of the world as described in the Book of Genesis; and the date was set down as 4004 B.C. During the 19th century facts were discovered which suggested a different theory of creation and a different time scale. These facts could be better explained by the theory that there had been a gradual succession of changes in the various forms of living creatures from the earliest living matter to the animals of the present day, and that of the many types produced by these changes, those which gave the best chances of survival were perpetuated, while others died out.

GEOLOGICAL EVIDENCE. The most striking evidence in support of the theory of evolution is found in the rocks. Geologists can trace the history of life in the world from its earliest beginnings by the fossils which have been preserved in layer after layer of the earth's crust. They tell us that at one time, millions of years ago, the crust would have been too hot for any animal to live, but that later it cooled down and crumpled up, the surface becoming separated into masses of land and vast sheets of water. Ever since those early times the world has been changing. Earth movements have raised up the sea-beds into mountain ranges and tilted the land under new seas. Rain and snow, wind and water, rivers and ice have been and still are at work on the surface (*see* EARTH, HISTORY OF, Vol. III). In the course of time and under

great pressure, gravels, sands, and mud harden into rocks, and the bits of plants and animals embedded in them are preserved as FOSSILS (q.v. Vol. III). From these fossils we can see that changes were slowly taking place in the forms of animals and plants and that, while some types of life become extinct, others survive.

GEOLOGICAL PERIODS. The earth is perhaps some 2,000 to 3,000 million years old. Of this immense time there has probably been life upon the earth for about 500 million years. Traces of man only go back between 500,000 and a million years. Man has left written record of his existence for only 6,000 years, a period which in a time-chart of the whole history of the earth would hardly show at all. In the very oldest rocks there are no certain fossil remains of living things. In the next stage fossils are found of early forms of plants, fishes, insects, and reptiles. The next stage, sometimes called the Age of Reptiles, shows traces of flowering plants, buds, early forms of mammals and the huge reptiles such as ichthysaurs and dinosaurs (*see* PREHISTORIC ANIMALS, Vol. III). But as yet there is no direct ancestor for Man to be found. It is during the following Tertiary Age, or Age of the Mammals, that we find creatures that can be said to be of direct concern for the study of our own origins.

For convenience, Man, together with the Apes, Monkeys, and Lemurs are said to belong to one group—the Primates—distinguished by the possession of highly developed hands, eyes, and, above all, brains. This does not mean that Man is descended from his nearest living relatives, the existing species of ape, but only that apes and men are descended from common ancestral stocks now long extinct. This idea of descent from a common stock is often illustrated by a tree in which the trunk represents the ancestral line, the branches the different species which develop from it.

The nearest ancestors of the primate group were the tree shrews, little creatures that spent their lives darting among the branches in pursuit of insects. The earliest-known primates, in which the brain is already well developed, are lemurs belonging to early tertiary times (Eocene) and species of tarsius, that nervous wistful-looking little animal with huge staring eyes; these in turn lead on to the most primitive of the monkeys, the marmoset. During the last two stages of the Tertiary Age (Miocene and

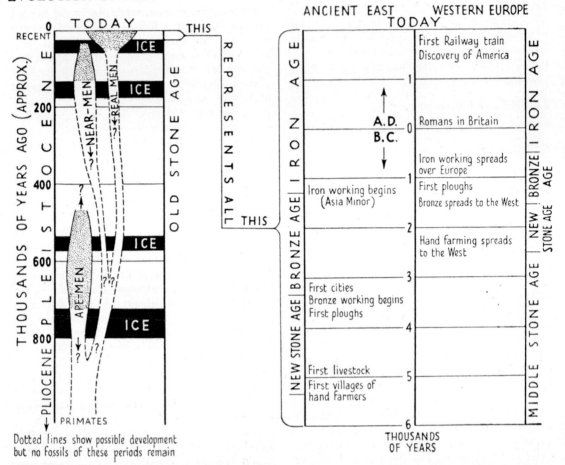

Dotted lines show possible development but no fossils of these periods remain

Pliocene) a group of apes emerged that have features suggesting that they may be directly ancestral to man. The remains of these apes have been found mainly in India. In South Africa several finds have been made of primates with even more distinctively human features, particularly in their teeth and limbs. It is hard to know whether these should be called ape-men or men-apes—that is to say whether we are their direct descendants or whether they represent an independent branch which failed to survive. They were living either at the end of the Tertiary Age (Pliocene) or at the beginning of the period of the great ICE AGES (Pleistocene) (q.v. Vol. III).

With the great Ice Ages we reach the period when human species certainly appear and can be studied, not only from their fossil remains but also from their stone tools. These early men are described more fully in another section (see FOSSIL MAN); here we need only say that during

the greater part of the Ice Ages two main types of human being seem to have developed side by side: one of these was more ape-like and ended in the Neanderthal men; the second, which seems to have included the Piltdown and Swanscombe men, was already approaching very closely to modern man far back in the Ice Ages. By the last Ice Age the modern type was fully developed (hunters of this period could hardly have been distinguished from living races of to-day), while the old ape-like Neanderthal stock had disappeared.

This, then, is how during several million years the wonderful and still not perfectly understood processes of evolution have led from small insect-eating animals skipping among the tree-tops to ourselves, with our complicated civilizations, our scientists, artists, and philosophers.

See also FOSSIL MAN; PREHISTORIC MAN.
See also Vol. II: EVOLUTION; Vol. V: C. R. DARWIN; T. H. HUXLEY.

F

FABLES. These are stories in which an animal, tree, or some other object speaks and acts like a human being. They generally have a moral. The best known are those of Aesop, a Greek who lived about 550 B.C. His name became attached to a collection of stories, although some of the stories were in reality much older and originated in India. Fables make their point clearly and briefly, helped by the fact that each animal represents a certain characteristic, so that a long explanation is unnecessary. Everybody knows, for example, that the fox represents cunning and the lamb innocence. Many later writers have written moral stories in the form of fables, the most famous being the French writer Jean de la Fontaine (1621–95).

See also FAIRY-TALES; FABULOUS CREATURES; FOLK-LORE.

FABULOUS CREATURES. In some of the myths connected with religious ritual, strange creatures such as DRAGONS (q.v.) are mentioned. Such monsters are sometimes symbolic figures representing the forces of nature which the ritual dramatized, and their shapes express this symbolic meaning. So, for example, the dragon's wings suggest its supposed connexion with the rain clouds. Animals have commonly been thought of as possessing special characteristic attributes —the fox is cunning, the lion strong and noble, and the lamb gentle. When the symbolic creature was intended to represent the attributes of more than one animal, it was made up of their parts. Thus the GRIFFIN (q.v.) is part lion and part eagle, the former signifying noble courage and the latter majesty. Sleipner, Odin's horse in the Norse myth, had eight feet to show that he was fleeter than an ordinary horse. Hydra, the many-headed snake, who was able to grow another head as quickly as one was cut off, represented an evil difficult to overcome (*see* MYTHOLOGICAL MONSTERS).

Such creatures are to be found in the mythology of every nation and were often taken over from one by another. The DRAGON (q.v.) is found in Chinese mythology as well as in countless Western stories of all ages. The Great Sphinx of Egypt stands guardian before one of the Pyramids. Its head is a portrait-statue of King Khafra, whose remains were preserved in the Pyramid, but its body is that of a lion. The Sphinx of Greek legend was represented with the head of a woman and wings on its lion body. She is said to have posed a riddle to her victims, devouring those who could not solve the riddle. The PHOENIX (q.v.) came originally into the West from Egypt. The Anglo-Saxon monster Grendel represented a type to be found widespread in Scandinavian folk-lore. He was a huge giant-like creature who raided by night a king's hall where the warriors slept. He seized and ate a number of victims and stuffed the rest into his sack and carried them off. The hero Beowulf undertook to destroy him. He tore off his arm in wrestling and pursued him to his cave under water, where he fought and destroyed him, as well as his equally horrible mother.

Other monsters owe their origin to travellers' tales. India and Ethiopia seemed very remote to the Greeks and peoples of the Near East. They were believed to be peopled by many strange creatures, both human and animal. The few travellers who reached such distant places

OEDIPUS AND THE SPHINX
The Greek hero Oedipus answered the riddle of the Sphinx, and so rescued the city of Thebes. Painting from a Greek vase, 5th century B.C. *Alinari.*

came back with stories of the strange things they had seen, mixed up with the myths and legends they had been told. Artists and writers interpreted their stories as best they could, and the results were often fantastic. So little was known about the animals of the world that the travellers' tales could not be checked by scientific observations.

In the Middle Ages new meanings were given to the fabulous creatures. Instead of studying the natural history of animals, men tried to discover in their nature or supposed habits some religious significance or moral lesson. Books about animals, called 'Bestiaries', were written, in which real animals were mixed up with the traditional creatures of Greek, Roman, and other myths and legends. Animals were not only imagined to have human characteristics, virtues, or vices, but were used to illustrate religious doctrines. For instance, it was supposed that lion cubs were born dead and remained so for three days until breathed upon by their father —this was symbolic of the Resurrection. The UNICORN (q.v.) became a symbol for Christ, its single horn representing the Gospel of Truth.

Some stories were obviously simply exaggerated accounts of real animals. The whale was described in stories as being so huge that sailors, finding one basking on the surface,

MARINERS MISTAKING A WHALE FOR AN ISLAND
Illumination from a 13th-century Bestiary. *British Mus.*

mistook it for an island. They landed on its back and started to make a fire, and only discovered that they were on a sea monster when it became restive on account of the irritation caused by the fire. The salamander is a real creature, a kind of lizard, but a series of queer ideas became connected with it until people came to believe that this animal had supernatural powers. The Greek scholar, Aristotle, wrote that the salamander 'not only walks through fire, but puts it out in doing so'. A later writer, Galen, contradicted him, but still the fire-resisting powers of the salamander were believed for centuries. The idea also arose that asbestos, which does resist fire, was salamander skin. About A.D. 700 an English bishop stated that the salamander lived in the fire, and later writers added

SALAMANDER

the idea that it lived on fire. So the fable grew until an Elizabethan author, Nashe, further elaborated and confused the story by getting what the Roman writer Pliny had said of the salamander mixed up with what he had said about the basilisk. Nashe said that the salamander 'with his very sight blasteth the apples on the trees'.

The sciapod was a man with one leg, but with a foot so huge that he could lie down and use it to shield himself from the sun. The idea of the basilisk arose from a Greek translation of the Hebrew word for serpent. People, being uncertain what kind of creature it was, imagined strange things about it. The Roman writer, Pliny, in the 1st century A.D. said that its poison was so strong that it could break stones, and that if a man on horseback killed one with a spear, the venom would pass up the spear and kill both horse and rider. A basilisk could kill a man with its look—a form of the widespread belief in the evil eye (*see* WITCHCRAFT). A 13th-century scholar called Neckam stated that very aged cocks sometimes lay an egg which is hatched by a toad and from which emerges a basilisk. This supposed connexion between the basilisk and the cock may have arisen from the ancient notion that the basilisk dies when a cock crows. In Tudor times writers, including Shakespeare, often referred to the basilisk. From the 14th century it was sometimes called the cockatrice, and Shakespeare represents the cockatrice as having the same evil powers as the basilisk. The creature was sometimes depicted with the head and wings of a cock and a serpent's tail. Nowadays the name basilisk is applied to a family of Central American lizards which have scaly crests on head, back, and tail.

COCKATRICE

With the growth of modern science, belief in fabulous creatures disappeared, but their symbolism remains: we still speak of sphinxlike or inscrutable behaviour; the lion still represents strength and nobility. Many of the fabulous creatures, such as dragons, griffins, and unicorns, survive in HERALDRY (q.v. Vol. IV).

See also FABLES; MYTHOLOGY; MYTHOLOGICAL MONSTERS; SACRED ANIMALS.

FAIRIES. Nowadays most people think of fairies as tiny, dainty beings in human form with insect-like wings. It was Shakespeare who made this idea popular. In *Romeo and Juliet* he described Queen Mab, the Queen of the Fairies, as:

In shape no bigger than an agate-stone
On the forefinger of an alderman,
Drawn with a team of little atomies
Athwart mens' noses as they lie asleep.

It is quite unusual to find such diminutive fairies mentioned in ancient tales, but one of these exceptional stories of the 'Tom Thumb' type, composed about A.D. 1100, tells of fairies so small that the close-cropped grass reached above their thighs. As a rule fairies are said to be about the size of children, though some are as big as full-grown human beings. Shakespeare thought of fairies as being of this kind too, for he describes how Falstaff was deceived by Mistress Page dressed up as a fairy (*Merry Wives of Windsor*, Act V, Scene 5).

'Fairy' is a term which includes elves, brownies, goblins, pixies, trolls, and banshees. In different places the 'little people' have different names —either local names, which have come into general use, or the names of particular kinds of fairy. The brownie, for instance, is the house fairy; the banshee is a woman fairy connected with a particular family, who announces death with loud wailing; the Irish leprechaun is a shoemaker fairy who knows where treasure is to be found.

We hear of fairy-like beings in many parts of the world. Outside Europe the Arabian fairies are the most like ours. Here we will describe the characteristics typical of most European fairies, especially British, French, German, and Norwegian.

These fairies are small people who dwell underground in ancient earthworks, inside the hills, or beneath the water of river, lake, or sea. They may live quite close to man's dwellings— sometimes they call at cottages and request the housewife not to throw water out of the door as it goes down their chimneys! Their palaces are usually very grand, but the light in them is dim, as the sun, moon, and stars are absent. Here they live a life very like that of human beings, the women spinning, sewing, and weaving. They spend a great deal of their time dancing and are excellent musicians. According to some accounts their voices are sweet and soft; but in Scandinavia their singing is said to be mournful. People listening at the fairy hills hear the music and remember the tunes, for some folksongs and lullabies are said to have been learned from the fairies. Births, weddings, and funerals occur as with human beings. The fairies are divided into clans, with a king or queen over each, and sometimes the clans fight each other or come forth to join in the wars of human beings. They tend cattle and live on a milk diet. Some say they are clothed in green, but more usually they wear red caps or jackets. A North of Ireland man once met an army of them, some in green and some in red. They are often said to have red hair. At night they come out of their underground homes and dance in the meadows—and folk may see the fairy-rings (really caused by a fungus) where they have been frolicking. In Ireland they disport themselves round clumps of rag-weed. Sometimes a human being is attracted into the dance, loses all sense of the passage of time, and is carried off to fairyland, whence, so they say, if he partakes of fairy food, he can never escape. There is a saying that if a person has a meal out of doors he should leave some of it for the wee folk.

It is very unwise to interfere with a fairy hill. In Ireland a farmer, who started ploughing a fairy hill, found that a cow died after the first day's work, another after the second day, and yet another on the third day—so he gave up and admitted that the fairies had won. A Norse farmer managed affairs more astutely. He wished to cultivate a field where a troll lived, so he arranged with him that they should share the produce, and that they should have, turn about, what grew above ground and what grew below. When it was the elf's turn to have what grew above ground the farmer grew carrots, and the next year, when it was his own turn the farmer grew corn. The troll did not object to this scheme, and so he and the farmer got on well together.

Solitary thorn bushes are connected with fairies, and it is believed that anyone who up-roots or cuts a fairy thorn will suffer for it. It was stated at the trial of Joan of Arc that the parish priest of Domremy, her native village, sang the Gospel each year near a fairy tree in order to drive the fairies away. This belief is connected with the world-wide belief in tree SPIRITS (q.v.).

It is at the witching times of Midsummer Eve and Hallowe'en that 'the gentle folk' are most

AN ELF
Sketch drawn by a Welsh peasant to describe the creature he had seen.

active. They swarm out of the fairy hills, and mortals are then in danger. In the Hebrides they say:

Hallowe'en will come, will come,
Witchcraft will be set agoing,
Fairies will be at full speed,
Running in every pass.
Avoid the road, children, children.

At such times bold men may peep into the hills and see the hoards of fairy treasure, and the fairies may be friendly enough to reveal secrets to people.

Some fairies help in the house and do good turns—though they are rather 'touchy' and leave if they are rewarded or the nature of their help is disclosed. When asked about them an Irishman once said, 'If we knew how to be neighbourly to them they would be friendly and neighbourly to us.' They dislike untidiness. 'Grant that the sweet fairies may nightly put money in your shoes and sweepe your house cleane' is an old-time good wish. Trolls, living under a Norwegian cow-shed, once complained to the dairymaid that there was too much dirt. She did nothing to improve matters, so they set her on a hayrick and departed to a meadow. They were seen moving off in a great hurry with their king riding in a magnificent coach. Fairies are apt to be mischievous. There is a German fairy who delights in setting people quarrelling but is kind enough to remove all dangerous weapons from their reach. They steal children and leave horrid changelings in place of them. As they are supposed to prefer boy babies, people in some places in Ireland, even up to the present day, sometimes try to deceive them by dressing boys in girls' clothes. When cattle suffer from disease they are said to be 'elf-struck', and those which die suddenly are 'shot-a-dead' with a 'fairy dart'. But when a child is born the fairies confer gifts on it. In spite of the tricks they play and the damage which they may do, on the whole fairies are thought to do more good than harm. In some places in Ireland, where it is believed modern inventions and ideas have driven the fairies away, the people say: 'It was better for the country before they left.'

Fairies have very definite dislikes. Above all, in common with WITCHES (q.v.) and DRAGONS (q.v.), they hate iron. When forges were built in Germany they departed. A pin fixed in a child's dress or placed in a keyhole will keep them away. Two Highlanders going home on Hallowe'en once mistook a fairy hill for a house, and as there were sounds of music and dancing they went in. One joined in the dance without thinking of danger, but his companion, being suspicious, stuck a needle into the door. He managed to escape, but when he passed that way a year later there was his friend still caper-ing. When they dragged him out he was found to be nothing but skin and bones, as he had

A KNIGHT VISITING A FAIRY CASTLE
Woodcut from Olaus Magnus, *Historia de Gentibus Septentrionalibus*, 1555

been dancing all the time. Another story tells how a Donegal man threw a nail at a fairy who had raised a great wave which threatened to overturn his boat, and managed to hit her. The little people sent for a woman to visit their under-water palace and cure the wounded fairy. The woman returned safely because she avoided touching any of their food. A fairy once offered another man a pot of gold if he would marry her, but he refused. Fairies of all kinds may be driven away by books or other objects connected with Christianity. Priests have escaped from them by throwing a prayer-book at them. When people have attempted to baptize them by throwing water over them, they have vanished with screams. The sound of bells is enough to make them leave a country-side.

It will be noticed that some fairies are good, some bad, and some have both good and bad in their character. There are honest and dishonest, helpful and harmful fairies. They may bring blessing and fertility, or disaster and death. They have more than human powers, yet they often send for human help or try to marry human beings. Their actions are rather unpredictable, and they are sometimes annoyed when people are kind to them. The practice of calling them 'the gentle people', 'the gentry', or 'the good people' is an example of the widespread custom of giving a pleasant or kindly name to a spirit or power which you fear or feel cannot be relied on to be good-natured, in order to avoid offending it. The Arabs speak of the fairy spirits or 'jinns' as 'blessed ones', for they are liable to steal what they fancy or even to spirit away human beings if they are displeased. The mixed harmful-helpful character of fairies is connected with their belonging to the realm of MAGIC (q.v.), for it is a common idea amongst people who use magic that the same spirit or power may either help or hurt.

There are similarities between fairies and the old Greek divinities and spirits of the woods and waters. Pan was a musician, and Dionysus frightened Greek sailors by transforming himself into various shapes—like Puck or Shakespeare's Ariel in *The Tempest*. The fairies' fear of anything connected with Christianity shows that they are associated with beliefs held by people before Christian times; and the German fairies' dislike of caraway seed, which was brought by the Romans, is an indication that the fairy-faith goes back to before the Roman invasion of Germany.

Some people think that the belief in fairies is, at least in part, a recollection of some early, primitive, dwarf folk who sought refuge in the hills from invaders and lived in caves and underground dwellings. They say that this explains many ideas about them, as for example that they live in prehistoric earthworks, use flint arrow-heads (which country people call 'elf-bolts'), steal children, and kidnap women to act as nurses. On the other hand, fairies are believed in where no dwarf people are known to have lived.

On the whole, though there may be some truth in the theory that fairies acquired some of their characteristics from ideas about nature spirits or real dwarfs, or from dream experiences, it is most likely that the belief in fairies arose through fear of and respect for the spirits of ancestors. In many places, including Ireland and China, food is sometimes left where the spirit of the dead person is thought to come for it. In the same way people leave food at night for the fairies. The belief that fairies steal the bodies or souls of mortals appears to be connected with widespread beliefs that the spirits of the dead sometimes drag away the living to the land of the dead. There is a story which tells how, when the Irish hero, Cuchulain, drowned one of his opponents, women in green appeared and bore the body away into a fairy mound. An old Scottish writer, one of the first to describe beliefs about fairies, says quite plainly that people believe that the souls of their forefathers live in the fairy hills, and we know that some of the earthworks in which the fairies dwell are, in fact, ancient tombs. In Scandinavia there is a belief in 'hill-people' who are partly elfish and partly human. They are said to be sad folk, and the belief in them may linger from the days when the first converts to Christianity thought that their heathen forefathers were doomed to wander, sighing, in the lower regions.

Whatever the explanation of the fairy faith may be—and the problem still puzzles learned men—it is largely due to the belief which people everywhere hold, that in the woods, meadows, and mountains there are beings in some ways like themselves, which they are seldom able to see, but which make their presence known by their activities.

See also FOLK-LORE; SPELLS AND CHARMS.

FAIRY-TALES AND TRADITIONAL TALES.

Before the times of which there is any written record people told each other stories in their huts or by their camp fires. These stories were often passed down from generation to generation, so that some of the stories now told round nursery fires have come to us from very long ago. An Italian, Giovanni Straparola, was the first European to bring out (in 1550) a book of nursery tales—which included *Puss in Boots*. In France Charles Perrault (1628–1703) collected together a number of stories such as *Cinderella* and *Little Red Riding Hood*. The translation of *The Arabian Nights* into French at the beginning of the 18th century made people realize the wonders of Eastern story-telling. The most famous of all collectors of fairy tales were the German brothers, Jacob and Wilhelm Grimm (1785–1863; 1786–1859). Nearly every book of nursery tales contains some of their stories, such as *Hansel and Gretel*, *Tom Thumb*, and *Rumpelstiltskin*. Hans Andersen, the Danish shoemaker's son (1805–75), is the next great name amongst the tellers of nursery tales, but he made up most of his stories out of his own imagination, while the brothers Grimm collected theirs from the lips of country people. Hans Andersen's tales are delightful, but the ancient traditional tales are more interesting to those who study folk-tales because they are so much older. Many other writers, such as the mathematician, 'Lewis Carroll', whose real name was Charles Dodgson (1832–98), have followed Hans Andersen's example.

The story-teller's business in the past (and still amongst primitive people) was mainly to remember stories passed on to him and to pass them on to others; whereas the modern

RUMPELSTILTSKIN

The little man stamped so hard in his fury that his leg stuck in the floor and he could not release it. Illustration by G. Cruikshank in the earliest English edition of *Grimm's Fairy Tales*, 1823

THE BABES IN THE WOOD
Woodcut illustrating a ballad, 1595. *Roxburghe Ballads, l. 284*

story-teller uses his imagination to compose new stories. Primitive people still cling to the old ways and are very particular that their tales should be told correctly. West African folk tell what are called 'Spider Stories', in which a spider, full of trickery, is the main character; but if a man makes a single slip in relating them, he is at once corrected. In Russia old story-tellers used to have contests in which they clasped hands and each recited long pieces of ancient poetry. The man whose memory failed first slackened his hold.

In islands off New Guinea the fairy-tales are 'owned' by particular people. Nobody has a right to tell a tale but the owner, though he may give it to somebody else. In these islands three kinds of tales are told: (1) stories recounting imaginary happenings such as the adventures of a man and his two daughters who sail away to another island, are captured by an ogre, and manage to escape by cutting the ogre in two while he is asleep; (2) legends or traditional tales—for instance about huge fish, visits to the land of the dead, how queer rocks got their shape, historical tales of other times, hearsay stories about things and people around them; (3) myths, which were once connected with rites and customs, but have lasted on as stories long after the ritual has died. While the first kind of tale is told round the fire for amusement, and legends are related in ordinary conversation and at any time when people are inclined to listen to them, myths have great importance in the people's lives, as they form a background of ideas justifying and strengthening their religion, customs, and way of life (*see* MYTHOLOGY). The tales told in all countries may be roughly divided into these groups. Our nursery tales belong mainly to the first two kinds. Many of them deal with supernatural beings or with people, such as WITCHES (q.v.), animals or things having supernatural powers—as, for instance, animals which speak, as in *Red Riding Hood* (*see* FABULOUS CREATURES). They are not stories about divinities or gods: the long hero tales are called epics or sagas, though we sometimes use the words 'fairy-tale' rather loosely. A fairy-tale is a story about which we don't ask, 'Is it true?' We just enjoy it.

Our old fairy-tales are full of ideas which are

based on notions and customs still to be found amongst primitive people. These folk often believe that men can turn into animals and animals into men, that magicians can fly through the air, and that good fortune can come suddenly by magical means as it did to Aladdin when he rubbed the lamp. Such ideas are common in fairy-tales, partly because they are so old, and partly because ideas that appealed to our forefathers are also interesting to us and especially to children—though sometimes what they took quite seriously we enjoy for amusement. Thus witches in fairy-tales only give us a nice creepy sensation, but two or three centuries ago they were considered really dangerous. We cannot, however, be sure because a story mentions some savage custom such as cannibalism—as in *Hansel and Gretel*—that it originated in the days of that practice, for the tale may have had old hearsay memories included in it. Some fairy-tales, such as those about some badly treated person like Cinderella who escaped from oppression, are stories which are likely to be popular amongst down-trodden people. Life becomes more bearable for them if they can delight in the mighty being outwitted or overthrown, even if only in a story.

In studying fairy-tales, scholars collect as many versions as possible and compare them with each other. It may then be seen that details in a story as it is told in one part of the world are similar to details in the story as it is told somewhere else, and it becomes clear that somehow the story has been passed on from one place to the other. There are several hundred versions of the story of Cinderella. Here and there people have added to or subtracted something from the original story, but the main theme remains the same. We now know that while the earliest Cinderella tale was recorded in writing in Europe in 1558, it was written down in China 700 years earlier. As told in China, Indo-China, and Egypt the story is most like the Russian version. What we do not know is whether the Cinderella story first went from China to Europe or from Europe to China, or whether it was first told in Egypt or India and went both East and West. By studying fairy tales scientifically we are able to solve problems of this kind and gain insight into how ideas and inventions spread in early times.

See also MYTHOLOGY; SAGAS; FOLK-LORE; FABLES.
See also Vol. V: GRIMM; HANS ANDERSEN.

ST. NICHOLAS

The saint is throwing golden balls into the house of a poor family. Italian painting of the School of Gentile da Fabriano (*c.* 1370–*c.* 1428). *Vatican, Rome*

FATHER CHRISTMAS. On 5 December, the eve of St. Nicholas's Day, it was customary in olden times for people to bestow gifts without revealing who gave them. The practice was connected with St. Nicholas—the patron saint of children and travellers—because this 4th-century Bishop of Myra in Lycia was famous for his kindness in giving presents secretly. Dutch emigrants to America kept up the custom on New Year's Eve in the name of San Nicolaas, San Klaas or Sint Klaas, as they called the saint. Eventually the gift-giving was transferred to Christmas Eve, and the names Santa Claus or Father Christmas became the most popular titles for the mysterious person who brings presents in the night. From America 'Father Christmas', as we now know him, came to England not much more than a century ago, for in 1827 an English writer referred to the tradition as 'unknown with us'.

See also FOLK-LORE.

FESTIVALS. In most religions, ancient and modern, particular times and seasons are set apart for the observance of rites or ceremonies, and these times are known as festivals. When the forces of nature were supposed to be directly controlled by supernatural powers, seed-time and harvest—spring and autumn—were the times when the most important festivals were held; and many of these ancient customs have gone on through the ages in some form or another, especially in country villages and towns. For example, on the Monday after 6 January (the Feast of the Epiphany), in some villages in Yorkshire, Lincolnshire, and elsewhere, plough boys may be seen with blackened faces, decorated with ribbons, and wearing masks and cowhides, going from house to house cracking whips, singing and dancing with swords in their hands and occasionally dragging along a plough with them. These Plough Monday ceremonies were originally held for the purpose of drawing away evil spirits from the ground where the new crops were to be sown. Like so many seasonal rites, they often included the offering of a sacrifice, and the sword dance is a reminder of this.

In nearly all seasonal festivals the struggle between life and death was enacted in order to get rid of evil (famine, disease, and death) and secure good (food, health, and wealth). When supplies were scarce and so much depended on the weather, hunger and barrenness had to be driven away by performing rites of this kind at each and every point in the year whenever a fresh crisis arose. The first festival was Plough Monday, when the earth had been prepared for the sowing of the new crops. The next festival came at the beginning of spring and coincides with our Shrovetide. For this festival a man was chosen to represent the creative spirit of nature. In order that his life might be set free to make the ground fertile, this victim had to be killed, or to undergo a pretence ritual death. This is the origin of the old English custom at this season in which a Wild Man is dressed up in the bark of trees—bark being essential to the life of a tree—and is pursued by a crowd until he falls down. Underneath his clothes he carries bladders filled with blood which burst when he falls to the ground, giving the impression that his own life is poured out on the soil to give life to the newly sown crops. The next day a straw man is made to look like the Wild Man and thrown into a pool; this represents the drowning of winter, the season of death and decay.

In some places in England the struggle between life and death at the turn of the year takes the form of contests arranged on Shrove Tuesday between two sections of the town. Examples of survivals of this type of spring festival are to be found in the great tug-of-war at Ludlow and the Shrovetide football matches at Ashbourne, Chester-le-Street, and other places. The parish

MAY FESTIVITIES
Illumination from an early 16th-century Flemish Book of Hours. *Victoria and Albert Museum*

divides into two groups, Uptowners and Downtowners, and engages in a rough and tumble with a ball in an endeavour to throw it, or prevent its being thrown, into a river outside the town. The ball in this case represents winter, which one side (the good forces) is trying to drive away and the other (the evil forces) to retain.

These seasonal rites and customs reached their climax in the Annual Festival, which was usually held about Eastertide or in the autumn. This was the centre of all the religious activities of the year, and although the details were not the same everywhere, the underlying meaning of the ceremonies did not vary very much. As in the sacred drama, a divine hero was represented as fighting with an enemy. He was killed and was brought to life again; and his victory was celebrated by a procession and a ritual marriage, to ensure the fruitfulness of the earth during the forthcoming year and the increase of men and animals. In the course of the festival, which generally occupied about a week, the story of

ROGATION SUNDAY CEREMONY
The Rector blesses the fields at Hever, Kent. *The Times*

creation was often retold or re-enacted, in the belief that by repeating in word or act the things that were done at the beginning of the world, creative energy could be released to recreate nature. At the end of the season when the crops were safely reaped, festivals were again held.

In addition to festivals connected with the sowing, growing, and reaping of the crops and the changes of the seasons, there are those associated with the dead—in Europe these are usually held in the month of November. When the days were shortening as autumn passed into winter, and men's minds were turned towards death and decay, the departed were thought to return to their old homes and haunts and assemble round the fireside. Bonfires were lighted to renew the energy of the sun, lest it should burn itself out and leave the world without its light and warmth.

Death and fire festivals are usually held at All Hallows-tide on 1 November—a day which is still very closely connected with the Feast of All Souls (2 Nov.). Guy Fawkes Day customs (5 Nov.) are also a relic of the same rites, which were given a new meaning for political reasons in the reign of James I. Some of these November rites have been transferred to Midsummer Night's eve when, as Shakespeare reminds us, the other world is very active and the sun has also reached a critical moment in its course, being at the height of its power. Others have become associated with Christmas, the Winter Festival, since the sun was thought to be reborn on 25 December. That is why at Christmas the Yule log is burned, candles and lamps are lighted, ghost stories are told in a darkened room as we sit round the fire, and many similar customs are observed, all connected with fire and the dead. A gigantic sort of fair, known as the Saturnalia, used to be held in Rome at this season: it included games, dances, the giving of presents, and such customs as the reversal of the position of servant and master, children and grown-ups. A mock king, originally representing Saturn, the god of the seed and sowing, was elected to preside over the revels. The merry side of Christmas has been largely derived from the Saturnalia—the deeper meaning being added when the Church took over the festival and made it the birthday of Christ.

This is, in fact, what happened to most of the ancient festivals when Europe adopted Christianity. Some of the old customs which could not be reconciled with Christianity were suppressed; but most of them, so long regarded as gleams of sunshine in the dull routine of everyday life, were retained, either as frolics and social festivities—such as the maypole dance, bonfires at midsummer or November, and the yule-log at Christmas—or transformed into Christian rites with new names and new meanings. It is interesting to notice that when an objectionable custom was suppressed, it tended to become a sort of 'underground movement' and to emerge, centuries later, in medieval witchcraft. The only sure way of destroying bad customs is to put something better in their place, and this is precisely what the Church did in most cases from the 4th century onwards. In the same way the Spring Festival became the chief feast in the Christian calendar, celebrated in honour of the death and resurrection of Christ, and illustrated by the earlier idea that the new life in nature broke forth from the grave of the earth at this season of the year. Similar festivals had been held at the end of March for this purpose in some of the secret mystery religions in the Roman Empire (*see* MITHRAISM). So, like Christmas, Easter was not a Christian innovation, but the development of all that had gone before with a new meaning.

Rogation-tide and Ascension Day also come from old festivals. Processions had long been held about the end of April to secure supernatural aid for the newly sown crops. The Church turned the occasion into a season of prayer for the blessing of God on the work of the farmers in the fields, and of thanksgiving for Christ's victorious return to heaven as the triumphant King from whom all blessings flow. Whitsuntide brought to an end the Spring Festival as the season of rebirth. On 15 August, when the fields were 'white to harvest', the Falling Asleep or Assumption of the Mother of God was celebrated at what was sometimes called the Feast of our Lady in Harvest. On this

occasion some of the rites that had been held in connexion with the Great Mother of pagan times were changed into acts of devotion to the Blessed Virgin. The celebration of the feast of All Hallows, All Saints Day, on 1 November, marks the beginning of the month of the dead. In this way all the main festivals of the old pagan beliefs have been taken over, and reanimated and reinterpreted in the festivals of the CHRISTIAN YEAR (q.v.).

See also RITUAL; SACRIFICE.

FIJIANS, *see* PACIFIC ISLANDERS; MELANESIANS.

FILIPINOS, *see* INDONESIANS.

FINNS. Very little is known of the history of the Finns before the 12th century. They belong to the group of Finno-Ugrian peoples whose original home was probably in the lands between the Ural Mountains and the river Volga. They show no signs of being physically related to the Mongols, nor are they originally related to the Germanic peoples or the Slavs. Their only original racial connexion appears to be with the Estonians and Magyars (Hungarians).

The Finns, who live in the country which they themselves call Suomi, but which the Swedes called Finland, have gradually developed from a collection of tribes into a single people. The main influence in this development was Swedish rule which began in the 12th century and lasted 600 years. Swedish rule was not oppressive, and it brought the Finns in contact with Western civilization. In 1809 Sweden ceded Finland to Russia, and the Tsar of Russia became Grand Duke of Finland. The country, however, kept a great deal of freedom, continued to develop its own institutions, and had its own army and parliament (called a Diet) and its own currency. In 1917, following the Russian Revolution, the Finns declared their independence, which was recognized by Soviet Russia in 1920. In 1940 Finland was attacked and defeated by Russia, and this brought them into the Second World War on the side of Germany. They lost some territory in consequence, and have come once more under Russian influence, though they still follow their own way of life.

The Finns have intermixed with the SWEDES (q.v.) so much that there does not now appear much physical difference between them. The Finns generally have very fair skin, fair hair, and blue or grey eyes. Those living to the west

ŠORTAVALA TIMBER MILL, FINLAND. *Roy. Geog. Soc.*

and south-west (the majority of the population) are taller, and they have longer shaped heads than those from the east and north-east, where there is some mixture with the LAPPS (q.v.). Their character, often described as dour, stolid, and slightly melancholic, can well be attributed to the kind of country they live in and the kind of life they lead. All around them there are the lonely rocky, forest country, the numerous and extensive lakes—Finland is known as 'the country of the thousand lakes' (in fact there are over 60,000)—and the long Polar nights. In these surroundings they earn their living by the arduous labour of cutting and preparing timber, or by the patient cultivation of a very difficult soil. Farming and forestry are often combined in one holding, the latter occupying the winter months. Those who work in factories to-day often have to ski many miles to reach them. (Incidentally, ski-ing was a Finnish invention.) Working conditions such as these require a vigorous constitution and a tenacious mind. These are qualities which have made the Finns leading athletes: not only have they produced the famous runner,

Paavo Nurmi, but they have been second in the Olympic Games six times since 1912, winning thirty-seven Olympic Gold Medals.

Although Finland is the seventh largest European country (twice the size of England and Scotland), the population numbers only about 3,887,000 (1940 census), and was only a quarter the size 100 years ago. To-day the Finns are, by ancient tradition, a nation of peasant proprietors. Large estates are the exception, about one-third of the holdings being less than 25 acres, and nearly two-thirds under 50 acres. Peasants have been able to buy their land and to bring new land under cultivation because of a system of state loans introduced in 1927.

In the rural districts the wooden houses are scattered and seldom close enough together to form streets. Each farm consists of separate wooden buildings which are often of a high architectural standard. The buildings are kept separate from each other, mainly as a safeguard against fire. The living-room is unusually large because the farmers have to be indoors a good deal during the long hours of darkness in winter.

There is always a separate building for the steam-bath, which is one of the oldest Finnish institutions and a very healthy custom.

Livestock is the principal wealth of the farm, and half the arable land is used for growing animal fodder. In normal times the Finns exported a good deal of butter, cheese, eggs, hides, and skins, which amounted to nearly a third of the total exports, almost all the rest of which is timber. Much of the work is done by machinery. Like the Scandinavian peoples, the Finns have built up an efficient co-operative system. In 1939 there were 7,000 co-operatives, with a total membership of over 900,000, which handled about 40% of the wholesale and 25% of the retail trade. They therefore play an important part in the life of the agricultural producer, and of the consumer, all over the country. A Finn (Väinö Tanner) was President of the International Co-operative Movement for many years.

The vast forests of pine, spruce, and birch are known as the 'green gold' of the Finns. Timber provides the farmer with fuel and building material, and the sale of timber forms an important part of his income. Timber constitutes two-thirds of the export trade of the country and is the basis of her principal industries. Coal being scarce, everything that can be, even trains, are run on wood. This makes the trains extremely smoky. The carriages have double windows, but even then, at every principal station, the carriages have to be aired and cleaned.

Finland is a republic with a parliament or Diet of 200 members elected for a term of three years. The President is chosen by an Electoral College of 300 members, who are elected by a direct and secret vote. The President appoints the cabinet. The first President of independent Finland was Field-Marshal Mannerheim, who retired in 1946. Finland in 1906 was the first European country to give women the right to vote. The Finns have a high standard of education: less than 1% of the population are illiterate; there are three universities, and for a small country they publish a great many books. The problem of language creates some difficulty owing to the 10% Swedish minority living in Finland. In one district Swedish is the official language. Ninety-eight per cent. of the people of Finland belong to the LUTHERAN CHURCH (q.v.), and this is the state religion.

See also Vol. III: FINLAND; Vol. IV: FINNISH AND ALLIED LANGUAGES.

FIRE WORSHIPPERS, *see* ZOROASTRIAN; PARSEE.

FLEMINGS, *see* BELGIANS.

FOLK-LORE. Folk-lore is the branch of the study of man (Anthropology) which deals with local customs, tales and traditions—for these things can be scientifically studied just like anything else. Everybody is a store-house of folk-lore, though not everybody realizes it. Often, indeed, those who have never even heard the word folk-lore have the greatest store of it, for the people with least book education commonly cherish most firmly old ideas and superstitions which have been passed on by word of mouth for generations, and it is they who carry on faithfully the customs of their parents and grandparents. Everyone has heard stories of GHOSTS, WITCHES, FAIRIES, and GIANTS (qq.v.). We all know some proverbs and have heard some old songs. We are sure to have come across such ideas as, for example, that it is lucky to see a black cat and unlucky to see a single magpie. We keep certain seasons of the year as festivals, such as Christmas, and we are familiar with the special customs connected with weddings and funerals. It would be hard to find anybody who had not played games such as Ring-a-Ring-a-Roses or Blind Man's Buff. All such things are of interest to those who study folk-lore.

People who are studying folk-lore put out of their minds the inclination to criticize as silly, childish, or old-fashioned, the old beliefs and practices they come across. They first of all try to collect accurate records of them, then see how these are connected with other ideas and customs of other places or times. By comparison with what is known of olden times or the folk-lore of other countries, they endeavour to discover how certain beliefs and practices came into being, and what purpose they serve now or used to serve in the past. Often we find that the beliefs which seem most peculiar and unreasonable, and the customs which appear least practical, are of the greatest interest and importance because they are commonly the oldest. Sometimes they were part of an ancient ritual or served a useful purpose when people's way of life was different from what it is now. So we not only learn about what people thought and did in the past but are better able to understand present customs. People often keep up customs

MODEL OF A CHINESE WAR JUNK
The painted eye can be seen on the prow
Pitt Rivers Mus.

derived from the old practice of bowing to the cross which was carried at the head of a funeral procession.

If we are interested in some traditional custom and wish to find out its origin and meaning, there are definite methods of setting about it. We discover all we can about similar customs observed by people near or far; and we often learn a good deal by noting how these vary, and by comparing the customs of primitive peoples with the survivals of similar customs amongst more civilized folk. We also try to trace back details of the custom in which we are interested in old books and records of all kinds, especially in Greece, Egypt, and other early civilizations. In these records, which include sculptures and pictures as well as written descriptions, we may find information preserved from the time when people carried out the custom more completely or remembered more correctly its original meaning. When we have collected all the knowledge possible by these two methods, we compare all the facts, and it often happens that we find that the two sets of facts taken together enable us to understand the significance of the custom. To give an example: if we ask a Chinese sailor why he paints an eye on the prow of his junk he will, perhaps, say, 'No have eye, no can see'. He has no useful information to give us, except that his forefathers did the same. But when we look around we note that eyes are painted on ships in other places, including India and islands in the Mediterranean. Greek records show that the eye appeared on Greek ships of 2,500 years ago. We eventually discover that eyes were first painted on ships in Ancient Egypt, where the sign of the god Horus was a falcon's eye. Thus it became plain that the long-forgotten reason for painting eyes on ships is because Horus, according to the myth, when on a voyage, stood on the prow of his ship looking out.

Another example of a widespread custom is the 'bull-roarer'. In Ireland boys still play with this toy, which is simply a lath of wood with notched edges, swung round on a string, thereby making a buzzing, booming noise. Old people there sometimes say it is unlucky if someone whirls a bull-roarer. To Australian natives, who use it in their INITIATION CEREMONIES (q.v.), it is much more than a toy; it is sacred and its sound is believed to be the voice of their sky god. No woman must ever be allowed to see one. There are similar rules in New Guinea and West

when they have forgotten the original reason for them, and in course of time a fresh reason gets attached to the custom. Thus, when some joker ties an old shoe to the back of the taxi taking the bride and bridegroom to the station for their honeymoon, he would say it was 'for luck', but actually a shoe is an old fertility symbol and has a place in the wedding customs of China and Palestine (*see* MARRIAGE CEREMONIES). In Ireland people explain the old custom of hunting the wren on St. Stephen's day by saying that, when James II and William III were fighting in Ireland, a wren, tapping on a drum, alarmed a sentinel of William's army, and so enabled his men to beat off a surprise attack. But this is only a comparatively recent explanation; the custom itself goes back to far earlier times. Men and boys take off their hats when a funeral passes 'in respect for the dead', as they say; but the present custom is really

Africa. The bull-roarer was also used in ceremonies in Ancient Greece. Some American Indians use it in rain-making ceremonies, and in other tribes it must be made of wood from a tree which has been struck by lightning. Its use in many parts of the world almost certainly arose from the belief that, because the noise it made was somewhat like thunder, therefore it could cause rain to fall. A great anthropologist said of it, 'This insignificant toy is perhaps the most ancient, widely spread and sacred symbol in the world'.

The practice of hanging mistletoe in the house at Christmas is an example of a custom with an ancient origin. In Norse mythology mistletoe possessed magical powers, as is shown by the story of Balder who was slain with a twig of mistletoe. In places as far apart as Italy and Japan, to carry or eat some mistletoe was supposed to help a woman to have a child. According to an old tradition in Britain, mistletoe should not be used in the decoration of churches, because it is a plant connected with heathen ideas. Ancient writers tell how the Druids cut the mistletoe with a golden knife as part of their religious ritual. The mistletoe, growing so strangely on the sacred oak-tree, was thought to be a supernatural spirit with wonderworking powers.

Thus the study of folk-lore can reveal the original and earlier meanings of many customs and superstitions by comparing them with the practices of primitive folk and tracing them into the past. English people have a distaste for horse-flesh, which really is quite good to eat, because the horse was an animal sacred to the sun in northern Europe, and so its flesh was once taboo or forbidden. The Chinese do not drink cow's milk for a similar reason. The cow was once sacred amongst the Chinese as it still is in India. Even the little custom which some people have of saying 'God bless you' when someone sneezes, reminds us of the time when

BULL-ROARER
From British New Guinea. *British Mus.*

people thought the breath was the soul, and if you sneezed you might lose your soul for good and all.

The science of folk-lore deals with myths, fairy-tales, legends and proverbs, as well as with customs and rites. Myths are not just imaginary tales which someone in the past has concocted. Often they have been originally a 'book of words' to ritual or a description of it. Fairy-tales contain many strange and ancient ideas. Local legends frequently preserve some historic fact in a veiled form. For instance, according to the legend, it had been intended to build Bisley church on a different site from that which it now occupies, but a supernatural power carried the material away every night. It has now been discovered that the place pointed out as the original site contains the remains of a Roman villa, and that materials from the villa, including an altar, were built into the church. So it is clear that the materials for the church were indeed carried away from another site, though not by any supernatural power. Thus the legend preserves some truth.

Nursery rhymes sometimes contain unexplained mysteries. The rhyme:

Snail, snail, put out your horn,
Or I'll kill your father and mother the morn,

has a version of one kind or another in England, Scotland, Germany, France, Italy, Romania, Russia, and China.

The folk-lore of games is full of interest. Many games originated as religious observances. Often they represented the struggle between summer and winter and were supposed to help the prosperity of the country-side and its inhabitants in various ways. In Morocco ball games are played with the idea of altering the weather. At Haxey in Lincolnshire, every Epiphany, a crowd of villagers join in a game in which different gangs try to carry a kind of ball of sacking or leather into their particular village. This ritual game has been played at Haxey for 600 years.

The study of folk-lore shows how closely connected are peoples' ways of thinking in different parts of the world, so that similar ideas, though with a different dress, are to be found among peoples widely separated from each other. Folk-lore studies throw light on many other aspects of man's life, such as religion, history, literature, and various arts and crafts.

See also MAGIC; MYTHOLOGY; FAIRIES.

FORTUNE TELLING, see DIVINATION.

FOSSIL MAN. In the article EVOLUTION OF MAN (q.v.) it is explained how fossils of extinct animals and plants come to be found in rocks. After being embedded in soft sands, clays, and similar substances in very remote times, they have slowly hardened into rocks over millions of years. Fossil remains, not only of many animals which are now extinct, but also of men, have been found in deposits which are comparatively recent when considered in relation to the many millions of years of the earth's existence, though they probably go back something like 600,000 years. These first men belong to types long vanished from the earth but who are the ancestors of the physical type known as Modern Man to which we, and all living men the whole world over, belong. These ancestral types of men are often very unlike Modern Man in details of bones, especially the skull and the brain-case. They show clear relationship with the higher apes which still survive, and even more with fossil apes now extinct, as might be expected if man and the apes have evolved from a common stem (see Chart, p. 166).

There are comparatively few of these early human fossils, considering that they cover a period of some 400,000 years at least. The colonies of earliest man must have been very small and widely scattered—spreading, in fact, all over the Old World from Britain to China. They are usually called after their place of finding (e.g. Peking Man or Neanderthal Man). In scientific language they are classified according to the international system of double names made up from Latin and Greek roots (e.g. *Pithecanthropus erectus*, the Erect Ape Man).

The earliest known human fossils come from east Asia, from the island of Java and from near Peking in China, and have strong resemblances to certain features in the skeletons of apes. The earliest fossil of Java Man (*Pithecanthropus erectus*) is a child's skull dating from the first interval between the successive great ICE AGES (q.v. Vol III), perhaps about 570,000 years ago. Other human remains from Java belong to the same species of primitive man and to a slightly later period—the Second Ice Age. They all represent a type of being whose skull with a low forehead has very close similarities to the apes. His limbs, however, are not really strikingly different from those of Modern Man, so that he walked upright and did not shuffle, crouched up, as a large ape does. That is why he is called 'The Erect Ape Man'.

Near Peking remains have been found in a cave-shelter of no less than forty skeletons usually known collectively as Peking Man (*Sinanthropus pekinensis*, or the Chinese Man from Peking). The most recent opinion among the experts is that these Peking men were really very closely related to those from Java—as closely as two races of Modern Man—so that a better scientific label would be *Pithecanthropus pekinensis* (the ape-man from Peking). All the remains of Peking Man (dating from between the second and third Ice Ages, about 300,000 years ago) show that there were considerable variations among this group of early men, though they all show the same ape-like characteristics in the skull and the modern type of limbs. A fact of enormous importance is that remains of hearths and fires and numbers of implements chipped out of quartz were found with the human bones in the cave. This means that Peking Man (and presumably his relatives in Java) had found a method of fire-making and could manufacture tools, and this represents a very important stage in the development of human control over nature.

From all this material we can form a picture of the Ape Man of Peking or Java as a man of rather short stature, with beetling brows, sloping forehead, powerful jaws with strong teeth, and heavy neck-muscles, but with limbs like those of Modern Man. His standard of intelligence was probably low, but he was definitely a man, not an animal. All the recent discoveries have emphasized this.

Some of the types of ape-man found in the Peking cave show similarities with the remains of another race of fossil man whose remains have been found in Europe, in Palestine, near Tashkent in Russian Turkestan, and even in Java itself (though distinct from the Ape Man of Java). The name given to this group of skulls and other bones is Neanderthal Man (*Homo*

SKULLS OF (1) PEKING MAN, (2) NEANDERTHAL MAN (LA CHAPELLE), (3) HOMO SAPIENS (CRO-MAGNON). The third skull, that of *Homo Sapiens*, has much more room for the developed brain of modern man than have either of the others

neanderthalensis), from a place in Germany where one of the discoveries was made. This name, however, covers a wide range of variations, and the fossils range in time from perhaps as early as 200,000 to 100,000 years ago, the earlier being more like Peking Man than the later. Although they are later than the Java and Peking men, the Neanderthal people show a curious line of development in which the apelike features did not die out but went on until the race became extinct, like a sort of dead end. We know a great deal about Neanderthal Man's competent flint-work. One man of this race was found to have been carefully and deliberately buried in a grave dug in the earth of a cave floor. He was provided with flint implements and the bones from a joint of beef, which must surely mean that he was expected to make use of these offerings in some form of a future life. This burial may be attributed, like the majority of Neanderthal remains, to the beginning of the last Ice Age (about 115,000 years ago). Types of humans actually or nearly those of Modern Man were evolving at the same time as Neanderthal Man. These are our real ancestors who, by reason of their better brains, proved serious competitors to the more dull-witted Neanderthalers, and so survived when Neanderthal Man died out.

Thus from the general type of primitive man evolved from Ape Man and giving rise on the one hand to Neanderthal Man, there also seems to have developed the earliest representatives of Modern Man—our own direct ancestors. The most important discovery of this type of fossil man so far made is from the gravel-pit in Kent, where a skull known as Swanscombe Man was discovered in a river gravel. He is associated with flint implements which date from the period between the second and third Ice Ages, perhaps about 300,000 years ago, and contemporary with Peking Man, though later than Java Man. There was no need for archaeologists to invent a scientific name for Swanscombe Man, because he belonged to the same species as we do ourselves—*Homo sapiens* (Wise Man), the name used by archaeologists for Modern Man.

There are two other well-known finds often mentioned in archaeological literature. The first is the Mauer Jaw, found in Germany. It is a single lower jaw, and its owner is called by anthropologists *Homo heidelbergensis*—Heidelberg Man. He is perhaps a contemporary of the Ape Men of China. He belongs to the same type as modern man, and he may be related to the main human line of ascent to Swanscombe Man. The second find is a skull discovered in 1911 in a gravel pit in Sussex. This is called Piltdown Man, or *Eoanthropus dawsonii*—Dawson's Dawn Man, so named from the discoverer. Piltdown Man puzzled archaeologists for many years, but modern scientific methods of investigating and dating bones have recently revealed the find to be a fraud. It is now known that the cranium is a fairly ancient human skull of modern type and that part of the lower jaw belongs to a modern ape.

By the middle of the final Ice Age Modern Man (*Homo sapiens*) was established as the only surviving human species. The Neanderthal groups must have become extinct by this time (about 70,000 years ago), and the types of man hereafter peopling the globe differed no more among themselves than do Chinese and Negroes and Europeans of to-day.

See also PREHISTORIC MAN; ARCHAEOLOGY; EVOLUTION.

FRANCISCAN, *see* FRIAR.

FRANKS, *see* FRENCH.

FRENCH. When the Romans conquered the land we now know as France, most of the country was inhabited by a Celtic people whom they called the Gauls. Gaul remained part of the Roman Empire until the 5th century A.D. when various Germanic peoples—the Goths, the Burgundians, and the Franks—invaded the country from the East, and of these the Franks eventually established their supremacy. During the 9th century the north of France was invaded by the Northmen, who by 911 had got possession of the country we know as Normandy. It can thus be seen that the modern French (like the English) are of very mixed racial origin in which the Latin and German elements prevail.

Towards the end of the 8th century there arose a great leader, the Frankish king CHARLEMAGNE (q.v. Vol. V), who subdued the German tribes and conquered most of the western Roman Empire. He was the first really strong and great ruler of the Franks, and he attempted to establish order and peace, and to bring culture to western Europe. But after his death there was no great leader to follow him, and his empire fell to pieces. It was not until the 16th century that France again became a strong united country with an effective central government. France is a rich and fertile land, but open to attack from land and sea, so that her history tells of almost constant war with her neighbours.

Until the last century France and Britain have been in constant rivalry. From the time of the Norman Conquest of Britain, the British kings were also barons of a part of France, and their claims on France increased, including even a claim to the throne itself. From 1337 to 1453, the period of the Hundred Years War, there was continuous warfare between the two countries. In 1429 JOAN OF ARC (q.v. Vol. V) started the campaign which finally drove the British out of all France, except for the town of Calais which remained in British hands until the 16th century. During this period France was often split by civil war between king and powerful barons, and so was unable to stand strongly against outside enemies.

From the middle of the 15th century, however, the fortunes of France improved. By the time Louis XIV came to the throne in 1643, she was a rich, united, strong, and cultured land. The riches and the power were all in the hands of the king and great lords, and the court at Versailles was the most splendid in Europe. This too was the golden age of French literature—the age of the verse tragedies of CORNEILLE and RACINE, and the comedies of MOLIÈRE (qq.v. Vol. V) in which he shocked and delighted his audiences by his mockery of all that was foolish and hypocritical in the life of the day. At the same time LA FONTAINE (q.v. Vol. V) wrote his animal fables which French children have learnt by heart ever since.

The 18th century—the age of reason—produced in France the great political philosophers, VOLTAIRE and ROUSSEAU (qq.v. Vol. V), and Montesquieu, whose ideas concerning individual liberty and social justice had a tremendous influence on the political thought of the time and undoubtedly prepared the way for the French Revolution. When the Revolution came in 1789, its motto was 'Liberty, Equality, Fraternity'. The wealth and power of the Crown and aristocracy were swept away, the King and nobles were sent to the guillotine, and a republic was formed. The country, so much weakened by internal troubles, might well have fallen victim again to conquering neighbours, had not NAPOLEON (q.v. Vol. V) become her military leader and, in 1804, her Emperor. His wars brought poverty and suffering to the people of France, and finally also defeat, culminating in the Battle of Waterloo in 1815. But the systems of justice, administration, and education which he established or strengthened did much to make the next generation of Frenchmen sturdy and prosperous.

During the 17th and 18th centuries the rivalry with Britain continued—a competition in colonial expansion which resulted in struggles for supremacy in Canada, India, and elsewhere. Since the 19th century, with the rise of Prussia and the growth of a powerful united Germany, France's greatest rival has been Germany. In 1870 France was defeated and financially crippled in the Franco-Prussian War; by 1914 she had recovered and shared in the victory of the First World War. In 1940, during the Second World War, she was occupied by Germany and did not recover her freedom till 1945.

Though it is difficult to generalize about any people, one might say, perhaps, that the most outstanding characteristics of the French people as a whole are their realism, their sense of logic,

PEASANTS AT WORK IN THE FIELDS

The whole family are at work. The boys in their typical French 'berets' are preparing leeks for the market. *Fox Photos*

and their industry. By English standards they are vivacious and passionate—like all peoples with Latin blood—and they love gaiety. Their realism sometimes tends to make them sceptical, but they are not without true depth of feeling. They are passionately devoted to their land. As a whole they are an intellectual people: whereas the great interest of the English is sport, the French are more interested in pursuits of the mind—literature or the arts, for example. It is interesting to compare the space given to these respective topics in French and English newspapers. The French appear to lack the *esprit de corps* of the English: their education does not lay the same emphasis upon it. They are a race of strong individualists. This is apparent in their politics where solidarity is often lacking and the fall of a French government a not uncommon event.

The life of the peasant before the Revolution was one of ceaseless hard work with very little comfort or pleasure. Although things have gradually become better, the generations of hardship have left their mark on the French people. The countrymen in particular will work themselves, their families, and their servants unsparingly to wrest prosperity from the land. The aim of this labour is often to amass money and property which will give them security and power among their neighbours. With this aim they sometimes become hard and avaricious, taking pleasure in little but their own success. The French recognize this spirit in themselves, and it forms the theme of many novels and plays. Fortunately the more attractive side of the same characteristic is never far to seek in France, and we find many who take pleasure in hard work for its own sake, and who are most generous and kind.

One cannot be long in France without noticing how much importance is attached to family life, and how much the head of the family is

A PARIS CAFÉ NEAR THE ARC DE TRIOMPHE. *Fox Photos*

respected. In their choice of a husband or wife, in their choice of a profession, and even in small matters of everyday life, children are expected to be obedient to their parents. The older people are proud of this tradition and try to preserve it.

The French housewife is usually most skilful and thrifty. Her interest is rather in feeding and clothing her family than in her house and garden. France has taught Europe much of its best cooking, and French cooks are employed in good hotels and restaurants all over the world. In the homes and restaurants of the middle classes the food is very varied and excellently cooked. In poorer homes, the cooking is as careful even though the food is simpler: the family usually has coffee and bread for breakfast and a good vegetable soup at supper. A great deal of bread is eaten, and everyone, even the children, drink the wine of the country with their meals. Most families have vegetables, cheese, eggs, and lettuce dressed with oil and

vinegar either at mid-day or in the evening. They very seldom have puddings of the English type, but on special occasions they eat rich cakes and sweets. French women of all classes have excellent taste in dress and are good needle-women, so that the poorest French girls look smart and well-dressed, however little they spend. In dressmaking and fashions for women Paris leads the world.

The French are very proud of their language, which is particularly rich and lucid. As a whole they speak it very well, much better than the majority of English people speak English. The school children work extremely hard and reach a high standard in the French language and literature, foreign languages, history, mathematics, and philosophy. Handicrafts and sport are not so much stressed in the schools. Public examinations are given much importance, and training for professions such as law, medicine, or teaching is long and severe. There is no national French sport apart from the Basques' traditional game of pelota, played in the Basque country of the Pyrenees.

When the ordinary Frenchman is not at work, he often likes to sit at one of the little tables on the pavement outside a café, slowly sipping coffee or some alcoholic drink and talking to a few friends. On Sundays and public holidays the villages and small towns often arrange fishing competitions. On great occasions the town band plays, and in the evening there are processions with lanterns and fireworks. 14 July (the date of the fall of the Bastille and a great national day) is the gayest of public holidays.

The religion of France is Roman Catholicism, but many Frenchmen take little share in the life of the Church. In the country, however, religious duties and ceremonies are much more conscientiously observed. This is especially true in Brittany, a part of the country which speaks its own language, and has kept its own costumes and customs more tenaciously than any other district of France.

See also Vol. III: FRANCE; Vol. IV: FRENCH AND ROMANCE LANGUAGES.

FRIAR (Latin *frater*, French *frère* = brother).

A member of one of the mendicant or begging religious orders, so called because of their emphasis on poverty, an emphasis lost by many of the prosperous monasteries of the 13th century.

There are four great orders of friars, and six lesser ones. The great orders are:

The Franciscans, or Lesser Brothers, founded by ST. FRANCIS OF ASSISI (q.v. Vol. V) 1209. They were called 'grey' because they wore the peasants' homespun.

The Dominicans, or Brothers Preachers, founded by ST. DOMINIC (q.v. Vol. V) 1215. They were called 'black' because of their black cloaks.

The Carmelites (called 'white' because of their white cloaks), founded on Mount Carmel in Palestine during the Crusades, became Mendicants in 1245.

The Augustinians, hermits who looked back to ST. AUGUSTINE (q.v. Vol. V) for inspiration, and were made into an order in 1255.

By the end of the 12th century people were beginning to criticize the worldly wealth of the Church and its lack of zeal in teaching the faith. There were many monasteries, but the monks were often quite out of touch with the lives of the ordinary people, especially those living in

A FISH MARKET IN BRITTANY
Lubinski

towns. Sects were arising in opposition to the Church, and they often taught false doctrines. It was to meet this situation that Francis and Dominic founded their orders.

Francis was the son of a rich cloth merchant of Assisi in Italy. He had lived a gay life until a grave illness caused him to think more seriously. He gave up his possessions and, like the Apostles, went out without money, shoes, or staff. His followers, 'the Lesser Brothers', clad in a dark-grey habit and bare-foot, preached to the people, helped the poor and sick, worked with the peasants, and spent much time in prayer. A small band of Franciscans came over to England in 1224, where they soon set up friaries. Over each friary ruled the Father Guardian. The friaries were grouped together into provinces, over each of which ruled a Minister. Franciscans went out as missionaries, not only in Europe but also to North Africa and to Asia. They wrote prayer books in the language of the people and translated parts of the Gospels.

Franciscan

Dominican

Carmelite

HABITS OF FRIARS

(The Bible and prayer books of the Western Church had hitherto been only in Latin.) They also wrote much religious poetry. Here were men really preaching and living Christianity among the poor. Before long, religious houses for women were founded by Saint Clare, the friend of Francis. These belonged to the order of Franciscan Minoresses.

Dominic was a Spaniard. Unlike Francis, he was studious and a priest. He was alarmed at the ordinary people's ignorance of the Church's teaching, and so he founded his order of preachers, the Dominicans, to study and to teach. Dominicans from the start were learned men. Soon they were not only winning men from false teaching, but influencing the great centres of learning, Rome, Bologna, Paris. The greatest medieval theologian, THOMAS AQUINAS (q.v. Vol. V) (d. 1274) was a Dominican.

These orders were not shut off from the world like the monks, but wandered abroad in it. As Matthew Paris, a Benedictine monk, said of the friars: 'They have the world for their cell and the ocean for their cloister.' As new routes across the world were opened, the friars sent out missionaries. A Franciscan mission was founded as far afield as China by 1294.

The Friars continued in later centuries as preachers and teachers, servants of mankind in works of mercy, and one of the chief agents of the Church's missionary expansion (see MISSIONARY WORK).

See also CHRISTIAN CHURCH; MONK.

FRIENDS, see QUAKERS.

FUNERAL CEREMONIES, see DEATH CEREMONIES.

G

GAELS, *see* IRISH; SCOTS.

GAULS, *see* FRENCH.

GAUTAMA, *see* BUDDHISM. *See also* Vol. V: GAUTAMA.

GERMANS. These are the largest group of people of central Europe. Their homeland lies between the Slav territories of eastern Europe and those of the Latin nations, the French and the Italians, to the west and south. On the north it is bounded by the Baltic and North Seas and by Denmark.

The Germans, like other European groups, are of mixed racial origin. The typical German is taller, more fair-haired, and more round-headed than his neighbours, but there are many exceptions. The early inhabitants of south Germany and Austria were of Alpine stock, and their descendants are smaller and darker than the Germans of the north. Along the Polish–Lithuanian borderlands considerable intermarriage has taken place through the centuries. The most useful guide to German nationality is not race, but language. There are about 80 million Europeans whose mother-tongue is German. Some 7 million of these are AUSTRIANS (q.v.) who claim a separate nationality. At the end of 1945 about $65\frac{1}{2}$ million were living within the new frontiers of Germany; the remainder were in eastern Europe.

The earliest accounts we have of the Germanic, or Teutonic, peoples come from Roman times. Julius Caesar described their strength and bravery in battle, and the historian, Tacitus, praised the simplicity and honesty of their tribal customs. The Roman legionaries invaded the borders

THE PRUSSIAN EAGLE

of their territory, establishing a military frontier along the Rhine and the Danube; but the tribes living beyond these rivers were never subjected to Roman rule.

From Roman days right up until relatively recent times, there was no united German nation. When the primitive tribal divisions disappeared, they were succeeded by small kingdoms, principalities, bishoprics, free cities, and so on, each with its own separate government. At the end of the 8th century CHARLEMAGNE (q.v. Vol. V) managed to unite most of central and western Europe under his rule, but this Empire fell to pieces soon after his death. From time to time throughout the Middle Ages ambitious rulers tried to unify central Europe in the HOLY ROMAN EMPIRE (q.v.), but without lasting success.

In the 16th century the LUTHERANS (q.v.)—the German Protestant movement led by MARTIN LUTHER (q.v. Vol. V)—broke away from the Catholic Church. The German people were about evenly divided between the old and new religions, and there followed a terrible civil war—the Thirty Years War (1618–48)—conducted with great persecution and bitterness. The war did not establish religious unity. North Germany became firmly Protestant, while the south and west remained Roman Catholic—a distinction which is roughly true to-day.

The leadership in the struggle for unity was taken by the small north German kingdom of Prussia. From the 17th century onwards Prussia was served by an exceptionally able line of rulers, the most outstanding of whom was FREDERICK THE GREAT (q.v. Vol. V), who established toleration of race and religion, a fair and incorruptible system of justice, and a good educational system. Her great weakness was that all this was brought about by royal dictatorship and not by the will of the people. In 1741 Prussia, under Frederick the Great, fought the first of a long series of wars which were eventually to establish her ascendancy in Europe. Many Germans, however, were reluctant to accept unity at the price of Prussian military domination, and an attempt was made to create a liberal Germany by co-operation among the smaller states and peoples. But the influence of

Prussian efficiency was too strong. The great Prussian Chancellor, BISMARCK (q.v. Vol. V), finally achieved German unity after bringing Prussia triumphantly through three wars—against Denmark in 1864, Austria in 1866, and France in 1870–1. King William of Prussia was crowned first German Emperor at Versailles in 1871. Only the Austrian territories remained outside this new German Empire.

It helps to explain the almost hysterical emphasis which modern Germans have put upon their national unity if we remember that this nationhood, which Englishmen or Frenchmen have taken for granted for centuries, was achieved in Germany only at the end of the 19th century.

When William II came to the throne in 1888, Germany began building a navy and threatening to expand her overseas colonies. It was this challenge to the British Empire which was one of the causes of the First World War of 1914–18 in which all the great Powers were involved. In 1918 Germany was defeated, stripped of her colonies, partially occupied, and ordered to pay reparation to the victorious Allies. In the hour of defeat the German people revolted against the Prussian system of government and set up a republic.

From 1918 to 1933 the Germans endeavoured to establish a parliamentary democracy.

THE MARKET-PLACE, EISENACH, THURINGIA

Unfortunately the republic, inexperienced in this form of government, faced continual economic difficulties. These were partly caused by the reparation payments to the Allies, and partly by the great economic depression and widespread unemployment which in the 1930's affected most countries of the world to a greater or lesser degree. In 1933 the Nazi Party, under the leadership of ADOLF HITLER (q.v. Vol. V), introduced an openly anti-democratic programme.

Hitler's ambition was the same as the Emperor William II's—to increase the power and territories of the German nation. To do this he believed that the country must be really united from within, and he achieved unity by the ruthless suppression of all criticism of the government. He taught the German people to consider themselves a master race, superior to all others, whose destiny it was to dominate Europe. Racial hatred was stirred up, particularly against the Jews whom the Nazis tried to exterminate by torture and massacre. Propaganda in schools, in literature, in radio, and in the strictly censored press, was used to instil Nazi ideas. In 1938 Germany invaded Austria and Czechoslovakia, and in 1939 attacked Poland. This started the Second World War which in course of time involved almost every country. Germany had prepared for war with such thoroughness that it took the United Nations six years to defeat her. After the war the task remained of eradicating Nazi teaching from the minds of the people.

The character of the German people presents some curious contrasts. Many English people find it easier in normal times to fit in with the German way of life than with, for instance, that of the French. The individual German is usually polite and open with foreigners; he is a good linguist, likes travelling, and enjoys discussing other countries. In business he is honest and reliable. As a workman, he is exceptionally industrious and efficient. As a family man, he is homely, fond of children and of animals. German women, who are less independent and more respectful of male leadership than the average English woman, are domesticated and hospitable. The German word *Hausfrau* is used in England to describe a woman whose interest is centred in her home and who is proficient in the arts of home-making. Most Germans eat *Schwarzbrot* (black bread), and the *Wurst*

A BEER HALL IN BAVARIA. *D. P. Wolff, Frankfurt a. M.*

(sausage) is rarely absent in their daily diet. The Germans drink large quantities of beer, and the *Biergarten*, like the English public house, plays an important part in their social life. As a nation the Germans are well-educated, somewhat sentimental, and almost universally fond of music. Many of the greatest musicians, such as BEETHOVEN, BACH, MOZART, and SCHUMANN (qq.v. Vol. V.), were German or Austrian.

Unfortunately, in spite of these good qualities, history shows that Germans have a greater capacity than most peoples for turning a blind eye to cruelty and persecution carried on in their midst. They also tend to enjoy military display and uniforms and to applaud the successful use of force. A study of their history shows how subservience to authority has become deeply engrained in the modern German character. Luther taught unquestioning obedience to political rulers; and from Frederick the Great down to Bismarck and William II, Prussian power was founded on rigid, detailed control from above. Under Hitler the most dangerous characteristics of the German people were deliberately glorified and exploited.

A most important problem for the future peace of Europe is to ensure that the better qualities of the German people, their industry, honesty, appreciation of education, and love of music, should develop and be used for the common good, while the uglier qualities disappear.

See also Vol. III: GERMANY; Vol. IV: GERMANIC LANGUAGES.

GHETTO. Members of the same race living in a foreign country tend to herd together, and to reside in the same locality. This is specially convenient if they happen to need the same kind of food, not easily obtainable elsewhere, or if they possess the same religious and social habits. They are bound together also by their language. Thus there is a block of streets in Marseilles entirely inhabited, not by French people, but by Arabs in blankets and red fezes; Soho in London is noted for its Italian quarter, and there is the Irish Roman Catholic quarter in

Liverpool and Chinatown in San Francisco. It is not surprising to find that so distinctive a people as the Jews have always tended to form separate communities wherever they live.

'Ghetto' is the name given to the area of a town inhabited by Jews. The word is short for *borghetto*, an Italian word meaning 'a little town'. So far as is known, it was not used until the

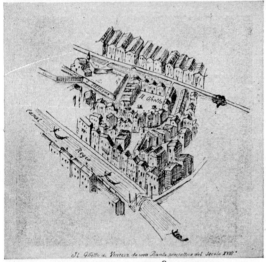

VENICE GHETTO IN THE 18TH CENTURY
The houses form a wall enclosing the ghetto and shutting it off from the rest of the city

year 1611, and then at first only in Italy; but now it applies to any Jews' quarter in any city. The institution existed before the name, although the degree and object of living apart has varied according to time and place. It was at first a convenient arrangement freely accepted by the Jews, and later even a favour granted by well-meaning rulers who respected the claim of the Jews to seclusion. Thus one German bishop, who founded one of the first ghettos in Germany, did it, as he said, 'to enhance the town's renown'; and he had it surrounded with a wall 'to protect the Jews against the impertinence of the mob'. The same arrangement is said to have been made at Prague by a king of Bohemia, and the Jews were given keys so that they could lock the gates of the ghetto and live in security and peace. Elsewhere, in parts of England for example, the Jews lived where they pleased.

Right through history the Jews have been subjected to waves of persecution. They often became unpopular simply because of their money-lending activities. During the time of the Crusades hostility against them increased because they were said to be the 'descendants of the murderers of Christ'. For this reason the followers of Peter the Hermit ravaged the Jews' quarters in central Europe. The ghettos became objects of contempt and loathing, and were attacked and broken into. Jews were compelled to wear a distinguishing dress or badge, they suffered civil disabilities and loss of liberty, and were treated as outcasts from society. Many Jewish persecutions and massacres took place in the 13th and 14th centuries. After 1290 no Jews were officially allowed to live in England until the time of Cromwell, and there were similar expulsions of Jews from France in 1394, and from Spain in 1492. At the time of the Black Death the unpopularity of the Jews increased still further. Their better sanitary laws and their sober habits made them less liable to infection than their Gentile neighbours, who became jealous, and even accused them of causing the plague and of poisoning wells. Thousands of Jews were exterminated, especially by the fanatical order of flagellant friars. The one country which gave them a haven of retreat was Poland, and this is why the ghettos of eastern Europe have been so large.

During and after the First World War a great many of the Polish Jews moved into Germany, thereby greatly increasing the Jewish element in that country. The Germans feared and suspected the Jews because of their skill in commerce and finance, and the Nazi Government played on this fear as a means of arousing a national spirit based on racialism. There followed the Nazi anti-Jewish agitation and massacres. The Zionist movement has withdrawn many Jews from the eastern European ghettos to Palestine, where they have settled under British mandate, and since 1948 to the independent state of Israel. Meanwhile, although they can hardly be called ghettos in the strict sense of the term, new Jewish quarters have developed in such cities as Manchester and New York, creating fresh problems. In Russia, under Soviet rule, the walls of the ghettos have fallen, and liberty for travel and residence has been granted to all Jews.

See also JUDAISM; JEWS.

GHOSTS. The supposed appearance on earth of spirits of dead people. The belief in ghosts is very ancient, probably far older than the belief in Heaven and Hell. Many peoples have believed that on one day of the year the dead come back to visit their old homes. In Europe this day is known as the Feast of All Souls. At all times of which we have knowledge certain people have claimed to possess special powers enabling them to see or communicate with spirits, and even to make these visible or audible to others. Thus in the Bible story Saul employed the witch of Endor to conjure up the ghost of Samuel before him, and, to-day, many believers in SPIRITUALISM (q.v.) use the services of 'mediums' who, they think, are able to put them in touch with the spirits of the dead. But the best-known type of ghost is that which appears uninvited, perhaps in some 'haunt' of its lifetime, perhaps on a certain anniversary, perhaps at the time of its owner's death many miles away from the relative or close friend who perceives it.

Most people wish so strongly for life after death that they tend to accept eagerly and not too critically any evidence suggesting that it will be fulfilled. Also, people think that the possession of supernatural powers is a sign of superiority, and, indeed, many mediums find such powers can be very profitable. We may be inclined to think, therefore, that all ghostly apparitions are due either to imagination or deliberate fraud. But in recent years attempts have been made to explore ghostly phenomena by strict scientific methods, and the results so far achieved suggest that they can not be dismissed quite so lightly. Up to the present no ghost has been photographed or had its voice recorded under conditions strict enough to satisfy unbiased scientists of its genuineness. This suggests at least that the visions have no existence outside the minds of the observers. The reality of a ghost might be proved if it should impart to a living person some piece of information which could only have been known by the dead person. But an absolutely indisputable case of this has never been recorded, although some extraordinarily interesting cases have been investigated. The one possible exception lies in the class of death-bed apparitions— but here the person appearing in ghostly form is actually still alive, though perhaps at the very point of death, so that the explanation may rest in telepathy.

In 1889 a committee of the International Congress of Experimental Psychology undertook an inquiry, in the course of which some 17,000 people were asked if they had ever had any supernatural experience. Of these almost one in ten answered 'Yes', about two-thirds of them having 'seen something'. Three hundred and eighty-one people had seen the ghost of a human being—sixty-five of these having appeared within a few hours of the death of their owners. After making generous allowance for errors and exaggerations, the committee came to the conclusion that about one ghost out of every forty-three seen was a death-bed apparition, whereas the normal chance of the vision coinciding with the time of death would be only one in 19,000. As in no fully authenticated instance did the vision appear after death, the most probable explanation of such cases is to be found in 'telepathy', or the power of one brain or mind to communicate with another through some channel other than the usual sense organs. Telepathy is an easier subject to investigate under strict laboratory conditions than apparitions of the dead, which usually require seances in darkened rooms and various other paraphernalia making exact observation impossible. The proofs of the existence of telepathy are so numerous and unanswerable that they must now be accepted—as indeed they are by many eminent scientists who are far from being spiritualists or even, in many cases, convinced of human survival after death.

Telepathy, then, furnishes a satisfactory explanation of death-bed apparitions, being itself 'supernatural' only to the extent that science does not yet know a great deal about it. It may very possibly be at any rate partly the explanation for all ghosts which are not mere hallucinations in the mind of the beholder. If we sleep in a room which we think to be haunted, our imagination may conjure up the ghost in some form perceptible to our senses; if we sleep there not knowing its reputation, our brain may still receive by telepathy impressions from someone not so ignorant—and the result be the same. There are, however, instances less easy to explain by telepathy, as, for instance, of apparitions seen in lonely places or in empty houses when no one would be expected to be present to see them; but the possible ramifications of telepathy are so wide and so unexplored that it is wise to withhold judgement in such cases, even in that small proportion of them which seem to be unassailably authentic. Almost nothing is known of the nature of thought itself: it is accompanied by electric disturbances in the physical brain—it may or may not itself be electrical in origin. If it is, one brain may, under certain conditions, pick up waves of thought from another, as a wireless set picks up the sound of an electric lift or of a flash of lightning. It is not beyond possibility that in places where intense emotion has been experienced, as at the scene of a murder, some sort of static charge of thought-electricity may have been deposited, capable at times of influencing the minds of people visiting the place even years later. But these are mere speculations.

That people see ghosts we need not doubt; that the ghosts have any existence outside the minds of living persons still remains unproved and, on the whole, unlikely. A whole host of so-called 'supernatural' phenomena, many of them undoubtedly genuine, await scientific investigation. We should resist the temptation to see proof of the return of the spirits of the dead in the mere occurrence of events which cannot at present be given a natural explanation. Whatever other views we may hold on the after-life, we are safe, so far as modern scientific knowledge can guide us, in believing that the dead do not return to this earth.

GIANTS. The myths and legends of peoples all over the world tell of the doings of giants. There are many stories in Greek mythology of fights between giants and gods. The giants were supposed to be the sons of Uranus (Heaven) and Ge (Earth), so they were only half-human. They fought against the gods, were defeated, and were imprisoned under the earth. One of them, Enceladus, was held down by Mount Etna whose volcanic eruptions were caused by the giant. In order to invade Heaven, two giants—the brothers, Otos and Ephialtes—piled mountains on top of Mount Olympus. They were destroyed by Zeus, the king of the gods. The Titans, six sons and six daughters of Uranus and Ge, also attacked the gods, who were helped by three friendly giant-like monsters, Briareos, Kottos, and Gyes, who each had a hundred hands and fifty heads (*see* MYTHOLOGICAL MONSTERS).

The size of these legendary giants varies a great deal. Some of them are said to have been not a great deal taller than ordinary men, but others are thought of as gigantic beings with powers more like gods than men. Goliath, who was slain by David with a stone from his sling,

was 9 ft. 6 in. in height (1 Sam. xvii). People nearly always exaggerate when they tell of giants or dwarfs, making giants rather taller and dwarfs somewhat smaller than their actual height, so perhaps those who told the story of the fight between these two champions added something to Goliath's height. Once your enemy is defeated it is pleasant to think how powerful he was. In Scottish and Irish folk-lore giants are described as very mighty, but local heroes are nearly always able to vanquish them.

There is no evidence that men were ever much higher than they now are. The tallest man of whom we have definite records—a Russian called Machnow—measured 9 ft. 3 in. He came to London in 1905 when he was twenty-three years old. An Englishman, John Middleton, born in Lancashire about 1572, is said to have reached the same height. There is a portrait of him in Brasenose College, Oxford. Ireland has produced a number of giants, including Cornelius Magrath (7 ft. 5 in.); Charles O'Brien (8 ft. 4 in.), whose skeleton may still be seen in the Royal College of Surgeons in London; and Patrick Cotler (8 ft 7 in.), who died in 1802. Cotler used to go for walks at night in order to avoid attracting too much attention. One night, at Bath, a watchman was frightened nearly out of his wits when he saw this man reach up to a street-lamp, lift off the cover and light his pipe at it. A Russian girl, Elizabeth Lyska, who came to London in 1889 when she was twelve years old, was already 6 ft. 8 in. The average height of a tribe in Patagonia in South America is 5 ft. 10–11 in., though individuals may be several inches taller. But the early Spanish travellers who saw these people, reported that their own heads hardly reached the Patagonians' waists. This sort of exaggerated traveller's tale is the origin, no doubt, of many reputed giants.

Most real giants, like the giants of fairy-tales, are rather stupid. Growth is controlled by the pituitary gland under the base of the brain. If the gland becomes enlarged during childhood, the boy or girl grows unusually big; if it is damaged, he or she becomes a dwarf. The abnormality of the gland is believed to cause both the growth and the stupidity.

People came to believe in giants, not only through exaggerated stories of unusually big men, but also because of things found in the countryside, which they supposed to be the work

GOG AND MAGOG
Statues of London's giants which take part every year in the Lord Mayor's Show. *The Times*

of giants. In many countries there are great stone monuments, such as circles of immense blocks of stone, built by people long forgotten. STONEHENGE (q.v.), which used to be called 'The Giants' Dance', is the most famous example in England. The people living in the neighbourhood of such monuments very often tell stories of how giants built them. It is also likely that people's experience of storms and earthquakes encouraged the belief that enormous giants caused these disturbances. Sometimes, when bones of some large animal have been dug up, people have jumped to the conclusion that they were human bones. Saint Augustine once saw on the sea-shore what he took to be a human tooth, a hundred times larger than any normal tooth. This he felt sure, was evidence of the existence of the giants mentioned in the Old Testament (Gen. vi. 4). Some large bones found in England were taken for giant's bones until the scientist, Sir Hans Sloane (one of the founders of the British Museum) examined them and

proved them to belong to the backbone of a whale. Even natural objects, if they are large and odd looking, have been supposed to be the work of giants. Near Portrush, in the north of Ireland, there are numbers of five-sided and six-sided columns of volcanic rock, created by the cooling of lava. This strange place is called 'The Giant's Causeway', and legend relates that it was built by the Irish giant Finn MacCool, to bridge the channel between Ireland and Scotland. In England and Germany there are places where, according to the legends, two giants played games with each other, throwing bowls or a hammer several miles across a valley; and at Turton, in Lancashire, strange grooves in a rock are said to have been made by a giant's fingers when he used it as a plaything.

While some of these huge giants, connected with immense boulders and queer features in the landscape, are supposed to have been playful, others belonging to mythology are described as savage cannibals—like the one-eyed monster Polyphemus who captured Ulysses and his men. This belief in barbarous and wicked giants may be due to the natural idea that what is huge is likely to be dangerous. However these notions arose of monsters outwitted and defeated by men, we may be sure the stories were told, generation after generation, because it gave people a kind of gruesome pleasure to think of mighty beings who could yet be overcome by men. The tale of Jack the Giantkiller is an example of this type of story, and John Bunyan made good use of the idea when, in Part II of *Pilgrim's Progress*, he described Mr. Great-heart killing Giant Maul who had sought to prevent him from continuing with Christian's wife and family, on their pilgrimage to the Heavenly City.

JOHN MIDDLETON, THE 'CHILDE OF HALE'
This giant, who lived from *c*. 1572 to 1623 was 9 ft. 3 in. tall. *By courtesy of Brasenose College, Oxford*

Various cities have their own giants. Thus Gog and Magog are connected with London, and giants support the coat of arms of Lucerne. It is said that they owe their presence there to the fact that a doctor, who examined some animal bones which were discovered near Basle in 1577, decided that they belonged to a giant about 16 feet in height. In London giants used to walk in the Lord Mayor's Show. Like the giants which sometimes appear at pantomimes, they were disguised men walking on tall stilts. There is a record of such giants appearing in the May games in St. Martin's-in-the-Fields, London, in 1555.

See also FOLK-LORE; FABULOUS CREATURES.

GOBLINS, *see* ELVES.

GOD. The word 'God' is used to describe any divine being who is given religious worship, whatever form or shape he may take, be it that of a man, an animal, a mysterious mountain, tree, or stone, or the One Supreme Creator and Ruler of all things. It is also used sometimes to mean a divine principle running through everything in the world. This shows that there are and have been many ways of thinking about the idea of God, and these have changed and developed as people's notions about things in general have altered. Thus, to people living under primitive conditions God seems to be the highest, wisest, and most powerful Person or Thing of which they can conceive, and so they make 'God' a great chief in the sky or some very wonderful animal or natural object. At the other end of the scale people who think of God as the ground and support of the entire universe realize that no bodily shape or form could adequately describe Him. Nevertheless, people have to try to form some picture or idea in their minds, whether it be concrete or abstract, to make the notion of God intelligible to them. Thus, for example, when the Greeks pictured a god called Atlas holding the pillars on which the universe rested, this was only a picturesque way of describing a very profound truth, namely, that God who is perfect and complete in Himself 'holds up', so to speak, everything that exists.

All these various ideas about God fall roughly into three main divisions which are commonly classified as follows: (*a*) polytheism, or the belief in more than one god; (*b*) monotheism, or the belief in only one God; (*c*) pantheism, or the belief that everything is God.

(*a*) POLYTHEISM. In many parts of the world, especially in the great ancient civilizations like those of Egypt, Babylonia, Greece, and Rome, and among many primitive races it has been commonly supposed that there is a multitude of gods and spirits inhabiting natural and mysterious objects like the sun, moon, and stars, running water, peculiar trees, stones, and animals, and sacred mountains. These may be either friendly or harmful to man, but, for good or ill, they are thought to be responsible for making things behave as they do. When the unseen powers show themselves in terrifying events and are thought to be the cause of misfortune, they are propitiated (*see* SACRIFICE). But often they are imagined to be bearers of good gifts and the authors of all that man needs for his well-being—food, children, rain, sunshine, &c. As such they are often looked upon as glorified mortals who live in the sky or on the top of a mountain under a Supreme Being or Powerful Chief. Thus in Scandinavia, Odin, the highest of the Norse gods, was regarded as the all-wise ruler of heaven and earth who lived in his palace in the sky. He was also the god of war and, therefore, he had his seat in the warrior's paradise, Valhalla (*see* HEAVEN). As the source of all life in the world, he had many different names and numerous wives and children. His queen, Frigga, was the mother of the mildest, best, and most cunning of all the gods, Balder the Beautiful. Balder apparently kept his soul safely stored away in the mistletoe, but when this secret was discovered, he was killed by a blow from a branch of this plant sacred to him. His death brought terrible misfortune on gods and men and was believed to hasten the day when the whole earth would be destroyed, because he was the god who gave life and prosperity to everything (*see* NORSE MYTHS).

In Greece the principal god was Zeus, a name that may originally have meant the 'sky'. He too was the source of all life and light, the god of thunder and lightning and of rain. All mountain-peaks were sacred to him, but his chief home was Mount Olympus in Thessaly, where he ruled over eight other gods as their overlord. There they feasted, drank, played music, and quarrelled with one another, just like the old warrior chieftains and princes on whom they were modelled. Therefore, Zeus and his companions (collectively called the

ZEUS
He is preparing to throw a thunderbolt. Bronze statue, *c.* 470–460 B.C. *Ashmolean Mus.*

Olympian gods) were gods made in the image and likeness of men (*see* GODS OF GREECE AND ROME).

In the religion of Ancient Rome Zeus had his counterpart in Jupiter who was a personification of the sun and the sky. He controlled the weather, manifested his power in thunder, lightning, and rain, and came to earth in the form of a thunderbolt. Both Jupiter and Mars looked after the crops, especially the vine, but neither of them was so strongly associated with the fertility of vegetation as Osiris in Egypt. In no country has the cultivation of the soil seemed to be more miraculous and supernatural in its origins than on the banks of the Nile, where the life-giving waters annually turn desert into very fertile land. Egypt, in fact, has been described as 'the gift of the Nile', and the god believed to be responsible for all this was called Osiris. It is suggested that he was really the first man who discovered the secret of growing barley, or of cutting the canals through which the waters of the Nile were carried to the fields. Therefore, the Egyptians looked to him for sustenance on earth and, since he was also the judge of the dead, for a joyful resurrection hereafter (*see* EGYPTIAN MYTHS).

In Egypt each district had its own special local god or gods; but when Upper and Lower Egypt became a single kingdom, the god of the capital of the kings—Heliopolis, near Cairo— rose to great importance and was worshipped all over the country. In this way the Sun-god, Re, worshipped at Heliopolis, became widely recognized as the creator of the universe and the source of all life. Around him were grouped eight other gods; and these nine deities of Helio- polis collectively made up the most important of the Egyptian assembly of gods. But in early times in Egypt there were also other gods who were thought by their respective worshippers to have created the world, such, for instance, as Ptah of Memphis. In the end, however, the worship of Osiris eclipsed that of the Heliopoli- tan Sun-god, Re. One of the Pharaohs, Akhna- ten (about 1375 B.C.), attempted to bring Egypt to recognize one supreme and only creator and father of mankind—the Sun-god, Aten. When Akhnaten died, however, the power of Aten declined, and Egypt returned to her polytheistic beliefs in many gods.

(*b*) MONOTHEISM. In early times it was only among the Jews, Moslems, and Christians that the entire universe was thought to be the crea- tion of a single deity controlling all things in heaven and earth. In Persia, about the 7th century B.C., Zoroaster, or Zarathustra, taught that over and above all the good and evil spirits and gods, there was one supreme Creator of the universe, called Ahura Mazdah, the all-wise, all-powerful, and wholly good God. But soon after his death this idea was lost, and his fol- lowers divided up good and evil into two groups of gods, with their respective spiritual armies, fighting against each other. His attempt at monotheism was as temporary as that of Akhna- ton in Egypt (*see* ZOROASTRIAN).

The great prophets in Israel declared that JEHOVAH (q.v.), the god of Israel, was the one and only God who has created the earth, and orders everything that happens in the world to His own ends and purposes, however long these may take to work out. They thought that Jeho- vah's chief interest was with His own nation, but, nevertheless, they believed that through the Jews all mankind was to come to a knowledge of Him and worship Him alone in His temple at Jerusalem. They believed that He was guiding the ups and downs of their history to this goal, and then at last they would fulfil the purpose for which He had chosen them and separated them from the rest of the nations of the earth (*see* JUDAISM).

From the Jews CHRISTIANITY (q.v.) took over the belief in the unity of God; but since Chris- tians believed that Jesus was the human embodi- ment of God in the relation of Son to Father, and that the work He began was carried on on earth by the divine Spirit, Christian mono- theism was rather different from that of Judaism or Zoroastrianism. God is one; but He was manifested in Christ, and is active in the world and in human beings in the Holy Spirit. This God is thought to be a Trinity, i.e. that He exists as 'three Persons' in one God. Moreover, He is thought of not only as a Ruler but also as the God of love, who not only rules His people with perfect wisdom and justice, but is eternally mer- ciful towards them. This was a new conception.

A third form of monotheism arose in Arabia in the 7th century A.D., when Mohammed, the prophet of ISLAM (q.v.), proclaimed that there is no god but Allah, 'the strong' or 'mighty one'. As the Arabs were polytheists when Mohammed began his mission, he had to insist on the abso- lute unity of the one true God. So high and unique is Allah, he declared, that He is quite separate and apart from man, whose only duty is to submit to His commands. Nevertheless, the Arabs think that God is 'merciful' and 'compassionate', although man in His hands is like a pawn in a game of chess.

(*c*) PANTHEISM. In India, among followers of HINDUISM (q.v.), polytheism has moved in a different direction. In very early times a female vegetation goddess was worshipped, together with sacred trees, horned cattle, and snake- spirits, and a god of vegetation later known as Shiva. Then came the Aryan invaders from the north (*see* INDIAN ANCIENT CIVILIZATION), who brought with them a whole collection of nature gods not unlike those of the Vikings of Scandina- via. The greatest was Brahma, a rather remote god who was less popular than the fair-haired and bearded Indra. Indra rode into battle on a great chariot, wielding the thunderbolt as his weapon. He represented the energy dis- played in the thunderstorm, and was a god of the air, just as Agni was the god of fire, the hearth, and the altar. Then there was Varuna, representing the heavens that stretch across the

THE HOLY TRINITY WITH SAINTS
Painting by Pesellino (1422–57). *National Gal.*

sky. He became a universal monarch, king of gods and men, and established the heaven and the earth, made the sun to shine, kept the moon and the stars in their courses and gave to nature and mankind their law, which he upheld. As he was all-seeing, he guarded the moral order of right and wrong and, like Jehovah, he punished evil and rewarded good.

Later these gods were brought together and conceived of as a single divine principle, controlling the whole of nature and man, so that the idea of God became that of an indwelling power that orders and animates all things—Brahma—so that everything is God (Brahma) and God is everything (*see* BUDDHISM). As Brahma comprehends all existence, so in every individual there is an invisible part, the 'self' or 'spirit', which is identical with the Great Self of the universe (Brahma). Thus God ceases to be regarded as a 'person' but is an impersonal principle pervading all things. In practice, however, most Hindus have continued to worship the earlier gods, such as Vishnu, the preserver, and Shiva the destroyer, of life, while Brahma has remained the remote Absolute, so great that He (or It) is beyond all understanding and yet is in everything.

See also RELIGION; THEISM.

GODS OF GREECE AND ROME. 1. GREEK
GODS. These began by being merely forces of nature thought of by the Greeks as personal and divine, each having his own history and special ceremonies of worship (see GREEK MYTHS). By the time of Homer, about 750 B.C., the original connexion of the gods with the phenomena of nature had faded, and they were thought of in the shape of men and women with many of the needs, desires, and characteristics of mortals. The poems of HOMER (q.v. Vol. V) gave much more definite shape and uniformity to these ideas.

The gods and goddesses lived in a community on Mount Olympus and were ruled over by Zeus. They directed the affairs of men, but their power was limited: they did not, for instance, know everything, they could be in only one place at a time, and they needed food and sleep like mortals. They were also subject to the decrees of Fate, a power never clearly explained. They governed mankind according to their own inclinations, not according to any ideas of morality or standards of right or wrong (such ideas came gradually into Greek religion as Greek civilization developed). They quarrelled and interfered with each other; they were moved by jealousy and revenge as well as by pity and

HERMES

kindness. The justice of a cause did not influence them much. Humans, therefore, were compelled to conciliate them by prayers and offerings.

The chief of the gods of Olympus was Zeus, the god of the sky. He was the son of Cronos and Rhea (or Cybele) the great Earth Mother, descended from the giant Titans. Zeus' sister Hera was his wife, the queen of heaven. His two brothers, Poseidon and Hades, ruled respectively the sea and the underworld. Poseidon lived in a golden palace in the depth of the sea. Bearing his mighty trident he drove over the sea in a chariot drawn by swift-footed steeds and around him frisked all the monsters of the deep. The underworld, the kingdom of Hades (or Pluto), was separated from the land of the living by the rivers Styx and Acheron. This land, also called Hades, was inhabited by the dead who were ferried across the Styx by Charon, the ferryman. Hades was grim but just and, unlike Satan, in no sense a personification of evil. He seized and took to the underworld to be his queen Persephone, the daughter of Demeter, the goddess of corn and agriculture. The myth of Persephone is one of those myths about the spring common to many religions. Persephone was destined to spend half the year with Hades in the underworld, but for the other half she might return to her mother. As she came back into the land of the living, the grass began to grow and the flowers to spring up at

ATHENA
Relief of the 5th century B.C. *National Mus., Athens*

her feet: spring was returning to earth. In autumn, when she had to return to Hades, all growing things began to fade and die.

Athena, or Pallas Athene, the daughter of Zeus, was the goddess of wisdom, the patron of all towns, and Athens in particular, and of all town crafts. She is depicted as severely beautiful, clad in armour. Apollo was the god of medicine, poetry, and music, and especially of prophecy. At Delphi he had a shrine with a priestess whose replies to questions put to her by the Greeks were supposed to contain the answers of Apollo himself. This was the Delphic Oracle. Dionysus was the god of fertility, especially of the vine. Being a god of the earth, Dionysus, like Persephone, disappeared in the winter and returned or was reborn in the spring.

Aphrodite was the goddess of love, judged by the mortal prince of Troy, Paris, to be the most beautiful of the goddesses. She was the mother of the little winged god of love, Eros. Artemis was the goddess of hunting, and the patroness of all very young things. She was identified with the moon. Hebe was the handmaiden of the gods, pouring out nectar for all to drink. She was the spirit of perpetual youth. Hermes, the god of luck and wealth, was the gods' messenger and was responsible for conducting souls to Hades. He was also the god of roads. He had wings on his feet, a broad-brimmed hat, and a staff round which serpents were twisted.

The god Pan of flocks and shepherds, unlike the rest, was not entirely manlike in form, but had the legs and horns of a goat. He had the reputation for exciting sudden terror in the lonely wanderer in the forests—hence the word 'panic'. He invented the musical pipes, which he was said to have made from a reed into which a nymph, fleeing from his love, had been changed.

It is interesting that the Greeks' god of War, Ares, is comparatively unimportant and takes a much less prominent place than does his Roman counterpart, Mars.

PAN

APOLLO

The central figure of the west pediment of the temple of Zeus at Olympia. Beside him are fragments of other figures from the same pediment. *c.* 460 B.C.

2. ROMAN GODS. Roman religion began much as did the Greek, but the ideas in it developed in a different way. The Greeks endowed their gods with real and individual personalities: the Romans, although they personified their gods, thought of them rather as abstract powers. In early times they did not make images of their gods, but represented them by symbols—a flintstone for Jupiter, a spear for Mars, and fire for Vesta, the goddess of the hearth. As well as the principal gods and goddesses the Romans had a great number of lesser gods, especially for the earth, fields, and woods, and for house and home. The Lares and Penates, the gods of the house and family, were important objects of worship. Every individual had his own protector, his Genius.

The religion of the Romans was gradually influenced and very much altered by the Greeks. The Romans introduced shrines for their gods and began to think of them as having human characteristics. Three gods—Jupiter (or Jove), the supreme god, Juno, the goddess of women, and Minerva, goddess of wisdom—were recognized by the state as supreme, and given a temple at the Capitol. The principal Greek gods were adopted by Rome and identified with native gods. They were as follows: Jupiter (Zeus),

Juno (Hera), Neptune (Poseidon), Minerva (Athena), Mars (Ares), Venus (Aphrodite), Cupid (Eros), Diana (Artemis), Ceres (Demeter), Mercury (Hermes), Bacchus (Dionysus).

See also GREEK CIVILIZATION; ROMAN CIVILIZATION, Section 5; INDEX, p. 137.

GOLDEN HORDE, see TARTARS.

GORGONS, see MYTHOLOGICALS MONSTER (a).

GOTHS. The origin of this Germanic people is still a matter of uncertainty. They were first known of for certain in the 3rd century A.D., in the lands north of the lower Danube. They began to move westward, no doubt because of

THE GOTHIC INVASIONS

the attacks of the HUNS (q.v.), and they became the leading Germanic people of the 4th to 6th centuries A.D. They adopted a form of Christianity, called Arian, which the Roman Church refused to accept as true Christianity. Their history is closely connected with the history of the last period of the Roman Empire. They first appeared in the east of the Empire, and moved across it to the west, playing a considerable part in its final downfall. In 410 Alaric, king of the group called the Visigoths, made his third attack on Rome and finally captured the city. After this, the break-up of the Western Roman Empire was only a matter of time. All through their history, however, the Romans exercised great influence over the Goths, who showed an almost superstitious reverence for things Roman.

The Goths came into Europe in two main groups—the East or Ostrogoths, and West or Visigoths. After various migrations and a long and complicated history of wars and alliances with the Eastern and Western Roman Empires, the West Goths settled in Spain and southern France, and the East Goths in Italy. At the end of the 5th century Theodoric (A.D. 455–526), King of the East Goths in Italy, had gained control of all Italy, both Gothic and Roman, although the Romans continued to be governed through their own ancient institutions. After Theodoric's death in 526, however, the Gothic rule in Italy ended, and the power of the East Goths vanished, leaving very little trace.

The West Gothic kingdom in Spain lasted much longer. The Goths became very much romanized, but their power outlived that of the Romans. The Visigoth kingdom in Spain lasted until A.D. 713, when their king Roderick was finally defeated by the Moslem Arabs, and the Goths only remained as scattered groups.

It is remarkable that a people who played such a part in history for nearly three centuries should have left so little trace behind them. They have never given an abiding name to any part of Europe, as did other early peoples such as the Franks, Angles, and Saxons. Their only legacy is a title, Gothic, applied to a style of art, especially architecture. Gothic Art does not mean the work of the Gothic people, but rather a style of art in the later Middle Ages which did not follow the classical style of the Greeks and Romans. In the Renaissance the word 'Gothic' was used as meaning 'barbaric', since anything which was not derived from Greece or Rome was thought of as barbarian and therefore inferior.

See also Vol. IV: GERMANIC LANGUAGES.

GREEK CHURCH, see ORTHODOX EASTERN CHURCH.

GREEK CIVILIZATION. 1. Greece has given so much to the glories of civilization, in art, science, literature, and philosophy, that only the briefest idea of her contribution can be given in an article of this length. The source of the greater part of this richness is the city of ATHENS (q.v. Vol. III) where Greek civilization reached

THE ERECTHEUM, ATHENS

The Acropolis, rising steeply above the city, was the ancient Athenian citadel. The Erectheum built in the 5th century B.C. was a temple dedicated to Athene, Poseidon, and Erectheus. Through the Ionic columns of the peristyle can be seen other 5th-century ruins and the distant view across the Athenian Plain. *Peter Jones*

its summit. In consequence, much of this account will be concerned with Athens. But Sparta, the age-long rival and foe of Athens, had also a share in the glory of Greece. To understand the character of Greek civilization we must know a little about the Greeks themselves and how Greece came into being.

2. HISTORY. The deepest roots of Greek civilization go back to Crete and Mycenae (*see* MINOAN and MYCENAEAN CIVILIZATIONS), but at present no one is certain where the various peoples who settled in the mainland of Greece originally came from. According to early Greek traditions, the first Greeks who invaded the mainland and drove out the pre-Greek inhabitants were called Pelasgians. Why they were so called is unknown, but their home seems to have been in northern Greece whence they moved southward. They remained to form part of the original stock of the Athenian people and were at their most prosperous in the 13th and 12th centuries B.C. Apart from these early people, there were, according to Greek tradition, three main elements in Greece—the Achaeans, the Dorians, and the Ionians.

(*a*) *Achaeans.* It is now thought that there is some connexion between the Achaeans and the people known as HITTITES (q.v.) who dwelt in Asia Minor. The Achaeans also gained a foothold in Crete, and are mentioned in an Egyptian inscription of the 13th century B.C. as helping the Libyans to invade Egypt. The tradition of an Achaean expedition to the Hellespont is to be found in the story of Jason and the Argonauts. In the picture drawn by Homer of the various petty states of Greece and the Aegean, the Achaeans occupy by far the most important place. And they were responsible for much in the political and social organization of Athens.

(*b*) *Dorians.* The Dorian invasion of Greece was part of a great movement of peoples which took place during the 12th century B.C. and profoundly affected the whole of the ancient Near East. The Dorian invasion, coming from the north, drove the Achaeans into the more remote parts of Greece, and it ultimately spread as far as Crete, Rhodes, and even into the south-west corner of Asia Minor. The principal Dorian centres of classical Greece, however, were Sparta, Argos, Corinth, and Megara. Partly because the Dorians held their territory by right of conquest, all Dorian states had the same kind of three-class social and political structure. The foundation of the State was the slave class, called 'helots', who were the property of the State; next came a class of freemen who had no political rights, but engaged in commerce and menial crafts which were forbidden to the upper class; the highest class were the pure-blooded descendants of the Dorian invaders, the true Spartans, whose business was to govern, to make war, and to train their minds and bodies to endurance and strength.

(*c*) *Ionians.* The origin of the Ionians is also obscure, but the name is very ancient. It occurs in a very early Egyptian inscription, and also in the Old Testament, and is the name by which the early Semites knew the Greeks. The Ionians appear to have migrated across the Aegean to the west coast of Asia Minor where they founded many prosperous settlements, the most important of which was Miletus. They mingled freely with the non-Greek peoples of Asia Minor, and, because of this wider contact, developed a free and inquiring spirit which made them the pioneers of early Greek philosophy and science. They played an important part in the great struggle against the Persians which was followed by the most glorious period in the history of Athens.

These three peoples—the Achaeans, the Dorians, and the Ionians—with their various dialects and their different customs and ways of life, contributed each in its own way to that complex thing which we call Greek civilization, and which we must now attempt to describe.

First, something must be said about what is the foundation of almost all civilizations—the art of writing. Evidence shows that by the 8th century B.C. the Greeks had an alphabet which was directly derived from the early Phoenician script in use in Canaan and Syria in the 14th century B.C. So they were very early equipped with the most important tool of civilization, the **alphabet**, which was unknown to the scribes of Mesopotamia and unused by those of Egypt (*see* WRITING, HISTORY OF, Vol. IV). From the Greek alphabet all our Western alphabets are descended. The principal material used for writing was the prepared inner tissue of the papyrus reed, though books were also written on tablets of lead and on leather. But papyrus is a perishable material, and so it was gradually ousted by a more durable material—a form of prepared sheepskin called parchment. Practically all existing manuscripts of ancient authors are written on parchment.

3. ART. The Dorian invasions in the 12th

century B.C. brought to an end the Mycenaean Civilization and started a period which was from the point of view of arts and crafts a Dark Age. In the 8th century B.C. a revival began which led to the full flowering of Greek art, above all in Athens. The pottery of this transition period was decorated with a formal, geometrical type of design. But in the 7th and 6th centuries B.C. we can see how much the Greeks had developed a feeling for form and proportion from the fine Attic vases of that period with their vase paintings illustrating early Greek myths. In the following two centuries—the greatest period of Greek Art—most of the well-known achievements of the Greeks were created—the Parthenon, for instance, and the work of the great sculptors such as Phidias and Praxiteles. The influence of Greek architecture is still seen in many of our public buildings.

4. POLITICAL THOUGHT. Great as were the achievements of the Greeks in the fields of architecture, sculpture, and painting, their greatest contribution to European civilization lies in the fields of political thought, philosophy, and the drama. The Ionians, Achaeans, and Dorians, when they invaded Greece, were organized on a tribal basis. The poems of Homer give a picture of a number of petty states ruled over by a king, who was himself a vassal of a more powerful king. That was the relation of the Achaean chiefs to Agamemnon; they were entitled to sit in council with the king and share in the direction of affairs. In fact the king's control over his more powerful vassals was often far from firm. The Dorians retained their tribal system more unbroken than the rest of the Greeks. In Sparta, for instance, the most purely Dorian part of Greece, all political power was at first in the hands of a small military caste headed by two kings, equal in power. Later, the main power passed into the hands of five officials, called *ephors*, who were elected annually by the assembly of the Spartans. These officials managed all the affairs of Sparta except religion (*see* SPARTANS). On the other hand, from Athens sprang the idea of political freedom and that special form of government called democracy; and this is the most important development to consider.

The old Greek story about Midas, the Phrygian king whose touch turned everything into gold, illustrates the actual situation in the beginning of the 7th century B.C. The exploitation of

ATTIC VASE

The painting, in black and white, shows Achilles slaying the Amazon, Penthesilea. Late 6th century B.C. Brit. Mus.

the gold- and silver-mines of Phrygia and Lydia and the invention of a coinage led to the growth of a new class, the merchant princes of Ionia and Greece, who were able by their wealth to seize political power and become what the Greeks called Tyrants. During the period of the Tyrants the tribal structure of society underwent a gradual change. The old aristocracy was based on the possession of land, and only those descended from one of the ancient tribes had the right to call themselves citizens of Athens. But the growth of these new commercial and manufacturing interests, and the consequent immigration into Attica of artisans and other workers, broke down and transformed the old exclusive tribal system. The Attic tribes were increased in number from four to ten, and Attica was divided into *demes* or parishes, each of which was a political unit with an elected chief called a *demarch*. Every male in the deme, except the slaves, had the right to vote as soon as he came of age. At the time of the first reform movement in 593 B.C. a Council of Four Hundred was set up, and this was later increased to five hundred, the members being elected by lot. In addition fifty members from each of the ten tribes acted in rotation, month by month, as a standing committee of the Council. The same method of election by lot was soon used for appointing the highest officers of state, the *archons*, but only holders of property could be elected as archons, so that the poorer classes were excluded. This, in short, was the political machine created by the Athenians, and the way in which it worked was called by Aristotle 'democracy'. It had two important defects: first, it excluded the lower classes from office and was really the outcome of a middle-class revolution; secondly, the working of the machine depended on the existence of a large body of slaves without any political rights at all. But the Athenian system of government, together with Aristotle's penetrating analysis of it, remains a permanent monument to the political genius of Athens (*see also* ARISTOTLE, Vol. V).

5. PHILOSOPHY. Next, something must be said about what the Greeks accomplished in the field of philosophy and science. It was natural that the impulse to explore the meaning of the universe should come from the free and restless minds of the Ionian Greeks, and most of the early philosophers of the 7th and 6th centuries B.C. come either from the Ionian settlements in Asia Minor, or from the Greek colonies in Italy. The earliest of these was Thales of Miletus. His answer to the question 'What is the universe?' was that all things were made of water. A hundred years later Heraclitus of Ephesus declared that fire was the basic element of the universe, and maintained that the particles which compose the universe are in perpetual motion. All these thinkers were occupied with the nature of the physical universe and so have been called the Physicists. But the most vital figure of Greek philosophy was SOCRATES (q.v. Vol. V). He was born about 470 B.C. in Athens, and was put to death in 399 B.C. on the charge of impiety. Socrates wrote nothing himself, but his portrait has been drawn for us by his disciple, PLATO (q.v. Vol. V), in the *Dialogues*, and by another disciple, XENOPHON (q.v. Vol. V), in the *Memorabilia* and the *Symposium*. It is possible that much of the philosophy in the *Dialogues* which is attributed to Socrates is really Plato's. We know that Socrates was passionately interested, not in what the universe was made of, but in the nature of man—in such questions as 'What is justice?' or 'What is courage?' He tried to make people realize that they used many words without any knowledge of their meaning, and his method of teaching was by asking questions. This method is now known as the Socratic method, and was used by Plato in the *Dialogues* in his attempt to learn about and analyse the nature of reality. From these great Greek philosophers has grown the study of Moral Philosophy and Ethics, and Socrates is the first in a long line of great thinkers.

Plato was succeeded by his pupil ARISTOTLE (q.v. Vol. V), born at Stagira in Thrace in 385 B.C. He was intensely interested in classifying everything, and the study of his terms and logical methods still has an important place in a classical education. He wrote a large number of books, not many of which have come down to us. Other famous schools of

THEATRE AT EPIDAURUS
The audience sat on stone seats rising in a semicircle above the central space where the chorus danced and sang. On the right can be seen the ruins of the stage building with the low stage in front of it. *B. Ashmole*

philosophy sprang from the great Athenian thinkers, especially the Epicurean School (*see* EPICURUS, Vol. V) and the great Stoic school which played an important part in Roman life. The names of Stoic philosophers are ZENO (q.v. Vol. V) and Chrysippus, and its central doctrine was the idea of living according to nature. The great Roman emperor MARCUS AURELIUS (q.v. Vol. V) was a follower of the Stoic philosophy.

6. DRAMA. Lastly a word must be said about that most splendid and distinctive of all the achievements of Attic genius, the Greek drama. It is through the drama that we get closest to the true spirit of ancient Greece, because the drama grew directly out of the great rituals which expressed Greek religious feeling at its deepest. In the drama we find expressed the triumphant surge of patriotic emotion after the repulse of Persia in the 5th century B.C.; there too we find all the stories of ancient GREEK MYTHOLOGY (q.v.) and tradition transmuted into splendid poetry; and in the brilliant and bitter satires of the comedies of Aristophanes we find reflected the passions and prejudices of contemporary political life in Athens. There were many dramatists in Athens in the heyday of the drama, but the three great names which will always be numbered among the immortals are those of AESCHYLUS, SOPHOCLES, and EURIPIDES (q.v. Vol. V); and for the reader who does not know Greek, no better introduction to them can be found than the translations of Gilbert Murray.

See also ANCIENT CIVILIZATIONS; Vol. IV: GREEK LANGUAGE.

GREEK HEROES.

GREEK MYTHOLOGY (q.v.) is full of stories of the heroic adventures of legendary heroes whose fortunes were often either helped or hindered by the participation of the gods in their affairs. These heroes were themselves sometimes descended from the gods, and came to be worshipped almost as gods.

Perhaps the greatest of the Greek heroes is Heracles (Hercules is the Roman version of his name). He typified the virtues of courage and endurance, and he was a symbol for strength. According to the legend, he strangled two serpents when still a child in his cradle. Heracles won immortality by performing the twelve labours set him by Eurystheus, King of Tiryns. These included cleaning within one day the Augean Stables of the accumulated filth of huge herds of cattle. This he achieved

ATLAS BRINGING HERACLES THE GOLDEN APPLES
Heracles, helped by Athena, holds up the firmament for Atlas while he fetches the apples. Metope from the temple of Zeus at Olympia. *c.* 460 B.C.

by diverting the river Alpheus, so that it flowed through the stables. Another labour was to catch alive the Erymanthian Boar, which he did by driving the boar into a snowfield, where it became so exhausted that he could catch it in a net. Hera, the wife of Zeus, always opposed Heracles, bringing disasters upon him, because he was reputed to be the son of Zeus by another mother.

In many of the legends the Greek heroes are engaged in overcoming some MYTHOLOGICAL MONSTER (q.v.) which is causing harm to mankind. Perseus, another son of Zeus, set out to fetch the head of Medusa, the Gorgon, who had the power of turning to stone all who looked on her. In this enterprise he had the help of the gods. Pluto gave him a helmet which made him invisible, Hermes gave him wings, and Athene provided him with a mirror which prevented his having to look directly at the Gorgon. With these aids he slew Medusa. On his way back he rescued Andromeda from a rock where she had been chained, and married her.

Theseus, the Athenian, delivered his country from the fearful yearly tribute to Crete of seven youths and seven maidens to be sacrificed to feed the monster, the Minotaur. Theseus found his way through the labyrinth in which the Minotaur lived, slew the monster, and, with the help of Ariadne, daughter of the king of Crete, found his way out again. Jason set forth with some fifty of the chief heroes of Greece, the

JASON DELIVERED FROM THE DRAGON OF COLCHIS
The Golden Fleece can be seen on the tree behind the dragon. This painting from an Attic Vase of *c.* 475 B.C. illustrates an unusual version of the myth. *Alinari*

Argonauts, in the ship *Argo* to recover the Golden Fleece from the King of Colchis. To gain the fleece he had to perform a number of apparently impossible tasks, all of which he achieved with the help of the magic arts of Medea, the king's daughter.

The Greek heroes often behaved in a way which seems dishonourable and mean according to our ideas of heroic conduct. Theseus, after receiving the help of Ariadne, deserted her, leaving her heart-broken. Jason also deserted Medea. The behaviour of the Trojan hero, Aeneas, to Dido, Queen of Carthage, seems to us heartless and contemptible.

Many of the legends of the Greek heroes are connected with the war between the Greeks and the TROJANS (q.v.). Agamemnon was the leader of the Greeks. He sacrificed his own daughter, Iphigenia, to the goddess Artemis, to bring good fortune to his fleet; and in the end he was killed by his own wife, Clytemnestra, in revenge. He had a great and disastrous quarrel with Achilles, the hero of the Trojan wars. Achilles had been plunged as a baby into the river Styx by his mother and made invulnerable, except for his heel by which she held him. He slew the Trojan hero, Hector, and was himself killed by being shot in the heel by Paris. He was of a fierce and implacable temper—a contrast to Hector who was noble in victory and

defeat and was represented by Homer as a man of human affections.

Odysseus (Ulysses in the Roman version) after the Trojan wars was detained by the goddess Calypso for seven years, and then started on the long journey back to Greece and his faithful wife, Penelope, during which so many misfortunes and adventures befell him.

Homer's epic poems are the source of our knowledge of many of the Greek heroic legends (*see* HOMER, Vol. V). Many of them formed the subjects of the great Greek dramas. Some of the heroic characters may have begun with real people, around whose name there had collected many legendary tales until the real person was lost in the legend.

GREEK MYTHS. Until about a hundred years ago Greek mythology was the only mythology of which European scholars had any considerable knowledge; and so until quite recently all theories about mythology have been based on Greek mythology. We now know a great deal about other mythologies—Egyptian, Babylonian, Indian, Chinese, and Japanese, as well as of those of lower cultures; and we find that in all these the myths are, or were, closely connected with religion (*see* MYTHOLOGY). In Greece, on the other hand, we find many myths which seem to have no connexion with religion, and many others which seem to be at variance with the religious beliefs of the Greeks.

To take an example, we know that Zeus was regarded by the Greeks as the king of the gods and the ruler of the world, and was revered and worshipped as such. Yet many stories were current which told of his making love to women on earth, going about disguised as an animal, quarrelling with his wife, and behaving generally in a manner quite unsuited to his divine character. Probably these stories have grown from very early religious beliefs of which little is known. Most of our ideas of Greek religion have been derived from the more highly civilized Greeks, so that we tend to forget that even in the 5th century B.C. it retained many primitive features. And many of the myths date back to the period much earlier than the 5th century, when writing was first introduced. If writing had not been introduced when the best of the Greeks were still rather barbarous, these earlier elements might well have been lost.

It is probable that the Greeks originally had

A GYPSY ENCAMPMENT

few myths of their own but borrowed freely from their neighbours, both civilized and savage, sometimes perhaps without adopting the religious beliefs with which these myths were associated. Such myths, or those which had lost their religious associations, could be used by philosophers or poets to point a moral or adorn a tale.

Thus, we may find in Greece three types of myths: firstly those connected with Greek religion as it is known to us; secondly those connected with religious practices such as are found elsewhere but are not certainly known to have existed in Greece; and, thirdly, those which had no connexion with Greek religion.

THE JUDGEMENT OF PARIS
Attic Vase painting early 4th century B.C. *Ashmolean Mus.*

As an example of the first we have the story of Iphigenia: when the Greek fleet was ready to sail for Troy, the goddess Artemis kept it from sailing by sending contrary winds. The Greeks consulted Calchas the seer, who said that the goddess must be appeased by the sacrifice of Agamemnon's daughter, Iphigenia. The girl was brought and was about to be sacrificed when the goddess snatched her away, and, according to one story, put a bear in her place. This was supposed to have happened at Brauron in Attica, and was obviously connected with the worship of Artemis there. A leading feature of this worship was a dance by girls in the character of bears. We may suppose that at one time it was the custom to sacrifice a girl of high rank, that later a bear was sacrificed instead, and that finally they just danced a bear dance, and that names familiar from Homer were put instead of those in the original myth.

An example of the second type of myth is a story in the *Odyssey*. Odysseus, when he wishes to talk to the spirits of the dead, has to dig a trench, kill a sheep, and let its blood run into the trench. The spirits come to drink the blood, and he then talks with them. The Greeks in historic times did not feed their dead with blood: either they must have borrowed this idea from their neighbours or it must have come from an old religious custom of the Greeks of which we have no record.

For the third we will take the judgement of Paris. The story tells how a golden apple, labelled 'for the Fairest', was thrown among the gods and goddesses when they were feasting. Three goddesses claimed it, and Zeus, being unwilling to decide between them, told Hermes to take them to Paris, a Trojan prince, and tell him to award the apple. All three goddesses tried to bribe him, and he decided in favour of Aphrodite, who promised him the love of Helen, fairest of women. It is impossible to say how this story arose, but it is difficult to connect it with any religious cult.

This story draws attention to a remarkable feature of Greek religion and mythology, the important part played by goddesses. In historic Greece women played no part whatever in public affairs; yet the Athenians had a goddess, Athene, as protector of their city, and a myth tells how she reached this position by overcoming the god Poseidon. Other goddesses, such as Hera and Artemis, were very prominent both in myth and religion. It would seem either that the Greeks greatly changed their social customs after their religion had been formed and their myths recorded, or that they had taken these over from some other people, perhaps the Cretans, among whom women played a much greater part in public life.

In this, as in many other respects, Greek mythology offers many problems which have not been solved.

See also GREEK CIVILIZATION; GODS OF GREECE & ROME.

GREEKS. The Greeks to-day proudly claim that they are the descendants of the Ancient Greeks—people who have had more influence on Western civilization than any other race. How far this is true has been a matter of much dispute among scholars.

Although towards the end of the 2nd century B.C. the Romans conquered Greece, Greek culture remained supreme, and no young Roman would have considered himself well educated unless he had read the Greek philosophers. In A.D. 328, when the Emperor Constantine built his new capital, Constantinople, in what is now Turkey, the centre of the Greek world was gradually transferred from Athens to this new imperial city. During the Middle Ages the Crusaders from western Europe tried to set up a feudal system in Greece, and even to-day their ruined castles may be seen on many a hill-top. In 1453 disaster overtook the eastern Mediterranean, when the Ottoman Turks, after a long period of gradual conquest, captured Constantinople and spread over the whole Balkan Peninsula. In Greece, however, the ORTHODOX EASTERN CHURCH (q.v.) resisted oppression and kept alive in the minds of the people their faith, language, and national consciousness. The Greek struggle for freedom from the Great Ottoman Empire in the early 19th century, in which the English poet Byron took part, received sympathy and help from all Europe: and in 1829, with the support of Great Britain, France, and Russia, Greece again became an independent state. At first a Bavarian prince was made king, but in 1863 George I, son of the King of Denmark, became king and founded the dynasty to which the present King George belongs. In 1940, during the Second World War, the Greeks were attacked by Italy and later by Germany. Their fierce patriotism and love of freedom inspired them to resist in a spirit fully worthy of their Athenian and Spartan ancestors.

The Ancient Greeks were passionately interested in political discussions, and this characteristic has certainly been inherited by their modern descendants. They will sit all day outside cafés, clicking their strings of amber beads through their fingers, arguing hour after hour about politics. But, unfortunately, they do not find it easy to combine for the good of their country, and in the last 100 years they have tried many different forms of government. The

THE PLAIN OF ARGOLIS
The sheep can barely get enough to eat from the stony ground. *Boyce Allen*

Greek people are very able merchants and traders, and they love travel. They are to be found all over the world, buying, selling, working hard; and in all parts of Greece there are people who have visited the great cities of Europe and America. They are also very friendly towards travellers in their own country, receiving them with the most hospitable welcome and lively interest, especially in the more out-of-the-way villages.

Except for a comparatively small number of town dwellers, the Greeks are mostly farmers and sailors. There are no large industries in the country, but recently a number of small local industries have sprung up. In 1920–1 there was an exchange of populations between Greece and Turkey, and, in consequence, over a million people (descendants of Greek colonists who had been settled in Asia Minor for more than two thousand years) returned to Greece. Although at first this enormous increase of population was a great strain on the resources of a poor country and gave rise to an acutely difficult refugee problem, the new-comers were, in the long run, an asset. They were largely craftsmen and artisans who brought their skill with them. They set up small factories round the towns and also introduced new methods of agriculture, especially in the cultivation of tobacco.

The majority of the Greeks live in little fishing ports on the coast, or in villages situated in the fertile inland valleys between mountainous ranges. The villages consist mainly of small stone houses, and are often reached by very rough winding tracks more suitable for mule and mountain pony than modern transport. They are surrounded by rough pasture, maize fields, olive groves, and vineyards. The life of the peasant is still simple and laborious—as one foreign observer remarked, 'the crops are still planted and harvested as in the days of Homer'. Nor has the food changed very much—a lamb or kid on feast-days, otherwise bread, yoghourt (a kind of sour junket), cheeses made from goats' or sheep's milk, honey, olive oil, grapes, and figs. The ordinary Greek wine is mixed with resin and, to the foreigner, tastes like turpentine.

The peasant women are to be seen sitting outside their houses weaving the rough home-spun garments which form their everyday wear. On special occasions they still often wear their gay national dress—white dresses for the women,

beautifully embroidered in bright colours; for the men, white kilts, sleeveless coloured jackets over white shirts, and red caps.

See also Vol. III: GREECE.

GRIFFIN. This fabulous creature, usually depicted with an eagle's head and the hind quarters of a lion, is one of the most famous of the various imaginary beasts which combine the

GRIFFIN
Bronze figure, about 10 in. high., 4th century B.C.
British Mus.

nature and characteristics of two or more animals. A number of the four-footed creatures in ancient sculpture, such as are shown on the bas-relief carvings in Persia, were represented with the wings and beaks of eagles. These beasts represented to people who thought in pictures the idea of several kinds of power united in one being. Like the eagle, the griffin was connected with the sun. They were also said to guard gold-mines and hidden treasures. The griffin became popular as an heraldic emblem and appears on many coats of arms. The bird known as the griffin-vulture is named after the fabulous creature.

See also FABULOUS CREATURES.

GUATEMALA, PEOPLES OF, see CENTRAL AMERICANS.

GUIANAS, PEOPLES OF, see WEST INDIANS.

GURKHAS, see INDIAN HILL TRIBES, Section 3; INDIAN PEOPLES.

GYPSIES. The word is a contraction of Egyptian, and should, strictly speaking, be applied only to members of the Romani race, who, when they first came to Britain, called themselves Egyptians. But nowadays it is used, quite inaccurately, to describe all wandering people other than tramps, whether they be Romani or not.

The Romani are a distinct people, with their own language, their own customs, and, in many parts of the world, their own laws. Their original home is not known for certain, but it seems likely that it was somewhere in the region of the Indus valley in India. The first definite records of them in Europe date from 1417, but it is certain that they were well established in the Balkans long before that date. They are first heard of in this country in Scotland in 1505 under the name of Egyptians. From then on they are mentioned frequently, for they soon began to make themselves a nuisance, and laws were passed for their expulsion from the country. Every country in Europe has at some time passed laws for the expulsion of the Gypsies, but no country has ever succeeded in getting rid of them. Persecution in Britain (up to about a hundred years ago one could be hanged just for being a gypsy) had little effect on numbers, and gradually they came to be accepted as part, even if an undesirable part, of the population.

Even to-day persecution of the Gypsy has not ceased in England, though it is not so blatant as it used to be. And the view of them as an undesirable part of the population has not decreased at all. Gypsies are not tramps. In England, at least, they are regarded with more distrust than any tramp. Usually they have a very bad reputation as thieves, but they are also credited with all sorts of other crimes from child-stealing to witchcraft. This reputation is founded not so much upon fact (as a matter of fact major crime is rare among Gypsies in Britain) as upon fear. No matter how long they may have lived in Britain, they are Orientals. Their dark skins, their shabby clothes and love of bright colours, their strange speech and use of gesticulation, above all their way of living—these things, rather than any pronounced leaning towards lawlessness, have given them a reputation they do not wholly deserve, but which they are not likely to lose.

Much of their life, it is true, is not strictly honest. Their ideas of property rights, especially in the matter of food, such as pheasants, partridges, and rabbits, are peculiarly their own. And they earn a good deal by trickery. Most of their fortune-telling is pure trickery, but so is fortune-telling everywhere (see DIVINATION). Against this must be placed some excellent work in the making of clothes-pegs, baskets, and such crafts, and some of the best work in the world in the mending of china, and as coppersmiths. Even so it must be admitted that it is a characteristic of the race to earn an easy living rather than to work if it is possible, though there are many exceptions to this rule.

Much of the fear with which they are still regarded in country districts springs from their fortune-telling, which is always done most impressively and which is very often correct in its forecast, since it is largely a matter of character-reading at which most Gypsies are adept. Some of the women seem to have what is called 'second sight', and are able on occasions to foretell the future in the most uncanny manner. There have been some astounding and well-authenticated forecasts of events in the future by Gypsy women, but it must not be thought that they all equally have this gift: it is most uncommon. Gypsy women, too, are expert herbalists and have a wide knowledge of the medicinal properties of plants. Some of them are also expert animal doctors, although this is work that is usually done by the men.

It will be seen from the above that Gypsy women are very important in the life of the family. They are, as a matter of fact, the chief earners of the family income, and they do most of the work. It will not be surprising, therefore, to learn that they are the rulers of the family, and often of much more than the family. This is not apparent on a casual visit to a Gypsy camp, but is so nevertheless. The women hold the purse strings, and in any great event it is their decision that counts for most in the councils of the family. Moreover, though 'Kings of the Gypsies' are as common as blackberries, it is the Gypsy Queen who is important and who is acknowledged by the Gypsies everywhere. The dominant position of women in their lives is, perhaps, being gradually broken down by the stress of modern life—for example, descent always used to be through the mother, and children used to take the name of the mother and not of the father. This is not now the case, but it is very far from being altogether lost.

The Romani language is also being broken down by the stress of modern life, but is not by any means dead. Romani, a much-corrupted

A GYPSY CAMP ON EGDON HEATH, DORSET. *The Times*

Indian language, is the same language all over the world, though naturally it differs a little (and the differences are getting bigger every year) from country to country, just as the English spoken in America, Australia, Scotland, or Wales is not identical. Pure Romani speakers are very rare in Britain now, and many Gypsies use only a few words of their language in their ordinary talk; though probably all true Gypsies speak much more Romani than they will admit to doing. But if most Gypsies speak English rather than Romani in their daily life, we use quite a number of Gypsy words in our ordinary everyday life without realizing that we do. 'Dad' is the most common: it is the Romani for father. And we often speak of children as 'shavers', derived from the Romani word *chaver*, meaning a child (*see* INDIAN LANGUAGES, Vol. IV).

It has been the custom of the Gypsy everywhere to take the names of people in his adopted country and to use them for his own. Thus most of the Gypsies in Britain bear English surnames —but not all of them, for the love of travel has never deserted the Gypsy, and there are usually some Gypsies from other countries in Britain, just as British Gypsies are to be found all over

the world in ordinary times. The names of the most influential Gypsy families in the country are Burton, Cooper, Boswell, Stanley, Smith, Lovell, Wood, Faa, Gray, Young, Lee, and Buckland. There are, of course, many others. Some men with Gypsy blood in their veins have risen high in the life of the country. The late Earl of Birkenhead was half a Gypsy—his name was Smith—and he became Lord Chancellor of England. Sir Richard Burton, the famous explorer, was half a Gypsy. And it is very probable that John Bunyan, the author of *The Pilgrim's Progress*, was a pure-blooded Gypsy.

Wherever one goes in the world one will find Gypsies. Despite all the persecution (and they have been persecuted every whit as much as the Jews), they have never lost their national characteristics. Indeed, these two landless, wandering, persecuted peoples have maintained their identities better than any others, and of the two the Romani have remained the purer. For though marriages with *gorgios* (i.e. non-Gypsies) are not uncommon now (a half-bred Gypsy is called a *diddekai*, pronounced diddecoy), the Gypsy on the whole clings fanatically to his way of life and is very proud of his Romani blood.

H

HADES, *see* HELL; GODS OF GREECE AND ROME.

HARPIES, *see* MYTHOLOGICAL MONSTERS, Section (*b*).

HARVEST FESTIVALS. Nearly all peoples who grow corn celebrate the end of harvest in some way. In many parts of Europe, particularly Scotland and Germany, it was the custom to attach great importance to the last sheaf. This was cut with special ceremony, carried home in triumph, and often, dressed as a woman, hung up in the room in which the harvest supper was held. Elsewhere it was widely believed that when the last of the corn was cut, its spirit went into some animal such as a cock or a hare. This animal was then killed and eaten as part of the harvest feast.

Among peoples who believe in divine kings or chiefs it is a common practice to offer some of the new crop at their tombs, to thank them for the harvest, and to pray for a good harvest next year.

In many parts of the world it is, or was, the custom to celebrate the feast of the dead at the end of the harvest. A feast of food and liquor is prepared and the spirits of the dead are invited to come and partake of it. Their way is made easy by leaving the windows open (as in France), by clearing the paths (as in Assam and California), or by providing them with miniature boats to travel in (as in Borneo). The houses are lit with lamps or torches. When the spirits are supposed to have eaten and drunk their fill— usually after three days—they are bidden to depart, and the living then fall to feasting.

A survival of some of these customs is found among ourselves. It is still usual to decorate the church for the Harvest Festival with choice specimens of all the crops, and it is, or was, the custom in some places to place a sheaf of corn or a miniature cornstack in the church, and leave it there till the following harvest. When the Christian thanksgiving festival is over, the harvest gifts are often given to the local hospital.

See also FESTIVALS.

HAUSA, *see* NEGRO AFRICANS.

HAWAIANS, *see* POLYNESIANS.

HEAVEN. This word when used in the plural means the sky where the sun, moon, and stars are to be seen: in the singular it is the name given to the abode of God and His angels, or the state in which He exists. Most peoples have thought of the earth as only part of a much larger scheme in which there are other worlds where the gods and spirits live, and from which come the souls of men (and sometimes of animals and other 'animated' objects) when they are born, and whither they will return after death. The Ancient Egyptians, for instance, believed that the sun, moon, and the sky were gods, and that, since these heavenly bodies were in the sky, all life came from and would eventually return to the sky. At first, however, they thought that only the Pharaoh was immortal and at his death he would return to the home of his father, the Sun-god, while everybody else continued to live on in a nondescript sort of way under the earth. But when Osiris, who ruled over the underworld, was raised to the sky, then it became possible for all whom Osiris declared to be 'true of heart and voice' (i.e. properly qualified) also to enjoy immortal life in the heavens. The necessary qualifications for heaven were mainly of a magical nature, though they did include good behaviour on earth (*see* EGYPTIAN MYTHS). In the neighbouring civilization in Mesopotamia, on the other hand, no one went to the sky. Good and bad, rich and poor, high and low, spent the next life without any distinction in a dreary underworld (*see* BABYLONIAN MYTHS).

The first gods of the Greeks, we are told by Plato, were the heavenly bodies, and their chief, Zeus, was the sky-god. They lived in great splendour where Mount Olympus towers up through the clouds into the mysterious heavens. In fact, in Greece there were some twenty or more mountains called Olympus, and probably they were regarded as all pointing to the heavenly home of the gods, who lived there like fighting chiefs, playing music, eating, drinking,

PARNASSUS
A Renaissance artist's conception of the classical heaven. Painting by Raphael (1483–1520) in the Vatican, Rome. *Alinari*

and marrying, and conquering and deceiving one another in a very ungodlike manner (*see* GODS OF GREECE AND ROME). But human beings did not go to Olympus after death. On the contrary, they were said to pass to a dismal underground region (Hades), ruled by Pluto and his wife Persephone. There, all the souls of the dead, good and bad alike, mingled together as shades. Later, however, Hades was divided into two compartments. Good people all went to Elysium where they lived in great comfort, enjoying plenty of everything desirable, with no rain or violent storms but only cool refreshing showers from the west. The other division was Tartarus, the place of the wicked (*see* HELL). The Greek poets developed a great variety of ideas about the character of the next life. Some pictured Elysium as a highly delightful abode, either below ground, in mid-air, or in the centre of the earth, or as Isles of the Blest in the western sea, reached only by a few highly favoured individuals. Homer, on the other hand, painted a sombre picture of the state of departed souls—for instance, Achilles, though in Elysium, is made to envy the life of the poorest man on earth (*see* GREEK MYTHS).

About the 6th century B.C. a belief arose in Greece that ordinary people, as well as heroes, could go to heaven, if they were helped by elaborate rites—purifications, stately processions, hilarious dances, and solemn dramatic performances held in very strictly guarded secrecy. Those who passed through these stirring experiences felt that they had entered into communion with the god of the mysteries and so gained an assurance of a happy life beyond the grave as well as peace and security on earth. They had, as it were, died to live again—not really, but in a kind of make-believe or ceremonial manner.

In Scandinavia it was thought that those who fell in battle, instead of descending to the underworld, went to a special 'hall of the slain', or Valhalla, where they were honourably received by their god, Odin. At first the abode of Odin may have been in the hills, like that of Zeus in Greece, because the souls of dead warriors were often supposed to return from the mountains. But in the mythological poems of Iceland, called the *Edda*, Valhalla is represented as being in the sky, and brave warriors are said to have been taken there by the Valkyries—the divine maidens who were sent by Odin through the air

DANTE'S VISION OF PARADISE

In the *Divine Comedy* Dante visits Hell and Purgatory, and then Paradise, where Beatrice, whom he loved on earth and who is now an angel, guides him. The drawing shows Beatrice and Dante talking with SS. Peter, James, and John whose souls, like those of the other blessed, are flames of light encircling the godhead. Drawing by Botticelli (1444–1510)

during a battle to collect the slain. When they arrived there, they were entertained by Odin and served with wine by the Valkyries in the great hall which was decked with shields and coats of mail. From it they went out every day, through one of its 540 doors, to engage in combats with each other, and at night returned to feast, drink mead, and amuse themselves (*see* NORSE MYTHS).

Besides Valhalla we are also told in Teutonic mythology of a heroes' paradise on a glass mountain. Below the mountain there were beautiful meadows reached through a well, where the souls of the dead fluttered about like birds or butterflies, surrounded with elves. The ruler of the 'glittering plains' was Gudmund, a divinity who had banished from his country all weakness, old age, and death; only those, however, who had performed deeds of daring were allowed to enter it. Ordinary mortals presumably lived under much less ideal conditions in and around their tombs. In fact, Heaven—in the sky, in one

of the planets, on a mountain or a magic island —was nearly always a privileged abode reserved for rulers, warriors, or semi-divine heroes. Entrance to Heaven was generally accompanied by special funeral rites, such as cremation, so that the soul might get to the sky in the smoke of its own body: sometimes the corpse was sent to the Isles of the Blest in a canoe or boat attended by slaves (*see* DEATH CEREMONIES).

The ancient Hebrews, like the Babylonians, do not seem to have adopted these beliefs and practices so common in other civilizations. The word 'Heaven', in fact, is seldom mentioned in the Old Testament except as the place where God lives. The dead were thought to go to a dreary underworld called Sheol (translated into Greek as Hades), where kings and commoners dwelt in darkness, huddled together, eating the dust and cut off from their God. Only one or two heroes like Enoch and Elijah were translated to the sky and 'went up by a whirlwind into heaven' (Gen. v. 24, 2 Kings ii. 11) which was situated in the upper firmament, or roof of the world, supported by the mountains as pillars. But heaven was shut against ordinary mortals, who only brought disaster upon themselves when they tried to reach it by building a tower to the sky (Gen. xi. 4 ff.).

After their exile in Babylonia, however, when the Israelite people returned to Palestine and re-established themselves in and around Jerusalem, the Jews were no longer content to regard the grave as the end of all their hopes. Jehovah had restored them to their own land, and surely He would not forsake them in death. And so they came to believe that 'God will redeem my soul from the power of Sheol', 'for He shall receive me', as the Psalmist continually declared. They began to look forward to that great day when the Messiah should come, and the dead would be raised up to share in His just rule on a restored earth (Isa. xxvi. 19, Dan. xii. 2). (*See* JUDAISM.)

Although there is no mention in the Old Testament or in the early Christian writings of Paradise as a beautiful garden with wonderful trees and orchards like Eden, this is the picture that is drawn of the home of the righteous in some of the Jewish books. Sometimes it was said to be the final abode, sometimes only a temporary place where they stayed while they were waiting to pass to the many mansions in the sky after the Day of Judgement. In the New Testament Paradise is only mentioned three times, and in none of these is anything said about what it was like and what happened there. Heaven was the abode of God where the angels beheld the face of their heavenly Father (Matt. xviii. 10, Luke xxiv. 51), and whither Jesus Himself expected to return. There the angels rejoiced when a sinner repented, and there would be the scene of the final reward of the faithful on earth (Matt. v. 12, Luke vi. 23). St. Paul described it as 'a house not made with hands, eternal in the heavens', and regarded it as the final home of the righteous (2 Cor. v. 1 f.).

In these Christian Scriptures Heaven is thought of, not as the scene of endless banquets and amusements as in the ancient religion, nor as a place where everything is exactly as we should like it to be on earth. It is where God is, and there is joy, peace, goodness, beauty, and truth in all their fullness. The Kingdom of God, as understood and taught by Christ, could only be realized when and where human beings do the will of God and obey His commandments, whether it be on earth or anywhere else (*see* CHRISTIANITY).

The Heaven to which Moslems look forward is described rather simply and crudely in the Koran, the sacred book of ISLAM (q.v.), as a place of abundant pleasures for the senses. 'The pious shall be in gardens and pleasure, enjoying what their Lord has given them.' Heaven is a place where the pious shall have 'fruits such as they deem the best, and flesh of fowl as they desire'. A soul's claim to Heaven depends upon the will of Allah and the results of the great judgement day.

See also RELIGION; GOD.

HEBREW CIVILIZATION. The history of the people whom we call the Hebrews is mainly known to us from their own literature which is contained in the Old Testament (*see* BIBLE). In this important collection of ancient documents we have the HEBREW MYTHS (q.v.), sagas, laws, religious poetry, histories of the kings, and other materials, from which a picture can be drawn of the gradual growth of the political and religious life of this strange people who have exercised an influence upon the history of the world out of all proportion to their political importance. Indeed, their main contribution to human history was made after they had ceased to be of any political importance whatever. Besides the information gained from these Hebrew documents, we can learn a great deal which supplements and corrects what they say of themselves, from records of Assyrian kings, from Egyptian inscriptions, and from correspondence between the rulers of various states of the Near East.

The Hebrews formed part of a series of migrations from the Arabian steppes, which ultimately peopled the greater portion of the Near East with a large group of nations closely related in speech and custom. This group is called the Semitic group or family of nations. Its common bond is language, and it includes Hebrews, CANAANITES, SYRIANS, BABYLONIANS, ASSYRIANS, PHOENICIANS, ARABS (qq.v.), and a number of smaller peoples such as Moabites, Edomites, and Ammonites. All these peoples spoke languages which were very much alike. When, for example, David took refuge from Saul in the country of Moab, he found himself among a people who spoke practically the same language as himself.

The Hebrews began to settle in Canaan about 1750 B.C. They did not enter the land as a united nation and at one definite period, but in different tribal groups, from different directions, and at different times. According to their own tradition, the earliest group, under the leadership of Abraham, came in from Mesopotamia and finally settled in the south of Canaan round about Hebron. Other groups of tribes continued to come in at intervals from the east and the south, and the settlement was probably complete about 1200 B.C. But the various tribal groups remained separate and independent, often fighting with one another, much as the Bedouin tribes of Arabia have done for many centuries. About 1000 B.C., however, the threat of Philistine conquest forced them to unite under an elected king, and they began to develop a national consciousness. Under Saul, DAVID, and SOLOMON (qq.v. Vol. V), the Hebrews became a state with some kind of political organization, ruled by a despotic monarchy, like the rest of the small kingdoms of Syria and Palestine. The united monarchy only lasted for about 100 years, and after the death of Solomon a split took place which divided the Hebrews into two unequal and independent kingdoms, the larger in the north being known as the kingdom of Israel, and the smaller kingdom in the south, named after its most important tribe, the kingdom of Judah. The northern kingdom came to an end in 721 B.C., when the Assyrian king Sargon took Samaria and carried away most of the northern Israelites to Mesopotamia, replacing them by settlers from other parts of the ASSYRIAN Empire (q.v.). The southern kingdom of Judah continued to exist for another 150 years, until Nebuchadnezzar II of Babylon took Jerusalem in 586 B.C. and carried away a large part of the population of Judah to Babylon. In 539 B.C. the Persian king, Cyrus, took Babylon and allowed the various deported peoples to return to their own countries. A small number of the exiles from Judah, henceforth known as JEWS (q.v.), returned to Judah. They rebuilt the Temple in Jerusalem, restored the ruined city and, for the next 500 years, continued to exist, with a certain amount of self-government, as subjects of Persia, Greece, and Rome successively. Their political existence came to an end

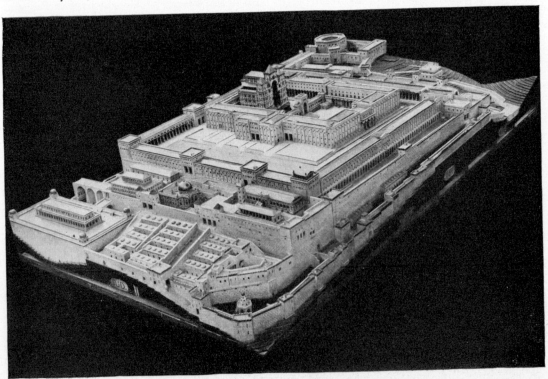

RECONSTRUCTION OF SOLOMON'S TEMPLE
Berlin Mus.

JEHU DOING OBEISANCE BEFORE SHALMANESER III (859–824 B.C.)
Part of an Assyrian relief showing the conquered Hebrews paying tribute. *British Mus.*

in A.D. 70, when, after a siege whose heroism and horror stirred the imagination of the ancient world, Jerusalem fell before the armies of the Roman, Titus. Since then the Jews have been a scattered people, maintaining their religion and distinctive way of life among nearly all the nations of the world.

Although this article is called 'Hebrew Civilization', there is in fact no such thing as a distinctively Hebrew civilization. It is possible that the kind of life lived by any BEDOUIN tribe (q.v.) to-day may give us some idea of how the Hebrews lived before they left their original home in the Arabian steppes. But the earliest group of Hebrews to enter Canaan had already lived in Mesopotamia for at least one generation, in contact with the urban and agricultural civilization of that country. Hence it is misleading to think of the Hebrews as being still a simple nomad people when they entered Canaan. When a country has been invaded and conquered by a foreign people, archaeologists can often find evidence to show whether the invaders were of a higher or lower culture than the people they have conquered. For example, the excavation of such a site as Colchester shows a clear break between the levels of Roman and British civilization. But it is well recognized that excavation in many sites in Palestine shows no violent break between the Canaanite and the Hebrew civilization.

Some of the earliest Hebrew legislation is found in what has been called 'The Book of the Covenant', in Exodus xx–xxiii. Here we have a picture of the way of life of a settled agricultural people: there are laws relating to straying cattle, to the damage of corn-fields by fire or a neighbour's cattle, to damage done by a vicious bull; the three great festivals of the year are agricultural festivals; there is nothing to suggest a nomad way of life. Further, by comparing the early Hebrew laws with the far earlier Babylonian Code of Hammurabi, it is easy to see that the Hebrew law and custom was largely based upon early Mesopotamian law.

Again, excavation has shown that when the invading Hebrews occupied a Canaanite city, such as Beth-shan, for example, they took over the temples which they found there, and adapted them to their own use. Not long ago there were found in the excavation of Samaria some pieces of carved ivory, known as the 'Samaria Ivories', which may have formed part of the decoration of a bed belonging to the time of King Ahab, and which were probably the work of a Hebrew craftsman. These have a decorative pattern which is clearly borrowed from Egyptian designs. All these examples of borrowings in Hebrew law, temples, and craftsmen's designs go to suggest that Hebrew civilization was almost wholly derived from Babylon, Egypt, or Canaan. From representations on Assyrian and Egyptian monuments we can see that Hebrew dress and arrangement of the hair is the same as that of other inhabitants of Palestine or Syria. The patterns and material of Hebrew pottery are Canaanite. When King Solomon wanted an architect and master-craftsman for the building of his temple he had to send to Phoenicia to get one, and the general plan of domestic and public architecture was based on foreign models. The Hebrews even practised human sacrifice like their Canaanite neighbours. When Jeroboam, at the time of the split into two kingdoms, set up new sanctuaries for his northern kingdom, the Hebrew god was represented by bull-images, as was the common practice in agricultural religions in the Near East.

If, then, the civilization of the Hebrews was so lacking in originality and so indistinguishable from that of their neighbours, what was it that in the end made them so distinct from all the other small peoples of Canaan, and caused them to have such a profound and enduring influence upon the history of the world? The answer is not to be found in the material aspects of their civilization, but in the fact that one element, a non-material element, of their civilization developed in a way which has no parallel elsewhere. The class of sacred persons variously known as 'seers' or 'diviners', whose function it was to interpret omens and dreams and to perform certain important ritual ceremonies, was by no means peculiar to the Hebrews (*see* PROPHECY). But only among the Hebrews did it produce a succession of great religious figures whose utterances and writings have been preserved in the collection of Hebrew literature, and whom we know of as 'the Prophets'. As the result of a religious experience which is vividly described in their writings, these men arrived at a conception of God, and of the relation between man and God, which gradually transformed the old nature-religion, with its conception of a storm-god or a fertility-god who might be represented under the form of a bull-image, into a religion whose vital centre was the belief in one God who was a spiritual being, who could not be represented by any man-made image. Under their influence a code of conduct was developed with, as its standard, the character of the God whom their religious experience had revealed to them. History bears witness that, during the closing centuries of their existence as a nation, there was a widespread recognition in the ancient world of the unique character of what the Jews called their *Torah*, that is their Law, especially their moral code; and in the century

before and after Christ many Gentiles were attracted to the Jewish worship (*see* JUDAISM). But this process was suddenly interrupted by an event which, strangely enough, was the crowning achievement of what we may call Hebrew civilization—the birth of Christianity. Christianity in its beginnings was wholly Jewish; its central figure was a Jew, its earliest adherents were Jews, its conception of the Kingdom of God and of the Messiah were Jewish, and its moral standards were Jewish. Whatever opinions may be held about the truth of Christianity, it cannot be denied that it has played a very profound part in the growth of Western civilization, and in this fact lies the final judgement on the contribution of Hebrew civilization to the world.

See also ANCIENT CIVILIZATIONS; JUDAISM; CHRISTIANITY; Vol. IV: HEBREW LANGUAGE.

HEBREW MYTHS. Myth is a word which has, so to speak, come down in the world. To-day, if we say that a statement is a myth, we mean that it is false and unworthy to be believed by intelligent people. Hence many people are unwilling to admit that there are myths in the Bible. But in the early stages of human history, myths were not only regarded as true, but they were an essential part of religion.

Long before the appearance of the Hebrews on the stage of history, the Sumerians and Egyptians on the banks of the Euphrates and Nile had learned the arts of agriculture and how to live together in cities. They had learned how to control their environment and make it serve their needs. In doing this they had found that they were surrounded by forces whose nature they did not understand. They did not know why the buried seed sprang up to new life, nor whether the miracle would be repeated the next year; what made the life-giving flood of the Nile come with such marvellous regularity, nor what caused the destructive and incalculable floods of the Tigris and Euphrates. So in an attempt to control these unknown forces surrounding them, the dwellers in Egypt and Mesopotamia had developed a system of RITUAL (q.v.), that is, a set of actions performed in a fixed way, at regular times, by authorized persons (priests). The ritual consisted of a dramatic representation of the acts which they believed had brought their civilization into being, in other words, the drama of creation. As the priests performed the drama, they chanted

THE CREATION OF MAN
Painting by Michelangelo (1475–1564), a detail of the Creation on the ceiling of the Sistine Chapel in the Vatican, Rome
Alinari

or sang the story of what they were acting, and this was the 'myth' or spoken part of the ritual. At the most important point of the great Babylonian New Year Festival the priests chanted a myth, known as the Epic of Creation, which told how the god Marduk had died and risen again, how he had conquered the chaos-dragon, Tiamat, and how he had separated the heavens from the earth, created the heavenly bodies, and finally made man out of clay and the blood of a god. All this was repeated every year in the spring, because they believed that the ritual, and the myth which was part of it, were necessary in order to keep creation going. In the earliest form of the creation-myth, which goes back to the SUMERIANS (q.v.), the creation is connected with the story of a great flood from which one man was saved in a specially constructed boat, built by the orders of a god, so that the 'seed of life' should be preserved. There are other early BABYLONIAN MYTHS (q.v.), all having some connexion with ritual. These myths with their ritual spread to those neighbouring countries which came under the influence of Babylonian civilization, and especially to Canaan and the Hebrews.

When the first Hebrew settlers came into Canaan they had already, according to their own tradition, lived for some time in Mesopotamia and come under the influence of BABYLONIAN CIVILIZATION (q.v.). In Canaan they found the same type of religion and civilization in altered forms. The Hebrew traditions of their origins were collected by the editors of the Old Testament in the 5th century B.C. and woven into the story which we have now in the first eleven chapters of the book of Genesis. This contains the creation-story, the stories of the garden of Eden, the Fall, Cain and Abel, the Flood, and the Tower of Babel. There are other fragments of myth scattered about the Old Testament, such as the myth of the slaying of the dragon in Ps. lxxiv. 12–14 and Isa. li. 9, and another form of the Paradise-myth in Ezek. xxviii. 11–19. It is clear that there is a close connexion between the stories in Gen. i–ii and the Sumerian and Babylonian myths of Creation and the Flood: for instance, the Hebrew word for the chaos of waters in Gen. i. 2 is *tehom*, and this corresponds to the Babylonian name of the chaos-dragon Tiamat. In the Babylonian myth the character corresponding to Noah sends out birds to find out how far the waters of the flood have gone down, just as Noah does in the Hebrew story; and there are many other striking parallels and resemblances. Hence it seems certain that the Hebrews drew their myths from the common stock of myths which formed a part of the religious ritual of the ancient Near East. Also, whereas we can see the Babylonian and Egyptian myths in their original setting as an essential part of the ritual to which they were attached, the Hebrew stories have been separated from the ritual and completely transformed by the influence of the religious ideas of later writers who gave the Old Testament its present form. In the minds of these writers the myths of Creation, Paradise, the Fall, and the Flood came to be thought of as history—the history of the Hebrew people, intended to teach them that everything that had happened from the beginning was a part of the plan of God for His people. By the 5th century B.C., when the Old Testament took its present form, the religious ritual of the Hebrews, as well as their idea of what God was like, had greatly changed, and so these stories became entirely separated from the ancient ritual to which they had originally belonged. But the sacred character of the stories was not lost. The story of the slaying of the dragon disappeared save as a picturesque image to be found in the poetry, but the other stories were retained and added to, so that they should convey religious and moral teaching; and these are the stories to be found in the familiar narrative of Genesis.

See also HEBREW CIVILIZATION; MYTHOLOGY.

HECTOR, *see* GREEK HEROES.

HELEN OF TROY, *see* TROJANS.

HELL. The word comes from the name of the Scandinavian goddess of death, Hel, Queen of the Lower Regions.

In English the word Hell is usually used to mean either the place of torment of the wicked after death, or, as in the Apostles' Creed, the place of departed spirits, like the Greek Hades or the Hebrew Sheol. In the more primitive beliefs, however, the idea of rewards and punishments after death is not inspired by any ethical or religious consideration. The next life, it is thought, will be either better or worse than that on earth, but only in a material sense. That is to say, there will be more opportunities for exciting fighting, good hunting, excellent harvests, and perfect weather, or there will be none of these things, and life will be just a dreary, shadowy, ghost-like existence, as the Greeks and Hebrews pictured it (*see* HEAVEN). In neither case is the lot of the dead fixed by right or wrong conduct in the moral sense in which we understand these terms. It is all pre-arranged according to a general plan, every soul going to its appointed place either below ground, in the sky country, in the western paradise where the Sun sets, or to the Isles of the Blest. Virtues like bravery and conspicuous service to the community, or vices such as blasphemy and breaking the rules of society, often play an important part in the ultimate fate of the soul; but, generally speaking, it is not until people begin to understand the idea of a holy and righteous God, that right and wrong in the higher meaning of good and evil are made the test. The more primitive ideas are by no means confined to savages—we find them in all the great ancient civilizations, and many have survived in most countries to this day, even where higher beliefs prevail.

In Greece the abode that corresponds to hell was called Tartarus and was represented as a deep, sunless, underground region where those who rebelled against the gods were confined behind closed gates and afflicted by a variety of punishments. Sisyphus, for instance, was condemned to roll an immense stone from the bottom to the top of a hill. Whenever it reached the summit, it rolled down again to the bottom, and so he had to begin his wearisome task all over again. Another notorious 'sinner', Tantalus, a son of Zeus who had betrayed the secrets of the gods, had to stand

HERMES LEADING A SOUL TO THE STYX

The Greeks believed that dead people were rowed over the River Styx by Charon on their journey from earth to Hades. From an Attic Vase, *c.* 450 B.C. in the National Mus., Athens. From W. Reizler, *Weissgrundige attische Lekythen*

THE LAST JUDGEMENT

The Souls are weighed in the balance by the archangel Michael. The saved climb the ladder of Heaven, while the damned are cast down to everlasting torment. From a 12th-century painting in Chaldon Church, Surrey

Victoria & Albert Mus.

parched with thirst in a lake, the water of which receded every time he tried to drink. Over his head grew clusters of fruit, but always just out of his reach. Another victim was Tityos who was preyed on by vultures. In one branch of Greek beliefs Tartarus was the name of the place where those who had not been purified of their sins on earth endured torments before they were reborn into this world.

In Indian mythology those who did not perform the proper rites or disobeyed the commands of the priests were hurled into a prison of great darkness and sat among streams of blood chewing hair. According to the beliefs of HINDUISM (q.v.) there are between twenty and thirty hells which are reached after a terrible journey. On arrival at one of these the wicked man is plunged into a heated cauldron, or a lake of blood or of stinking mud; or he may be driven through a dense jungle full of plants with leaves as sharp as knives; or he may have to walk over a plain paved with iron spikes. After these tortures have been endured for a time, the soul is

reborn in another body and given a chance to do better and to reach heaven at last. To this end some Hindus put their whole trust in a divine saviour such as Vishnu, Krishna, or Shiva, but others think that the process of reincarnation (i.e. rebirth in a series of bodies) works according to fixed laws based on the principle that what a man sows in this life he reaps in the next.

In the Scriptures of BUDDHISM (q.v.) eight hells are described. These are situated below the earth, and there murderers, liars, persecutors, infidels, and those who have killed their parents or a religious teacher or certain animals undergo grim punishments. Attached to each great hell are sixteen lesser hells, some of which are very hot, others intensely cold. As among the Hindus, the punishments are thought to come to an end when the soul has been purified, though it may take several thousand years before release is secured. And that is not the end: peace at the last can only be secured when all traces of earthly contacts and activities (*karma*) have been removed through a series of lives.

In Persia ZOROASTRIANISM (q.v.) abandoned the idea of reincarnation in a series of different bodies. Those whose deeds were named as evil, when their actions had been weighed in the balances, were led away to the 'house of the Druj', where they were condemned to live in endless darkness surrounded with demons and wicked souls, and to eat loathsome and poisonous food until the resurrection. Then, after three days of further punishment in a restored body, there would come a great flood of molten metal which would purify even hell itself. So that, at the last, God (Ahura Mazdah) would reign supreme everywhere, and the Devil and all his works would be destroyed.

The Jews, who borrowed a great many of their later religious ideas from the Persians, when they gave up thinking of Sheol as the place where all the dead went (Heaven), gradually changed that gloomy underworld into a sort of 'waiting-room' for either the good Israelites before the final resurrection, or for both the righteous and the wicked. It was also sometimes called 'the pit' and was sometimes a prison-house with barred gates where evil kings and bad angels were sent for punishment. But when it came to be thought of as a place of torment, it came to mean the same as Gehenna, the name given to the Jewish hell. This place derived its name from the valley of Hinnom on the south-west of Jerusalem, where all the refuse of the city was burnt, and children were offered in sacrifice to the god Moloch (Jer. vii. 32, xxxii. 35). Such a spot would readily suggest the unhappy lot of those who because of their sins were cut off from God and were condemned to live in a fiery abyss where 'their worm dieth not and the fire is not quenched'.

This is the meaning attached to it in the New Testament, where Jesus Himself is said to have used the name Gehenna in this sense. But although He spoke of the wicked being consumed in everlasting fire, He was careful to explain that it was the *spiritual* consequences of wrongdoing that were experienced on the other side of the grave. Every man has before him the choice of two ways, the one leading to life in the Kingdom of God, the other to destruction in Gehenna. In the end, however, all evil, it was said, would be conquered and the devil and his angels would be consumed (Matt. xxv. 41; Rev. xx. 13 ff., xxi. 8). But even when the heavens and the new earth have been created, and the wicked have been cast into the lake of fire, there will still be evil-doers who will have to dwell outside the city of God (Rev. xxi. 15).

Islam borrowed most of these Jewish and Christian ideas. According to its teaching, when Jesus descends from heaven, the Anti-Christ will be destroyed, but unbelievers and demons will remain in hell for ever, tormented by huge serpents, fire, and boiling water. When their bodies have been burned up new ones will be created to suffer more torment. No one, however, will be eternally damned who believes in the prophet Mohammed; and as some think that in the end everybody will become Moslems, it should follow that eventually all will be saved. But the Koran teaches that those who go either to Paradise or to Hell will dwell for ever in whatever abode they reach.

If these beliefs seem to-day to be rather crude and materialistic, it has to be remembered that they are attempts to put into words and pictures, as in the parables in the Gospels, truths about the awful reality and far-reaching consequences of evil in a world which, nevertheless, has been created and is controlled by a good God who is just as well as loving. The evil as well as the good that men do lives after them, and if the one carries with it consequences in the eternal world, so must the other.

See also RELIGION; SATAN.

HELLENES. A term used by the Greeks to describe, not a Greek nation or state, but all Greek-speaking peoples, as opposed to non-Greek-speaking peoples whom they called 'barbarians'. The Greeks liked to think they were descended from a common ancestor called Hellen.

See also GREEK CIVILIZATION.

HERA, *see* GODS OF GREECE AND ROME.

HERACLES, *see* GREEK HEROES.

HERMES, *see* GODS OF GREECE AND ROME.

HINDUISM. This means the religion of Hind or India. Yet it is not the only religion of all the 400 million inhabitants of India. There are altogether about 216 million Hindus, apart from 9 million people following primitive animist beliefs of their own, many of whom are gradually being absorbed into Hinduism. The rest of the population of India are mainly either Moslems, Christians, or PARSEES (q.v.).

Although as a system of belief Hinduism is extremely tolerant, and will make room for almost any sort of religious idea or practice, it is also extremely national, especially of recent years, and does not normally make converts of foreigners. As we shall see, it has quite a distinct way of thinking about life, but when it seeks to spread this attitude outside India, it ceases to be Hinduism, and becomes something else, as, for example, BUDDHISM (q.v.), a religion which first grew up in the mind of a Hindu. Hinduism is indeed rather a form of civilization than a religion, as we understand the term in the West. To be a Hindu you must properly be a member of some CASTE (q.v.), and it is expected that Hindus will not live outside India except as visitors—strict Hindus of high caste will seldom cross the ocean. If some non-Hindu group of people in India or near its frontiers seeks to be included in Hinduism, it is said that this is only possible by the formation of an additional caste. Hinduism is not a state-controlled religion, and in this respect India is very different from China or Japan.

A Hindu accepts five main general ideas as the framework of his spiritual life.

(1) The Hindu's idea of the highest way of living is that of the holy ascetic (*see* ASCETICISM), the hermit who lives a very frugal (vegetarian) and solitary life. Although it is recognized that during his life a man may become in turn a student, a householder, and the father of a family, sooner or later he is expected to pass on into the final stage of the hermit. There are many different sorts of 'holy' persons besides the *purohit*, or priest, who is in charge of a temple or shrine. There is the *guru*, who is a spiritual teacher and adviser, and who has one or more disciples. Then there is the *sādhu*, or wandering ascetic, who may be also a teacher; and the *bhagat*, or emotional devotee, who is greatly in request by villagers for casting out demons. Although their occupations may vary, they have in common the possession of a mental and bodily technique for putting and keeping themselves in a state of consciousness which not only claims to unite the soul with God, but also makes for calmness and good health. This technique is known as *yoga*, a word meaning much the same as our word 'yoke', and coming from the same root. The weakness of *yoga* is its tendency to make the devotee identify himself with God. One *sādhu* said with great arrogance to a European

THE HINDU GOD VISHNU, THE PROTECTOR AND RESTORER
13th-century sculptured relief from Konarak, India

spectator: 'You can look on me, for I am God.' It would be unjust to condemn all ascetics on this account, but the Hindu mystic is usually unlike the Christian in just this respect.

(2) The Hindu does not believe, as most Europeans do, in the importance of historical events or historical accuracy. He does not much care whether a story is true, so long as it contains an inward and spiritual meaning. The reason for this is that he does not usually believe that God acts with a purpose in history, nor does he believe that a single human life could express any important purpose. Hence he is not interested in such things as the record of important events, or the biographies of great men, or keeping a National Portrait Gallery. He believes

THE HINDU GOD SHIVA, THE DESTROYER
Copper figure from South India. *Mus. of Fine Arts, Boston*

others sing emotional hymns. Some would kill human beings in sacrifice if the Government did not prevent them; others believe in *ahimsā*, or harmlessness, which is a reverence for life so intense that it makes them even strain the liquids they drink to avoid killing any small organisms that may be floating in them. There is, in fact, among Hindus a toleration of opposites, and they seem able to accept contradictory ideas at one and the same time.

(4) Hindus usually believe that living things have a succession of lives, past and future—reincarnation. This chain of births and re-births, called *samsara*, or 'migration', is governed by a law or principle called *karma*, or 'action'. Thus the result of virtuous deeds is to be re-born in a higher state, while the result of vicious action is to be re-born in some unpleasant state, as a worm, a moth, or a pig. It must not be supposed that Hindus like this idea of reincarnation. Far from it. The most earnest of them seek, and have ever sought, to escape from its dreary round into a condition of peace and of freedom from the passions which vex and disturb humanity, and to be swallowed up in the life of God. Yet even this does not satisfy all of them. One sage remarked, 'I like the taste of sugar, but I should not like to become sugar.' There are also Hindus who believe in a future life not unlike that expected by Christians, in which the soul will enjoy the presence of God and the fellowship of other human beings, without entirely losing its own self.

(5) Lastly, Hinduism teaches that whatever Being lies behind and above this physical world that Being is not concerned with morality—with questions of right and wrong, good and evil, and so on. A Hindu would not be likely to have written the Ten Commandments.

It is rather hard to describe what it is like to be a Hindu, in view of the great variety of beliefs and practices which Hindus acknowledge; but in the main there are two broad types.

The first type does not believe in any personal God, whether one or many. 'We philosophers are above it', they would say. For simple people it may be useful to make acts of worship or devotion to such a Being, but for those who claim to have climbed from the lower to the higher knowledge this idea seems childish and even foolish. There is really one Existence and one only, and the soul is identical with it. About this Existence you can really say nothing,

life to be due to the surplus and abundant energy of the Supreme Being, rather than to any plan on His part.

(3) At the same time Hinduism seems to allow beliefs or disbeliefs of almost any kind, so long as the framework of caste is preserved. Thus there are Hindus who are virtually atheists, others who are believers in many gods, and yet others who put their faith in a single god—one not entirely unlike the God of Christians, who comes from time to time and lives in human (or animal) form on earth. Almost all Hindus think that there are a number of divine beings, gods and goddesses, such as Vishnu, Shiva, Kali, and so on, who are different aspects of the Supreme Being, known as Brahma, Himself beyond description, since He embraces and constitutes *everything that is*. Some Hindus might be called idolaters; others will have nothing to do with idols, though they generally acknowledge that the use of images is helpful to many people. Some are meditative philosophers;

knew as Hittites, and whose civilization is here described, were the second of these groups —those who dwelt in Asia Minor and north Syria between about 2000 and 1200 B.C.

At first the king of the Hittites was elected, and his power was limited by the existence of a council of nobles—a kind of feudal system rather like that which existed among one of the early groups of Greeks. But after a period of struggle between the king and the nobles, a struggle which is described in an early Hittite text, the kingship became more after the pattern of the kings in the ancient Near East. In the early period the bare title 'king' was always used, but after about 1600 B.C. the king was addressed by the title 'my Sun'. This shows that the position of the king was becoming much more elevated and powerful. The early feudal system also disappeared; instead, the king governed by means of local officials whom he could dismiss at will—a system also to be found in Egypt at much the same period. An interesting feature of Hittite civilization was the important place held by the queen, a position independent of the king and with a special religious significance. This is to be connected with the fact that a goddess, the Sun-goddess, and not a god, held the chief place among the Hittite deities—a state of things also to be found in Cretan religion, where the Mother Goddess was the centre of the worship (see MINOAN CIVILIZATION).

At the end of the 14th century B.C. the Hittite Empire was organized into a kind of federal state made up of a number of small conquered states. These had some stand in the government, but the central Hittite kingdom had always the decisive voice. From the valuable documents found at Boghaz-Koi we have been able to learn a great deal about the foreign treaties of the time and we can see the beginnings of what might be called international law. Among these documents was a Hittite code of criminal and civil law. Compared with the codes of other Near East peoples, such as the Assyrians or Babylonians, the Hittite code was much more humane: it was quite without the more brutal forms of punishment used by their neighbours, and the death penalty was limited to certain capital offences and could only be inflicted on a freeman by sentence of the king's court.

Our knowledge of the religion of the Hittites has been gained partly from carvings and inscriptions found in certain ancient Hittite holy

since it is beyond definition, and you yourself are part of it. Hindus call this idea of everything being part of a Single Substance *Advaita*, which means 'only one thing really exists, i.e. God, and we are all part of God'.

The second type of believer generally tries to live in a gracious personal relationship with one single deity, generally Vishnu or Shiva, though there are admitted to be many others. This means saying prayers, singing hymns, and offering sacrifices to one or other of these gods. The worshipper uses images and symbols freely, and makes often quite simple gifts such as rice or marigold flowers, or a kid or calf. Vishnu is a kindly god who protects and restores, but Shiva represents the ruthless force of tropical nature. Neither have the clear-cut personality of Jesus Christ, and they do not give moral and spiritual teaching as he does (though Vishnu is sometimes said to do so); yet both are adored by the pious Hindu with something not unlike the earnestness of evangelical Christians. Followers of Shiva carry on the forehead, breast, and arms three parallel lines called the

tripundram ☰. Followers of Vishnu carry on the forehead a sort of V-shaped sign, ⩗.

Hindus, especially in southern India, have built a great number of large and richly carved temples, which are thought of as the earthly palaces of the gods, whose images are treated as though they were actually princes or nobles, having to be waked, washed, fed, amused, taken for drives, and presented with petitions. Besides the temples there are many outdoor shrines, some of them connected with lesser deities concerned with special human needs. Thus there is a goddess of small-pox. On one festival in the year, the *Ayudha puja*, everybody worships and makes offerings to the tools of his trade or profession. Thus a student may sacrifice to his books, his pen, or desk, or to the goddess of learning, and a mill-hand in Bombay may offer a kid to the machine which he minds. When it is remembered that Hindus believe that everything is part of God, it is easier to understand the reason for this practice, also found in other old religions. In the Old Testament (Habakkuk i. 15 and 16) there is an account of some people

A SADHU, OR WANDERING ASCETIC, AND TWO BRAHMINS OUTSIDE A HINDU MONASTERY. *Paul Popper*

who sacrificed and burned incense to
fishing-net.

Hinduism to-day is being deeply affec
contact with Europe and America: educa
spreading, and new ideas are destroyi
customs and beliefs. Some Indians are
up their religion altogether, others are I
ing followers of some substitute-religic
communism or nationalism, and many
become, if not entirely and openly Chris
least influenced privately by Christian te
Some are even at work reforming Hinduis
trying to bring features of other religions
—yet without ceasing to call themselves I
Hinduism is, in fact, not a fixed and imm
system of beliefs, but the extremely vari
tolerant spiritual culture of a subcor
which has changed much and is still cha

See also INDIAN PEOPLES.

HITTITES. The importance of the Hi
the ancient history of the Near East h

THE HITTITE GOD HADAD
Sculptured figure found in the Hittite City of (
mish. *Dr. D. G. Hogarth*

HITTITE KING PRESENTING HIS SON TO HIS ARMY
Behind him are his younger children and the Queen. Sculptured relief from the King's Gate at Carchemish, *c.* 800 B.C.

model for the kind of historical records which
we have of the Hebrew kings.

Hittite art is seen at its best in the stone
carvings in deep relief, and in statues of gods
supported on lions or sphinxes. They show
the influence of Egypt and Mesopotamia in the
choice of designs and mythological subjects; but
the treatment shows a rough vigour which is
peculiarly Hittite. Further excavation will no
doubt throw fresh light on the civilization of
this remarkable and important ancient people.

See also ANCIENT CIVILIZATIONS.

HOLY COMMUNION, *see* SACRAMENT; SACRI-
FICE.

HOLY ROMAN EMPIRE. Europe in the
Middle Ages was not divided into nations as it
is now, but was split up into countless small
provinces ruled by dukes, princes, and kings.
Yet there was a sense of unity which knit
Europe together. The members of each state
were also members of Christendom and believed
in the brotherhood of all Christians and in the
authority of the Pope as head of the Church.
The Pope's authority was real and binding,
covering not only spiritual matters but some
temporal ones as well.

The idea existed that there should be a
temporal power corresponding to the spiritual
authority of the Church, to which all the feudal

lords would owe allegiance. The Roman Empire
had been this unifying power, and men still
looked back on the greatness of the Roman
Empire under which Christianity had developed. In A.D. 800 CHARLEMAGNE (q.v. Vol.
V), who sought to revive the culture of Ancient
Rome and to unify the peoples he had conquered, was crowned Holy Roman Emperor by
the Pope in Rome. He was a great and powerful
leader and had conquered most of what is now
western Germany, Austria, France, Belgium,
and Holland. But after his death there was no
leader, until the German Otto 200 years later,
with vision or power enough to give reality to
an idea so unfamiliar to many of the peoples of
Europe. Otto and his successors held the title
for a short time while they remained powerful,
and then followed a period during which Holy
Roman Emperor was no more than an empty
title. Nevertheless, although it was impossible
to give real meaning to the Empire, the ideal
of a single temporal power ruling Christendom
as a counterpart to the spiritual rule of the
Church persisted throughout the Middle Ages.

At the end of the 13th century Rudolph of
Hapsburg, the ruler of Austria, became so
strong that he was elected Emperor. From that
time the title was usually held by the Hapsburg
family until its dissolution in 1806. In theory the
title was not hereditary, the Emperors being

chosen from among the rulers of German states by seven Electors—the Archbishops of Mainz, Cologne, and Trier, the King of Bohemia, the Duke of Saxony, the Ruler of Brandenburg, and the Count Palatine of the Rhine. But in practice the heads of the Hapsburg family were elected Holy Roman Emperors because they were the most powerful German princes.

The Empire was administered by a diet or parliament to which the subject states belonged, but they only acknowledged its authority when it suited their convenience. As it depended on the various states for its army, it had little real power. Rather, the states used the diet to further their own ends, and the electors often sold their votes to the highest bidder.

In the 16th century many states were developing into powerful nations over which the Emperor had no control, and the Empire lost entirely its original significance. By the nineteenth century it held authority only over the Hapsburg territories of the Austrian Empire, and in 1806 the title was finally abolished.

HOMO SAPIENS, see Fossil Man.

HONDURAS, PEOPLES OF, see Central Americans.

HOROSCOPE, see Astrology.

HOTTENTOTS. This was the name given by the Dutch to certain groups of natives whom they found in Cape Colony in the 17th century. These people speak mainly in words of one syllable, most of which, as in the Bushman language, begin with a click, which makes their speech sound jerky and staccato. The Hottentots once occupied the greater part of Cape Colony and, although many have been driven out, a number of tribes still survive in South-West Africa. Not only in language but in appearance the Hottentots are somewhat like the Bushmen (q.v.). They have slightly narrower faces, are taller in stature, and have a more yellowish skin, but they have the same 'peppercorn hair', growing in little tight spiral tufts. The main difference between them is that, while the Bushmen were always hunters and collectors of wild food and never gave up their hunting life in the mountains and gorges, the Hottentots occupied the plains and kept cattle and sheep —and this influenced their way of life, their food, their clothes, their huts, and their fate.

For while the frontiersmen relentlessly shot down the hunting Bushmen, like any other animals that attacked their cattle, they encouraged the Hottentots who were useful to them as herders, and therefore more of them survived. Their clothing originally consisted of garments of skin, the men wearing a loin-cloth, the women aprons, while a kaross, or sheepskin cloak, kept them warm in winter. Nowadays most Hottentots wear European garments. Their social organization is also more complex than that of the Bushmen. They are divided into a number of groups or clans—the head of the senior clan being chief of the group. Marriage is marked by the exchange of cattle between the families of the couple, and a special feast is held. There are also elaborate ceremonies for Birth, Initiation, and Marriage (q.v.), though some of the original initiation ceremonies for boys, which were concerned with hunting, are no longer held.

The Hottentots still rely mainly for their living on their cattle, sheep, and goats, and these are dependent on pastures and water. But they cannot always find pasture, and water is often scarcer than grass. So the group cannot long remain in one place but must be always ready to move, wandering from pasture to pasture and from water-hole to water-hole. Milk is their chief food which they drink sour and store in skin bags. They do not kill their animals for food except on special occasions such as feasts, births, or marriages. They obtain some meat by hunting and snaring wild game, by fishing, or by catching lizards and mice. Vegetable food is obtained from wild plants, roots, fruits, and grasses. In recent times, with the restrictions on hunting, these wandering groups are obliged to supplement their food-supply by growing crops such as wheat, maize, millet, and beans, and in consequence they are beginning to lead a more settled life.

The Hottentots' huts are exactly suited to their wandering way of life—made of materials ready to hand, easy to set up, take down, and transport, yet strong enough to resist a storm. A number of light poles—twenty to sixty, according to the size of the hut required—are collected and planted in a circle some 3-5 yards in diameter. These are then bent over and tied at the top to make a skeleton framework which is strengthened by intertwining rods and sticks, as in making a basket. Then they thread reeds into mats by means of bark string, and tie these

A HOTTENTOT FAMILY

The woman is preparing locusts which she stews in the large pot. *Dorian Leigh*

mats on to the cross-sticks of the hut to make an excellent covering. If it rains the reeds swell and make a waterproof roof; in hot sunshine they shrink and let in the air. In cold weather a lining of skins makes the inside warm and snug. The main entrance is away from the direction of the wind and is covered by a mat which will roll up or let down. A hollow in the centre of the floor is the fire-place, and round this are the mats or skins on which the family sleep. When they move on, they merely have to untie and roll up the mats, pull up the poles, tie them up with ox-hide thongs, and pack the bundles on the backs of the oxen, who plod off with them to the next camping-ground. The whole encampment is surrounded by a fence of thorn bushes.

The culture of the Hottentots is more advanced than that of the Bushmen. Their arts and crafts are more skilled, and they know how to smelt iron. They make vessels of wood and bags of skin for water.

Music and dancing—religious and non-religious, or a mixture of both in pantomime—play a large part in their lives. They have a musical bow, and they also form orchestras of reed pipes which are conducted by a bandmaster.

Their religion has been very much influenced by missionaries, and little is known of their original beliefs. But they worshipped the moon as well as certain mythological heroes, some of whom were especially prayed to for rain.

See also NEGRO AFRICANS; SOUTH AFRICANS.

HUGUENOTS. French Protestants who followed the reforming movement of CALVINISM (q.v.) in the 16th and 17th centuries. In the latter half of the 16th century there were no fewer than eight minor civil wars (known as the French Wars of Religion) between the Huguenots and the Catholics, and a terrible massacre of Huguenots took place in Paris on the eve of St. Bartholomew in 1572. However, this strife was ended in 1598 when, by the Edict of Nantes, King Henry of Navarre gave full liberty to the Huguenots to worship as they pleased. Nearly a hundred years later, in 1685, the edict was revoked by Louis XIV, and Huguenots for a time were forbidden to worship in public places.

As a result many thousands fled abroad and took refuge in England and other countries, which benefited from the Huguenots' skill in craftsmanship and trade.

HUNGARIANS. The origin of the Hungarians, or rather the Magyars as they call themselves, is not known for certain. That they came into eastern Europe from south-west Asia is now generally agreed; but most of the nomadic peoples who came from that part of Asia are Slavs, whereas the Magyars are quite a different people. There are no certain records of them till they raided eastern Europe in A.D. 894. For a hundred years the land they held depended on their success in battle, until at last, in A.D. 997, Stephen I, a great statesman and soldier and the most famous figure in Hungarian history, became king. He established his authority over the warlike tribes in the country we now call Hungary, welded them into a nation, completed their conversion to Christianity, and invited settlers from the west to teach them the arts of peace. He died in 1038 and was canonized by the Pope in 1083. In the centuries that followed the countries of eastern Europe were too busy fighting among themselves to realize their great danger from the highly disciplined forces of the Ottoman Turks. In 1547 the Turks conquered Hungary and settled in the rich central plains, and there they remained as rulers for about 150 years. In 1686 they were driven out, and Hungary became part of the Austrian Empire. For nearly two centuries the Magyars struggled against the Austrians, who ruled the country from Vienna, until in the middle of the 19th century they forced the Austrian Emperor to recognize Hungary as a self-governing kingdom. From then, the Emperor of Austria was also crowned King of Hungary at Budapest (the capital) with the crown of St. Stephen. After the First World War, in which Austria-Hungary fought on the side of Germany, Hungary was separated entirely from Austria and also lost much of her territory. In 1941 she again joined Germany in the Second World War, in the vain hope of recovering this land.

A review of the distracted history of the Magyars is necessary for any understanding of this proud, romantic, passionate people. They will speak proudly of their kingdom, which lasted for a thousand years, forgetting how often the kings were deposed and the country overrun. They dislike and despise their neighbours, and regard themselves as the bulwark of civilization in eastern Europe. Until recently the nobles wore their magnificent historic costumes of velvet and brocade with the 'slung jacket' and the jewelled sword, on all state occasions.

Before 1914 most of the land was owned by the great nobles, but these estates have been gradually broken up. Over 55% of the population is engaged in agriculture, southern Hungary being one of the great granaries of Europe. The Magyars who live on the Great Hungarian Plain have been for generations stock-rearers and breeders of horses. They are practically a community of their own, living very simple, isolated lives, except when they round up their horses, cattle, or sheep and drive them to the big stock-fairs. Until recent days they wore a special most picturesque costume—wide-skirted trousers, leather aprons, and felt hats with broad brims. They are spectacular horsemen, and very skilled with the lasso, which they use to catch and bring in animals from the herds on the plains. Old methods of stock-breeding are being

HUNGARIAN PEASANT COSTUME
These gay national costumes are still worn in the country districts on Sundays and holidays. *Roy. Geog. Soc.*

replaced by modern ones, however, and the picturesque cowboy is disappearing.

Gypsy encampments are a common feature of Hungary. The gypsies have great musical gifts, so that, in spite of their vagabond, thieving way of life, they are welcome with their violins and guitars at village festivals, at cafés in Budapest, and even at the great houses; and their wild music and dancing form part of every festivity (*see* Gypsies). Budapest (Buda on the west bank of the Danube and Pest on the east) used to pride itself on being one of the gayest capitals in Europe; no restaurant or café was too small to have its gypsy orchestra. On the hot summer nights most of the population sat out or strolled on the long promenade beside the Danube, the lights sparkling in the water and the old castle of Buda on the far side glowing like a stage set.

See also Vol. III: Hungary; Vol. IV: Finnish and Allied Languages.

HUNS. These were a nomad people once scattered widely in Asia in the steppe country, north of the Caspian Sea. They were probably akin to the Mongols and the Turks, and were short in stature with black hair, yellow skins, broad noses, and small, deep-set eyes. In the 4th century A.D. they began to move westward across the Danube into Europe, spreading panic before them. They rode small, swift, tireless horses and made surprise attacks with such ferocity that no one could withstand them. Their wild, ferocious appearance, and the cruelty with which they enslaved or exterminated the peoples they overran, filled Europe with terror.

They later settled north of the Danube in the lands which are now Austria and Hungary, and dominated the peoples for a wide area around them. In the 5th century, under their ruthless leader Attila (q.v. Vol. V), they reached the height of their power, their dominions stretching from the river Rhine to the Urals and the Caucasus. Attila attacked the territories of the Roman Empire, and for a time it looked as though he would overrun all Europe; but in A.D. 451 he was defeated by a combination of the Romans, Goths, and Franks in a very bloody battle on the plain of Châlons, south-east of Paris. The next year, however, Attila struck south and advanced on Rome, destroying everything on the way. Rome was not sacked, partly because Attila's armies were stricken with pestilence, and partly because the Pope, Leo I, went out to make a personal appeal to him and bought him off with large sums of money.

Soon after Attila's death in A.D. 453 the Hunnish Empire destroyed itself by internal quarrels and fell to pieces. The main body of the Huns moved back to the Urals, where they remained as a nuisance to the Byzantine Empire for some seventy years.

The present Hungarians have no connexion with the Huns, in spite of their name: they are a Magyar people who came into Europe at a later date, after the Huns had disappeared. The word 'Hun' as applied to Germans has no reference to their racial descent, but is used to denote ferocity and destructiveness, and was not applied to them until the 1914–18 war.

HUSSITE, *see* Moravian Church.

HYDRA, A many-headed snake, *see* Fabulous Creatures.

I

IBERIANS, *see* SPANIARDS.

ICELANDERS, *see* Vol. III: ICELAND.

INCA CIVILIZATION. When the Spaniards conquered Peru in 1533, they found a vast Inca empire extending from Ecuador in the north to about the middle of Chile in the south, a distance of over 2,000 miles. It also included a considerable part of the highlands of Bolivia and Argentina, but to the eastward it stopped short at the tropical forests of the Amazon basin. These Incas (so-called after their king, the 'Inca') were a highland folk, having their capital at Cuzco, 11,000 feet above sea-level. Their empire followed roughly the lines of the Andes mountain range, but included the narrow strip of lowland on the Pacific coast.

The Incas were not, however, the first inhabitants of this part of South America (*see* PERU, ANCIENT). From small tribal beginnings their dominion had grown by conquests in the course of about five centuries, attaining its full extent at the end of the 14th century A.D. At about this time, having gradually extended and consolidated their power in the highlands, the Incas swept down to the coast destroying or absorbing all the older cultures. The Incas represent the last phase of the old civilizations, and we know much more about them than about the earlier cultures, since their civilization was seen by the Spaniards and described with much detail by historians and writers of the 16th century.

The Inca state was very highly organized, socialistic in some respects, but dominated by one supreme ruler, the Inca, and the members of his royal clan. The Inca himself was worshipped as the divine representative of the Sun, and lived in magnificent state. The ordinary people lived a simple, industrious life; they were provided with the necessities of life, but had very little liberty and owned no property. All their work was regulated and controlled by state officials, and a fixed amount of all that they produced was allotted to the Inca and to the Sun for the maintenance of the priesthood and the

WALL AT OLLANTAYTAMBO, NEAR CUZCO IN THE ANDES
It is made of large irregular blocks of stone, accurately fitted together without the use of mortar. *Bennet Greig*

WATER BOTTLE

It was carried on the back by means of a cord passing through the handles and round the forehead. *British Mus.*

temples. Writing was not known, and no form of money was in use; yet accurate accounts were kept by means of elaborately knotted and coloured strings called *quipus*. Even to this day knotted strings are used by Indian shepherds in the Andes to keep a tally of their flocks.

The Incas showed great skill in the construction without machinery of roads, aqueducts, and reservoirs, suspension bridges, and other public works. Two main roads ran from north to south, one through the mountains and the other along the coast. In some places they were paved or raised on causeways, in others hewn out of the solid rock: their excellence excited the admiration of the Spanish conquerors of South America. The Incas also showed great ingenuity in the vast system of terraces which they built with much labour along the steep slopes of the valleys for the cultivation of their crops, and which are still in use. For solidity of construction the walls of their fortresses and temples surpass anything ever achieved elsewhere. With extraordinary skill they handled huge blocks of hard stone, such as granite, weighing many tons, cutting them into irregular shapes with many angles, and then fitting them accurately together like the pieces of a jig-saw puzzle. These walls are practically indestructible, and have resisted the shocks of earthquakes for centuries. Many

of them still form the foundations of Spanish buildings in Cuzco to-day. The Incas had discovered the art of casting bronze, but the chisels which they made from this alloy were not hard enough to cut the tough rock used in some of their buildings, and these must have been shaped with stone tools. The roofing, which has long perished, was constructed of timber and thatch, for the principles of the arch and the vault were unknown.

While the Incas surpassed the earlier coast peoples as builders, they were inferior as artists. Their pottery was well formed but severe in style, and the painted designs were mainly geometrical. The realistic painting and modelling of the early cultures is never found in Inca vases; nor did they produce sculpture to any extent. Their textiles were of fine quality, and often beautifully coloured; but the designs tend to follow geometric forms even when they are based on motives borrowed from nature. They knew a great deal about astronomy, and had calculated the length of the solar year by means of 'observatories' with stone pillars used as sundials. But in this respect they were inferior to the ancient MAYA (q.v.) of Central America. In surgery also they had made advances and were able to perform difficult operations with some success.

If we try to assess the position of the Incas in the scale of civilization, we notice that they had failed to make a number of important discoveries known to the Old World, such as writing, money, wheeled transport, and the smelting of iron. They also retained some cruel and barbarous practices, including occasional human sacrifice. On the other hand, their skill and refinement in many of the arts and crafts, as well as their remarkable social organization and engineering achievements, were such as to arouse our admiration. Among the useful contributions which they have made to humanity one might specially mention the potato, and the coca plant from which cocaine is obtained.

The conquest of the Inca Empire in 1533 by less than 200 Spaniards led by Pizarro was an astonishing feat of arms. The Spaniards succeeded in capturing and putting to death the Inca himself; and the people, who had believed their ruler to be divine, lost heart and gave up resistance. And so Peru became a Spanish colony. But although the old civilization was destroyed, the Indians, speaking their own languages, survive as the chief element of the

TAPESTRY STRIP

Woven in four colours. Coast style. *British Mus.*

RUINS OF THE FORTRESS TOWN AT MACHU PICCHU, NEAR CUZCO IN THE ANDES
Note the stone terracing of the precipitous mountain slopes. *Bennet Greig*

population, and in spite of European influence retain many native beliefs and customs, especially in the remoter highland regions. Women can still be seen spinning by hand on the way to market, and men cultivating the ground with the old type of digging-stick; potato mash is still prepared in the ancient way; the llama carries its load along the rough mountain paths. But the glory of ancient Peru has departed never to return (*see also* AMERICAN INDIANS, CENTRAL AND SOUTH).

The motives of the Spanish conquerors were various. Love of adventure and fame, and the desire to convert the Indians to Christianity played their part. But one of the main incentives was certainly the quest for gold. *El Dorado*, which means 'The gilded one', was originally the name given to a Colombian chief, who covered his body with gold dust at certain ceremonies. But later in the 18th century the name was used for various imaginary places in the far interior of South America which were believed to contain fabulous riches, and many ill-fated expeditions have set out in the hope of discovering 'the Inca gold'.

See also ANCIENT CIVILIZATIONS; PERU, ANCIENT; Vol. IV: AMERICAN-INDIAN LANGUAGES.

INDIAN CIVILIZATIONS. 1. PRE-ARYAN. The existence of the earliest known pre-Aryan civilization of India was only brought to light between 1920 and 1930, when excavations at the site of Mohenjodaro in Sind and Harappa in the Punjab showed that there had been cities in northern India going back to a date between 3000 and 2500 B.C. Like the ancient civilizations of Mesopotamia and Egypt, these very early peoples developed their civilizations in river valleys, especially in the valley of the Indus. They may have been at some time connected with the SUMERIANS (q.v.): indeed some of the finds in their cities resemble the finds at Ur.

The ruins excavated show that these ancient cities had wide streets, with an elaborate drainage system and substantial buildings of burnt brick. Houses were of more than one storey, and had flat roofs, and baths and latrines on the upper as well as on the ground floor. Kitchens

had serving-hatches; drains were built into the thickness of the wall and led into covered sewers running down the centre of the streets. The houses had narrow, steep stairs of brick to the upper floors, and nothing in the plan of them suggests that women were secluded, as they have been later in India. Large pottery jars were used, as they still are in that region, for storage, and it appears that wooden chests, beds, and seats were also used, since fragments of carved legs and bone or shell fasteners have survived. Houses had their own wells, and there were public as well as private baths. Indeed, frequent washing seems to have been an important feature of the life of the ancient Indians.

For tools and weapons, copper and bronze were used—copper for fish-hooks and copper-headed arrows, bronze for razors and for mirrors. Pottery was made on the wheel, and some of it, particularly candlesticks, has a most modern appearance. The painting on it is generally in black pigment on a polished red surface, designs being predominantly geometric but sometimes more naturalistic with animal figures. They kept domestic animals—dogs, sheep, goats, fowls, and cattle which were used

RUINS AT MOHENJODARO OF AN ANCIENT INDIAN CITY
The building in the centre was a bath. *Indian Railways*

to draw vehicles. They probably kept song-birds as pets, and they used ivory, stone, or pottery dice for their games, and perhaps also in their religious ritual. Women wore short, scanty petticoats, and men a cloth worn over the left shoulder and under the right arm. Their clothes were made of cotton and possibly also of other materials, such as linen or wool. They had ornaments made of gold, electrum, silver, copper, bronze, shell, and semi-precious stones such as jade, cornelian, and lapis-lazuli.

The religion of these early Indians seems to have been a fertility cult—that is, its main purpose was to encourage increase, especially of crops. Certain animals, such as the bull, the goat, the snake, and the crocodile, were held sacred, and perhaps also the fig-tree or *pipal*, which Hindus still hold sacred. They worshipped a god rather like the god Shiva of modern Hinduism, and a mother goddess surrounded by sacred doves. It is also probable that their ritual required regular and plentiful washings.

This civilization seems to have been overwhelmed somewhere about 2500 B.C., probably by invaders from the north-west. At some time during this period India must have been invaded by strangers from the Persian plateau, and this invasion may perhaps have first brought into India some branch of the Aryan languages. The invaders, however, were not the same physical type as those who came into India with the main Aryan invasion about 1500 B.C.

2. ARYAN. This term really refers to language only, not to race. The Aryan invaders who came about 1500 B.C., are most important as they brought with them a branch of the INDO-EUROPEAN languages (q.v. Vol. IV), which has profoundly affected all the languages with which it has come into contact, and which is the basis of most of the languages spoken in India to-day, except in the south. In race these Aryan invaders were probably an offshoot of the peoples who, besides migrating north-westwards and populating northern Europe, invaded Mesopotamia and Asia Minor to the south-west and gave rise to such peoples as the Philistines and the Dorian invaders of Greece (*see* ARYAN).

It was their possession of the horse and the bronze and, later, iron sword which ensured the Aryans their conquests; but the bow also was an important weapon, being used probably from a chariot. Their mode of life was primarily pastoral, great value being set upon herds of cattle. They also kept sheep, pigs, and dogs. Agriculture by means of the plough was also practised, possibly with irrigation. They made garments from skins and from sheep's wool. They sacrificed cattle, sheep, and goats to the gods and also slaughtered them for feasts. Milk and grain were important foods, and intoxicating drink was brewed from grain. Chariot-racing, gambling, dancing, and music were popular as recreations.

The religion of these Aryans was a form of NATURE WORSHIP (q.v.) in which the great natural phenomena such as the sky, earth, dawn, the sun, fire, and thunder were thought of as deities in human form, and worshipped as such. There were minor deities such as water-nymphs, the titans who opposed the gods, and demons who were evil and destructive. There were a great many popular stories, songs and poems about these gods and godlings. The gods were worshipped in the hymns now collected together and known as the *Rig-Veda*, in the latest book of which there is a tendency to change over from simple nature worship to the kind of philosophy found in later Indian religions. In the end HINDUISM (q.v.) completely supplanted the Rig-Vedic religion, reducing its high god Indra to a mere doorkeeper in the house of the god Shiva, one of the chief gods of Hinduism. It seems probable that Hinduism was a good deal influenced by these ancient religions, and that it inherited many of its ideas from them.

The Aryan society was divided into four classes: the nobles, who were the rulers and leaders in war, the priests, the common people, and the serf or slave class. These social divisions became greatly modified, largely no doubt as a result of mixture with the earlier inhabitants and absorption of their ideas. From this developed the CASTE system (q.v.), which is the basis of Hindu society. While the nature worship and the religious feasts and sacrifices practised by the Aryans have disappeared in Hinduism, some ceremonies of social importance, in particular the marriage ceremony, have survived.

Of the material civilization of the Aryans little trace has been discovered: no work of art, no building, and few weapons or utensils that can be attributed to them. Of their history for ten centuries nothing certain is known. Traditions survive of wars, leagues, battles, and a grand all-India fight that lasted eighteen days, During these centuries the priesthood became

PILLAR SET UP BY THE EMPEROR ASOKA (273–232 B.C.) AT LAURIYA-MANDANGARH It is 32 ft. high, made of polished sandstone. *Indian Mus., Calcutta*

more powerful, and the Brahmins, originally kings' servants, became king-makers, and laid the foundation of their supremacy, social, political, and intellectual, which has dominated Hinduism ever since.

With the dawn of history in the 6th century B.C. this priestly power was challenged in the east by the rise of BUDDHISM (q.v.) and the rise, or more probably the resurgence of JAINISM (q.v.), the founder of Buddhism and the champion of Jainism both being of noble lineage. In the west, 'India' (which at that time meant no more than the Indus valley) became a province of Persia and continued so for nearly two centuries. Then a Greek army under ALEXANDER THE GREAT (q.v., Vol. V), having overthrown the Persian Empire, marched into India to claim it as their own (327–325 B.C.). Alexander advanced across the Punjab until his troops refused to go farther, and he had to withdraw.

3. BUDDHIST AND HINDU INDIA. Within a few years of Alexander's death an empire known as the Mauryan arose which drove the Greeks from the Indus valley, and brought most of India under one rule. This Empire lasted at its height for about ninety years, under three great rulers, the best known of whom is ASOKA (q.v., Vol. V). Its founder, Chandragupta, managed his enormous empire with unscrupulous and autocratic power, but his organization was highly efficient. He built up a strong army consisting of four parts: elephants, chariots, cavalry, and infantry. He built a magnificent royal city which stretched nine miles along the river to a depth of two miles. It was defended by a massive timber palisade, strengthened by 570 towers and surrounded by a deep moat, filled from the river. There were sixty-four great gates. The royal palace was also built mainly of timber, with gilded pillars and fine stone sculptures. The king himself appeared in public carried in a golden palanquin or mounted on an elephant with gorgeous trappings. He wore fine muslin embroidered with purple and gold.

Asoka must have been as efficient and strong a ruler as his predecessors, since he held together his great empire. But he is known to us for his preaching of peace and gentleness, courtesy to the aged, the poor, the servant, and the slave. Horrified by the suffering caused by his one and only war, he accepted Buddhism and devoted the rest of his life to spreading its doctrines. He set up inscribed and carved pillars in places associated with events in Buddha's life, and along the pilgrim roads which led to them. He carved sermons on rocks, and sent missionaries to countries beyond his Empire, to the independent Tamil kings of south India, to Ceylon, and kingdoms of the Greeks. Till Asoka's conversion Buddhism was little more than a sect of Hinduism; he made it a state religion. But his peace plans failed, as peace plans so often do, and not long after his death in 232 B.C. his Empire vanished, and India reverted to her normal condition of perpetual war.

Some 600 years later, in the 4th century A.D., another great Hindu Empire, the Gupta Empire, arose in north India. This period, which reached its climax in the 5th century, is often called the Golden Age or the Hindu Renaissance.

ENTRANCE TO A CAVE TEMPLE AT AJANTA

There are 29 caves at Ajanta; some are Buddhist temples and others monastries. They are elaborately decorated with sculpture and paintings which date from the 3rd–6th centuries A.D. This is a 6th-century example

The greatest Empire since the days of Asoka was governed with efficiency, and yet without the ruthlessness of the Emperor Chandragupta. During this period, religious ideas developed and changed without persecution. This was the golden age of SANSKRIT literature and music (q.v. Vol. IV). The scientific ideas of Greece had influenced Indian thought, and mathematics and astronomy were studied. Many of the large buildings of the Gupta age were destroyed later by the Moslem conquerors; but enough remains to show that their architecture, sculpture, and metal-work were outstanding, as also were their paintings in the Ajanta and other cave monasteries and temples. The great intellectual vitality of this period resulted in the exchange of ideas with other lands, both east and west, particularly with China, Persia, and Rome.

4. MOSLEM INDIA. THE MOGUL EMPIRE. Towards the end of the 5th century and through the 6th century, the Gupta Empire suffered continued attacks from hordes of HUNS (q.v.), and then Turks. During the 7th century there was a short revival of power under the strong rule of the Emperor Harsha; but after his death the Empire broke up before the attacks of Moslem tribes of Afghans, Mongols, and Tartars. For many centuries kingdoms rose and fell, and India endured endless warfare. The Moslem power increased, and the Hindus suffered cruel suppression. In the 16th century the first of the great Mogul Emperors established his power, and founded an Empire which lasted, though in a weakened state, until the British took control in the 18th century.

The greatest of the Mogul Emperors was AKBAR (q.v. Vol. V) who reigned from 1555 to 1605. He built up a great Empire embracing all northern and central India, and he gained control over a great part of the continent. He ruled his Empire with justice and efficiency. His grandson, Shah Jahan, was as renowned a ruler, and during his reign some of the most magnificent of the Mogul building was carried out. The Imperial palace at Delhi and the famous Taj Mahal at Agra are among the most splendid of India's Moslem monuments.

During the 16th century began the first European trade settlements in India. The Portuguese came first, and then the Dutch and the English, and later the Danes and the French. They settled along the coast of India, forming companies to trade with the Indians and to send merchandise to Europe. In 1600 the East India Company was formed. From that time on, the European powers, and in particular France and England, took more and more part in Indian politics, until the French were driven out, and England became the predominant power in India.

See also ANCIENT CIVILIZATIONS.

INDIAN PEOPLES. To write of the peoples of India is rather like writing about the people of Europe, except that the differences of race, language, and religion, as well as of physical conditions of life are even greater. Moreover, Indian civilization is much older than that of Europe. In the valley of the Indus there was an advanced civilization as early as 2000 B.C., when most of Europe was still primitive (see INDIAN CIVILIZATIONS). In India to-day there are to be found cultured and educated people as advanced as any in Europe; others have never progressed beyond the most primitive stages. The particular way of life of the Indian hill tribes and also of the Indian villages is described in separate articles, as are also the main Indian religions.

The population of India in 1941 was 390 millions—about equal to that of America and Africa combined, or one-fifth of the human race. It has increased greatly since then, but is not evenly distributed: in some parts there are 1,500 people to the square mile, in other parts only two. The density of the population depends mainly on the annual rainfall, which varies from 450 inches in the east to 3 inches in some parts of the west. There are about 150 different languages spoken in India, belonging in the main to two language families. The one, Indo-European (to which European languages also belong), is spoken by about two-thirds of the Indians in the north and north-west; the other, Dravidian, is spoken over the greater part of south India. Of all these many languages only about fourteen are spoken by more than 5 million people. Indians are clever at learning languages—even those who can neither read nor write can often speak two or three.

The two main religions of India are HINDUISM and ISLAM (qq.v.). There are 216 million Hindus (excluding the 50 million 'untouchables'), and 95 million Moslems, as well as less than 6 million SIKHS (q.v.), about $1\frac{1}{4}$ million JAINS (q.v.), some 100,000 PARSEES (q.v.), and rather more than 6 million Christians. BUDDHISM (q.v.), which was

BATHING GHATS, BENARES

The waterfront is lined with *ghats* (steps) where Hindu pilgrims wash and drink the muddy water of the sacred Ganges
Indian Railways

founded in India, has spread east, and has now only a relatively small following in the land of its origin. There are also about 25 million aboriginal tribes who are neither Moslem nor Hindu but follow primitive beliefs.

From the time of the Mogul Empire in the 16th century, until the coming of the British in the 18th century, the Moslems were the ruling power, although the Hindus were vastly in the majority. In 1947, when British rule in India ceased, a separate Moslem State, Pakistan, was established in the east and west, and the remaining area became the State of India, or Bharat. This division left large minorities of Moslems in India and Hindus in Pakistan, and, in spite of mass migrations, there are still considerable minorities in each country. At the time of partition there were many Indian States ruled by their own princes, some large, such as Mysore and Hyderabad, others only a few square miles in area; but these have now all joined either India

or Pakistan. In India the present nineteen political units are mostly made up of people speaking the same language.

India is a land of villages. Agriculture is by far the most important industry: the chief crops grown are cotton, rice, sugar, wheat, barley, or millet, according to differences in climate and soil. In the last thirty years there has been a move to the towns, partly because of improved services of lighting, water, amusements, &c., the better chances of employment in the industries, and the pressure of population on the soil. India is no longer content to import all manufactured goods: factories are increasing in number and output (chiefly cotton, jute, and sugar mills), and rivers are utilized to generate electric power and light. A good example of this development is the city of Jamshedpur: in thirty years, as the result of Parsee initiative and capital, it developed from a little townlet to a model city of 150,000 inhabitants, containing a very large steel plant.

North-west India is a vast plain of silt deposited by the River INDUS (q.v. Vol. III) and its tributaries. It is dry, horribly dry in parts, with large tracts of desert. There are frosts in winter and a temperature of 115° in the shade in June. Moreover, the north-west frontier, teeming with truculent tribesmen, gives easy access to invading armies from Persia and central Asia. Life is hard, and the Punjabi, the inhabitant of the Punjab, is necessarily a doughty fighter; in fact two-thirds of the Indian Army was made up of Punjabis. Most of this area, which is largely Moslem, is now in Pakistan. The population is generally sparse, especially to the south in Sind; but in the central Punjab better rainfall and colossal irrigation works which divert the rivers to the fields have made the land support more people. This is the homeland of the SIKHS (q.v.) who, though outnumbered by Hindus to the east and Moslems to the west, would like to call the province their own.

North-east India is the most densely populated and richest part of India, owing its richness to better rainfall and the River GANGES (q.v. Vol. III). The martial spirit, so strong in the west, dies out in the east—for the Ganges Plain is protected from outside invaders by the Himalayas and the hills on the Burmese border. The people of the west and centre speak Hindi, the nearest language to the Sanskrit of Hindu Scriptures. The Ganges Plain is the Holy Land of Hinduism and the Ganges their holy river. Although Moslem conquerors swept through it and founded many kingdoms, Islam took no deep root but in Bengal, which is now part of Pakistan.

The Peninsula is a plateau high in the west—the Western Ghats—with the main rivers flowing eastwards. Population is densest near the coasts, the interior for the most part being thinly populated. From the west coast there has been an age-long sea trade with the West to which it owes its settlements of Abyssinians, Jews, Portuguese, half-Arab Moslems (Moplahs) of Malabar, and others. There is, for instance, a community of over a million 'Syrian' Christians who claim that their Church was founded by the Apostle St. Thomas. Moslems have for long ruled the state of Hyderabad, and have built splendid mosques and palaces in many other places; but in the Peninsula they nowhere outnumber the Hindus. In the north-west live the Mahrattas, once brave fighters who overran almost the whole of India. The shrewdest and most enterprising of the Dravidian-speaking Indians are the Tamils, who have played an important part in the development of Hinduism. They have emigrated to many other countries in south-east Asia, Guinea, Natal, and even as far as Fiji, and these countries owe much to their intelligence and industry.

See also Vol. III: INDIA; Vol. IV: INDIAN LANGUAGES.

INDIANS, AMERICAN, see AMERICAN INDIANS.

INDIANS, HILL TRIBES. 1. These peoples are interesting for several reasons. Those of the borderland region are influenced by the civilizations of adjacent countries: Persia and Islam on the north-west, Tibet and Buddhism on the north, and Burma and south-east Asia on the north-east. The central and southern hills preserve some of the most primitive elements in all Asia. Population is sparse, for the peaks and glaciers of the Himalayas, and the rocks and jungles, wild beasts and malaria elsewhere, make cultivation difficult or impossible and limit the food-supply. Further, on account of the difficulties of access from the plains, and from valley to valley in the hills, the people are split up into small isolated communities, and there is a bewildering multiplicity of dialects and customs.

A WHEELWRIGHT IN MADRAS. *Pitt Rivers Coll.*

PATHAN FARMER THRASHING WHEAT. *Indian Railways*

2. NORTH-WEST BORDER OF PAKISTAN. This region, bordering Afghanistan, is very harsh country consisting of tracts of rock and stone with scanty rainfall and temperatures ranging from 120° in the shade to 15° below zero. Across it, at all stages of history from prehistoric times, traders and raiders have pressed into India.

From Quetta northwards, up and across the Kabul river and then eastwards to the Indus, the hills are held by tribes of Pathans, some of the fiercest and least tractable of the hill tribes. The Pathan sense of kinship is strong, each tribe tracing its descent from a common ancestor; they do not welcome outsiders as members of their clans. They have a bad name for treachery and bloodshed: an insult, real or fancied, may involve a whole village in a blood-feud. They have little respect for their chiefs. Fanatical Moslems, they are easily stampeded into a war against 'unbelievers'. They are, on the other hand, hospitable and rarely refuse protection to those seeking refuge; and they are very brave. Their control is a serious problem, as no government can tolerate their robberies, kidnapping, and murders, or neglect the defence of this vulnerable frontier.

South of the Pathans, the hills belong to a confederacy of tribes called Brahui. They speak a language like those spoken in south India (Dravidian) though they are otherwise quite unlike the south Indian people. The Brahui tribe is not based on blood-kinship; it is made up of groups of families who happen to live in the same locality, and they willingly accept newcomers. In the past the tribal chiefs were responsible to the head Khan at Kalat in Baluchistan, and each tribe supplied its quota of armed men for state service. The name Baluchistan is taken from the Baloch tribes who came from Persia. Although they outnumber the Brahui they are not masters in Baluchistan. They have swarmed down into the Indus valley making settlements in Sind and the western Punjab. Their tribes are composed on the same lines as those of the Brahui, and they are organized on a military basis. These peoples are not fanatical, like the Pathans: they respect their chiefs and are much easier to control.

3. NORTHERN TIBETAN BORDER. The peaks and glaciers of the Himalayas between the bend of the upper Indus in the west and the Brahmaputra in the east are a stiff barrier between India

BHIL HILLMEN WITH THEIR BOWS
They are skilful archers and shoot with their feet. *Paul Popper*

on the crest of a mountain ridge, are stockaded for defence. The approaches to a village bristle with short bamboo spikes, so sharp that they can pierce a leather boot. Head-hunting is, or was, a predominant sport. The tribesmen believed that a human head taken from another village would bring prosperity: no girl would consent to marry a man who had not at least one head to his credit.

Boys at about the age of ten leave home and live together in a club-house where they learn to be good tribesmen. In some villages girls too are trained in the same way (*see* INITIATION CEREMONIES). For the most part their methods of cultivation are simple —they cut and burn a tract of jungle and sow seed in the ashes. But some tribes have learnt to terrace their fields and irrigate the crops. Most tribes love dancing and have extremely picturesque dancing costumes. On the whole there is much about these tribes which is very attractive, and they are reasonably amenable to control.

5. CENTRAL AND SOUTH INDIAN HILL TRIBES. These tribes are very different from the frontier tribes: they are much darker, and some of them still follow a very primitive way of life—they are mere food-gathering jungle folk clad in aprons of leaves. In south India the tribes are few in numbers; some of them have customs similar to those of the more primitive of the Malayan tribes—such as their methods of fire-making, of building houses in trees, and of chipping the front teeth (*see* MALAYA, PEOPLES OF).

The biggest tribal communities are in the fever-stricken hills of central India, from the borders of Gujarat in the west to Bengal. The western group include a number of distinct tribes known generally as Bhil. They vary greatly in their degree of development. They have little sense of community and have lost their tribal languages, speaking instead dialects of the languages of their Hindu neighbours. In some Hindu states where Bhils are numerous there was an old custom that the Bhils should publicly recognize a new rajah (king or ruler) by marking his brow with blood from a tribesman's thumb or toe.

and Tibet. Yet Tibetan races, language, and religion are found on the Indian side of the frontier, in the far north of Kashmir, in Nepal, and in the Buddhist states of Sikhim and Bhutan. Most of the people are Mongolian, but Indians from the Plains long ago invaded the hills, married hill women, established many little principalities, and remodelled society on the lines of Indian CASTE (q.v.). Some of these little chieftaincies survive, especially round Simla; but in the 18th century many of them were absorbed by the Gurkhas and formed into the independent kingdom of Nepal, and others by the Sikhs in Kashmir. The composite character of Himalayan society has resulted in a multitude of languages and dialects. In Nepal, where tribal distinctions are still alive, there are at least a score. From two of the Nepal tribes come the Gurkhas, some of the best soldiers in the world.

4. NORTH-EASTERN BURMESE BORDER. Except in the Hindu state of Manipur, the hill tribes of Assam have more in common with Burma and Tibet than with India. They are for the most part Mongolian both in physical type and language, and in customs they are in some ways like the hillsmen and islanders of south-east Asia. The best-known group are the Nagas; but even among the Nagas customs differ from tribe to tribe. Their villages, usually large and perched

Tribes of the eastern group have a stronger sense of tribal solidarity, and their languages, Dravidian and Munda (an ancient south-east Asian language), still thrive. These eastern peoples, like the tribes of Assam, are keen dancers, they train their boys in club-houses, and their traditional agriculture is by jungle-burning. They are also courageous hunters, but they do not decapitate their neighbours. The best known, Santals, Oraons, and Mundas, have migrated in tens of thousands to the tea plantations of Bengal and Assam or wherever jungle needs to be cleared.

Farther south are the tribes called Khonds who were notorious for their custom of human sacrifice. They believed that the bodies of human victims were needed to fertilize their fields. They kidnapped their victims, fattened them, and then hacked them to pieces so that they might bury the bits in fields. About a century ago they were persuaded that the bodies of buffaloes would do instead of men. 'Hook-swinging', once widespread throughout south India, is undoubtedly a relic of the old custom of human sacrifice; the practice is now prohibited, and puppets are swung from the hooks instead of men.

See also Vol. IV: INDIAN LANGUAGES.

INDIANS, VILLAGE LIFE. The majority of the INDIAN PEOPLES (q.v.) live in villages and are occupied in some way upon the land. The villages vary a good deal in different parts of India: in the Peninsula, for instance, on the west coast the houses are scattered, while in the Deccan they are often crammed inside a small fort for defence against marauders, and again, in parts of the east they are neatly arranged in streets. The houses themselves also differ according to the climate of the area and the building materials available. In areas of heavy rainfall the houses have sloping roofs; in dry areas the roofs are flat. In some parts wood is available; in others stone. Mud is used everywhere—either as plaster or made into burnt or sun-dried bricks.

Although conditions vary, the life of the villagers is much the same all over India. A Tamil village in the south may be taken as an example.

The Tamil word for our word 'build' means 'tie', and indeed their houses are tied together. The simplest house is a circular one-roomed hut of bamboos, tied together with string and thatched with grass, straw, or palm-leaves. Rectangular houses, however, can be divided into

A VILLAGE WEAVER IN RAJPUTANA
He uses a primitive loom and works in the road outside his hut. *Paul Popper*

several rooms and added to when necessary, and the better houses in a Tamil village have several rooms opening on to interior verandas surrounding a small, square courtyard. There is also usually a veranda on the street side. The houses are sometimes tiled but generally thatched, and are almost always of one story only. The floors are of beaten earth, and there is very little and very simple furniture. The household equipment consists of vessels of earthenware or brass, a grain-bin or two, and perhaps a chest. Chairs, tables, bedsteads, knives, forks, and spoons are rare, for Tamils prefer to sit and sleep on the floor and to eat with their fingers.

The villages are largely self-supporting: each village has its own potters, blacksmiths, carpenters, tanners, barbers, washermen, herdsmen, and fishermen. Particular kinds of jobs belong to particular families, for under the CASTE system (q.v.) no one is allowed to do a job which does not belong to his family.

Wages are usually paid in grain instead of money. The peasant cultivators, the largest section of the community, have, therefore, to grow enough food to feed their own families and their field labourers, and also to have enough

WOMEN HUSKING RICE
Pitt Rivers Coll.

any rain at all, and the rivers run nearly dry. Storing water and irrigation are therefore very important matters, since without water the rice will not grow. They dam the rivers and make artificial lakes called tanks, from which run channels to take the water to the fields. They also raise water from wells by various devices, the commonest being a sort of see-saw. There is a long rod and bucket at one end of the see-saw and a weight at the other; a man stands in the centre and raises or lowers the bucket in or out of the well by shifting his weight.

The Indians plough with oxen and light wooden ploughs. They thresh the rice by driving a row of half a dozen bullocks tied together by the neck round the threshing-floor till all the grain is trodden out. They winnow the grain by shaking it gently in a sort of dust-pan-shaped basket; the heavy grain falls to their feet while the chaff is carried away by the wind. The Indian bull or *zebu* is different from an English bull, his horns point backwards, a flap of skin hangs loosely from his neck and chest, and there is a convenient lump over his shoulder which prevents the yoke from slipping along his neck. Bulls and cows are sacred and must not be killed: in consequence old and useless animals go on eating up the precious fodder needed for young and useful beasts. The buffalo is not sacred. It produces a rich milk and is a very useful draught animal. Some of the buffalo carts have solid wheels without spokes.

Some of the games of an Indian village, such as hop-scotch, prisoner's base, and leap-frog, are very ancient and are to be found among many peoples, including ourselves. Indians also play a kind of backgammon, using the ground marked out as a board, bits of stone or pot for 'men', and split beans shaken in the hand for dice. They do not dance but are very fond of their own music, which is not attractive to European ears. Bargaining and gossiping in the weekly market, domestic celebrations, such as weddings, and the regular rotation of religious festivals are their main forms of entertainment.

Each village is like a little municipality with a council of elders and officers. The headman is a magistrate and he collects the taxes; the accountant keeps a register of all the land, the extent and owner of each field, the tax to be paid, and other details. The strength of the village is its unity—every member must do his best for the welfare of the whole. For instance,

to sell so that they can pay for their rent, taxes, and other expenses. The field labourers are mostly pariahs (untouchables) and live apart in separate hamlets or streets. In most villages there is a money-lender, who is also a grain merchant and perhaps a shopkeeper too. A weekly open-air market is held at some convenient centre to serve a number of villages. There the villagers can buy the few things they do not produce—salt, for instance, and cloth.

In southern villages, where the climate is always warm, people wear little clothing. A man wears a white cotton loin-cloth, a girl wears a long piece of bright-coloured cloth, part of which she winds round her waist to hang below the knee, the rest goes across her breast, over her left shoulder, and tucks in behind.

The principal food is rice in the wetter parts or millet in the dryer, except in north-west India where wheat is grown. In the Tamil country it rains heavily from October to December, and after that for six months there is hardly

in the rainy season, if the tank dam starts leaking, every man, woman, and child must help to prevent a breach which would ruin the year's crops and bring starvation. Without this co-operation disaster would never be avoided.

See also Vol. III: INDIA; Vol. IV: INDIAN LANGUAGES.

INDO-CHINESE.

The total population of Indo-China was in 1939 about 23 millions, a little under half of that of Great Britain. About 43,000 of these are Europeans, the rest being of very mixed descent, for large numbers of people have come to settle in Indo-China at various times from the neighbouring countries, China, Burma, and Siam. In consequence there is a good deal of variety in physical appearance and way of life. In general, however, the people belong to the Mongolian division of mankind. They are rather short, have brown skins, rather flat faces, and straight dark hair. They wear very wide round hats—almost like small parasols—in order to protect them when they are working all day under the hot sun. Several different languages are spoken in the different parts of the country, the principal ones being Annamite, Cambodian, and Siamese (*see* CHINESE AND ALLIED LANGUAGES, Vol. IV). The chief religion is BUDDHISM (q.v.), but many of the people follow CONFUCIUS (q.v. Vol. V), and ANCESTOR WORSHIP (q.v.) plays a large part in their lives.

The whole of Indo-China came under French control by the end of the 19th century, but it is now divided into three states—the Vietnam Republic, and the two kingdoms of Laos and Cambodia, all of which achieved national sovereignty in 1954. During their rule the French had done a great deal to develop the country, especially in building good roads and railways in the lowlands and round the coast. Communications across the mountains, however, are difficult, and the people living in the mountain villages still live very isolated and simple lives. The great majority of the people live in the rich lowland plains and along the coast, where the population in some areas is very dense.

By far the greater part of the population lives by cultivation of the land, especially the growing of rice (or paddy, as the rice is called before it is milled). The importance of rice to the peoples of the East is easy to realize when one remembers that bread and potatoes, so vital a part of the diet of Europeans, are almost unknown to them. Domestic animals are kept almost solely

A MOÏ WOMAN CLIMBING UP TO HER HOUSE
The Moï are aborigines living in the interior of Indo-China. They build their houses on posts as a protection against animals and floods. *Paul Popper*

as draught animals, for the people are too poor to be able to kill cattle for meat. To make up in part for the lack of meat, the Indo-Chinese catch large quantities of fish in the country's many rivers, in the lakes, and even on the rice-fields themselves: fish traps, built of stakes and wattles, are much used.

The main towns of Indo-China have grown up on the lower reaches of the two great rivers, the Red River and the Mekong. Hanoi, the capital, and the port Haiphong, are the main towns of the north, and in the south, in Cochin-China, there is the largest town and port of the country, Saigon. In old days there used to be a great city at Angkor Thom in Cambodia, and near the site still stands a huge temple called the Angkor Wat which is one of the wonders of the East. Its walls are elaborately carved, some of the scenes representing ceremonial dancers in curious costumes. Dancing figures are still a feature of Indo-Chinese art.

See also Vol. III: INDO-CHINA.

INDO-EUROPEANS, *see* ARYANS.

INDONESIANS. Indonesia is another name for the East Indies, and Malaya, or the Malay Archipelago; the Indonesians are the peoples who live in the peninsula and islands of Indonesia, excepting New Guinea and Halmahera, both of which are peopled by Melanesians and Papuans. Indonesians differ considerably in appearance, customs, and ways of living. There are some groups of Australoid and Negrito peoples, such as the Sakai and Semang in Malay (*see* MALAYA, PEOPLES OF). But these are not usually regarded as Indonesians, who are dark-skinned but delicately featured peoples, probably of mixed Indian and Mongoloid ancestry (*see* INDONESIAN LANGUAGES, Vol. IV).

A few are primitive, living by hunting or by gathering berries and roots in the forests. Others practise shifting cultivation. This means that they clear a small area in the forest, cultivate it for one or two years, and then, as the soil loses its richness, move on to another area. Round the coasts are fishing peoples. They fish from boats by lines, spears, and nets. In the Moluccas the line is often attached to a kite which is flown from a boat. Traps are also used —the most common type being formed by a fence of bamboo built at right angles to the shore and leading to a pen at its seaward end. The fish, swimming along the shore, come to the fence, turn along it, and enter the pen. Some of the people are highly civilized. The Javanese and Balinese, for example, had developed an intricate system of agriculture long before Europeans came to the islands, terracing hill-sides to form small fields and draining parts of the marshy coastal plains.

Indonesian houses are often built on poles, with the floor about 5 feet above the ground. The poles go up through the floor and are used to divide the house into rooms. A ladder leads up to the living-room. The Javanese have a different type of house. It is on the ground and has a floor of flattened earth stamped hard. Both types of house have walls of bamboo and a roof thatched with palm-leaves. They are grouped in villages and are surrounded by gardens of vegetables, fruit-trees, and coco-nut palms.

The more backward tribes wear few or no clothes. A cotton skirt, the sarong, is the principal garment in most of the islands. It is ankle length, but is often tucked up to give more freedom of movement. Men usually wear with it a short jacket, while women wear a jacket or a broad scarf. Sometimes shorts are worn instead of the sarong. Sarongs, especially in Java, are often patterned by batik work. A design is drawn with wax on the cloth, which is then put into a dye bath where the unwaxed parts take the dye. The wax is then removed

MAP OF INDONESIA

Showing the relation between the islands of Indonesia and the south-east of Asia, Australia, and New Guinea

A VILLAGE LAW COURT IN JAVA
The chief sits in the centre of the village square while the defendant pleads his case. *Mrs. T. Muir*

and a fresh pattern drawn and another colour of dye used. This process is repeated several times. In Java and Bali there is a wealthy aristocracy, and the princes have very elaborate costumes of stiff silks and brocades with heavy and costly embroideries. In the towns, however, many Indonesians now wear European clothes. The craftsmen are often highly skilled, and their silver-work and wood-carving are of very beautiful workmanship and design and are in great demand by visitors to the islands.

Indians colonized parts of Indonesia between the 2nd and 8th centuries A.D. From the 5th to the 7th centuries immigrations from India led to the foundation of Hindu and Buddhist kingdoms on the Malay Peninsula, Java, and elsewhere. The ruins of one of the mightiest Buddhist temples in the world are at Boroboedoer in Java. A modified form of Hinduism is still practised, especially by the Balinese. But to-day the dominant religion is ISLAM (q.v.) of the Sunnite sect, tinged with magic and spirit worship. There were Moslem settlements at various times in Indonesia. Marco Polo reported, however, in 1292 that he found Moslems only in one small area in north Sumatra. But by the mid-15th century there was a large Moslem area centred in Malacca, and by 1526 Java was completely Moslem. Since then Islam has spread much farther.

The Portuguese, in 1511, were the first Europeans to visit Indonesia. They were followed by the Spanish, the Dutch (1595), the French, and the English, all seeking spices and establishing trading stations. By 1684 the Dutch East India Company was the chief power in Java, and from there it expanded its influence through the islands. In 1798 the Dutch Government took over the administration of the islands, and has governed them since then, except for a short period, 1811–16, when Java, part of Sumatra, Macassar, and Dutch Timor came under British rule (*see* RAFFLES, Vol. V).

To-day Portugal governs part of Timor, Britain governs British North Borneo and British New Guinea, Australia governs the Mandated territory of New Guinea, while the rest, and by far the greatest part of the region forms the independent Republic of Indonesia. Dutch rule had long been opposed, especially in Java, by a strong nationalism, a movement much encouraged by the work of a daughter of one of the princes, who died in 1904 at the age of twenty-five, after four years of pioneer work in the education of native women. Complete independence was granted after the Second World War.

See also Vol. III: EAST INDIES; PHILIPPINES.

INITIATION CEREMONIES. It is a very widespread custom amongst peoples of varying grades of civilization to make young people undergo initiation ceremonies by which they become full members of the community. The age at which they undergo the rites varies a great deal, but it is usually only after initiation that young men and women are allowed to marry. Initiation rites are also performed for adults when joining secret societies or when moving from one age-group to another. Witches and

IVORY MASKS WORN AT INITIATION CEREMONIES
These small masks represent the old life of the initiate which ends when he begins his new life. Belgian Congo.
British Mus.

witch-doctors are initiated into the mysteries of WITCHCRAFT (q.v.) by other sorcerers.

There are usually three stages in initiation ceremonies, though they may not always be definitely marked off from one another: seclusion from most of the other members of the community, especially from the other sex; preparatory ceremonies by which the boy or girl qualifies for admission into the community; and acceptance by, or graduation into, the community. These ceremonies may last for several months. All through many of them there is also the idea of education—of teaching those who are being

initiated the rules and customs of the tribe or group.

The suggestion that a person is being reborn to another kind of life underlies the ritual celebrated at initiation, as well as at BIRTH, MARRIAGE, and DEATH (qq.v.). The original purpose of such rites was not only to celebrate the change from one kind of life to another, but also to bring about the new life. In order to understand this one must remember that primitive people think that acting what you want to happen is a way of magically making it happen (*see* MAGIC).

How strong was this idea of rebirth will be seen if we consider a few of the rites which form part of initiation ceremonies. Among some Australian natives a scene of death and rising from the dead was enacted. The boys were placed beside a grave in which a man was concealed as if dead. A procession of men then approached, chanting invocations, and suddenly the apparently dead man jumped up. During the initiation as witch-doctors the boys of an African tribe, the Azande, are actually partly buried, as in a grave, and then jump out, feeling rather dizzy and out of breath.

In some tribes boys to be initiated are put into what is supposed to be a magic sleep: when they awaken in the morning they are regarded as having become men. The idea of entering a new life is sometimes emphasized by giving a new name at the initiation. The main initiation ground of a North Transvaal tribe is called 'the place where things are forgotten', and the Indian boys of Virginia were given a medicine which was believed to blot out all memory of the past. It is not unusual for boys after initiation to pretend to have forgotten their early life and how to do the simplest things, even how to talk.

In some communities of Eskimoes, the magician, when initiating someone into the mysteries, pretends to kill him; his soul is believed to fly off and find out the secrets of the earth and sky while he lies still on the ground. Then he is 'revived' and becomes a magician in his turn. Before a man becomes a Benedictine monk he is laid on the ground, covered with a sheet, and the service of the burial of the dead is performed. This idea of rebirth is expressed in the New Testament: (1 Pet. ii. 24) 'that we, being dead unto sin, should live unto righteousness'. The words are quoted in the Church of England baptismal service. At confirmation in the

AN AUSTRALIAN INITIATION CEREMONY

The initiates crawl through the legs of the men in the central group. Kakadu Tribe, N. Australia. *Pitt Rivers Coll.*

Roman Catholic Church the candidate is given a new name to mark his or her new life.

Hindus emphasize the idea that at initiation a boy undergoes spiritual rebirth—becomes one of the 'twice-born', as they say. The ceremony in which a young Hindu is 'girded with the sacred thread' is a most important occasion. When he is eight years old, musicians play at the house, which has been specially cleaned and in which an altar facing the east has been erected. He is anointed and his head is shaved, leaving only a topknot. His mother takes him on her lap to feed him and for the last time eats from the same plate with him. At the 'lucky' moment the priests and guests throw red rice over him, and the priest puts the sacred thread over his left shoulder and below his right arm. On the fifth day after this ceremony he goes in his best clothes to the temple to worship.

As with marriage ceremonies, it is probable that many initiation ceremonies are derived from a very ancient ritual in which the king at his coronation or enthronement was thought to die and be reborn as a god. Thus, at initiation, an Indian boy is anointed like the king of England at his coronation, and the Indian's sacred thread corresponds to the girdle which the Dean of Westminster places around the king. The Indian boy receives a yellow cloth to wear, shoes and a staff; the king is vested in a robe of cloth of gold and given spurs, sceptre, and a rod. The boy takes his seat on a stool, the king on his throne.

There is the notion that people are centres of magical power at the times when they change their status in the community, and that at such times the powers of evil are particularly active. Therefore those to be initiated are secluded and isolated. As initiation is a time of education there are practical advantages in isolating the candidates. The responsibilities, duties, arts and crafts of men and women are so different that the instruction in adult life is different for boys and girls, as also is the sex instruction. Girls during initiation may be taught basket-making and cooking, and lads cattle-herding or hunting technique, as well as being instructed in the traditions and marriage customs of the tribe.

In many East African tribes there is a series of initiations at different ages. Amongst the Didinga, for instance, there are initiations at the ages of eight, thirteen, eighteen, and twenty-eight—and others later on. After the ceremony, at the age of eight, a boy may carry a spear and is trained to use it. He is taught dances and songs, good manners, and the duty of obedience to his elders. At thirteen he is instructed in rain ceremonies, shown how to hunt, and taught the use of herbs as medicine. At eighteen he begins his period of about ten years' service as a warrior of the tribe. During these initiations a youth gains a wider outlook by mixing with others of different clans. The system serves somewhat the same purpose as our junior and senior schools, universities, and military service.

During the period of initiation boys and girls often have to undergo various frightening, painful, or otherwise unpleasant ordeals to impress them with the importance of the occasion and give them the opportunity to show that they can undergo hardship manfully and are fit to be full members of the community. They may have to submit to circumcision, tattooing, or earpiercing. Candidates, both boys and girls, may have to fast, eat nasty or dirty food, keep silence, and observe various TABOOS (q.v.) and rites of purification. Boys are told that they must now behave with dignity as men and no longer in a childish manner. Various customs are often reversed during initiation. In a North Transvaal tribe the boys wear their loin-cloths the wrong way round; some Australian tribesmen tell the candidates the opposite of what they mean; and some initiates are made to walk backwards and turn their plates upside-down.

In many ways initiations serve useful purposes. We are told, for example, that amongst the Australian blacks each lad is given, 'by one of the elders, advice so kindly, fatherly, and impressive, as often to soften the heart, and draw tears from the youth'. An Indian in North Carolina told a European that initiation meant the same to them as it did for Europeans to send their children to school 'to be taught good breeding and letters'. When Basuto boys are initiated they are told: 'Be men, fear theft, fear adultery, honour your father and mother, obey your chiefs.'

We can understand the part that initiation plays amongst primitive people only when we remember that they have no schools, and no way of writing down or recording their customs and laws. The traditions of the tribe must be passed on from old to young, by word of mouth and example, and with care and solemnity, or what knowledge and organization the tribespeople possess would be lost and they would perish. Therefore they make every effort to impress the new generation with their duty to be loyal to tribal traditions and to carry on its religious practices, its code of conduct, and its way of life.

INQUISITION. In the later Middle Ages, from about the 13th century, people began to question the authority of the Church; and a number of heresies arose which resulted in the breaking away of groups of Christians from the Church. The priests tried to control men's beliefs by force. They felt so certain that those who disagreed with them would not only be damned themselves but lead others to damnation, that they thought it their Christian duty to force men to accept their way of salvation. They thought that no measures, even the most brutal tortures, were too drastic in order to save men's souls from burning in hell for eternity.

It had always been the duty of the bishops to discover and punish heretics. With the great increase of heresy, the kings of some countries passed laws that heretics who would not recant should be burnt at the stake. In 1233 the Pope set up a special tribunal to suppress heresy, and appointed official inquisitors to do the work previously done by the bishops. This tribunal, the Inquisition, was controlled largely by Dominican and Franciscan friars—often pious men who believed they were doing God's will. At a later stage the Jesuits also were very active inquisitors, especially in Spain.

Some of the kings of Europe feared the Reformation, not only because of its threat to the authority of the Church of Rome, but also for political reasons. The struggles for freedom in religious beliefs became mixed up with struggles for political freedom. The Inquisition therefore was often called in for reasons which were by no means only religious. The kings of Spain made great use of it in the 15th and 16th centuries in helping to keep their great Empire together. In the 15th century the Inquisition took part in Spanish attacks on the Moors, and enormous numbers of heretics were burnt at the Autos-da-Fé, the public burnings of heretics. The Inquisition was also used in the Netherlands against the Dutch Protestants in their struggle for freedom, and in South America to help in converting and subjugating the Indians.

Most of the worst horrors of the Inquisition are connected with the history of Spain. In 1483 Tomas de Torquemada, prior of a Dominican monastery in Spain, persuaded the King of Spain to call in the Inquisition to combat heresy. Torquemada became the Inquisitor-General in Spain and began an attack on heretics which has left his name a byword for pitiless

name being the Congregation of the Holy Office: it is one of the executive organizations of the Roman Catholic Church responsible for investigating false doctrine. But now that the right of the individual to believe as he thinks fit is generally recognized, the Inquisition no longer uses force in carrying out its duties.

See also ROMAN CATHOLIC CHURCH.

IONIANS, *see* GREEK CIVILIZATION, Section 2 C.

IRANIANS, *see* PERSIANS.

IRAQI. Mesopotamia, through which run the great rivers the Tigris and Euphrates, was the home of one of the earliest civilizations of the world—the SUMERIAN (q.v.), which flourished over 6,000 years ago. This was followed by the civilization of the BABYLONIANS and the ASSYRIANS (qq.v.). From about 1700 B.C., however, a series of invasions began which subjected the country to foreign domination—Egyptian, Persian, Mongol, and Turkish—until in 1924 Iraq became a kingdom under British mandate with King Feisal, father of the present king, on the throne.

The people of modern Iraq number nearly four millions. Of these a large majority are Arabs, inhabiting the great plains of the Tigris and Euphrates and the surrounding deserts. The next largest element in the population are the Kurds, about 750,000 of them in the northern plains and hills north of Mosul. Other minorities are the Turkomen, descendants of tribes who invaded Iraq in the 15th century; the Persians, whose settlements are mainly in Bagdad and Basra; small groups of Christians near Mosul; and in the north-west the tribes of Yezidis, a nature-worshipping people descended from very early invaders.

Their long history of subjection has resulted in a poor and backward people who cling to ancient ways of life and have as yet little sense of nationality. They think of themselves as members of tribal or religious groups (which are usually mutually antagonistic) rather than as Iraqi. The Arabs and the Kurds have a deep-rooted racial antagonism which is aggravated by the hillsman's traditional contempt for the plainsman. The Kurds have a proverb: 'A camel is not an animal, an Arab is not a human being.' The Arab's reply to this is: 'There are three plagues in the world, the Kurd, the rat, and the locust.' Ninety-three per cent. of the people

AN AUTO-DA-FÉ

Heretics are being burned at the stake while others, with ropes round their necks, await their turn. Painting by P. Berruguete in the Prado, Madrid. *Vernacci*

cruelty. The suspected heretic, when brought before the Court of the Inquisition, had hardly any chance of escape, even if he were innocent. Witnesses were bribed and their names kept secret; prisoners were tortured to make them confess their guilt or recant their heresy; hundreds were burnt at the stake.

The Inquisition also played a part in the suppression of the Knights Templar in Cyprus, the main motive for which was jealousy of their great wealth (*see* KNIGHTS, ORDERS OF). Joan of Arc was condemned for heresy and witchcraft with the help of the Inquisition. But apart from these special attacks, the medieval Inquisition in France and Italy was usually fairly inactive, only burning an occasional witch or religious fanatic.

The Inquisition is still in existence, its official

SILVERSMITHS IN THE BAZAAR AT BAGDAD
Associated Press

follow the ISLAM faith (q.v.); but some belong to the Sunni sect of Moslems and some to the Shia sect, and this is another cause for antagonism.

The Arab of Iraq has as a rule brown hair and eyes, a sallow complexion, and average height. He is lively and imaginative, subtle and quick to learn, but he despises manual work and does not accept new ideas willingly. The *fellahin*, the peasants, live in mud or reed huts; the *Shawiya* or shepherds and the BEDOUIN (q.v.), the nomad camel-breeders, move about in search of pasture and live in their brown camel-hair tents. The Arab's normal dress is a long cotton shirt buttoned to the throat, and a cloak of brown camel-hair or wool called an *aba*. On his head he wears a length of cotton cloth tied with a coil of rope.

The Kurds are generally smaller than the Arabs, and have brown hair, bright eyes, and long aquiline noses which give them a rather fierce appearance. They are hardier than the Arabs, more hot-tempered, and less quickwitted and genial. They are generally thought of as treacherous, but they are loyal and hospitable to their friends. They are more thrifty and hard-working than the Arabs: many of them leave the hills and work as porters, labourers, policemen or soldiers in the cities of the plains. Much of the labour of the oil fields near Mosul is Kurdish. They are organized in tribes between whom there are often blood-feuds. They live in houses built strongly of stone, with few windows so that they can be easily defended. They wear brightly coloured clothes—long baggy trousers tied round the waist with a girdle on which are hung knives, for use as well as decoration, wide-sleeved shirts, dark-coloured, thick, felt waistcoats and short jackets. On their heads they wear brightly coloured, striped, loose turbans, and on their feet leather slippers with peaked toes.

From ancient times the inhabitants of Iraq have depended on agriculture and stock-breeding. The ancient Sumerians carried out irrigation works in the valley of the great rivers, which brought fertility to the responsive soil. Both Arabs and Kurds to-day depend largely on sheep, camels, and the crops grown in the fertile river valleys. The Government of Iraq has the task of welding their country into a unified whole. Racial and religious antagonisms, the long history of subjection, and the lack of education make this a slow and difficult task.

See also ARABS.
See also Vol. III: IRAQ.

IRISH. Ireland is divided into two parts—Northern Ireland and Eire. In 1921, after a long and bitter rebellion, the twenty-six southern counties of Ireland broke away and declared themselves an independent state, now called the Republic of Ireland. Mr. De Valera, later Prime Minister, took part in the revolution, defending a flour-mill against British troops. In 1949 the country left the British Commonwealth, so now coins have on them, not the Queen's head, but horses, salmon, greyhounds, hens, and pigs. In Eire soldiers wear green uniforms, notices are written in Irish, and a national flag of green, white, and orange flies over the public buildings. This is because Eire is no longer part of the United Kingdom. But the six counties round Belfast, in the north-east corner of the island, preferred to remain in the United Kingdom and are now called 'Northern Ireland'.

To understand why this happened we must go back into Irish history. The rebellion ending in 1921 was the last of a long series of risings, disturbances, and troubles in Ireland, dating back hundreds of years to the days of Queen Elizabeth, when the English first conquered and occupied all Ireland. One of the real causes of the whole bitter tragedy was that England became a Protestant country in the 16th century while the south of Ireland remained Roman Catholic, looking to the Pope as head of their Church. The peasants were always at loggerheads with their landlords — usually English Protestants, and in every generation a new Irish leader appeared to stir the people into another rebellion. These rebellions were usually

4852

put down with great bloodshed, burning of houses, and hanging of the leaders in the cold dawn. At one time the Catholics were forbidden to practise their religion, and no Catholic might inherit land or own a horse worth more than £5. All these years of unrest caused much bitterness and, worse still, the country became very poor. During the great famines of the 19th century when the potato crop (on which many of the peasants lived) failed, thousands died of starvation. In valley after valley, whole families with their children, their dog, their donkey, and their pig, died and lay around their little cottages with no one to bury them. We must remember all these things in trying to judge the history of Ireland.

The history of the North is quite different. During the reign of James I and afterwards, many English and Scots farmers and merchants settled there, and the country became predominantly Protestant. Their descendants refused to unite with the Catholic South; so they are still part of the United Kingdom.

The Irish are a Celtic people of the same racial origins as the ancient Britons and akin to the Bretons, Cornish, Welsh, Manx, and Gaels of Scotland. When the Angles and Saxons invaded Britain from the east in the 5th and 6th centuries, they drove the Britons westward, and many of them took refuge in Ireland as well as

A 'TURF' (PEAT) SELLER IN CONNEMARA. *Vincent Brennan*

K

PREPARING FLAX IN NORTHERN IRELAND
The plants are steeped in the retting dam before being sent to the linen mill. *Irish Linen Guild*

in Wales, Cornwall, Scotland, and Brittany. The Irish, therefore, are of quite a different racial origin from the English people. Their stormy history has made them very patriotic, with long memories for what has happened in the past. Since 1922 the Government of Eire has been trying to reinstate the ancient Celtic or Irish Gaelic language, sometimes called Erse, which died out about a hundred years ago except in remote country places. All the children have to learn Irish Gaelic at school, but almost all speak English as well, and often more easily than their national language. But the English that the Irish speak is peculiarly their own and full of poetic phrases, some of them really translations from the Gaelic. Very strong tea, for instance, may be called 'strong enough to trot a mouse on'; they will say that a thin person is 'no thicker than a thrush's ankle', or that something that is lost has disappeared 'like a daisy in a bull's mouth'.

Apart from Dublin, capital of Eire, and Belfast, capital of Northern Ireland, Ireland has few large towns. The great majority of the Irish people are farmers living in the country. Every peasant keeps pigs and hens which he sells in the country markets for ready money to buy clothes and other necessaries. Even the poorest labourer can fatten a pig on potato-peelings, and since in the past the rent was the main item for which money was required, the pig was often called 'the gentleman who pays the rent'. A farmer's work is hard, but except in the poorest parts he gets a good livelihood and is usually able to keep a horse or two for his favourite sport of fox-hunting. The Irish are passionately fond of horses and know a great deal about them.

In the Donegal Highlands and in Connemara, in the north-west and west of Eire, the land is poor and rocky, and the peasants have a hard struggle for existence. Life is very primitive and simple. The peasants live for the most part in little whitewashed, one-storeyed cottages, generally of only two rooms. Pigs and chickens are apt to get very much mixed up with the family, and all live mainly on potatoes. The family sit round the table in the evenings with a bowl of boiled potatoes before each person, and a bowl of milk and salt in the middle, so that everyone can dip in turn. The fuel for their fires is mostly peat dug from the bogs. Their clothing is very poor—the children often go barefoot, and the women wear shawls with kerchiefs on their heads. In these poor and more remote parts the lives of the people are much influenced by the priest, who is himself often a very simple and credulous person. Life is bound by superstitions, connected partly with their religion and partly with their lingering folk-lore beliefs.

The two most exciting occasions in the country are the market-days and the *ceilidhes*. A *ceilidhe* —pronounced 'kaylee'—is an evening party for all the people of the district. After the market, or on a church holiday, everybody gathers in a village hall or large farm-house, bringing with them baskets of tobacco, bacon, tea, whisky, and a sort of bread with raisins called 'barm-brack'. The old people sit round the fire, talking and smoking, while the others dance jigs and other Irish dances to the music of a violin and accordion. Then they all take turns at singing or reciting poetry or listen to an old folk-tale told again by a young man. Outside in the dark the horses and donkeys wait patiently till the *ceilidhe* is over and the people set off for home along the lonely country lanes.

But the greatest holiday of all is St. Patrick's Day (17 March), a whole holiday for all the schools. This is the feast-day of the national saint, ST. PATRICK (q.v. Vol. V), who converted the Irish to Christianity in the 5th century. His emblem, and consequently the emblem of the country, is the shamrock, a small, green, three-leaved plant rather like clover, which will only grow in Ireland; people have planted it in other countries, but it has always withered and died.

Since most Irish farms are small they cannot be divided amongst the family, so only one son, normally the eldest, can inherit his father's land. The other sons, when they grow up, must try to find work in the towns. There are very few jobs in Dublin or the country, so most of these young men emigrate to America or England or the Empire. That is why the population of Eire remains very low—nearly three millions—while in every American and English city you find large numbers of Irish emigrants. In North Ireland, however, since the Industrial Revolution, a good deal of industrial life has grown up, especially connected with linen, breweries, distilleries, and tobacco. In consequence, the population of North Ireland is nearly twice as dense as that of Eire.

Irish emigrants always think of themselves as exiles and plan to return to Ireland when they have made enough money, but they do not always manage to do so. A very great Irish poet, W. B. YEATS (q.v. Vol. V), expressed his feeling of home-sickness in the poem he wrote from London, 'The Lake Isle of Innisfree'.

See also Vol. III: IRELAND; Vol. IV: IRISH LANGUAGE.

IRON AGE, *see* PREHISTORIC MAN, Section 6.

ISLAM. 1. This is the religion of the Moslems, founded in the 7th century by Mohammed in Arabia. It is followed by almost all Arab peoples, as well as by many other peoples, mostly in the countries of the old World not far from the Equator. In 1920 there were said to be 221 million Moslems in the world, but since then the numbers have probably shrunk, especially in Turkey and in the areas under the influence of the Soviet Union.

2. BELIEF AND PRACTICE. What is the religious life of the average devout Moslem like? In a large community there are likely to be considerable differences of belief and observance, and it is certainly the case that in many parts of the Islamic world (for example in Morocco) there are people who, though they call themselves Moslems, are really ANIMISTS (q.v.) or who, as in parts of the East Indies, hold two religions at once. The main point, however, about the person who treats Islam as a serious creed is his almost white-hot belief in the supreme majesty of the one and only Deity in the universe, Allah. Allah is Power and Mercy, but not, it seems, necessarily Goodness or Love. Or rather, in the case of Allah, good and evil mean whatever Allah at his own discretion chooses. 'Allah is not to be inquired as to what he does.' 'It shall be as Allah pleases.' These are typical phrases, and they certainly make for a submissive and even a fatalistic habit of mind. The first duty of a Moslem is unquestioning obedience and submission. He is the *abd* or slave of Allah, not a child of God. There is no talk of 'co-operating with Allah', and such a passage as 'No longer do I call you servants, for the servant knoweth not what his lord doeth, but I have called you friends', &c., would not occur in the Koran (the Moslem sacred book). The Moslem is not encouraged to think of Allah as 'loving', in the manner that Christians think of God, though some educated Moslems explain this away, and lay stress on the passages in the Koran which speak of the mercy of Allah or of the beautiful and excellent names of God. (On the other hand, in spite of Jesus Christ's teaching, Christians in the Middle Ages both taught and believed whole-heartedly in the most terrible torments of the lost souls in hell, while Calvinistic Christianity seems to represent God as being quite as arbitrary as Allah.) It is easy to see that Islam is a good soldier's creed, and Moslem soldiers, such as we find in India, are generally good ones.

The recitation of the creed 'There is no God but Allah' is called the *Kalimah*, and it is the first observance due from a good Moslem. There are four other duties which he must perform as part of the outward expression of his belief: Prayer, Fasting, Almsgiving, and Pilgrimage, and some would add as a fifth, the Holy War.

(*a*) *Prayer*. Moslems can pray in any place so long as it is clean, and they often carry a mat with them on which to stand and kneel. Each complete set of prayers consists of eight distinct acts, and the object is to form in the worshipper the habit of surrender, and the constant remembrance of the power of Allah. Bowing his head to the ground, he has to repeat, 'Glory to Allah the Most High; Allah is greater than all else.' These prayers are taught to little boys at an early age before they can understand their exact meaning, so as to develop in them the right habits. Men should pray facing in the direction of Mecca—the birthplace of Mohammed—(at first they prayed facing towards Jerusalem), and on Fridays and festivals they should pray in the mosque. There are no priests—only teachers: any Moslem can lead prayers in the mosque. On Fridays there is a sermon which is often political. Friday is not a day of rest except in certain areas where it is treated like a Christian Sunday.

The first meeting-place for Moslems was very simple, and was called *Masjid-al-nabi*, or prayer-house of the prophet. *Masjid* in Italian became *Moschea*, and in French—*Mosquée*; the accent got rubbed off in English and so we get 'mosque'. Some of the big mosques, such as the Pearl Mosque at Agra and the Mosque of Kaid at Cairo, are very magnificent buildings. The great Byzantine church of St. Sophia at Constantinople became a mosque after the Turkish conquest. The only real essentials in a mosque are an enclosure with a sort of pulpit or stage in the middle for the leader or preacher, and a niche in one wall to mark the direction of Mecca. Part of the enclosure or courtyard may be covered in and have a colonnade running round it. Times for prayer are generally announced by a crier known as a *muezzin* from a tower, called a minaret.

(*b*) *Fasting*, especially voluntary fasting, is considered of great religious merit—Monday and Thursday in each week are special fasting days, also the three middle days of each lunar month. During one month, Ramadan, it is compulsory for all Moslems to fast from dawn till sunset.

(*c*) *Almsgiving* takes the form of a tax which is levied on all property that has been held for at least a year, with certain exceptions such as the tools of one's trade. The tax varies from one-fortieth to a fifth of a Moslem's property, and is expended on the relief of Moslem poor.

(*d*) *Pilgrimage*. If it is within his power, every Moslem should make a pilgrimage to Mecca once during his lifetime, and during the proper month. When he reaches Mecca, the pilgrim has to wear sandals and a special new costume consisting of two white cotton cloths. Among other things, he visits a special hill outside Mecca, and he makes the circuit of a sacred shrine in the centre of the city, called the *Kaabah*, where he must kiss a sacred black stone which has been built into a corner of the wall. At the end of the pilgrimage he shaves his head, pares his nails, and again puts on his ordinary clothes. Most pilgrims also visit the tomb of the Prophet at Medina. One sect of Moslems, the Shiahs, allow the pilgrimage to be made by proxy.

(*e*) *The Holy War* used to mean 'military service against non-Moslems', but there are those to-day who take it to mean 'spiritual warfare against evil', very likely owing to the influence of Christian or modern pacifist ideas.

Moslems' conduct is in the main guided by what is set out in the Koran, by what tradition has laid down, and in case of doubt, by the agreed opinion of certain Moslem leaders. Playing games of chance for money and loaning money at interest are forbidden, and also the consumption of pork and alcohol. The remittal of loans is recommended as a form of meritorious almsgiving. Women are supposed to have the same privileges as men, but until lately, at any rate, they have had an inferior status. This seems to be allowed by the Koran, which in the fourth *sura* (chapter), officially permits husbands to punish their wives by beating and to marry

THE GREAT MOSQUE AT MECCA
Pilgrims are visiting the sacred Kaabah. *Paul Popper*

more than one wife, four being the maximum. Good and evil deeds are believed to be recorded by the angels in Heaven and balanced against one another to determine how much purification the believer must undergo before entering Heaven; but it is believed that no Moslem can go permanently to Hell, which is apparently reserved for unbelievers and apostates. One of the central beliefs taught by Mohammed throughout his life and constantly repeated in the Koran is that of the Resurrection of the Body, with a final Judgement Day, followed by the dismissal of mankind to Heaven or Hell. Mohammed also taught that Abraham, Moses, and Jesus were true prophets, but that he himself was the last and greatest.

3. REFORMING MOVEMENTS. Very early in the history of Islam there was a split in the movement which came about over the question of succession to the leadership and which still remains to-day. The larger section, called Sunnis, supported a kind of elected Khalifa (Caliph or successor) drawn from the Prophet's tribe, the Quraish: the smaller section, the Shiahs, mostly to be found in Arabia and much more intolerant and narrow in their outlook, would only accept Ali, Mohammed's nephew, and his descendants as leaders. Islam is now naturally affected by twentieth-century ideas and dis-

coveries. Some Moslems are trying to modernize their faith and perhaps bring it closer to Christianity. A movement to this end began in India, but it has also come to England, and its followers have a mosque at Woking in Surrey.

Other reform movements have been started in Egypt and, lately, among the Javanese Moslems of Indonesia. These hold that the principles of the Koran should be interpreted and adapted to meet special cases as they arise by following the guidance of the Caliphs and other great Moslem leaders. Other Moslems, especially in Arabia, wish to go back in all details to the exact teaching of the past. 'Back to Mohammed and the Koran' is their cry.

The attraction of the Islamic faith probably lies in five main features: its simplicity and directness; its accommodation to the facts of nature and the eastern way of life, especially in matters of sex and authority; its setting of a standard not too exalted for the average man to reach; its very practical insistence upon the brotherhood of all Moslems; and its promise of a Heaven of material delights.

4. HISTORY. The history of Islam is very closely wrapped up with that of the ARAB people (q.v.). At the time of Mohammed's death in 632 there were in Arabia a large number of unquestionably sincere men, like his friends Abu

SULTAN HASSAN MOSQUE, CAIRO. *Paul Popper*

Bakr and Omar, who believed passionately in Mohammed's teaching. These men formed the driving power of Moslem Arab expansion. It was they who inspired and led the vast armies that poured out to conquer the world for Allah. Every Moslem soldier was assured of salvation in the next world, besides the advantages of a successful campaign.

There were three main waves of Moslem advance. First there was the Arab movement proper, from 632 to 800, which carried Islam to Persia, Syria, North Africa, Sicily, and Spain. Then a little later, after the conversion of the various groups of Turks, came the second wave, 1080 to 1480, carrying Islam through Turkistan, eastward to India and China, and northward with the Ottoman Turks across the Balkans up to Vienna. Constantinople, the centre of the Byzantine Empire, fell to the Moslem Turks in 1453. The third wave was social and economic rather than military. After an interval of some four centuries, Islam once again moved forward, and by means of the Arab trader, the returned pilgrim, and the colonist from India, it advanced through Negro Africa, and also through Malaya and the Dutch East Indies. It is still making converts, especially among the pagan African tribes.

In the 7th and 8th centuries Arabia became one huge depot for the breeding and training of soldiers, and for a time there seemed almost no limit to the size and efficiency of the armies which ranged over Asia and the Mediterranean countries. It is hard to say whether these Moslems were better or worse than many other military leaders of their day. The Moslems would offer safety to their enemies if they would accept the Islam faith, a crude method of conversion, which did at least put a limit to slaughter. It was, in fact, also used by the Christian emperor, Charlemagne, in the 8th century, when he offered the heathen Saxons massacre or conversion to Christianity. The modern Moslem will admit that the victims of forcible conversion are unlikely to be sincere, but he adds 'Their children will be'. And since he has no doubts about the truth of his own creed, this point of view seems to him reasonable. At the time of Mohammed, and for some long time on, the idea of Holy Wars and the conversion of people by force was generally accepted as right by Christians quite as much as by Moslems. The wars were, no doubt, demoralizing, as wars usually are. Yet so stale and degenerate was the world into which Islam entered that for a time the Arabs did bring with them a new and vigorous life, a new reorganization of society and a fresh outburst of art and literature. It is said that the institutions created by the Arab Moslems were remarkable for their good sense and humanity, and that justice was frequently well administered. Even Jews and Christians, so long as they paid tribute, received the protection of the Islamic state. The modern world also owes a debt to Islam for keeping alive and fostering the arts and sciences through the Dark Ages, in the great centres of Arab civilization at Bagdad, Cairo, and Cordova.

Moslems to-day are in the main a religious rather than a political body, scattered in various countries from China to Morocco, from the Pacific Islands to Pakistan. Their missionary activities are very great, especially among more primitive peoples in the equatorial countries. But they have no visible head. The formation of the Arab League is a step in the direction of a big political federation of Moslems under an Arab leader.

See also ARABS; DERVISHES; SACRED BOOKS.
See also Vol. V: MOHAMMED.

ISRAELITES, *see* HEBREW CIVILIZATION.

ITALIANS. In order to understand modern Italy it is important to remember her long and troublous history. The Italian nation as we know it to-day only started a united existence in 1870. Before that the country was composed of several different states governed independently, often by foreigners and often at war with each other. Italian history is therefore very complicated, for every great Italian city has its own distinct history. This has led to a tendency among the inhabitants to think of themselves first as Romans, Venetians, Florentines, Neapolitans, or whatever they may be, and only secondly as Italians, and thus it is not easy for them to understand and attain that kind of national unity which has been our birthright for centuries.

Differences of racial origin have produced differences in character among Italians which also hinder national unity. Italians claim that they are the most mixed people in Europe, for during the course of their history wave after wave of invaders have visited or settled in the country. Generally speaking the northern Italians are more Germanic and the southern more Latin in origin, and the differences between them are very marked. As a whole, the northerners are more practical, industrious, progressive, and efficient than the southerners, who, living in a hotter climate, are more happy-go-lucky and inclined to be lazy.

Although it is dangerous to generalize, there are certain characteristics which are common to most Italians. They are great lovers of beauty and intensely proud of their ancient civilization, their art, and their music, especially opera. On the whole they are content with simple pleasures, are gay and talkative, passionate and quarrelsome, and extremely sensitive to any slight. They love to gather in the streets, make a noise, and talk for hours. Until recently Italian girls led a secluded life in the home and were not allowed out unless escorted by a member of the family. Now they are becoming much more emancipated and may go to the universities and take up professions. Women doctors or lawyers are as yet rare in Italy, however. Italian women do not play games very much, but the men are particularly good at any sport which demands speed rather than endurance: they are good pilots and motor-racers, for example. Italians are clever engineers and mechanics—the pioneer of wireless, Marconi, was an Italian. They are not militaristic, though Mussolini tried to make

them so. They have little respect for law, for they are a race of individualists who wish to be left alone to manage their private affairs in their own way.

Italy has been inhabited since the Old Stone Age, and the remains of settlements of all periods since then have been discovered by archaeologists. The Etruscans, early settlers who probably came from Asia Minor, were not only great architects, but sculptors, painters, and craftsmen, and their influence is to be seen, after more than 2,000 years, in the small industries and crafts of central Italy. Colonies of Greeks settled on the coasts of southern Italy, and some of the most beautiful of the Greek temples are to be found at Paestum, south of Naples, at Agrigento, and near Palermo in Sicily. The establishment of the Roman Empire brought fresh incursions of foreigners. Rome itself attracted scholars, merchants, and adventurers from all over the known world, and these strains mingled with the original inhabitants (*see* ROMAN CIVILIZATION).

After the fall of the Roman Empire successions of invaders, particularly from the north, came either to plunder and depart or, like the Lombards, to settle down and establish kingdoms in what is now known as the Plain of Lombardy. In Sicily and the south there were invasions of Saracens in the 9th century and of Normans in the 11th, and these occupations, as well as that of the Spaniards in later times, have left their mark, especially upon the Sicilians—a people distinct from their neighbours in many ways. In A.D. 800 the HOLY ROMAN EMPIRE (q.v.) was founded—the Emperor to be head of the temporal world as the Pope was head of the spiritual. In the late Middle Ages a great rivalry grew up between the Holy Roman Emperor and the Pope. The Pope was not only head of the Western Church but was also ruler of certain Italian states called the Papal States. Some of the great Italian families supported the Emperor and some the Pope, and there was continual warfare between them.

Most of the city states were governed by despots who were often tyrannical in their treatment of the people and who did not hesitate to assassinate those who threatened their positions. In the Republics of Florence and Venice there were constant intrigue and murder amongst the great families who controlled the states. But these wealthy families, such as the Medici in

GENOA HARBOUR
Since the Middle Ages Genoa has been an important port. *Sport and General*

Florence, the Visconti in Milan, and the Este in Ferrara, encouraged learning and the arts, and fostered an individualism which allowed genius to develop freely. In the 14th century the poet DANTE and the painter GIOTTO (qq.v. Vol. V) foreshadowed the Renaissance of the 15th and 16th centuries. The 15th century was one of the most brilliant periods of artistic achievement, and Florence was the chief centre of activity. Stimulated by the revival of classical learning, poets, painters, architects, sculptors, and scientists were developing new ideas, exploring new countries, and devising new forms of expression. The genius of these men was not confined to one subject but ranged over many. LEONARDO DA VINCI was a scientist as well as a painter and sculptor, and MICHELANGELO (qq.v. Vol. V) was a sculptor, painter, architect, and poet. The wealth of the Papal Court in Rome drew artists from all over Italy for such great works as the building of St. Peter's. Milan, the most important commercial city, also attracted artists though it did not produce many noteworthy ones of its own. The Venetian State, the greatest of the maritime states, drew its wealth from its trade with the East. There is an Eastern richness in Venetian architecture and painting, which reached its greatest height in the 16th century with the painter TITIAN (q.v. Vol. V).

In the 16th century and for the following three centuries Italy was ravaged by the invading armies of France, Spain, and Austria, and most of her cities came under the power of one foreign conqueror after another. The Reformation in northern Europe had reduced the power and wealth of the Popes, and there was no one with sufficient power to unite the country against the invaders.

After the Napoleonic wars in the 19th century a movement for a united Italy, inspired largely by the idealist MAZZINI (q.v. Vol. V), began to take shape. The King of Sardinia, Victor Emmanuel, of the House of Savoy, became its leader, and after a series of wars, revolutions, and much clever diplomacy, in which the brilliant statesman CAVOUR and the romantic soldier GARIBALDI (qq.v. Vol. V), played important parts, Italy was finally united in 1870 and Victor Emmanuel crowned in Rome as the first king.

After the First World War political unrest and bad social conditions allowed MUSSOLINI (q.v. Vol. V) to establish himself as the dictator of a Fascist régime. Although he brought efficient organization into Italy and inspired the Italians with a sense of unity and pride in their country, he misled them into a policy of military aggression.

ASSISI
Orchards and vineyards surround the little town which is built on the top of a hill. *E. B. Hoyton*

With dreams of a second Roman Empire he became more and more militaristic, finally involving Italy in the Second World War on the side of Germany, with disastrous results both to himself and his country.

In 1946 the country decided by plebiscite to become a Republic. With a democratically elected Parliament, the Italians are now striving to make good the ravages of war and to achieve political stability. But even now the strongest unifying force in the country is the ROMAN CATHOLIC CHURCH (q.v.) to which some 97% of Italians belong.

Modern Italy has a population of over 47 millions, of whom nearly 70% are employed on the land. The industrial quarters in the large cities in the north, such as Turin with the Fiat motor works, are much like those in other countries. Farming conditions vary from the big dairy farms in Piedmont in the north-west to tiny patches of land on the mountain-sides of central and southern Italy. The well-to-do farmers live in large stone-built houses with inner courtyards, and only slits of windows on the ground floor. The agricultural labourers generally live in crowded tenements in the little towns and villages and go out to their work every day. This is especially the custom in the south and in Sicily where the low-lying farm land is still the breeding-ground for the malaria-carrying mosquito.

Education is free and compulsory—nearly all the children go to the same State schools, though there are a few boarding-schools run by the teaching orders of the Roman Catholic Church. The people still cling to their local dialects, which are almost different languages, especially in the country districts.

The popular holidays are the saints' days of each town or village. The day begins with Mass, then in the country there is a fair with stalls and side-shows, and people sit about all day and most of the night eating and drinking in the restaurants and cafés. Each district prides itself on its cooking and local delicacies, but the most popular dishes are *pasta*, that is, macaroni or spaghetti, and *minestrone*, a soup of vegetables and meat stock, and eaten with grated cheese. Practically every Italian midday meal begins with an enormous plate of *pasta*, with either gravy or tomato sauce poured over it. Everyone—even the small children—drinks the local wine with meals; coffee is a popular drink, but tea is an expensive luxury. Olive oil is used a great deal for cooking, especially in the south.

See also Vol. III: ITALY; Vol. IV: ITALIAN LANGUAGE.

J

JAINS belong to a relatively small religious community in India, numbering, in 1921, only about one million members—now perhaps about a million and a quarter, as compared with 216 million Hindus and 11 million Buddhists. One might think of them as a mere survival, of no special importance, were it not that they are educated people (495 males and 50 females per thousand can read and write—a higher percentage than that of any other group in India). Crime among Jains is scarcely ever heard of.

Jainism began rather earlier than BUDDHISM (q.v.) but in the same period of Indian religious history, and apparently for much the same reason; and the two movements to some extent resemble one another. The founder, properly called Vardhamana, but by his disciples Mahavira (the great hero), was, like Gautama (Buddha), the son of a nobleman of princely rank, and was born somewhere about 599 B.C. When he was twenty-eight his parents died, and he became entirely devoted to the quest for spiritual enlightenment. Like Gautama, he began by joining an already-existing order of ascetics (*see* ASCETICISM); but at this point the likeness ceases. Gautama lost confidence in the extreme forms of the ascetic life, and pursued what he called 'the Middle Way'. Vardhamana sought even more severe forms of discipline. He gave up clothes entirely and taught that to 'fast unto death' was meritorious. He also taught the greatest respect for all forms of animal life, so that if crawling animals bite the body of a Jain monk or nun, the sufferer must not kill the vermin or even rub the affected part. Jains carry this care for organic life to such extremes that they strain all liquids before drinking them to avoid swallowing any living objects in them. They also carry brooms when walking to sweep the ground in front of them, and wear veils over their mouths. They even screen lamps to keep insects from burning themselves at the flame.

Yet extreme asceticism and kindness to animals are not the most important doctrines of the Jain religion. Both Vardhamana and Gautama gave up the idea of a personal God—a God who was in any real way like a more exalted kind of human person. At this stage of religious thought in India the really advanced thinkers had come to give up the belief in this kind of God. In place of this Vardhamana taught that the Universe was eternal and made up of six substances, space, time, units of matter, laws of merit (of which there seem to have been two), and souls. The goal of life, and also its final stage, is a sort of Paradise called Jiva, in which those souls which have gained enough merit to win release, live happily for evermore. The word 'Jain' means a conqueror or one who lives victoriously.

Vardhamana's disciples seem in one sense to be more truly atheists than the Buddhists, whose idea of the Universe takes the place of God. But in recent years a famous Jain preacher has publicly denied that they are atheists, and says that they believe in a Supreme Spirit, whom they call Paramatman. If this is true, it means that the Jains have been misunderstood for many years. But it may also mean that the Jains are themselves altering their faith and changing its balance.

Jain temples are clean and beautiful, with much white marble and bright colours. Their chief features are statues of Jain saints, who are numerous. Jains believe in a succession of spiritual leaders called Jinas or Tirthankaras, who have all been members of the warrior caste (*see* CASTE). The ordinary people are encouraged to take an interest in them, though (as with Buddhism) to be a real Jain it is necessary to be either a monk or a nun. Every fully professed Jain has to take five vows—not to kill, not to lie, to take nothing that is not given, to abstain from all sex-experience, and to take no pleasure in any material thing. There are two divisions of Jains—those who, like their founder, wear no clothes and deny that women can reach Jiva, and those who wear a white robe and say that women can attain salvation. The former are split into four sects, the latter into as many as eighty-four. But even the stricter Jains now, for the most part, wear a cloak and only take it off when they are eating. Perhaps the best work

JAIN TOWER AT CHITOR, RAJPUTANA
One of the most famous examples of Jain architecture, built in the 15th century

which the Jains do is to maintain hospitals for animals, and they make a practice of collecting and rearing young animals which have been discarded by their owners. The worship in the temples consists partly of acts of silent meditation, partly of simple offerings of flowers, incense, and lights in front of the images of the Jinas, accompanied by the singing of hymns.

See also INDIAN PEOPLES.

JAPANESE. The original inhabitants of Japan were the Ainus called the 'hairy Ainus' because they were big, rather ape-like men, hairy-chested, and long-bearded. Of these aborigines less than 20,000 now survive, and they are to be found in the bleak, mountainous island of Hokkaido, the most northerly part of Japan.

The Ainus were driven northwards by successive waves of invaders from overseas, one wave of Mongolian people coming from China, another from Malaya, and another from the South Sea islands. The present Japanese, therefore, are a mixed race; they are not so tall as Europeans, and they have small bones, sallow skins, and dark, straight hair.

Civilization came late to Japan, as compared with China, and then came with great suddenness. In the 7th century A.D., when CHINESE CIVILIZATION (q.v.) was at its height under the T'ang Dynasty, the Japanese were so much

AINU WOMEN AND CHILDREN
Paul Popper

impressed that they adopted for themselves all its main features. The Japanese had no writing, so they borrowed the Chinese characters and used them for their language. They studied the classics of Confucius and the scriptures of Buddhism; they refashioned their whole system of government, their social habits, rules of behaviour, and even their style of dress in imitation of the Chinese. About a thousand years later, in the 19th century, they took over Western civilization in the same wholesale way and, with great rapidity, made themselves comparable to Western nations in modern science, especially military science.

In spite of this tendency to borrow new ideas wholesale, all except the more highly educated Japanese still cling to primitive tribal beliefs, such as other nations once had but have long outgrown. They see themselves as a master race, sons of the Sun, born of the gods, with their own rules of right and wrong, and appointed by the gods to discipline the world, if necessary by force. It was this spirit (very like that of the German Nazis), combined with fanatical loyalty to an Emperor whom they thought of as semi-divine, which made them so formidable a foe when they set out in 1940 to conquer the Far East.

From the earliest days of Japanese history the country was divided into military clans, practically independent and always fighting one another. The clan-chieftains, called *Daimyos*, like the great barons in England at the time of the Wars of the Roses, commanded hosts of armed retainers, called *Samurai*, who were bound in loyalty to their chief by the strictest code of honour, but were utterly ruthless and contemptuous in their treatment of the wretched peasant serfs. At the end of the 16th century, however, one clan, Tokugawa by name, made themselves masters over the rest and established a firm rule under which Japan remained at peace for over 250 years. The position of the Emperor during this time was very strange. He became a mere puppet, kept like a bird in a golden cage, the centre of a brilliant court, worshipped almost as God by his people, but with no political power. All authority lay with the Shoguns, the heads of the clan.

The Shoguns at the end of the 16th century grew disturbed at the influence in Japan of the increasing number of European merchants coming to trade, and also of the Catholic missionaries who were converting the people to Christianity. The Shoguns wished to preserve the old feudal state of affairs and to keep the people submissive, and so they decided completely to shut out the outside world, especially the West. Foreigners were expelled, Christians massacred, no ships were allowed to sail to or from foreign ports, returning Japanese were beheaded. For 250 years, from the time of Queen Elizabeth to the time of Queen Victoria, the Japanese people lived in almost complete isolation.

This artificial state of affairs was brought to an end by force from the European nations, starting with an American naval expedition under Commodore Perry in 1853. From then on the Japanese reversed their policy and borrowed all they could from the Western World. The last Shogun resigned, and the Samurai (the armed retainers) were abolished. The Emperor was restored to power, and a parliamentary system of government was adopted. But although superficially westernized, the Japanese still retained their old belief in the master race. The population of Japan had been increasing very fast. They began to need more room for expansion and to cast greedy eyes on the territory of their neighbours, especially China. In 1932 they invaded the Chinese province of Manchuria, thus starting a policy of military expansion which culminated in their attempt in 1940 to master the whole Far East. After their defeat in the Second World War the Emperor publicly resigned any claim to being divine, and a more constitutional form of government was set up. But it is likely to take some time before the mass of the people will change a way of thinking which they have followed for hundreds of years.

So much of Japan is covered with mountains and forests that the Japanese have to make the best of the remaining land, cultivating it intensively and building their houses close together. The houses are for the most part built of wood, on platforms raised above the ground, with walls that can be pushed back to let in light and air or to convert several small rooms into one large one. There is little furniture: the people sit on padded mats on the floor, using low tables for their meals. Bedding is kept in a cupboard and spread on the floor at night. The only heating is generally a pot of smouldering charcoal; and as Japanese winters are cold, the people wrap themselves in a great deal of thick, padded clothing. Most Japanese now wear European

A JAPANESE GIRL WRITING A LETTER
Paul Popper

dress, at any rate for business. At home, however, they generally wear the national kimono (a 'wearing thing'), cotton socks, and, out of doors, wooden clogs. Women wear wide stiffened belts called *obis*. The best clothes of a Japanese woman are beautiful—she wears a kimono of rich silk crêpe and an obi of patterned brocade.

The Japanese live chiefly on rice and fish. Food is served in sets of little bowls and eaten with chopsticks. Tea from small, wide cups is drunk, not only at meals, but all through the day. Milk is rare and butter even more so. The Japanese avoid eating imported foods, such as bread which has to be made from imported wheat flour.

The Japanese year is marked by many festivals which are the public holidays. First, there are the great New Year festivals lasting a week. March 3 is the feast-day of girls, at which the family dolls are set out—tiny figures of the old emperors and empresses and their courtiers, beautifully dressed. In May is the boys' festival with more dolls—this time figures of famous

A JAPANESE HOUSE

The windows have been drawn back so that the family can enjoy the water garden beneath them. *Paul Popper*

warriors in armour. Huge cotton fish are flown like flags from the roofs: the boys' fish is the carp because it swims upstream against difficulties as a boy should do. In July is the feast of the dead, when offerings of food are carried to graveyards, and tiny, frail boats, carrying a cargo of food and a light, are launched on lakes and rivers (*see* ANCESTOR WORSHIP). The different flowers—plum, peach, iris, and wistaria—have each their own festival: in cherry-blossom time the whole country goes on holiday. Every temple has its festival days with praying, acting, and holiday-making. In summer people go on pilgrimages to famous shrines on the mountains and beside lakes. The theatre is also very popular: the Japanese will sit for hours watching their own immensely long classical plays as well as translations of Shakespeare's plays. Professional wrestlers will collect large audiences; and recently young Japanese have taken up what they call 'foreign-style' games and sports.

The Japanese as a whole are a cheerful, busy, courteous, and good-tempered people: the women in particular are patient, hard-working, and long-suffering. But for generations they have been taught to think their country superior to all other countries and to think the individual of no importance compared with the country or the family. Even marriages are arranged by the family rather than by the individual: a bride may

perhaps never meet her husband until the wedding-day, and then she returns with him to his father's home where, instead of living an individual life, she becomes part of his family. The Japanese have not been taught to think for themselves, but rather to believe what their rulers have told them and to obey their orders. Their religions, BUDDHISM (q.v.) and SHINTO (q.v.), encourage this attitude—the former to think little of the importance of this life, and the latter to glory in the greatness of their country. They have therefore been willing to work long hours for small pay in unhealthy factories, or to die fighting in wars which were certain in the end to bring disaster.

See also Vol. III: JAPAN; Vol. IV: JAPANESE LANGUAGE.

JAPANESE RELIGION, *see* SHINTOISM.

JASON, *see* GREEK HEROES.

JAVANESE, *see* INDONESIANS.

JEHOVAH. This is really a mis-spelling in English letters of the Hebrew name for God. Hebrew is frequently written with consonants only and without the markings or 'points' which indicate the vowels. Thus the Hebrew name for God is written יהוה or, as near as we can give it in English block lettering, YHVH or YHWH. The vowel-pointing is usually judged to give a form varying from YAHOH or YAHU to YAHWEH. Some think that YAHU or YAHOH is the oldest, and that it may have been the name for an ancient wind-god of the early Semites (Arabic, *hawah*, to blow). But the Bible story in Exod. iii seems to show that by the time it was written YHWH had become connected with the Hebrew verb, HVH, 'to be', and that YAHWEH properly means 'He Who is', or, as we might render it, 'The Supreme or Self-Existent Being'. This Name was held so sacred that the Hebrews, from motives of reverence, would not say it if they could help it, but substituted another word

ĂDONAI, or Lord. This word had different vowel-points, and JEHOVAH is the result of trying to write YHWH or YHVH with the vowels of ĂDONAI. 'Jehovah' is not used earlier than the Protestant Reformation (1520).

See also JUDAISM; GOD.

JESUIT, *see* MONK. *See also* Vol. V: LOYOLA, IGNATIUS.

JESUS OF NAZARETH. During the reign of Tiberius Caesar, about the year A.D. 29, a religious movement began in Palestine which soon spread through the Mediterranean countries, penetrated in a few centuries as far west as Britain, and as far east as China and south India, and is still growing and developing. Since the wide extent of this movement, both in area and duration, argues that in some special way it meets human needs, it is natural to ask what kind of man its Founder was, whence he came, and what he said and did.

Most people assume that the birth of Jesus of Nazareth took place in A.D. 1, but it has lately been calculated that it occurred four or even six years earlier. At that time Palestine was under the supervision of the Roman Government. In 37 B.C. the Romans had put over it a puppet king, Herod, who, although he professed the Jewish religion (*see* JUDAISM), was by birth an Edomite, one of a neighbouring race intensely hated by the Jews. His sympathies also were Greek rather than Palestinian. In 27 B.C., when Augustus became Emperor, the area of Herod's government was enlarged, and Herod became very rich, and built a magnificent new temple at Jerusalem. Herod kept a strong army, and was quite ruthless in putting to death any rebels. In 4 B.C. he died, and the Jews, sick of his tyranny, begged to be put directly under Roman rule. At first this request was not granted, but after nine years, when as many as 2,000 Jews had been crucified for revolt, the Emperor saw that direct administration was the only expedient. So in A.D. 6 he left Galilee under the rule of one of Herod's sons, but put Judaea and Samaria under an official called a procurator who was responsible to the imperial legate for Syria. Of these procurators Pontius Pilate was the fifth.

Naturally the Jews were unhappy under alien domination, but they were divided in their reactions to it. The high-priestly party or Sadducees were on the whole tolerant of both Rome and the Herods, to whom they owed their hereditary power. The Pharisees, on the other hand, were strict Jews; they were intensely religious, though narrow in their interpretation of the law, and on the whole non-political. The Zealots were fanatical nationalists, ready to use armed force in order to gain independence of Rome, and if possible, to set up a federation or Empire of the Middle East under Jewish leadership.

This was the background to the life of Jesus. (His name means 'rescue' or 'deliverance', the Greek form of the Hebrew name, Joshua.) His first public appearance was, it seems, during a curious kind of revival mission, held in the Jordan valley by his cousin John. The latter was a picturesque figure, rather like one of the ancient Hebrew prophets. The key-word of his message, as given in Greek, means 'Repent', or 'Change your mind'. Everyone who came to John was invited to give a sign of a new start and to be cleansed from sin by washing in the Jordan, much as Hindus wash in the Ganges. Hence John's nickname—'the Baptist' or 'Washer'. Among the pilgrims who came to the mission was Jesus himself. He also came to be washed in the Jordan, and he must afterwards have told his cousin of a spiritual experience which he had had at the time. A white dove settled on his shoulder, and he heard a voice from God saying: 'Thou art my Son, the Beloved; in Thee I am well pleased'—meaning: 'You have a special and intimate relation to Me.'

Immediately after, Jesus went away into solitude beyond the Jordan, to think things over. The only possible evidence for what happened to him there can be what he must have told his friends. It was a severe trial. Alone with his thoughts, and conscious of his special relation to God, he was three times tempted to use it for wrong purposes, and every time he rejected the temptation. First, he was tempted to use his power for worldly ends, and to work mere conjuring tricks with matter. Secondly, he was tempted to copy the oriental saints who claimed to be able to float through the air, and by a magical trick to compel the allegiance of the crowds by 'coming on the clouds of heaven' and soaring down into the Temple courts during worship. Thirdly, he was tempted to become a political leader, and to found an earthly empire. Although he chose none of these ways of winning success, his admiring followers afterwards could not resist the desire to glorify him by attributing to him some of the very actions which he had refused to perform. This was no doubt partly due to their awareness that he was a unique Personality. Had he been an ordinary sort of man, there would not have been the inducement to describe him in such a way.

At the end of his time of solitude Jesus returned to begin his special task as he had come to picture it. We may pause a moment to ask who (speaking humanly) he was. He is described as 'the son of Joseph and Mary', whose home was at Nazareth in Galilee. He, like Joseph, was by trade a 'carpenter and builder', and this was natural, since all Jews believed industrious work to be a sacred duty, and every Jewish boy was taught some handicraft.

Extremely little is known about his early life, but what is recorded is of great interest and beauty and must have come from the memories treasured up by his mother. From these we learn that before his birth she had a message or premonition that she would bear a child who would be of great and decisive importance, a Deliverer sent from God. The birth took place when Joseph and Mary were visiting Joseph's native town, Bethlehem, because of a census, and the place was so crowded at the time that they had to encamp in the yard of the inn. Thus the circumstances of his birth were humble, not to say those of poverty.

Two different accounts of the parentage of Jesus are to be found in the New Testament. On the one hand, he is described as the son of Joseph and Mary, and, on the male side, descended from David—that is, of the royal family. On the other hand, it is said that he had no human father, and that his mother was a virgin. This statement occurs in the first and third Gospels. It is quite easy to say that this second account belongs entirely to the realm of pious romance; and it is certain that any number of famous persons in antiquity, both legendary and historical, have at some time been called 'virgin-born', to account for their seemingly superhuman qualities. It is also probable that the Greek version of Isaiah vii. 14 (where the Hebrew word for 'young woman' has been incorrectly translated by a Greek word meaning 'virgin') may have encouraged the actual shape of the Gospel stories.

But what if *in essence* both accounts are true? There is no reason for doubting that Joseph and Mary may have had some deep spiritual experience about the birth of their first-born,

which convinced them that in and through him God was acting uniquely in the world. The exact nature of this experience we can now never know, nor need we wish to know. At any rate, it is a fact that as he grew to manhood people found no difficulty in saying 'In him dwelt all the fulness of the Godhead bodily', and in representing him as saying: 'He that hath seen me hath seen the Father.' He spoke with authority and not as the scribes. Whatever, then, the circumstances of his birth, it is plain that in the last resort people found it impossible to regard him as 'just one more prophet', but treated him as in a supreme way the centre of the history of God's dealings with the human race, and that there were features in his life and personality which made them do so. They thought of him as God's great Act or Initiative.

Now this does not mean that Christians belittle the divine element in every human life and specially in the world's heroes and saints. Far from it. The fourth Gospel begins by declaring that God's Word or Activity enlightens every man, and one early Greek Christian, in writing about this, said that God's Word had acted in Socrates and many other famous men, so that 'whatever men have said or done well belongs to us Christians'. Then the Gospel says that in Jesus, who is fully human, both body and soul, the Word of God was present to a unique degree and in a unique manner from the moment of his conception, and this is the official belief of orthodox Christians to-day. It is known as the doctrine of the Incarnation, and it is expressed in the Gospels by the use of the language of the Psalm about the Messiah—Ps. ii. 7—'Thou art My *Son*; this day have I begotten Thee'. When speaking of Jesus as 'the Son of God' the word 'Son' is hardly used in the ordinary human sense. In any case, since Christians believe that all human beings are children of God, it must, in referring to Jesus, have had a special meaning —namely, that the Being who acted in the world through union with the human nature of Jesus of Nazareth is Himself fully and completely Divine. 'God's mercy took the homespun of our flesh.'

What was Jesus like? No actual portrait of him has survived. The Gospels refer to his commanding (almost *royal*) presence and to the effect of his eyes when fixed upon people. There is one tradition that his beard was slightly forked, but not long, his hair parted down the

THE NATIVITY

Painting by Sandro Botticelli (1444–1510). *National Gallery*

Achille e Nereo

On ceiling
Much delapidated — in
Many parts scarcely to
be distinguished — This
type they have (badly
executed) on I beard

Others cut though
in stone

Forms one of many
decorations in the
same chapel
some of which are
cut though

Fresco 2nd century
Catacombs of Achille e Nereo

AN EARLY PORTRAIT OF JESUS

This 2nd-century painting from a catacomb in Rome may
preserve the likeness of Jesus. From a copy by Thomas
Heaphy (1813–73). *British Mus.*

middle, his face oval, with bright eyes, his
complexion olive-tinted, his attitude slightly
stooping; and there are at the British Museum
representations copied from early Roman catacomb paintings, since destroyed, which are of
this type, and may preserve a genuine tradition;
but probably most of the pictures seen in books
or art galleries have little resemblance to the
original.

The stories of the visits of the shepherds and
of the Zoroastrian magi (or wise men) to the
home of Jesus during his infancy may well be
founded upon fact and perhaps related by
Mary. A male child of the house of David
would have been a centre of attraction both
to Syrian peasants and to foreign astrologers.

The public ministry of Jesus lasted probably
for a little less than two years. Part of the time
he was at Jerusalem, teaching in the temple
courts. What impressed everyone was the commanding presence of the teacher, strong and decisive, with a sureness of touch far superior to
that of the Jewish clericals of his day. His hearers
felt it to be so. He was positive, not negative. He
laid down no legal code, but instead he set forth

great principles; and he put the emphasis upon
constructive action. There can be no denial
that through his followers he has made God a
Living and Gracious Reality to more inhabitants
of the globe than any other being who has ever
lived upon it. He accompanied all this teaching
with practical works of mercy, and he showed
remarkable power in the mental cure of diseases.
At first the Pharisees favoured him, inviting him
to their houses, but they gradually drifted into
opposition, and the synagogues closed their doors
to him. He was too revolutionary for the orthodox conservatives. The worldly Sadducees feared
and hated him.

His ministry divides into two parts, and the
dividing line comes towards the end of the first
year. At first he moved about attracting large
crowds which may, at the height of his popularity, have sought to persuade him to make an
attempt to establish himself as king. This he
would not do, and he saw he was in danger of
being misunderstood. So once more he went
away into retirement—this time not alone but
with his intimate friends—and he remained for
nine months outside Israelite ground. At the
beginning of his retirement a memorable conversation took place in which he challenged his
disciples to say who he was, implying that he
was the 'Man' spoken of in Daniel vii, or, as
Peter said, the Messiah, or Christos, yet not a
political adventurer bent on restoring the Jewish
monarchy, but someone with a far wider mission. This mission he had now come to believe
he could only fulfil by freely offering himself to
die in the cause for which he stood. In the long
quiet months of that summer and autumn spent
in retreat he had come to know more fully who
he was, and to understand that he could not
bring in his kingdom, which was 'not of this
world', except by complete personal sacrifice. So
at the end of the nine months he resolutely went
up to Jerusalem, followed by a half-admiring,
half-terrified band of disciples whom he had
done his best to instruct in the mystery concerning himself.

He gave his teaching, apparently, in two
main ways, both easy for memorizing: first, by
short pithy sentences, and later by means of
stories to illustrate his points. He always had a
tendency to drop into the form of Hebrew
poetry, with its rhythms and parallel clauses,
sometimes rising in steps, sometimes drawing
contrasts. So far as we know, he always spoke

in his native tongue, Aramaic, never in Greek or Latin. He probably repeated himself with slight variations, and, like the Hebrew prophets, he sometimes used action to symbolize a truth. This may well be the explanation of the feeding of the multitude or of the riding into Jerusalem on an ass; but his whole life was an illustration of the truth which he came to give. He admitted ignorance on some points, and showed growth and development during his life, even to a change in policy. He was, in fact, a real human being.

What of the substance of his message? It is, of course, centred upon the intense and vivid reality of the One Supreme Good God, whose activity is concerned with the whole universe, and to whom the entire human race stands related as one family. His picture of this Supreme God is given with great clearness and originality in the opening passages of the parable of the Prodigal Son, where he describes the character of God as being like that of a generous householder who divided the whole of his property during his lifetime between his two sons. God is thus the ungrudging bestower of free will upon his creatures, and he is prepared to take the risk of its misuse. He is also the eternally loving parent who, when humanity in its wretchedness sees its errors, takes the initiative and goes forth to meet and rescue. Against this background Jesus built his great idea of the Commonwealth or Kingdom of God. In the Sermon on the Mount and in other parables he gives in poetic language a picture of the ideal character which its citizens should have (*see* CHRISTIANITY).

At first Jesus may well have hoped from his large and attentive audiences that his task of proclaiming a New Order would be an easy one. But as the first year of his ministry passed by, he saw difficulties and obstacles arising, until he became convinced that the programme, appealing as it may have seemed to the crowds at first, could only be realized by the Cross. Nothing less could deliver mankind from its wrongheadedness. He must act as well as preach.

The story is only too well known. One of his own associates, Judas of Kerioth, disappointed no doubt that Jesus would not become a political leader, betrayed him to his enemies for a bribe, under the pretence that he was a seditious person and a heretic. He was arrested by night when he was at prayer in an olive-garden.

There followed a series of rather irregular trials, his display at daybreak by Pilate to the fickle crowd in the streets, and then, in the end, Golgotha— a criminal's death by crucifixion between two brigands.

Yet it seems that it was not the end. All four gospels tell how after three days he rose from the dead and appeared to his followers.

At his crucifixion most of the followers of Jesus had scattered, some even going back disillusioned and broken-hearted to their former occupations. But in a very short while they rallied, confidently declaring that he was neither dead nor defeated, and that they had evidence of this in his continued life and Spiritual Presence in their midst. That confidence, instead of waning, as perhaps might have been expected, has gone on, and has even gained in strength, so that, whatever may be thought about the future and the truth of Christianity, the historical fact remains that its greatest expansion has actually taken place during the last 150 years, and has carried it all over the world, from Cape Horn to the Arctic Circle.

See also CHRISTIANITY; CHRISTIAN CHURCH.

JEWS (from 'Judah')—the descendants of the southern branch of the Israelite tribes who settled in what is now called Palestine, probably in the 15th century B.C. (*see* HEBREW CIVILIZATION). In the year A.D. 70 they were utterly defeated after a revolt against the Romans, and their capital Jerusalem was destroyed. Their political hopes being crushed, the Jews reorganized their lives in a new fashion under intellectual leaders or Rabbis whom they recognized henceforth as their supreme authority in all things, much as other people recognize their government. They began to study their traditional lore based on the Bible with an ever-increasing passion. The Talmud—the edition (about A.D. 200) of the Jewish law and the discussions based on it—is one of the most remarkable productions of the human mind, and includes, in what seems a rather haphazard and confusing form, every conceivable human interest. This great work afterwards formed the main subject of Jewish studies in every land, and made it possible for a Jew to carry about with him, as it were, in all the lands of his exile, the very atmosphere of the ideal Jewish life of long ago. It was this, together with his burning religious conviction, that enabled the Jew to preserve his individuality during so many centuries.

A great deal of the intellectual activity of the Talmudic period took place in Mesopotamia (Iraq) where the descendants of the Jews, deported from Palestine by Nebuchadnezzar hundreds of years before, still survived and maintained a throbbing intellectual life.

The Jews, taken prisoners by the Romans in increasing numbers every time they revolted against the harsh Roman rule in Palestine, were scattered as slaves throughout the Roman Empire, until in the end, only a tiny handful remained in Palestine. But the Jews, though scattered, were held together by their common faith, their common literature, and their common hope of a restoration to their Promised Land, and never surrendered their individuality. Minorities who refuse to be absorbed may well be a difficulty in a country and are often disliked. Moreover, in the Middle Ages people actually thought that the Jews of their own day were responsible for the crucifixion of Jesus many centuries before, and were inclined to forget that Jesus himself was a Jew, as were most of his early followers. Therefore a period of Jewish persecution began: they were forced to live in a separate quarter of the town, later known as the GHETTO (q.v.); they had to wear a disfiguring badge to mark them off from other people; they were not allowed to own land, to practise handicrafts, or to be physicians; they were compelled to earn their living as pawnbrokers and moneylenders, and if they became rich at these callings they were hated all the more. All manner of incredible charges were made against them, for example, fanatics often accused them of the 'ritual murder' of Christian boys at Passovertide. From time to time they were attacked by mobs, and appalling massacres took place: e.g. in the Rhineland in the period of the Crusades, when it was actually believed by the ignorant that the murderer of a Jew was secure of a place in Paradise; or in England in 1189–90, when an exceptionally terrible onslaught took place in York; or all over Germany at frequent intervals. Conditions in the Moslem countries were not quite as bad, for the indignities were not enforced quite so systematically.

Such experiences as these could not fail to leave their trace on the Jewish character, which has inevitably suffered as the result of being despised and ill-treated for generations. But in spite of this, many Jews were able to continue their high standard of intellectual achievement. In every place where they lived they had not only their synagogue but also their House of Study. They collaborated as far as they could in the intellectual life of their neighbours. They did great work in medicine, science, and philosophy, especially where conditions were more favourable, as they were in Spain during the period of Moslem influence. Some of the important names of this period, such as those of Rashi, the learned French Biblical commentator (1040–1105), Moses Maimonides, the greatest of Jewish philosophers (1135–1204), and Judah haLevi, the sweetest singer of Zion (1186–1241), are among the most famous in Jewish history: all are scholars and artists rather than soldiers or men of action.

The medieval persecutions culminated in the total expulsion of the Jews from country after country—from England in 1290, from France in 1306, from Spain in 1492, and so on. By the close of the Middle Ages no Jews were left in western Europe, except in parts of Germany and Italy where the number of independent states made concerted action impossible and some Jews managed to exist but under degrading circumstances. The great mass of the Jews lived in the East—in the hospitable Turkish Empire then at the height of its power, and in Poland, where the kings had realized how valuable the Jews were for economic life and had therefore encouraged their immigration. The great majority of Jews at the beginning of the 20th century were still living in eastern Europe.

At the close of the 16th century and during the 17th there was more toleration of the Jews in the West, especially in the rising seaports of the Atlantic, where people were beginning to be more interested in developing trade than in religious prejudices. Thus, Amsterdam and Hamburg became great Jewish centres; while the Jews were readmitted to England largely through the broad-mindedness and keen practical sense of Oliver Cromwell. With the triumph of liberalism in the 19th century, the Jews received emancipation everywhere in central and western Europe. In Tsarist Russia, however, which had by now absorbed the greater part of Poland with its huge Jewish population, there took place after 1881 an appalling number of massacres of Jews ('pogroms' they were called) which drove hundreds and thousands of Jews out of the country. The vast proportion of them went to America where there are now more Jews than in any other country of the world. A certain number also went to England and the Dominions.

In every country the Jews took advantage of the new opportunities that emancipation brought them. It is enough to mention people like ALBERT EINSTEIN (q.v. Vol. V), author of the theory of Relativity; Paul Ehrlich, a very great physician; or persons of Jewish birth though professing Christianity, like FELIX MENDELSSOHN (q.v. Vol. V), the musician, or BENJAMIN DISRAELI, the English statesman (q.v. Vol. V). While other countries valued the contribution which the Jews could make, the Germans became jealous of it and considered it a national menace. At the end of the 19th century there

A JEWISH SETTLEMENT IN PALESTINE. *Paul Popper*

started in Germany a new anti-Jewish movement, based on what they called 'racial' grounds and termed therefore 'anti-Semitism'. From 1933 onwards the Nazi party in Germany used the anti-Semitic movement as a means of rousing German national emotions, and the Jews were useful scapegoats for all Germany's difficulties. This persecution caused a terrible amount of misery in central Europe where Jews were thrust out of their positions, incredibly maltreated, and forced to leave the countries where their ancestors had lived for centuries. During the Second World War this persecution developed into a homicidal mania on the part of the Germans who attempted to exterminate the Jews in all the countries they occupied. There were on the Continent (outside Russia) in 1939 something like 7,200,000 Jews. By 1945 about 5,700,000 had perished; only some 1,500,000, or one in five, remained; in many countries nine persons out of ten had disappeared. It was the most brutal tragedy that had ever happened to any people throughout the course of human history.

Only one thing kept up the Jewish morale in this terrible time. Throughout their history the Jews had preserved, together with their faith, the hope of being restored one day to the land of their fathers, Palestine. When anti-Semitism began to sweep Europe at the end of the 19th century, a Viennese Jew named Theodore Herzl had launched the Zionist movement, with the object of making a Jewish national home in Palestine. The British Government expressed sympathy with this in 1917 (the 'Balfour Declaration') and in 1920 was assigned the 'mandate' for administering Palestine under the League of Nations. Thousands of Jews have been admitted into Palestine and in 1948 an independent republic, Israel, was set up. The Israelis have done much to improve methods of cultivation. They have also developed industries, founded a Hebrew university, and established all-Jewish towns. Parts of Palestine have become centres of Jewish settlement, where they have tried to establish a better order of society. Jews throughout the world take pride in this achievement. It now remains for the conflicting claims of the Arabs and Jews in Palestine to be settled on a basis satisfactory to both.

See also JUDAISM; Vol. IV: HEBREW LANGUAGE.

JOVE, *see* GODS OF GREECE AND ROME (Zeus).

JUDAH, *see* HEBREW CIVILIZATION.

JUDAISM. In many large towns there may be seen a strange building which looks much like a church or chapel, but which is of a rather different shape. It does not have the sign of the Cross anywhere on it, but may carry over its entrance an inscription in strange lettering, something like this, יהוה, and possibly a Star. This building will be a Jewish synagogue, and its presence is a reminder that what is called Judaism is still a living religion, and that there exists in the vicinity a colony of JEWS (q.v.). In Palestine, where the Jews are establishing a national home, Israel, there are a num-

ber of synagogues, but in other parts of the world these buildings only occur where a colony of Jews is in the neighbourhood, since the minimum for a synagogue meeting is a *minyan*, or gathering of ten male Jews.

To understand why the followers of Judaism, though belonging almost entirely to the Jewish people, are now spread all over the world, it is necessary to know something of their history. Five hundred and eighty-six years before Christ the Jews in Palestine were most of them taken away into exile in Mesopotamia, in much the same way that the French, Russians, and Poles were deported in recent times by Hitler Germany. This separated them from their native land, and deprived them of the centre of their public worship, Solomon's temple at Jerusalem. When Mesopotamia was conquered by the Persians, the latter treated the Jews well, and allowed those of them who wished, to return to Palestine. Some did, but others stayed behind, while large numbers went to live among other nations round about. But, wherever they lived, Jews who remained true to their national faith and traditions used to meet together at least once a week, and the place of meeting was called a כנסת (*Keneseth*) or congregation. Later, after the conquest of the Middle East by Alexander the Great of Greece, the name 'synagogue', from the Greek word meaning 'meeting-house', began to be used instead. Sometimes the Jews met in private houses for prayer and reading of the scriptures, especially on the eve of the Sabbath, and these gatherings were called *Chaburoth* or Brotherhoods. Jews outside Palestine were supposed to avoid living more than ninety days' journey from Jerusalem, to pay a half-shekel tax annually for the upkeep of the restored temple, and to visit it at least once a year.

Now in addition to their strict belief in One Holy and Invisible God (*see* JEHOVAH) who had given them the Law or *Torah* (lit. 'direction' or 'instruction') as their way of life, the Jews from the time of their exile had come to expect the approach of a Divine Agent, a sort of priest-king sent by God, who would restore independence to them, and set up a great religious Empire of the East. Some thought of this more in political, others in more spiritual terms, and their ideas as to the exact character of the Deliverer were vague, but they believed Him to be of great importance, not only for themselves, but for the entire world, and they spoke of Him by a name

THE WAILING WALL, JERUSALEM

Jews come here to mourn their departed glories. The wall is built on the site of Solomon's Temple. *Vincent Brennan*

INTERIOR OF A SYNAGOGUE

On the left is the *almenar* or reading desk. Behind the curtain decorated with the Star of David is the ark, a cupboard containing the scrolls of the Law. *Matson Photo Service*

usually now spelt Messiah, which means the Anointed or Consecrated One (Greek, *Christos*). When Jesus of Nazareth appeared, those who became His disciples were soon called Christians or followers of Messiah, though at first in ridicule. The nickname was only afterwards accepted by the disciples as a serious title.

Jews who did not become Christians declined to believe that Jesus was the expected Messiah, and, though some of them might revere him as a teacher, they would not accept him as the Supreme Revelation of the One True God. To do so would have meant a serious blow to their national pride and an admission that their previous religious beliefs had been mistaken, since Jesus refused altogether the role of political leader and declared that his kingdom was not of this world but was a spiritual kingdom. After the destruction of the Temple in A.D. 70, during the first Jewish war against Rome, there was a sharp division between Christians and Jews. This increased in bitterness, especially when the Jews aided in the persecution of the early Christian Church. From then onwards Judaism cut

itself off completely from Christianity, the Jews still hoping for a future worldly triumph. Here and there at times individual Jews were on friendly terms with their neighbours and even influenced their thought, as was the case with a famous Spanish Jew, Maimonides, who lived at the same time as Thomas à Becket (from 1135 to 1204) and who was a wonderful scholar, astronomer, and physician.

The five main religious principles of Judaism may be described as follows:

(i) That there is no need of any mediator or go-between so far as God and man are concerned, and that therefore the idea of Incarnation is a false one. The Messiah will be entirely human, even if he is God's Agent.

(2) That all members of the Jewish community have equal rights and duties before God. There is no aristocracy, no priesthood or clergy as a superior caste. The rabbis are not priests, only teachers.

(3) That justice, and the observance of the Law given to them by Jehovah, are the central ideas and aims of life.

(4) That knowledge gained by reason is of supreme value, so that the learned and righteous scholar takes first place in the community. In some parts of eastern Europe, however, Jewish scholars (*Chassidim*) do claim a spiritual knowledge which is mystical rather than purely rational.

(5) That the righteous will find his reward in this life, and that there is no promise of a personal future existence. This, however, seems to ignore some of the ideas in the Psalms.

These principles are held by almost all Jews, whether they observe orthodox Judaism or no. If, however, they are strict Jews, they hold themselves bound also to certain pious practices. These are mainly practices connected with the prayer-life and the reading of the Hebrew Scriptures, and they centre round the synagogue which is also a place of religious instruction for the young. They also include certain physical ceremonies, such as the circumcision of infants, and the eating of only certain kinds of prepared food, called *kosher* or 'correct'.

Here is the typical career of a Jewish child, let us say, in Poland. Eight days after birth it is circumcised at home, and the father performs certain ceremonies in the synagogue on the following Sabbath. If it is a girl it is simply given a name. If a first-born son, it has also to be redeemed within a month by a payment of five shekels to the synagogue. As soon as the child is old enough to wear it, it is given a square woollen garment with four tassels at the corners, and a hole in the middle for the head to go through. This is in remembrance of the order given to the Israelites in Numbers xv. 38–41, where its meaning is given. On the doorpost of the house there may be a *Mezuzah*, or small roll of a text, and the children will be held up to kiss it as they enter. The first sentence the child is taught to repeat is the *Shema*—'Hear O Israel, the Lord our God, the Lord is One'. At the age of four or five the child goes to a school, and will learn by heart the Law in Hebrew. At thirteen the boy is admitted to the Congregation and becomes a Son of the Covenant. This is in some ways similar to the Christian rite of Confirmation. Every morning he is supposed to get up early and go to the synagogue to say his prayers. Three times a day he should go through the form of prayer in the Jewish prayer-book. The eve of the Sabbath is observed with certain ceremonies which include a benediction of bread and wine before the evening meal. On the Sabbath the boy will go with his father and mother to the synagogue, though when they get there the men and women sit separately. The rule against work on the Sabbath is strictly kept, though there may be ingenious ways of keeping food hot without breaking the rule, and sometimes a Gentile is hired to do extra jobs forbidden to the Jew. In all there are six services on the Sabbath which it is possible for the Jew to attend. There are, of course, special feasts and days of penitence and mourning during the year. The feasts are Passover, Pentecost, and Tabernacles. The most important fast-days are the ten days with which the Jewish New Year opens, leading up to the Day of Atonement. There are no longer, of course, sacrifices of animals on the Day of Atonement, but there is a general confession of sins. At the beginning of the New Year and at the end of the Day of Atonement a ram's horn or *shophar* is blown solemnly. Passover is still kept with a special evening meal, and the children will be carefully instructed as to its meaning—a commemoration of the leading of the People of Israel from out of the land of Egypt.

The end of life is marked by an impressive burial service, which is preceded by a very careful and reverent preparation of the body for interment. This is performed by a special guild of Jewish men who regard the duty as a solemn privilege. One prayer at the burial—the *Hashkabah* or laying to rest—shows a more definite belief in a future life in the Paradise of God than might have been expected from the official doctrines of Judaism.

A large number of Jews do not take the trouble to observe the whole of this scheme of life, but those who do develop an old-fashioned and intense piety of great beauty. Others who keep the ceremonies in a superficial manner sometimes become proud and self-righteous and satisfied with the externals of religion—a danger which, alas, is not confined to Jews. Some become reformers and liberals and seek to adapt Judaism to the needs of the modern world, while others are free-thinkers and make no pretence of holding to Jewish beliefs or customs.

See also HEBREW CIVILIZATION; JEWS.

JUNO, *see* GODS OF GREECE AND ROME (Hera).

JUPITER, *see* GODS OF GREECE AND ROME (Zeus).

K

KENYA, PEOPLES OF, *see* EAST AFRICANS.

KNIGHTS OF THE ROUND TABLE, *see* ARTHURIAN LEGEND.

KNIGHTS, ORDERS OF. The romantic idea of knights fighting for their faith against the powers of evil was a common one in the medieval world. The ARTHURIAN LEGEND (q.v.) consisted mostly of stories of such knights. When in 1096 the call came to free the holy places in Palestine from the infidel Turk and to protect pilgrims from molestation, the response was enthusiastic. Some of the Crusaders wanted not only to fight for Christianity but to dedicate themselves to its service for the whole of their lives in the same way as the monks did. They formed themselves into Military Orders, following the same rule of poverty, charity, and obedience as the monks practised, but pledged also to fight the Saracens and protect pilgrims. The Orders of Knights Templar and Knights Hospitaller were founded at the beginning of the century, and the Order of Teutonic Knights in 1190.

1. KNIGHTS TEMPLAR. The First Crusade succeeded in recovering Jerusalem and parts of the coast of Syria and Palestine from the Turks; and many of the knights from Europe seized land and settled there. But the Saracens still continued to harass pilgrims on their way to Palestine. Nine knights therefore formed themselves into a brotherhood to defend the pilgrims, calling themselves 'poor fellow soldiers of Christ Jesus', and setting themselves to follow the monastic rule. Later they were called Knights Templar because they established their headquarters in a house near Solomon's Temple in Jerusalem. The appeal of the Order was strong to adventurous knights who joined in great numbers, while kings and wealthy people gave money and lands. The knights wore white tunics with a red cross.

The Templars built strongholds from which to defend the Holy Land and fought valiantly against the Saracens, often with great losses. But much of the crusading effort was spoilt by bad organization and quarrels between those who should have been uniting against the Turk. At one time the rivalry between the Knights Templar and the Knights Hospitaller grew so bitter that open fighting broke out, and most of the Templars in Palestine were killed.

The Knights Templar also established houses in many parts of Europe where they accumulated great wealth and lived in idleness. In England their headquarters was the Temple Church in London. This and other churches which they built were round, in imitation of the Church of the Holy Sepulchre in Jerusalem.

In the 13th century, when Palestine was lost, the Templars established themselves in Cyprus. Their wealth and possessions aroused envy and hatred, and they were accused, quite falsely, of idolatry, heresy, and immorality. The Pope was persuaded to suppress them, and horrible tortures were inflicted on them to make them confess their guilt. Almost all were exterminated,

THE TEMPLE CHURCH, LONDON
The round church was built in the 12th century and the chancel on the right was added later. *Crown copyright by permission of the Controller of H.M.S.O.*

KNIGHT TEMPLAR

KNIGHT OF ST. JOHN

TEUTONIC KNIGHT

a few remaining in Spain where they continued for some time to fight the Moors.

2. KNIGHTS HOSPITALLER. As early as 1023 a 'hospital', dedicated to St. John the Baptist, was founded in Jerusalem to help poor and sick pilgrims. The medieval meaning of the word 'hospital' was a place of refuge for the needy, not only for the sick. In the next century the Hospital of St. John was organized into a military order on the same lines and for the same purpose as the Knights Templar. Their uniform was a black tunic with a white eight-pointed cross on it. In the 13th century when the crusading spirit was weakening, crusaders returning to Europe sold their lands to the knights, so that the Hospitallers grew as wealthy as the Templars. When Palestine was retaken by the Turks, the Hospitallers went with the Templars to Cyprus; but instead of suffering the same fate, they conquered the island of Rhodes and remained there for 200 years. They built strong fortresses and kept the Turks at bay until 1522 when at last the island fell. The knights retreated to Malta where they became known as the Knights of Malta. Again they withstood the attacks of the Turks with magnificent

valour, finally breaking the Turkish power in the Great Siege of Malta in 1565. After this the Order disappeared. Their badge has been adopted by the modern organization, the St. John Ambulance Brigade.

3. TEUTONIC KNIGHTS. In 1128 some German merchants founded a 'hospital' in Jerusalem which survived until the city fell sixty years later. During the Third Crusade, in 1190, the hospital was revived by German knights who formed themselves into a military order. Their uniform was a white tunic with a black cross. This Order also became strong and wealthy. When crusading came to an end, they turned their attention to the heathen in east Prussia. Under pretence of spreading Christianity, they attacked the Lithuanians and Russians, seizing their lands and treating the people with great cruelty and barbarism. In 1525 the Grand Master, Albert of Brandenburg, converted their possessions into a duchy for himself, and the Order came to an end.

See also CRUSADES.

KORAN, see SACRED BOOKS, Section 8; ISLAM.

KURDS, see IRAQI; SYRIANS.

L

LAKE DWELLINGS (PILE DWELLINGS). Mention is often found in books dealing with ancient man (especially the older books) of 'Lake Dwellings', and often of 'The Swiss Lake Dwellings', as if they were some kind of settlement made by a special group who lived only on the edges of lakes or rivers. This is hardly true, for primitive

dwellings are rather striking and, of course, very important to the archaeologist. So many things made by primitive man, such as woodwork, baskets, cloth, and even such food as bread or buns, have been found preserved in the peat at these waterside settlements, that they have become very important in reconstructing the life of ancient peoples. On drier sites the remains of similar peoples consist only of imperishable things like stone or bronze tools and perhaps the post-holes of their timber houses.

Some of these riverside houses seem to have been set up above the level of marsh or water on piles or posts. Houses built in a similar manner are to be found to-day in New Guinea, for instance, and indeed in most old farm-yards in England the granary is built up on little pillars to keep it free from damp and safe from rats. It so happens that some of the earliest of these

LAKE DWELLING
From a reconstruction in the Ashmolean Museum

man in many places and times (up to a couple of centuries ago, for instance, in Scotland or Poland) has built dwellings in or near the water for protection from his enemies or for convenience in fishing. Since the wet peat that forms in such places in the course of time preserves wooden structures and objects that would otherwise rot away, the remains from such lakeside

'pile dwellings' of the New Stone Age period dating from about 2500 B.C. were discovered in Switzerland: others of about the same date have been found in Germany. Besides the timberwork of the lower parts of the houses, objects have been found such as remains of woven cloth, basketry, wooden tools, horn and bone implements, fish-nets with their floats, and even apples and plums that had been gathered for food. On the Federsee Lake in Germany, where the houses are very well preserved, their plans are just like those whose foundations can be faintly traced on hilly sites. It is known that both the houses on the lake and on dry land were built by the same group of people.

Later in prehistoric times, various groups of peoples who were working in bronze, and had built up a more complicated kind of trading and agricultural life, still continued to make water-side dwellings in various places, often on the same sites as those of earlier settlers, whose houses by that time would have been in almost unrecognizable ruins in the marsh. Late in the Bronze Age a settlement was made in the Federsee Lake already mentioned: an artificial island was built up of mud and timber, with a strong palisade round it and a village of houses inside—it was in fact a 'water-fort' which could be reached only by boats. The first village, built about 1000 B.C., consisted of about forty square houses set round the edge of the island, inside the palisade and with an open space in the middle; but two or three centuries later the village was rebuilt and contained only nine big farm-houses, each forming three sides of a court-yard, with several barns or storehouses beside them. There was a rather similar 'water-fort' dating from a little later (about 700 to 400 B.C.) in western Poland, at Biskupin, and a very famous settlement of the Iron Age was found at a place called La Tène (which means The Shallows) at the north end of Lake Neuchatel in Switzerland, where remains of houses and bridges, traced along the banks of streams at the outlet of the lake, mark a trading station of about 350 B.C. Bronze Age waterside dwellings have also been found in northern Italy.

In England very fine examples of the 'water-fort' type of village have been excavated in the Somerset moors at Glastonbury and Mere. The Glastonbury village consisted of an artificial island with a timber-built landing-stage (a wooden canoe was found too) and with over seventy circular houses which must have had domed-over thatched roofs and walls all in one. Posts for supporting granaries above the general rather damp level of the island's surface were also found there. Inside the houses were hearths of clay, and as the island gradually settled and sank slightly, these were always being remade, so that the excavators found several layers of hearths built one on top of the other. All manner of timber-work was found—mortised beams, hurdles, planking, a door in one piece of solid oak, a ladder, cart-wheels, tubs, ladles, and various hafts for iron tools—also remains of food such as peas, beans, barley, and wheat, as well as little cakes or buns of wheat grains almost certainly mixed with honey. These Somerset villages were built and lived in from about 100 B.C. onwards for a century or so.

At least one waterside settlement in Ireland dates from the Iron Age and may be about the same date as Glastonbury, and both in this country and in Scotland 'water-forts', usually called 'crannogs', continued to be built in the traditional manner until the 17th and 18th centuries A.D.—indeed for as long as the primitive and tribal organizations of these regions made it necessary for chieftains to live in such strong-holds.

See also PREHISTORIC MAN.

LAMAISM, see TIBETANS.

LAPPS. These are people who live above the Arctic Circle in what is marked in most maps as Lapland, but which actually is territory divided among Norway, Sweden, Finland, and the Soviet Union. The Lapps call themselves *Samen*, which means people of the marshes, and their country is called *Lappmarks* (Lapp Marshes).

Their early history is a mystery. They may have come originally from the Ural Mountains or the Volga, and thus be related to the West-Finn division of the Finno-Ugrian speaking peoples; or perhaps they are the remnants of a distinct race of men who once upon a time inhabited north-eastern Europe, and which may have been conquered by a Finno-Ugrian people whose language they adopted. They themselves believe that they were the first people who lived so far north, and they have certainly been there for many ages. Originally they lived farther to the south-east, but they withdrew northwards when the FINNS (q.v.) and Scandinavians penetrated these areas.

To-day there are about 32,000 Lapps all told. Most of them—about 21,000—live in Norway, another 7,700 in Sweden, 1,600 in Finland, and 1,700 or thereabouts in the Kola Peninsula in Russia. Exact numbers cannot be given for they have mixed with Norwegians and Finns to a considerable extent over the centuries. Hence, not all Lapps have the characteristic physical features of their race—a short stature and small body not more than 5 feet tall, a broad head which, although small, is large in proportion to the body, and predominantly dark skin, hair, and eyes. Actually many of the Norwegian Lapps have light skin and eyes and brown hair, and only a very small proportion of this group have pure dark eyes. The typical Lapp is mainly to be found amongst those who are still reindeer-herders, for reindeer-herding is believed to have been the original occupation of those Lapps who first entered Scandinavia. To-day the great majority of Norwegian Lapps have settled down to fishing, and the number of reindeer-herding Lapps has shrunk to 5,000, of which 3,000 live in Sweden. The other half of Swedish Lapps are farmers or work in forests. The Russian Lapps divide their time between herding reindeer during the winter and moving to the coast to fish during the summer. In Finland some are fishermen and others are reindeer-herders.

Of those Lapps who to-day make their living by reindeer keeping, some are mountain or nomad peoples and others forest peoples. The mountain Lapps have the larger herds and follow them regularly every year into the mountains. This is an occupation which requires a strong and sturdy physique. The herdsman has to withstand the snow, the dark autumn and winter months, and the fact that the domesticated reindeer is not a faithful animal like the horse. The forest Lapps have by no means an easy time either. They have to guard those reindeer which remain in the valleys and whose grazing-grounds are among the low-lying forests and swamps. They worry lest the mountain reindeer pass through their grazing-grounds on the way to the mountains. For in contrast to the forest reindeer, which do not spoil the plants but only nibble at the grasses and shrubs, the mountain reindeer tear up roots and thus ruin the pasture lands. Another difficulty is the pest-fly or gad-fly which the Lapps call *Kurbma*.

The reindeer-keeping Lapp depends on his animals for almost everything—transport, food, and clothing. A reindeer hitched to a light sled takes him on his long journeys or carries his belongings to fresh pastures. Reindeer meat is eaten fresh, and some of it is frozen or cured so that it can be stored or sold. Milk and cheese are obtained from reindeer. Each reindeer gives only about half a cup of milk at a time, but since

A LAPP COUPLE
Behind them is the tent in which they live during the summer. *Swedish Tourist Traffic Ass.*

the average family possesses several hundred animals, their requirements can easily be met. Reindeer cheese is sometimes taken stirred in coffee, rather like the Mongolian custom of mixing rancid butter in tea. There is hardly an article of Lapp clothing which does not come from the reindeer. Winter clothing is made out of the long-haired fur from the backs of the animals and leggings from the short-haired fur from their legs. Both men and women wear trousers. Knives with handles and sheaths, possessed by every boy, are made out of reindeer horn. Soft reindeer leather is used to make loose-fitting shoes, lined with dried grass to keep their feet warm.

The mountain Lapps sometimes live in tents which are easily transported. Otherwise they build little turf huts or sometimes occupy small wooden dwellings for part of the year. Lapp families find it easier to move their herds all together, and these groups or 'wandering villages' are called *sidas*. Each *sida* elects a leader who directs the route of the journey.

All Lapps are now Christians, though it took missionaries a long time to find many of the groups of wandering Lapps. Strong Puritan influences have practically destroyed the old Lapp culture—their dances, feasts, games and

A LAPPLANDER WITH HIS REINDEER
Paul Popper

songs, legends, and art. The Russian Lapps belong to the Orthodox Eastern Church, but they are said to have retained some of their old beliefs.

The Lapp language is related mainly to the FINNISH (q.v. Vol. IV) and Estonian, but there are about fifty dialects, so that Lapps from one region often cannot understand those from another region. The Lapps have full rights of citizenship in the various countries in which they live. A modern electric railway which runs from Lulea in Sweden across Lapland to Narvik in Norway has broken down a good deal of their former isolation, and so also has the busy Norwegian seaport of Hammerfest—the most northern city in the world—where many fishing Lapps live.

It is doubtful whether the Lapps, considering their small number and their increasing contact with modern life, will remain as a separate people much longer. They will, however, remain important as an influence on the European peoples with whom they are mixing.

LATVIANS. The small Baltic state of Latvia includes the old province of Livonia which in the 13th century belonged to the Teutonic Knights (*see* KNIGHTS, ORDERS OF). The Knights defended their territory from all their neighbours until the middle of the 16th century. By 1721, after a long struggle, the country became part of Russia and remained so until, in 1918, an independent republic was formed out of Livonia and three other provinces. In 1940 Latvia and the two other Baltic states, Estonia and Lithuania, became part of the U.S.S.R.

The original Livonians (people akin to the Finns) have almost entirely died out. Latvia (or Lettland) is now inhabited mostly by Letts with considerable groups of Russians, Jews, Germans, Poles, Lithuanians, and ESTONIANS (q.v.). They are mostly foresters and farmers, particularly dairy farmers. In 1920 the large estates were all broken up and divided among the peasants. Riga, the capital, is an important Baltic port connected by railway to Leningrad, Moscow, Warsaw, and Berlin. It is ice-bound, however, most of the winter.

See also Vol. III: LATVIA.

LEBANESE, *see* SYRIANS.

LEGEND. The word 'legend', like the word 'lesson', which once had the same meaning, is derived from the Latin *legendum*, 'intended to be read'. The original legends were the stories appointed to be read to monks and nuns at meals. These stories were taken from the lives of the saints and often told how the saints had been tempted or attacked by evil spirits and had triumphed over them. In time the word 'legend' came to be used for any miracle-story, especially one connected with a particular place.

LETTS, *see* LATVIANS.

LEVITES, *see* PRIEST.

LITHUANIANS. In the 13th century a Lithuanian prince called Ringold gathered together into one nation the scattered tribes of Lithuanians in the lands north of Poland. After a century or more of fighting, especially with the Teutonic Knights (*see* KNIGHTS, ORDERS OF), their prince, Jagiello, married the heiress of Poland. From that time Lithuania was ruled by grand-dukes appointed by the Poles until, in 1569, it was incorporated into Poland. When Poland fell under the power of Russia, Lithuania also became Russian. A strong spirit of nationalism developed, and in 1918, after the First World War, Lithuania became an independent republic. In 1940 the republic became part of the U.S.S.R. (*see* SLAVONIC LANGUAGES, Vol. IV).

The Lithuanians are generally fair and blue-eyed, with good features and fine physique. They are mostly farmers and foresters. The great forests, marshes, and lakes which cover much of their country have played their part in forming the national character. Although most Lithuanians are Christians, the peasants still cling to ancient heathen customs—religious ceremonies carried on in the forests and including the veneration of great oak-trees. In times of danger they have relied upon the forests and marshes for protection. National folk-lore and songs are full of the peacefulness and melancholy loneliness of the vast forests, and their literature draws its inspiration from the country rather than the town.

See also Vol. III: LITHUANIA.

LOGIC, *see* PHILOSOPHY.

LUCIFER, *see* SATAN.

LUTHERAN. This large branch of the Christian Church was founded in the early 16th century, and was one of the breaks from the Medieval Church which took place in most parts of Europe between the 15th and 17th centuries. Martin LUTHER (q.v. Vol. V), the founder of the Lutheran Church, was Professor of Theology at the small German University of Wittenberg. An abuse had grown up in the Church of allowing people to pay a sum of money to gain absolution and cancel punishment for sin. This cancelling of penance was called an 'indulgence'. To a man of Luther's deep religious experience the idea of the Church selling the forgiveness of sin was abhorrent, so when finally aroused in 1517 by a particularly flagrant case, he made a public protest against the whole system. He expected to raise a keen theological argument; the result was far greater—a revolution which cut off most of northern Europe from the control of the Papacy, and the formation of a Church which now includes in all its branches some 90 million people.

The heart of Luther's teaching was the subject of Christian salvation. The medieval Church had come to look at the matter mostly from the point of view of discipline: those who were obedient to the doctrines of the Church were sure of salvation. Luther, like St. Paul, St. Augustine, and all the greatest teachers, went deeper. He regarded salvation as a change in the relationship between man and God. The Church taught that man is saved from sin by a gradual process guided by the discipline of the Church: man is saved by the grace of God —that is, by the new power given him through the sacraments; man's part is to make use of the grace and try to benefit by it. Luther, on the other hand, taught that man is saved from the wrath of God caused by his sin and taken back as a son again. This is not a gradual process but immediate and brought about by God's graciousness. Man has no part in it at all, except to have faith in that which God does. This is the main Lutheran teaching—justification by faith alone —and is the basis of much Protestant doctrine. This doctrine was set out in a creed called the Augsburg Confession in 1530.

The modern Lutheran Church is most active in Germany, the countries of the Baltic, Iceland, and those parts of America, especially the Middle West, where peoples from these countries have settled. Lutheran missions have planted churches in many parts of Africa and Asia. There is a good deal of variety in church organization within this great number. In Germany the Church, reorganized after it was freed from Nazi interference, is now called the Evangelical Church and is independent of the State. In Denmark, Norway, and Sweden it is the national State Church, including most of the population in its membership. In Sweden the Church has preserved the succession of bishops from pre-Reformation times.

There is also much variety in the form of service. Luther made the sermon the central feature; he also encouraged congregational singing of hymns, many of which he composed himself. In many German and Danish churches Holy Communion is a special service rarely held, whereas in the wooden village churches in Norway, Communion with much medieval ritual crowns each Sunday morning's worship. The most elaborate form of Lutheran service is to be found in the Church of Sweden.

See also CHRISTIAN CHURCH.

M

MAGIC. This is a word which many people use without knowing definitely what they mean by it. 'It worked like magic', they say. Most of us do not take magic seriously, but to a great number of people all over the world it is a very serious matter. Even amongst educated people there are some who believe in magic more than they would like to admit: they carry mascots about with them and believe in certain days or things as 'lucky'. When a professor at an American university once asked how many students carried any object supposed to have magic-working powers, nearly half of the class admitted that they did. Belief in magic does not easily die out, and amongst primitive people it is very much alive. It is important for all who have to work among such people to understand their ideas about magic.

In order to get a better idea of what magic is, let us imagine ourselves watching a native witch-doctor making magic in one of the South Pacific islands. He is trying to bring about the death of another man. First he spies on his proposed victim, getting to know his habits. When he is away from his hut the witch-doctor creeps in and finds some object belonging to his victim, such as a hair from his head. He puts the hair into a tube made of a section of bamboo, and in order to keep it warm he places it under his arm-pit. Having returned to his own hut he makes a fire of sticks, selected because the sap in them blackens when they are cut, just as blood from a wound blackens as it coagulates. He lays the bamboo with the hair in it on the fire and says:

> Eagle and Hawk. Ye both, here is your prey. Seize it with sharp claws. Rend his body and tear it in pieces.

Again and again he repeats the spell, while his assistant turns the packet on the fire. All this time the witch-doctor acts as if he were the victim of his own magic, writhing as if in terrible agony and uttering groans and loud shouts. He cries for help and pleads for sympathy. At last he collapses, pretends to draw his final breath and lies down as if dead.

As this illustration shows, a man working evil magic may try to secure something connected with his victim—hair, clippings from his nails, or even dust from a footprint—because to possess such things is believed to give the magician power over the person he wishes to injure. Secondly, we note that here, as in practically all cases of magic-making, the operator has a definite aim and object, something good or bad which he is intent on bringing to pass. He may be called in to cure a man or to kill him, but his magic is always for a precise purpose. Thus magic is often used to change the weather. If rain does not fall at the proper season the crops may fail, so rain-makers beat drums or perform other ceremonies to bring rain. Natives know very well that they must cultivate their gardens or fields if the crops are to prosper, but they believe that magical ceremonies are also necessary. Since no one dares to leave out these ceremonies, the natives never have any proof that they are useless, and they prefer to be on the safe side. If rain happens to fall after rain-magic has been made, then it seems that the magic has been effective; and as the rain-making goes on for months if necessary, there is usually rain sooner or later. The victim of evil magic does sometimes die because he is so completely scared. So we need not be surprised that those who believe in magic are not easily persuaded that it is useless.

The sorcerer on the South Pacific island whom we have been describing recites various words expressing his hatred, and such words used in this way make a spell. The spell or charm is a very important part of magic—few magical ceremonies are performed without the use of spells. The sorcerer says what he wants to happen, though not always aloud; but there are occasions when the spell is made up of meaningless words or syllables, for makers of magic sometimes feel that the magic will be more powerful if it is mysterious even to themselves (*see* SPELLS AND CHARMS).

Not only does the magician say what he wants to happen, but often he also acts it. In so doing he causes it to occur—so he believes. In the South Seas a rain-maker paints his body black and white because white clouds become black

A WITCH DOCTOR IN ZULULAND DRIVING OUT EVIL SPIRITS
South African Railways

when rain is coming. He thinks if he paints himself in the colours of a cloud it will help to bring rain. The rain-maker usually beats a drum to imitate thunder, for he knows that rain accompanies thunder and thinks that if he makes thunder there is likely to be rain. People in some places jump as high as they can, believing that thus they assist the crops to grow tall. A Zulu in love with a girl will chew a piece of wood to soften her hard heart. In many parts of the world there is the belief that you can injure your enemy by making a figure of him and ill-treating it. A Malay mixes his enemy's nail-parings or hair into a figure of wax and scorches it over a lamp every night for seven nights saying,

It is not wax that I am scorching,
It is the liver, heart, and spleen of So-and-so that
    I scorch.

In Scotland pins are stuck into a clay model, and a spell said which begins, 'As you waste away, may she waste away; as this wounds you, may it wound her.'

Also very widespread is a belief in the 'evil

eye'. It is supposed that by magical means a person, envious or jealous of another or for some other reason wishing him ill, can bewitch or magically injure him by looking at him. This belief is thousands of years old. It is fear of the evil eye which makes some ignorant people frightened of the camera—they see its glass eye pointing at them and run away or cover their faces. About fifty years ago, when a Somerset woman's pig became sick, she assumed that it had been 'overlooked' and sent for a white witch to cure it. The witch ordered a sheep's heart to be stuck full of pins and roasted over the fire while a group of people chanted this incantation:

It is not this heart I mean to burn
But the person's heart I wish to turn,
Wishing them neither rest nor peace
Till they are dead and gone.

Iron in many parts of the world is believed to have power to counteract magic. This is why horseshoes are supposed to be 'lucky'.

Amongst many peoples there are individual sorcerers or groups of witch-doctors who are

L

regarded as being the great experts in magic. The tribesmen go to these magicians to get them to foretell future events (*see* DIVINATION) or to perform magic on their behalf. But it is usually recognized that ordinary people may perform magic or witchcraft without being 'professionals', and in some tribes anybody may be suspected of casting spells, though no one would own up to being a witch. Even at the present day in the Scottish Highlands and Islands there are spells and charms which anybody might use, but only a comparatively small number of people are believed to have 'second-sight' and other such mysterious powers.

A person who believes in magic is not necessarily stupid. He argues, as we do, that when something happens, or some action or ceremony is performed, certain things follow, but he makes the mistake of thinking that, because things are connected in his thought, therefore they must be connected in actual fact. He hears the wind whistling as it blows his boat along and realizes that wind and whistling go together, but he then jumps to the conclusion, or more usually believes it when he is told, that if he whistles like the wind he can get it to blow. He hears a bird call, and then rain begins to fall. He accepts the explanation that it was the bird's call which made the rain fall, and thinks, 'If I make a sound like the bird it will bring rain'.

How is it that the magic-maker does not realize that magic does not work? We must remember that, according to his ideas, magic may be opposed by more powerful magic. If the sorcerer is not able to kill or cure a man—whichever he wishes to do—he may conclude that it is because he is up against a greater sorcerer. Also it is often difficult to decide between success and failure; and, still more significant, successes are remembered after failures have been forgotten.

Belief in magic often occurs mixed with religious ideas, but there is one great difference between magic and religion as these are

AN ENGLISH GIRL'S LOVE CHARM
Putty figure of a man in a box with rosebuds. *Pitt Rivers Coll.*

commonly understood. In performing magic a person tries to control events by what he does and says. He does not humble himself in reverence towards a divine being, praying the god or gods to do this or prevent that. His magic is often meant to work his will contrary to the well-being of someone in the community. He acts as one who has skill in an art and performs his magic as if, by his skill, he could force what he desires to happen. He believes that his magic has power in itself to do what he wants, unless he performs it incorrectly or it is baffled by greater magic. In religion a person does not trust in himself and his own powers in this way, but relies on higher and greater powers to aid him. We must remember, however, that primitive people do not see clearly the difference between magic and religion. Indeed, even in England there are people who do not realize that their beliefs about mascots and lucky charms do not fit in with their religion.

Witch-doctors and sorcerers may sometimes practise their art in groups, yet there is always something secret about magic-making. There are such groups in one tribe in the southern Sudan—the Azande; they will allow other people to learn and perform their dances, but they will allow only those who are, or are learning to be, witch-doctors to know their lore about plants and the medicines, poisons, and magic preparations which can be made from them. The secrets of the magic art are passed on privately or revealed in the INITIATION ceremonies (q.v.) of the witch-doctors. While the tendency in magic is towards secrecy, the tendency in religion is towards publicity. People, of course, have their personal prayers and religious experience; also some religious ceremonies are only for those who have qualified by a special rite or a series of rites; but as a rule, in religion, people seek the good of everybody and are glad when the whole community joins in, and this is particularly true of primitive people. At their festivals all rejoice together. Religion gives a feeling of unity to the group taking part and thus helps to weld the community together. The effect of magic is often to make people suspicious of one another and to create bad feeling within the community.

See also FOLK-LORE.

MAGI, *see* ZOROASTRIAN.

MAGYARS, *see* HUNGARIANS.

MAHRATTAS, *see* INDIAN PEOPLES.

MALAYA, PEOPLES OF. The word 'Malays' refers strictly to one only of the many people who inhabit the Malay peninsula. This article, however, deals with all peoples who now live in Malaya.

The Semangs and the Sakais appear to have been the original inhabitants of the Malay peninsula. Both these peoples still live in the dense hot jungle; they are extremely primitive in their ways. The Malays themselves, who are the predominant race of Malaya, probably came to the Malay peninsula from the mountains of Sumatra about 500 years ago. Chinese and Indian traders used to find their way down the coasts of Malaya, settle there, and trade with the Malays. Arab missionaries of the Moslem faith also visited Malaya and succeeded in converting most of the Malays to ISLAM (q.v.), to which religion the majority of them still belong. The Siamese, too, exercised some influence on Malaya, and the sultans of the old native states used to offer allegiance to the king of Siam.

The first Europeans to settle in Malaya were the Portuguese who established themselves at Malacca in 1511. By about 1640 the Dutch took Malacca and other small trading posts from the Portuguese and occupied them for about 150 years. The British influence started with the acquisition by the East India Company in 1786 of the island of Penang, off the middle of the west coast of the peninsula. In 1819 the island of SINGAPORE (q.v. Vol. III) was occupied for the East India Company by Sir Stamford RAFFLES (q.v. Vol. V) and in 1825 the Company acquired Malacca from the Dutch in exchange for various small trade posts in Sumatra. These three areas, Penang Island, Singapore Island, and the town and surrounding land of Malacca, form what is often known as the 'Straits Settlements' and were the first British links with Malaya. Beyond these British trading posts were

SEMANGS IN THEIR LEAF-COVERED SHELTER
Pitt Rivers Coll.

poor and backward native states, organized on a feudal basis, under the absolute power of their sultans. Eventually, after fifty years of British influence, four of these native states (Perak, Selangor, Negri Sembilan, and Pahang) requested British protection, which they were granted, and these states became known collectively as the Federated Malay States, F.M.S. The rest of Malaya was still governed feudally by its Sultans. In 1909, however, the Siamese ceded the four native states (Kedah, Perlis, Trengganu, and Kelantan) to the British. Johore was added to the F.M.S. in 1914. They were placed under British protection, the native sultans remaining in power with British advisers to assist and to some extent control them.

The tin and rubber industries developed immensely under the British. Consequently the number of Chinese and Indians increased greatly. Since then, apart from the Japanese occupation during the Second World War, Malaya has been part of the British Empire. At the beginning of 1946 a new constitution was offered to Malaya and a Malay Union was set up. This met with considerable opposition, especially from the Malays, and the Union was replaced in 1948 by a Federation of all the Malay States and British

SAKAI WITH A BLOWPIPE. *Pitt Rivers Coll.*

Settlements, excepting Singapore which became a separate colony.

The total population of Malaya is over five millions; this is about the same as the population of Scotland. Roughly, for every three British people in the country there are about 150 Malays, 120 Chinese, and 45 Indians. About two-thirds of the British live either in Singapore, on Penang Island, or in Kuala Lumpur—the capital of the Federation: a third probably lives away 'up country', possibly looking after a plantation, or in charge of the building of a railway or a tin-mine. A big proportion of the Chinese live on Singapore Island. The Malays are scattered all over the country; the primitive peoples—the Sakais and Semangs—live in small numbers in the densest forest areas; the Indians mostly work on rubber plantations.

The Semangs and the Sakais, the primitive inhabitants of the peninsula, are interesting people. The Semangs look rather like dwarf negroes. They move around in bands of twenty to thirty strong and live on wild berries and roots, such as the wild yam which they collect in the forest. They live in simple huts quickly made from palm leaves, and they cook their food in thick bamboo tubes which withstand flames just long enough. They add to their meals by shooting birds, monkeys, and other small animals with bows and arrows, poisoned with a juice called 'Ipoh' made from the gum of the Upas

tree. They also fish by spearing the fish with a sharply pointed leaf-stem. For such clothes as they have, they use the bark of trees which they soften and form into a kind of girdle.

The Sakais are a little taller than the Semangs and look less like negroes. They move around much less and build rather more permanent huts, which are frequently raised on trees so as to get protection from the damp and from animals and snakes. Instead of bows and arrows for hunting they use blowpipes—pieces of bamboo, 8 to 12 ft. long, through which they blow light poisoned palm darts about the thickness of a knitting-needle. The Sakai is very accurate with his blow-pipe at a range of 25 to 30 yards.

The Malays—the most numerous people in Malaya—are for the most part an agricultural people, and many are also excellent fishermen. Rice, their staple food, is their main crop, but they also grow sugar-cane, maize, and tapioca, and they keep groves of coconut palms and fruit trees near their dwellings in their *kampongs* or villages. They are an easy-going, pleasure-loving people with considerable charm. They dress in *sarongs*, long strips of cotton (or perhaps silk) twisted round the body. Some sarongs are woven in Malaya, but most are imported from India and Japan.

Most of the manual work in Malaya, especially on the rubber estates, is done by Indians and Chinese, who are more industrious than the

Malays, and this gains them little admiration from the natives. The trade is mostly in the hands of the Chinese who are the merchants and shopkeepers of Malaya and have made much money out of this rich country. They also supply the semi-skilled labour for the tin-mines. The administration and development of the country and the management of the industries and big estates is in the hands of the British. British people do not as a rule stay very long in the country at a stretch, as the climate is most unsuitable for Europeans: it is like living in a permanently overheated greenhouse.

Malaya is rich in natural resources. It produces more natural rubber than any other country and, before the war, about one-third of the world's tin. Its wealth has attracted many immigrants, particularly Chinese and Indians. The British, struggling against a climate which they are not able to sustain for long, appreciate the vast economic possibilities of this country, but appreciate too a moral obligation to improve the living conditions of the people and are doing everything possible to promote this end.

See also Vol. III: MALAYA; Vol. IV: INDONESIAN LANGUAGES.

MALTESE. The people of Malta—the smallest of European nations— have their own language, their own traditions, their own recognizable physical characteristics, and a history which is one of the longest of any people now existing. Malta has been since 1814 a British colony; and it is one of the most densely populated areas in the world, with a population of well over 2,000 people to the square mile. Its key position in the middle of the Mediterranean has given it an importance altogether out of proportion to its size.

The history of the Maltese goes back into prehistoric times. The Stone Age temples of Malta and Gozo (two of the three islands that make up the Maltese archipelago) are some of the most interesting in Europe. Many fossil remains have been found of prehistoric animals which migrated southwards during one of the Ice Ages when northern Europe became uninhabitable. During this time the Mediterranean was a series of freshwater lakes, and Malta one of the bridges between Europe and Africa.

Malta was colonized in the 5th century B.C. by PHOENICIANS (q.v.) who came from their colony at Carthage near the modern town of Tunis in North Africa. The modern Maltese speak an ancient SEMITIC LANGUAGE (q.v. Vol. IV) which is recognized to be much like that spoken in ancient days by the Phoenicians, but on to which have been grafted words and phrases borrowed from Arabic. At later stages Italian, Spanish, French, and, more recently, English words and phrases have been added. The framework and grammar of the language has, however, remained Semitic in spite of all European influences.

St. Paul, we are told, was wrecked on the shore of the bay now called after him. The Maltese are proud of the antiquity of their Church and of the fact that Publius, the Roman governor of Malta, who was converted to Christianity by St. Paul, became the island's first bishop. The Church is now a part of the Roman Catholic Church.

After the break-up of the Roman Empire, Malta was occupied for some 200 years by the ARABS (q.v.). Then, for a time it became a Norman stronghold and later was in the power of the Aragonese and Castilians of Spain. Then for two and a half centuries from 1530 to 1798 it was ruled by the famous international Crusading

BRINGING ROUND THE MILK
Though goats can still be seen in the streets, the milkman with his bottles is becoming more usual. *Paul Popper*

Order of the Knights of St. John of Jerusalem (*see* KNIGHTS, ORDERS OF). This wealthy and splendour-loving group of men built massive fortifications and magnificent palaces and churches, many of which survive to-day. After they had successfully resisted the attacks of the Turks in the 16th century, their Grand Master, La Valette, built the capital city, Valetta, named after him. In 1798 Malta was taken by the

THE GRAND HARBOUR, VALETTA, MALTA
Ph. Sir Harry Luke

French under Napoleon, who broke up the power of the Knights of St. John; but in 1814, with the consent of the Maltese, the island became part of the British Empire.

Italian influence has for long been strong in Malta. During the Fascist régime of Mussolini the Italians organized much unscrupulous propaganda to undermine the loyalty of the Maltese and make them believe that they should belong to the Italian rather than the British Empire. In spite of this, however, Malta remained loyal to Britain and played so heroic a part in the Second World War that the whole Maltese people were awarded the George Cross by the King—the first time that a community has been collectively awarded with a British decoration.

Malta was famous in the past for its honey and cotton (the name Malta—Melita—is derived from *mel*, meaning honey), and even to-day the chief occupation is pastoral. The islands are so rocky that most of the soil has had to be imported. There is not enough pasture for cows,

so the Maltese depend for their milk on goats. Herds of goats abound all over the island and have earned for Malta the name of 'the island of goats'. They are driven along the streets and milked from door to door. Fishing and sea-faring are other pursuits. The naval dockyard, however, and the work connected with supplying the Royal Navy give employment to the majority of the population and form the principal source of their income.

See also Vol. III: MALTA.

MAN, EVOLUTION OF, *see* EVOLUTION.

MAN, PREHISTORIC, *see* PREHISTORIC MAN.

MAN, RACES OF, *see* RACES AND PEOPLES.

MANCHUS, *see* CHINESE PEOPLES.

MAORIS. Like most Polynesian peoples, the Maoris of New Zealand say they came 'from Hawaiiki', from which comes the name Hawaii; but their latest migration seems to have been from the Cook Islands, some 2,000 miles north-west of New Zealand. They arrived about the year 1350 in large double sailing-canoes, helped by the wind and swell from the west which is usual in summer. When CAPTAIN COOK (q.v. Vol. V) landed in 1769 among the descendants of these fearless navigators he was struck by their fine appearance and warlike temper. Their skin colour is often light brown or olive and their features like those of Europeans, though some have darker skins and flatter noses, showing a mixture of race. Cook's interpreter from Tahiti had no difficulty in understanding their Polynesian dialect (*see* OCEANIC LANGUAGES, Vol. IV).

When Cook first discovered them they had no knowledge of metals or pottery. Their tools were of stone, bone, or wood, yet they managed to fell big trees and shape the trunks into canoes or frames for their large meeting-houses. They had brought with them to New Zealand the sweet potato and the root called *taro*, and they also ate a native fern-root and berries. Other vegetable foods were few, but fish and shell-fish were plentiful on the coasts, and they snared birds. Their only domestic animal was the dog, which they brought with them. They ate dogs and a kind of rat, but it was perhaps scarcity of animal food which encouraged CANNIBALISM (q.v.). They feasted on their enemies after a battle, and continued to do so for some time after the coming of European settlers.

AN OLD MAORI WITH HER GRANDCHILDREN
The older generation still wear native dress, but the younger Maoris have adopted western clothes
High Commissioner for New Zealand

For clothes they had mats made from the fibre of New Zealand flax, which was also used for making ropes and lines. They wore birds' feathers and a rare green stone as personal ornaments; but their chief ornament was tattooing—done by a slow painful process. After a design had been sketched on the skin, grooves were punched through it with a narrow bone chisel, and a charcoal pigment was rubbed in to leave permanent patterns. Women were usually tattooed on lips and chin; men, especially those of high rank, were very elaborately tattooed on face and body. Tattooed and smoke-dried heads, of both friends and enemies were carefully preserved after death. Some were brought to Europe as curios, and this started a brisk and scandalous trade. Even slaves were tattooed so that their heads could be offered for sale. With the latest generations tattooing has gone out of fashion.

Their huts were quickly made of reeds bound to wooden frames, and were so small and stuffy that they preferred to sleep in the open in fine weather. But each village had a large meeting-house with richly carved posts where guests were received and the affairs of the tribe discussed. All free members of the tribe might speak but they were guided by the leading men, especially by their hereditary chief, and customary law was strong. They believed in spirits of trees and birds, as well as in the spirit of the sea, and there were also lesser spirits, usually malicious. Fear of displeasing these spirits ruled their lives—the anger of the spirits being usually brought on by breaking, as they thought, some Taboo (q.v.). Certain people, things, and acts—such as a burial-place, a man while being tattooed, a chief, especially his head and also any food he had tasted—were taboo or sacred, and must not be touched. To eat such food, even by accident, was thought to bring death. The rule of the chiefs and priests was largely maintained by these taboos.

The Maoris were great hand-to-hand fighters

though they had no better weapons than stone clubs or axes and wooden staves, for they had not even bows and arrows. Before a battle the fighting-men worked themselves up in a war-dance, shaking the ground by their perfect time, rolling their eyes hideously, and poking out their tongues to an amazing length. They built hill-forts, protected by wooden stockades and trenches, against which European fire-arms proved to have little effect. There was constant fighting between tribes over land, fishing rights, ancient feuds, or fresh insults. When the white men introduced guns and steel weapons it seemed as if the native tribes would wipe one another out; and the small number of Maoris living in the colder South Island were almost exterminated by invaders from the North.

The white men also brought strong drink and new ways of living, to which the Maoris were unaccustomed, as well as new diseases. It was thought that their gradual disappearance or absorption was certain, but in recent years, against all predictions, the Maori population has increased rapidly and at about 137,150 is probably larger than ever in the past. Until 1871 there were many local wars against the Euro-peans, who came first as whalers, sealers, and traders, later as gold-seekers, and who stayed permanently as farmers. But the Maoris were divided among themselves, and the influence of the missionaries for peace was strong, so that finally the two races settled down well together. Part of the credit for this unusual success is due to the humane attitude of the British Govern-ment during the troubled period before the settlers and the Maoris learnt to respect one another. Part is due to good New Zealand laws which secure them plenty of land to live on, recognize their rights and customs, give them schools, and encourage them to be equal citizens. The Maoris, being very intelligent people, have been able to profit by all these opportunities, and have produced eminent doctors, lawyers, and even Cabinet Ministers, and have shown their loyalty and their old fighting spirit in the two Great Wars.

See also POLYNESIANS; NEW ZEALANDERS.
See also Vol. III: NEW ZEALAND.

MARRIAGE CEREMONIES. The marriage of individuals in a community affects the lives of many others in various ways, so both primitive and more civilized peoples, both in the past and present, have always made regulations and cere-monies in connexion with marriage. When a man and a woman marry, their position in society changes, each of them becomes 'related', as we say, in a new way to other people, and the question of the status of their children arises. Amongst most peoples there are strict rules as to whom a person can marry. In many primitive tribes, like the AUSTRALIAN ABORIGINES (q.v.), men and women must marry someone outside their section of the clan. Civilized peoples, too, have their rules of this kind. At the back of the Church of England Prayer Book there is a long list of those 'forbidden in Scripture and our laws to marry together'. These regulations are part of the system of rights and duties among kinsfolk on which so much in primitive society depends, and they are backed up with all the force of religious authority.

Amongst a great many peoples marriage is a religious rite or attended by religious obser-vances. It is very natural that the joining together of a man and woman to bring up a family should be regarded as an occasion for ceremonial when blessings are sought. Bride and bridegroom are making a momentous change in their way of life, so people do all in their power by prayers, religious ceremonies, and magical practices, to enlist the aid of good against the forces of evil.

As law, tradition, and religion regulate the conditions of marriage to a large extent, it is not surprising to find that 'arranged' marriages are the rule in many parts of the world. The Japanese, for example, employ a 'go-between' as match-maker. In Persia and many other countries the match is brought about by the parents and friends. Wedding preliminaries often take a good deal of time, and the cere-monies connected with marriage may cover a period of weeks or months; indeed, the com-bined betrothal and wedding ceremonies may be spread over a number of years. Often various devices are used to try to discover a lucky date for a wedding. There were such practices amongst the Greeks and Romans, and even now astrologers are often consulted before a Chinese wedding is arranged. The exchange of gifts is one of the most widespread marriage customs. Amongst many peoples a girl is very useful to a family or clan because of the work she does, so she is not given up without some return. Usually it is the man or his family who gives the presents,

THE MARRIAGE OF PRINCESS ELIZABETH AND LT. H.R.H. THE DUKE OF EDINBURGH, R.N.
The scene in Westminster Abbey, 20 November 1947. *The Times*

but amongst more cultured societies the bride or her family also send gifts, though generally less valuable ones. The bride-price in cattle of an African girl may be of great value. In many societies the bride is expected to bring a dowry with her—her contribution to their joint establishment.

Although there are innumerable differences in the details of marriage ceremonial, yet many marriage rites have main features which are similar to those occurring in the coronations of kings and queens. This marriage ritual is in fact derived from extremely ancient coronation ceremonies. In these rites the kings and queens were thought to represent the gods of heaven and earth respectively. Present-day wedding ceremonies often include customs which remind us of these ideas. In ancient Greece bride and bridegroom were crowned; in Rome they wore wreaths; in Yugoslavia at the present day crowns are placed on their heads, and so also in Russia, where the wedding is called 'the matrimonial coronation'. In an ancient Indian ceremony the bridegroom used to say to the bride, 'I am the heaven, you are the earth; let us unite and have

children'. In Malaya, even amongst the poorer people, bride and bridegroom are called 'sovereigns of a day'. At the coronation of our king a ring is placed on his finger, just as the bridegroom in the wedding service places a ring on the bride's finger. An ancient Roman wedding included the giving of presents and a ring, the joining of hands, veiling, crowning with flowers, prayers, and partaking of a sacrificial cake. Our Christian wedding service follows much the same pattern.

In general, wedding ceremonials are designed to achieve these main ends: (*a*) The transition from one family or condition of life to another. (*b*) The banishing or subduing of evil influences. (*c*) The stressing of the idea of fertility. (*d*) The stressing of the unity of the married couple. These ends are achieved in many different ways, some of which we will describe.

(*a*) MARKING A TRANSITION. It used to be the custom in Scotland when the bride left her home to throw an old shoe after her to signify that her father no longer had a legal right over her. Amongst the INCAS OF PERU (q.v.) the bridegroom placed a sandal on the bride's right foot

A WEDDING IN MALAYA

The bride and bridegroom, in their ceremonial dress, have to sit still for hours or their luck is broken. *Paul Popper*

as a sign that he accepted her as his wife. Shoes play a part in many wedding ceremonies, usually representing that the wife must be submissive to her husband, although they may have an older meaning as fertility symbols. The custom of lifting the bride over the threshold of her new home, which is observed in England, Algeria, Palestine, Java, and China is probably a way of marking the change from one home to another, though it is sometimes explained as a means of preventing the bride from stumbling on the doorstep, which would be unlucky. Amongst various peoples, such as the tribe of the Amaxosa in South Africa, a mock fight is staged at a wedding, apparently symbolizing the resistance of the bride's family to the carrying off of one of its members. A Chinese bride marks her coming to her husband's house by worshipping at his ancestral shrine. At English weddings the bride's father or some relative is present to 'give her away'—thus marking the transition from one family to another.

(*b*) BANISHING EVIL. Before the Chinese bridal sedan-chair leaves the house, it is searched for evil spirits by women who use lighted spills of red paper—red being the Chinese lucky colour and therefore also the colour of the bride's costume. Then they go over it again with a mirror, for they believe that if an evil spirit catches sight of himself in a looking-glass he gets such a fright that he hurries away. At some African and Indian weddings arrows are discharged to transfix any evil spirits which may be about. In Palestine and elsewhere guns are fired with the same idea, and a similar custom was observed in the north of England until recently, though the old significance of it had been forgotten. An English bride sometimes carries a horseshoe of silver paper. Horseshoes are considered lucky because they are made of iron, which is believed to have the power of driving away evil spirits. The bride's veil was originally a means of intercepting evil influences such as the 'evil eye' (*see* MAGIC). One of the most widespread practices before a marriage is for the parties to undergo ritual purification by taking ceremonial baths or exposing themselves to incense. When a Matabele bride arrives at the bridegroom's house she pours water over him as a ceremonial purification

(*c*) FERTILITY. In Ireland oatmeal used to be scattered on the bride, and in the north of England she was sprinkled with bits of cake; in Greece she was showered with nuts and figs and in Minorca with almonds. An old Spanish song referred to the pelting of the bride in these words: 'All down the street the ears of corn are flying.' In Persia the officiating priest sprinkles the couple with rice during the wedding service. Our custom of throwing confetti at weddings is a recent change from the older practice of casting rice. At Jewish weddings the guests used to shout 'Increase and multiply' as they threw corn over the bride and groom. In north China the third day after the wedding a mother of a thriving family empties a vase containing rice and millet into the laps of the bride and bridegroom. In the Slav nations a boy is placed in the bride's lap. All these customs signify the desire that the marriage should be fruitful, and the idea underlying them is to make it so by sympathetic magic.

(*d*) UNITY. In south Celebes the bride and groom are sewn together by their clothes and one garment is put over them to show that they are united. During the Persian marriage ceremony a symbolic knot is tied. Part of our marriage ritual is the joining of hands, and the exhortation in the service quotes from St. Paul the meaning of such rites—'They two shall be one.'

In modern marriage emphasis is increasingly laid on wedded life as a state in which husband and wife share rights and duties. Christian marriage involves a solemn pledge of lifelong faithfulness, which will make it possible to provide children with the best chance of continuous loving care. True love in marriage involves a spiritual relationship, and the essentials for a happy marriage are mutual physical attraction and the sharing of similar ideals.

See also FOLK-LORE.

MARS, *see* GODS OF GREECE AND ROME (Ares).

MARTYR, *see* SAINT.

MASAI (AFRICANS). These are a cattle-keeping people of East Africa who live in the central part of the highland zone east of Lake Victoria in Kenya and Tanganyika. They are tall and slender in appearance with long limbs and skin-colour varying from light chocolate-brown to dark brown.

They live in homesteads, consisting of a series of oval huts made of brushwood and mud, set round in a circle. In the centre are kept the cattle, and the whole encampment is surrounded by a thick fence of thorn-bush to keep out wild animals and cattle raiders.

The group in a homestead, which consists of a man, his wives, his sons, and his son's wives and children, may often be quite large as a man may have several wives. Each wife has a hut for herself and her small children.

The young men live apart from their families as warriors. They have to defend the herds of their district and to add to them by raiding their neighbours' cattle. They have spears, swords of iron, wooden clubs, and shields of ox hide. The weapons are made by skilled blacksmiths who form a distinct caste and hand on their craft from father to son. The smiths marry among themselves and are both feared and despised by the Masai.

Men in Masai society are divided into a series of age-groups. The main groups are the boys, the warriors, and the elders. Boys from the ages of thirteen to seventeen are formed into sets for training and INITIATION (q.v.) to the warrior class. After about four years they are admitted by a special ceremony to the warrior grade, and their group receives a special name. The different age-sets pass through the warrior grade and finally leave it to marry and become elders. Throughout their lives the members of the same age-set give help and assistance to one another.

The Masai have no supreme chief or king, but the chief priest (the *Laibon*) of one of the clans is a recognized religious leader who unites the different groups. The Masai believe that he has the power to provide war magic for success in raids, that he is able to prophesy the future, interpret dreams, and avert ill luck. He is also

MASAI WARRIORS
Their decorated shields are made of coloured hide. *British Mus.*

supposed to hold the remedies for various cattle diseases.

The Masai, like the NUER (q.v.) and most of the peoples of this part of Africa, value cattle above everything else. Each cow has its own personal name, and the herdsman has his favourites among them. But they do not kill cattle for meat except on ceremonial occasions. Their main food is maize and millet, while the warriors live mainly on milk and blood.

They have no developed arts and crafts or markets as, for instance, the neighbouring Baganda people have. Their clothing is made of skins and the young warriors often wear elaborate ornaments. The warriors wear a skin wrap, the women goatskin aprons. On ceremonial occasions the warriors wear elaborate feather head-dresses. Girls of rich families wear long coils of iron wire wound round their necks, lower arms, and legs.

See also NEGRO AFRICANS; EAST AFRICANS; Vol. IV: AFRICAN LANGUAGES.

MATABELE, *see* RHODESIANS; SOUTH AFRICANS.

MAYA CIVILIZATION. The highest civilization in North and Central America before the coming of the Europeans was developed by the Maya people in the tropical forests and mountains of Guatemala, Honduras, and the south of Mexico. These people had a very great influence upon the culture of their neighbours, especially in Mexico (*see* MEXICAN ANCIENT CIVILIZATION).

The Maya probably came down from the north-east about the beginning of the Christian era. Their history falls into two principal periods called the Old and New Empires. The Old Empire flourished for about 500 years between the 2nd and 7th centuries A.D. or possibly rather later; the New Empire was established about A.D. 1000, and lasted until the arrival of the Spaniards in the early 16th century.

The Maya of the Old Empire were remarkably fine builders and sculptors. They built many large cities with fine stone buildings, some of which, though overgrown and damaged by tropical vegetation, can still be seen in a fair state of preservation. At a few of the most important sites the forest has now been cleared away, and many of the buildings have been thoroughly restored. The result is extremely impressive. In a typical Maya city there was a spacious religious and civic centre which consisted of courts enclosed by pyramidal platforms. On some of

these platforms stood temples and palaces which were probably occupied by the rulers and priests. The temples were built of well-dressed stone and concrete, and were approached by steep and lofty stairways. Inside they contain a number of rooms, generally on one story only, with sloping roofs which were surmounted by high roof crests to give them strength. They were richly decorated with sculptured or stucco figures, generally of gods, priests, and worshippers. There were also other strange symbolic figures among which the most usual were serpents conventionalized into complicated and often beautiful patterns. The feathered serpent or 'serpent bird' was the symbol of one of the chief Maya gods, the god of the arts and crafts, and this creature is to be found in other places where Maya influence spread, especially in Mexico.

Another characteristic feature of the Maya cities was the massive stone pillar or 'stela', generally rectangular and entirely covered with

SCULPTURED STONE PILLAR OR 'STELA'
The figure is wearing ceremonial costume. At the sides are hieroglyphic inscriptions. Old Empire: Copan, Honduras
British Mus.

sculptured figures and hieroglyphic inscriptions. The tallest of these single-stone pillars is 25 ft. high. Many of them have colossal figures in ceremonial dress carved in relief on one or two sides. But the most interesting thing about them is their inscriptions. These record the dates on which they were set up and certain astronomical calculations. At present only part of these writings in stone can be deciphered. The Maya had invented a kind of picture writing in which many of the symbols stood for the days and months of the year, and others for numbers. For numbering they also used a system of bars and dots—a bar standing for 5 and a dot for 1. Instead of a decimal they used a system of counting by twenties, and were thus able to make advanced mathematical calculations. Their knowledge of astronomy was also so good that they had worked out a calendar with leap year corrections almost as accurate as our own Gregorian calendar. They knew the movements of the planets and were able to predict eclipses. In fact, in astronomical and mathematical science they were far ahead of any of the other American Indian civilizations and of many of the ancient civilizations of the Old World. They had many religious books or 'codices' written on lengths of folded paper, but unfortunately all except three of these were destroyed in the 16th century by the Spaniards as works of the devil.

The life of the Maya people was dominated by religious ceremonial, and most of their more permanent buildings were connected with it. (The houses or huts of the ordinary people were built of timber and thatch and have perished.) They worshipped a large number of different gods, among which were the SKY-GOD (q.v.), regarded as the Creator, the gods of the earth, the moon, rain, maize, and death. The god of arts and crafts, symbolized by the feathered serpent, and the rain-god with a trunk-like nose, were the two most often to be found in the sculptures, and therefore must have been of great importance. There were many religious festivals, accompanied by the music of drums and flutes, at which animal sacrifices and gifts of crops were offered to the gods. The gods were also offered human blood collected by piercing the tongue or ears, but human sacrifices seem to have been rare at this period, though they became more common later.

The early Maya were not a warlike people. Their various city-states were probably not

SCULPTURED STONE LINTEL

The standing figure is a priest, and beside him is a worshipper making a blood-sacrifice by drawing a cord with thorns through his tongue. Old Empire: Minchi, Chiapas
British Mus.

united under a single ruler, although they must have been closely associated. They must, however, have organized their labour effectively to have been able to construct such large buildings and to clear the dense forest for agriculture, which was their principal occupation. When we remember that they had no metal tools and no wheeled transport, it is all the more astonishing that they should have achieved so much.

Their food consisted mainly of maize which they ground and baked into bread and cakes. But they also grew yams, beans, and other food plants, and they made a chocolate drink from the cacao bean. They domesticated turkeys, geese, and bees, hunted deer, and fished from sailing canoes. They grew tobacco and smoked it in pipes. They were masters of the art of flaking and polishing stone tools, and their tools were as fine as any in the neolithic age of the Old World (*see* PREHISTORIC TOOLS AND WEAPONS). They made beautiful pottery without the potter's wheel, and many of their jars,

STONE TEMPLE, KNOWN AS THE CASTILLO, ON THE SUMMIT OF A LOFTY PYRAMID
It is dedicated to Kukulkan, the god of life and crafts. It has now been restored. *British Mus.*

bowls, and dishes were richly decorated with paintings or incised figures and designs. The costumes carved on the stone figures show that they had reached a considerable degree of skill in weaving and embroidery. They made various small ornaments, such as pendants and beads, cut skilfully from jade and other hard stones, and later they worked gold and copper ornaments. Altogether Maya art must be given a high place. Even though it is sometimes over-elaborate, and its symbolic character often makes it difficult to understand, the sculpture shows great dignity and the paintings and reliefs a strong sense of design. Their technical skill in dealing with difficult materials with such simple tools is quite admirable.

The Old Maya Empire collapsed for unknown reasons soon after A.D. 600. The people left their great cities and gradually migrated northwards, finally settling in part of the south Mexican state of Yucatan in about A.D. 1000. Here there was some revival of Maya civilization during what was called the Later or New Empire. New influences were introduced in the style of art; the decoration of buildings became more formal with geometric patterns; the use of columns in architecture appears for the first time. Another

innovation was the building for the ball game of large courts, the finest of which is still to be seen at the important town of Chichén Itza in Yucatan. The ball game was a semi-religious game played with a large solid rubber ball; one of the chief objects was to knock the ball through stone rings fixed high up on the sides of the court. A simplified form of this game is still played in parts of Mexico to-day.

The period of the second Maya Empire was not wholly peaceable, for there were civil wars and invasions by the Toltecs from Mexico. It lasted, however, until the beginning of the 16th century when the Spaniards conquered the country.

See also ANCIENT CIVILIZATIONS; Vol. IV: AMERICAN-INDIAN LANGUAGES.

MEDES, *see* PERSIAN CIVILIZATION.

MEDUSA, a Gorgon, *see* MYTHOLOGICAL MONSTERS (section a).

MEGALITHS (MEGALITHIC MONUMENTS) **1.** The name (from the Greek for large-stones) is given to a variety of monuments built, not in ordinary masonry, but with huge blocks of stone. They are found all the way from the Mediterranean round western Europe to Scandinavia, and most of them were built in New Stone and

Early Bronze Age times, perhaps between 2400 and 1800 B.C. The fact that in most countries they are very much commoner near the coasts than inland suggests that the people responsible for them had arrived by sea. There is little doubt that this kind of architecture was spread by sea-farers, coming originally from the Mediterranean, who gradually pushed their way along the coasts of the Atlantic from Spain to Brittany and Britain, thence northward by Scotland to the Scandinavian countries.

2. CHAMBERED TOMBS provide some of the most strange and interesting examples of megalithic architecture. In these a burial chamber built of great stone blocks was covered with a mound of earth or stones which made it quite dark and cave-like. An entrance passage leading into it from outside the mound allowed burials to be made one after another over a long period of time—just as family vaults may be used to-day. Sometimes (most often in Brittany and Ireland) the stones were carved with curious magical patterns, and there are other features which suggest that these megalithic tombs were centres where men would go to perform rituals, probably always connected with the dead who lay buried inside. Sometimes the chamber stands with all its great stones uncovered, but this only means that the mound has either been robbed for building stone or has gradually been worn away during the 4,000 or so years that have passed since it was first piled over the grave.

Monuments of this kind are often called 'cromlechs' or 'dolmen'; the term 'chambered tomb' has a wider meaning for it includes also other burial vaults which, as they are cut in the solid rock or built with small masonry, cannot be called megalithic, yet are very similar in plan and were the work of closely related people.

3. CIRCLES of standing stones (*see* AVEBURY *and* STONEHENGE) are probably all of the Bronze Age, as none that has been excavated so far has been found to be earlier than about 1900 B.C., while others belong to later centuries. Smaller examples, which may be little more than the edging of cairns for individual burials, belong to the middle Bronze Age (about 1500–1200 B.C.). There are very few stone circles outside Britain. Sometimes lines or avenues of standing stones lead up to circles, or occur by themselves.

4. STANDING STONES or 'menhirs' are very common in west and north Britain and may be of almost any date from the Early Bronze Age

LEGANNANNY DOLMEN, COUNTY DOWN, N. IRELAND
G. M. Boumphrey

onwards right up until the Dark Ages after the collapse of Roman Britain in the 5th century A.D. Stones of the Dark Ages sometimes have inscriptions on them in debased Roman letters showing them to be a form of tombstone, and burials have frequently been found at the foot of pre-historic standing stones.

See also PREHISTORIC MAN; BARROWS AND CAIRNS.

MELANESIANS. This name applies to the dark-skinned native inhabitants of many of the western Pacific islands (*see* PACIFIC ISLANDERS, Map). As might be expected, there are many local differences in physical appearance and way of life between the inhabitants of different islands and island groups scattered over so wide an expanse of ocean. The following account gives a general picture which has to ignore many of these differences.

Racially the Melanesians are a part of the great negroid stock. Their ancestors many generations ago reached the islands by migrating from south-east Asia. They have frizzy or curly hair, dark chocolate or black skins, and though they vary in height, they are generally rather short—about an average of 5 ft. 2 in. The shape of their heads also varies: most are long-headed, though in some islands many broad-headed types are met with. Their noses are generally very broad.

INTERIOR OF A HUT IN SANTA CATALINA, SOLOMON IS.
Haddon Lib., Cambridge

Before Europeans persuaded them to dress in cheap cotton fabrics, most Melanesians went almost naked. The men wore kilts or loin-cloths made from a kind of cloth prepared from the bark of a tree; the women wore skirts made of grass—frequently half a dozen skirts at a time. The old forms of dress are still worn in the Solomon Islands, the New Hebrides, and the Bismarck archipelago.

Melanesians live in villages varying from a few dozen to one or two hundred inhabitants. On many of the larger islands we can distinguish between the 'salt-water people' and the 'bush people'. The 'salt-water people' are expert fishers and canoe-men who live in coastal villages and depend on their fishing for a livelihood. The 'bush people' live in inland villages and specialize in gardening. At regular intervals they come down to the coast and barter vegetables for fish with the 'salt-water people'. The coastal villages are often larger and more permanent than those of the inland people, who frequently move their villages in order to cultivate fresh land, a method called 'shifting cultivation'. They build small rectangular houses made of a framework of poles covered on the walls and roof with palm-leaf thatch. Consequently a village looks rather like a group of hayricks. The houses are scattered about among palm- and fruit-trees. Villages in many parts of Melanesia each have

a large finely made building which serves as a club-house for the men. The timbers of these buildings are elaborately carved to represent spirits and creatures who figure in the local religious beliefs.

Close by the village in the jungle are small garden plots where the people grow their crops of taro, yams, sweet potatoes, and sugar-cane. The land is seldom owned by one man or family, but generally by the whole village or by the local clan, though the use of the land is shared out between individual men and families. The men do the heaviest work in chopping down and clearing the jungle ready for planting, and the womenfolk generally do all the planting, hoeing, and weeding. Relatives and neighbours help one another. A man can always count on the support of his kinsmen in cultivating his plot and gathering and storing the harvest, and he in his turn must assist each of them. A newly married young man wishing to build a house can obtain help from his kinsmen and neighbours in preparing and erecting the timbers for the frame and in putting on the thatch covering; the women among his relatives meantime busy themselves in cooking a feast for the workers.

In some ways family life in a Melanesian village is not so different from our own. The family generally live together in one house; though where there are European plantations the grown-up sons often leave home to go to work as labourers and to earn money with which to buy European goods. Where Christianity has not forbidden it a wealthy man may have more than one wife.

Throughout Melanesia society is organized in clans, which vary very greatly in numbers. These clans are social groups whose members trace their relationship to one another through either the male or the female line. Members of a clan tracing its descent through the male line (patrilineal) belong to the same clan as their brothers and sisters, father, father's brothers and sisters, father's father, and so on. Members, however, of a clan tracing descent through the female line (matrilineal) belong to the same clan as their mothers, mother's brothers, and sisters, and so on. Therefore sons and daughters belong to a different clan from either their father or their mother. It is a general rule that a member of a clan must marry someone of some other clan than his own. In some Melanesian societies a man is free to choose a wife from any clan except

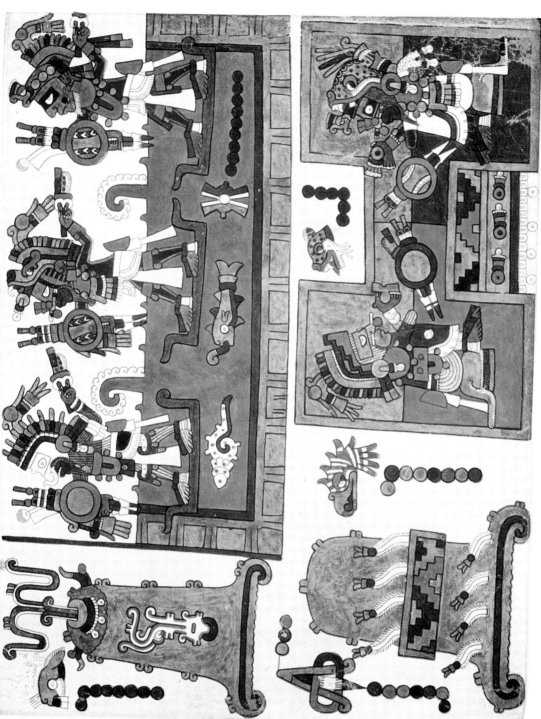

A PAGE FROM THE ZOUCHE (NUTTALL) CODEX

An ancient Mexican book printed on deerskin. This page is part of the story of a chief called Eight Deer. At the top he is seen with two other warriors in boats and below he is exchanging gifts with another chief. On the left are the symbols of a smoking volcano (above) and a town, with date glyphs beside them.

NATIVE HUT ON THE SHORE OF MALAITA, SOLOMON ISLANDS
Haddon Lib., Cambridge

his own; but in Fiji it is customary for a man to ask for a daughter of one of his mother's brothers as wife. This system of marriage of first cousins is known as cross-cousin marriage.

Marriage between members of different clans is looked on as a link between the respective clans. Throughout most of Melanesia the custom of 'bride-wealth' was in force, though European influence has caused it to disappear in some parts. A young man intending to marry seeks the support of members of his own clan in accumulating valuables to be presented to the members of the girl's clan. Wealth in Melanesia takes the form of pigs (especially boars with long curving tusks—the longer the more valuable), the teeth of many other animals, and strings of shell beads and other kinds of shell 'money'. Large quantities of food are also produced for the wedding-feast. This system of bride-wealth is not thought of as purchase money for the wife, but as a proof that the young man's clan approve his choice (otherwise his kinsmen would not help him in collecting the bride-wealth); it is also a stimulus to work hard to save the necessary wealth; above all it is a ceremonial which binds together the clans concerned.

In many parts of Melanesia clans have also a religious aspect: all members of a clan are held to be descended from some mythical supernatural ancestor who to-day is thought to dwell in the body of some species of bird or animal from which the clan takes its name. This animal is sacred and must not be killed or eaten by the clan members; thus, all members of the Eagle clan are forbidden to eat eagles (*see* TOTEMISM). In some areas each clan has an hereditary priest whose duty it is to make sacrifices to the spirits of the clan ancestors. The animals in which the spirits dwell, the priests who commune with these spirits, and other exceptional people and things are said to have a supernatural power known in many Melanesian languages as *mana*. Success in love-making, in gardening, fishing, or trading is held to show that a man has mana. All these vital activities are also assisted by the performance of appropriate magical spells (*see* MAGIC).

Clans also have political functions. In some parts of Melanesia political decisions and the maintenance of law and order rest with the hereditary chief of the clan. In others a council of old men rule the clan. In Fiji and locally in the other main island groups several clans are bound together under one chief to form a tribe. The tribe lays claim to a definite territory over which in old days it frequently went to war. CANNIBALISM (q.v.) used to accompany warfare in Fiji and some other parts of Melanesia. It apparently began as a religious rite but was later indulged in just to gratify a taste for human flesh. In the Solomon Islands whole districts were terrorized by raiding bands of head-hunters. The belief in mana was the basis for head-hunting: if a man killed an enemy and collected his head, he believed that the mana of his enemy was added to his own mana.

See also ANCESTOR WORSHIP; ANIMISM; Vol. IV: OCEANIC LANGUAGES.

MERCURY, *see* GODS OF GREECE AND ROME (Hermes).

MERMAIDS. These are fabulous beings, half-woman and half-fish, believed to live in the sea, rivers, or lakes. People have always imagined strange beings to exist in unexplored places, such as mountain peaks and deep waters. The belief in such beings is not surprising, for some of the natural animals of the waters are very strange. Moreover, water is both beautiful and treacherous. A calm pool can swallow up a man who cannot swim, and a stormy sea is much to be feared. Whirlpools, currents, and tides are difficult to understand. So the imaginary beings which live in the water are thought of, some-times, as being beautiful and helpful, but more often as being weird, elusive, and tricky, and bringers of misfortune. Some FAIRIES (q.v.) are believed to live in palaces at the bottom of the sea. In Greek mythology the naiads were connected with brooks and fountains, and the nereids were sea-nymphs. The kelpie is a spiteful Scottish water-fairy; the nixe lives in German streams; and the rusalka is a Russian sprite somewhat like a mermaid.

The name 'mermaid' is derived from *mere*, a lake, so although we now think of mermaids as inhabiting the sea, it seems that they were originally believed to live in lakes. The usual idea of a mermaid is a very beautiful woman with the tail of a fish instead of legs, but on the Continent mermaids are sometimes depicted with two tails. The notion of a being, partly fish and partly human, is very ancient. The Babylonian god Oannes, the Phoenician god Dagon, and the Greek Nereus had tails like fish. However, our mermaids did not originally have tails. People's imagination added them in later times. The mermaids and mermen which, according to the Chinese, inhabit the southern seas, are also without tails. They are white-skinned and spend their time weaving. When they weep their tears become pearls. The idea of mysterious and lovely water-women, only partly human, who lure men to destruction, is also many centuries

ST. NICHOLAS PROTECTING A SHIP IN A STORM
The mermaid, which has almost caused the destruction of the ship, is seen swimming away at the approach of the saint.
Painting by Bicci di Lorenzo (1373–1452). *Ashmolean Mus.*

old. Ulysses had to be tied to the mast of his ship so that he might not be enchanted by the sweet singing of the sirens; and the Lorelei, a maiden who, forsaken by her lover, was turned into a siren, is said to sit on a rock in the Rhine and to drive men who see her out of their wits.

Dealings with a mermaid or merman usually lead to trouble. Legend relates that when a man marries a mermaid they may live together for years, but sooner or later he breaks some promise and she leaves him and returns to the water. In one form of this story he promises not to inquire what she does on Saturdays, but at length his curiosity gets the better of him, and he finds his wife in a bath with her tail clearly visible. This story is closely connected with a very widespread type of tale in which a seal or a swan lays aside her sealskin or feather cloak, marries the man who steals it, and escapes later. Other stories tell of how a mermaid marries a man and lures him to live with her in the sea. After many years he manages to return. In some cases mermaids foretell the future, give marvellous powers to human beings, or punish people who do them harm. There is a Norse tradition that they have no souls.

Occasionally, so legend relates, women are transformed into mermaids. In north Ireland a tale is told of Liban who swam the sea for 300 years, together with her lap-dog which was transformed into an otter. Having attracted the attention of men by her singing, which was like the chanting of angels, she announced that she would come ashore at a certain place in a year's time. So she was baptized and honoured as a saint. In the case of at least one mermaid story, we know that it was people's imagination which turned a woman into a mermaid. A monk recorded that in 1403 a wild woman came through a dyke into a lake in Holland and was taught to spin. A later writer argued that she could not have been a woman because she could live in the sea, nor was she a fish for she could spin —so she must have been a mermaid. The story of this 'mermaid' was repeated for centuries.

Probably glimpses of sea-animals have helped to keep alive the belief in mermaids. Seals are inquisitive, and when one of them hears strange sounds, such as men in a boat talking, it may thrust its round head above the surface and gaze around. In a mist or a poor light, people seeing such beasts might easily imagine mermaids were watching them.

See also FOLK-LORE.

MESOLITHIC AGE, *see* PREHISTORIC MAN.

MESOPOTAMIAN CIVILIZATION, *see* SUMERIAN; BABYLONIAN; ASSYRIAN.

METAPHYSICS, *see* PHILOSOPHY.

METHODIST. A member of a Nonconformist Church which began within the CHURCH OF ENGLAND (q.v.) in the 18th century and gradually became a separate denomination. The Methodist Church has now about 800,000 members in the British Isles, and some ten times as many in the U.S.A. Altogether, including the Churches in the Dominions and in the mission fields, the membership is nearly twelve millions.

Methodism began with John WESLEY (1703–91) (q.v. Vol. V). As he described it himself: 'In November 1729 four young gentlemen at Oxford began to spend some evenings a week reading, chiefly the Greek Testament.' Other young men joined them, and the nick name 'Methodist' was given to them because of the regular and methodical way in which their religion led them to conduct their lives. These early followers of Wesley did not wish to break from the English Church, but only to lead people to take their religion more earnestly. They began to preach, often in the fields and market-places, and to organize their many converts into societies under local leaders who carried on after the preacher had passed elsewhere. These local groups held their own meetings for inspiration and discipline in their new religious life, but continued to use the Sacraments and Sunday worship of the parish church. It is natural that in many places the meetings of the 'Society' counted for more with its members than the services of the Church.

The break with the Church of England came in 1784. Wesley was sending a group of preachers to look after the Methodists in America, and he thought it necessary that they should be ordained priests before they went. The Bishop of London refused to ordain them, and therefore Wesley, who was a priest, ordained them himself. In the Church of England only bishops can ordain priests, so in doing this Wesley broke with episcopal church order.

Methodist worship is rather like that of other Free Churches, but their set services, including their Communion service (generally held once a month), are almost the same as those of the English Prayer Book. Methodists claim to hold the Apostolic Faith of the Creed and the doctrine of the Protestant Reformation, with special emphasis on two doctrines—first, that a man not only needs to be saved but to have a sense of salvation in his own heart; secondly, that salvation should result in a life of victory over sin. They particularly emphasize that the Gospel is for all men, and therefore they have been pioneers in the modern missionary movement since 1786 when they started work among the slaves in the West Indies. The Methodist Missionary Society was founded in 1813, and it and the Church Missionary Society are the two biggest British Missionary Societies. Its American counterpart is bigger still.

The organization of Methodism is close-knit and efficient, and it has a strong sense of solidarity. Instead of being organized on the parish system, as is the Church of England, the basis is the 'circuit', that is, a group often of twenty or more churches in one area. The circuit is served by a team of three of four ministers and a number of local voluntary helpers who are trained and led by the ministers as local preachers and class leaders. A group of circuits form a 'district' under a chairman who, in America, is called a bishop. The districts form the nation-wide Church, which has an annual Conference and an annually elected President.

See also CHRISTIAN CHURCH; REFORMATION.

MEXICAN ANCIENT CIVILIZATION.

America is spoken of as the New World, and its existence was not really known to the Old World until the discoveries of Columbus in the 15th century. But the beginnings of civilization had been growing among the American Indians for hundreds of years before this, especially in the centre of the continent, with particular centres of culture in Mexico and Peru (see PERU, ANCIENT CIVILIZATION). The earliest traces of American Indian culture are not as old as those in Mesopotamia or Egypt, but they almost certainly go back to many centuries before Christ. We do not know at what point these higher forms of culture first arose or how far they were due to a common inspiration. But

PAINTED TERRACOTTA WHISTLE FIGURINE
The mouthpiece of the whistle projects at the back. *British Mus.*

it is most likely that there was some interchange of trade between Mexico and the countries lying to the south of it, and that in consequence ideas and fashions passed between them. In some ways these ancient Indian civilizations reached heights worthy of comparison with the early civilizations of the Old World—in their stone-carving and modelling, their building, their hand-made pottery and weaving, and in their social organization. But right up to the time of the arrival of the Europeans they were without some inventions known for centuries in the East—the most obvious of these being the use of metals and the wheel. When the Spanish conquerors, Pizarro and Cortes, led their small forces against the INCAS (q.v.) in Peru and the AZTECS (q.v.) in Mexico, the possession of fire-arms and horses gave the Spaniards overwhelming advantages.

The earliest-known culture in Mexico is called the 'Archaic'. It was very widespread, extending, though not quite continuously, from Mexico through Central America to Panama and beyond. We cannot date its first beginnings at all precisely, but these Archaic people had clearly outgrown the stage of wandering hunters and had settled down to grow maize and other food-plants some centuries B.C. Much of our knowledge of them is derived from the little terra-cotta figures which they made. These were rather crude with the features modelled from clay pellets stuck on to the head; but they have plenty of character and give us a good idea of the dress and ornaments of the time: for instance, they show that the art of weaving cloth was already known. These little figures, some of which seem to represent gods, are often found buried at a great depth, and are always underneath the remains of later cultures (*see* ARCHAEOLOGY). A great many ancient undisturbed graves, sealed off long ago from the upper strata by a flow of lava, have been excavated, revealing skeletons and objects of stone and pottery lying as they were originally placed. A large oval altar-crowned pyramid built of clay bricks faced with stone has also been uncovered near Mexico City. This was clearly a religious building which must have

SUNK COURTYARD AND FAÇADE OF PALACE II AT MITLA, NEAR OAXACA
The walls both inside and outside are adorned with stone mosaic patterns in relief, originally coloured. Zapotec culture, 15th century A.D. (Restored.) *H. J. Braunholtz*

been used for a long period. Pyramid building is a characteristic of many Indian civilizations of North America.

The Archaic period of Mexican civilization had for the most part come to an end by A.D. 500. The cultures which followed it were all to a greater or less degree influenced by the Maya people of Central America, who developed the most advanced civilization to be found in North America (*see* MAYA CIVILIZATION).

In southern Mexico an important centre grew up at Monte Alban, a long mountain ridge, near the modern town of Oaxaca, where the Zapotec Indians lived. The remains of massive temple pyramids and other buildings are now being excavated and restored on the flat top of Monte Alban. A great many walled chamber tombs have been found there, containing urns modelled in the shape of figures in ceremonial dress, much fine pottery, alabaster vases, gold ornaments, jade amulets, and other precious objects. The gold work with its delicate filigree is particularly beautiful. The insides of the tombs were often painted in bright colours with religious and mythological scenes. The influence of the Maya is clearly seen in much of this art as well as in the calendar system and the character of the

hieroglyphic writings on stone. Another famous Zapotec site not far away is Mitla, 'the place of the dead', where chiefs were buried in cruciform tombs. The most remarkable monument is a large stone temple or palace, unusually well-preserved, containing many groups of rooms and open paved courts. The walls were decorated with stone mosaics in geometric patterns, while the outer surfaces were painted red and adorned with frescoes of religious ceremonies.

This Zapotec culture probably lasted for at least a thousand years. As well as their building and art the Zapotecs had sacred books of picture-writing. These were much like the books of the Aztec people, who conquered them at the end of the 15th century. There are Zapotec Indians in large numbers in Mexico to-day, speaking their own language and preserving many features of their ancient art.

On the south-east coast of Mexico, in the state of Vera Cruz, another Indian people called the Totonacs were building up their own culture—a mixture of the Archaic and Maya styles. They spoke a language much like that of the Maya. In fact it is quite possible that the Maya came originally from this region and developed their early culture here. The Totonacs were particularly

GREENSTONE RITUAL AXE IN HUMAN FORM. Totonac or Olmec culture. *British Mus.*

skilful at making painted pottery. They also made finely modelled heads with a peculiar smiling expression, elaborately carved stone objects shaped like yokes and apparently used in burials, and large paddle-shaped stone slabs carved in relief with animal or human figures. They built large pyramidal temples rising in a series of terraces and faced with rows of niches like windows built of stone. Stone columns inscribed with hieroglyphics have also been found.

Perhaps the most remarkable of the Mexican Indians were the Toltecs, who succeeded the Archaic people in the high-lying valley of Mexico and flourished from about A.D. 500 to 1100. They were the forerunners of the Aztecs, with whom they were connected both by race and language. Soon after they settled in Mexico they seem to have come under the influence of the Maya, possibly through the Zapotecs.

The Toltecs are called the 'Master Builders' and are best known for the enormous pyramids (the largest in America) which they built as bases for their temples. The largest pyramid at Cholula, near the modern town of Puebla, measured 1,000 ft. square at its base and was over 200 ft. high. At the Toltec capital and religious centre, Teotihuacan, not far from Mexico City, there was another enormous pyramid called the 'Pyramid of the Sun'. This also rose to a height of 200 ft. in four great terraces connected by stairways. It was built of clay bricks (adobes) faced with stone and plaster, and it was surrounded by the priests' houses. The temples which must have stood on top of these pyramids were not built of stone like those of the Maya, and no trace of them now remains.

The capital city of Teotihuacan must have been a most imposing sight. Great buildings stood on either side of a broad, straight road which ran for over a mile through the city. The most interesting building is the temple thought to have been dedicated to Quetzalcoatl, the god of art and learning, or possibly to Tlaloc, the rain-god. The front of the temple and the stairway were adorned with magnificent stone figures and reliefs, painted blue, white, and red, and portraying the god's emblem, the feathered serpent and other symbolic objects. This feathered serpent—the serpent bird—appears in other Toltec temples, as does the figure of the popular rain-god with his trunk-like nose. They are also typical figures of Maya religious art and show the connexion between the Toltec and Maya culture.

Like most of the ancient peoples of Central America, the Toltecs were great potters and decorated their vases beautifully in various styles of painting and engraving. They also made, for religious purposes, a vast number of small terracotta figures with admirably modelled features. They were very skilful at flaking a kind of natural volcanic glass called obsidian which they used for their tools and weapons. They cultivated most of the known domesticated plants of Mexico, including maize, beans, and chili peppers. They grew cotton for spinning and weaving. For clothing the men wore robes and breeches and sandals of plaited fibre; the women wore sleeveless blouses and skirts as they still do to-day. Some of these details come from the fresco paintings which have survived in one of the temples. Like many other Indian tribes, both ancient and modern, the Toltecs made use of steam baths as aids to health and cleanliness.

At the height of its power the Toltec Empire extended more than half-way across Mexico from east to west and as far south as Yucatan. But their civilization perished during the 12th century, partly owing to religious strife and civil war; and the old cities fell into decay before the Aztecs rose to power. The Aztecs, the last people in this series of Mexican civilizations, are much better known to us than their predecessors because their civilization was found at its height by the Spaniards in the early 16th century, and we have therefore contemporary accounts of what the Spaniards found. An account of the Aztecs is given in a separate article. The Aztec civilization perished when the Spaniards invaded Mexico and from then on the Indian peoples of Mexico came under the domination of European culture.

See also ANCIENT CIVILIZATIONS; AZTEC CIVILIZATION; Vol. IV: AMERICAN-INDIAN LANGUAGES.

PYRAMID OF THE SUN, ON WHICH A TEMPLE FORMERLY STOOD, AT TEOTIHUACAN

About 700 ft. square at the base and 200 ft. high. Toltec culture. (Restored.) *Mantel*

TEMPLE OF QUETZALCOATL OR TLALOC AT TEOTIHUACAN

Part of the stairway flanked with serpents' heads and, in the recessed panel, painted feathered serpents, masks, shells, and other emblems. Toltec culture. *H. J. Braunholtz*

MEXICANS. Mexico is the most northerly country of Latin America—just south of the United States. But it is misleading to think of it as Latin, for Mexico is largely an Indian country. Its Indians are akin to the Indians of North America, whence they originally came. The majority of the Mexican people are of mixed Indian and European blood; about a third are pure Indian; and only a comparatively few are white. It was the home of the only native Indian civilization in North America before the Europeans came (*see* MEXICAN, ANCIENT, *and* AZTEC CIVILIZATIONS), and to-day Mexico is more and more remembering its Indian traditions.

But the three centuries during which Mexico was part of the Spanish Empire have left a deep impression. Indeed, Mexico has a certain resemblance to Spain. Like Spain, it consists largely of barren plateau and has great mineral wealth. It is like Spain in its stormy and passionate history, and in the courtesy, poverty, and idealism of its people. The two countries have about equal populations, though Mexico is four times the size of Spain. But there is one great difference. Like France and Russia, but unlike Spain, Mexico is the country of a revolution. To understand this it is necessary to know the outline of its history.

The modern history of Mexico began when CORTES (q.v. Vol. V) landed on the shores of the Gulf in 1519 and burnt his ships so that there should be no retreat for him and his 500 Spaniards. By 1521 they had conquered the Aztec Empire and taken possession of its capital, which is now Mexico City. Thus Mexico became part of the Spanish Empire, and was given the name of New Spain. The Spaniards tried to convert the Mexicans to Christianity, but they were even more eager to gain the wealth of the Mexican silver- and gold-mines. Their rule was greedy, oppressive, and inefficient. The land was divided up into large estates, and the Indians were reduced to slavery. Very soon the Church became so powerful that it owned half the property in the country.

Mexico was ruled from Spain for exactly 300 years, from 1521 to 1821. The Spanish colonists, as elsewhere in Spanish America, revolted against Spain when Spain was conquered by Napoleon; but in Mexico the movement for independence soon became something deeper, a revolt by the Indian peasants against the Spaniards. This, however, was not successful, and when Mexican independence was finally gained in 1821, it simply meant that the Spanish colonists had won freedom for themselves alone, and that the Indians had changed their masters.

The history of Mexico since its independence is one of the most dramatic of modern times. It is full of exciting episodes, romantic figures, and tragic failures. In the 19th century the country was reduced in size, and slowly gained in unity. Its frontier with the United States on the north was vague and undefined. In 1845 Texas, which had been part of Mexico, revolted and joined the United States, and in the war which followed (1846–8) the United States defeated Mexico and annexed all the country north of the Rio Grande together with California. In this way Mexico lost more than half its territory.

Foreign war was followed by civil war. At the same time as the great American Civil War (1861–5), another civil war was raging in Mexico (1858–67) in which the French took part in the hope of winning a colonial empire for themselves. The hero of the American War was Abraham Lincoln; the hero of the Mexican War was Benito Juarez (1806–72). He was an Indian who became president of Mexico, and the greatest statesman Mexico has had. He has often been compared with Lincoln for his honesty and his belief in democracy; and like Lincoln he saved his country, driving out the French and restoring peace.

Civil war was followed by dictatorship. Five years after the death of Juarez, one of his lieutenants, named Diaz, seized power and ruled Mexico with an iron hand from the year 1877 to 1911. He developed the wealth of the country, but did nothing for the welfare of its people. Then came the revolution. It began in 1910, and all the governments since then have continued its work, in a long slow effort to reorganize the country. The three chief objects of the revolution have been to reduce the power of the Church, to divide up the great estates and give the land to the peasants, and to develop the wealth of the country for the benefit of the Mexican people and not of foreigners. Like every revolution, it has brought new struggles and new sufferings, and has committed many mistakes and crimes. But it has given a new hope to the Mexican people, and especially to the Indians. For the first time they have a government which they feel is concerned with their welfare. For all its ugly and disturbing

A MARKET IN MEXICO. *Mrs. T. Muir*

features, the Mexican Revolution is the most important event that has happened in Latin America since the winning of independence from Spain.

The revolution is interesting because in some ways it is an attempt to modernize Mexico, but in other ways it is a harking back to the Indian traditions which existed before the white man came. In the main thoroughfare of Mexico City there is an imposing monument to the last of the Aztec emperors, but in all Mexico there is no statue of Cortes to be found. This shows how the Mexicans look at their past. And indeed, in spite of independence and the revolution, life has changed little for the Mexican peasant since Aztec days. He wears the same brightly coloured square blanket; he eats the same 'national dish' of red, brown, or black beans; he drinks the same 'national drink' of *pulque*. He has the same festivals, though these have now become the Christian holidays; he uses the same simple

tools; he tills the same fields. The Aztecs used knives made of obsidian, a glassy volcanic stone. The Mexican peasant to-day sometimes uses razor-blades made of the same material.

The full name of the country is the United States of Mexico. It consists of twenty-eight states, and has a constitution modelled on that of the United States of America. The language of the country is Spanish, but many Indians speak only their own various tribal tongues (*see* AMERICAN INDIAN LANGUAGES, Vol. IV); and most of the people can still neither read nor write. But Mexico is rich in popular arts and crafts, in folk-songs and folk-stories. The peasant expresses himself in beautiful potteries, tapestries, woodcarvings, and leather-work. The chief art of Spanish colonial times was architecture, which filled the cities of Mexico with splendid churches. But since the revolution the supreme art has been painting. The two most famous Mexican painters are Rivera and Orozco; their frescoes

are found on the walls of buildings all over
Mexico; and they rank among the greatest of
living artists.

See also Vol. III: MEXICO.

MICRONESIANS. These people, as their name
implies, live in the 'small' islands north of the
Equator in the western Pacific Ocean. The
Micronesian Islands include the Caroline,
Mariana, Marshall, and Gilbert Islands (*see*
PACIFIC ISLANDERS, Map). Most of these are low
coral atolls providing a poor living from the
coco-nuts and other trees growing on the sandy
soil, and from the fish which abound in the
lagoons. A few of the larger volcanic islands of
the Carolines and Marianas offer greater scope
(*see* PACIFIC ISLANDS, Vol. III).

The Micronesians are brown-skinned like the
POLYNESIANS (q.v.), but show signs of mixture
with other races. Some have frizzy hair like
MELANESIANS (q.v.); others, in the west, are more
like MALAYS (q.v.), and their language is a mixture of Malayan and Polynesian. It is believed
that the Polynesian voyagers, passing through

A NAVIGATIONAL CHART USED BY MARSHALL ISLANDERS
Small shells represent islands and curved sticks the swells
set up by intersecting currents. By following the ripples
caused by the swells the Islanders can find their way when
out of sight of land. *British Mus.*

the islands on their way eastwards many centuries ago, left some groups behind them, and
that other peoples from Indonesia, the Philippines, and perhaps New Guinea moved in behind
and mixed with the survivors. In 1668 the
Marianas were settled by the Spaniards who
introduced Western ideas and customs. The rest
continued a primitive way of life till the Japanese
mandatory government began to develop the
islands in 1920. Ever since, they have resisted
Japanese attempts to change them, but inevitably, especially during the Second World
War, much of their old way of life has disappeared. More of it remains in the Gilbert
Islands which are under British rule.

Before the Japanese and others changed their
way of life, the people of the Micronesian Islands
lived in scattered groups along the coasts of the
coral atolls, or in more regular villages in some
of the bigger islands. On two of the Caroline
islands they built stone causeways, jetties, and
sea-walls, as well as large ceremonial club-houses
in which the young unmarried men slept, and
where visitors could be lodged and important
village meetings held. In two places the traces
of larger towns with canals running through
them have been found, which probably belonged
to the ancestors of the present people. The
buildings of these towns were simple structures
made of rough, natural, six-sided blocks of basalt
found nearby.

The island people for the most part grew yams,
taro, sweet potatoes, and coco-nuts; they kept a
few pigs and chickens and caught all sorts of fish.
They lived in simple wooden huts with mat
screens for walls and palm-leaf thatch for roofing.
They used tools made of stone or the ground-
down shells of the giant clam. Their weapons
were slings and spears and, especially in the
Gilbert Islands, weapons edged with sharks'
teeth; their armour consisted of thick coco-nut-
fibre matting. They, and some Melanesians,
were the only Pacific peoples who knew the art
of weaving on simple breast looms with strips of
pandanus fibre; but they did not spin. The
women wore grass skirts and the men loin-cloths.
They had necklaces, belts, ear-rings, and combs
made of wood and shell. Other works of art are
spoons made of turtle-bone and beautiful wooden
bowls inlaid with white shell to be found in one
Caroline island.

The Micronesians excelled as sailors and
navigators. They built single sailing-canoes with

A VILLAGE BESIDE THE LAGOON, BUTARITARI, GILBERT ISLANDS. *Pitt Rivers Coll.*

an outrigger float on one side—probably the fastest craft in the Pacific. They used to hold a yearly canoe race round the island of Babel-thuap, the winner of which was held in great honour. In the Gilbert Islands to-day native regattas are common, and there are elaborate rules of etiquette to be observed when sailing. In the Marshall Islands they made charts on strips of bamboos with shells to show the position of the islands, and curved strips of bamboo to indicate the swells and ripples caused by the meeting of ocean currents. In the Gilbert Islands they navigated by the stars.

The islanders had several kinds of currency (money). In the island of Truk, for example, small cakes made of powdered Turmeric root known as *taik* had an exchange value—an axe-blade cost ten pieces of taik, for instance. In the Marshalls strings of black and white shell-beads were used. The most extraordinary money was that of the island of Yap. It consisted of large stone disks, some as much as 8 ft. across.

Micronesian society was, and largely still is, divided into many classes. The clan relationship with its obligations spread over many villages and islands, so that a man visiting a strange island could be sure of obtaining hospitality from members of his own clan. A man had to seek a wife from some other clan than his own.

See also Vol. IV: OCEANIC LANGUAGES.

MIGRATION OF PEOPLES. Mankind has wandered over the earth since the beginning of time. At first, the wandering of peoples was prompted by the need to satisfy hunger and thirst, and to find shelter. Man was still in many ways close to the animal world and so the migrations were widespread, continuous, and unplanned. That is how the earth gradually became peopled, and why we find evidence of prehistoric cultures all over the world (*see* PREHISTORIC MAN). As the more favourable parts of the world filled up and man learnt how to grow food rather than hunt it, migration had less point and therefore became less general. In the course of time, the original motives became obscured by others more complex, and the physical and geographical factors that had determined the migratory routes became overshadowed by political and commercial considerations.

We know a good deal from the Bible records about the wanderings of the ancient HEBREW people (q.v.) during the course of their migrations from the Arabian steppes to their new home in Palestine. And they were only one of many Semitic tribes in that part of Asia who were moving through the countries of the Near East. The migration of people from Ancient Greece or Phoenicia to other parts of the Mediterranean area was more of a colonizing venture than an aimless wandering. The pressure of population in a small infertile country induced many Greeks to seek their livelihood by commerce. The settlements that were founded on the coast of Asia Minor, in Sicily, Spain, and North Africa were as much trading posts as colonies.

Another type of migration in classical times was that of military movements of armies as empires rose and fell. ALEXANDER THE GREAT (q.v. Vol. V) led one of the greatest military migrations in history, and with his soldiers went a knowledge of Greek civilization; whilst the legions of Rome reached the four corners of the then known world, and laid the foundations of western European culture.

From the 4th to the 7th centuries A.D. successions of barbarian hordes swept at intervals from the East into Europe, breaking through the defences of the Roman Empire, and finally settling in the lands they conquered. The reason which made these peoples—HUNS, GOTHS, VANDALS, MAGYARS, and TARTARS (qq.v.)—leave their eastern homes is not certain. It is probable that a gradual change in climatic conditions made life precarious on the marginal grasslands of central Asia, whilst the attraction of better land and a superior way of life to the west and south helped to set them on the move.

In the 9th and 10th centuries the remarkable sea-migrations of the Vikings (see NORWEGIANS) peopled Iceland and Greenland and affected events in Britain, France, and even the Mediterranean countries, and it is now widely believed that America was originally discovered by these Norsemen. In time, though, all these peoples were absorbed into the populations they assailed or overthrew.

In Asia, also, there were periodic mass movements of people, the reasons for which are not always easy to tell. China throughout her history has been subject to periodic inflows of foreign conquerors—the MONGOLS (q.v.), for instance, who were akin to the Huns who came to Europe, and the Manchus (see CHINESE CIVILIZATION). Similar movements have taken place in India and Ceylon. One of the most remarkable of all was the astounding migration of POLYNESIANS (q.v.) from Asia which probably

took place at the beginning of the Christian Era. These people travelled enormous distances in long, light craft, each carrying up to 100 people, with only the stars to steer by, and settled in the islands of the Pacific including, in course of time, New Zealand.

One of the other most remarkable migrations, about which practically nothing is known for certain, is the great movement of people of a Mongolian type from Asia across the Behring Straits into North America, and from there right through the American continents. These were the ancestors of the people we now call the AMERICAN INDIANS (q.v.). This must have happened thousands of years ago, shortly after the Ice Age.

When America was rediscovered by Europeans in the 15th century, another period of migration began. During the following 200 years many Spanish, Portuguese, Dutch, English, and French sought their fortunes in the Americas. The motives were mixed: greed for gold, lust for power, genuine missionary zeal, and a desire to find a new route to Asia. But these ventures had as their aim exploration and exploitation rather than permanent settlement. The first colonies that were founded were based on slave labour. It was not until the 17th century that the New England settlements were founded by English Puritans, driven from their country by religious persecution. Emigration to these settlements was steady but did not reach great proportions until the 19th century. Between 1820 and 1914 approximately sixty million Europeans emigrated to the Americas, South Africa, and Australasia. More than 60 % of them went to the U.S.A. Before 1880 the majority of these emigrants came from Britain, Germany, and Scandinavia, where the economic and social effects of the Industrial Revolution and the increase in population had brought about great social distress and unrest. These people saw in the open spaces of the New World the hope of a better life.

Of the twenty million people that entered the U.S.A. after 1880 the majority came from Italy, Poland, and Russia. By 1921 the U.S.A. had introduced restrictions on immigration and since then the flow of peoples to the Americas and elsewhere has been strictly controlled and limited. The entrance of Orientals into the U.S.A. and also into Australia has been especially restricted, since, in recent times, the need for emigration has been felt chiefly amongst the overpopulated countries of the Far East.

After 1933 began the emigration of thousands, of political refugees from the Fascist-controlled countries of Europe, and this has caused a serious international problem. The JEWS (q.v.), who form the majority of the refugees, are a people apart. Their migrations during the centuries have generally been the result of persecution, often caused by their determination to remain a distinct group of people and not to be assimilated by the people among whom they lived. 'The Wandering Jew' is a historical fact.

Apart from migrations between countries, there are also migrations that take place within a single country, as for example, the northward movement of the AMERICAN NEGRO (q.v.) from the south of the U.S.A. in search of a better job and a higher standard of living. This can be paralleled by the drift of the rural population in Britain to the towns, and the migration of people from the Scottish Highlands to the industrial areas farther south.

Akin to the wanderings of nomadic herdsmen after fresh pasture, are seasonal migrations, such as the annual exodus of families from London's East End for fruit picking and the hop harvest, and the migration of the Scottish fisher-girls to the east coast fishing ports in the start of the herring season.

From this brief survey it is obvious that human migrations are due to a variety of causes and are of several kinds; but all migrations lead to a mingling of peoples and cultures and so contribute to the civilization of mankind. Perhaps there is something fundamental in man's nature that makes him at heart a wanderer, always ready to believe in something better somewhere else. There are still some large areas of the world relatively unsettled, notably the great expanses of Canada with their riches still unexploited.

See also RACES AND PEOPLE; POPULATION.

MINOAN CIVILIZATION is the civilization which flourished in Crete for some 1,500 years, from about 3000 to about 1400 B.C. The legends of Greece told how there had once been a Golden Age of splendour and prosperity connected with the name of King Minos. That the legends were based on historical events has been proved by Sir Arthur Evans's excavations of Minoan remains on the island of Crete. The two chief centres of this civilization were Knossos (Cnossus)

THE SNAKE GODDESS
From a facsimile of the faience statuette found at Knossos
Ashmolean Mus.

on the north side of the island, and Phaestus on the south side. Our knowledge of Minoan civilization used to rest entirely on the evidence of excavation for, although various systems of writing were used in Crete, no modern scholar knew how to read them. In 1953, however, two scholars published a decipherment of a writing called Linear B, and many written tablets can now be understood.

The history of this brilliant island civilization falls into three main periods which, for convenience of classification, archaeologists have labelled Early, Middle, and Late Minoan. It is possible that the first impulse to the development of civilization in Crete came from Egypt which was also at this time in the early stages of her civilization. In fact a number of ivory seals have been found of which the material could only have come from Africa, and the designs resemble those on Egyptian seals of about the same time.

The first or Early stage of Minoan civilization

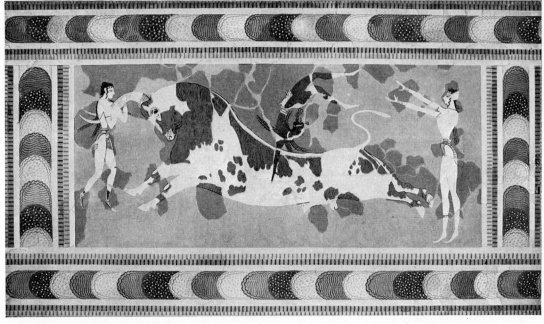

THE BULL SPORT. A fresco in the Palace of Knossos. From a copy in the Ashmolean Mus.

covered the period from about 3000 to 2000 B.C. The people of this period lived in small rectangular houses gathered into villages. They made gracefully designed pottery, decorated with geometrical designs on a glazed surface. They also made beautiful polished stone vases, like those made in Egypt at an earlier period. In the graves of this period have been discovered bronze daggers, axes, knives, pincers, and other implements showing a high degree of skill in craftsmanship; also gold armlets, diadems, pendants and crystal, amethyst, and agate beads. The presence of amber suggests trade with Sicily or the north. The number of small towns on the east coast and on the adjoining islands points to a very active foreign trade.

The Middle Minoan period began about 2000 B.C. or a little later, coinciding with one of the greatest periods in Egyptian history, and ended about 1600 B.C. The cities Knossos and Phaestus, with their magnificent palaces, were evidently the two great centres of power in Crete, whether as the seats of two rival kingdoms we cannot tell until we are able to read their documents. In this period the Cretans and the mainland Greeks (*see* MYCENAEAN CIVILIZATION) developed an elaborate system of writing their old Achaian language by using signs, some standing for syllables and others for objects such as wheels, houses, and men, a writing not unlike that found in Cyprus. The documents (i.e. tablets) found at Knossus undoubtedly deal with trade, particularly trade in horses and chariots; and the use of hieroglyphs for various commodities, side by side with signs indicating the inflections in the language, suggest that the former were used as a kind of commercial shorthand. Almost certainly the Cretans had worked out an elaborate system of finance such as could only be found in a highly developed civilization. There was certainly a vigorous trade going on between Crete and Egypt during this period. The Egyptian inscriptions frequently mention a people called the Keftiu (probably their name for the Cretans), and there are pictures showing Keftiu or Cretan messengers bringing presents of vases and blocks of metal to the Egyptian king.

The walls of the Cretan palaces were decorated with coloured frescoes, the brilliant colours and natural freshness of which are characteristic of Minoan art at its best. In this period the potter's wheel was introduced, and geometric decoration gives place to a style of decoration based on floral motives and intricate patterns of curved lines. In addition to this advance in pottery, the metalwork and fine gem-cutting show a high degree of artistic skill.

The Middle Minoan period ended with a general destruction, possibly brought about by earthquake shocks. Whatever the cause, the revival was rapid, and the two great palaces at Knossos and Phaestus were rebuilt almost at once. The last period, the Late Minoan period, lasting from about 1600 to about 1400 B.C., ushered in an age of greater splendour and prosperity than Crete had yet known.

The Late Minoan civilization shows no sharp break with the preceding period, but the palaces and houses were rebuilt on a larger and more luxurious scale. The palace frescoes give a vivid picture of various aspects of Minoan life: particularly interesting are the pictures of the bull-games which are the origin of the Spanish and Mexican bull-fights. On the frescoes may be seen the figures of the athletes, young women as well as young men, engaging in this exciting sport: they are shown awaiting the bull's charge, grasping the bull's horns, and somersaulting over his head. The representations are full of life and naturalness, a characteristic of all Minoan art. The Minoan artists were very fond of depicting scenes from nature: cows and goats suckling their young, a monkey hunting lizards among the rocks and flowers, and very fine and delicate representations of marine life. No art of the ancient world can show anything approaching the freedom and joyousness of feeling, and the sureness of execution of these artists—in both frescoes and crafts such as seal-cutting and jeweller's work. From the frescoes we learn what the dress of the Minoans was like. The women's dress was very elaborate; a full, flounced skirt, a short-sleeved blouse or bodice, cut very low in front to show the breasts, and the whole surmounted by a high conical hat; the hair was worn long and flowing on the shoulders. This seems to have been the ceremonial dress for processions and court occasions. It is also the dress of the Snake Goddess, who is represented in wall-paintings and statuettes as grasping snakes in both hands, while a snake is coiled round her high ceremonial hat. The ordinary dress of the men consisted merely of a short kilt, but they wore elaborate robes for court occasions.

The principal deities of Cretan worship were goddesses. The Mother Goddess is frequently represented standing on a mountain, attended by lionesses and young male priests. The Snake Goddess was evidently much worshipped, and many of her shrines have been found in caves and underground chambers. The bull was an object of worship: bull's horns, the symbol of the bull cult, are found everywhere—on altars and decorating the walls. The myth of the Minotaur bears witness to the bull's importance. The myth tells how the monster, with a bull's head and man's body, was concealed by King Minos in the Labyrinth and fed once in nine years with seven boys and seven girls from Athens. The legend of the Labyrinth may have arisen from a memory of the winding passages of the palaces of Knossos and Phaestus. It seems that during this last period of Minoan culture the rulers of Knossos controlled the sea-routes of the Mediterranean, and the prosperity of the Minoan Empire rested, not on conquest, but on commerce.

About 1400 B.C., invaders from the mainland of Greece, possibly the Mycenaeans, finally destroyed the greatness of Knossos and the power of the Minoan Empire. Minoan civilization survived, but under altered conditions, and gradually passed into the stage of Hellenic (Greek) civilization known as MYCENAEAN (q.v.).

See also ANCIENT CIVILIZATIONS.

MIRACLE. If by miracle is meant a marvellous event due to the exercise of supernatural power, then to the primitive mind almost any remarkable happening may be and generally is miraculous. The savage, in fact, has no word for 'nature' or 'natural'. He thinks that everything that arrests his attention or requires an explanation is the work of supernatural forces—spirits or gods from 'the other world' (see RELIGION). Since he explains in this way nearly every mysterious and inexplicable object or occurrence he thinks that the whole universe is filled with influences and actions beyond the understanding and control of men, and therefore miraculous. Thus, simple folk are so surrounded with what seems to them marvellous and unaccountable that they see supernatural agencies at work all around them.

This, in fact, is how the natural order and the course of human history have been interpreted everywhere until recent times. Modern science has taught us that the universe is governed by fixed laws which always act in the same way under the same conditions. Thus, for example, in the Bible, especially in the Old Testament, many events which we should explain in terms of natural laws, such as thunderstorms, volcanic eruptions, healing by auto-suggestion, &c., are

THE MIRACULOUS DRAUGHT OF FISHES

Cartoon by Raphael (1483–1520) for a tapestry. *By gracious permission of H.M. the Queen*

represented as miraculous acts of divine intervention. The same is true of all the other ancient civilizations where the gods were thought to be responsible for everything out of the ordinary that happened in the world. The Jews, however, differed from their neighbours in placing the main emphasis on God's direction of the history of their nation as a whole to predestined ends. For instance, the miracle that stands out above all others in their traditions is the deliverance from Egypt, because it was a turning point in the fortunes of the nation. This they thought was the Lord's doing and it was marvellous in their eyes.

Human beings have gradually come to know that natural processes follow orderly laws. As far as they have discovered natural law they have learnt to control nature and have therefore changed the whole face of the earth since they first appeared upon the scene. This human stage of development has been reached by a process of evolution from the most primitive stage of life to the human beings of the 20th century. At each higher stage new powers are revealed which produce results that are perfectly 'natural' at that level but would be regarded as supernatural and miraculous at the lower levels. If a piece of rock could think, it would doubtless look upon the power of growth in the tree as a miracle. The tree similarly would look upon the power of primitive man to run and throw as miraculous; and primitive man in his turn naturally thinks of the modern inventions of the motor-car, the aeroplane, or telephone as miracles. It is not surprising therefore that human beings should still explain in much the same way situations and achievements which are still outside their normal range of knowledge and experience. Many extraordinary events, therefore, that used to be called miracles we now know to be perfectly natural happenings because we understand the natural law which caused them.

Sometimes stories of miracles which have grown up round a sacred place have in fact developed from very slight origins, but have been encouraged because they gave the sacred place greater importance in the eyes of the worshippers. In other cases the great actions of famous people have, after their death, been exaggerated and recounted as miracles. It was, for instance, thought that a saint, holy man, or hero must have had miraculous powers: even as late as the time of the Stuarts our own kings were thought to be able to cure certain diseases by touching those suffering from them. Then there are traditions of extraordinary happenings which, at the time when they occurred, seemed to be so unusual and arresting that they could not be explained except as supernatural events, and have been handed down the ages as such by subsequent generations. The story of the crossing of the Red Sea, when the Israelites fled from Pharaoh, may be quoted as a familiar example of this type of miraculous tradition. To-day, volcanoes in eruption, avalanches, typhoons, severe droughts, and the appearance of comets have ceased to be explained as miraculous happenings because we understand the underlying causes. Nevertheless, there are still times when, to many quite intelligent people, it seems that forces from another world intervene to restore the balance of our own world. We speak, for instance, of the 'miracle of Dunkirk'. Similarly, hundreds of sick people every year in modern Europe make a long and difficult journey to Lourdes in the Pyrenees in the hope and belief of receiving miraculous cures of their complaints.

Whether or not miracles do really happen, those who believe they do, if they are intelligent folk, do not think of them as arbitrary acts of an all-powerful God who plays fast and loose with His creations according to His whims and fancies like a despotic king. If He is the Creator of the universe He must control the forces of nature and guide the fortunes of the world in the way in which He wills. But having made and set in motion the laws and processes of nature He must, as it were, play the game according to the rules He has drawn up. Otherwise everything would be in a state of chaos and confusion. So He could not be continually interfering in the orderly course of events. But, on the other hand, since man is able to use the forces of nature for his own purposes, it must be possible also for the divine mind and will behind the universe to make use of them.

MISSIONARY. From the days of the Apostles (a Greek word meaning Missionary) the Church has had the commission to 'preach the Gospel (good news) to every creature'. Every period of revived zeal in the history of the Church has been accompanied by a return to this, the Church's central charge. The main missionary activities of the Church are described in the articles on the various branches of the Christian Church. The other great world religion which takes part in missionary activity is ISLAM (q.v.).

Besides the work of spreading the Gospel, missionaries have often been instrumental in enlightening primitive peoples, and bringing new life and vigour to some ancient civilizations. Mistakes are inevitable in all great enterprises, but taken as a whole, missionaries have played a leading part in spreading literacy, raising the standard of life, enriching culture, reforming society, combating disease, and contributing to international and inter-racial understanding and goodwill. On the whole, the missionary works for the good of the people and upholds the importance of the individual person, whatever his race or colour. This was an attitude of mind often entirely lacking among the conquerors and traders in whose wake the missionaries generally came.

From the time that Bishop Ulfilas in the 4th century devised a script for the language of the Goths so that they might have the Bible in their own language, translations of the Bible have been the means, again and again, of giving illiterate languages a script (see TRANSLATIONS, Vol. XII, Section 2). Modern medicine was first introduced to most parts of Asia and Africa chiefly by missionaries. For instance, nearly all China's doctors and nurses began their training under missionaries, and two-thirds of China's hospitals to-day are mission hospitals. All over the world those suffering from the terrible disease of leprosy have depended for help almost entirely on mission homes and settlements (*see* Father DAMIEN, Vol. V). Wherever modern missionaries have gone, schools and colleges have been established. Such men as Alexander Duff in India and Timothy Richard in China did much to determine government educational policy. In

China many of her great modern leaders were educated at one of the fourteen universities founded by Protestant Churches. In Africa as much as 80% of negro education is in mission schools.

In the 16th century during the time of Spanish and Portuguese imperialism in South America, it was such missionaries as Las Casas in Spanish America who opposed the exploitation of the natives. In the 19th century missionaries such as David LIVINGSTONE (q.v. Vol. V) played a large part in exposing and finally abolishing the slave-trade in Africa and the West Indies. To-day missionaries are combating the evils of the colour bar in Africa and facing the problems of advancing industrialization in the East.

See also CHRISTIAN CHURCH.

MITHRAISM. Mithras was a god of the ancient Persians representing the light of the day and bright heaven. He was retained in the Persian religion of ZOROASTRIANISM (q.v.), where he was one of the lesser gods surrounding Ahuramazda, the Great God and 'Lord of Wisdom'. Later, Mithras was apparently worshipped as a sun-god who overcomes the demons of darkness; and by the 4th century B.C. he seems to have become a god of purity, moral goodness, and wisdom— a warrior-god always fighting with the powers of evil on behalf of mankind. His followers became 'soldiers of Mithras': they had to take part in the struggle and obey commandments demanding purity, loyalty, and fraternity among comrades.

Mithraism spread into the Roman provinces in the 1st century B.C. and became a popular cult with the Roman army—the warrior-god appealing to the soldier's mind. With the Roman legions it spread all over the Roman Empire even as far as Britain: remains of Mithraic cave temples have been found at York and on Hadrian's Wall in Northumberland. Mithraism was encouraged by some of the Roman emperors and flourished in Rome during the 2nd to 4th centuries A.D. Indeed, the Emperor Constantine, before finally adopting Christianity, is said to have leaned towards Mithraism. In A.D. 378, however, the Mithraic mysteries were prohibited in Rome, and the holy cave there destroyed.

Mithras was always worshipped in a cave— either natural or artificial. The relics found in these caves show Mithras as a young man in Persian dress in the act of stabbing a bull with a dagger. This represented a perpetual mystic sacrifice which Mithras was conceived as performing on behalf of mankind, and through which he achieved the triumph of good over evil and the ascent of the human soul to God. The bull, it is believed, was therefore not thought of as evil but as a noble beast from whose blood came life. In this idea of sacrifice for mankind Mithraism had something in common with Christianity, though the conception took a much cruder form.

Not a great deal is known with any certainty about the beliefs and practices of Mithraism. It appears that a candidate, before being admitted to the secret mysteries, had to undergo a series of trials of increasing difficulty. Those initiated as soldiers of Mithras had continually to undergo periods of fasting and penance considered essential for the purification of the soul.

MITHRAS SLAYING THE BULL
Relief from an altar from the Capitol, Rome, now in the Louvre

THE COURT OF THE LIONS, ALHAMBRA, GRANADA
This Moorish Palace was built in the early 14th century. *Courtauld Institute of Art*

the Gothic king, Roderic. They came, led by Târiq, who captured Gibraltar and gave it his name, Jebel Târiq. They defeated Roderic and overran the whole of southern Spain. The large numbers of Jews in Spain, having been persecuted by the Goths, welcomed the Moors, and even the Christians were not sorry to see the last of the Goths. The Moors then pushed into south-eastern France and in 732 captured Bordeaux. They advanced north from there but were decisively defeated in a battle at Poitiers and made no further attempts to advance out of the south-west corner. They were not finally ejected from France until the end of the century. The Moors in Spain fought so much among themselves that the Christians in the north were able to avoid being conquered, but they were too disunited themselves to drive the Moors out.

The Moors brought not only their armies to Spain but also the arts of peace, and for several centuries Moorish Spain was the most civilized and enlightened part of western Europe. To Cordova, its capital, came men from all parts of the Moslem world, as well as Christians from France and Italy, to study the arts and sciences. Astronomy, geography, chemistry, and natural history were studied there at a time when the rest of Europe was sunk in barbarism. The ideas of chivalry, and the love of poetry and music spread from there northward, chiefly by means of the Troubadours of Provence. Many of the beautiful buildings of the Moors are still to be seen in southern Spain as well as in North Africa.

The Moors' most flourishing period was in the 10th century. After that came a time of gradual decline. More and more of the country fell into the hands of the Spaniards, till in 1260 the kingdom of Granada alone remained to the Moors. GRANADA (q.v. Vol. III) continued as a Moorish centre of the arts and sciences till 1492 when it was forced to surrender to the Spaniards. The Moors remained as subjects to the Spaniards, but were reduced by persecution and massacres till the last of them were expelled in 1610, and so the flourishing and magnificent civilization of the Moors came to an end.

See also ARABS; ISLAM; SPANIARDS.

MORAVIAN CHURCH. This community, which calls itself *Unitas Fratrum* (the Unity of Brethren), was founded in the late 14th century by John Huss of Bohemia, and its members are sometimes called Hussites. Huss was one of the earliest Protestant reformers of the medieval Church (*see* REFORMATION). He was much influenced by the English pre-Reformation reformer, John WYCLIFFE (q.v. Vol. V); and like Wycliffe he wanted to reform people's beliefs by turning their minds back to the teaching of the Bible. Huss was opposed by the Church and was burnt to death in 1415. His followers were persecuted as heretics but they struggled on with varying fortunes in Bohemia and Moravia (now parts of Czechoslovakia). In the year 1722, when they were being severely persecuted, a party of refugees found welcome in Germany on the estate of Count von Zinzendorf, a pious LUTHERAN (q.v.); and there they founded a settlement which they called *Herrnhut*

(Lord's Watch). This was the beginning of the revival of the Moravian Church.

The Moravian Church to-day is a small one. There are not more than 3,000 members in the British Isles, about 10,000 on the mainland of Europe—chiefly in Germany and Denmark—and nearly 30,000 in America. In proportion to its size, however, its missionary work is tremendous: as many as 154,000 people have been baptized in its mission-fields in North India, South Africa, Alaska, Labrador, the West Indies, and Central and South America.

See also CHRISTIAN CHURCH.

MORMONS. A sect of Christians mostly confined to the state of Utah in the United States of America. They were founded in 1830 in western New York State under the title of the Church of the Latter-day Saints, by a certain Joseph Smith. Smith claimed to have had heavenly revelations, and also to have received some ancient records of American history inscribed upon plates of gold. What is supposed to have been graven on these plates was translated by Joseph Smith and written down in a book called the Book of Mormon, which his followers hold to be as sacred as the original Bible.

The Mormons soon migrated westward, and they met with some remarkable adventures which they faced with great courage. Eventually they settled in the Salt Lake Valley in Utah, where they maintain themselves as a self-reliant and well-organized community, ruled by the Church, but within the jurisdiction of the United States. Smith's successor, Brigham Young, for a time declared the right of Mormons to have more than one wife, but polygamy among them is today a thing of the past—and nowadays the members of the Mormon Church conform to the marriage laws of America.

Mormon Christianity professes belief in the Trinity as three separate and distinct persons, and in the universal resurrection of all mankind through Christ. It looks forward to the Second Coming of Christ and to His personal reign on earth. It has a voluntary mission system worked mostly by young men and women who go to all parts of the world, to Asia as well as to Europe, for periods of two to three years at their own expense, to make known their beliefs. Although, through lack of training and ignorance of the appropriate languages, they may not make many converts, they say that their own faith and loyalty are much strengthened by this work. There were in 1945 about 1,600 Mormon churches in all, with a total membership of nearly 900,000.

See also CHRISTIAN CHURCH.

MOSLEM, *see* ISLAM.

MOZAMBIQUE, PEOPLES OF, *see* EAST AFRICANS.

MUSES. Greek goddesses of learning and the arts, especially poetry and music. They were thought of as nymphs whose favourite haunts were certain springs, near which temples and statues were erected in their honour. Apollo, the god of music and poetry, was their leader, and they shared with him knowledge of the past, present, and future.

The Muses were generally supposed to be nine sisters—the daughters of Zeus and the goddess Mnemosyne (Memory). Calliope, the Muse of epic song, was the noblest of them, and she was depicted carrying a tablet and pencil. Clio, the Muse of history, carried a scroll; Euterpe, the Muse of lyric song, carried a flute; Thalia, the Muse of comedy is shown with a comic mask, wreath, and shepherd's staff; Melpomene, the Muse of tragedy, had a tragic mask and wreath; Terpsichore, the Muse of dancing, carried a lyre; Erato, the Muse of love poetry, had a smaller lyre; Polyhymnia, the Muse of sacred songs, is usually veiled and pensive; Urania, the Muse of astronomy possesses a celestial globe.

Greek and Roman writers often begin their work with a call to the Muses, and there are allusions to them in works of many later poets, especially those influenced by classical ideas. The word 'museum' originally meant a place dedicated to the works of the Muses.

MUSLIM, *see* ISLAM.

MYCENAEAN CIVILIZATION, called after the great city of Mycenae on the mainland of Greece, is important because it forms a link between the brilliant MINOAN CIVILIZATION of Crete and the early stages of the GREEK CIVILIZATION (qq.v.) which succeeded and grew out of it. During the last period of its history, Minoan power and influence had extended far into the mainland. It is not impossible that the 'Shaft-Grave' dynasty of Mycenae may have been founded by some great Cretan family who, bringing Minoan civilization in its finest form

GOLD CUP DECORATED WITH LIONS IN COURSE
From a facsimile. *Ashmolean Mus.*

to the mainland, settled in Mycenae, and ruled over Greece from that city. Hence the beginnings of Mycenaean civilization, perhaps about 1500 B.C., overlap the close of the Minoan civilization.

Our knowledge of early Mycenaean civilization has been gained from the excavation of a remarkable group of tombs in Mycenae called the 'Shaft-Graves'. This form of grave consisted of a sloping or perpendicular shaft cut in the rock, leading to a burial chamber. These were evidently the burial-places of kings and members of the royal family. The objects found there are of great richness and show that the Mycenaeans had reached a high degree of artistic skill. Gold is very conspicuous: in the two richest graves the bodies had gold masks, gold diadems and breast plates, gold bracelets and signet-rings. Buried with them were long swords, richly decorated with gold, and large numbers of gold and silver cups. One of these was a libation-cup, that is, a cup for pouring ritual drink-offerings, upon which was embossed an interesting scene depicting the repulse of a pirate-raid on some Mycenaean stronghold. There were amber and amethyst beads, alabaster vases, great copper cauldrons, ostrich-eggs mounted for use as libation-vessels, and an inlaid gaming-board. Among the most beautiful objects are the bronze daggers inlaid with gold, depicting hunting-scenes which include spirited lion-hunts. The vividness and naturalness of these works of art is much like that of the late Minoan art. The kings buried in these tombs ruled in Mycenae for about a century, dominating the islands and most of the mainland of Greece.

By the beginning of 1400 B.C. the Shaft-Grave kings were succeeded by a succession of kings who were buried in tombs called *tholos* graves—buildings of great blocks of stone surmounted by domes. The influence of these kings extended over almost all southern Greece and also stretched northwards. The people of this period made better pottery than the earlier Mycenaeans; the decoration is more luxuriant and unrestrained. Two famous gold-embossed cups, found in one of the tholos tombs, depict the capture and taming of wild bulls, and are so much like the best Minoan work that they have been thought to be the work of a Cretan master craftsman. The Mycenaean masons and builders of this period were very skilled in the handling of stone blocks, some of which were of great size—a remarkable achievement for workmen with no iron tools, iron being as yet unknown in Greece. The huge tomb known as the Treasury of Atreus is a famous example of this skill in the use of immense blocks of masonry. It was built for a king of Mycenae when Mycenaean civilization was at its height. With its magnificent decoration in gold, bronze, and ivory, it is a monument to the power and splendour of the kings of Mycenae in the 14th century B.C. Another great tomb of the same period, and almost as splendid, has been discovered at another Mycenaean site in the Peloponnese.

The Mycenaean rulers kept up the trade relations established by the Minoan Empire: for instance, they must have got ivory by trade with Egypt; Mycenaean objects have been found in Spain and Sicily; and there were Mycenaean colonies on the coasts of what are now Turkey and Syria. One form of pottery specially characteristic of the Mycenaeans is the 'stirrup' vase, apparently used for the export of oil or wine, and this is found everywhere in the Mediterranean area among the civilizations of the Mycenaean period.

The religion of the Mycenaeans was very much the same as that of the Minoans. The principal deity was the Mother Goddess, as in Crete, and her symbol, the double-axe, is frequently found in excavations. The snake also was sacred, and the bull occupied the same place in Mycenaean ritual games as in Cretan. The Mycenaeans being more war-like than the Cretans, there is a development of armour, richly decorated with gold, not to be found in Crete. Homer's description of the shield of Achilles is a witness to the skill of the Mycenaean craftsmen: indeed there is a great deal in the *Iliad* on the customs and general way of life of the Mycenaean people.

About the 12th century B.C. there was a general movement of peoples in the Ancient Near East which caused many changes in political power. Greece, at this time, was invaded by the Dorian peoples; and it was probably this invasion which brought to an end the Mycenaean civilization. There followed in Greece a dark age which lasted until about the 8th century B.C., when there arose the brilliant civilization of Athens, the roots of which, however, are to be found in Crete and Mycenae.

See also ANCIENT CIVILIZATIONS.

THE LION GATE, MYCENAE
One of the strongly fortified entrances to the Mycenean Citadel, *c.* 1500 B.C.

MYSTICISM. The word 'mystic' comes from the Greek, and meant originally someone or something connected with the 'mysteries'. The *mustēs* was one who had been made a member by a ceremony of a secret religious fellowship or 'mystery', which possessed some private religious knowledge. But in time the word 'mystic' changed its meaning, and it has gradually come to mean anyone who, in his private life, is very closely and immediately united with a supernatural being. For example, a Christian becomes in mystical union, as it were, 'one with God'.

Now it is possible to reach this feeling of union in different ways and by different methods. By one method which takes a great deal of self-sacrifice to practise, the mystic tries to become detached from the world around, and to treat it as unreal or unprofitable compared with God, who is the only completely real and satisfying Object in the whole universe. By another method the mystic tries to see God in and behind everything in nature, so that nature leads on to God, or explains God through signs.

Mystics of different religions are aiming at different goals. Some mystics, as for example Hindu mystics, think that the right aim is to see everything, including themselves, as part of God, with the object of ceasing to be individuals, and becoming simply part of God. Christian mystics always distinguish carefully between God and human beings. They say, as St. Paul says: 'I live, yet not I, but Christ liveth in me.' They draw near to God through Christ, and because of their union with Christ they find themselves acting in daily life as Christ would act himself if he were in their place (as indeed they believe he is). This may make the Christian mystic very practical, and he may be fully engaged in an active or constructive life. Some of the greatest leaders in social service have been Christian mystics, for example, Elizabeth Fry (q.v. Vol. V).

A great many mystics, however, are people so full of the sense of God's presence that they want to dwell on it the whole time. Anything except thinking about God, speaking to or watching God at work seems to them waste of time and energy. These people are called contemplatives. There are not many of them in the Anglo-Saxon world of to-day, but in India they are common.

All mystics, it is probably true to say, believe that the visible world is not the whole world, but that it is like a veil hiding us from another but invisible world, which is as real as, or more real, than the world we see. The difference between mystics at this point seems to be that some of them love nature, and find God through nature, while others think of nature as unreal and unsatisfying, and not worth troubling about except to escape from: some mystics also find it hard to

ST. FRANCIS RECEIVING THE STIGMATA
The Saint attained such close mystical union with Christ that his body bore the marks of the Passion. Painting by Sassetta (1392–1450). *National Gal.*

think of God as a Person at all, and prefer to use some other word, like 'the Absolute', or 'the Godhead', or 'the Self-Existent'.

Mystics generally find that their sense of the unseen needs training. The methods used by mystics of some religions may seem rather strange. They include such physical devices as breathing in a certain slow fashion, or taking a special drug (as among Indians in New Mexico) or gazing at a red flower, or sitting in a special position, or saying a particular word a number of times. But these devices are only steps on the way, and as soon as the mind and body are quieted, then the real meditation begins.

The methods of Christian mystics are all simple and straightforward compared with these others, with nothing extravagant about them— their chief object being to bring about union with Christ by using the imagination to picture scenes in his life or sayings uttered by him. Yet it is improbable that any mechanical technique will bring about by itself a mystic vision. Perhaps God gives and withholds such visions as and when He pleases, for the flash of insight which some people have spoken of is not something that we can command when we choose.

Mystics have their own special troubles. Sometimes they come to feel that nothing is of any value, and that God has completely deserted them or does not exist. This 'dark night of the soul' often distresses people very much, especially if they have not been forewarned to expect it. For those, however, who can endure it with patience, there follows the period of peace and brightness when they have won through to the sense of God's presence.

See also RELIGION.

MYTHOLOGY. The word 'myth' has come to be used for any fable or invented story, especially for an obviously untrue or improbable story. Its proper meaning is very different. The word is derived from the Greek word *muthos*, which means word or speech, and is akin to our word 'mouth'. Properly speaking, a myth is the spoken part of a religious or magical rite: a rite consists of two parts—the things done and the things said—and it is the latter which form the myth.

In very early times, it seems, people came to think that they could get what they wanted by pretending that they had got it: that they could cause rain by pouring out water, wind by blowing or waving fans, sunshine by lighting fires, and could kill animals or enemies at a distance by pointing weapons in their direction, or drawing pictures of them with weapons sticking into them. Many primitive peoples still perform such rites to-day. Later on they went further and came to believe that nothing that they wanted to happen would happen unless they first acted its happening. They thought, for example, that the sun would not keep on its course unless they rolled a burning wheel along, and that the corn would not grow unless they first planted and carefully tended a little seed in a pot. In time they came to think that it was not enough merely to do such things, if they were to be quite sure that all would go well, they must do them in a special way, the way that, as they supposed, had always brought success. So that everyone should know what was being done, and should be sure

that everything was being done in the proper way, they made up songs which told how they were setting the sun on his course, or causing the crops to grow. In these songs the people who took the various parts were given names, and in course of time it came to be believed that these names were those of heroes of the past who had been the first to grow corn, or perform the rites. These songs were the first myths.

Later still it came to be believed that it was not enough to act what you wanted, you must also act the destruction of what you did not want. Finally a complex ritual arose, in which pretence was made first of destroying the old world, with all its deaths, diseases, and failures, and then of creating a new and perfect world. In one of its forms there was a human sacrifice of a victim who represented the bad old world, followed by the coronation of a king and queen who by their joyful union would bring about a time of happiness and plenty. The persons who were candidates for the throne had to go through a number of tests to prove their fitness for their important task. Perhaps the reason why, in many myths, the hero and heroine have so many dangers and difficulties to overcome, and are always successful, is that the myths tell only of the chosen couple. The unsuccessful drop out of the myths, as they dropped out of the running. In any case, as time went on, the tests became largely a matter of form; but the myths went on speaking of them as if they were real. Similarly, though the king and queen had to perform many ritual acts, the myths did not describe what they actually did, but what they were supposed to be doing. The king put on a golden crown, and, mounting a chariot, drove men dressed as demons before him; but the myth told how the sun was driving away the demons of darkness. The king waved a glittering sceptre while drums were beaten; but the myth told how the lord of the sky was thundering, and would cause rain to fall. The king roared through a lion mask, and the myth told how his enemies fell before him as the other animals before the king of beasts. The queen represented the earth; she pretended to sleep until the king embraced her, and the myth told how the earth sprang to life with the kiss of the sun. Or she was the moon, alone in her white robe till rescued by the sun from the powers of darkness. There were many such rites, which took different forms in different places; but the ideas were always the same.

SONNENAUFGANG

THE RISING SUN AND SETTING MOON

Helios, the sun-god, rises in his chariot from the waves into which the setting stars are diving. Eos, the dawn, is chasing
Kephalos, while the moon-goddess retires on horseback. Greek vase, 5th century B.C., in the British Mus. From Furtwängler-Reichhold, *Griechische Vasenmalerei* (Bruckmann)

Traces of these rites survive among ourselves.
We have the King and Queen of the May, and
they have their myths in such stories as those of
Robin Hood and Maid Marian. Robin Hood
is the god or king of the spring. In his suit of
green he fights the old demons who keep happiness from the people.

We must realize that the people who spoke
these myths had no idea of being romantic or
poetical. They were priests saying what, according to their beliefs, was necessary to make their
people prosperous. They spoke in verse because
verse is easier than prose to remember and
repeat. It was only when the myths had lost
their connexion with the rites that people turned
them into romantic or moral tales. We must
also realize that though we may be fairly sure
that myths arose in the manner outlined above,
we cannot be sure of the actual steps in their
growth, because the few myths which have been
known to arise in modern times have merely
followed the lines of the old myths, and these
arose long before there was anyone who could
write them down. But though our ideas about
these myths and rites are based on careful study
of ancient times, this study is fairly recent.

In former times myths were studied as if they
existed entirely on their own, and very different
views were held as to how they arose. According
to one of these views, myth is a kind of history,
the kind of history which was told by people who
cannot read or write. It was supposed that these
people told and retold the stories of how their
ancestors had won battles, or moved from one
country to another, and that to make them
simpler and easier to remember they spoke of
tribes as if they were single men. One objection
to this view is that most myths are nothing like
real history. A well-known Greek myth, for
example, tells how Zeus took the form of a bull
and carried off Europa. Nobody can suppose
that anything like that really happened in Greek
history. It can, however, be explained as the
account of marriage ritual in which the king
wore the horns of a bull, the emblem of strength,
and the priests sang of how the mighty bull had
come to wed the queen. There are many pictures of early kings partly disguised as bulls.
Another objection to the view that myths are a
kind of history is that people who cannot read
generally forget everything about the past
that has not something to do with the present.

THE RAPE OF EUROPA
Roman fresco from Pompeii. Museo Nationale, Naples
Anderson

fair maiden pursued by the sun, who was a man in a chariot. The chief objection to this view is that early man, if we may judge him by modern savages, was probably not in the least interested in the wonders of nature, and felt no urge to explain them. He took them all as a matter of course, just as most of us do when our curiosity is not aroused by what we read or learn. Some early men did take an interest in nature, but it was a purely practical one as they thought they could make it work as they wanted. Another objection is that the sun is not in the least like a man, for instance, or the dawn like a maiden; and nobody would think they were, unless he had seen people pretending to be the sun or the dawn, or had been told that the sun and the dawn were really people. It has often been supposed by those who do not know savages, that savages naturally think of stars, animals, and trees as if they were human beings; but those who have studied savages have never found a savage who thinks in the least like that.

Yet another view of myths which has been suggested is that they are the result of day-dreams. It has been supposed that all over the world people have had the same sort of day-dreams, in which they pictured themselves as heroes and heroines, and that these have led to the same sort of myths. People nowadays draw the matter of their day-dreams largely from novels and fairy-tales; but in the days when there were no books, people must have confined themselves to their own experiences, and it is most unlikely that they would have made up their day-dreams out of things they could not possibly have seen, such as enchanted castles, fire-breathing dragons, talking animals, and two-headed giants. Yet such things are found in many myths. Nor are myths everywhere the same. The Romans and Greeks were closely related in race and language; yet the Greeks had many myths and the Romans very few. Are we to suppose that the Greeks went in for day-dreaming but the Romans did not? The fact is that the Greeks, living close to Asia, took over many Asiatic rites and myths.

We see then that myths are not untrue, in the sense of having no connexion with fact, nor are they true, as history is true, in the sense of being accounts of things that happened once only. They are true as things that happen on the stage are true. It is not true that there was a real boy called Peter Pan who really flew in through a

We do the same ourselves unless we write it down. We may remember most of what has happened in our own lifetime (though we forget a great deal of that), but we know what happened before only if we have looked it up in a book. We may remember a few odd bits of what our parents told us; but that will not take us very far back unless our parents happen to be readers of history. Many people in this country do not know what their grandfather's Christian name was or where he lived, and they do not care. We are taught in school to take an interest in the past; but savages have no interest in the past for its own sake, they take an interest in their myths because, as has been explained, in their view these myths belong to the present even though they may speak of an imaginary past.

Another view of myth once widely held is the opposite of that just mentioned. It is that there is no truth in myths at all. According to this view, early man looked about him and, seeing the wonders of the heavens, of the changing seasons, and of birth, growth, and death, felt he must explain them. He knew nothing of science, however, and so his explanations took the form of fanciful stories, such as that the dawn was a window; yet it is true that Peter Pan did, and does, fly in through a window, for you have seen him do it.

It is in this sense that myths may be said to be true; and it is for this reason that while the facts of history are forgotten, myths are remembered because they have been spoken and acted again and again.

See also RITUAL; BABYLONIAN MYTHS; EGYPTIAN MYTHS; GREEK MYTHS; HEBREW MYTHS; NORSE MYTHS.

MYTHOLOGICAL MONSTERS.

Mythology, especially NORSE and GREEK MYTHS (qq.v.), contains accounts of a great variety of monsters, both in human and animal shape. They were not so popular with the Romans. These monsters are of three main types: (*a*) humans, either of exaggerated size or possessing some extraordinary feature; (*b*) monsters, half human and half animal; (*c*) animal monsters often combining the shapes of two or more animals.

(*a*) HUMAN MONSTERS. The most common and widely spread are the GIANTS (q.v.). Some of these were merely huge in size, like the Titans, Tityus of Hades, and the Norse giants, Ymir, and others. Others had some extraordinary characteristic, for example the Hundred-handed Giants, or the one-eyed Cyclopes. Other human monsters included Argus, the herdsman, who had eyes all over his body. When Hermes killed him his eyes were transferred to the feathers of the peacock's tail. The Gorgons were female monsters with serpents in their hair and round their waists. They had hideous faces, and their gaze had the power to turn to stone anyone on whom it fell.

(*b*) HALF-HUMAN, HALF-ANIMAL MONSTERS. There were a great many of these in Greek mythology. The Sphinx was a winged woman with a lion's body. Sphinxes were also to be found in Egypt and probably originated in Mesopotamia. The Satyrs were goat-footed, and had horns and tails; the Centaurs were human as far as the waist with the body and legs of a horse; the Minotaur had a human body and the head of a bull. (There was a Phoenician god, Baal-Moloch, who took this form.) Of sea monsters the best

CENTAUR

known are the Tritons and Scylla. The Tritons were sons of Poseidon, lord of the sea. They had human bodies and fishes' tails like MERMAIDS (q.v.). Scylla, according to Homer, lived in a sea cave in the Straits of Messina, and had

PEGASUS

twelve feet and six heads on six long necks, each with three rows of teeth. According to Virgil, the Roman poet, Scylla was less fearsome, possessing a woman's body and a dolphin's head, with a girdle of dogs' heads. In the Greek myth Scylla seized and devoured sailors passing up the Straits. The sailors, in endeavouring to escape her, fell into the whirlpools of Charybdis. The Sirens and the Harpies had women's heads and the bodies of birds, a common form of fabulous monster in many parts of the world. The Sirens lured men to destruction by the attraction of their song. The Harpies, or snatchers, may have been connected with the idea that the souls of the dead were snatched away from the living.

(*c*) ANIMAL MONSTERS. The most widespread of these were DRAGONS and GRIFFINS (qq.v.). Cerberus, the watchdog of Hades, had three heads and hair composed of snakes. The terrible monster, the Chimaera, had the head of a lion, the body of a goat, and a dragon's tail. It was finally destroyed by the hero, Bellerophon, who rode to attack it on

CHIMAERA

Pegasus, the flying horse. The Greek sea-gods had a horse with a fish-like tail: the Norse God, Odin, rode a horse, Sleipnir, which had eight legs to carry him swiftly over the world. Serpents are common, one of the most remarkable being the huge earth serpent, Jormungand, of Norse mythology, who lay curled round the whole world.

The myths, particularly of Greece, are rich with stories of these monsters, most of whom were harmful to mankind, and had to be fought and overcome by the heroes.

See also FABULOUS CREATURES; GREEK HEROES; GREEK MYTHS; NORSE MYTHS.

N

NAGAS, *see* INDIANS, HILL TRIBES, Section 4.

NATURE WORSHIP. Until people come to understand how the laws of nature work, they tend to think of everything that is strange and mysterious as being due to supernatural causes and therefore as sacred. A peculiar mountain, rock, or tree, an unusual animal or plant, a bubbling stream, a great cataract, a dangerous crossing of a river, or a devastating storm, may all be looked upon as belonging to the 'other world' (*see* RELIGION) and so not to be carelessly approached (*see* TABOO). The natives of the Melanesian islands of the Pacific Ocean use the word *mana* to describe the power which shows itself in the unfamiliar, powerful, and puzzling, whether it be in a person, event, or thing; and

RAINMAKER'S DANCE IN UGANDA
The woman on the left is the witch doctor making rain. She sprinkles the others with water from a gourd. The drummer is seated behind the drum in the centre
Pitt Rivers Coll.

this term is now sometimes used to describe the attitude of mind lying behind the worship of nature in its simplest form.

Worship means the approaching with reverence, veneration, and awe that which has sacredness or supernatural power, and this generally finds expression in a ritual act or ceremony of some kind (*see* RITUAL). Thus in Greek Legend the Trojans regarded their sacred river, the Skamandros, as containing supernatural power, and so they threw live bulls and horses into it as an offering, very much as Jacob anointed with oil the sacred stone at Bethel (Gen. xxviii. 18). Later, when they had come to think of the river as the home of a spiritual being with an independent life of its own, they built altars on the banks for the sacrifice of bulls, because they believed that the god or spirit of the river would leave the stream to partake of the offering in the holy place on the shore (*see* SPIRITS).

Probably it was not until man became aware of himself as a living being that he thought of nature also as having a spirit or soul. But once he arrived at this idea he peopled with a multitude of spirits certain trees and flowers, rocks and mountains, streams and rivers, wind and storm, and every cloud and heavenly body which seemed to be alive, active, and, as he believed, able to do things like himself. Rivers and clouds moved, trees and plants grew, thunder rolled, lightning flashed, mountains quaked, rain fell, the sun and moon gave light, and stars twinkled. Moreover, he himself was so dependent upon nature for his food, shelter, and general wellbeing that he regarded it as a sort of Providence and therefore as an object of worship. He thought that by sharing in food sacramentally with nature and its spirits and gods, he shared in its providence and so would enjoy in greater abundance the fruits of the earth.

But nature is not always kindly and generous with its gifts. It can be hostile and unfriendly and produce famine, blight, and pestilence. Therefore people feared and tried to propitiate it (*see* SACRIFICE) so that its destructive powers might be avoided and rendered harmless. Thus the worship of nature has two aspects; on the one side it seeks to maintain favourable relations with the mysterious forces and supernatural powers controlling nature, on the other side it endeavours to appease their wrath when they are angry and spiteful. There is also a third element in it. Not only do human beings depend upon nature for their food and protection, but in primitive society it is believed that if the gods and spirits in nature are to do their good work properly and not become weak and resentful, they in their turn must be given sustenance by man. The sun, for instance, must be strengthened and its energy renewed by the sacrifice of human or animal victims, or by the burning of fires at the turn of the year (*see* Festivals). In the same way rain is made to fall, storms are driven away, and the fruitfulness of the earth is increased by rites performed by man in the belief that the gods and spirits of nature, like human beings, need to be nourished in order that they can do their work properly and efficiently.

See also Animism; Religion.

NEGRILLOS, *see* Pygmies.

NEGRITOES, *see* Andaman Islanders.

NEGRO AFRICANS. Africa has long been known as the Dark Continent because so much of it remained unknown until the 19th century. Many people had sailed round the coast and trading settlements had been established, but few travellers had been able to penetrate far inland because of the thick forests. The only easy routes into the interior were the rivers, but most of these were obstructed by falls or rapids and some by sandbanks at their mouths. Explorers were also deterred by the hot climate and the dangers of diseases such as malaria and yellow fever.

The African continent has an area of $11\frac{1}{2}$ million square miles, greater than the whole of Europe, India, China, and the United States. Physically it can be pictured as a great table-land with a narrow coastal edge. This table-land is highest in the south and east where the land is over 6,000 ft. in height. As the continent is so large there is great variety in the types of climate and vegetation—the hot, wet, forest region of the Congo and West Africa, with dense bush and very tall trees; steamy mangrove swamps on the west coast; open savannah and grassland with abundance of game; high plateaux as in East Africa, where the climate is suitable for European settlers; and barren deserts like the Kalahari in the south and the Sahara in the north which cuts off the Mediterranean peoples from Negro-land.

The inhabitants of Africa south of the Sahara are mainly of the Negro race. They have dark

A FULANI MILKING A COW
Prof. D. Forde

skins, woolly hair, thick lips, and broad, flat noses. But just as there are many types of white people in Europe, so there are many types of Negroes in Africa. The most typical Negroes are those found in West Africa, the Ashanti (q.v.) of the Gold Coast and the Yoruba and Ibo of Nigeria for example. They are fairly tall, broad shouldered, and of slender build with ebony black skins and oval faces. It is mostly from these regions that the American Negroes (q.v.) originally came. In the savannah country farther north, but south of the Sahara, we find people known as the Fulani who have lighter coloured skins, narrower noses, and facial features more like those of southern Europeans. Farther east in the regions of the upper Nile live very tall thin people like the Nuer or the Dinka, who are often over 6 ft. in height, with long limbs, narrow shoulders, and very black skins; while, in contrast, in the Congo forests are the Pygmy people who are only about 4 ft. 8 in. in height. The Bantu peoples of East and South Africa seem to be of mixed racial origins and show great variation in skin colour and body build.

The Bushmen and Hottentots of South Africa are a different racial type. They are small with yellowish-brown skin, and hair which is rolled into small tangles (peppercorn hair). Their faces have prominent cheek-bones and their noses are broad and flat.

The majority of African Negroes are small farmers or herdsmen, but we find examples of

A DINKA

These immensely tall, dark-skinned people, live in North-east Africa. *Haddon Lib., Cambridge*

every type of life—from the hunter living in the forest, to the clerk in the modern city who travels up to his work each morning by bus; from wandering herdsmen to labourers earning wages in the gold-mines; from farmers who do not know how to read and write, to lawyers, doctors, ministers, and government officials; from people who use no money and exchange goods by barter to business men engaged in trade with overseas countries.

The African peoples speak very many different languages and dialects. The exact number is not certain, but it is probably about 700, and of these 200 or 300 have been written down. Some languages are understood over wide areas and serve as a common language between different tribal groups. Such are Hausa in West Africa and Swahili in East Africa. But many languages are confined to quite small tribes.

The Bushmen and the Hottentots of South Africa speak languages which have peculiar clucking sounds—rather like the sounds we make when urging on a horse. In the north the languages are mainly of the Hamito Semitic families (*see* SEMITIC LANGUAGES, Vol. IV)—a group which includes languages like those of

the Berber people in North Africa and the ABYSSINIANS (q.v.). The languages spoken by the Negro peoples are divided into three main groups: The Nilotic group—spoken in the region of the upper Nile by peoples such as the NUER (q.v.) and Dinka; the Sudanic group—spoken in the area between the Sahara and the Equator, from the upper Nile to the Gambia and Senegal, typical languages being Twi in the Gold Coast and Yoruba in Nigeria; and the Bantu group—spoken in Central, South, and East Africa, which includes languages like those of the ZULU (q.v.) and Xhosa peoples of South Africa.

In spite of the great variety of race, language, and culture, we can divide up the peoples of Africa into a number of distinct groups according to their general way of life and their geographical distribution.

In the first place we have the PYGMIES (q.v.) (Negrillos) who live in the forests north and south of the Equator. They are very small in height, dark skinned, with roundish heads, big noses, and wide mouths. They have no cattle and grow no crops but live entirely by collecting and hunting, for which they use bows and poisoned arrows. They live in small bands and move about after game. They have no fixed dwellings but make themselves shelters of branches fixed in the ground. They are very timid people and are rarely seen, but sometimes they come out of the forest to exchange the game they have killed for foodstuffs grown by their Bantu neighbours.

Another people who live entirely by hunting and gathering food are the BUSHMEN (q.v.) who live in the Kalahari desert in South Africa. They differ from Negro peoples in race and language. They live in small bands which vary in size from 20 to 100 people, each band having its own tract of territory for hunting. The men, who use bows and arrows, are expert hunters, very skilful in tracking down and following animals. Some-times they dress up in animal skins so as to get near the animal they are stalking. The women go out to collect roots and berries for food, using for this purpose a long digging stick which is pointed at one end.

The HOTTENTOTS (q.v.) resemble the Bushmen in race and language but differ from them in being a cattle-keeping people with herds of long-horned cattle and flocks of sheep. They also know how to smelt iron and make arrow-heads and blades of spears. They build better huts than the Bushmen—beehive shaped and constructed of pieces of wood stuck in the ground, bent over and tied at the top. In former days their clothing was made of skins, though nowadays they generally wear European clothes. The women wear ornaments of shells. The men formerly wore loin-cloths, the women aprons, and both men and women had ornaments of copper, and painted their bodies with ochre and fat.

The inhabitants of North-east Africa are mainly cattle-keeping peoples, but they also know something of agriculture. They are generally tall, their skins lighter and their facial features finer than the other African peoples. The Somalis, not strictly a Negro people, are typical of the pastoral peoples of the north-east. They live in tribes, and their affairs are managed by elders appointed by the tribesmen. They have beehive-shaped huts which they carry with them. They are normally armed with a spear; but they are much less warlike than formerly, and bows and poisoned arrows are no longer seen.

The NUER (q.v.), Dinka, and Shilluk of the upper Nile region live in villages during the rainy season and move to cattle camps during the dry season. They have a little agriculture but their main attention is devoted to their cattle. Some of these peoples have a very elaborate religious organization with a king at their head who acts as the chief priest.

In East and East Central Africa are the Nilo-Hamitic peoples such as the MASAI (q.v.), most of whom are herdsmen and warriors. What little agriculture there is is done by the women. The men of the tribe are divided up according to age —children, warriors, married men, elders. When the boys grow up they enter the age-grade of warriors, becoming fighters and cattle-raiders. Each age-group protects the country and carries out cattle raids for about ten years. The young warriors live by themselves and have their hair dressed in a special style. They carry spears and oval leather shields and live mainly on meat, milk, and blood.

The Bantu people in the east and south of Africa are also cattle-keeping people. They value their cattle above everything else and use them as a means of displaying their wealth. In the region near Lake Victoria, when these cattle-keeping people invaded East Africa, they conquered an agricultural people, and the distinction between them still remains in their

BOPOTO CHIEF AND HIS FAMILY
The Bopoto are a Bantu people living in Central Africa.
Haddon Lib., Cambridge

present-day society, the cattle-keeping people often being a distinct ruling class.

In South Africa the Bantu peoples are grouped into a very large number of tribes each under a chief. In the 19th century a chief called Chaka conquered a number of these tribes and established the ZULU (q.v.) nation.

These people generally live in *Kraals* or homesteads. In the centre is the cattle fold in which the cattle are herded at night, and round this are the huts of the various members of the household. In this way they protect their cattle from wild animals and cattle-raiders. The huts are either beehive-shaped or round with conical roofs. They live mainly on milk (drunk sour), maize, and vegetables such as peas and beans. Cattle are killed only on special occasions. The cattle are herded and milked by the men; women are not allowed to have anything to do with them.

In West and Central Africa—the Congo Guinea area—the people are nearly all farmers. They live in permanent villages, but practise 'shifting cultivation', that is, they burn down the bush to make a farm and then after a year or two let the bush grow up again and make a new farm elsewhere. Their chief crops are the yam (a root crop tasting like potato) cassava, and plantain, which is like a large banana. Most of the farm-work is done by the women, though the men help with the heavy work of clearing the bush, preparing the land, and harvesting. When they are not at their farms, the women spend a great deal of their time in trading and are very fond of going to market to sell their foodstuffs. There they can gossip with their friends and hear all the latest news. In this area there is great variety in the size and kind of political organization, ranging from small independent villages to great native states under a Paramount chief, with populations of more than a million and an organized system of payments of tribute. Age-grades are not so much developed here as they are in East Africa, but secret societies or clubs exist everywhere, and for these there is usually an elaborate ritual of initiation. They often play a very great part in the religion and government of the people. It is in this part of Africa too that arts and crafts have been most highly developed—the carved ivories, wooden and ivory masks, and the bronze work of Benin in Nigeria being specially famous.

See also Vol. III: AFRICA; Vol. IV: AFRICAN LANGUAGES.

NEGRO AMERICANS, *see* AMERICAN NEGROES.

NEOLITHIC MAN, *see* PREHISTORIC MAN.

NESTORIAN CHURCH.
A branch of the Christian Church sometimes known as the East Syrian Church. Nestorians prefer, however, to call their church the Church of the East. There are now only about 60,000 members, spread over Iraq, Syria, Persia, Russia, and America. The Nestorian Church has never gained the protection of any state but has always consisted of minority groups, scattered through the countries of central and western Asia.

It is called Nestorian because it has retained some theological ideas derived from the teaching of Nestorius, a Patriarch of Constantinople. Nestorius was condemned at a general Church Council in A.D. 431 for teaching a heresy about the nature of Christ—that Christ was both God and Man, and that it was important to keep separate His divine and human natures. Nestorius was deposed from his position and kept in prison till he died twenty years later.

The Nestorians separated from the Church of the Roman Empire because they were being persecuted by the Persians for their Roman connexions. They were ruled by their own Patriarch, or 'Catholicos', from Sileucia in Persia. Their Church language, instead of being Greek or Latin, was Syriac, as it still is. For some time they spread widely in the East. The Syrian Christians of south India date from about A.D. 300. In 635 a Persian bishop reached Ch'ang-An in China where the Nestorian Tablet, a carved granite slab set up in 781 and bearing their history, is still to be seen. In the 8th century a Nestorian bishop of Tibet was appointed. By the 9th century there were twenty-five Nestorian bishops scattered over Asia. At one time it even looked as though the Mongol emperor, Kublai Khan, might adopt Christianity; but, however, in the 13th century the Mongols chose ISLAM (q.v.). From then on the Nestorian Church has declined.

See also CHRISTIAN CHURCH.

NEW STONE AGE, *see* PREHISTORIC MAN.

NEW ZEALANDERS.
Europeans first came to New Zealand in 1642 when Tasman, the Dutchman, discovered it; but no landing was made until James COOK (q.v. Vol. V) visited the country more than 100 years later. Even then little was known about New Zealand except that the MAORI natives (q.v.) were fierce and unfriendly to sailors. Early in the 19th century, however, large numbers of whalers and sealskin and flax-traders began to establish themselves there. Escaped convicts from Australia also took refuge there. This kind of colonization was naturally without law and order, and it was not till 1840 that the British Government rather reluctantly took over control, partly to prevent the French from making a settlement. The treaty of Waitangi was signed with the Maori chiefs, and in this the rights of the Maoris to their land were fully recognized.

Missionaries led by the Rev. Samuel Marsden came to New Zealand with the early traders, and they played a very important part in the early development of the country.

The history of New Zealand since 1840 has been the history of the development side by side of two races—the whites (or *pakeha* as the Maoris call them) and the Maoris. There were wars between them from 1840 to 1850. These were mainly over the question of land, for the whites wanted to buy and some Maoris wanted to sell

A NEW ZEALAND HOMESTEAD
The High Commissioner for New Zealand

in defiance of their tribal law by which all land is communally and not individually owned. The war of 1860 went on for nearly ten years, by which time both Maoris and whites were exhausted. Since then the two races have lived together in peace, and the original distrust has died away. The Maoris are now progressing vigorously, and their numbers are increasing. They live mainly in the North Island, and there are very few in the South.

The Maoris themselves originally came to New Zealand somewhere in the 14th or 15th centuries. Before then it is thought that New Zealand was inhabited by some aboriginal people called the Morioris who were either killed off or driven out by the Maoris. Some of them fled to island groups near New Zealand, especially the Chatham Islands, where they existed until quite recently.

To-day the population of New Zealand is about 2 millions, of whom some 137,150 are Maoris. This is roughly the same as the population of Philadelphia, or twice that of Birmingham, a fact which should be kept in mind in estimating the many social and physical achievements of the people. The white New Zealanders

are nearly all of British stock—and are the least mixed of all the Dominion peoples.

The way of life in New Zealand is very much governed by its climate and situation. Its climate is ideal for stock-farming and fodder-growing: its isolated position, very far from the rest of the civilized world except Australia, and its small, mainly agricultural community, make it peculiarly suitable for social experiments which can be carried out without fear of outside interference. At first the country was ruled, like most other countries, by the big landowners, but at the end of the 19th century power was transferred to the people by peaceful election, and since then the government has been predominantly radical socialist. To-day New Zealand has a highly developed social legislation—old-age pensions, unemployment benefits, medical, health, and dental services, and their road, rail, and air communications are developing in spite of the difficult shape of the country.

New Zealand is a free Dominion, linked to Britain under the Statute of Westminster of 1931. It has an elected House of Representatives on the English parliamentary pattern, with majority government and a Prime Minister.

Its Legislative Council roughly corresponds to the House of Lords. The Sovereign is represented in New Zealand by a Governor-General.

Though many New Zealanders have close connexions with the mother country which they call 'home', they have a social and a farming tradition peculiarly their own. They have even developed a system of co-operative production among farmers, somewhat like that in Denmark, different from the systems of co-operative buying as carried out by the Co-operative Stores to be found in this country and others. Although about half the population now live in the four big towns, they are mainly a country people. This is natural in a land where nearly everyone has to do with farming directly or indirectly. To an outsider there is a sameness about them, though South and North Islanders would hotly deny this. They have the same speech and the same stocky build. There are no great extremes of wealth and poverty, and an Englishman would be struck by the fact that there are no beggars and practically no slums. The only group which is a little apart from the others is the 'squatocracy' or holders of huge sheep runs, who were the original landholders. New Zealanders are a healthy, practical, and cheerful race, very well off for the material things of this world, especially food which is excellent and cheap, but they have, possibly, a rather low aesthetic and artistic standard. Excellent libraries are, however, being built up and the New Zealanders are great readers. Radio programmes carry more classical music than in Great Britain, and although there are no professional acting companies in the country, there are flourishing amateur societies which fight the all-penetrating influence of the cinema. Their picture galleries have good collections of reproductions and modern paintings. They live in well-constructed wooden houses, brightly painted, with corrugated iron or shingle roofs; nearly all are supplied with electricity. Their manners are informal and friendly and they are kind and hospitable, but their outlook is perhaps a little parochial because they are far away from the centre of things. They follow the same religions as in England, the largest Church being that of the Church of England with over half a million members.

Primary education is free, secular and compulsory between the ages of seven and fifteen years. Most children go to state schools, but there are some private schools. There are also many excellent secondary and technical schools, both state and private. Maori children may attend the state schools, but there are also native village schools for their primary education. Finally there is New Zealand University with its four colleges at Auckland, Wellington, Christchurch, and Dunedin.

New Zealand is a sportsman's paradise. There are excellent opportunities for yachting, mountain climbing, ski-ing, fishing, golf, and tennis. Everyone is especially keen on racing and there are many racecourses, while football is almost a religion. New Zealand is also a gardener's paradise, and flowers which have to be grown with great pains under glass in Great Britain flourish out of doors there. New Zealand will also one day be a paradise for the tourist, and places such as Rotorua, where there are famous GEYSERS (q.v. Vol. III) and hot springs, are already well known to the outside world.

New Zealand is a young country, only at the beginning of its history; but, with a population of only $1\frac{3}{4}$ millions, great areas of land have been farmed, towns, roads, and communications built, and an advanced social system set up. What traditions it has are those of the rule of law, of personal freedom and justice, and of democratic government. It will develop these in its own way in the future.

See also Vol. III: NEW ZEALAND.

NICARAGUA, PEOPLES OF, *see* CENTRAL AMERICANS.

NONCONFORMIST, *see* CONGREGATIONALIST; BAPTIST; METHODIST.

NORDIC, *see* RACES AND PEOPLES (Europe).

NORMANS, *see* FRENCH.

NORSEMEN, *see* DANES; NORWEGIANS; SWEDES.

NORSE MYTHS. Our knowledge of Norse mythology comes from more or less obscure allusions in poems of various dates, the later ones at any rate having been written under Christian influence. It is impossible to get from them a clear idea of what the pagan Norsemen really believed. This is not surprising when we remember that myths were originally accounts of religious rites, and that these rites had mostly, if not entirely, ceased to be performed before the poems about them were written down.

In the beginning, according to Norse mythology, was the Yawning Gap which had on one
side of it the world of cold and on the other the
world of heat. In this gap lived the first being
in human form, the giant Ymir. He drank the
milk of the cow Audumla. This cow licked the
salt rock, and as she licked it there gradually
emerged a being called Buri. Whom he married
does not appear; but his son Bor married a
giantess and had three sons, Odin, Veli, and Ve.
These three slew Ymir, and his body filled the
gap, and his blood overflowed, causing a great
flood which drowned all the giants except one,
Bergelmir, who with his wife took refuge in a
cunningly made boat.

Space was now void and drear. The new gods
did not like this state of things; so, in accordance
with the will of Allfather who dwelt somewhere
in the abyss, they began to create. They made
the world of Ymir's body, the sky out of his
skull, the trees out of his hair, and so on.

The chief feature of the world was the ash-
tree Yggdrasil. Its boughs stretched to heaven
and overshadowed Valhalla, the hall of heroes.
Its three roots reached down to Hel, to the land
of the giants and to Midgard, the home of men.
On its branches browsed various animals including the goat Heidrun from which flowed the
mead which the dead heroes drank.

According to another version Midgard was in
the centre of the world, and above and in the
midst of it stood Asgard, the home of the gods.
Round it was the sea, and round that was curled
the huge earth serpent, Jormungand. Outside
was the land of the giants, and from there to
Asgard stretched the Rainbow Bridge at the end
of which stood Heimdal, the watchman of the
gods. The sound of his horn could be heard over
the world, and it was his duty to give warning
should the giants attempt to invade Asgard.

At first there were no people in the world; but
one day the gods Odin, Veli, and Ve, when
taking a walk, found two lifeless bodies whom
they endowed with life. These became Ash and
Alder, the first man and woman and the
ancestors of all mankind.

Somewhere to the south of the world was the
land of heat, where Surtur of the flaming sword
reigned over the sons of Muspel. These were
among the chief enemies of the gods.

On the highest point of Asgard stood the
throne of Odin or Woden, father of gods and
men. As he sat on his throne he was visited by
his two ravens, Hugin and Munin, who brought
him news of all that was going on in the world.
But he was already possessed of all knowledge of
the past, present, and future. This knowledge
he had gained by pledging one of his eyes for the
right to drink from the well of Mimir, underneath the world: he is therefore always represented as one-eyed. At times he left his throne

ODIN

to go about and direct the affairs of men. He
went barefoot, with a long cloak, and a wide hat
or hood over his eye. Sometimes he went on
foot, sometimes on his horse, Sleipnir, which
with its eight legs carried him at lightning speed.
At times, with a train of horsemen and hounds,
he went hunting through the air—in parts of
northern Europe the peasants are said still to
believe that they see Odin's wild hunt in the
storm.

According to one version, Mimir had his head
cut off, but his head continued to prophesy,
and from it Odin learnt the runes and the Norse
alphabet which were some of the sources of his
power. He knew runic songs that would give
victory in battle, quicken the tempest, and win
the love of women. He often went among the
giants in disguise and engaged in various kinds

of contest with them; but though he sometimes got into difficulties, he always emerged victorious.

Beneath Odin's throne the other gods lived in twelve palaces. The largest palace—540 stories high—seems to have been that of Thor, the son of Odin by Mother Earth. Thor was also called Thunar and was the god of thunder which he caused with his hammer, Miolnir. This hammer not only caused thunder but also fixed landmarks, sanctified marriages, and consecrated the funeral-pile. Thor was thought of as upholder of all laws and proper customs, and was more widely worshipped, perhaps, even than Odin. We can judge of his popularity among our ancestors from the number of names that begin with Thor-, Thur-, or Thir-, such names as Thorolf or Thorkel, belonging to men who took their god's name as part of their personal name.

Many stories are told of Thor's adventures and contests with the giants. Once they stole

THOR

his hammer and demanded the goddess Freya as the price of its return. Thor disguised himself as the goddess and got his hammer back.

Freya, when she is the wife of Odin, is also called Frigg. At other times she is a separate goddess, the sister of Frey and the goddess of spring and love. In her gorgeous palace Frigg sat spinning on her golden distaff and her spinning-wheel. She bestowed her silken thread on the most worthy housewives. She was the goddess of marriage; and among the Germans her day, Friday, was regarded as fittest for a wedding. But in the Norse myths Freya appeared rather as the goddess of spring and of the earth, and as such wore Brisingamen, the necklace of stars, jewels, or spring flowers which shone as brightly as the sun. She had a falcon dress which she sometimes lent to the other gods.

Another of the palaces was occupied by Bragi, the god of poetry, and his wife Iduna. She had charge of the apples of immortal youth, one of which she gave daily to the gods for breakfast. Once she was captured by the giants, and until she was recovered the gods got daily older and greyer.

Baldur dwelt in the palace of Wide Outlook in which no evil could be done. He was the god of everything that is young, bright, and fair, and was beloved by all the gods except the jealous Loki. One night he dreamed that he must go down to Hel. The gods were much disturbed, and it was decided that his mother Frigg should make everything swear not to harm him. The gods then amused themselves by shooting arrows and throwing spears at him, and these did him no harm. But Loki found out that Frigg had left out the mistletoe, so he made a dart of it and put it into the hand of the blind god Hodur. Hodur aimed it at Baldur and killed him. His body was burnt on his ship with his faithful wife Nanna and went down to Hel, there to await Ragnarok and the renewal of the world.

Of the other gods not mentioned as having palaces the most important and the bravest is Tyr or Tiu, the god of war. He had only one hand as he lost the other in a fight with the Fenris wolf.

Loki is the most mysterious of the gods. He is both the cunning adviser of the gods and their bitter enemy. It must be remembered that all these stories are myths—that is, stories connected with the rites—and that the rites are repeated at regular intervals. There is therefore a sense in which all these incidents happened in the past and another sense in which they will all happen in the future. Loki's dual character is due, at least in part, to his being the god of fire which both helps and hurts mankind. He often travelled about with Odin and Thor, sharing in their adventures, sometimes helping them and sometimes playing tricks on them. After the death of Baldur, however, the gods decided to make an end of him, and after a long chase caught him in the disguise of a salmon. He was chained to a rock, with an adder fastened above him in such a way that its poison dripped on to his face. His wife caught the poison in a bowl; but whenever she had to empty the bowl the poison fell upon him causing him such agony that he shook the earth to its foundations. This was said to be the cause of earthquakes. By his wife, Sigyn, Loki had two sons, one of whom was changed into a wolf and devoured the other. By the giantess, Angurboda, he had three children, Hel queen of the underworld, the Earth Serpent, and the fierce Fenris wolf.

One of the palaces in Asgard was Gladsheim, the home of the glad, in which was Valhalla, the hall of the heroes. It was roofed with spearshafts and thatched with shields, and the benches were strewn with chainmail. The Valkyries, the maidens who chose the slain, rode about the battlefields in splendid armour on white horses and brought to Valhalla those who had died bravely. The heroes spent their days in fighting and their evenings in feasting, waiting for the great day of Ragnarok and the renewal of the world.

At last came a terrible winter which lasted for three years. All the trees and plants perished, men died of cold and hunger, and the world was full of treachery and bloodshed. Two huge wolves swallowed the sun and moon, and a great earthquake shook the earth so that all chains were broken. Loki and the Fenris wolf were set free. They were joined by Surtur with his flaming sword, by his followers, the sons of Muspel, and by all the giants and monsters. Heimdal, the watchman, sounded his horn; the gods and heroes assembled, and the last battle began. The heroes and the giants slaughtered each other. Odin was killed by the Fenris wolf, Thor slew the Earth Serpent but was killed by its poisonous breath. All the gods and monsters perished except Surtur, who grew till he reached the heavens, and then with his flaming brand plunged the whole world into a sea of fire. When the fire went out everything was dark and dead. Eventually a new earth appeared and was warmed by a new sun; so that the trees and flowers grew again. The gods assembled and built a new golden palace where they dwelt in love and peace. From out of a wood came a youth and maiden, Lif and Lifthrasir, whom Allfather had miraculously preserved. They came into a world full of fruits and crops which no human hand had tended. There they lived happily and became the ancestors of the new race of men.

See also MYTHOLOGY.

NORWEGIANS.
Members of the Nordic race, as are most peoples of northern Europe. Typical Norwegians are tall, fair-haired, and blue-eyed. Like their Viking ancestors, many of the men are half sailors, half farmers. In proportion to its small population of about three millions Norway has the largest number of merchant seamen in the world: their mercantile marine has ranked fourth after Great Britain, U.S.A., and Japan. The farmer-fishermen of the coast come ashore for the sowing and the harvest, and spend the rest of the year at sea. During the dark winter months they may be absent on distant voyages for long periods.

It is part of their tradition that Norwegians should be bold and adventurous sailors and great explorers. From about A.D. 800 the Vikings launched their 'long ships' in the early spring and late summer and sailed away to raid and loot their neighbours. Their raids grew more frequent and bolder and they reached farther and farther afield—as far as Spain, Morocco, and the Balearic Islands. In one year they sailed up the river Rhône in south France, and the next year they captured Pisa in north Italy. One of the boldest of them, Eric the Red, discovered the island of Greenland. In the year 1000 his son, Leif Ericson, with a band of followers sailed across the Atlantic in the small open Viking ships without compass to steer by and with no maps or fresh food, and reached a land they called Vinland, which was almost certainly part of North America. In 911 a Norwegian earl founded the Dukedom of Normandy, and it was his descendant, William of Normandy, with his 'Northmen' or Normans who finally conquered England in 1066.

Meanwhile in Norway itself a 'united kingdom' was established in 1030, and in 1319 the country became a member of the Scandinavian Union. At the end of the 14th century Norway and Denmark became a single kingdom, but in the resettlement of Europe after the Napoleonic wars, the Danish–Norwegian kingdom was broken up and Norway was united to Sweden. This union lasted till 1905 when the two countries became independent kingdoms.

The Norwegians believe in the principle of an hereditary constitutional monarchy and they are intensely democratic: all titles of nobility were abolished in the 19th century, although many of the farms have been in the possession of the same family for hundreds of years. All education is free from the elementary schools to the universities; everyone is taught English for

In the extreme north, especially at Hammerfest, the most northerly town in Europe, there is great activity from May to July, when the sun never sinks below the horizon. This town is the headquarters for the fleets which hunt whales, walruses, seals, and polar bears, as well as for the big cod fisheries. The narrow streets of the town are alive with bronzed seamen, Norwegians,

HERRING FISHING AT SALTSTRØMMEN, NORWAY
Norwegian Official Ph.

two years. The languages of all three Scandinavian peoples—the Norwegians, Swedes, and Danes—are so much alike that they can understand each other, though the spelling, grammar, and pronunciation differ (*see* GERMANIC LANGUAGES, Vol. IV).

Since one-quarter of Norway is covered with forests, everything possible is made of wood. In the south the wooden farm-houses, painted white or brown, grey or yellow, have slate roofs, while in the north there are log houses with turf roofs. In the summer when the cows, sheep, and goats are sent to the high pastures, the elder boys and girls, or perhaps the farmer's wife with her small children, are sent with them. There the small log cabins with their low blue-painted doors and the little byres and milking-sheds all look rather like the illustrations to a fairy story.

Swedes, British, Germans, Finns, and Lapps, and the smell of cod-liver oil fills the air. In much of Norway outdoor work is impossible in the snow-bound winter, so the women are busy with their looms and embroideries, and the men, unless they are working in the saw- or paper-mills, make and mend the farm implements or fishing nets or do beautiful wood-carving. All Norwegians, even the very little children, can ski and skate, and when everywhere is thick in snow, ski-ing and sleighing are the natural ways of getting about. Even Norwegian townsmen never lose touch with the land; they return as often as they can to the farms, travelling great distances in winter on their skis to spend week-ends with their families.

See also LAPPS.
See also Vol. III: NORWAY.

NUER (AFRICANS). A people belonging to the Nilotic group of NEGRO AFRICANS (q.v.) who live in the flat country watered by the White and Blue Nile in the south of the Anglo-Egyptian Sudan in north-east Africa. They speak a language which belongs to the Nilotic group of AFRICAN LANGUAGES (q.v. Vol. IV), and their way of life is typical of the upper Nile peoples, such

During the rainy season from June to December, when the rivers overflow their banks and flood most of the grassy lowlands, the Nuer live in villages situated on high ground or on small ridges. Sometimes, if the ground is suitable, the houses are close to one another; at other times they may be strung out along a ridge for a considerable distance. The houses are round with

A NUER FAMILY OUTSIDE THEIR HUT
British Mus.

as the Dinka and the Shilluk. They keep cattle, practise a little agriculture, and hunt and fish.

They are generally tall and thin with very dark skins and woolly hair; they often have well-shaped features, thin lips, and noses with high bridges. They are a very proud and haughty people who have no wish to adopt European ways. They wear very little clothing, generally only a loin-cloth.

The only occupation which they consider worthy of a man is cattle-keeping. The deep attachment which a man feels for his cattle or a boy for the bull which his father gives him amounts almost to a religion. Each cow has its own name and the herdsman knows its personal characteristics. Until recently the chief sport of the Nuer was to make raids on their neighbours to capture their cattle.

a conical roof of grass, reeds, and leaves. While living in the villages the Nuer cultivate the land, growing corn and millet.

In the dry season from January to May they leave the village and take their herds down to pasture in the grasslands. Here the young men who look after the cattle make temporary huts of straw. At night they drive the cattle into large enclosures of thorn-trees, and a fire is kept smouldering to protect them from the bites of the mosquitoes. Here, in the lowlands and near the rivers, the Nuer also fish and hunt the hippopotamus.

See also Vol. III: ANGLO-EGYPTIAN SUDAN; NILE.

NUN, *see* MONK.

NYASALAND, PEOPLES OF, *see* EAST AFRICANS.

O

ODYSSEUS, *see* GREEK HEROES (Ulysses).

OLD STONE AGE, *see* PREHISTORIC MAN.

OLYMPUS, *see* GODS OF GREECE AND ROME.

ORTHODOX EASTERN CHURCH. This branch of the Christian Church consists of ten self-governing churches: these are the ancient churches of Constantinople, Alexandria, Antioch, and Jerusalem, and the later ones of Russia,

GREEK MONKS IN A MONASTERY ON MOUNT ATHOS

Serbia, Roumania, Bulgaria, Greece, and Cyprus. There are also 1¼ million 'Orthodox' Christians in North America, and smaller groups in several lands of western Europe.

The Early Church was organized under five Patriarchs (Father-Rulers), the bishops of Constantinople, Alexandria, Antioch, Jerusalem, and Rome. When the Roman Empire accepted Christianity, the Roman Patriarch became particularly important and tried to assert authority over the others. With the split of the Roman Empire into West and East and the development of the Eastern or BYZANTINE EMPIRE (q.v.) with its headquarters at Constantinople, the Roman Patriarchate became even more separate from the four eastern ones. The Roman Church used Latin as its official language; the others retained Greek—which is why the Eastern Church is often referred to as the Greek Church. The separation into two distinct churches came gradually and was not complete until 1054.

The Arab invasion of Egypt, Palestine, and Syria in the 7th century and the Turkish invasions in the 15th century reduced the old Patriarchates to minority communities in the midst of Moslem countries. In the meantime the Russian Orthodox Church had grown up, and in 1589 the Bishop of Moscow was declared a fifth Patriarch to take the place of Rome. Russia became the centre of the Eastern Church and remained so until the Revolution of 1917. Two further Patriarchs were later added, those of Serbia and Roumania. Since 1830, when Greece won her freedom from Turkey, the Greek Church has expanded and is now the most important centre of Orthodox Eastern Christianity.

The word Orthodox means right teaching. The Church claims to hold the faith as revealed by Christ to the Apostles, as found in the Holy Scriptures and as set forth by the early Fathers. The two Fathers of the Church in whom they put most trust are St. Basil (d. 379), whose Rule fixed the way of life for eastern MONKS (q.v.), and St. John Chrysostom ('Golden-mouthed'; d. 407), the great preacher and bishop of Constantinople. The four Patriarchs are the ancient heads of the Church, and of these the Patriarch of Constantinople has the title 'Ecumenical Patriarch' (Universal Father Ruler); but he holds no such position as the Pope does in the Roman Church. Except for the bishops, often chosen from among the monks, the clergy may

THE PATRIARCH OF MOSCOW BLESSING THE CONGREGATION AT THE ASSUMPTION CATHEDRAL, MOSCOW
S.C.R.

many. Both monks and clergy have beards. Their churches are often rich and beautiful and contain many icons—paintings or mosaics of the saints which are held in great honour. The chief service is the Eucharist, a beautiful service with much ritual. There is no organ, but the choral singing is generally magnificent. The congregation is much less formal than in an English church: people move about, kneel to pray or stand to watch, as they think fit. There is little emphasis on preaching.

See also CHRISTIAN CHURCH.

OSIRIS, *see* EGYPTIAN MYTHS.

OTTOMANS, *see* TURKS.

OXFORD MOVEMENT, *see* CHURCH OF ENGLAND. *See also* Vol. V: NEWMAN.

the use of metals, and used mainly stone for their tools and weapons. They were all dependent on fishing and gardening for a livelihood, and on canoes for transport.

Civilization has come to some extent to almost all, except certain tribes in the interior of New Guinea and of some of the larger islands of the New Hebrides.

See also MELANESIANS; MICRONESIANS; POLYNESIANS; Vol. III: PACIFIC ISLANDS; Vol. IV: OCEANIC LANGUAGES.

PALAEOLITHIC MAN, *see* PREHISTORIC MAN.

P

PACIFIC ISLANDERS. The islands of the Pacific, varying from tiny coral atolls to large islands like New Guinea, almost of continental size, were found by the early explorers from the

PAN, *see* GODS OF GREECE AND ROME.

PANAMA, PEOPLES OF, *see* CENTRAL AMERICANS.

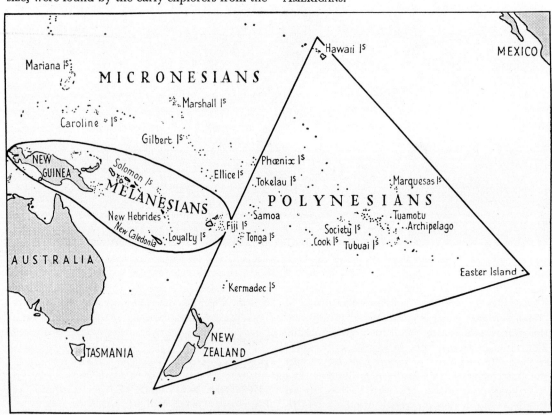

THE PACIFIC ISLANDS

time of Magellan onwards to be inhabited by three main groups of peoples—Melanesians, Micronesians, and Polynesians (*see* Map).

While there were local differences, the islanders had many things in common. They all lived a stone-age life—that is, they had not discovered

PANTHEISM (all-god-ism) is a belief about the nature of God and the Universe held by large numbers of Hindus, though some peoples in other parts of the world believe it also, even if they do not express themselves quite so definitely. The Supreme Being is by Hindus called Brahma, and a Hindu who is a pantheist will say that his bowl and his chair are Brahma, as well as the food he eats, and everything he can see around him. It is not simply that these things proceed from Brahma or are created by him, but that they actually *are* Brahma. As has been explained elsewhere (*see* HINDUISM), this belief is called by Indians *A-dvaita*, which means 'non-duality' (*a* = not; *dvaita* = twoness), in other words that there are not two separate items in existence in the universe, but only one, and that the universe *is* Brahma. There are other folk in India who hold a modified form of this belief, and say that everything is *in* Brahma, but is not actually Brahma's Self—though it may be on its way to becoming more closely united to Brahma. There is a third group which is called *Dvaita*, which says that Brahma and the world are to be sharply distinguished from each other. Although these examples have been taken from India, there exist similar types of thought, by means of which people all over the world conceive of the universe, though they may use different words for them. Even Europeans, though mostly *Dvaita*, have sometimes come very near to being *Advaita*, and so to being pantheists.

One difficulty about accepting pantheism is that it fails to account properly for distinctions between good and evil, right and wrong. In *Advaita* there is no distinction between the criminal and the saint: both are equally Brahma. Christians have generally held that, although both are created by God, and both in a sense fulfil God's purpose by being alive, the saint fulfils it more completely than the criminal. And again, pantheism does not seem to distinguish between beauty and ugliness. We say that a lily is more beautiful than a sundew, an Arab horse more than a centipede, and a Red Admiral butterfly more than a liver-fluke. But if all are God, this distinction loses meaning. Yet people believe it to be a real one. This is a problem which needs to be thought out.

See also GOD.

PAPUANS, *see* MELANESIANS.

PARAGUAYANS. Although Asuncion, the capital of Paraguay, is one of the oldest South American cities, founded by the Spanish invaders in the early 16th century, Paraguay is one of the most backward republics in South America. A large proportion of the people cannot read or write, and though the government is making

A PARAGUAYAN VILLAGE
South American Miss. Soc.

strenuous efforts to combat the illiteracy, many of the children in the scattered rural areas have no opportunity to attend school. Progress is made more difficult by the fact that the old Indian language, Guarani, is still widely spoken, and the newspapers often carry part of the news in Spanish, and the rest in Guarani. The mixture of virile Guarani blood with that of the Spanish colonists has produced in the rather isolated Paraguayan a remarkably patriotic fighting spirit. Early in its history of independence from Spain the little republic was at war at one and the same time with Argentina, Brazil, and Uruguay. The president at that time, Francisco Lopez, though a thorough-going dictator, was a great leader of men. So fierce was the fighting that, at the close of the war, there were very few men left alive, and to-day, seventy years afterwards, the republic is only just beginning to recover from this loss of man-power. The Paraguayans still love to gather in the starlight, after the day's work is done, and, to the accompaniment of the guitar, an instrument well suited to these old-time patriotic airs, sing the old songs of the Lopez war.

The Paraguayans are a hard-working, happy people, and seem quite content with a very low standard of living. The women and children do much of the field work. Two meals a day, eaten at midday and at sundown, are the custom of the country, with a drink of maté in the early morning and after the siesta rest in the heat of the day. Yerba maté, or Paraguayan tea, is a mixture of crushed dried leaves with a proportion of stalk from the yerba plant. It is not made in a tea-pot, neither are cups used; but a cow's horn, or a gourd, is partially filled with yerba maté, and boiling water is poured on it. A silver tube with a filter at the lower end, called a *bombilla*, is inserted into the brew which is sucked up, piping hot. More boiling water is then poured on, and the next person takes a draw, and so on until all have drunk. It is a point of etiquette that the host always takes the first drink to show his visitors that there is no poison in the maté, a relic of the old days when such suspicion was often well founded.

The Paraguayans are great meat eaters: they will tell you that if there is no meat it is not a meal. The ration of meat issued to the cowboys is 2 kilos a day (roughly 4½ lb.). When a cow is killed, much of the meat is dried in long strips called *charqui*, which needs soaking and long boiling before it is fit for the table. The Paraguayans are fine horsemen, and take great care of their horses. A Paraguayan has to be in serious financial need before he will sell his horse. In times of prosperity the bridles and saddles are often ornamented with silver.

On the Chaco side of the river Paraguay there are still Indians living their old tribal life of hunting; but these are now rapidly coming into contact with civilization and learning to become citizens of the Republic.

See also AMERICAN INDIANS, CENTRAL AND SOUTH; Vol. III: PARAGUAY; Vol. IV: AMERICAN-INDIAN LANGUAGES.

PARIAH, *see* CASTE.

PARSEE. This is the name of an Indian religious community, the members of which are descendants, at least in spirit if not entirely by kinship, of Persian followers of ZOROASTER (q.v.), who are said to have fled into exile from their native land 1,200 years ago, in order to escape from its Moslem invaders. It has also been said that they came to India mainly for trade reasons; but this cannot be proved. For whatever reason, they landed not far from Bombay: and to-day there are about 50,000 of them in that city, about 30,000 in other parts of India, as well as smaller settlements in other places such as Colombo, and about 200 in London. In Persia itself there are still about 10,000 Zoroastrians, mostly in either Yezd or Kirman. They are said to be fairer and rather different in build from the Parsees in India, who call them Iranis.

Till about the end of the 18th century the leaders of the Persian Zoroastrians were regarded as a kind of central authority, to whom reference could be made by those in India concerning problems of religious procedure.

Although the ancient Zoroastrian sacred books are known and their teaching reverenced, Parsee piety to-day is really more concerned with its ceremonial. It has a priesthood which, in the main, descends from father to son. (These priests are not very highly educated and are often content to memorize sacred texts without understanding them.) It is a strict religion, but not a missionary faith. The chief ceremony is connected with what has been called fire-worship. This in itself is not peculiar to Parsees. They have, in fact, merely preserved and fixed their interest upon something which they have inherited from the very distant past. The Romans had a sacred fire, tended by the Vestal Virgins. Hindus preserve a fire ceremony, and there is even a Christian fire-ceremony—the blessing of the holy fire—which is held in Jerusalem on Easter Eve at the Church of the Holy Sepulchre, and is no doubt a relic of something pre-Christian. The connexion between a fire and the sun is fairly obvious, and reverence for fire is akin to reverence for the sun, which Parsees also observe. But educated Parsees will declare that the reverence for angels, fire, and sun, are only symbolical ways of approaching the one Wise Lord.

Religious Parsees visit the fire-temple almost daily, and on four days of the month the attendance is very large. As soon as the worshipper gets to the temple, he washes and repeats a short prayer which he was taught when as a child he was vested with the sacred thread or girdle. (This custom is also held in common with Hinduism.) After that he goes barefoot through an outer and an inner hall, till he comes to the sanctuary where the Fire is burning. Here he stands on the threshold (for only the priest goes into the sanctuary), and hands to the priest a piece of sandalwood to burn, and some money. The priest brings him ashes from the sacred urn in a ladle, and with these he anoints his forehead and eyelashes. After some prayer he retires backwards to where he took off his shoes and then goes home. Apart from two or three set prayers the worshipper may pray in his own words.

The Parsee disposal of the dead by exposure to vultures has grown up since the time of Zarathustra, the founder of Zoroastrianism. It

THE DEATH OF MAJNUN ON THE GRAVE OF LAYLA

Persian painting from the Nizami MS., a book of five poems, written in 1495 for the Sultan of Samarkhand. One poem tells how Layla is prevented by her father from marrying her lover Majnun. He remains faithful to her, and at Layla's death he also dies, heartbroken, on her grave

is derived from a belief that the cause of death is the work of a malignant spirit which has somehow to be prevented from harming the survivors. The quickest and most effective way of getting rid of a corpse is either to burn it or to let birds of carrion devour it. Since the Parsees hold fire to be sacred, they cannot use it for such a purpose as cremation, and they are left with the alternatives of either burial, which they reject, or the *dakshma* or Tower of Silence. This is a round, open, brick or stone structure placed on rising ground, with a floor inside, sloping down to the middle and divided into three sections, for men, women, and children. A special class of professional corpse-bearers—who have to live apart from other people and are not allowed inside a fire-temple—carry the body to the *dakshma*. When it has been laid down, a furrow is drawn round it with a piece of metal, and two priests, having their mouths covered with a cotton cloth making them look rather like surgeons in an operating theatre, recite a sacred text. Then the body is left, and in half an hour it is stripped to a skeleton by the vultures. As soon as the bones are dry, they are raked into a central well, where they gradually crumble away. There are only sixty places where there are enough Parsees to make it possible to maintain a *dakshma*; but Parsees only very reluctantly resort to burial, while hardly any have dared to advocate cremation.

Parsees are a highly educated, rich, charitable, well-behaved, and industrious body of people. But their birth-rate is shrinking; and since the 18th century they have been a closed community, opposed to the making and admitting of converts. Probably this is partly from fear that needy individuals may pretend to become Parsees in order to benefit by the large endowments which exist for the relief of their poor. It has in fact been declared illegal by an Indian court of law to initiate any foreigner as a Parsee.

See also ZOROASTRIAN.

PARTHIANS, *see* PERSIAN ANCIENT CIVILIZATION.

PATHANS, *see* INDIANS, HILL TRIBES, Section 2.

PEGASUS, *see* MYTHOLOGICAL MONSTERS, Section (*c*).

PERSEPHONE, *see* GODS OF GREECE AND ROME (Proserpine).

PERSEUS, *see* GREEK HEROES.

PERSIAN ANCIENT CIVILIZATION. During the 9th century B.C., there came into Persia tribes of Iranians, a people connected with the Indo-Aryans who migrated into north India; and the history and civilization of ancient Persia, which shows some likeness to the ancient INDIAN CIVILIZATION (q.v.), is almost wholly theirs. We know little of the peoples that inhabited the country before the 9th century, and even less of their culture. There have been found beautiful bronze figurines and other objects, which show that a high standard of civilization had been reached before the Iranians came.

Iranian tribes spread into Afghanistan, Baluchistan, Russian Turkestan, and the Steppes north and west of the Caspian Sea, as well as into Persia. The most important of the Iranian tribes who found a home in Persia are the Medes and the Persians. The Medes settled in central and northern Persia, the Persians in the south in the province called Persis. As the Persians were the more powerful, the whole country came to be called Persia. Recently, however, the more comprehensive term Iran has come back into frequent use.

The Iranians, and in particular the Persians, excelled as administrators. The Medes had already created a powerful state; but when it was taken over by the Persians, under CYRUS (q.v. Vol. V) in 550 B.C., the Persian Empire reached dimensions never before attained by any

SEAL OF DARIUS THE GREAT (521–485 B.C.)
British Mus.

empire. When it reached its height under DARIUS and XERXES (qq.v. Vol. V) it stretched from Greece to India, from Russian Turkestan to Upper Egypt. The Persians no doubt learnt a good deal about empire-building from the ASSYRIANS (q.v.); but instead of massacres they brought peace to their subjects, and religious freedom and cultural independence in the place of repression and slavery. They encouraged trade,

THE RUINS OF PERSEPOLIS, BUILT BY DARIUS THE GREAT (521–485 B.C.) *J. V. Harrison*

instituted a postal service and, like the Romans in later times, built a network of good roads. With their administration they introduced the art of writing into even the remotest provinces. They did what they could to bring together the different cultures of their subject nations (Babylonians, Syrians, Egyptians, Lydians, &c.) into a unified and living whole, without destroying the individuality of the separate groups. When, in the 4th century B.C., the Persian Empire fell under the domination of ALEXANDER (q.v. Vol. V) and the Greeks, Alexander continued their work, but added the elements of Greek clearsightedness and adventurousness of spirit.

Even the consummate statesmanship of the Persians was unable to keep together this great empire for much longer than two centuries. In a moment of weakness it fell an easy prey to Alexander the Great (330 B.C.). Soon after his death the grand Persian Empire was broken up. The Greeks continued to rule in Afghanistan, but were expelled from Persia by the Parthians.

Persia, therefore, did not remain under Greek influence as did most of the countries of the Near and Middle East. Although weakened within, it was just able to maintain its political and cultural identity even against the Roman Empire, at a time when no one seemed strong enough to resist the march of the Roman legions.

At the beginning of the third century A.D. there was a great renaissance of Persian power. The movement began again in the province of Persis, the ancient home of Cyrus and Darius. The Parthians had been bad administrators, and the power had become divided among many small potentates, who warred against each other and thought only of their private interest. Their Persian successors, a family of rulers called the Sassanids, created a strong state which became a leading world power from the 3rd to the 7th centuries A.D. The Sassanids regarded themselves as the rightful heirs to the ancient Persian Empire, the state of Cyrus and Darius, and imitated its administration with great success.

Neither before nor after did Persia attain so high a level of civilization. The irrigation systems, on which all agriculture depends in Persia, were kept in good order; social measures of tax alleviation and land assessment were introduced; commerce and industry flourished in the cities, several of which boasted more than a million inhabitants; traders went out to China, India, Arabia, and Byzantium. The law courts could be relied on to give justice irrespective of the person; books were translated from Greek and Sanskrit, and were widely read by the large section of the population who had been through the schools; there was a good university for the study of medicine; Greek philosophers, expelled by the Christians of Byzantium, found a refuge in Persia, where a learned man was allowed to have an opinion of his own.

Unfortunately, the strength of the Sassanian state was sapped by the unending wars in which its rulers indulged. Much defensive warfare had to be carried on against the raids of nomad tribes from Turkestan; but the senseless and destructive battles, lasting for some four centuries against the BYZANTINE EMPIRE (q.v.), in which neither side was strong enough to gain a decisive victory, brought no permanent advantage to Persia. By the 7th century both the Byzantine Empire and the Persians were so exhausted that they fell victims to the Moslem Arabs, who, fired by the message of Islam, carried everything before them. The Arabs, whom the Persians should have been able to defeat without difficulty, crushed the mighty Persian state in the course of a few years. For a long time Persian culture became merged in the comprehensive Islamic civilization (see ISLAM).

The importance of Persia in the general history of civilization lies, not so much in its original creations, as in the fact that it carried eastern civilization to the west and western civilization to the east. It was due mainly to the Iranians that the links between China and India on the one hand and Europe on the other were never broken, and that progress in cultural development was in many ways uniform and sustained for the whole of the Eurasian world. The most original contribution of Ancient Persia was in the field of religion. In literature they produced nothing of real importance. Later, however, especially from the 10th century onwards, Persian poetry is particularly fine. The famous Persian miniaturists drew their inspiration from

A SASSANIAN KING HUNTING STAGS
4th-century silver dish. *British Mus.*

the painting of Sassanian times, especially from the admirable illuminated manuscripts. Throughout the ages the Persians have been celebrated for their skill in the weaving of tapestries and rugs. In architecture, as in other aspects of civilization, the Persians derived most of their ideas from elsewhere, but carried them out with great magnificence. In the splendid city of Persepolis, built by Darius, the enormous terraces on which the palaces stood were imitated from the Babylonians; the magnificent stairways leading to the palaces, as well as much of the stone carvings and relief sculptures, were learnt from the Assyrians; and the vast colonnades and the brilliantly coloured walls of enamelled brick were borrowed from ancient Egypt.

The primitive religion which the Iranians brought to Persia from their homeland was in essence similar to that brought into India in ancient times. By a process of subordination of the many gods to the one, a form of monotheism (belief in only one god) was developed in Iran at an early date. The originality of Persian religious thought shows itself in the way in which the monotheism was transformed into a dualistic system—a dualism of Good and Evil. All monotheistic religions were and are troubled by one problem: how did evil and suffering come into the world? If God is good, if the world was created by Him, why is the world so imperfect? why do the good suffer and the wicked flourish? The Persians answered that the world was dominated by two Powers—the good God and the evil anti-God—both equally strong and eternal. The one had created all that was beautiful, good, and pleasing, the other all that was ugly, evil, and displeasing. The two Powers fought their never-ending battle in this world, and the final decision would lie with mankind. Man, possessed of free will, could join either Power, and his support would secure ultimate victory to the one side or the other. This belief was first taught by Zoroaster who lived at the beginning of the 6th century B.C., and lies at the basis of all Persian religious thought. With the coming of Islam the ancient belief disappeared: only the PARSEES (q.v.), religious refugees who found a home in India, and a few villagers in remote districts of eastern Persia, still adhere to it (see ZOROASTRIAN).

See also ANCIENT CIVILIZATIONS.

PERSIANS. Persia is a country with a long history (see PERSIAN ANCIENT CIVILIZATION). The author of the book of Daniel in the Bible wrote of 'the law of the Medes and Persians which altereth not', which shows how high was the prestige of the Persians some 2,500 years ago. Although the country has been conquered more than once in her long history, her people have each time conquered their conquerors and emerged again an independent people.

PERSIAN NOMADS MIGRATING TO NEW PASTURES
J. V. Harrison

In 1932 the population of Persia was just over fifteen millions. The great majority of the people are of the Iranian race—indeed Persia is often called Iran (see PERSIAN LANGUAGE, Vol. IV). But the north-west is largely inhabited by people of Turkish origin, and in the south also there are Turkish-speaking tribes. Most of the people are now Moslems (see ISLAM). Until the Moslem conquest of the country in A.D. 636, the Persians had been ZOROASTRIANS (q.v.) for 1,300 years. But as a result of savage persecution by their conquerors, most of them abandoned their old faith and accepted Islam. To-day there are only a few Zoroastrians in the country, most of whom live in Yezd and Kirman in the centre of Persia. The only Christian community of importance is that of the Armenians.

The poverty of the people is extreme, particularly in the villages where life is still very primitive. The good roads and railways run only to the main centres, and the villages are connected by rough tracks, camel and donkey being used for transport. Many of the tribes, especially in the south, are nomadic, spending the winter in the warmer valleys and coastal land, but moving with their flocks on the approach of summer to the high country, where the air is cool and the grazing good. They live all the year round in tents made of black goat-hair.

At the head of the Persian state is the king, or Shah. There is an elected Majlis or House of Commons, and a ministry responsible to it. All male citizens of twenty-one and over are entitled to vote. The country is divided into ten provinces, each under a governor general. In these ten provinces there are altogether forty-nine shahrestans or counties, each of which has a town of some importance as its seat of administration.

For centuries no attempt was made by the rulers to educate the common people or to develop the resources of the country; but when Shah Riza came to the throne in 1925, he began to develop and modernize his country. He recognized that Persia was, and would continue to be. mainly an agricultural country, and he determined to establish industries based on raw materials, especially oil, which the country already produced, or could be made to produce. The result was the establishment of some 150 factories, producing a large variety of articles from sugar, soap, and paper, to aeroplane bodies. The carpet-making industry, for which Persia is famous, has its centre at Tabriz in the north, and

BAZAAR AT ISFAHAN
National Geographical Magazine

there in the streets of the carpet-makers the craftsmen can be seen at work. The women spin the camel and sheep wool, which has been dyed with a variety of fadeless vegetable dyes. The big carpet looms are for the most part worked by men and boys, who sit cross-legged on a platform before the carpet on which they are working.

Shah Riza began to establish a general system of schools, at least in the towns, and to improve the position of women. He ordered men to adopt European dress, and then directed that women and girls should lay aside the Moslem veil, which for many centuries had hidden their faces from all men save those of their own family. The veil, in fact, had been little used by women in the villages. It was made illegal also for a girl to marry under the age of sixteen, whereas before this it had been fairly common for girls to be married even as young as nine years old. The position of women, however, is still inferior according to European standards. Shah Riza, unfortunately, though many of his reforms were good, was himself a corrupt ruler, and in 1942 he was deposed in favour of his son.

See also Vol. III: PERSIA.

PERU, ANCIENT. When the Spaniards came to Peru in the 16th century, they found a well-developed civilization already established by the Inca people (*see* INCA CIVILIZATION). But the Incas were comparatively late-comers in the history of South America. Many centuries earlier, certainly as early as A.D. 500, and perhaps even before the Christian era, other remarkable cultures had grown up and reached a high level, both on the coast and in the highlands of Peru.

Our knowledge of these early peoples comes from archaeological evidence, since there are no written records and no surviving oral traditions to guide us (*see* ARCHÆOLOGY). All these people were living essentially in the Stone Age. They had indeed learnt to smelt and work gold and copper, but used it chiefly for making ornaments, as they did not know how to harden the metals enough to make useful tools. Their weapons consisted of bows and arrows, darts thrown with a 'throwing stick', clubs, battle-axes, and slings. For defensive armour they wore quilted helmets and tunics, and carried shields.

There is evidence that the people followed some organized religion, since temples and pyramids remain. On the coast the principal deities seem to have been connected with the moon and the sea, while the highlanders believed in a SKY GOD (q.v.) as their creator. A number of lesser gods in the form of natural objects were also worshipped, and there was a cult of clan ancestors in the guise of various birds and animals whose masks were worn in the religious dances. These early people certainly believed in a future life, for the bodies of their dead were carefully wrapped up in fine cloths and buried in pits, which were sometimes walled, in caves, or in stone chambers in the highlands. With them were placed earthenware vessels containing food and drink, and many other objects for use in the next world.

1. EARLY COAST CULTURES. On the coast the climate is very dry and the land a desert, except for a number of small river valleys coming down from the Andean foot-hills to the Pacific. The early inhabitants, though they lived in the fertile valleys, buried their dead with many of their possessions in the sandy deserts nearby. In these cemeteries, often very large, even the most fragile and perishable objects, such as baskets and woven materials, not to mention mummified bodies, have been wonderfully preserved by

MOCHICA VASE

It represents a water-bird sitting on its nest among reeds with fishes below. *British Mus.*

desiccation—just as they were in ancient Egypt. In consequence, we have been able to gain detailed knowledge of the arts and crafts of these people.

The coast peoples lived chiefly by agriculture; but they ate also a good deal of fish. They cultivated a number of crops, including maize, beans, squashes, potatoes, and cotton. To regulate and increase the fertility of their land by irrigation they constructed great waterworks and built stone aqueducts which brought a perennial supply of water down from the mountains, converting, as one writer wrote, 'a coast desert into an earthly paradise'. For their

WOVEN FABRIC: NASCA STYLE

With a design of birds in several colours. *British Mus.*

buildings, they generally used sun-dried clay bricks (called adobe), with which they built many large flat-topped pyramids, on which were placed the temples of their gods.

Owing to the nature of the country, which made communications between the valleys difficult, a number of different local cultures developed. These can often be most conveniently distinguished from each other by the kind of pots the people made. The coastal regions show two principal styles of pottery in the earliest days. One, in the north near the modern town of Truxillo, is known as Early Chimu (or Mochica), and is distinguished by the realistic modelling and painting of its vases. The other, in the south, called after its chief site at Nasca, shows a more conventional style of painting, using a wide choice of colours. Early Chimu vases give us a vivid picture of the appearance and life of the people. Some are realistically modelled in the form of human heads or figures; others depict animals, plants, &c., in a most lifelike and often humorous way; others, again, show scenes of warfare, religious ceremonies, hunting, or fishing. The vases of the Nasca people, though beautifully shaped and coloured, do not tell us so much about ordinary life. Many of them depict strange supernatural figures, although others use plants, birds, and fish for their designs. All these vases were modelled from the clay by hand without the use of the potter's wheel; but the ware is hard and of fine quality.

The art of weaving and spinning had also reached a high degree of perfection: in fact, both in the technical excellence and variety of the fabrics and in their decorative designs, they have hardly been surpassed.

2. EARLY HIGHLAND CULTURES. The most important of the pre-Inca highland cultures, at about the same period as the early coast cultures, was centred near Lake Titicaca, at a height of nearly 13,000 feet, where the climate was wet and cold. The most striking achievement of these peoples was their stone monuments, many of which were destroyed or mutilated in colonial times. The architectural remains, however, consisting of massive walls and huge blocks of stone cut with mathematical precision, are most impressive. Most famous is the single-stone gateway, 'the Gate of the Sun', measuring 12 × 10 feet and weighing at least 12 tons. One side of this great gateway is carved with panels in relief, showing in the centre what is probably the sky god with rows of winged attendants on either side. The gateway leads into a large square enclosure, surrounded by monoliths and colossal stone statues, evidently forming a kind of temple. The carving of the figures is formal and angular, a style characteristic also of the painted pottery found there.

The climate of this high region is too cold for maize to ripen; but potatoes and fish from the lake would have been available, and other kinds of food may have been transported from lower-lying lands. These people undoubtedly established a powerful dominion, and eventually extended their influence right down to the coast of central and southern Peru, if they did not actually conquer the whole country. Farther north there were other centres of highland culture, but none so extensive. These highlanders had domesticated the llama and the alpaca, using their wool to weave *ponchos*—a kind of loose sleeveless tunic. The llama, which was introduced on the coast, was also used as a beast of burden.

The early highland cultures seem to have fallen into decay before the rise of the Incas, who knew nothing about them. On the coast, however, the early cultures continued, though they changed and deteriorated in some respects. In the south the Nasca pottery was replaced by an inferior type with rather mechanical geometric patterns. In the north and centre a blackish

MOCHICA POTTERY PORTRAIT HEAD
British Mus.

pottery made in moulds became fashionable. A remarkable achievement in this period was the building of the capital city, Chan Chan, which was very large and excellently planned. Its ruins cover some twelve square miles. This shows that there must have existed a powerful and well-organized state.

But the Incas by this time were gaining power, and by about A.D. 1400 they had conquered the whole coast, and made it part of their empire.

See also INCA CIVILIZATION.

PERUVIANS. The Indian people of Peru have a very ancient history, perhaps dating back to before the birth of Christ (*see* PERU, ANCIENT CIVILIZATION). Later followed the civilization of the INCA people (q.v.) who, before the arrival of the Spaniards, had developed an elaborate and efficient form of government under their emperor, the Inca. They cultivated the fertile land, building a wonderful system of terraces up the foothills of the Andes Mountains. They built roads and organized their society so that unemployment and poverty were unknown. This was the civilization existing in Peru when the Spaniards under PIZARRO (q.v. Vol. V) invaded and conquered the country in 1531.

NASCA VASE
The coloured design represents a demon figure with a border of heads below. *British Mus.*

PERUVIANS WITH THEIR LLAMAS. *Dorian Leigh*

The Spaniards were lured on by greed for gold and the rumours of *El Dorado*, the Man of Gold; and indeed they found much gold and other riches, as well as an intelligent Indian population whom they forced to work for them. In consequence, with an idle aristocracy of Spaniards and an Indian population in a state of serfdom, the colony developed quickly, in contrast to the slower, sounder, more democratic methods of the CHILEANS and ARGENTINES (qq.v.). The government is still undemocratic; but the white minority have now an increasing sense of responsibility for the welfare of their Indian subjects, who form by far the majority of the population.

As the republic of Peru divides itself into three natural regions, so the people divide into three types, living approximately in the three regions. In the coastal strip live the majority of the pure-bred Spaniards, descendants of the old colonists. The climate here is temperate because of a cold ocean current. Most of the principal towns, including Lima the capital, are built in this strip, and traffic between them is very largely sea-borne.

In the highlands of the Andes are found the 'tame' Indians and the mestizos (half-breed Spaniards who have intermarried with Indians and speak Spanish): they are rather backward as a result of their isolated position, the poverty of much of the country, and low standard of living. The Indians of the highlands are mainly of the Quechua and Aymara tribes, descendants of the Incas.

On the eastern side of the Andes, down in the Amazon jungle, live many wild tribes of Indians, still little touched by modern civilization. These Indians still live by hunting and fishing, with little attempt at agriculture, and they are often hostile to travellers. They still speak their old tribal languages, most of which have never been written down. Some tribes still follow the custom of the Inca ruling classes, piercing holes in the lobes of the children's ears and stretching the holes so that, in time, quite large disks of wood can be inserted. Other tribes possess the curious art of treating the head of their slain enemies by a secret process so that they shrink and are preserved. These shrivelled heads can be found in curio shops near the coast.

Means of transport are still primitive over large parts of Peru. There are few railways, except in the coastal region, and many of the villages are only reached by mountain tracks, transport being provided by pack-animals—mules, donkeys, and the tough, sure-footed llama—or by Indian porters. The coming of airways will do much to open up these isolated regions of South America.

See also AMERICAN INDIANS, CENTRAL AND SOUTH; Vol. III: PERU; Vol. IV: AMERICAN-INDIAN LANGUAGES.

PHARAOHS, *see* EGYPTIAN CIVILIZATION.

PHILISTINES. A Mediterranean people who migrated from the island of Crete in the 13th century B.C., and settled in the south-west corner of Palestine. In fact, the name Palestine is simply another form of the word Philistine. The Philistines formed a highly civilized and warlike nation, and proceeded to press the Hebrews, who were finding it difficult to unite into a nation. In spite of the Hebrew legend of the young David's victory over the Philistine hero, Goliath, the Philistines defeated King Saul and routed his army. But a few years later, when David became king, he succeeded in beating back the Philistines and ruling over a united Hebrew kingdom.

The word Philistine is now often used to denote an uncultured person, and sometimes with the sense of an outsider or an enemy—for example 'to fall among the Philistines'.

See also HEBREW CIVILIZATION.
See also Vol. V: DAVID.

PHILOSOPHY. Originally a Greek word meaning love of wisdom. Among the ancient Greeks there were a number of great philosophers of whom PLATO (428–347 B.C.) and ARISTOTLE (385–322 B.C.) (qq.v. Vol. V) were pre-eminent. Among the Greeks and in the Middle Ages philosophy included the study of many subjects that are now included in science, and even in Victorian times science was often called natural philosophy. But from its beginning philosophy was largely concerned with questions with which science does not deal; and it is this kind of question that interests philosophers to-day.

These questions spring from the impulse that comes to most thoughtful persons at some time to inquire into beliefs that are ordinarily taken for granted. There are a great many beliefs which we use in our everyday life and accept without question. For example, we believe that some actions are right and others wrong, that democracy or government by the people is a good thing, that each of us is free to choose his own course of behaviour. When habitual ideas of this kind are criticized or challenged, then we are led to think about them. Now when we begin to think carefully about these customary beliefs, we find that we are obliged to ask ourselves what the general ideas underlying these beliefs mean. Let us take the first example mentioned above. We use every day the word 'right', and many words that are equivalent to it, such as decent, proper, fitting. We say 'it is right to be honest' or 'a man ought to do his job well'. What precisely is the meaning of 'right' and 'ought'? When we try to give an answer to the question, we are entering upon the work of philosophy. We may come to the conclusion that 'right' means obeying our conscience; or we may decide that it means helping to make ourselves and other people happy; or we may decide on some other definition of this familiar word. The fact that different people give different accounts of the idea is a reason for pursuing the question farther, in order to find out which account is nearer the truth. Now books on philosophy show us that a great deal of careful thinking is required in order to reach a satisfactory description of such an idea as 'right'. They examine numerous accounts that have been given by different thinkers at different times, and in considering these accounts they work methodically towards a deeper understanding of the idea. The branch of philosophy that deals with ideas such as 'right', 'good', 'duty' is called Moral Philosophy or Ethics, from the Greek word meaning moral.

Philosophers, in a similar way, inquire carefully into the meaning of ideas that are used, often carelessly, in political discussions. Examples of such ideas are democracy, the State, liberty, and 'rights' (in the sense of the right to property, or the right to free speech). This branch of philosophy is known as Political Theory.

In all these inquiries into the meaning of ideas there is an important point that must be made quite clear. When philosophers consider ideas—such as right, good, liberty, and so on—they are not trying to advise people what they ought to do, or how they can become better persons, or what political party they should vote for. Advice of this kind must be sought for from persons with practical experience of life. Of course a philosopher may also have considerable experience, and be able to give good advice about practical problems. But when he is making philosophical inquiries into the meaning of ideas such as goodness or duty, he is trying only to understand and truly describe these ideas: his aim is to think about them clearly, not to make himself or others better men. Nevertheless the knowledge that he arrives at about the ideas that are used in our ordinary beliefs is bound to affect practical life. When we have made a critical inquiry into our beliefs, we are less likely to be led away by false theories, and we shall have a deeper understanding of the principles that should guide our actions.

Let us glance at a quite different field of philosophy. Among the most obvious of our everyday beliefs are beliefs about the world of things that we see around us—furniture, houses, trees, clouds. We believe that the chairs and table, the curtains, and the carpet in our room, are really there before us just as we see them, and we believe that another person coming into the room sees the same things as we do. Few of us ever dream of questioning these beliefs until we read a book on philosophy. Philosophers show that these common-sense beliefs about the world of things that surrounds us are not as obvious or certain as they seem. A careful reading of any good introduction to philosophy, such as Bertrand Russell's *Problems of Philosophy*, will make clear what difficulties there are. The critical inquiry into common-sense beliefs about the world that we see and hear and touch, found in such books, shows that it is extremely difficult to give good reasons for beliefs that we usually suppose to be beyond dispute. And they show, too, that the world that appears to us obvious may, in reality, be very strange. Philosophy keeps alive the sense of wonder.

The critical methods of philosophy are applied to many other fields, for example to science, to art, and to religion. Science takes many ideas for granted in order to carry on its work. It takes for granted, for example, the idea of cause. Philosophers try to make as clear as possible what we mean when we speak of one thing being the cause of another thing. They are not trying to find out what particular cause produces a particular effect, such as what causes the rise of mercury in a thermometer: that is a question for

science. The questions the philosophers ask are, what is cause and what are the reasons for believing in it? These are wider questions than those with which science deals. The philosophical questions about science start farther back, in order to try to understand ideas that science uses. There are many other very general ideas besides the idea of cause, such as the ideas of time, space, and law. Since the time of LOCKE (q.v. Vol. V), whose *Essay on Human Understanding* appeared in 1690, philosophers have considered in great detail the nature of knowledge and what kind of subjects it is fitted to understand. This part of philosophy is called Theory of Knowledge. Another study that is connected with the theory of knowledge, and indeed with all parts of philosophy, is the science of Logic, which discusses the ways of correct reasoning. Many other subjects are examined by philosophers. They ask what the nature of the mind is, and how it is related to the body. They inquire into the meaning of beauty. They consider the kind of knowledge that is contained in the study of history.

This, then, is one side of the work of philosophy —a cool and thorough inquiry into the convictions and beliefs that we usually accept without question, in order to reach a clearer and more precise understanding of the meaning of these beliefs and of our reasons for holding them. This is obviously an important task: it helps to free ideas from vagueness and confusion, and brings a deeper understanding of the universe.

There is another great task that is undertaken by philosophy. Men have a profound impulse to connect the different sides of their experience together, to see the world as a whole. Human beings have many different interests. They are concerned with their families and friends, and with their daily work; they are interested in art and literature and history; they seek truth in science, and they respond to the call of religion. Men who think seriously about life feel a desire to see the relation between all these different interests. They desire to reach a coherent and unified way of looking at experience; they want to know whether the universe has a plan and, if so, what it is. Some philosophers try to meet these desires. They try to show how the material, the moral, and the spiritual aspects of the universe are systematically related to one another. The great constructive philosophers describe what each of the main interests, science, art, religion, and others, contribute to our knowledge of the system of reality. In making these very wide inquiries these philosophers show how methods and ideas that are useful in special fields cannot be applied to other fields or to the universe as a whole without confusion. Some scientists, for example, have thought that science was the only kind of truth, and they have tried to interpret the moral and religious sides of the universe in the same way as they describe the material sides.

In the history of philosophy there have been many attempts to carry out this great task of surveying the plan of the universe in its varied aspects. The names of the philosophers AQUINAS (1225–74), SPINOZA(1632–77), KANT(1724–1804), and HEGEL (1770–1831) (qq.v. Vol. V) may be mentioned. We may add the names of two Englishmen of our own time, S. Alexander and A. N. Whitehead. The accounts that all these philosophers give of the scheme of things differ markedly from one another; but no one can study these great structures of thought without gaining deeper insight into the wonderful complexity and grandeur of the universe. This aspect of the work of philosophy is often called Metaphysics or Constructive Metaphysics. The Greek word *meta* means 'after', and the term metaphysics is derived from the fact that Aristotle's work on philosophy was arranged by early editors to follow his lectures on physics.

Anyone who wishes to pursue philosophy should begin on those sides in which he is interested. It is necessary when studying philosophy to read slowly and critically, taking instances of one's own to illustrate the arguments. It is no use disguising the fact that philosophy calls for considerable mental effort. But the effort is supremely worth making.

The individual contributions of the great philosophers are described in the biographies of these men in Vol. V. To those already mentioned we might add ST. AUGUSTINE, HUME, and KARL MARX (qq.v. Vol. V).

PHOENICIAN CIVILIZATION.

This civilization developed in the narrow strip of coast along the eastern shore of the Mediterranean, from Mt. Carmel northwards as far as the mouth of the Orontes. There was never a kingdom of Phoenicia. The name Phoenicia is a Greek word meaning 'red Syrians', probably used by the Greeks to distinguish these people from the

GOLD DISH FROM RAS-SHAMRA (UGARIT)
First half of the 14th century B.C. *Editions 'Tel'*

Hittites, whom they called 'white Syrians'. This strip of coast contained a number of ancient and important city-states, such as Tyre, Sidon, Byblos (Gebal), and the recently discovered Ugarit (Ras-Shamra). These cities were prosperous trading centres, and as early as the 12th century B.C. their inhabitants had founded colonies on the north coast of Africa, the most famous of which was the Tyrian colony of Carthage.

The people of these cities spoke a SEMITIC LANGUAGE (q.v. Vol. IV), closely resembling Hebrew; but the populations of the sea-coast were by no means all Semites, since many other peoples had settled along the coast at various periods. Our knowledge of Phoenician civilization was, until recently, mainly drawn from north-Semitic inscriptions, from the Old Testament (where there is a vivid description of the wealth and glory of Tyre), and from the Greek writers, such as Herodotus, and Philo of Byblos. But the discovery of the Tell el-Amarna Letters in Egypt in 1887 threw much new light on the history and politics of the cities of Phoenicia in the 14th century B.C., and the excavation of the site of Ugarit by French archaeologists, which began in 1929 and is still proceeding, has revealed a great deal about the way of life of a people living in the extreme north of the Phoenician part of Syria.

The people of the city-states of Phoenicia were seafarers, and were much influenced by their

BAAL

Bronze figure from Ras-Shamra (Ugarit), 14th century B.C. *Editions 'Tel'*

the alphabetic principle but, owing to their intense conservatism, had not made use of it; but in Phoenicia two experiments in alphabetic writing were made, possibly about the same time, one of which survived to become the parent of all the Western alphabets. In the excavations at Ugarit there were discovered a large number of tablets written in a different kind of writing from any found before. The writing made use of twenty-nine signs, and therefore was obviously alphabetic; and the language proved to be a Semitic dialect, not unlike Hebrew. However, when Ugarit fell in the 13th century, this form of alphabetic writing seems to have come to an end. The second alphabetic experiment, probably almost as early as the Ugarit alphabet, is generally known as the Phoenician script. An example of this script—the famous Moabite Stone, containing an inscription of a king of Moab in the 9th century B.C.—had long been known to scholars. But when Byblos was excavated in 1924, an inscription was found in the tomb of an early king of Byblos belonging to the 13th century B.C., which differed very little from the writing on the Moabite Stone. Therefore it seems that alphabetic writing, one of the most important of all human inventions, may be credited to one of the vigorous merchant-cities of the Phoenician coast. It was carried by the Phoenician traders to Greece, and thus became the ancestor of all the Western alphabets.

The excavations at Ugarit showed that there existed in that city, in about the 15th century B.C., an elaborate religious organization in which the king played a central part, as in Egypt and Mesopotamia. There were temples, an organized priesthood, sacrifices, great seasonal rituals connected with harvest and vintage, and an extensive mythology. The names of some of the gods occur in the Old Testament: there is the high god, El; his wife, Asherat-yam (that is, Asherat-of-the-sea); his son, Baal, whose sacred animal is the bull. Baal was worshipped also at Tyre under the name Hadad, and in Syria. There are a number of lesser gods, among whom is the craftsman god Hiyan, a parallel to the Greek Hephaestus and the Roman Vulcan. Among the myths recorded is that of the conflict between two lesser gods, Aliyan and Mot, which is not unlike the Egyptian myth of Osiris and Seth. Aliyan is slain, descends into the underworld, and returns in the spring. This is the familiar

contacts with the other Mediterranean countries. Egyptian temples and inscriptions, as well as many objects of Egyptian workmanship, have been found in cities like Byblos and Ugarit. In Ugarit there was a Mycenaean quarter containing houses and tombs of Mycenaean architecture, and among the objects found were some magnificent silver bowls of Aegean workmanship, embossed with spirited hunting-scenes in the Cretan style. The trade of Tyre, Sidon, and Arvad was mainly with Egypt and the Aegean; but Ugarit, owing to its special position, was not only a centre of the Mediterranean trade, but was the meeting-place of important trade-routes from Asia Minor, Cappadocia, Assyria, and northern Syria. Until its destruction by the Sea-peoples in the 13th century B.C., it was probably one of the most important and prosperous cities of Phoenicia.

The Phoenicians were the first people to make use of an alphabetic mode of writing instead of the cumbrous systems of writing used in Egypt and Mesopotamia (*see* WRITING, HISTORY OF, Vol. IV). The early Egyptians had discovered

pattern of the dying and rising god, so widespread in the ancient Near East. Another of the myths tells of the fight between Baal and the dragon, who has the same name as the mythical Hebrew sea-monster, Leviathan.

We have already said that the civilization of the Phoenician cities was based on sea-going trade. In the vivid description of the wealth of Tyre in the Old Testament (Ezekiel, cc. 26–8), written about the time of Nebuchadnezzar's siege of Tyre, which lasted for thirteen years, 585–572 B.C., there is a catalogue of the places with which Tyre traded, and of the varied merchandise in which she trafficked. The account gives the sources of her shipbuilding materials: fir trees for the deck-planks from the Amanus, cedars for the masts from Lebanon, and oak for the oars from Bashan. Linen for the sails came from Egypt, while her seamen were drawn from many sources. She is represented as trading with Tarshish in Spain, with the Ionians of Asia Minor, with Armenia and the Caucasus, with Arabia, with the Red Sea ports and India. The goods in which she trafficked were precious metals and precious stones, purple embroidered woven stuffs, wheat, spices, wine, wool from Miletus, and iron from Asia Minor. No doubt she largely imported raw materials and exported finished articles. It is a picture of great wealth and prosperity—a prosperity shared by the other cities of the Phoenician coast as well as Tyre.

During the early period of Phoenician history the government of each city-state was in the hands of a king and council of nobles. Ezekiel's description of the king of Tyre shows that the king was regarded as a divine person, perhaps as the result of Egyptian influence. But later on, at the time of the Punic wars, we know that Carthage was governed, not by a king, but by an oligarchy, whose members were called *suffetes*—a Semitic word meaning 'judges'.

The Phoenicians were the most daring sailors and explorers of the ancient world. They were the first to venture beyond the Pillars of Hercules (Straits of Gibraltar) in search of precious metals, and they have left traces of their presence on the west coast of Brittany and the Cornish coast (where Semitic place-names still survive), and they may even have reached Ireland.

See also ANCIENT CIVILIZATIONS.

PHOENIX. The story of this mythological creature, which was said to be born from the ashes of its parent, arose in Egypt, and grew as details were added from time to time throughout the centuries. As the phoenix provided an illustration for sermons and was popular with poets, its fame has lived on until the present day. The Greek historian Herodotus who visited Egypt about 459 B.C., gives the earliest account of it. He confesses that he never saw one and did not believe the story; but refers to pictures of the phoenix in which it was like an eagle, but with red and gold plumage. He said that, according to the Egyptians, it appeared out of Arabia once in every 500 years, carrying the dead body of the father-bird in a ball of myrrh to the temple of the Sun. Actually it was to an egret or heron that the Egyptians gave the titles 'the soul of the sun' and 'the heart of the renewed sun'; so either Herodotus or his informants seem to have been mistaken or to have strayed away from the original idea. The egret has beautiful glistening white plumes radiating from its breast, which may have suggested the rays of the sun, and the purple heron's plumage is tinged like sunset clouds. One or other of these birds, being connected with the worship of the sun which 'dies' at sunset and rises again next day, may have

PHOENIX
Engraving from Arnold Freitag, *Mythologia Ethica*, 1579

given rise to the fable of the phoenix. The story was retold in an old collection of animal stories, called the *Physiologus*. According to this book, the phoenix lives on air for 500 years, and then, carrying spices, flies to the temple of the sun and is burnt to death on the altar. A tiny worm appears in the ashes, and by the next day a young phoenix has grown up; by the day after that it is fully fledged, salutes the priest and flies away. Another version records how the bird makes a nest of spices, which is set on fire by the sun's heat. The phoenix dies, fanning the flames with its own wings. Because of these stories the phoenix became a symbol of rebirth to new life, and was regarded as the king of birds. It was believed that there was never more than one phoenix alive in the world, and it was said to be surpassingly beautiful.

There is a Chinese mythological bird, which is commonly known as the Chinese phoenix, but should be called the 'love pheasant'. It is a very frequent emblem in Chinese art. According to Chinese ideas, the love pheasant appears now and then in the course of centuries to indicate that a happy state of affairs will presently occur. The descriptions and pictures suggest that, like the DRAGON (q.v.), it grew up in people's minds by a process of adding together the characteristics of a variety of different creatures.

See also FABULOUS CREATURES; FOLK-LORE.

PILGRIMAGES. Anyone who has read Chaucer's *Canterbury Tales* will know about the journey of a group of people to Canterbury to visit the tomb of Thomas à Becket. But the idea of such journeys is much older than Christianity, and occurs all over the world The actual word 'pilgrim' comes from the Latin *peregrinus*, which means 'a stranger' or 'wanderer'. We may not think of ordinary churchgoing as a pilgrimage: in any case it is usually a very short one. But it certainly does mean breaking off one's ordinary occupation and leaving one's home to go, perhaps as a family or with a friend, to a place called 'holy'—that is set apart—in order to make contact in it with what is sacred and to feel in touch with the Power of the Universe, by whatever name we may call that Power. Another common kind of pilgrimage is that of people to cemeteries where their kinsfolk are buried. This may seem a purely human affair, but even there the idea of the sacred enters in. The cemetery is 'consecrated ground'—the old Anglo-Saxons called the churchyard 'God's acre'.

A pilgrimage, then, is a movement of people to a sacred spot where they are able to make at least temporary contact with the supernatural world. People expect to benefit by making a pilgrimage—whether bodily, by cure of sickness, or spiritually, by forgiveness of sins, or by inspiration from seeing or touching some object which

recalls to them a wonderful work of God. Not unnaturally pilgrimages came to be associated with holy days, which were holidays when all ordinary work stopped. Social life came to centre round pilgrimages to distant holy places. There is a real gain, a true refreshment in the interruption of ordinary life by such a break, in which perhaps one comes to live in fellowship with other folk who are bent on a journey to the same spot. Of course some pilgrimages are made in solitude.

Sometimes the holy place is made by nature, such as the great RIVER GANGES in India, or MOUNT FUJI YAMA (qq.v. Vol. III) in Japan, or the Mount of Transfiguration in the New Testament. Sometimes, however, it is connected with a great historical event, or a human life in which the working of the Deity seems visible—such, for example, as the group of places in India associated with the earthly life of the good king Rama, who is believed to have been an incarnation of the god Vishnu; or, in Arabia, the two cities of Mecca and Medina, so closely linked with the deeds of the great religious leader Mohammed; or, in China, one of the four specially sacred shrines connected with Buddhist saints; and for Christians, the Holy Land of Palestine with Jerusalem as its centre; or, in England, the place where some famous Christian lived and died or was martyred. Jews at the time of Christ were expected to make a journey to Jerusalem once a year, even if they lived outside Palestine: Jerusalem is still their Holy City.

Christian pilgrimages to the Holy Sepulchre began in the 3rd or 4th century; and Helena, the mother of the Emperor Constantine, was one of the first to make the pilgrimage. The Romans had built a pagan temple over the Holy Sepulchre; but Constantine had this removed and erected a church in its place. We learn a great deal about these early pilgrimages from a diary kept by a lady from southern Gaul, called Etheria, who went to Palestine somewhere about A.D. 534 and who visited, besides Jerusalem, Sinai, Horeb (the burial-place of Job), and the brook Cherith (the place where Elijah was fed by ravens). Later on, the Knights of St. John of Jerusalem organized pilgrimages to the Holy Land, owning the ships in which the pilgrims travelled from Venice, and providing hostels for them (*see* KNIGHTS, ORDERS OF).

But not every one could afford to visit the Holy Land, and after its capture by the Turks, it was for a time quite cut off from the West,

PILGRIMS AT LOURDES. *Planet News*

until the crusaders restored communication (*see* CRUSADES). Places in the West, where famous Christians were buried, also became places of pilgrimage—the most important being Rome, where the tombs of the Apostles, Peter and Paul, were reputed to be. Throughout the Middle Ages thousands of pilgrims visited Rome every year, not only to visit the tombs of the Apostles, but to be blessed by the Pope and to obtain pardon for sins.

The body of the Apostle St. James was believed to have been buried at a town in Spain, Compostella (Sant Jago Apostola), and his shrine became even more popular than Rome for English pilgrims, who used to sail thither from Winchelsea in Sussex. Frenchmen favoured the shrine of St. Martin at Tours. There were other shrines all over Europe and more than sixty in England alone, visited by people who could not afford long journeys. The shrine of St. Thomas of Canterbury was visited by foreigners as well as by English—the road from Southampton to Canterbury is still called the Pilgrims' Way. Other roads called Pilgrims' Way in other parts of England showed the routes to other shrines—to Glastonbury in Somerset, for example, and Walsingham in Norfolk. Maps were drawn specially to show the pilgrims' routes, and guidebooks written telling pilgrims what they must do, and what lesser shrines to visit on their way. Not

everyone went willingly: some were ordered to do so as reparation for an offence. Sometimes they were ordered to walk barefoot and be scourged or wear chains. Even kings might be sent in this manner. Henry II for example went to Canterbury, and Henry VIII, before his break with the Pope, went to Walsingham. But it was often possible to pay a money fine instead of making the actual journey.

Pilgrimages played a very important part in European medieval life. People from all parts travelled great distances together. Many spoke Latin, and this common language and their common purpose gave them a sense of the fellowship of all Christian people, which was stronger than any feeling of separate nationality. Chaucer expresses something of this in his *Canterbury Tales*. It is true that his pilgrims are all English; but though they are drawn from almost every walk of life, they live together and travel as equals. Each one is called upon to tell his or her story to enliven the journey, and the variety and jollity of the stories show clearly that, besides the religious purpose of the pilgrimage, it was considered a delightful holiday—indeed to some of Chaucer's characters this was plainly the more important aspect.

Pilgrimages were, incidentally, a means of spreading new ideas and of fostering trade. Travellers would bring back home with them books and works of art, such as paintings, ivory carvings, and silk hangings, and from these, native authors and artists would get new inspiration.

Pilgrims were supposed to wear grey cowls down to their ankles and broad-brimmed hats, and only to carry a staff, a sack for money, and a gourd for water. (Chaucer's pilgrims did not dress in this way, if we may believe his description.) They organized themselves under a master who made all arrangements. Coming home, they wore an emblem to show which shrine they had visited. They lodged in hospices built specially for them along the route. These could charge no fees, but the rich pilgrims made gifts to them.

The travellers also gave large sums of money to the shrines and churches which, in consequence, became very rich. The shrines themselves were decorated with gold and jewels, sculpture and paintings, and the churches often had to be enlarged to make room for the procession of visitors round the shrine. At Canterbury

THE EARL OF WARWICK STARTING ON A PILGRIMAGE
15th-century drawing (MS. Cotton Julius E. iv. 205)
British Mus.

the place where the choir had to be widened for this purpose can clearly be seen. The monks and priests realized how profitable it was to possess a shrine, and in some cases they bought, or even forcibly removed, relics from another place— either the bones of a saint or a reputed piece of the Cross from the Holy Land—and set it up in their Church, claiming that it had miraculous powers.

The English shrines were destroyed at the time of the Reformation, and pilgrimages were no longer allowed. They have, however, revived somewhat in recent years, and people once again go to such places as Lindisfarne, the spiritual home of St. Cuthbert, to St. Albans, to Edward the Confessor's chapel at Westminster Abbey, and in recent times to Little Gidding in Hunts., the former home of the saintly Nicholas Ferrar, who lived in the reign of Charles I, and built there a specially beautiful little church for his household to worship in.

For Roman Catholics Rome remained the chief place of pilgrimage until the 19th century, though a good many went to Chartres, to the shrine of the 'black Virgin'. Since 1850 one or two new places have become very popular, especially Lourdes on the French slope of the Pyrenees, where a little girl is said to have had visions of the Virgin. It is now visited every year by thousands of invalids, because of the reputed healing quality of a spring which flows from the ground close to the grotto where the visions were seen.

PILGRIM FATHERS, *see* CONGREGATIONALIST.

PLUTO, *see* GODS OF GREECE AND ROME (Hades).

POLES. Several Slav races first emerged into the light of history between A.D. 800 and 1000, and settled in central Europe. The Poles were one of these. The earliest Polish State, which came into being about A.D. 960, stretched from the Vistula to the Oder. Its capital was at Gniezno, near Poznan, in the extreme west, and the Archbishop of Gniezno is still regarded as the Primate of Poland. At the beginning of the 12th century Poland's western frontier lay even farther west than the line made after the Second World War in April 1946.

Though all the western Slavs, including the Poles, were frequently fighting the Germans to resist their eastward expansion, Christianity came to them through German bishops. The Poles became Christians about A.D. 970 under their first historic king, who married a Christian Czech princess. In spite of their fear of German aggression, the Polish kings remained faithful to the Roman Church, and all through its history of nearly a thousand years, until recent times, Poland has been in sympathy with the ideas and ways of life of western Europe.

Late in the 11th century Cracow became the royal capital. During the second half of the 12th century and the 13th century Poland was divided and weak; but from that date onward it grew steadily in extent and wealth. In 1386 the Queen of Poland married Ladislas Jagiello, the Grand Duke of Lithuania, who, with his whole people, became Christian. Lithuania

A POLISH VILLAGE. *Paul Popper*

was at this time a vigorous militarist state which had conquered several of the larger but weaker eastern Slav states. The union of Lithuania and Poland was a strong protection against the danger of being overwhelmed by the advance of German rule along the Baltic coast. Under the Jagiellonian kings (1386–1572), some of whom were outstanding statesmen, Poland, at the height of her power and prosperity, shared in the great intellectual movement of the RENAISSANCE (q.v.). Unfortunately, the Jagiellonian kings were followed by a weak and inferior ruler at a time when Russia and Prussia were rapidly gaining strength, and Poland became even further weakened by wars with Sweden. In spite of this, it was a Polish army, under King John Sobieski in 1683, which triumphantly came to the rescue of Vienna, the capital of Austria, and thereby saved south-central Europe from being overrun by the Turks.

In 1772, when the First Partition of Poland took place, and Russia, Prussia, and Austria seized vast tracts of her territory, Poland had hardly any effective government at all. This was the lowest point in her history. By two further partitions, in 1793 and 1795, her three great neighbours put an end for the time being to Poland's independent existence. From 1795 to 1918 Polish history is confined to the efforts of the Polish people to secure, sometimes by armed revolt and sometimes by collaboration, conditions of existence which would make it possible for them to preserve their national individuality. The end of the First World War finally saw the re-creation of an independent Polish State. It is probable that modern Poland will cover much the same area as it did in the first centuries of its existence—namely, the lands drained by the Oder and the Vistula.

In no race is the spirit of national solidarity stronger than among the Poles. All the efforts of their oppressors to destroy their national individuality only resulted in uniting them far more than before. Their national consciousness became wider and deeper until, by 1900, it had permeated all classes of the population and all districts inhabited by Poles, except Silesia and Mazuria (East Prussia). The possession of a common religion and of a language with hardly any dialect differences no doubt contributed to the growth of national solidarity. All Poles feel that their membership of the Roman Catholic Church distinguishes them from Protestant Germans and Orthodox Russians. Any Pole from Wilno in the far north-east feels at one with any Pole from Cracow, because both of them speak the same language, no matter what their social class. Even in Silesia, which Poland lost in the 14th century and only partially recovered in 1921, the vast majority of the working-class population has always spoken Polish at home, even if forced to learn German at school and to speak it with German foremen in mines and factories. The ruined castles, which still exist in many places in Silesia, have always been called, even by the Germans, 'Piast castles', after the Polish dynasty of the early Middle Ages, under whom they were originally erected.

Poland is predominantly an agricultural country: even the working classes of the towns are only separated from the peasantry by one or two generations. Indeed, during the economic crisis of the early thirties, many of the factory workers, who lost their employment, found refuge with farmer relations and thus survived the bad years without great hardship. Even to this day it would hardly be an exaggeration to say that every Pole, whether he works with his hands or with his brain, looks forward to the day when he will settle in the country on a piece of land of his own. In Poland everything which has to do with the land is respected. A great Polish poet, Wyspianski, in his most famous play, *The Wedding*, first acted in 1901, has extolled the dignity of the farmer's life in verses of extraordinary fire. PADEREWSKI (q.v. Vol. V), the great Polish musician and Prime Minister, had meant to do the same in music had he not died suddenly. This universal love of the country and of country life has helped to strengthen the spirit of national solidarity, and has also fostered the individualism which is the most marked and perhaps the most valuable feature of the Polish character. All attempts to suppress and bully them in the past have proved useless. They are not militarists, like the Germans; but none the less they are proud to serve in their country's army. That they make first-class soldiers is well known to all who have fought by their side in the Second World War. Our knowledge of the Poles gained during the Second World War has shown us that they are in some ways very like the English, and that the things which they cherish and for which

they are ready, if necessary, to die, are held in equal honour by ourselves—family life and ties, love of country and religion. In spite of their tendency after the Second World War to turn towards the East rather than the West, the Poles follow the same code as the Western world has followed for more than a thousand years.

See also Vol. III: POLAND; Vol. IV: RUSSIAN LANGUAGES.

POLYNESIANS (the people of the many islands).

These are the people of the eastern Pacific islands within a triangle bounded by Hawaii in the north, New Zealand in the south, and Easter Island in the east (*see* PACIFIC ISLANDERS, Map). They are a tall, brown-skinned race of seamen, who might be called the Vikings of the Pacific. At some unknown date, perhaps about the beginning of the Christian era, they sailed into the Pacific in long out-rigger canoes, generally one canoe at a time, from their forgotten homeland known as 'Hawaiiki'. Some authorities think they came from India—indeed traces of ancient Polynesian writing found in Easter Island, but at present undeciphered, are thought by some experts to be connected with northern India.

What is known of their history before the arrival of the Europeans towards the end of the 18th century has been learnt from the Polynesian chiefs. Family pride directed that the young members should learn by heart their family tree, even as far back as twenty generations or more, and also the principal exploits of their more important ancestors. From these records in the memories of the chiefs we learn of the discovery of many islands, of romantic voyages over long distances in search of wives or to wreak vengeance on enemies. One New Zealand legend of the MAORIS (q.v.) suggests that they went as far south as the Antarctic ice, and there is also a possibility

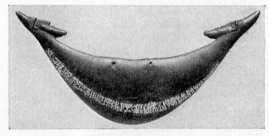

WOODEN NECK ORNAMENT FROM EASTER ISLAND
The little figures carved round the edge are in the Easter Island script. It is not proper writing, for each symbol represents an idea, not a sound. Nobody can read them to-day. *British Mus.*

that they reached the west coast of South America. It is indeed true that they cultivated the sweet potato, a plant which originated in America.

When the Europeans arrived, the Polynesians had not discovered metals: they still depended on stone tools for cutting down trees, making planks, and hollowing out canoes, and on sharks' teeth for finer carving. When the early explorers showed them iron, they were quick to see its value, even before they understood its nature. They were known to steal ships from the Europeans for the sake of the nails in them; but then they planted the nails in the ground hoping to grow more nails. Their principal weapons of war were clubs and spears. They used slings and sling-stones; but, though they possessed bows and arrows, they only used them for sport.

The Polynesians, like another Pacific people, the MICRONESIANS (q.v.), depended for their food largely on a combination of gardening and fishing. They grew yams, taro, and sweet potatoes, and also bread-fruit, coco-nuts, and bananas. They also grew pepper root from which they made a drink called *Kava* which, especially in western Polynesia, was drunk with great ceremony often accompanied with an exchange of gifts. CANNIBALISM (q.v.) was not unknown, especially in the Marquesas Islands, where there was continual fighting for the possession of the narrow valleys in these rocky islands.

Their houses varied a good deal from island to island. They were sometimes square and sometimes round, but nearly always were supported on stout poles with matting for walls and a palm-leaf thatched roof. In New Zealand, where timber was plentiful and the climate colder, the greater part of the house was built of elaborately carved planking, and the eaves came down almost to the ground. Their clothing was mostly of bark cloth made from the inner bark of a special tree, beaten out and painted with various designs. For important occasions the chiefs of Hawaii wore the most gorgeous cloaks of red and yellow birds' feathers sown on to a coco-nut-fibre net foundation. In New Zealand the chiefs wore cloaks of flax made by a sort of basketwork. The Polynesians, unlike the Micronesians, had not learnt the art of weaving. But they had a rich sense of art. As well as the finely painted and printed designs on the bark cloth, their wood carving was developed and elaborate. They made strange images to represent their

WOODEN FIGURE OF THE HAWAIIAN GOD KUKAILIMUKU
Some people have seen a resemblance to classical antiquity, but the crested helmet is probably of native origin.
British Mus.

gods. Stone carvings were to be found in many islands, but most commonly in Easter Island, where large ancestral figures were carved out of the volcanic stone with stone chisels. In New Zealand, particularly, the pillars and lintels of their houses, as well as the prows and sterns of their canoes, were beautifully carved.

The priests were a powerful body, exercising their influence by imposing TABOOS (q.v.). The Polynesians worshipped many chief or high gods, among whom were Tane, a creator god, Tangaroa, the god of fishing, and Oro, the god of war. As well, they worshipped many lesser deities—spirits of natural forces, such as Pele, the goddess of fire (the volcano goddess in Hawaii), and spirits of trees and other natural objects, and also family gods. Sacrifices, including human sacrifice, were made to these gods.

The people of the Polynesian islands are, and always have been, a cheerful, friendly people, fond of music, singing, dancing, and athletic pursuits. They possessed flutes, blown with the nose instead of the mouth, wooden gongs and bamboo cylinders with which they beat time on the ground. Among their games and sports was surf-riding on flat boards, and they were excellent swimmers.

With the coming of the Europeans their numbers declined sharply; but now, especially in New Zealand, they appear to be increasing again. They are all now nominally Christians and in most places wear European clothes. In Hawaii they are intermarrying with Europeans and other Pacific peoples so much that soon no pure-blooded Hawaiians will remain. The only independent native kingdom now surviving in the Pacific is the kingdom of Tonga, a British Protectorate. The kingdoms of Hawaii and Tahiti belong respectively to the U.S.A. and France.

See also MAORIS; Vol. IV: OCEANIC LANGUAGE.

POLYTHEISM, see GOD, Section (a).

POPE, see ROMAN CATHOLIC CHURCH.

POPULATION. It is estimated that there are about 2,000 million people in the world. If they were all spread out evenly over the earth's land surface, the density of population would be fifteen people to the square mile; but, in fact, there are open spaces where a man can travel 100 miles and not meet a soul, whilst in crowded cities he can live in a block of flats on an acre of land, and know that there are several hundred people living there besides himself.

Most of the blank spaces shown on the map are desert lands, where the climate is either too hot or too cold. Other scantily peopled areas include the high mountain ranges where rugged relief and inaccessibility do not favour settlement, the northern coniferous forests, difficult to reach and with a harsh climate and poor soil, the temperate grasslands with their problems of distance and communication, and the impenetrable forests of the tropics.

Because of these unfavourable regions, more than one-half of the world's population lives on one-thirtieth of the earth's surface, concentrated in three great areas—western Europe, eastern U.S.A., and the Asiatic countries of India and China.

In western Europe and eastern U.S.A. the climate is temperate, the soils are varied and suitable for growing a wide range of crops, power resources of coal, oil, and electricity are available, as well as the mineral wealth essential for modern industry, and transport by road, rail, river, and canal is comparatively easy. Because of these advantages, 520 million people live in western and central Europe and 100 million in eastern U.S.A. In some parts the density of population is very great and leads to overcrowding in large cities.

In INDIA and CHINA the population is concentrated in the river basins, where the astonishing fertility of the soil can support 350 million people in India and 500 million in China. In parts of the GANGES valley (qq.v. Vol. III) the density of population is 1,000 to the square mile; but it must be remembered that the standard of living of the people is very low compared with that of Europeans.

There are two other areas in the world where the population is dense, and they are the lands round the Mediterranean Sea and south-eastern Asia. The Mediterranean lands were the cradle of Western civilization, and had many advantages for the settlement of early man. They have little coal or iron on which modern industry depends, and so to-day are still mainly countries of farmers and shepherds. The MALAY Peninsula and the islands of south-east Asia (see EAST INDIES, Vol. III) have their hot, wet climate modified by the sea and by highlands, so that Java, the richest region of them all, has an average density of 700 people to the square mile.

With this concentration of population in a few regions of the world, there is over-population in certain countries. A country is said to be overpopulated when it can no longer support its people at a reasonable standard of living. A densely peopled country can try to prevent this either by MIGRATION (q.v.), or by industrialization. In the 19th century large numbers of British and other European people migrated to North America and the Southern hemisphere. To-day the over-populated countries are India and China, and numbers of Indians have settled in East and South Africa, whilst Chinese settlers have migrated to Malaya, the Pacific Islands, and South America. That is one reason why the development of industry is advocated in India and China, so that the surplus population may be absorbed.

When the pressure of population increases in the favourable areas of the world, the less favourable areas are brought under cultivation.

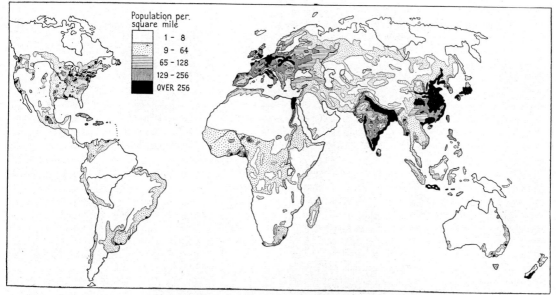

Population per square mile

	1 - 8
	9 - 64
	65 - 128
	129 - 256
	OVER 256

DISTRIBUTION OF POPULATION THROUGHOUT THE WORLD

Owing to the development of scientific knowledge, crops are now grown beyond the arctic circle in Siberia and North America; advances in medical knowledge have made life in the tropics easier; irrigation and dry-farming methods have brought arid lands under the plough; whilst the use of hydro-electric power has led to the building of factories in mountainous regions.

Only two-thirds of the countries of the world regularly take a census of their peoples—so complete statistics are not available; but it is thought probable that the world could, with our present knowledge and resources, support a population of between 3,000 and 7,000 millions. There seems no danger of the world as a whole becoming over-populated, for, although in India and China the population is increasing, this is not true of western Europe or of eastern U.S.A.

An increasing population may be due to more births or fewer deaths or to migration. In the 19th century, when Britain's population grew from 12¾ millions in 1811 to 40½ millions in 1911, the increase was due, not so much to an increase in the birth-rate, as to a decrease in the death-rate. Owing to increased medical knowledge and better sanitation, the average span of a man's life increased from forty years in the 18th century to fifty years in the 19th century and to sixty years in the 20th century.

To-day in Britain the death-rate has been brought to a low level, but the birth-rate has fallen slightly, as it has in the rest of Europe, North America, and the Dominions. An increase or decline in the birth-rate is important because, not only does it affect the prestige of a country, where numbers mean political and military power, but it also has an effect on the country's internal life and economy.

In India and China the death-rate has yet to be reduced to the level of the West, and this should result in an increase of the population. But on the other hand, it is now realized that as the standard of living improves, people, both for biological as well as psychological reasons, tend to have fewer children. So, as the masses of Indian and Chinese peasant peoples get raised above a semi-starvation level, it is probable that, in the long run, their birth-rate as well as their death-rate will decrease.

PORTUGUESE. The Iberian Peninsula is the only country in Europe where the present population belongs basically and almost entirely to the Mediterranean race. The Portuguese are more Mediterranean than the SPANIARDS (q.v.), as the high mountainous borderland between Spain and Portugal prevented their being invaded, like Spain, by the Goths, Vandals, and Moors. This very isolation has made them, however, proud and conservative, and much of the old way of life has remained alongside modern innovations,

PORTUGUESE WOMEN AT COIMBRA. *Paul Popper*

The Portuguese have always been great sailors and, in the days of exploration in the 15th and 16th centuries, the Portuguese explorers led the way. PRINCE HENRY THE NAVIGATOR, BARTHOLOMEW DIAZ, VASCO DA GAMA (the first man to sail round South Africa) (qq.v. Vol. V), Americo Vespucci (who gave his name to America) and many others, were sent out by the King of Portugal to find new trade routes and fly the Portuguese flag in new countries. Brazil was first colonized by Portuguese, and it is now a Portuguese-speaking country (*see* BRAZILIANS).

There are just over seven million Portuguese in Portugal, almost all being slender and short, with wavy hair and brown eyes. About three-fifths of them are engaged in agriculture, cultivating especially vineyards, orange groves, fields of wheat and maize, and the cork-producing evergreen oaks. Many more live north of the river Tagus than south of it, since the northern provinces are broken up into small holdings, while in the south there are larger estates. The

Portuguese are also great fishermen, and the innumerable fishing villages along the coast of Portugal are scenes of very busy and colourful life.

The conservative individuality of the Portuguese is expressed in many ways. In the province of Alemtejo in the south-east many farmers still wear cow-boy trousers with sheepskin chaps (or overalls), and shepherds wear brown fleeces and carry blue umbrellas; while in the Douro valley raincoats and leggings of reeds are worn. Their pottery expresses their individuality too. Estremoz produces red and brown pottery; the region of Estremadure produces green and brown and buff; while in Tras os Montes and Beira Alta, farther north, the pottery is black; and in the west, from Coimbra to Caldas da Ramha, there is cream-glazed work with floral designs.

The Portuguese are a colourful cheerful people, delighting in pilgrimages to Catholic shrines (*romarias*), in *festas* and market days. In the town wine is sometimes carried in motor-lorries, but is just as likely to be carried in carts drawn by long-horned oxen with elaborately carved and painted yokes. The fishermen of the coast use double-ended boats, like Arab dhows, with bright coloured lateen sails. Bull-fighting is a national sport, but differs from Spanish bull-fighting in that the bull's horns are sheathed.

See also Vol. III: PORTUGAL; Vol. IV: FRENCH AND ROMANCE LANGUAGES.

PRAYER BOOK. The name by which the service book of the Church of England is generally known. Its full name is 'The book of common prayer, and administration of the sacraments, and other rites and ceremonies of the Church, after the use of the Church of England'. As this title shows, the contents are in three parts:

1. The Common Prayer, i.e. the daily services of Morning and Evening Prayer.
2. The Sacraments, i.e. Holy Communion and Baptism, along with Confirmation, Matrimony, and (added to the book in 1550) Ordination.
3. Other rites and ceremonies, i.e. Burial of the Dead, Thanksgiving of Women after Childbirth, &c.

The book was first issued under Edward VI in 1549, a few years after the Church of England had split from Rome. Archbishop CRANMER (q.v. Vol. V), a master of glorious English, was responsible for most of it. It was founded on the medieval church services; but these were simplified, and many things which were regarded as superstitious by Protestants were left out. The medieval Church had five books of services—the Breviary (containing the eight daily services which made a round of worship day and night), the Missal (the Mass book), the Manual (the priest's service book), the Pontifical (the bishop's service book), and the Processional (made up of anthems, &c.). The Edward VI Prayer Book reduced these to one book, and this was in the language of the people instead of in Latin. The preface to the new book said: 'The curates shall need none other books for their public service, but this book and the Bible.' In this book the eight daily services were reduced to two—Matins (Morning Service) and Evensong; though the eight are still used in Anglican monasteries, where the chief work in life is to maintain an unbroken chain of worship. This new Prayer Book was to be used, not only by monks and priests, but by the congregation of the ordinary parish church. It was based on the experience of worship through many centuries adapted to meet the demands of the new day. Whereas in the eight services of the Breviary all the psalms were gone through every week, the two daily services of the new Prayer Book took a month to go through the psalter. The Edward VI Prayer Book established one orthodox form of service for the first time in England. The preface says: 'Heretofore there hath been great diversity . . . some following Salisbury use, some Hereford use, and some the use of Bangor, some of York, some of Lincoln; now from henceforth all the whole Realm shall have but one use.'

The first book was revised in 1552 and as the result of Calvinist influence made more definitely Protestant. When Elizabeth came to the throne the third Prayer Book, the book in use to-day, was issued in 1559. Not many changes were made except that vestments and ornaments of the altar, which the more Protestant book had displaced, were now ordered to be retained, and an offensive prayer for deliverance from the 'Bishop of Rome and all his detestable enormities' was left out.

In 1927 the Prayer Book was revised again, bringing it back more nearly to the original Edward VI book. This new Prayer Book was rejected by Parliament but, in fact, some churches do now use the revised form, especially for the Holy Communion Service.

See also CHURCH OF ENGLAND.

PREHISTORIC MAN (WESTERN EUROPE). 1. It is impossible to say when the first men lived on this earth, though geologists give a date of some 600,000 years ago for humanly made implements in the First Ice Age (see EVOLUTION OF MAN). We cannot give exact dates for events that happened in Europe more than a few hundred years B.C., when written records and a fairly accurate calendar begin and the prehistoric period comes to an end. Just as we might call the age we live in a Machine Age, the prehistoric Iron Age marks the time when iron was first commonly used for making tools and weapons, between two and three thousand years ago, in central and western Europe. Before that the Bronze Age covers the period of another thousand years, when bronze was the most useful known metal for tools. But before the discovery of the use of metals there was the immensely long period of the Stone Age, when Man had no better material for his tools and weapons than stone, bone, or wood. Bones are brittle and crumble away; wood rots even more quickly; but stones can survive indefinitely. So where we find stone tools shaped by hand we know that Man must have existed, because Man is the only animal that has learnt to use his hands in this way.

In this Chart we see how the ages before the beginning of history can be shown in sections or layers, one above the other, with the earliest period at the base; so the chart is read from the bottom upwards. Each section or layer marks a change in the life of Man as shown by the working tools that he made. The historical period with written records begins during the Iron Age. The dates given here are, of course, only approximate.

Name of period	Main changes in the technique of living and of tool-making	Beginning dates B.C.
Iron Age	Use of iron for tools and weapons; horses for riding and draught; increased trade; small coins; villages and small towns.	1,000
Bronze Age	First use of metal for tools and weapons; wheeled vehicles; widespread trade; gold and amber ornaments.	2,000
Neolithic (New Stone Age)	Farming, stockbreeding, villages, corn-growing; polished stone axes for forest clearing; mining for flint, trading in stones for axes; tools of stone, bone, wood; pottery; weaving.	2,500
Mesolithic (Middle Stone Age)	Hunting and food-gathering communities, partly nomadic; boats, sledges, skis; stone tools, some axes for chopping; perhaps some pottery, bone harpoons; fish-nets.	10,000
Palaeolithic (Old Stone Age)	*Upper*: Small hunting communities; throwing-sticks and bows and arrows; summer huts and winter houses or cave-shelters; fine flint-work.	50,000
	Middle: Flint tools, first evidence of deliberate burials.	115,000
	Lower: First use of chipped stone tools; wooden spears; use of fire; very nomadic units of hunters.	500,000

2. PALAEOLITHIC (Old Stone Age). England was at this time part of the mainland of Europe, and remained so until about 6,000 B.C. (*see* ENGLAND, HISTORY OF, Vol. III). There were very long periods of intense cold when the Ice Cap, which now lies within the Arctic Circle, came as far south as the English Midlands. Alternating with these ICE AGES (q.v. Vol. III) were warm periods when semi-tropical animals, such as elephants, rhinoceros, and hippopotamus, were living side by side with early Man. Nearly everything used by man at this time has vanished except his stone tools.

The first definite stone tools made by early Man show great technical skill in flaking flint or similar materials—one has only to handle a stone tool to see that it has not been made by accident. If you take a block of flint, by hitting it at the right spot, you can strike off a flake. You can then make your tool from the flake by trimming its edges and shaping it; or you can go on striking off flakes from the block or core, and shape that into the tool you want. Some of the earliest people made their chopping or cutting tools from large flakes; but heavy hand-axes made from flint cores are more widely spread (*see* PREHISTORIC TOOLS AND WEAPONS).

The Palaeolithic or Old Stone Age lasted for thousands of years, and many important changes can be seen in the tools and the men who made them. The period is, therefore, subdivided into three parts—the Lower (the oldest), the Middle, and the Upper. The Lower Palaeolithic is so called because, when the archaeologists dig, they find remains of this period underneath those of later periods (*see* ARCHAEOLOGY). The human remains from Swanscombe (*see* FOSSIL MAN) belong to this period in western Europe, and show a very modern physical type of man. It is interesting that, although the Lower and Middle Palaeolithic lasted for an immense length of time—at least 400,000 years—during which there were huge fluctuations of climate from extreme cold to nearly tropical heat, very little advance in the technique of living was made by the first humans. They remained from first to last as wandering hunters, and their livelihood depended on the animals which they hunted, whose movements they had to follow with the seasons. Having secured the elements of mastery of nature—the use of tools and the use of fire—man for many thousands of years did not carry these essential beginnings any further.

PREHISTORIC MEGALITHS AT CARNAC, BRITTANY
These avenues of standing stones may commemorate victories, the accession of kings, or they may mark boundaries

In the Upper Palaeolithic we know rather more about the lives of these hunting peoples, who by now seem to have worked out a way of life in which semi-permanent settlements were possible, at least in winter. Some of these settlements found in Russia have large houses partly dug down into the ground, rather like the old Eskimo settlements in Greenland and elsewhere in the north. These houses were occupied by people who hunted the mammoth and the woolly rhinoceros—and mammoth tusks were in fact used to form part of the walling. Summer camps of reindeer hunters have also been excavated in north Germany.

In western France and in England similar groups of hunters, whose quarry was mainly reindeer, made their winter settlements in the convenient caves which occur in the limestone there. These settlements in caves (see CAVE MAN) have preserved considerable evidence of the arts and crafts of the peoples, so far as these are represented by less perishable materials such as stone and bone. The Upper Palaeolithic hunters were completely modern in physical type. Their flint-work included small blades,

with one of which a modern anthropologist cut up a small deer in less than half an hour—so they must have been very serviceable in the hands of their original owners. But perhaps the most remarkable feature is their art, which takes the form, in the caves, of painting and engraving on the rock face, and also in carving and engraving on small objects of bone or stone. The bone objects include many types of spear-points and harpoons, as well as needles and piercers.

3. MESOLITHIC. When the Ice retreated finally within the present Arctic Circle the tundra conditions in northern Europe began to change to woodland, and the Upper Palaeolithic hunters and their descendants had to change their mode of life. As well as stone and bone objects, remains of wooden arrows are found. From finds in north Europe we know that Mesolithic man invented sledges and skis for moving over the snow or frozen land, and boats with paddles are known to have existed, as well as fishing-nets with birch-bark floats and barbed bone points or 'harpoons'. These show that the people were seal-hunters and fished with spears; and the great accumulations of shells on the old shore-lines in Scandinavia represent the refuse from many meals of shell-fish on the site of summer camps on the coast. Britain was still joined to Scandinavia and north Germany at this date (from about 10000 B.C.) by land full of swamps and lagoons, and traces of Mesolithic folk have been found in eastern England. One harpoon was dredged up from the Dogger Bank, embedded in peat which must have formed in a freshwater pool on what was then land.

4. NEOLITHIC AGE. While these small groups of hunters were struggling for their livelihood in Europe, in other parts of the world new inventions and discoveries, altering the whole history of Man, were being made. In the lands from the Nile valley to the Indus and the Oxus, and especially in Egypt, Mesopotamia, and Persia, at some time between 6000 and 4000 B.C., the foundations of civilization were laid (see ANCIENT CIVILIZATION). Men and women learnt how to grow grain, how to tame and breed sheep and cattle, how to spin thread and weave cloth, and how to make pots. They made their stone axes by grinding and polishing; they built brick houses and temples; in course of time they learnt how to smelt metals and make ornaments and tools of copper and bronze. Men settled in groups, groups grew into villages, villages grew into towns, and new ways of maintaining law and order were introduced.

But the new inventions came very slowly into western Europe, and more slowly still into Britain. There were two main routes by which the new civilization of the Near East spread among the Mesolithic hunting folk of Europe. From Asia Minor Neolithic colonies were made in Greece and Macedonia, and the great river Danube afforded a thoroughfare up into central and northern Europe, passing through easily cultivated land where primitive agriculture could be carried on successfully. Some of the settlements on the lower Danube were almost small towns, and these Danubian Neolithic people built large villages farther north. The history of one village near Cologne in Germany is known in detail from excavation: the first settlers built a group of timber barns and twenty-five houses, and then put up a palisade and ditch for defence against wild animals. The village was later deserted, and new folk moved in and built more houses; their agriculture exhausted the land, and they had to move on to new regions; the land recovered and another group took over.

The second route was formed by the western sea-ways along the Mediterranean and Atlantic coasts. This move probably came from prehistoric Egypt, but at all events villages and groups of collective tombs (see MEGALITHS) were being built in Spain and the south of France by about 2600 B.C., and from these areas the Neolithic agriculturists spread to Britain, by now an island. Some groups crossed the Channel from the north of France to the Wessex and Sussex chalk downs, while others established themselves up the western coasts. The Neolithic colonists of southern Britain built hill-top earthwork enclosures (see EARTHWORKS) which appear to have been occupied, probably seasonally at the end of the summer. Quantities of beef-bones show that they killed off much of their stock before the winter; and actual grains of burnt corn as well as stone grinders show that they grew cereals.

In eastern England the descendants of the Mesolithic hunters seem to have formed a distinctive way of life for themselves, very much concerned, it appears, with the trade in stones for axe-making from the hard rocky areas of west Britain. They lived more in the river valleys than the Neolithic herdsmen, whose stock grazed on the relatively open and dry hills.

5. BRONZE AGE. While the Neolithic villagers of northern Europe still used only stone tools, the use of bronze and copper had been known for generations in the Near East. This knowledge slowly spread north and west. Since copper ore (and later tin which, mixed with copper, makes bronze) is only found in relatively few localities, unlike hard stones which occur almost everywhere, the use of metal resulted in far more organized trade. Communities became less self-sufficing as they began to want more things which could not be found and made in their immediate neighbourhood. In northern Europe and Britain, among the first metal users were probably the people who also manufactured rather distinctive vessels called beakers, and who invaded southern England somewhere about 1900 B.C. These Beaker people buried their dead in separate graves, often under a mound (see BARROWS AND CAIRNS), and they also built circular sacred sites surrounded by circles of standing stones or a bank and ditch (see AVEBURY and STONE-HENGE).

In the European Bronze Age there were village communities of farmers and peasants with cattle and fields of grain, linked to one another by regular trackways along which merchants and craftsmen travelled. The trade routes by land and sea brought new inventions which had originated in the East, and a return trade was done in Spanish or Cornish tin, Irish gold, or Danish amber. So we find new fashions in pots, improved forms of tools and weapons, gold ornaments, new ideas in religion, and new forms of burial. Round barrows covering individual graves, with skeletons or burnt ashes preserved in urns, are the usual kind of grave.

6. IRON AGE. In Europe this covers the thousand years before the birth of Christ, and links prehistory with history. Iron was known in the Ancient East for many centuries before its use spread into Europe about 1000 B.C. It was later still in reaching the extreme west—indeed the Late Bronze Age was only just beginning there after 1000 B.C., when general unrest on the Continent resulted in groups of invaders pushing their way across the Channel into south-eastern England. These invaders established some of the earliest British farming communities of which we have detailed knowledge—small villages or homesteads of round timber-built houses within a stockade, with arable fields around and large land divisions marked out with banks and ditches. These people who first brought iron were almost certainly the people later called the Celts, who spoke a language allied to Latin and Greek which was the ancestor of Welsh, Erse, Breton, and Manx (*see* CELTIC CIVILIZATION).

Because the times were warlike, these early Iron Age people built hill-forts which could be places of refuge for villagers around: some were probably more or less permanently inhabited. In south England there were, about 300 B.C., homesteads consisting of a large circular timber-built farm-house, granaries built up on posts out of reach of damp and rats, pits for corn storage, and racks for drying hay. Some of these were fortified by a bank and ditch, perhaps because of the many invasion scares of the times. Other groups of circular houses were formed into villages—stone-built in the west where they survive as 'hut-circles'.

We know from the evidence of classical writers that, in the two or three centuries B.C., tribes moved from what was to become Roman Gaul to Britain, taking with them their old Celtic tribal names—some of the Parisii from the Seine valley established themselves in Yorkshire for instance, and later, while the Roman conquest of Gaul was in progress, fugitives made their way across the Channel and carved out little kingdoms for themselves in England. The movements of one such tribe, the Belgae, resulted in the setting up of native kingdoms in south-east England, and we know the names of many of the princes in latinized forms, such as Cunobelinus or Tasciovanus.

At this time, just before the first Roman invasions, a vigorous barbaric civilization was established in England, as in Gaul. There were the farms and villages which had been established since early Iron Age times, with all the peasant industries of pottery-making, carpentry, weaving, metal-work, and blacksmithing: very fine work was turned out, often ornamented with splendid patterns in curves and swelling lines. The chieftains must have formed a warrior aristocracy, and faint traditions of their courts have come down in the ancient Irish and Welsh tales.

See also LAKE-DWELLINGS; PREHISTORIC POTTERY; PREHISTORIC TOOLS AND WEAPONS; RELIGION, PREHISTORIC. See also Vol. VI: AGRICULTURE, PREHISTORIC.

PREHISTORIC POTTERY. As long as Man was a hunter and collector of wild plant foods, wandering from camping-place to camping-place, he had few possessions. A hunter must travel light. When he moves camp he carries his

PREDYNASTIC EGYPTIAN POT. *Ashmolean Mus.*

BRONZE AGE BEAKER FROM SUTTON COURTENAY, BERKS.
Ashmolean Mus.

weapons, both for defence and to help him to get food on the way. His wife carries the baby and everything else. So when the homes of the earliest men are found, there is little in the way of furnishings, only a few stones, perhaps some bones, and the ashes of the hearth. But when men had learned how to grow grain and had tamed animals for food and for milking, they could store provisions and make a settled home: then containers and cooking-vessels became more useful and necessary. Gourds and skins in scooped-out wooden tubs and baskets were all used, but none of these could be put in the fire

CORDED WARE. *British Mus.*

for cooking, and it was the invention of pottery that solved this problem. In many parts of the world people plaster a basket with clay to make it watertight, and pottery may have developed from this. Suppose that the basket was accidentally burnt in the fire. It would be destroyed, while the clay lining, hardened in the fire, would be left in the shape of a bowl. Such an accident may have given a man, or more probably a woman (for women are usually the primitive potters, basket-makers, and cooks) the idea of moulding clay into useful shapes and baking it into hard pottery, capable of being placed over the fire—an invention which would enormously increase the possibilities of cooking.

To make good pottery is not a simple process. The clay has to be carefully collected, freed from stone and grit, mixed to the proper consistency by the addition of sand, charcoal, ground up shells, or bits of broken pots, and moistened with water. Then it must be worked up in the hands to the proper shape and baked in the fire. Sometimes the clay is made into a sort of pancake and moulded over a gourd, basket, or another pot; sometimes the clay is drawn out into thin, sausage-like lengths and coiled into a spiral, the surface being then polished smooth. Both methods have been used in many parts of the world, and both methods appear to have been used in early days.

Primitive pots were fired in an open hearth; but it was discovered that the clay burnt black where it was covered with ashes, and red where there was an open flame. Some control of colouring was therefore possible, even under very simple conditions of firing, and with the introduction of a closed oven or kiln for pot baking, the colour of the surface could be kept constant. The earliest pots were moulded by hand; but later the potter's wheel was invented, and pottery-making became a specialized man's craft as much as that of the blacksmith.

Some of the earliest pots, dating from about 5000 B.C., have been found in Egypt, and their shape suggests that they were copied from skin bags. Pots of much the same shape were made in western Europe some 2,000 or 3,000 years later. Some round-bottomed Egyptian pots seem to have been similarly shaped to imitate gourds and baskets, and the patterns are like the criss-cross of basketry; while from another Egyptian source the early pots suggest wooden models. It was probably from somewhere between Egypt and Persia that the art of pottery spread slowly throughout the world; though there are still many places where it is unknown. Although pots break easily, the fragments can be as indestructible as stone; so potsherds often survive on prehistoric sites, and their study can illustrate a good deal about the way of life of the people who made them—their migrations, their trade routes, their food, drink, and cooking—as well as revealing their artistic sense and sometimes their ideas of religion and a future life.

The simplest patterns were impressions made with the finger-tips or finger-nails. It was also found that effective strokes and dots could be made with a piece of stick or bone, and that these could be executed with endless variations of lines and zigzags, as in the Beaker pottery of western Europe, or with graceful curves, as in the New Stone Age ware of the Danube region. Especially in eastern Europe we find 'corded ware', so called because the clay, while still wet and soft, was impressed with patterns made with a cord or twisted thong, and other pots were evidently marked with the bone of a small bird. But while beautiful painted pottery was being made in early New Stone Age times in Egypt and eastern Asia, little

of the kind is found in western Europe before the introduction of copper, and none at all in Britain.

Pottery can be used for dating in the same way as stone tools are used—in fact, in Britain, several of the early groups of people are named from different types of pottery (such as the Beaker Folk of the Early Bronze Age).

The earliest pottery in Britain was introduced about 2500 B.C. by New Stone Age colonists from France, and consists of plain bag-shaped round-based pots. Wares connected with the east European cord-ornamented pottery were also made from about this date. Successive immigrants during the Bronze and Iron Ages brought with them new ideas of pottery-making from their continental homelands, and it is these changing styles in pots that form the basis of much of our archaeological classification.

See also PREHISTORIC MAN.

PREHISTORIC TOOLS AND WEAPONS.
Early Man had two great advantages which have given him dominion over the beasts of the field—brains and hands. No animal as small as Man has so large and complex a brain, and few other animals stand naturally on their hind legs, with

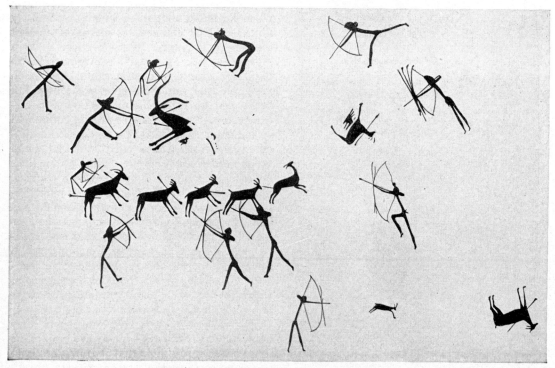

PREHISTORIC PAINTING FROM A CAVE IN VALENCIA, SPAIN
Ashmolean Mus.

their fore-limbs free from the work of feet. With his brains Man could make discoveries and inventions: with his hands he could make tools. Discoveries must have come first. Even apes, whose hands come nearest to Man's in dexterity, are said to pick up a stone or stick to threaten an enemy and, when trained, they can learn various handy tricks; but it is doubtful if they can invent anything new for themselves. Moreover, apes are still dependent on their hands for support; while Man gave up walking on all-fours at an early age, leaving his hands free for touching, handling, and experimenting. With his hands he could pick up and hold or throw sticks and stones which he could use in his daily hunt for food. He could dig up edible roots or tubers, hammer and pound up tough roots or stems, crack nuts or shellfish, break limpets off rocks, and in many other ways increase his supply of food—so important in his struggle for existence. With sticks and stones he could also defend himself against enemies or wild animals and, with well-directed shots, stun or kill animals and birds.

He soon discovered that a pointed stick would do more damage than a blunt one, and that a sharp stone was more useful than a round one. It was a great landmark in human development when he found that some stones, particularly flint, could be chipped by means of another stone so as to make a cutting edge. With a sharpened stone Man could lop off branches to build a roof for his shelter; he could dig holes in the ground for store-houses, or to make his hut larger and warmer; he could hollow out tree-trunks for a dug-out canoe; he could cut up and scrape hides for clothing. He could defend himself from enemies, attack and kill even large and fierce animals, carve up their joints, scrape their bones for meat, and break the bones for marrow. Sharpened sticks and worked bones were probably used too; but most of these have perished long ago, and as a rule only stones remain as records of the handicraft of Man. These earliest tools, a rounded stone for a hammer and a sharpened one for an axe, are the remote ancestors of all our present hammers, axes, adzes, chisels, knives, saws, planes, and other treasures of our tool-boxes and workshops.

The earliest tools or weapons—and they doubtless served as both—must have been of the simplest kind, so simple that it is impossible to decide with certainty if they have been shaped by Man or accidentally fractured by nature.

OLD STONE AGE TOOLS
1. Early Old Stone Age hand axe.
2. Late Old Stone Age harpoon.
3. Late Old Stone Age flint flake.
All half size. (1 and 3 from Hugo Obermaier, *Fossil Man in Spain*, Yale University Press)

When once Man had started experiments in chipping stone tools, it might be expected that he would provide himself with a varied outfit; but for thousands of years he seems to have continued making much the same tools in much the same ways. Among the most important of these are the so-called 'hand-axes' of the Early Stone Age, over 500,000 years old. To make these, the craftsman took either a lump of flint or a flint flake and chipped it at one end into a tool, shaped rather like a flattened pear. Such 'hand-axes' are found in Europe, Asia, and Africa; they vary locally because of the variety of rock, but they are much alike in general outline, though not all of the same age. Other peoples in Europe and Asia in this period made tools of different shapes out of heavy flakes that they chipped off a lump of flint.

We can trace a slow evolution in the craft of making flint tools: they became gradually smaller, lighter, and more carefully trimmed, and were worked all round instead of only at one end. They could be fixed in short handles and used as knives, or in longer ones and used as spear-heads. It is not known what the handles were like, nor how they were attached to the blades, but they were probably of wood or bone, lashed on with strips of hide.

Man's progress in handicraft was very slow, and even during the middle Old Stone Age, 150,000 years or more ago, he only made a small range of tools or weapons. He had 'points' serving, doubtless, for knives or spear-heads, small hand-axes, scrapers for scraping hides and trimming spear-shafts, and sharp flint flakes used as awls, probably for boring holes in skins to be sewn together. Late Old Stone Age Man, some 70,000 years B.C., made more use of thinnish, flat, flint flakes, sharpened along the sides or at the ends. Some of these were serviceable knives, some were tools for engraving. Towards the end of the Old Stone Age special tools, both in stone and bone, were made for special purposes. There is no doubt about the harpoons of reindeer antler or deer antler for fishing, nor about the bone needles with eyes threaded with sinews for stitching skins. Somewhere about this time men invented bows and arrows. They had already invented spear-throwers to increase the range of their weapons, and we can learn how they used them by seeing how the Australians or Eskimos use them to-day. The invention of the bow increased the range still farther. Among the rock-

paintings of eastern Spain there are pictures of men shooting and wooden arrow-shafts have been found in north Germany. Some of the arrows are pointed at the end, some are shaped to hold arrow-heads of flint. Similar flint arrow-heads were used down to historic times: when their origin was forgotten, they were called 'elf-darts' and treasured as charms.

After about 5000 B.C. great progress was made. The people of the New Stone Age still used stone as their principal material; but new discoveries in farming and a more stable way of life called

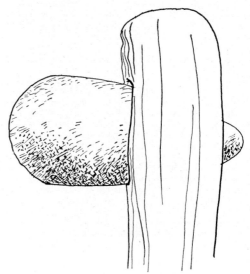

NEW STONE AGE AXE. Half size.

for new tools. Flint flakes were still used for knives, scrapers, awls and borers, spears and arrow-heads, and numbers of sharp little flints were fixed in a row for a sickle. The typical New Stone Age axes, instead of being chipped, were ground and polished to give a smooth surface and regular blade, and mounted in a hole in a wooden handle. Experiments have shown that a polished axe cuts down trees more quickly and easily than a chipped one. Sometimes a socket of stag antler was fitted in between the axe-head and the handle to prevent the wood splitting. Later, when methods of boring stones were invented, the wooden handle was fitted into the holed stone, instead of fitting the stone into the hole in the handle. Axes like these were the weapons of the bands of warriors of northern Europe in the Bronze Age.

When copper and bronze were discovered, and men discovered the possibilities of the new materials for tool-making, they began by imitating the stone forms in metal, and so the first bronze axes were solid. But as the craftsmen grew more skilful, they made improvements, and successive stages in methods of hafting can be

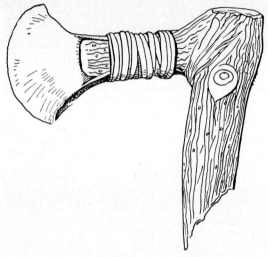

BRONZE AXE. Half size.

recognized. First they hammered up the sides of the blades to grip the handles; later they curved the edges round into a socket; finally socketed axe-heads with loops for attachment were cast in moulds. The steel axe of to-day has ancestors in copper in the ancient civilizations of the East, and its wooden handle differs little from that made by prehistoric Man.

Bronze took the place of stone for axes, chisels, and spear-heads; but arrow-heads of flint were still used, even in the Iron Age, perhaps because arrows are so often lost, and metal was scarcer than flint. Flint knives and daggers were imitated in copper and bronze, but the new weapons soon showed little likeness to their earlier ancestors—there were no stone models for the rapiers and swords with which our forefathers fought their battles in the Late Bronze Age.

The change from bronze to iron was a gradual one during the last centuries B.C., introducing us to historic times and to the tools and weapons which we use to-day. But we have not altogether emerged from the Stone Age as long as we still use stone pestles and mortars for pounding, or mill-stones for grinding our daily bread.

See also PREHISTORIC MAN.

PRESBYTERIAN, see CALVINIST.

PRIEST. An agent of a god, a person who offers sacrifice to the god or performs other religious actions on behalf of the people whom he represents. He differs from a medicine-man or magician because he does not claim to act for himself by his own control of supernatural powers (see MAGIC). He has to be set apart for his office by the gods or spirits whom he serves.

The office, which is given him by a solemn act of consecration or ordination, used often to be confined to members of a royal or priestly line. In Egypt, for instance, the Pharaoh was the high priest, because he was the son and incarnation on earth of the chief gods who ruled over the country and controlled the course of nature. But, although he spent most of his time performing ceremonies for the benefit of his people, he could not be in more than one place at once. Therefore he had to appoint others to act as priests on his behalf in the temple services and in carrying out the other priestly duties. In carrying out these duties priests also acted on behalf of the gods, of whom Pharaoh was the earthly representative, and therefore they frequently acted as though they were the gods. In the funeral rites, for instance, they dressed as Osiris and Horus, and behaved exactly as if they were these gods.

In Mesopotamia, too, the Babylonian king was the high priest; but, because his position as head of the nation kept him fully occupied, he, too, had to appoint priests in much the same way and for the same reasons as the Egyptian Pharaohs. It was these priests who had to decide whether it would be lucky to do a particular thing on a given day, and to act as intermediaries between the gods and the people in the offering of SACRIFICES (q.v.), explaining omens and oracles, and performing rites of purification and penitence when the gods were angry and spiteful. The priests were also seers or soothsayers (see PROPHECY), who foretold what was going to happen by such methods as inspecting the liver and gall-bladder of an animal slain as a victim at the altar.

In Israel, before the exile in Babylon, the priests were usually royal officials, and the king as the anointed of God offered sacrifices (1 Kings ix. 25; 2 Kings xvi. 12) and on occasions dressed and behaved as a priest (cf. 2 Sam. vi. 14) while his sons served in the priesthood. After the Israelites returned from exile to Jerusalem in 523 B.C. and began to re-establish their customs, beliefs and institutions, the high priest took the

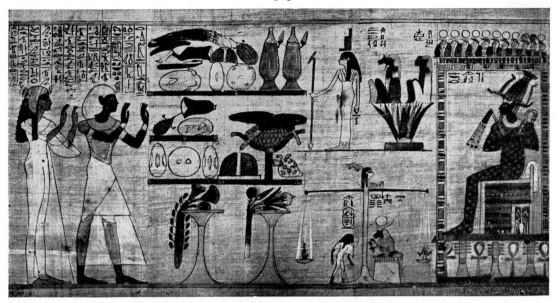

HER-HERU, THE FIRST EGYPTIAN PRIEST-KING, AND QUEEN NETCHEMET PRAYING TO OSIRIS
Painting from the *Book of the Dead*, 21st Dynasty (*c.* 1050 B.C.). *British Mus.*

place of the king in religious ceremonies, and the priesthood became quite separate and distinct from the royal family.

The priesthood, in consequence, became a very powerful body of men in the land. The priesthood is said to have started with Aaron, the brother of Moses, and the Levites to have been especially set apart to produce men suitable for the service of the sanctuary. In early days it was not necessary, though desirable, for a priest to be a Levite. In course of time, however, anyone who was attached to a shrine was treated as a Levite. But there were also other priestly families—the Zadokites and the Aaronites. Besides these priests engaged in the service of the Temple, there were the seers and in later Judaism the rabbis, doctors of the sacred Law, and teachers, who drew up very elaborate and complicated rules governing the way Jews were to live and behave among themselves and in relation to Gentiles. But they were lawyers rather than priests (*see* JUDAISM).

The Jewish priesthood was, in a sense, continued in the CHRISTIAN CHURCH (q.v.) when the worship of the Temple was transferred to the central act of Christian worship—the service at first called the Breaking of the Bread and later known as Holy Communion, the Eucharist, or the Mass. When this service was regarded as a sacrifice, the man who made the offering on behalf of Christ, the eternal High Priest in heaven (Heb. v. 5 ff., vii. 22 ff.), was spoken of as a priest and set apart for this purpose by a solemn act of ordination. This has been the custom in the Catholic Church all down the ages. At the Reformation in the 16th century, however, in many Protestant Churches the ancient line of bishops, priests, and deacons was brought to an end, and in its place a new order of ministers was established. Their chief work lay in preaching the Gospel, acting as shepherds of their flocks, and ministering to a congregation, rather than in acting as attendants at the altar.

In ISLAM (q.v.) there is no priesthood and no sacrificial worship. The faithful are called to prayer by the 'crier' or *muezzin*, from the top of the tower (minaret) of the mosque, where he stands facing the Moslem holy city, Mecca. Within the mosque (i.e. the Mohammedan equivalent of a church) a 'leader of prayer' (*imam*) is all that is needed to conduct the repetitions of portions of the Koran, the Moslem sacred book. On Fridays (the Moslem holy day) a sermon is preached or an instruction is read by a 'preacher' (*khatib*) who must be a man of good character and able to do what is required of him efficiently. But none of these officials is set apart by ordination as a member of a priesthood.

See also RELIGION; TEMPLE; GOD.

PROPHECY. Prophet is a Greek word which meant a person who uttered or interpreted an oracle. Therefore, at first, prophecy was concerned with foretelling events, and the methods used for finding out what was going to happen often included the prophet working himself (or herself) into a state of frenzy by wild dancing and strange music, in order that he might become 'possessed' by the god who made the revelation. In this condition of ecstasy or delirium he proclaimed the god's mind and will about things that were happening in the present or going to take place in the future. Sometimes, however, oracles were consulted by crystal-gazing, casting lots, and other such devices used in DIVINATION (q.v.), and the prophet then became a seer, like Samuel in the Old Testament.

The Hebrew word, *Nabi*, translated 'prophet' in the Greek version of the Bible, means a person endowed with second sight (i.e. a seer), who was consulted on all sorts of matters. But it also means a member of one of the wandering bands called 'sons of the prophets', who had their headquarters at such sacred centres as Gilgal, Bethel, Ramah, and Jericho. These people roamed about the country preceded by players on the harp, tambourine, flute, or zither. They worked themselves up into a frenzy by the help of the music, and so great was the state of religious excitement which they created that the people who stood by also became infected and themselves 'prophesied', being filled with the divine spirit. We read of an experience of this kind in the book of Samuel, when Saul at the time of his anointing went among the prophets (I Sam. x. 1–11). These prophets often practised divination and soothsaying, as well as their wilder methods, to obtain knowledge from heaven which ordinary people could not get.

In the 8th century B.C., however, a new movement arose in Palestine, in which a higher type of prophecy made its appearance. It was then that men like Amos, Hosea, and Isaiah declared the will and purpose of God in great pronouncements which they claimed to have received as a special revelation given to them by Jehovah, without the use of the magical methods adopted by the earlier seers, soothsayers, and dancers. They felt themselves moved by the spirit of God to deliver a message which very often was quite different from the beliefs, customs, and ideas of their own day. Indeed, it was usually an unpopular cry they uttered; but what they said was so original and spoken with such urgency that it sounded like a message straight from God. So they generally began with the words, 'Thus saith Jehovah'. Often the prophets attacked the priesthood of Israel because their sacrificial worship had got mixed up with the pagan cults of Palestine and those of Egypt, Babylonia, and Phoenicia; and they refused to associate themselves with their predecessors, the local seers and soothsayers. Their first and chief pronouncement was that God was holy and righteous and demanded of His people right living based on justice, goodness, forbearance, mercy, and love. They also declared that He was a jealous God and would not tolerate the worship of any other divine being, great or small. Whether at this time they really believed that there was only one God of all the earth is not quite clear. But by the end of the period of the captivity in Babylon, the writer of Isaiah xl–lv taught in no unmeasured terms, as did the priest-prophet Ezekiel, that there is but one Creator and Sustainer of all things beside whom all the 'gods' are mere idols. They also taught that each individual was of value in the sight of God and personally responsible to Him for the way he used his life; and that the Jewish nation as a whole was a holy people, chosen by God because, through them, God was working out His purposes for the world.

These were new ideas of religion which the prophets declared to be the direct word of God. When the Jews returned from their exile in Babylon, the prophets had done their work, and while their influence was very strongly felt in the restored kingdom, the Hebrew prophets had no real successors in Judaism from the end of the 6th century B.C. But, while the period of the prophets was short-lived and unique in the religious history of the nation, and indeed of the world, it had far-reaching consequences. In Persia ZOROASTER (q.v.) also started to preach the idea of only One God, and others also played some part in laying the foundations of modern ways of thinking and believing about God and His relation to man.

See also RELIGION; JUDAISM.

PROTESTANT, see CHRISTIAN CHURCH; REFORMATION.

PRUSSIAN, see GERMANS.

PUNJABIS, see INDIAN PEOPLES.

PURITANS, see CONGREGATIONALIST.

religion to supply the spiritual foundations on which the world may be rebuilt.

See also GOD; SATAN; AGNOSTIC.

RELIGION, PREHISTORIC (SUN-WORSHIP AND DRUIDS). Very little indeed is really known about prehistoric religion in Europe, though a great deal is often talked and written about it. That men had ideas of Another World we can see by the elaborate funeral rituals which they practised from late Old Stone Age times onwards: weapons, ornaments, and other objects buried with the dead must imply that they were intended for use in some sort of a life after death.

In the Early Bronze Age we find structures consisting of circular banks and ditches, combined with circles of standing stones or of timber uprights (*see* AVEBURY *and* STONEHENGE), which must have been some form of open-air temples, where we can guess, if we like, that a deity corresponding to the SKY-GOD (q.v.) of some early religions may have been worshipped. The fact that Stonehenge is planned so as to face the rising sun at midsummer, and that many other circles have a rough indication of an entrance or other feature towards the east, has led to the building up of a lot of theories about sun-worship, for which there is not otherwise much reliable evidence, except perhaps in the later Bronze Age. Statuettes from late Old Stone Age times suggest worship of a Mother Goddess connected with the idea of fertility and abundance, and similar beliefs about the growth of crops and the breeding of animals are likely to have been held in the agricultural communities of the New Stone Age and later times.

When the classical writers of Greece and Rome first came in contact with what were to them the barbarians of prehistoric Europe, in the first couple of centuries before and after Christ, they were particularly interested in the organized priesthood which existed among the Gauls and the Britons—that of the Druids. There are a number of scrappy and confused references to the Druids in Greek and Latin writers, but we really know very few facts about them. Certainly some of them practised rites which were savage enough to fill the Romans, who saw them, with horror. The archaeological evidence suggests that Druidism was already an ancient religion in Julius Caesar's time, when he encountered it in his Gaulish campaigns. It may have inherited

THE GREAT MOTHER
This figure probably represents the goddess of a prehistoric fertility cult

something from the Bronze Age for, although Druids can have had no original connexion with the great stone circles built nearly 2,000 years before their time, they may have carried out ceremonies, ritual dances for instance, in some of them. There are also little shrines on Iron Age sites in Britain which would be contemporary with the Druid religion recorded by the Latin writers.

The island of Anglesey is known to have been one of the most important Druid centres in western Europe, and a great treasure of Celtic metal-work found in a bog there may once have belonged to the priesthood. It included chariots, swords, trumpets, ritual wands, ornaments, and a great iron gang-chain that possibly was used to fasten victims intended for sacrifice.

See also PREHISTORIC MAN.

RENAISSANCE. 1. This is the name given to the civilization which began in Italy in the 14th century, reached its height in the 15th, and spread to the rest of Europe in the 16th and 17th centuries. The word means 'rebirth' and refers to the rediscovery of the ancient civilizations of Greece and Rome, which was one of the characteristic happenings of the Renaissance. But, in

STATUE OF GATTEMELATA AT PADUA

Bronze statue by Donatello (1383–1466). This figure of a Condottiere or General is one of the earliest Renaissance statues. The arrogant pose, the truthful portraiture, and the Roman costume all express the humanistic outlook. It is also a technical achievement, being the first full-size equestrian portrait to be cast since Roman times. *Alinari.*

fact, that was only one of the things discovered at that time, for it was a great period of discovery of all kinds—of new worlds, new scientific laws, new kinds of art, and, above all, new strengths and possibilities in man himself. It would be better to define the word Renaissance as 'new birth', and even that would not be quite correct, since the Renaissance grew naturally out of the Middle Ages and was not a sudden occurrence.

The Renaissance is the beginning of the modern world. It was then that people began to think as we think to-day, and the foundations were laid on which our philosophy and our knowledge of the universe and of science are built. The nations of Europe came into being, and with them national languages and literatures. The forms of literature and art which were invented then are still in use to-day, and the political, economic, and religious ideas which govern our lives were first formulated then.

In the early Middle Ages, when life was precarious and unsettled, man had lost faith in his own ability and judgement, and relied on the teaching of the Fathers of the Church and of the classical authors, in so far as they survived. It follows that the civilization of the Middle Ages is based on tradition, to which every new discovery and development was referred. Later, men's ideas grew beyond this rigid tradition, and, at the beginning of the Renaissance, it was finally overthrown. There followed a period of immense activity and brilliance. Never before nor since have there been so many men of genius or men with such universal talents. Never have men dared so much and achieved such great results. It was in Italy, which had not been so fully immersed in the ideas and traditions of the Middle Ages as had the people of northern Europe, that the Renaissance first flowered. The first scholars, explorers, scientists, and artists were all Italians, though other countries soon followed their lead.

2. THE NEW LEARNING. During the Middle Ages the works of some of the Greek and Roman writers and philosophers had been read. This happened particularly in the time of the Emperor CHARLEMAGNE (q.v. Vol. V) at the end of the 8th century, when he tried to revive the culture of the Romans by encouraging the copying of their books and works of art. But few of these manuscripts continued to be read, and by the end of the Middle Ages much of classical literature was unknown.

The first scholars of the Renaissance, such as PETRARCH (q.v. Vol. V), found in Latin writings an outlook much the same as their own. Therefore they began to search for manuscripts which had lain buried in the libraries of monasteries for hundreds of years, to study and copy them and to make them widely known. All educated people could read Latin because it was the common language of the Church and of scholars throughout Europe, but very few could read Greek. In the 15th century some Greek scholars came to Italy and taught the Italians Greek, and when the Turks captured Constantinople in 1453, more came as refugees bringing manuscripts with them.

The scholars, or humanists as they were called, found in the ancient writings authority for their new ideas. Most fundamental of these was a belief in the power and dignity of man, which led to a new interest in the physical world. This was very different from medieval philosophy, which emphasized that man was insignificant with no power of his own apart from God, and that therefore this life was unimportant, except as a preparation for the next. The humanists, however, believed that the new ideas were reconcilable with Christian belief; and the Church, too, encouraged the new learning until it led to the REFORMATION (q.v.) in the 16th century.

For some time the humanists were so devoted to the study of the classics that they considered that Latin and Greek were the only scholarly languages. Although Petrarch wrote poetry in Italian, he did not think it had the same value as his Latin works. In the 16th century the Dutch humanist, ERASMUS (q.v. Vol. V), wrote entirely in Latin or Greek, and the *Utopia* of Sir THOMAS MORE (q.v. Vol. V) was not translated into English until thirty-five years after it was written. Even in the 17th century Milton began to translate into Latin his great poem *Paradise Lost* in order that it might live.

Interest in the new learning spread so much that soon there was a demand for books in the national languages. In the 15th and 16th centuries poets and writers in all countries were producing works in their own languages. In Spain CERVANTES wrote *Don Quixote*, in France the best-known writers were RABELAIS and MONTAIGNE. In England SHAKESPEARE combined classical learning and the humanistic study of man with an interest in national history and character (qq.v. Vol. V). The invention of

THE SCHOOL OF ATHENS

Painting by Raphael (1483–1520) in the *Stanza della Segnatura* in the Vatican, Rome. This painting is a tribute to classical learning; Plato and Aristotle are discoursing in the centre while around are groups of classical scholars. *Alinari*

printing in the 15th century made an enormous contribution to the spread of learning. Instead of the great labour of copying manuscripts by hand, a very much quicker, cheaper, and more accurate method was available, and the possession of books became a practical possibility for many people (*see* PRINTING, HISTORY OF, Vol. IV).

3. THE AGE OF DISCOVERY. The new life of the Renaissance not only stimulated scholarship, but also influenced the practical affairs of life. The new sense of man's strength and power, as well as the growth of trade and wealth, made men look beyond the Old World of Europe and the Near East to the unexplored countries of south and east. The urge to explore was stimulated by the fact that the old overland routes from India and the Far East, by which the wealth of the East had been brought to Europe, had become dangerous on account of the spread of the Turkish Empire. New routes to the east which would by-pass Turkish lands were needed. Prince HENRY THE NAVIGATOR encouraged exploration, and BARTHOLOMEW DIAZ found his

way southwards round Africa. COLUMBUS and, later, many others sailed westwards to reach the east, and discovered the New World of America (qq.v. Vol. V). Later, English explorers tried to reach the east by sailing round the north of Europe. But they did not get farther than north Russia (*see* EXPLORATION, Vol. IV). These explorers were followed, as explorers nearly always are, by traders and missionaries who took Christianity to the heathen as well as bringing back treasures to their patrons.

4. SCIENCE. Every branch of science was developed in the Renaissance, for when men began to explore in one direction, they found their curiosity aroused in others. Little progress could be made in the study of ASTRONOMY (q.v. Vol. III) while men believed that the sun and stars moved round the earth; but when the Polish astronomer COPERNICUS (q.v. Vol. V), about 1500, demonstrated that the sun was the centre round which the planets and Earth revolved, the way was open to many new discoveries. Nearly a hundred years later the

Italian GALILEO (q.v. Vol. V) was able to show with his telescope what Copernicus had proved by mathematics.

Biology, medicine, chemistry, and physics were all studied with equal fervour. The human body was dissected and its organs studied. Plants and animals were collected, described, and grouped. Nothing was too large or too small to escape man's curiosity. The results are amazing when we realize that there were no instruments and no established methods by which to work. Modern methods of scientific research are entirely different from the way men thought and worked in the Middle Ages, and the scientists of the Renaissance had to break down the old traditions.

5. ART. Side by side with the humanists and scientists in 15th-century Italy were the artists, who were also stimulated by the new life of the Renaissance. The first great artists of the period, Brunelleschi the architect, Donatello the sculptor, and Masaccio the painter, laid the foundations of Renaissance art. Human character was studied in portraits, figures were made more lifelike by the study of anatomy, and settings more real by the use of perspective. Classical buildings suggested new forms for architecture. Art was of the greatest importance because it expressed the glory of man and his achievements, even when the subjects were religious. The great artists, ALBERTI, LEONARDO, and MICHELANGELO (qq.v. Vol. V) were not only architects, sculptors, and painters, but poets and scientists as well. In other countries the same spirit grew, though it was more limited than in Italy. In Flanders painters concentrated on the detailed representation of men and things, and the German HOLBEIN brought a similar interest to England. It was not until the 16th and 17th centuries that the full meaning of the Italian Renaissance was realized in northern Europe, when INIGO JONES brought classical architecture to England and RUBENS' painting in Flanders was based on his study of the Italian painters. DÜRER carried the spirit of the Renaissance to Germany and François I of France brought Italian artists to his court at Fontainebleau (qq.v. Vol. V).

RHODESIANS. The total population of the two Rhodesias is about three millions, and of this only about 95,000 are Europeans. The history of Rhodesia before the white man arrived is part of the history of the Bantu-speaking regions (*see* NEGRO AFRICANS; Vol. IV; AFRICAN LANGUAGES).

Boer trekkers (Dutch pioneers) from the Transvaal, and Scottish missionaries were the first Europeans to travel and settle in the country north of the Limpopo river. Some of these missionaries were also explorers—Moffat and LIVINGSTONE (q.v. Vol. V) were the best known of them. Other explorers, who helped to open up this part of 'Darkest Africa' in the period after 1850, were STANLEY (q.v. Vol. V), Burton, and the great hunter Selous.

But it was not until CECIL RHODES (q.v. Vol. V) used the money he had made at the Kimberley diamond-mines to develop this territory, that there was any settled European occupation. In 1889 he founded the British South Africa Company (or the Chartered Company) with the object of settling and developing the country between the Limpopo and the Zambesi and even farther north. This country was later called Rhodesia in honour of its founder, and 'Founder's Day' is its chief public holiday.

Lobengula, chief of the Matabele, who were the strongest native tribe in Rhodesia, gave Rhodes and his followers the right to prospect for minerals in his country, and to start with, most of the men who went north from the Cape did so in the hope of finding 'New Witwatersrand', or gold-fields. In 1890 Rhodes's friend, Jameson, took Mashonaland, where the town Salisbury was established, and in 1891 British prospectors got a 'concession' (or the right to look for gold) in Barotseland, north of the Zambesi.

It was soon found that, although there was gold, it was not in great quantities. The proud Matabele, like the ZULU (q.v.) before them, began to regret the white man's presence, and in 1893 and again in 1896 tried to drive him out. The latter rebellion was settled by Rhodes, personally, when he went unarmed into the Matabele territory to persuade the chiefs to make peace.

For its first thirty years or so Rhodesia was governed by a private company, the Chartered Company, just as Bengal in the time of Clive was governed by the English East India Company. In 1923 Southern Rhodesia became a self-governing colony with its own elected parliament; now it forms, together with Nyasaland and Northern Rhodesia, the Central African Federation. Northern Rhodesia is still a Crown Colony: that is, it is directly under the control of the British Government. This is because the European population of Northern Rhodesia is still

TOBACCO GROWING IN RHODESIA
The farmer inspecting the crop

very small—only about 37,000—while that of Southern Rhodesia is about 135,000. These Europeans are chiefly English speaking, although in Southern Rhodesia there are a number of Afrikaans-speaking immigrants from the Union of South Africa.

The Europeans work mostly in the mines (coal, copper, or gold), on farms, or in the Civil Service. In Northern Rhodesia, where the native reserves are larger, the Native Administration Department has a large percentage of Europeans.

In both colonies there is always the danger of malaria or other tropical diseases, so that most Rhodesians like to take a holiday in a cooler climate fairly often. Most government employees are obliged to do so once every three years. In many parts of the colonies, but especially in the north, the tsetse fly causes sleeping sickness, and no cattle can live in these districts. The spraying of such areas with D.D.T., among other methods, has been tried and has proved fairly successful, so that more land may in the future become available for settlement.

The Rhodesians are much like the South Africans (q.v.). They are fond of, and spend a lot of time at, open-air activities, such as big-game hunting, or playing cricket, rugby football, and other games. They are very sociable and friendly and, though their farms are sometimes 40 or 50 miles apart, visit each other regularly for games or 'sundowner' parties. The great distances, combined with the small population, make good roads difficult to keep up, and the main roads consist of two strips of asphalt, each about a foot wide and the distance of a car's wheels apart. Cars travel on these strips and have to leave them when they meet another car.

Native labour is plentiful, good, and very cheap, so that most European households have two or three domestic servants. Practically all the manual labour in mines is done by natives, the white man being the owner, manager, or foreman. This is also true of the farms, so that the white man, even more than in the neighbouring Union of South Africa, has a great deal of leisure, and has developed a lazy attitude towards manual labour.

School education is state controlled and well developed, but there is no university in either of the colonies. Rhodesians who want a university education get it either in South Africa or in England. While the ties between Rhodesia and England are still very strong, Southern Rhodesians, especially, are beginning to stand much more on their own feet, and the majority of them think of Rhodesia as their home and not merely as a place where they can make money before retiring to live in England.

See also Vol. III: Rhodesia.

RIG-VEDA, *see* Sacred Books, Section 2.

RITUAL. The way in which a religious observance, such as a baptism, wedding, or funeral, is carried out according to a properly prescribed order. The ritual of a wedding, for instance, includes the words spoken and the actions performed by the priest or minister and his assistants, together with the singing of the choir (if there is one), the responses of the congregation, the acts of the bride and bridegroom—such as the joining of hands, the giving and receiving of the ring, and in some countries eating from the same dish, and similar customs suggesting the idea of uniting two people together—and the bestowal of a blessing upon the union. Without some kind of ritual religious observances could not be carried on at all, since the whole routine and method of holding a service is, in the broadest sense, a ritual. The rite may be long and complicated,

THE DANCE OF THE ELAND BULL
Bushman ritual dance. The dancers pretend to stalk the prey while women sing and clap their hands
Haddon Lib., Cambridge

as in the coronation of a king or the singing of the solemn High Mass on Easter Day in the great cathedral of St. Peter's at Rome; or it may be very short and simple, as at Evensong in a village church. But whether the things done and said are elaborate or simple, the performance of them is a ritual.

In primitive society people find it easier to 'dance out their religion' than to talk about it, and so their rites consist mainly of actions. Since everywhere simple folk more readily express the things that affect them most deeply in actions than in words, they tend to rehearse their experiences, hopes, and fears in a sort of pantomime, in the belief that by so doing they influence what actually happens. They are not interested in the problems that perplex philosophers and profound thinkers, such as what are the causes that lie behind the universe and the way things behave in this world. They are quite content to seek and find a religious satisfaction for their emotions in the performance of rites which represent, by signs and actions, their inmost desires and wishes. And this applies to ordinary people all the world over and at all times.

Thus, for example, in Greece the common folk were not in the least attracted by the reasoning and speculations of Plato and Aristotle, and they had not much use for the stories of the gods related by Homer, except as good tales. What really thrilled and gripped them were the sacred dramatic performances, or mystery plays, held in secret, amid signs and circumstances calculated to produce an intense sense of wonder and awe, in which mysterious lights, sounds, objects, and processions played an important part. This ritual re-enacted the ancient myths of famous heroes, such as Demeter and Persephone, Dionysus, or Attis and Cybele (*see* GREEK MYTHOLOGY), who passed through death to a new and fuller life, in order that those who beheld these sacred sights and took part in the rites, might themselves undergo a similar experience—namely, be reborn as new creatures.

DIONYSUS RITUAL

At the rites held in honour of Dionysus, the god of wine, women danced themselves into a frenzy round the effigy of the god. Painting from an Attic vase, 5th century B.C. Furtwängler-Reichhold, *Griechische Vasenmalerei* (Bruckmann)

It was, in fact, in rites of this nature that the drama began. We go to the theatre to be entertained; the Greeks and other ancient people went for religious reasons—to obtain blessings on the country and renewal of their own spiritual life, such as we seek in the sacraments in church. The word 'drama' means 'the thing done' or 'performed', and originally the action was in honour of a divine being, like Dionysus the hero of one of the Greek mystery cults, or secret societies. In much the same way, in the Middle Ages, the mystery plays were part of church ritual, like the greatest of all sacred dramas, the Mass. These medieval plays, indeed, grew out of the words spoken and the actions performed at the altar in the church service, until gradually they became separate performances. But they never lost their ritual character. In Greek drama, comedy was the ritual of life directed to making the crops grow, while tragedy was the ritual of death and decay in nature and in human existence. Together comedy and tragedy told the story in a ritual manner of life emerging from the grave. This same theme is found again in the mumming

plays, and it lies behind Christian ritual in its most important and characteristic forms.

In this mystery type of ritual the general pattern is the same. A divine hero is born and, when he grows up, he fights an adversary, is himself killed or wounded, but is restored to life, often to fight again, this time victoriously. A sacred marriage follows with a triumphal procession in which the hero-king, dressed as God, with a train of lesser gods, is the chief figure. The details vary, but the outline and purpose are the same everywhere. Under the ritual form of the dying and rising god, supernatural power is set free to meet every kind of human need in this world and the next—birth, marriage and death, sowing and reaping of crops, and, in the higher religions, the corresponding needs of the immortal spirit of man in its passage from life through death to new life. At every turn life is needing a fresh outpouring of life, natural and supernatural (*see* SACRIFICE). It is this which ritual supplies. Therefore, an annual festival has been held from time immemorial, either in the spring or autumn, to secure by ritual, wealth, prosperity, and health throughout the coming

year. But man has never been completely satisfied to labour only for the good things of this life In the higher religions, therefore, while the general ritual pattern remains the same, it has been used to meet the needs of the spirit rather than those of the body. Ritual has, therefore, been used from the earliest times up to the present day to minister to the religious wants and cravings of human beings in their various stages of development.

See also RELIGION; FESTIVALS; MYTHOLOGY.

ROMAN CATHOLIC CHURCH. Members of this Church call themselves simply 'Catholics', and claim to belong to the whole Church, not to a sect which has broken away from it. (Other Christians deny that breaking from the Pope prevents them, also, from belonging to the Catholic Church.) There are about 330 million Roman Catholics, almost half the total number of nominal Christians.

The head of the Church is the Pope—Bishop of Rome and originally one of the five Patriarchs of the Early Church before the split between East and West (see ORTHODOX EASTERN CHURCH). The Pope is believed to be 'infallible'—which means that, when as Christ's Vicar (Representative) on earth he defines a doctrine, he can make no mistake. There are altogether 1,300 dioceses of the Roman Catholic Church, each ruled by a bishop who is usually nominated by the Pope himself. The clergy are required to remain celibate (unmarried). The Pope is elected by the Sacred College of Cardinals, who usually choose one of their own number. Cardinal means 'chief': they were originally the chief bishops, priests, and deacons in the diocese round Rome and, until 1946, have almost always been predominantly Italian. Their number is usually supposed to be seventy, though, in fact, as many as ten or even more of these positions are often kept vacant. In 1946 the Pope appointed thirty-two new Cardinals, making the Sacred College nearly complete—six cardinal bishops, fifty-nine cardinal priests, and four cardinal deacons—a total of sixty-nine out of seventy. The new Cardinals come from all parts of the world, including even the Chinese Archbishop of Peking, so that, as the Pope declared, the Sacred College should be 'a true reflection of the universality of the Church'.

The Roman Catholic Church has fourteen committees, called Congregations, of which the Cardinals are the chief members. Each Congregation is responsible for a certain section of the Church's work. The Congregation of the Holy Office, the Holy INQUISITION (q.v.), begun in the early 13th century, is responsible for dealing with any false doctrines. The terrible work of this institution in the 16th century, in its attempt to stamp out the growth of Protestantism, is well known. The Inquisition still exists to safeguard true doctrine and restrain those who try to depart from it. Its meetings are secret, but no longer terrible. The Congregation of the Consistory deals with the forming of new dioceses and with new appointments, and generally supervises the work of the Church. The Congregation of the Propaganda deals with missionary work. The Congregation of the Index, begun in the 16th century when the introduction of printing seemed to make it necessary, censors all books, listing those thought to be dangerous to faith and morals. The Congregation of Rites, among other things, investigates all the evidence for canonizing a new SAINT (q.v.).

The Roman Catholic Church holds that Christ instituted seven SACRAMENTS (q.v.) by which God's Grace comes to its members through Christ's sacrificial death on the Cross. This is why the central service is the Mass, or Holy Eucharist—the offering to God of the Sacrifice made once for all on Calvary. The services are mainly in Latin; and the official text of the Bible is not the original Hebrew and Greek, but the Latin translation, the Vulgate (see TRANSLATIONS, Vol. XII, Section 2). The Church plays a central part in the lives of its members; in the hustle of week-day cares men and women find time to go to church, say a prayer, light a candle, or go to confession. Church discipline and organization are strong and centralized.

The unity of the Church in the West was not seriously challenged in the Middle Ages. From the 16th century onwards, following the REFORMATION (q.v.), northern Europe became mainly Protestant. The Reformation was followed by a Counter-Reformation, in which the Roman Church reformed itself and gathered together its forces to resist attack and to spread Christianity farther afield. The Council of Trent (1545–63) reformed many of the abuses which had helped to cause the Reformation, and stated more precisely than before what were the doctrines of Roman Catholicism. In 1540 the Society of Jesus (Jesuits) was founded, and this powerful

THE POPE HOLDS A CONSISTORY

At a formal meeting of the Sacred College the Pope confers the hat on newly-elected Cardinals. *Associated Press*

and zealous, even if often ruthless, organization played an important part in attacking Protestantism in Europe and, above all, in carrying Christianity to the new countries, especially to America (*see* IGNATIUS LOYOLA, Vol. V).

From A.D. 756 the Pope was not only head of the Church, but also ruler of a part of Italy called the Papal States. When, however, the various states of Italy became united into one kingdom in 1870, this temporal power of the Pope came to an end. In 1929 the Vatican Palace became the Vatican City, a sovereign independent state of 109 acres: this meant that the Head of a universal Church was independent of the political control of any one state.

In the past, particularly in the 18th century, the Roman Catholic Church has been thought of as the enemy of political and intellectual freedom. This was because of its close alliance with those monarchies which seemed most likely to preserve the state of society in which the Church had been an unquestioned power. Like most established institutions, it has been slow to welcome change and new ideas; but, particularly

in recent years, it has adapted itself in many ways to meet the demands of modern life.

See also CHRISTIAN CHURCH.

ROMAN CIVILIZATION. 1. In a mechanized age such as ours, when the patterns of life are rapidly changing, it is well to remind ourselves occasionally of the foundations upon which our Western civilization rests. Roman roads, villas, baths, camps, and amphitheatres remind us that the Romans occupied this island for more than four centuries; our language and our laws are stamped with the impress of Rome, and when we speak of the French, Italian, and Spaniards as 'Latins', we bear witness to the extent of Roman influence upon European civilization.

Like most of the ancient civilizations, such as those of Babylonia, Assyria, or even Greece, the civilization of Rome had its roots in an older culture. The growth of the Roman Empire much resembles that of the ASSYRIAN Empire (q.v.). Like the Assyrian, the genius of Rome was not creative: most of the elements of its civilization were borrowed,

2. HISTORY. The traditional date of the founding of Rome is 753 B.C.; but while the Latins were still a small agricultural people settled in the country round the Alban Hills, an advanced Bronze Age civilization had developed in Italy. There were probably three main zones of culture in Italy during the Bronze Age and on into the early Iron Age. In northern Italy a civilization was planted by settlers from eastern Europe and the Danube, who brought with them a knowledge of metal-working and of agriculture. They lived in houses built on piles, called *terremare*, and they cremated their dead. Large cemeteries of cremation urns have been found outside their villages. During the Bronze Age other settlers entered also from the north-east, absorbed the civilization of the Terremare people, and built up flourishing centres of Bronze Age culture.

A ROMAN SENATOR
Statue supposed to represent Cicero
(1st century A.D.). *Ashmolean Mus.*

Between 900 and 800 B.C. came the Etruscans whose origin is still uncertain, though their language and writing indicate that they were probably connected with the HITTITES (q.v.) and southern Asia Minor. They settled in Tuscany in central Italy, and they exercised an important influence on the early stages of Roman civilization.

The second zone of settlement lay to the east of the Apennines along the southern Adriatic coast. Here dwelt the Samnites, a warlike people but without any great culture, who are often mentioned in the early history of Rome. The peoples here were part of Italy's earliest recorded population. They buried their dead in the earth, and with their dead they buried an array of weapons formidable enough to suggest that they were extremely warlike.

The third zone was in south Italy and is culturally quite distinct. Here, the Greek influence grew strong, owing to the establishing of many Greek settlements on the coast, and the coastal area came to be called Magna Graecia.

It was against this background that Roman civilization developed. In their beginnings the Latin farmers of the Alban Hills were barbarous and uncivilized by comparison with the highly civilized Etruscans, or the Greek inhabitants of Capua in the south. The story of the Romans is the story of their struggle against neighbours who were powerful and warlike and the heirs of an ancient civilization; how they forged themselves into a compact and highly trained fighting force and, having once begun their career of conquest, could not stop until they had created the ancient world's greatest empire. The empire won, it had to be governed; and in learning how to govern they developed that genius for administration which is the main characteristic of their civilization.

3. ROMAN CONSTITUTION. Rome, like Athens, began as a city-state. The earliest accounts we have describe Roman society as divided into two classes: the patricians, or wealthy aristocrats, and the plebeians, or common people. Both were ruled over by the king, who was judge, general, and priest, all in one, and who was advised by a council of 300 patrician elders, the senate.

By 509 B.C. the royal family, the Tarquins, had become so tyrannical that the Romans drove them out. The Senate then set up a new form of government, a republic. The king's priestly powers and duties were given to a number of priests headed by the high priest (*pontifex maximus*). His functions as judge and general were divided between two men, called consuls. These two men had to be patricians. They held office for one year only and had power to veto each other's acts. The Senate reserved the right to appoint in time of emergency a 'dictator' with all a king's powers except the priestly. And all these magistracies or chief offices in the state were open only to patricians.

At this time the chief assembly of the people for political purposes was a general assembly, which was called *comitia centuriata*, and in which they voted by hundreds or centuries. This body elected the consuls and voted proposals brought before it by the senate; but the voting was so arranged that the patricians could outvote the plebeians. Thus, at this stage, nearly all political power was in the hands of the patricians, who formed the senate, supplied the consuls, and dominated the assembly.

The internal history of Rome from now till the end of the Roman republic is a history of the struggle for power in the state. At first this was a simple struggle between patricians and plebeians. The plebeians' first important gain was the right to elect from among themselves officials called 'tribunes of the people'. These could veto the action of any of the magistrates, and could also summon assemblies of the plebeians to discuss public affairs and recommend to the senate changes in the laws.

The laws themselves were not at this time known to anyone, except the magistrates. But in 451 B.C. the plebeians enforced the appointment of ten men (the Decemvirs) who drew up the famous body of law called the Twelve Tables. These were displayed where they could be seen by all. This was a second important gain for the people.

By 300 B.C. the plebeians had won, by continual struggle, the right to hold all the great offices in the state, and in 287 B.C. the decisions of their assemblies were granted the force of laws.

But conflict continued. Many of the plebeians had become wealthy and had held important offices: and these, no longer shut out from privileges, now tended to side with the senate, which still represented the powerful and the well-to-do. So the conflict, though no longer between plebeians and patricians in the old way, was still between the few who had power and the many who had not.

Meanwhile the conquest of Italy had been going on, as well as wars with Carthage in North Africa and expansion overseas. These wars made the armies important: soldiers began to give their loyalty to their generals rather than to the state, and generals were tempted to use their power more for personal ambition than for public good.

In the end, rival generals in the army began to support opposite sides in the state, and civil war resulted. In 88 B.C. Marius, claiming to represent the forces of change, and Sulla, claiming to represent those of tradition, took up arms against each other. Sulla, the victor, propped up senatorial government for a time. But in the next generation the struggle was renewed under new leaders, JULIUS CAESAR and POMPEY (qq.v. Vol. V). With Pompey fell the cause of the senate. Caesar became all-powerful, but was murdered while still making good his success. Once again the struggle was fought, this time between Caesar's successor, Octavian, and the senate's champion, Brutus. Octavian triumphed and, with the title of Augustus, so arranged matters that he himself had all the essential powers, and yet the old form of things was on the surface preserved. Both people and senate had lost, and were too weak to prevent the power for which they had fought each other so long from passing into the hands of one man, the Emperor, and his successors.

4. ROMAN LITERATURE AND ART. In estimating the greatness of Roman civilization we must contrast what Rome achieved in government with what she contributed to the human heritage in the field of art, poetry, the drama, or philosophy. It is not unfair to say that in these Rome produced little which was original. True, what she borrowed bore her own stamp, but even the golden age of Augustus produced no such creative activity as made Athens glorious in the age of Pericles, or filled England with song in the spacious days of Elizabeth. The greatest Roman poet, VIRGIL (q.v. Vol. V), the Laureate of the Augustan Age, wrote an epic poem which, though a Roman work of genius, was nevertheless an acknowledged imitation of Homer's *Iliad*; and his *Georgics* follow the model of Greek pastoral poetry. The Roman lyrical poets, such as HORACE, Catullus, and OVID (qq.v. Vol. V), borrowed their metres, and to some extent their subjects, from Greece. The philosophical works of CICERO (q.v. Vol. V) expound Greek Stoic philosophy. The plays which still exist from the flourishing period of Roman drama, the comedies of Plautus and Terence, are wholly Greek in form and spirit. Roman historians also were inspired by Greek models, though they developed an original character: LIVY (q.v. Vol. V) wrote a rather uncritical history of the rise of the Republic; CAESAR wrote accounts of his campaigns in Gaul and Britain, which are models of military history; TACITUS (q.v. Vol. V) wrote the history of the

THE RUINS OF THE ROMAN FORUM
The Forum was the centre of Roman life where public meetings were held and business transacted. *P. Hart*

early Empire in a sombre and caustic style all his own. The Romans wrote a great deal, and their writings form part of the great classical heritage; but, as a whole, it is more a witness to the overwhelming influence of Greek civilization upon her neighbours than an original contribution (*see* LATIN LANGUAGE, Vol. IV).

In architecture the Romans, while borrowing many features from the Greeks, made an original contribution in solving the problems of roofing large halls and spanning wide spaces by developing the use of the vault and arch. By these means they were able to carry out their many remarkable engineering works, the aqueducts and viaducts, the public baths, and other large public buildings.

5. ROMAN RELIGION. In the beginning, the chief gods—the gods of the city and the state, Jupiter, Juno, and Minerva—probably played a far less important part in the life of the people than the little gods, largely nameless, concerned with the affairs of the home and the fields. Jupiter, Juno, and Minerva were probably taken over from the Etruscans; but the little gods of the countryside belonged to the original population (*see* GODS OF GREECE AND ROME). As Rome grew in importance, the Romans felt that the

fate of the city depended on the worship of the great gods and on the due observance of ritual. And so the chief priest (*pontifex maximus*) became responsible for carrying out the state religion, and he was assisted by various sacred persons to whom certain duties were assigned. The flamens attended to the sacrifices and cult of the various gods; the augurs took the auspices (*see* DIVINATION), while priestesses called the Vestal Virgins kept the sacred fire continually burning. But as Rome expanded into an Empire, foreign deities and foreign religious ideas were admitted to the city. The result was that these foreign religions with their priests, their rituals, and their mysteries, attracted many people to whom the state religion meant little. In the hope of providing a religious bond which might unite the provinces of the Empire, Augustus established the worship of the emperor as a divine person; but this new religion never had more than a political importance. It was into this strange mixed world that Christianity entered and gradually triumphed.

6. ROMAN EMPIRE. Outstanding in the achievements of Roman civilization was the practical skill with which it united peoples of widely varying languages, customs, and religions

THE PONT DU GARD, NEAR NÎMES, FRANCE
Ruins of a Roman aqueduct, built at the end of the 1st cent. B.C. or early 1st cent. A.D. *Levy et Neurdein, Paris*

into a political structure which withstood many shocks for nearly a thousand years. In the first place, Rome recognized the value of granting citizenship to conquered peoples as a means of securing their interest and co-operation in the good government and prosperity of their province in the Empire. A Jew of Tarsus could take a pride in being a Roman citizen without losing his pride in being a Jew. Then, following the example of the Persian Empire, Rome recognized the importance of safe and easy communication between all parts of the Empire. The magnificent system of Roman roads and viaducts served a double purpose: they made possible the swift movement of troops to any part of the Empire where disturbance or danger threatened; they made commerce, postal traffic, and civilian travel sure, smooth, and swift; and they thus created conditions which were essential if capital and provinces were to play their parts in relation to each other and remain prosperous and contented. Finally, the great fabric of Roman law, which had slowly developed to meet changing needs, embraced the whole of the Empire, so that a citizen in Palestine might appeal to the decision of the emperor and be sure of a hearing.

The roads, the viaducts, the orderly Roman villas tucked away in some remote corner of Britain, the great framework of law, the very vocabulary of our daily speech, all survive as witnesses of what is meant by Roman civilization.

7. DECLINE OF ROME. From the 3rd century A.D. Rome began to weaken. To defend her territories against barbarians from central Asia, she had to withdraw her troops from the outlying colonies in the west, until the territory she effectively controlled was reduced to the countries lying around the eastern Mediterranean. Rome was no longer the centre of the Empire, and in A.D. 330 the Emperor CONSTANTINE (q.v. Vol. V) moved the capital to Constantinople. In A.D. 410 Rome was sacked by the GOTHS (q.v.). In the middle of the 5th century the Empire was threatened by the HUNS (q.v.), and in A.D. 455 Rome was again sacked, this time by the VANDALS (q.v.). In A.D. 476 the last Roman Emperor laid down his imperial dignity, and the Roman Empire of the West came to an end. The Empire of the East, known as the BYZANTINE Empire (q.v.), with Constantinople as its capital, continued for some centuries longer.

See also ANCIENT CIVILIZATIONS.

ROUMANIANS. The people of eastern Europe are, for the most part Slavs; but the Roumanians are Latin people, a fact of which they are very proud. The Daci, a Thracian tribe, living between the Carpathian mountains and the Danube, were conquered by the Roman Emperor Trajan in A.D. 106. Roman colonists followed, and the country became the Roman province of Dacia. The name Roumania or Romania means land of the Romani or Romans. Later began a series of invasions by GOTHS, TARTARS, HUNS (qq.v.), and Magyars (*see* HUNGARIANS), all of whom left their mark on the Dacian people. The Roumanian language is still largely a Latin one, though with a great many additions from the languages of Roumania's various invaders.

In the 16th century the Turkish conquest of eastern Europe brought the people of Dacia under Turkish rule. It was nearly 300 years before they again became free, and during that time the country, lying as it does between Turkey and eastern Europe, was the battleground for wars between Turkey and Poland, Russia and others. The Danubian Principalities, as they were called, of Moldavia and Wallachia became partly independent in 1829. In 1878 they were united as the Kingdom of Roumania and recognized as wholly independent, under a German Prince of the Hohenzollern family, King Carol (Charles).

The Roumanians took part in the First World War on the side of the Allies. The Roumanians were defeated, but at the Peace Treaty the victors almost doubled the territory of Roumania at the expense of Russia, Austria, and Hungary. In these new provinces were included many people who were not Roumanian by race or language. Germans, Hungarians, Bulgarians, Ukrainians, and Russians were handed over to Roumania by the victorious Allies as part of the land they lived on. While almost all true Roumanians belong to the ORTHODOX EASTERN CHURCH (q.v.), these new Roumanians were, with few exceptions, either Roman Catholics or Lutherans. This same settlement left nearly a million Roumanians outside the borders of their own country, in Russia, Yugoslavia, Bulgaria, and Greece. Roumania has also a large Jewish population.

The Second World War saw Roumania again fighting, but this time on the side of the Germans. She was defeated and, in consequence, lost some of the territory gained in 1918.

A ROUMANIAN PEASANT
Everything is carried on ponies on the rough mountain tracks. *Roumanian Legation*

The great majority of the people of Roumania are peasants working on the land, in the forests, or in the oil-fields. The country peasants, men and women, wear brightly coloured picturesque native dresses decorated with coloured hand embroideries. They live in low one-storeyed wooden houses, also brightly coloured. Before the First World War and the break up of the estates that followed it, the gap between rich and poor was enormous. The rich landowners lived in great luxury in Paris or on the Riviera, while the poor were almost in the position of serfs, living mainly on maize and not able to read or write. They are still very poor, but modern methods of farming and better education have raised their standard of living. Many of them, however, have drifted to the towns and become part of a slum population.

See also Vol. III: ROUMANIA; Vol. IV: ROMANCE LANGUAGES.

RUSSIANS. The people of the U.S.S.R.—the Union of Soviet Socialist Republics—are usually referred to as the Russians. In fact, the Russians are but one of some 160 peoples that live in the U.S.S.R. Originally they were an Alpine people, but in the course of centuries they have mixed with the Mongolian peoples of the north-east (*see* SIBERIAN PEOPLES), with the peoples of the north (*see* LAPPS), and with the Turkic–Tartar peoples of Central Asia (*see* SOVIET CENTRAL

ASIAN PEOPLES). This mixing continues to-day as people come west from the remoter areas of the north and east for education and for training. However, the Russians make up over one-half of the population of the U.S.S.R., their province, the R.S.F.S.R., occupies almost three-quarters of the land, and their language is the official language. It is with them, the Russians proper, that this article deals.

As early as the 7th century B.C. a warlike people called the Scythians lived in the southern steppe country of Russia, north of the Black Sea. Much influenced by the civilizations of Greece and China with whom they traded, they developed a simpler but distinctive art of their own, and they were great horsemen—a characteristic which has continued with the people of the Russian steppes. A succession of tribes followed the Scythians, until the SLAVS (q.v.) first made their appearance. The original Russians were a Slav-speaking people, agriculturists and herdsmen who settled in the lands between the rivers Vistula and the upper Dnieper. They were driven from these lands by the HUNS (q.v.), and settled in the mixed forest lands of the east European Plain (the Great Plain of Russia), an area of low hills, marshes, lakes, and rivers, roughly triangular in shape, with its corners marked by Leningrad, Moscow, and Kiev.

To the north lay the thick coniferous forests and the tundra, with its nomadic population of hunters. To the south and east were the steppes, peopled by nomadic herdsmen who periodically invaded the southern areas of the plain in search of pasture. The Russians had to organize themselves against these invasions, and between the 5th and 8th centuries fortified towns were built along the Dnieper. These towns became the centres of states, and for long, Kiev, at a crossing-place of the Dnieper, was the most important of them. Among the northern invaders were enterprising bands of Vikings from Scandinavia called Varangians, who originally were attempting to reach Constantinople by the river Dnieper for trade purposes, but later came to settle. One of their leaders, Rurik, who was probably a Dane, was invited by the Russians to become ruler of Novgorod, the next most important city-state to Kiev. His successor, Oleg, the Prince of Novgorod, conquered Kiev in 882, and the combined lands of Kiev and Novgorod became known as 'Kievan Russ', the first kingdom of Russia.

Christianity came to Russia from the BYZANTINE EMPIRE (q.v.) with which the Russians did a good deal of trade. The richness and beauty of the ceremonial in the Orthodox Eastern Church appealed to the Russian love of colour and drama. In the 10th century the Russian princess, Olga, was converted to Christianity, and by the end of the century her grandson, Vladimir, accepted Christianity as practised by the Orthodox Eastern Church for himself and his people. In the 11th century many beautiful cathedrals and churches were built in Kiev and Novgorod. When Constantinople and the Byzantine Empire were later overrun by the Turks, Russia became the centre of the ORTHODOX EASTERN CHURCH (q.v.).

In the first half of the 13th century Mongolian tribes called TARTARS (q.v.) overran Russia and ruled till the middle of the 15th century. They became known as the Golden Horde, because Batu, their leader, had a tent of golden colour. Their purpose in conquest was not to settle, but to secure wealth. This eventually caused their downfall as, later, they allowed the armies of Russian princes, in particular the Grand Duke of Moscow, to collect tribute for them, and thus to become rich and powerful. In the 15th century, Moscow, under Ivan III, had grown so strong by these means that she conquered many neighbouring states and asserted her independence. In the 16th century Ivan IV, Ivan the Terrible, proclaimed himself Tsar of all the Russias. Moscow was in a central position in the new kingdom. Merchants came to its markets from western Europe, from Greece, from China, and from India.

The 16th to 19th centuries were years of expansion and much warfare under the Romanovs, a family who ruled Russia from 1613 until the Revolution of 1917. In the 16th century trade was begun with England, and a port was established at Archangel. Later, ports were seized on the Baltic. In 1703 PETER THE GREAT (q.v. Vol. V), who did much to bring Western culture to Russia, built St. Petersburg (now Leningrad) and made it his capital. Moscow did not regain this position till after the Revolution. In the reign of CATHERINE THE GREAT (1762–96) (q.v. Vol. V) the whole of the Ukraine became part of Russia, and ports were obtained on the Black Sea. Between the 17th and 19th centuries, routes were opened to the east, and the lands of central Asia exploited.

THE RED SQUARE, MOSCOW

Lenin's tomb stands on the right against the wall of the Kremlin. In the centre is the Vasiliev Cathedral built in the 16th century, now used as a Museum. *S.C.R.*

The last of the Tsars, Nicholas II, ruled a vast Empire which stretched from Warsaw to the western Pacific, and from Lapland to the Caspian Sea. In this Empire a small number of the Russians, often highly cultured and brilliantly artistic people, enjoyed a privileged position, while millions of peasants of varied nationalities endured a very low standard of living and a state of serfdom which was almost slavery. This minority—the landowning class—controlled directly or indirectly the army, the police, the Church, and the machinery of government.

By the second half of the 19th century the urgent need for reform was becoming understood. Alexander II, Nicholas II's grandfather, was an enlightened ruler, and began the work of liberating the serfs in 1861. In 1864 District *Zemstvo*, local government councils, were set up, and the national system of justice received much needed reform. It seemed that, in spite of the Nihilists and other revolutionary movements, reform might be carried through without violence and bloodshed. Unfortunately, in 1881, Alexander was assassinated, and the next government, under Nicholas II, turned against reform. The work of the revolutionary apostles, LENIN,

TROTSKY (qq.v. Vol. V), Alexander Kerensky, and others, an unsuccessful war with Japan early in the 20th century, and the inefficient and hated government of the weak Tsar, much influenced by the Tsarina (a German) and the vicious and dissolute monk, Rasputin, made revolution inevitable. In December 1916 Rasputin was murdered by nobles who loathed and feared him. But even the removal of the hated Rasputin could not save the situation. The disasters and fearful losses which fell upon the Russian army in the First World War brought things to a head, and in March 1917 the Revolution broke out. The Tsar abdicated, but he and his family were brutally murdered. In October 1917 (by the old Russian calendar, November by the new) Lenin, the leader of the Bolsheviks (majority party of the Social Revolutionists) became head of the new revolutionary government, the Council of People's Commissars. Civil war between the White Russians (the anti-revolutionary party) and the Bolsheviks raged till 1921, bringing with it terrible suffering and cruelty.

From 1921 to 1928 the government consolidated its position, extending its control, building up a new army, a new police force, and a new

SPRING SOWING ON A COLLECTIVE FARM
Huge tractors are used on the wheat fields near the Volga. *Planet News*

civil service. In 1928 Stalin, Lenin's successor, introduced the first of his five-year plans for agriculture and industry. The Empire of the Romanov Tsars had become a very much more unified structure—a commonwealth of sixteen Republics held together by a great centralization of power and an extremely thoroughly planned economy. So great was their progress in the next twenty years that, when in 1941 they were again attacked by Germany, they were able to withstand a fearful invasion, expel the German army from their country, and play a vital part in the Allied victory in the Second World War.

Their land and its climate have had much influence on the history of the Russians. The wide plains of eastern Europe and western Asia and the lack of sharp climatic changes (*see* U.S.S.R., Vol. III) permitted free movement and the development of a very similar type of people over a broad area. Russians tend to be stocky and dark. Their two most noticeable characteristics are an ability to remain cheerful while living frugally and enduring hardship, and a love of colour, music, and laughter. They have a strong sense of humour and a great kindliness, in spite of their tendency to disregard human suffering.

It has been said that they are natural socialists—many of their great novels deal with social problems of people *en masse* rather than with individuals; in their theatres the leading actor in one play is likely to have a small part in his next; and in ballet great attention is paid to the *corps de ballet*.

All their good qualities of patient endurance and humour have been needed in the past twenty-five years, for, in building up their country, much self-sacrifice has been needed. They have made great advances; but to western European eyes much still has to be done. Houses are very scarce—many families still cannot have a room to themselves; clothes are scarce, food is controlled. But much basic work has been done: industries have been built up, canals have been constructed, dams built, factories, hospitals, schools, kindergartens, and technical colleges have been set up, land has been reclaimed for agriculture.

More important even than these material things, the people of Russia have a sense of unity and common purpose in building up their way of life, and a pride in the part they play. The best of Russia's past is the foundation of the Soviet present and future, and this is recognized in the intensive building up of Soviet patriotism. Alexander Nevsky, Peter the Great, Catherine the Great, have become not only Russian heroes, but Soviet heroes.

See also COSSACKS; SIBERIAN PEOPLES; SOVIET CENTRAL ASIAN PEOPLES.
See also Vol. III: U.S.S.R.
See also Vol. V: CHEKHOV; DOSTOEVSKY; PUSHKIN; TOLSTOY; ALEXANDER II; MARX.

S

SACRAMENT. An outward and visible sign of an inward and spiritual grace. The word to-day is used of certain ceremonies of the Church, through which God gives his grace to man.

By the 12th century in the Western Church the ceremonies called sacraments had been fixed at seven. These were Baptism, Confirmation, Eucharist, Penance, Extreme Unction, Ordination, and Matrimony. The Eastern Church had a similar list. At the time of the Reformation the Protestants were determined that only those sacraments 'ordained by Christ Himself', i.e. those with definite New Testament authority, should be accepted as sacraments. They found only two with this authority behind them—namely, Baptism and the Lord's Supper. Though the Roman Catholic and Orthodox Eastern Churches still hold to the seven sacraments, they too regard these two as of paramount importance.

1. BAPTISM. Washing as a sign of spiritual purification is common in many religions, and was prominent in JUDAISM (q.v.), especially when a Gentile was converted. Just before the ministry of Jesus, John the Baptist called Jews themselves to repent and be baptized, as a sign of a new start in life. It was not enough to have been born into the Chosen People: they must be re-born, and baptism was the sign of this rebirth. Jesus took over this custom, and His disciples baptized those who believed (John iv. 2). Jesus added the idea that the new life, which began at baptism, was made possible by the coming of God's Spirit (Acts xix. 2–5). Baptism is the ceremony whereby a new member joins the Christian Church. The denomination called BAPTISTS (q.v.) oppose infant baptism.

2. EUCHARIST. This is also called the Lord's Supper, the Holy Communion, the Mass. The evening on which Jesus was betrayed he ate a

meal with his disciples, told them of his coming death, and broke and blessed bread and gave it to them saying, 'This is my Body', and offered them the cup of wine saying, 'This is my Blood'. He told his disciples to repeat this action in remembrance of Him. This meal ever since has been the central act of Christian worship. Many ideas are included in it: Christ's special presence; Man's communion with Him through receiving the bread and wine; and the offering of the sacrifice of Christ's death to God.

The idea of a fellowship meal to mark special occasions is found in many religions, the best known being the Jewish Passover. Christ came to fulfil, not to destroy, the Law and the prophets, and he brought to completion the ancient idea of SACRIFICE (q.v.).

3. CONFIRMATION. This is the sacrament through which a Christian is strengthened by receiving anew the power of the Holy Spirit, and by accepting personally the vows made on his behalf at his Baptism. In the west the outward and visible sign of this establishment of grace is the laying on of hands by the Bishop. The ceremony takes place when the child is thought to be old enough to take his own vows. In the Eastern Churches confirmation follows immediately on Baptism. Oil, consecrated by a Bishop, is used to 'seal' with the sign of the cross the brow, eyes, nose, mouth, and ears, as the sign that the Holy Spirit comes to the aid of all man's natural powers.

In most branches of the Church no Christian may receive Holy Communion until he has been confirmed.

4. PENANCE. Confession to a priest was advised in the early Middle Ages, as an aid to true repentance; later it became the rule, especially before communion. The priest fixes the penance —some act which will be a sign of repentance and, as far as can be, a putting right of the wrong done. Then he pronounces absolution.

5. EXTREME UNCTION. In the Eastern Orthodox Church this is the ceremony of anointing the sick with holy oil as a means of healing, and has come from a Hebrew custom. In the West it has, rather, the idea of forgiveness for the sins of the various senses (eyes, ears, lips, &c., which are anointed) in preparation for death.

6. ORDINATION. From the time of the Apostles, those who were to rule the local churches were appointed with the laying on of hands, the sign of a special gift of the Spirit for a special work.

In all episcopal Churches a bishop ordains deacons, priests, and also new bishops.

7. MATRIMONY. Christian marriage, as set forth in the New Testament, and always in the services of the Church, is marriage to one partner for life. 'Those whom God hath joined together let no man put asunder.' The outward and visible sign of this unity is the giving and receiving of a ring: the inward and spiritual grace is the power of the Holy Spirit to sanctify married life.

See also CHRISTIAN CHURCH.

SACRED ANIMALS. Belief in the sacredness of certain animals goes back into the distant past, and is still found amongst many primitive peoples. To them, some animals seem much more powerful and a great deal wiser than human beings, and therefore able to bring blessing or misfortune to men. These ideas have led to a great variety of beliefs and rites in connexion with sacred animals.

Primitive people live in a way which is much closer to the animals than our mode of life, gathering or hunting food and living much in the open, as animals do. Naturally they feel that some of their animal neighbours are somewhat like themselves. And they express this in myths and stories, in which animals behave like human

SACRED FIRE SNAKE
Aztec carving. *British Mus.*

beings and men turn into animals or animals into men. These very ancient ideas linger on in some of our FAIRY-TALES (q.v.) and myths, such as the swan-maiden legend—a story of girls transformed into swans, told amongst people in many places all over the world. In many of these stories an animal talks human language, like Balaam's ass (Numbers xxii. 28), and is regarded as wiser in some ways than men.

Stone Age men painted animals, such as deer, bison, and wild boar, on the walls of caves, sometimes depicting weapons sticking into them. Their purpose, probably, was to increase magically the number of these animals and achieve success in hunting them. As a hunter, primitive man learned to respect animals which could outwit or kill him, and when he was successful against them, he believed that he had been aided by supernatural powers. But primitive people, who are impressed by the strength or craftiness of an animal, often go on from this to think of it as having greater and stranger powers than it actually has. Very often they do not know the real cause of quite simple things, and so they think, for instance, that because frogs appear with the rain, therefore the frog is a rain-maker, or that when a bird, such as the swallow, appears in spring, it has brought the spring. If they see a frightened hare dash out of the corn as they reap the last sheaves, they suppose it to be the corn spirit. The ancient Egyptians may have come to believe in the jackal god of the dead, Anubis, because they sometimes saw jackals stealing away from the tombs; and no doubt the beetle was regarded by them as a sacred insect, because it was seen emerging from the ball of dried dung in which the egg had been laid—thus appearing to be life from the dead.

Men worship and regard as sacred things which may do them harm, as well as things which seem to bring them prosperity, and they treat them very carefully lest they should be aroused to do evil. Animals are amongst the strange things of this kind. A snake, for instance, appears mysterious as well as dangerous. People often exaggerate the powers of things they fear or which mystify them. Animals, therefore, are believed to have supernatural powers or to be themselves supernatural beings, requiring to be appeased with sacrifices or other forms of reverence.

Sometimes these ideas result in the belief that it is wrong to kill certain animals. Thus, in some

ANUBIS

Egyptian jackal god of the dead. Sculpture from Tutankh-amen's tomb, XVIII Dynasty. *Ashmolean Museum, Oxford*

Indian bazaars, the monkeys are a great nuisance, for nobody dares to kill them when they boldly steal food. Some peoples believe in a mysterious connexion between their various groups and certain animals, which goes back to the creation of the world. Such animals, called totem animals, are usually not killed or eaten by the group named after the totem animal. An Australian native, belonging to the frilled lizard clan, regards this creature as sacred and calls it 'father' (*see* TOTEMISM).

There are, however, many animals which have to be killed for food or in self-defence, and people feel that they ought to apologize to them or in some way appease their spirits, lest they avenge themselves on those who kill them. So the hunter often has to observe TABOO (q.v.) to prevent evil, supposed to be caused by the animal spirits, from befalling him. The Ainu of northern Japan and some Siberian tribes slaughter bears and feast on them, but always take the precaution of performing various ceremonies, so that the bears' spirits may not seek revenge.

Reverence may be shown to animals in other ways besides worship. Amongst Indo-Chinese tribes, for example, the tiger is spoken of with a specially respectful name. In Ancient Babylonian and other carvings there are human figures with animals' heads. It is thought that these represent dancers or people taking part in ceremonies with animal masks. There is a

Stone Age picture of what is believed to be a magician wearing horns on his head, and many primitive people have magical dances in which they imitate animals.

See also FOLK-LORE.

SACRED BOOKS. 1. Among the earliest sacred writings known to us are the spells and prayers which were inscribed on the walls of burial-chambers in the pyramids of Egypt, about 2600 B.C. These are called the *Pyramid Texts*. Some 600 years later, in Egypt, another collection of religious texts occurred on the lids and sides of coffins, and these may be considered the direct ancestors of yet a third collection—the *Book of the Dead*—which, from the later period of Egyptian civilization to the Roman period (about 1580 B.C. to A.D. 300), was frequently copied out on papyrus, or inscribed upon the walls of tombs.

In Greece, in the pastures of Thessaly, probably before 1000 B.C., songs were sung in which were woven vague memories of ancient wars and of the gods who were thought to have had their home on Mount Olympus. During the next three centuries, after the songs had greatly increased in number, they were finally put together and, in this form, have been handed down to us as the poems that bear the names of Homer and Hesiod. At that time the Greeks had no other sacred books, and so the Homeric songs—the *Iliad*, the story of the Trojan war, and the *Odyssey*, the tale of the wandering hero (Odysseus) on his return from Troy—became virtually the 'Bible of Greece'.

2. HINDU SACRED BOOKS. The oldest sacred books in the world are the collection of hymns known as the *Rig-Veda*, which were put together in India between 1500 and 1000 B.C., in honour of the nature-gods whom the Aryan-speaking peoples brought with them, when they first entered the Punjab about 1500 B.C. (*see* INDIAN CIVILIZATIONS, Section 2). The term *Veda* means knowledge or wisdom, and the Hindus believe that these hymns are inspired songs, which were revealed to the seers as magical words of power, like the Egyptian texts. The *Rig-Veda* is about five times larger than the book of Psalms in the Old Testament, and contains 1,028 hymns grouped into ten books, for recitation by the priests at the sacrifices. The tenth book is much later than the rest, and contains more profound thought. It is believed that the Vedic hymns had been handed down from father to son in the

PAGE FROM THE RIG-VEDA
From a 17th-century MS. *Bodleian Lib.*

families of the seers who composed them, and their contents were kept secret and never written down at the time of their composition.

Later, a number of instructions in matters of ritual were added to the hymns for the guidance of the priests or Brahmans, and these are called the *Brahmanas*. Since divine power was in the sacred words, the words had to be uttered quite correctly by the priests, otherwise the spell would be broken. Between 800 and 600 B.C., hermits began to try to find a way to escape altogether from the world, which they regarded as evil, by bringing their souls into tune with the divine soul of the universe. They began to break away from the old Vedic beliefs about nature-gods and magical spells, and became seekers after the absolute, eternal, divine principle, which is also the world-soul into which every individual spirit is merged (*see* GOD). This 'secret Doctrine' was set forth in the *Upanishads*—a word meaning 'sitting close to' or getting into communication with the inner meaning of life. These beliefs took a great variety of forms, and there are some 250 *Upanishads*, many of which represent different Hindu schools of thought about 'Brahman' as the world soul (*see* HINDUISM).

3. BUDDHIST SACRED BOOKS. These doctrines, however, did not satisfy GAUTAMA, the Buddha, (q.v. Vol. V) (born about 560 B.C.) who, as a result of his remarkable spiritual experience, which is called his 'enlightenment', discovered what he and his followers believed to be the true solution of the problem of existence and the mystery of pain and sorrow. The oldest books that tell of his life and teaching were not completely put into writing until about 500 years later. Very likely they go back in the oral memory of the Buddhist community much farther than this, and some of the materials from which they were formed may have come from the first disciples of the Buddha, perhaps even from his own lips. But how much of these scriptures called the *Tripitaka* or 'Three Baskets of Tradition', goes back to his time we cannot be certain. They were written in Pali, the dialect of the common people of north-west India, and contain twenty-nine subdivisions, ranging in length from 10 to 1,839 pages. Only some of them have been translated into English, but, when the text is complete, it will occupy probably 10,000 pages. Besides these authorized scriptures, there is also a large quantity of Buddhist literature in Sanskrit; but none of the writing claims to be a divine revelation, because in Buddhism there is no idea of a personal God who discloses Himself to man. Nevertheless, both in Hinduism and Buddhism a devotional movement arose in course of time, in which God was thought to have descended to earth in human form, as Krishna or one of the Buddhas. The story of these 'descents' is told in the great Hindu *Bhagavad Gita*, 'the Song of the Blessed One' (Krishna), and in the Buddhist *Lotus of the True Law* (*see* BUDDHISM).

4. CHINESE SACRED BOOKS. In China and Japan, the sacred books are mainly 'the records of ancient matters', as one of them is called by the Japanese, in which the history of the nation is traced back to the mythical 'age of the gods'. The Chinese venerate the words of good rulers and wise men, because they are believed to have been raised up by Heaven to rule and teach men how to live well. One of these great teachers, CONFUCIUS (q.v. Vol. V), collected the literature of China and put it into four books, which have ever since been the *Classics* of the Chinese. These are *The Book of History*, *The Book of Poetry*, *The Book of Ceremony*, and *The Book of Changes*. The only work that Confucius wrote himself was a short history of his state of Lu, which is the fifth of the *Classics*. The rest are accounts of the traditional history of China, rules of behaviour and worship, folk-songs, hymns, and a book of the Sayings of Confucius, known as the *Analects*. Another Chinese wise man, Lao-tse, who was born about 607 B.C., some fifty years before Confucius, became the librarian in the royal capital Loyang, and wrote in a short book all the wisdom that he had collected during his long life. He believed that the 'Way of Heaven' or *Tao* is the divine order that runs through everything, and that if one lived quietly and acted according to this principle, one would be happy and blessed.

So he wrote about the *Tao* (*see* CHINESE RE-LIGION).

5. ZOROASTRIAN SACRED BOOKS. We must turn, however, to Zoroastrianism, Judaism, Christianity, and Islam to find sacred books which are believed to contain a divine revelation through the written words of scripture. Thus, the *Gathas* or Psalms of the *Avesta*, the Zoroastrian Bible, are thought to contain the records of the visions and revelations of the great prophet of Persia (who lived about 600 B.C.). In fact, only seventeen of those that remain go back to his time. The rest of the Avestan sacred books are later hymns in praise of angels and ancient heroes, and accounts of ceremonial rules concerning purifications and protection against demons (*see* ZOROASTRIAN).

6. HEBREW SACRED BOOKS. In Palestine, after the return of the Jews from exile in Mesopotamia in 538 B.C., the leaders of the community collected the ancient writings and divided them into three groups—the Law, the Prophets, and the Writings. In doing so, sometimes they combined under one name documents which had been the work of different authors. Thus, the first five books of the Old Testament—*Genesis, Exodus, Numbers, Leviticus, Deuteronomy* (commonly called the *Pentateuch*)—were attributed to Moses, and formed the first section (the Law) of this literature. In the second subdivision (the Prophets) the pronouncements of the Hebrew Prophets—*Isaiah, Jeremiah, Ezekiel,* and the twelve Minor Prophets—were collected together with the books of *Joshua, Judges,* 1 and 2 *Samuel,* and 1 and 2 *Kings.* As the services of the restored Temple were developed, 150 religious songs were arranged as the *Book of Psalms,* and with *Proverbs, Job, Song of Songs, Ruth, Lamentations, Ecclesiastes, Esther, Daniel, Ezra, Nehemiah* and 1 and 2 *Chronicles,* formed the third section (the Writings). But it was not until the Christian era that the Jewish leaders combined all these ancient writings into a single book, which, translated into English from the Hebrew, is called the Old Testament (*see* BIBLE).

Besides these authorized sacred books, which make up what is known as the 'canon', or official scriptures, the Jews had other religious documents, described as *The Apocrypha,* portions of which, in addition to the canonical books, are appointed to be read in Christian churches. Some of these, such as *The Wisdom of Solomon* and *The Wisdom of Jesus, Son of Sirach* (*Ecclesiasticus*),

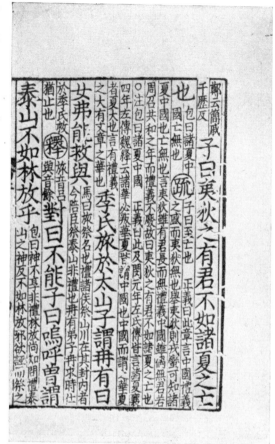

PAGE FROM THE 'ANALECTS' OF CONFUCIUS
One of the earliest printed copies, Sung Dynasty, *c.* 10th century A.D. *Bodleian Lib.*

are full of very beautiful literature. The books of the *Maccabees* describe the great struggle of the Jews for liberty in the 2nd century B.C., which played an important part in preparing the way for the events described in the New Testament (*see* JUDAISM).

7. CHRISTIAN SACRED BOOKS. As Jesus left no written records, the accounts of His life, work, and teaching have come down to us in the form of narratives (i.e. Gospels), collected from various sources during the second half of the 1st century A.D. It is commonly thought by scholars that some of His teaching was written down in the form of a lost document (now called Q), that was known to the writers of the first three Gospels, and from which they borrowed some of their material. To this they added stories about Jesus, His sayings and accounts of His mighty works, reserving for detailed treatment the sequence of events during His last

PAGE FROM THE KORAN
12th-century MS. *Bodleian Lib.*

few days on earth, from Maundy Thursday evening until Easter Morning. The first of these evangelists was St. Mark who wrote, about A.D. 65, the Gospel that bears his name. Then St. Luke retold the story with certain additions (e.g. the account of the birth and infancy of Jesus, and some parables and incidents not mentioned by St. Mark). Towards the end of the century came the First and Fourth Gospels as we know them—those bearing the names of St. Matthew and St. John. The writer of the first of these two included many of the discourses of Christ, like the Sermon on the Mount, and a number of Old Testament prophecies concerning the Messiah, arranged in a manner suitable for reading in church and for teaching purposes. The author of the Fourth Gospel, St. John, at the end of the century, retold the story in his own way to bring out the deeper spiritual meaning of the life and work of Jesus as the Son of God.

Of the remaining twenty-three books of the New Testament, most are letters written by St. Paul to local churches about matters of practical administration and questions of doctrine. Several of these letters (e.g. *Thessalonians, Galatians, Corinthians*) are earlier than the Gospels (*see* CHRISTIANITY).

All the books of the New Testament were written in Greek, some fifty fragments of early Greek manuscripts having been discovered in recent years. The famous *Codex Sinaiticus*, for example, dates from the early 4th century, and there is a fragment of *St. John's Gospel* which is thought to have been written before A.D. 150.

8. ISLAM SACRED BOOK. The *Koran* (Qur'an), the 'Bible' of ISLAM (q.v.), is believed by Moslems to contain the words of Allah dictated to Mo-HAMMED (A.D. 570–632) (q.v. Vol. V) in Arabic from a book kept in Heaven. Some Moslems think, however, that, while the teaching was revealed to the Prophet, the language was his own. The Koran consists of many stories borrowed from the Old Testament, later Jewish writings, and the Christian apocryphal Gospels. But it is generally believed in Islam that the revelation given to Mohammed has superseded the truth given in the Bible. Since these revelations describe things that the Prophet could not have learnt or known unless Allah (God) had revealed them to him, they are regarded as 'miraculous'. So the Koran is for Moslems the most sacred book in the world, containing, as they firmly believe, the last word of God to mankind.

SACRIFICE. The name given to the chief act of worship in most religions. It is the making of an offering to a divine being, in supplication for those who are making the offering. The sacrifice, however, can have a variety of purposes. Its purpose may be to establish a communion—that is, a joining of man and his god together in a very close bond of union. Its purpose may be to restore a relationship that has been broken by some improper act on the part of man (whether committed deliberately or accidentally) with harmful consequences. This driving away of the evil, or covering it up with purifying blood, often forms an important element in the ritual or ceremony. In some religions sacrifice may be an act of thanksgiving for blessings received. The highest offering of all is the giving of self on behalf of others.

In sacrifice of the communion type a sacramental meal is very often held, in which the worshipper, in order to receive spiritual strength and power, partakes of food and drink which is filled with the divine life of the god. Before receiving this gift, the priest usually offers to the god the life-giving blood of the victim—for primitive people believe that the gods need new life, just as they need it themselves. Looked at from this point of view, sacrifice becomes of vital importance for the well-being of mankind and the world; for, unless the gods are kept healthy and vigorous, they will not be able to bestow their gifts on man. Victims, therefore, are slain on the altar so that the setting free of their lives may produce more life on earth, as well as to drive away evil, expel death, and restore the bond that has been broken by sin. The two chief objects of the ritual of sacrifice are the making of (*a*) an act of communion, (*b*) an act of reparation and amendment for some wrong committed, either by an individual or by the community. Behind both of these intentions is the same desire, namely to enter into closer and more beneficial relations with the source of all strength and power, and to remove everything that hinders and spoils this relationship, so important for the well-being of mankind.

To bring this about the victim has to be somehow identified with the god, so that his life is the same as the divine life. In the ancient civilizations and in many savage tribes the king was regarded as a god, living on earth as a man, or at least having a divine life different from that of anyone else. By his supernatural powers he controlled the forces of nature. If he became old or weak, the people believed that the crops might fail. To prevent this calamity, kings were often killed before they lost their full strength. Thus, they were required to give their own lives as a kind of sacrifice on behalf of the community over which they ruled, in order to renew the vitality of nature. But various attempts used to be made to find a substitute for the royal victim. For instance, a strong and healthy prisoner of war might be made into a mock king for a time (generally a year), and then, at the end of his period of office, he would be sacrificed at the altar instead of the real sovereign.

This custom was prevalent in central America among people like the AZTECS (q.v.), and relics of it are to be found in most of the ancient civilizations, where human sacrifice was very common. Nevertheless, since the practice has always been against the natural instincts of man, there has been a tendency to replace human beings by animals on the altar, as in the story of the offering of Isaac in the *Book of Genesis*. Among the Hebrews it seems that at one time human sacrifice was practised, and then, no doubt, the divine command of the God of Israel, 'the first-born of thy sons shalt thou give unto me', recorded in *Exodus* (xxii. 29), was carried out quite literally. The numbers of skeletons of children found in the foundations of buildings in Palestine suggest that infants were often offered as sacrifices to strengthen the walls of houses and cities. The Feast of the Passover appears to commemorate a general massacre of first-born; but this grim event came to be celebrated every spring by the offering of a lamb or kid instead of human beings (Exod. xii; Deut. xvi. 1–8). The blood was then smeared on doorposts to drive away the forces of evil, which were supposed to be very active at that season of the year. For much the same reason, in the autumn a goat was slain, and its life-blood was sprinkled on the high priest, the sanctuary, and the whole congregation of Israel, while a second goat, the scapegoat, was sent into the desert, laden with the burden of the guilt of the nation, to carry it, like a dustcart, to a demon of the wilderness, called Azazel (Lev. xvi).

Thus, the institution of sacrifice centred in the idea of securing fresh life and driving away evil. As it has developed from these very crude beginnings, it has taken over other meanings, but they are all based on this general belief. For example, when the slaying of the first-born was no longer required among the Hebrews, they were allowed to pay a sum of money as an act of 'redemption' (i.e. buying back the victim that would have been offered) (Num. xviii. 15–16; Lev. xxvii. 27 f.; Ezek. xliv. 30). In this way the idea arose of paying 'tithe', or a tenth part of the first-fruits, in support of a sanctuary (Amos iv. 4; Lev. xxvii. 30, 32 f.). These offerings were made to the god or to his representative the king and were, therefore, holy (i.e. set apart), like the actual victim. But as soon as sacrifice became regarded as a gift of goods or money or the produce of the fields, it lost some of its earlier meaning, and it became very much easier for a rich man to buy off his sins by paying a sum of money, than by making a real act of sacrifice.

In Christianity this conception is lifted on to a higher spiritual plane, when God is represented as offering Himself to take away the sins of mankind and to bring the human race into a new and closer relationship with Him. Thus, according to Christian beliefs, Jesus, as the Incarnate Son of God, laid down His own life in a supreme act of sacrifice to draw all men to God. To give oneself for the sake of others is the highest form of love, and this is what Christ did on the Cross (John xv. 13). So the outpouring of His life's blood represents the climax of sacrifice in both its aspects of renewing life and removing evil. This has been commemorated ever since in the central act of Christian worship, called the Eucharist or Holy Communion; although there are different views about the way in which the death of Christ is 'shown forth' in this service. At first, it was mainly an act of thanksgiving before God for the blessing of Redemption. Later, it became more particularly a memorial of the offering on the Cross, repeated day by day at the altars on earth as an atonement for sin. Under the appearance of bread and wine Christ sacrifices Himself, as it were, in the same way that He offered Himself on Good Friday; and so the Mass became regarded as an act of propitiation to make God well disposed towards man. To some people this medieval view seemed to lay too much stress on the Eucharist as an act of sacrifice complete in itself, rather than as a memorial of what Christ had done Himself once and for all; and so, after the Reformation, the Eucharist was celebrated chiefly as a Communion service, in which Christians received the Body and Blood of Christ to refresh their souls. More attention now, however, is being paid to the sacrificial side of the rite, and it is generally agreed that in 'the Breaking of the Bread' (as the service was originally called by the Apostles) a memorial is made of the sacrifice of the death of Christ.

See also RELIGION; SACRAMENT.

SAGA. Icelandic for a tale, and used for a particular kind of tale written almost entirely in Iceland.

Iceland was settled in the 9th century by Norwegians, many of whom went there via Scotland and Ireland and took with them natives of those countries. In the 11th century the Icelanders were converted to Christianity, and their conversion was followed by an extraordinary outburst of learning: the classics were studied, and many books, including romances such as those of King Arthur (*see* ARTHURIAN LEGEND), were translated into Icelandic. All these influenced the sagas which were written down in the 12th and 13th centuries. They took the form of lives of heroes, who were supposed to have lived in the 10th century or earlier in Iceland or other parts of the north. They told how these heroes had triumphed over giants, monsters, and human enemies, and how at last they were slain fighting against enormous odds. Conversations make up a great part of the sagas, just as they do of modern novels, and many of them are very witty. When some of these sagas were first translated into English in the middle of the last century, it was widely believed that,

YGGDRASIL, THE TREE OF LIFE
Drawing by Sir E. Burne-Jones from William Morris's *The Story of Sigurd the Volsung*, Kelmscott Press, 1898

if the monsters and fabulous beasts were put on one side, the rest of the stories could be regarded as true history. Few now hold this belief, for it is recognized that long conversations cannot, in fact, be remembered for 200 or 300 years, and also that much of their matter is drawn from Norse and Irish myths. Like detective stories, the sagas conform to a fixed pattern, and though the heroes are often described as being in contact with historical personages, it is unlikely that they themselves ever lived. The sagas are now recognized for what they really are—very fine examples of the storyteller's art. Perhaps the best are those of Burnt Njal and Grettir the Strong, both of which can be bought in cheap editions. The hero-tales of countries other than Iceland are sometimes called sagas, but none of them are really in saga form.

See also NORSE MYTHS.
See also Vol. III: ICELAND.

SAHARAN PEOPLES (NORTH AFRICA). **1.** The Mediterranean lands of North Africa have been the scene of many migrations, settlements, and conquests, from prehistoric to very recent times. The Phoenicians, Greeks, and Romans colonized parts of the coast. The Arabs conquered it and converted the inhabitants to the Moslem religion. Later, they were conquered by the Turks, and the north-west coast, the Barbary States, became the headquarters of pirates who preyed on Mediterranean shipping. Finally the Turks were driven out by the French in 1830.

The dominating physical feature of the area south of the coast-lands is the Sahara Desert, the largest desert in the world, 1,000 miles from north to south and 3,000 miles from east to west. But this desert is not to be thought of merely as a 'sea of sand'. There are plains of hard sands, rock-strewn plateaux cut by deep wadis or dried-up water-courses, and series of mountain ranges. Where large depressions occur in the desert, underground water often comes to the surface and oases are formed. There, date-palms flourish, and fruit, vegetables, and millet can be grown. Some oases are small, but in many a sufficient quantity of food can be grown to support a very large number of people. The oasis of Tafilet, in Morocco, for example, has a population of 50,000 people.

The north-west coastal region has a series of high mountain ranges, the Atlas mountains, running from east to west, with a narrow coastal plain 50–100 miles wide. Here, the climate is like that of southern Europe, with hot, dry summers and mild, rainy winters. In this region there are two main groups of peoples, the Berbers, who practise agriculture in the fertile river valleys, and for the most part live in permanent villages, and the ARABS (q.v.), most of whom are nomads, moving from place to place in search of fresh pastures for their flocks.

2. THE BERBERS. The towns and villages of the Berbers have very narrow streets with high flat-roofed houses on each side. The Berber tribes with their flocks of sheep and goats often move up into the mountains after they have planted their crops. There they live in tents, and when the harvest is ripe they come down again to their villages. Some Berber tribes also travel south in the autumn to buy dates in the oases, so that they spend most of the year away from their villages.

The Kabyles are fairly typical of the Berbers as a whole. They live in villages which are independent and not under any central authority; though sometimes several villages join together in times of war, or a meeting of representatives from a number of villages may be held to settle disputes. The village is governed by a council of adult men (*djemaa*) which meets once a week. It settles disputes within the village, the elders (the heads of families and influential men) taking the principal part in the discussions. Each council has a president, an *amin*—generally a wealthy man from one of the leading families— who is elected by the council. The villages are also divided into two groups, known as *sofs*, at the head of which are rich and influential men. Members of a *sof* help one another in times of difficulty and when labour is needed for harvesting or house-building.

The villages are often built in the most inaccessible parts of the mountains for protection against raiders. The houses are made of mud and stone, and have flat roofs. Each family lives in one house. Ties between kinsfolk are very strong—a man's kinsmen used to be considered liable for crimes committed by him.

The dress of the men consists of a red fez, loose baggy trousers, a long loose shirt, and a long woollen cape. The women wear loose

A BERBER HORSEMAN
Dorien Leigh

cotton dresses, bright coloured headkerchiefs, and much jewellery.

The Kabyles are an agricultural people, but, except in the river valleys, they have to cultivate poor soil. They prepare the land with a plough and a short-handled hoe: a festival is held when ploughing begins. At harvest-time the grain is cut with a sickle, threshed by being trod out by oxen, and often ground by hand in a hand mill (a rotary quern). They have two important fruit crops—figs and olives.

They are good craftsmen. The women make pottery, some of it like that made by the ancient Egyptians, while some resembles that made in Cyprus. They also weave and embroider. Their jewellery work, some of it in silver enriched with coral, is excellent, and they wear ear-rings, necklaces, bracelets, anklets, and brooches.

The Kabyles are Moslem by religion, but they have retained many old pagan beliefs. They believe in evil spirits and in the power of the evil eye, and they wear amulets to protect themselves against harm.

Berber and Arab peoples are found also in Morocco, where the name MOOR (q.v.) is generally applied to the town dwellers.

Markets, known as *sugs*, play a very great part in the lives of these North African peoples. In some places large annual fairs are held, where goods from all parts of North Africa, the Sahara, the Sudan, and Morocco are exchanged. Weekly fairs are held in most tribal groups, many of these being associated with the shrines of saints. In these markets can be seen every kind of trader—traders in cottons and silks, sellers of groceries and fruit, grain merchants, dealers in cattle and sheep. Here also are to be found blacksmiths and barbers. Lawyers are present to witness important sales and advise on law cases. Entertainers—clever gymnasts, snake-charmers, and story-tellers—amuse the crowds. In the market friends meet, news is spread, and the commands of government announced and discussed.

3. THE ARABS. The most typical Arab peoples are found farther east. Some are still true nomadic peoples, such as the camel-owning tribes, the Kababish and the Kawahla of north-west Kordofan in the Sudan. Others, like the Baqqara, are cattle-owning. The nomadic Arabs generally look down on the settled peoples both Arab and Berber. Each Arab tribe is under the control of a head sheikh, and is made up of a number of groups, each with its own sheikh. Generally the position of sheikh is hereditary, though sometimes a sheikh is elected by the men of the group. A nomad Arab settlement consists of a series of long, black tents generally arranged in a circle, surrounded by a fence of thorny branches to protect the livestock from thieves and wild animals.

4. NEGROES AND TUAREG. Many of the oases of the Sahara are inhabited by negroid peoples—the Haratin, for example, who are descended from slaves brought from the Sudan; but most of the central Sahara is inhabited by the TUAREG (q.v.). While the Arabs in the north use horses, the Tuareg are a camel-riding people. They were formerly greatly feared as raiders, for they used to attack settlements to capture camels, and plunder caravans crossing the western Sahara. One of these large caravans crossing the Sahara might consist of as many as 5,000 camels. Tuareg men wear veils, without which they are never seen. These cover the lower part of their faces but not their eyes. They are Moslems by religion, but they allow their women much greater freedom than most Moslem peoples. The women do not wear veils, and take a larger part in public life.

5. THE TIBU occupy the Tibesti highland area farther east and south of the Libyan Desert. In former days they were a very powerful tribe, and were often at war with Tuareg peoples. They have dark skins and are more negroid in appearance than the other peoples of the Sahara.

The Tibu and other settled peoples in the oases of the Sahara practise agriculture. Their most important plant is the date-palm, which supplies them with dates to eat and wood to make bowls, camel saddles, tent-pegs, tables, and seats. They have developed many ways of obtaining water: sometimes they build dams across the beds of dried-up streams, so that when the rains fall and the streams fill up, the water can be caught; in other places they dig deep wells.

6. NILE VALLEY PEOPLES. The Nile valley was one of the centres of very early civilization. The peasants are Moslems; but many of the town dwellers are Coptic Christians. Most of them are small farmers, and their agriculture depends on a system of irrigation from the Nile. This now depends on great barrages and modern canals; but formerly the natural rise of the flood-water was used. The water is made to flow into

A VILLAGE ON THE NILE. *Roy. Geog. Soc.*

enclosures with high banks. When these are filled, the water is made to run into others farther down the valley. After the soil has been soaked by the irrigation, the crops are planted. The peoples live in houses of sun-dried brick with floors of beaten mud. Their villages are situated on small hills and elevated ground, so as to avoid the floods. The dress of the Egyptian peasant consists of a long, coarse cotton garment. The women wear a long black dress and a shawl to cover their heads. The Moslem women wear veils.

See also ARABS; ISLAM; Vol. III: SAHARA DESERT; NILE RIVER; Vol. IV: AFRICAN LANGUAGES.

SAINT. In the New Testament the word Saint is used as meaning followers of Christ—people made holy by their faith. Gradually the word came to mean selected Christians of outstanding holiness and courage. In A.D. 155 Polycarp, bishop of Smyrna, was martyred: his people buried him, and then gathered together every year to celebrate 'the birthday of his martyrdom'. This is the first example of the veneration of the relics of a saint, and the keeping of a Saint's Day. In the 4th century, when the Roman Empire accepted Christianity, the custom of venerating saints developed, because the idea of

paying honour to those who had suffered in the early struggles of the Church appealed to the people. The tendency to exaggerate the honour paid to saints led one Church authority to explain, 'We do not *worship* the saints, but venerate them as men of God.'

In the Early Church, when Christianity was brought to a new country, the missionaries sometimes turned the temples of the old religion into churches, and transferred heathen festivals to the honour of the saints. In this lay the danger that the saints might be worshipped as the local heathen gods had been worshipped—a state of affairs little different from polytheism, and quite contrary to Christian teaching.

In the Middle Ages relics (or reputed relics) of saints established in shrines were visited by pious people on PILGRIMAGES (q.v.). The countries of Christendom each began to adopt a patron saint, generally someone connected with their history. The patron saint of Ireland, St. Patrick, was the missionary who brought Christianity to Ireland in the 5th century. St. David of Wales was a 6th-century archbishop of Caerleon. The adoption of St. Andrew for Scotland is less obvious. According to tradition the Apostle St. Andrew preached to the Scythians, and so became Russia's patron. There was a

ST. LAWRENCE
The saint is holding the grid-iron on which he was flayed. Figure from King Henry VII's Chapel, Westminster Abbey, *R. P. Howgrave-Graham*

legend that a Greek bishop was directed by a vision to fetch a relic (an arm) from St. Andrew's grave in Constantinople. The bishop's ship was wrecked on the Scottish coast, and he landed and founded the Church and town of St. Andrews. A more likely reason is that a missionary went from an English church of St. Andrew in A.D. 732 to convert the Picts, and called the church which he founded by the name of his own church. St. George was martyred in A.D. 303 in Asia Minor. The Crusaders brought home stories of his aid in their battles; and this led to his being adopted in the 13th century as the English patron saint. His day, 23 April, is kept as the English national day.

Cities adopted a special saint as guardian, and so did trades and professions. Particular saints were thought of, generally as the outcome of a tradition or legend, as caring for man's welfare in some particular way. St. Christopher is the guardian saint of travellers, St. Nicholas cares for children, St. Anthony helps people who have lost things, St. Hubert looks after animals, and St. Blaise cares for those who have sore throats. People gave their children saints' names with the idea that the saint would look after the welfare of the child. The saint on whose day the child was born was considered as the child's patron saint (*see* INDEX, p. 123).

Martyrdom was the usual qualification for becoming a saint. A new saint only becomes officially recognized or canonized in the Roman Catholic Church after very thorough investigation by the Congregation of Rites, and an official announcement by the Pope. The veneration of saints plays an important part both in ROMAN CATHOLICISM and in the ORTHODOX EASTERN CHURCH (qq.v.). In any Roman Catholic church there are generally many images of saints and side chapels dedicated to them. In an Orthodox Eastern Church icons—pictures of saints, painted or in mosaics—take the place of images and are considered sacred. In both churches prayers to God are often made through the mediation of saints. The Protestant churches hold that Christ is the only Mediator between man and God; and at the time of the Reformation there was a strong move against the veneration of saints.

SALVATION ARMY, *see* Vol. V: BOOTH.

SARACENS, *see* CRUSADES.

SARDINIANS, *see* Vol. III: SARDINIA.

SATAN. 1. Satan is the name that has been given by Jews and Christians to the chief spirit of evil and the great enemy of God and man. Sometimes he is known in a more general sense as the Devil, while the followers of Mohammed call him Iblis. As he has many names, so he has a long history behind him, which goes back to the idea of a struggle between good and evil that has been going on ever since the world began. This conflict takes many forms, and we find examples of it in myths and fairy stories all over the world: the bad spirit engages in a fight or tussle of some kind with the champion of the friendly and helpful powers, who usually in the end defeat their wicked adversary.

2. THE DEVIL IN ANCIENT EGYPT. Ancient Egypt had long been divided into two kingdoms perpetually at war with each other; and the people were accustomed to live in a fertile oasis watered by the river Nile, and surrounded by a terrible desert. The distinction, therefore, between good and evil was a natural idea to them, and it found expression in their myths in the shape of two opposed forces—Set, around whose figure evil in its various forms had collected, and Osiris, the author of all life, who was connected with the life-giving Sun. Set murdered his brother Osiris, and became the model of the Devil as prince of the powers of darkness. The Egyptians, for instance, thought that Set tried to prevent the sun from rising in the sky at dawn; and as the enemy of mankind, they represented him as a huge serpent-dragon, having under his command all the fiends of the underworld. Night by night the never-ending fight between light and darkness went on, and in the changes in the seasons from winter to spring the same battle was fought between Set and Horus, the son of Osiris (*see* EGYPTIAN MYTHS).

3. THE DEVIL IN ANCIENT PERSIA. If the original idea of the Devil is seen most clearly in the Egyptian Set, it was in Persia that the picture of this struggle between good and evil reached its height in the imagination of the ancient world. There the central idea in religion was the warfare of the two opposed forces, who divided between them all the helpful and harmful powers in heaven and on earth, in nature and amongst men, as well as in the animal and vegetable kingdoms. Over and above these stood the good God called Ahura Mazdah. He alone had made the universe and he controlled it, but on a somewhat lower plane good and evil were arrayed against each other, represented by two primeval twin spirits, Good Thought (Spenta Mainyu) and the Lie (Angra Mainyu), with their respective followers. In course of time the twin spirits under one supreme God developed into a single author of evil, Ahriman or the Druj, who fought against, but was not as powerful as, the Creator, Ahura Mazdah. Unlike Satan in Christianity or Islam, the Druj was thought to have under his control a crowd of demons, or *daevas*, whom he had actually himself created, together with harmful creatures such as serpents, wolves, locusts, ants, and vermin. Men of diabolical character, disease, magic, witch-

SET, THE EGYPTIAN DEVIL
Hutchinson's

craft, and similar evils were thought to be his agents—so that there were really two creations and two creators, one exercising his powers for good, and the other for ill (*see* ZOROASTRIAN).

4. THE JEWISH IDEA OF SATAN. It was probably under the influence of these Persian ideas that the Jewish conception of Satan took shape. At first, however, the 'Satan' in the Old Testament was regarded as one of the servants of God who, as a divine agent, was permitted to bring evil upon Job to test this righteous man (Job i. 6 ff.). Next, he is represented as the accuser of Israel as a nation (Zech. iii. 1 ff.), and is made responsible for leading David astray (1 Chron. xxi. 1). From being 'the Adversary' and 'tempter', he very soon became thought of as an evil spirit; and then, after the exiles returned from their captivity in Babylon, and

Persian ideas had begun to spread in Palestine, he was transformed into the Devil, on the model of the Druj. Belief in evil spirits had been very prevalent among the Hebrews in ancient times, as among other Semitic people; and these included strange monsters, such as the winged serpents or seraphim, the satyrs, ghouls, and a great mythical dragon called Leviathan. The serpent, who had long been regarded as the enemy of mankind, was a powerful 'demon of the waste' with almost divine knowledge (cf. Gen. iii. 1; Isa. vi.). Therefore, when the world was supposed to be full of demons organized under the leadership of the Prince of Darkness, it was the serpent who was held responsible for having brought evil into creation by deceiving Eve in the Garden, although this was not the original meaning of the story in Genesis. But once the Satan and the serpent had been transformed into the Devil, the leader of the powers of evil was called by a great many different names, such as Lucifer, a fallen angel of light, Beliar (or Belial), Asmodeus, a Persian demon,

A MEDIEVAL SATAN AND DEVILS
Illumination from *Le Livre de la nostre Seigneur*. French, 15th century. *Bodleian Lib.*

and in the New Testament Beelzebub, an ancient god of flies. In later Jewish writings he was sometimes spoken of as a fallen angel, or as the great Prince in Heaven who came to earth to mislead the human race, and as an angel of death to take away their souls. Nowhere, however, was he said to be on the same level as God, and it was always believed that he and all his works would be destroyed. Then God would finally triumph (*see* JUDAISM).

5. THE CHRISTIAN IDEA OF THE DEVIL. Since the first Christians were Jews, they had been taught to think like Jews before they became followers of Christ and members of the Church. But while many believed that sin came into the world through the Devil in the guise of the serpent tempting Eve in the Garden of Eden, actually Christ Himself says nothing about this in His teaching. He is recorded as having described Satan as the tempter of mankind, and He spoke as though some diseases were caused by demons taking possession of human beings. Indeed, the whole world was like a field in which an enemy had sown tares among the wheat—a mixture of good and evil, the work of God spoilt by the Devil. But if Satan was 'the ruler of this world' (John xii. 31), Jesus had conquered him by resisting his temptations (Matt. iv. 1–12). In the last book of the New Testament, a striking picture is drawn of a war in heaven between God and his angels and 'the old serpent, the devil'— the deceiver of the whole world—and his hosts, in which Satan was cast out (Rev. xii. 7 ff.). At length he will be bound for a thousand years, imprisoned in the abyss or 'bottomless pit' (i.e. hell), and finally destroyed in a lake of fire and brimstone (Rev. xx. 2, 10). Borrowing the images and language of the late Jewish writers, the early Christians were expressing their own beliefs and hopes. Christ, they were convinced, had defeated the powers of evil, and although for a time Satan had been loosed and allowed to persecute the saints and martyrs, in the end his kingdom will be overthrown, and Christ and His Church will reign triumphantly for ever (*see* CHRISTIANITY).

6. SATAN IN ISLAM. In ISLAM (q.v.) the power of evil, called Iblis, is represented in the Moslem scriptures, the Koran, as an angel who was driven from heaven because he refused to prostrate himself before Adam when man was first created, believing that God (Allah) alone should be worshipped. But although Iblis is pictured as such a staunch upholder of monotheism (*see* God), he hates the human race, and therefore he has always tried to beguile men into serving other and false gods to their destruction. He cannot, however, compel the faithful to give up their faith. A man first becomes unfaithful, and then Iblis deprives him of the power to believe the truth about Allah. Among the other enemies of all that is good, Moslems recognize two persons in particular. One is Pharaoh king of Egypt, and the other Dadidjah the Anti-Christ, who will be destroyed at the second coming of Christ. Each of these three is said to work miracles; but, unlike Iblis, Pharaoh and the Anti-Christ claim to be divine.

See also Religion; God; Hell.

SATYRS, *see* Mythological Monsters, Section (*b*).

SAXONS, *see* British Peoples.

SCANDINAVIANS, *see* Swedes; Norwegians; Danes.

SCAPEGOAT, *see* Sacrifice.

SCOTS. The people of Scotland call themselves the Scots or the Scottish, but never the Scotch. Scotch is used of whisky and terriers, but never of people. The Scots are really rather different from the English, though the two peoples have lived as one nation for over 300 years. Their religion is different (*see* Calvinism), their law is different, their system of education is different, and their sense of humour is very different.

Some of the differences may be due to the fact that the Scots are basically Celtic. The north-west is much more Celtic than the south-east— Gaelic (q.v. Vol. iv), the language of the Celts, is still spoken there; but even in the south, Celtic place-names and customs and folk-tales persist to this day (*see* Celtic Civilization). The Gaels crossed from Ireland about A.D. 500, and gradually overcame the Picts of northern Scotland, converting many to Christianity. Their most famous prince, Columba, founded a Celtic Church at Iona, an island off the west coast of Scotland. In the centuries that followed peoples of many nations came to Scotland and mixed with the Celts, especially in the south and east. Norsemen, Danes, and, later, Flemings settled on the east coast; Saxons and Angles came from England. Mary Queen of Scots brought many French in her court when she returned from

A CROFT IN LEWIS IN THE OUTER HEBRIDES
H. D. Keilor

France in 1561. Spaniards, shipwrecked when the Spanish Armada was fleeing from Drake, settled in several parts of the country. But Scotland seems able to absorb foreigners readily— and to-day some of the most ardent Scottish nationalists are English by birth. The union of Scotland and England took place in two stages. When Queen Elizabeth died in 1603, James VI of Scotland was her heir and became James I of Great Britain. The two countries, however, had separate parliaments until 1707, when, by the Act of Union, the parliaments were united, and Scotland sent members to the Parliament in London.

The Scots are usually divided into Highlanders and Lowlanders; but of course these groups are not separated by a sharp line across the country. Neither of them is very like the typical 'stage' Scotsman, wearing a kilt, pronouncing his 'r's' in a very determined fashion, usually speaking with a Glasgow accent, and boasting of living on porridge. All Scots do not have a tartan to wear —very few of those who have the right to wear tartan wear a kilt. And a Glasgow accent is about as different from an Inverness accent as it is from a Devonshire accent.

The Highlander is the present-day Celt of Scotland, and a very much more colourful and romantic figure than the Lowlander. Usually he is quick-witted, well-mannered, courteous, and

CULROSS, FIFESHIRE. *L. & M. Gayton*

gentle in speech. To understand him it is necessary to understand the significance of the clan— a significance which continues in a modified form to this day. A clan in Scotland is a family grouping of those bearing the same name. The chief is the head of the family, and the relationship between chief and clansman is that between the head of the family and a brother or son, not that between master and man. The Highlander has a deep pride in the traditions of his clan and in its lands, but he was a hunter rather than a farmer, and he has little real love for the soil. His love and loyalty are for the spirit of Scotland rather than for the Scottish land. This love is the bond between the Highlander abroad and Scotland—very different from the point of view of the French peasant, whose love is for the soil which gives him his living. It is a joy and pride in being part of a tradition, and it is cherished by the many Scots who have sought their fortunes abroad, and made happy careers in every part of the British Commonwealth of nations.

The Lowlander is a much more **grim figure** than the Highlander. Long ago he had a hard struggle to gain his food as much of the land was not very fertile. And in the past 200 years he has lived for the most part in the toil and grime of coal-mines, iron and steel works, and big factories. Of course, there are some parts of the Lowlands which are not industrial—in fact some of the farmlands of the coast and the border valleys are relatively rich. The Lowlander is less impetuous than the Highlander, and also more determined and more ruthless. His speech is much less lovely, his manners are less pleasing, and he is argumentative. Abroad he is spoken of as 'dour'—a peculiarly Scottish characteristic. To be dour (it rhymes with moor) means to be uncommunicative, determined, severe, and unforthcoming. This rather forbidding exterior is only a shell, as has been proved by the large numbers of foreigners who have found great hospitality and friendliness from the Lowland Scots. The main body of Highlanders live in the north and west, while the Lowlanders belong to **the industrial central Scotland and the country**

AN ARAB WITH HIS CAMEL

to the south; but there are men with Highland characteristics in the cities of central Scotland and in the villages of the Borders, and men with Lowland characteristics in the towns of the north-east coast.

To-day many Scottish towns and villages look very much like those in England. But until fifty years ago, there was little brick or timber building in Scotland, for Scottish building is traditionally of the plentiful local stone. In all parts of the country crofters and farm-labourers lived in low cottages, originally thatched, but later roofed with slates or tiles. In the cities a very large proportion of the population lived in flats, or tenements as they are usually called. And in Edinburgh there still stand tenements eight to ten stories high, built more than 200 years ago round courts. They used to be the town houses of the Scottish nobles, and many of them bear the name of a former inhabitant. Now the district is one of the poorest in the city.

Deer-stalking and grouse-shooting have brought many visitors to Scotland, and the 'gillie' or gamekeeper is a particularly well-known and popular Highland character. Golf and fishing are national pastimes, 'soccer' and rugby are played as in England, and in the north-west men play shinty, a game which resembles a very violent type of hockey. Then in summer in many villages and towns there are Highland games, sometimes associated with the annual gathering of a particular clan. At these games Scottish dances are performed by individual dancers and teams of dancers to the rhythm of the bagpipes. There are running and jumping contests and a special Scottish contest called tossing the caber. There are competitions in bagpipe-playing: it is said that to appreciate the 'pipes' it is necessary to have Scottish blood—indeed, there is hardly a Scot who will not confess to being stirred by the sound of the pipes.

See also Vol. III: SCOTLAND.

SCYLLA, see MYTHOLOGICAL MONSTERS, Section (b).

SCYTHIANS, see RUSSIANS.

SELJUKS, see TURKS.

SEMITES. People who all speak a language which comes from a common origin (see SEMITIC

LANGUAGES, Vol. IV). According to Hebrew tradition, as set out in Genesis, the Semites are descended from Shem, son of Noah; but, in fact, the Genesis account includes peoples whose languages were not Semitic, and excludes others whose languages definitely were. Where the Semites originally came from is not known for certain, though it may have been Arabia. The main Semitic languages are Hebrew, Phoenician (very much like Hebrew), Aramaic (the language spoken by the Jews at the time of our Lord), Assyrian (which includes Babylonian), Arabic, and Ethiopic. Most of the peoples speaking these languages live in western Asia or north-east Africa, though the JEWS (q.v.) have spread very widely over Europe and America.

See also BABYLONIANS; ASSYRIANS; HEBREWS; PHOENI-CIANS; HITTITES; ARABS; ABYSSINIANS.

SERBIANS, see YUGOSLAVS.

SHINTO. Japanese religion is of three main sorts: Pre-Buddhist, Buddhist, and Christian. The second of these (see BUDDHISM) entered Japan from China about A.D. 404, but did not get a permanent footing there until some 150 years later. China was at that time probably the most powerful, the most advanced, and the best-administered country in the world, and had an immense influence on Japan.

But Japan had a native religion before that, which has continued right up to the present day. It is not clear what it was called before the Buddhist invasion; but the Chinese Buddhists called it Shin-to, which means the 'Way of the Spirits', as distinct from the 'Way of the Buddha', and it has borne that name ever since. Probably it was in many ways not unlike the religion of China before Confucius—a practical belief in many gods and many lords. A great deal of it was of the same type as the polytheism of Greece and Rome.

It is possible to distinguish three types of Shinto—first, the old Shinto which goes back long before European influence began; second, the state Shinto of the last fifty years, which is a revival of the old Shinto, but with certain differences, especially political; third, the sect Shinto, which is not under government control, and is of various kinds, some showing apparent Christian influence.

From A.D. 540 to 1700 Buddhism was very strong in Japan. It influenced Shinto, and most Japanese, like many Orientals, felt no difficulty

SHINTO PRIESTS. *Paul Popper*

about enjoying the consolations of both religions. But between 1700 and 1841, and again in 1870, nationalist revivals led to anti-Buddhist and anti-Chinese riots, with the slogan 'abolish Buddhism and down with the monks'. This violence died down after twenty years, and to-day Buddhism in Japan seems as much alive as ever, though state Shinto, at any rate up to the defeat of Japan in 1945, has seemed equally alive.

The central idea of Shinto seems to be that the Divine Spirit in nature, which is thought of in feminine terms, has produced the Japanese people as a strong race, with a divine origin and a great destiny. This idea used to be expressed by saying that the Sun-goddess, Amaterasu, is the original Mother of the line of Mikados (Emperors), so that the Emperor is a divine being. It also follows, said the Japanese, that since all human beings are the offspring of nature, whatever they think and do must be natural, and therefore right. Therefore, there is no such

thing as 'wickedness in the sight of God'. Whatever is, is right, and mankind stands in no need of redemption. This is a very comforting belief for realist statesmen, and also for those who have to obey them. It is said that those in high office in Japan, as well as the educated classes, did not really believe this mythology, and thought of it cynically as merely useful for keeping the superstitious masses of the people contented. Anyhow it seems clear that it has all been taught quite lately to the boys and girls in the State schools of Japan, and that every bit of it, including the legendary pedigree of the Mikado, was given in lesson-books, while the Mikado's portrait has had to be saluted with divine honours in the school playgrounds. In addition, Shinto includes the belief in a large number of minor gods and goddesses besides the great Sun-goddess, some of them fairly important *kami* or gods; others little more than small bogies, of whom there may be millions; others, again, unpleasant little animals like fox-gods, or female demons, who torment those who displease them and afflict them with illness.

Shinto shrines are often of great simplicity and beauty, and fit well into the landscape. Their shape is rather like that of the Hebrew tabernacle and, like it, they have two parts, an outer court and an inner or holy of holies. Shinto worship consists in keeping on good terms with the *kami*, and the Shinto priests also do a good business in consecrated objects, which are believed in as lucky charms. Vows are made and sacrifices offered to the various divinities. There are also pilgrimages to sacred spots (*see* FUJI YAMA, Vol. III).

Sect Shinto consists of a number of different groups, rather like Nonconformist churches in England. Most of them accept the usual Shinto ideas, but add others, such as the healing of the sick. Some show traces of European or American influence. Indeed, one sect believes in the idea of One Good God—so great a development from the ordinary Shinto beliefs that some have thought it to be modelled on the teaching of the Bible; though it is also possible that it may be independent, like the movement of Zarathustra in early Persia (*see* ZOROASTRIAN).

It is difficult to say what will happen to Shinto in the near future. It has been so much linked up with patriotic feeling and respect for the head of the State that it may not survive a change in the form of government. The Emperor, in a statement dated 31 December 1945, has publicly renounced the idea that he is a divine being, descended from the Sun-goddess. He declares his intention to abandon ancient superstitions, and to rule as the constitutional head of a democratic state. One thing now seems certain, that if belief in the Emperor's divine ancestry is abandoned, we may expect a fairly rapid break-up of Japanese nature-religion. It does not follow that the Japanese will of necessity adopt Christianity on a wide scale. Some form of Buddhism might be the gainer. It is true, however, that there are already a considerable number of Christians in Japan, and their influence seems likely to increase. Meanwhile Shinto, until recently, has been the nearest approach to a living survival of what Roman religion was like under the early empire.

See also JAPANESE.

SHRINE, *see* TEMPLE.

SIAMESE. The total population of Siam is about fifteen millions. This includes, besides the Thai or Siamese proper, considerable numbers of Chinese, Malays, and others, most of whom have acquired Siamese nationality, though they may have retained many of their own national characteristics.

The Thai are by far the largest and most important group, dominating the affairs of the country, and giving it its alternative name, Thailand. The Thai live mainly in the rich central region of Siam, and produce and control most of the country's agricultural wealth. They are slight in build and rather short. They have light-brown skins, broad faces with prominent cheek-bones but small chins. Their eyes are slanting and their noses broad and short, and they have straight black hair. In country districts, both men and women wear the *panning*, a length of cloth wound round the waist; but women also wear a scarf wound round the upper part of the body. In Bangkok, however, and to some extent in other towns, European clothes are worn.

The Siamese as a whole are a cheerful, friendly people and hospitable to visitors. They are very proud of their national independence. They are more hard-working than some Far Eastern peoples, and are quite good business-men and organizers. As in many Eastern countries, however, the Chinese, owing to their great industry, have come to occupy an important position in the country's trade.

The great majority of the people of Siam work on the land, and live in small villages. Indeed, there is only one large town, Bangkok the capital. The farmers are chiefly concerned with rice-growing—for rice is the main food of Siam, and is also their principal export. The way of life in a Siamese village is very simple, and according to Western ideas the standard of living is low; but the fertility of their country prevents them from suffering the great poverty which is suffered by the peasants of many Eastern countries.

Most Siamese follow the religion of BUDDHISM (q.v.), and Buddhist teaching plays an important part in their lives, especially of the children, who for the most part depend on Buddhist priests for their education. The Buddhist calendar is the official calendar of Siam: the year A.D. 1947 would be called in Siam the year 2489 of the Buddhist era. Although education is spreading, their ideas about health and sanitation are very

SIAMESE LOADING THEIR BOATS WITH FRUIT
Roy. Geog. Soc.

primitive in the villages, and the people suffer much from malaria and other tropical diseases.

The King of Siam was, until 1932, absolute ruler of the country. Now the King governs in accordance with laws made by a representative assembly elected by vote, and works through ministers with the advice of a council. The country is divided into districts which are administered for the King by local officials.

Bangkok is the centre of the government and the centre of culture. There Siamese art may be seen at its best, especially in the remarkable traditional dances. Each of these dances represents some episode in Siamese ancient folk-lore. They are executed with great skill by highly trained dancers, chiefly young girls, who are dressed in rich and beautiful costumes.

See also Vol. III: SIAM; Vol. IV: CHINESE AND ALLIED LANGUAGES.

SIBERIAN PEOPLES. 1. These are the in-habitants of an immensely large territory, about twenty times as great as France and nearly twice as large as the United States of America. But the number of people who inhabit this area is comparatively small—less than twenty millions in 1939. Most of these are colonizers from Russia proper who have settled in the newly founded towns, and are not the natives of Siberia with whom we are concerned here. The real peoples of Siberia consist of small groups, varying from the largest, the Yakuts, numbering about 400,000 and dispersed in the Yakut Auto-nomous Soviet Republic over an area equal to

two-fifths of Europe, down to the small group of Koryaks in the extreme north-east, of whom there are less than 8,000. These peoples of northern Asia have led for many generations the life of reindeer herders, and most of them have been isolated in small, widely separated groups, very much removed from the happenings of the rest of the world. Many of the peoples of Siberia have now accepted Christianity, others follow a kind of BUDDHISM (q.v.) called Lamaism, and some small groups still practise a pagan religion called Shamanism.

2. THE YAKUTS. This is a Russian name: the inhabitants call themselves *Sakha* or *Uriankhai Sakaalar*. They settled in Siberia towards the end of the 14th century, if not earlier, driving northwards the Yuagirs, Tungus, Lamuts, and others. They probably came from the Central Asian steppes or from Transbaikalia; they are of Turki origin with a strong admixture of Mon-golian blood, with high cheek-bones, slanting eyes, and black hair; their language belongs to the Turkic family of languages.

The Cossacks conquered them in the 17th century, and made them pay tribute in furs called *yasak*. This was changed to heavy taxes in cash under Catherine the Great. In addition, they had to provide transport for goods going overland to the far north-east or by boat along the rivers. They were bribed by relief from taxa-tion to accept Christianity and, consequently, by the middle of the 19th century most Yakuts were Christians. They also accepted Russian names, such as Ivanov or Petrov, and in this way some obtained Russian civic rights.

Formerly they were a nomadic horse-breeding tribe, and they still retain customs related to this

THE PEOPLES OF SIBERIA

way of life, such as the drinking of mare's milk (*kumiss*) on the Yakutian national holiday. They introduced horses and cattle in the region where they now live, and cattle-breeding is now their chief occupation: reindeer breeding has always been of secondary importance except in the Arctic north. Agriculture has only been developed of recent times.

The provision of sufficient food to last through the long severe winters is the main problem in the life of the Yakuts. Up to 70° of frost are sometimes registered. Many used to die during especially severe spells, and whole reindeer herds were sometimes wiped out. Trapping and hunting foxes, squirrels, and wild reindeer are vital occupations, since fur skins are one of the most important commodities which the Yakuts can exchange for stores to keep them through the winter. Yakutsk on the river Lena is the centre of trade in the short, hot summer. The people arrive from everywhere, mainly in boats. All food is delivered frozen—milk is sold in round slabs. Meat, fish, and vegetables are not only preserved frozen, but are eaten frozen.

Since the Yakuts keep only small reindeer herds, they often have to hunt wild reindeer. A man often kills thirty-five to fifty or even a hundred animals a year for their meat and skins— a wasteful custom, since much of the carcass is left for the wolves—and in consequence the reindeer are being reduced in numbers. Fishing —in particular herring fishing—is also an important occupation. Salting and storing of fish is still carried on in primitive and wasteful ways. How to keep the cows alive in the winter is a serious problem. Oblong-shaped log cow sheds are built, with wooden floors to protect the cattle from hoof-rot. The Yakuts themselves used to live at one end of the barn, in a square room like the original tent (*yurt*), with its fireplace in the centre, but with no wooden floor. This had such a bad effect on the health of the people that, in 1927, a government decree ordered the separation of the human dwelling-place from the animal shelter.

The Soviet Government has been trying to introduce many reforms, especially in the holding of land. After the establishment of the Autonomous Soviet Socialist Republic of Yakutia in April 1922, there followed nearly six years of disturbances, as the rich landowners, the *toions*, resisted the move to distribute pasture and arable land to the poorer peasants. As in the rest of

Russia, collective farms were introduced, and the people encouraged to give up a nomad life and settle in villages. Russian wooden houses were erected in place of the old primitive abodes, built below the ground level to keep out the winter cold. New methods were also introduced to increase the cultivable land, in spite of the permanently frozen subsoil, and vegetables and potatoes made their appearance. As well as the

BURYAT MONGOL CHILDREN
S.C.R.

main industry of fur-trapping, gold has now been discovered, and coal and iron are also mined. The problem of education is difficult to solve. The widely scattered and isolated communities are not easy to reach, especially in a country where there are no railways and no proper roads. Though the population was formerly nearly wholly illiterate, many can now read and write, Yakutian being the official language and Russian the second. As many of the children will be trappers and hunters when they grow up, they are taught by lessons and games to develop keen sight and hearing. Their way of life makes children self-reliant at an early age. They are such good skiers by six years old that they can be trusted to ski on an errand several miles away.

3. THE BURYAT MONGOLS inhabit the other Autonomous Soviet Socialist Republic in Siberia. They live in a crescent-shaped mountainous land south and east of Lake Baikal, one of the biggest fresh-water lakes in the world. To-day about half the inhabitants of Buryat Mongolia, some 300,000, are Buryats, most of the rest being

AN OSTYAK OF THE YENISEI DISTRICT
Pitt Rivers Coll.

Ude. Trapping, especially of the valuable types of squirrel and sable ('soft gold'), found east of Lake Baikal, is still an important industry. There is a State farm for breeding and preserving the sable. The Buryats live in less isolated conditions than the Yakuts and other Siberian peoples. They are near the important TRANS-SIBERIAN RAILWAY (q.v. Vol. IV): consequently they have integrated themselves better with the Soviet system. Education is spreading, and a Latin script has been adopted; Buryat women now wear the Russian peasant shawl, and the men wear felt hats.

4. OTHER SIBERIAN PEOPLES. All the other peoples of Siberia are far less numerous than the Yakuts and the Buryats; they live in areas difficult of access, and have changed their ancient mode of life very little. The main groups now live in National Regions in the northern part of Siberia.

The Ostyaks and Voguls belong to the same National Region: the Ostyaks, about 17,000, live on the right bank of the river Ob; and the Voguls, about 7,000, on the eastern slope of the Ural mountains. They live in tents and huts, and their occupations are hunting, fishing, and reindeer breeding. Formerly, they used to move about over many hundreds of miles, going in the summer to the vast treeless regions of the tundra, and returning to the pine forests (*targa*) in the early autumn, always in search of feeding grounds for their reindeer herds. Fishing is mainly the occupation of the older men, and they sell their catch to government trading-posts, which are often in very remote places. Some medical assistance, education, and radio are now reaching these peoples, in spite of their nomad existence. Some of the Voguls still wear their hair in two plaits hanging from the neck near the ears.

Some branches of the numerically small group of Samoyedes live in these regions, some in the northern tundra between the Urals and the Yenisei river, some on the tundra between the Yenisei and the Khatanga river; and others farther to the south. Except for the last, the Samoyedes are settled and keep horses and cattle, but no reindeer.

The Tungus tribes, originally a Manchu people, migrated at some unknown time from the Manchu country to Siberia. They are now spread all over eastern Siberia in small groups. Their correct national name is Evenki; they are found mainly in the northern forests, and they

Russian settlers. The Buryat Mongols are related to the Mongols of Outer Mongolia, and were converted to Buddhism by Mongolian lamas during the 18th century. They are considered the most intelligent of the MONGOLS (q.v.), possibly because closer contact with other peoples of Siberia has made them more alert.

The great majority of Buryats used to be stock-breeders and fishermen, a nomadic people living in large *yurta* (felt tents). This way of living has been changed under the Soviets, and most of them are now settled, mainly in collective farms; though many of them return to the old nomad tent life during the summer, when they move with their herds in search of fresh pasture. Livestock raising remains the basic industry. The growing of hay and other food for cattle now prevents the great losses among the herds which used to follow a very hard winter.

Since 1923 new industries have sprung up, such as the locomotive works in the capital Ulan

REINDEER TUNGUS CHILDREN IN THE NORTH-WEST MANCHURIAN WOODS. *Ethel John Lindgren.* Nov. 1931.

live by deer-breeding, hunting, and fishing. By trapping and hunting fur-bearing animals, they get not only their living and food, but the materials of their dwellings and clothing. Reindeer skins are used for tents. The fur supplies blankets, caps, and boots; blouses and trousers are made out of reindeer skins. They used to exchange their furs and fish for liquor, with disastrous results; but this is now forbidden, and all trading is done through co-operative societies.

The Yukagir, who live in the most remote parts of Yakutia, represent the remnants of a very early migration to the north. Before the arrival of the Russians they were numerous; but they are now nearly extinct, and those that remain have intermarried with the Tungus. Their own language, Yukagir, now very little spoken, is not related to any other known language, except perhaps to that of two other Siberian peoples, the Chukchee and Koryak. They are nomadic deer breeders, and their herds of reindeer number thousands. They train a few reindeer to pull their sledges, which they use even when there is no snow. They trade the ivory from mammoth tusks found in the tundra. In the very far north reindeer cannot live, since there is no fodder for them, and here the people depend on dogs who, like the men, feed on fish. Apart from ivory,

their only article of exchange is the skin of the white fox, and on the precarious success of the hunt depends the purchase of tea, sugar, and tobacco for the winter. The Yukagir are Christians, though they have preserved some of their old Shamanist customs.

The Chukchee, Koryak, and Kamchadal live near the far north-east coast. They resemble the most western North American Indians, mainly as regards the structure of their language and their fishing and hunting methods. The Chukchee, about 12,000 to 15,000 of them, live in the extreme north-east peninsula. Some of them are nomadic reindeer breeders; others live by the sea and fish and hunt seals and walrus. They love their independence, and resent interference in their way of life, which includes the practice of the pagan religion, Shamanism. The Koryak are divided about equally between Reindeer and Maritime Koryak, and number about 7,500. Salmon is their chief food, but they love tea, and the tongue of the deer is a highly prized delicacy. The Kamchadal live in the southern part of the peninsula Kamchatka. Few now speak their original native language, but use instead dialects which show strong Russian influence. They are a settled people, and live in little Russian block-houses in small villages, situated alongside a river which provides their main occupation, salmon and other fishing.

In the centre and north of Kamchatka live the Lamut, a branch of the Tungus, who hunt and breed reindeer. In contrast to their neighbours, the Koryak, they ride the reindeer and use them, as well as dogs, as draught animals.

In the northern part of the island of Sakhalin and on the mainland opposite lives the small Gilyak tribe, who are a people rather apart from the other Siberian tribes. They change their living places frequently, following the migrating fish along the rivers and the sea-coast.

See also Vol. IV: Turkic and Finnis Languages.

SICILIANS, *see* Italians. *See also* Vol. III: Sicily.

SIKHISM. This is a new religion which developed in India during the 16th and 17th centuries A.D. out of the contrast between Hinduism and Islam (q.v.). Its origin is as follows. A certain young orthodox Hindu called Nanak, born in 1469, and living near Lahore in the Punjab, became dissatisfied with his ancestral religion and interested in Islam. He set to work to learn Persian, and then read various Moslem writings. But the new faith failed to meet his needs completely; so he developed one of his own, which took what he felt was best from both Hinduism and Islam, and which, in particular, rejected the Hindu idea of caste, and the inferiority of women to men. Nanak taught the equality of all human beings, and the uselessness of extreme self-torture (*see* Asceticism), and he advised the eating of meat, and family life and marriage as the normal state for all. On the other hand, he urged temperance and simplicity, and forbade his followers the use of alchohol and tobacco. They were to rise early and take cold baths before morning prayer. All this sounds to us very sensible and familiar; and if Nanak had given up believing in the many Hindu gods and goddesses, he would have been rather like a Jew or a Puritan Christian in his religion. Indeed, at the beginning of the 20th century, one of the members of his movement, the famous Sundar Singh, actually crossed over to Christianity. There were, however, limits to Nanak's own reforms. He seems to have accepted the Hindu beliefs of his day about the various deities, except that he regarded them all as inferior to the one Supreme God, the idea of which he took from Islam. He invented a costume for himself, partly

A SIKH SOLDIER. *Indian Railways*

Hindu, partly Moslem, and travelled forth as a wandering preacher, using especially hymns as a means of teaching his doctrine.

Nanak journeyed all over India and Ceylon, and some say that he even went as far as Mecca. But most of his followers came from the people of his homeland, and this may explain, to some extent, the later development of the Sikh community. When he died in 1538, he appointed a successor who was called by the ordinary Hindu title of *guru*, which means spiritual teacher. He was succeeded by a second *guru*, who invented a special alphabet, and in this, which was used to express a dialect of Punjabi, called *Gurumukhi*, the sacred books of the new movement were written down. The followers of Nanak called themselves Sikhs, which simply means 'disciples'. The first four *gurus* were specially chosen, but after that the office became hereditary. The fifth *guru*, Arjun, was responsible for establishing Nanak's religion as an institution. He built the celebrated golden temple at Amritsar (which was destroyed in 1762 but rebuilt two years later). He also collected a volume of hymns, to which he added some of his own composition, and these form the

Sikh sacred book, known as the *Granth Sahib* or Master-Book.

At this point a remarkable development occurred. Hitherto the Sikhs had been a religious, not a political, community, and they had not been persecuted. But in 1606 a new and intolerant Moslem Emperor, a Mogul called Jehangir, succeeded his very liberal-minded father Akbar as ruler of north India. He tortured Arjun till he died, with the result that the Sikhs came to the conclusion that they would have to fight for freedom of worship and thought, if they were to survive as a separate religious body. By this time they had already become a numerous and highly disciplined community. The threat to their freedom knit them more closely together, and strict military training, in addition to their abstemious habits, soon made them into a formidable army. For over fifty years they held their own successfully against the Moslem Emperors. Then the Mogul Emperor imprisoned the ninth *guru*, Teg Bahadur, for having dared to invite him to forsake Islam in favour of Sikhism. The *guru* was executed— a second martyr—and thereafter the Sikhs, under Govind, the tenth *guru*, became literally a nation of warriors, a people apart in the midst of the Mogul Empire. Before he died Teg Bahadur uttered a curious prophecy, that the Mogul Empire would fall, and that a Christian army would come from Calcutta and join forces with the Sikhs; and something like this actually happened towards the end of the 18th century.

The Sikhs still survive in modern India; but, since they lost their political independence to the British, there has not been much to hold them together, and there has been a tendency for many to fall back into ordinary Hinduism. Indeed, most of their religious teachings can be found among the reforming sects of Hinduism. It is said that the younger generation of Sikhs do not read the *Granth* very much. But since 1910 there has been a certain revival of religious zeal, and the Sikh community has shown signs of increasing again in numbers. The membership in the 1941 census was given as about 5½ millions, four-fifths of these in the Punjab, with a steady rise in numbers from 1901 onwards. For some years after the partition of India most Sikhs lived in a group of states called PEPSU, but in 1956 these were merged in the Punjab.

Although most of the recruits for the Sikh army have come from the fighting tribes of the Jats, the Sikh movement is perhaps a unique example of a political unit, developed solely by religious influence, without the unifying power of common blood, in which the members have grown alike in appearance and manners. Supposing that the QUAKERS of Pennsylvania or the MORMONS of Utah in America (qq.v.) were to have grown into distinct peoples by strict intermarriage among themselves, and were to have adopted a distinctive costume and spoken a separate dialect of English, that would have given us something like what has happened in the case of the Sikhs.

See also INDIAN PEOPLES.

SINHALESE, *see* CEYLONESE.

SIRENS, *see* MYTHOLOGICAL MONSTERS, Section (*b*).

SKY-GOD. Many gods are in some sense sky-gods—although a few are connected solely with the Underworld. Gods are often connected with the sun or the moon, the rain or the thunder. They live somewhere in the sky, and come down to earth from time to time in the guise of men or birds or even clouds. Many peoples, however, believe in a supreme god, who lives in the sky and never comes down at all—who, in fact, takes very little interest in the affairs of men. It is supposed among such peoples that, after creating the world, he retired to the sky, leaving the world to look after itself, or to be looked after by inferior gods. Gods of this type are probably the reflection of the kind of divine king who performed, once a year, the creation rite, and for the rest of the time remained shut up in his palace. This kind of god is not found among peoples whose kings were more active, such as the Greeks and Norsemen.

See also RELIGION; GOD.

SLAVS. These include most of the peoples now living in eastern Europe and speaking languages which have a common origin. Slav-speaking peoples first came into Europe, probably from Central Asia, at a very early date, and settled at various times in the countries where they are now known as RUSSIANS, BULGARIANS, POLES, CZECHO-SLOVAKS (including the Slovaks and Moravians), and YUGOSLAVS (including Serbs, Croats, Montenegrins, and Slovenes) (qq.v.).

See also Vol. IV: RUSSIAN LANGUAGES.

SLOVAKS, *see* CZECHOSLOVAKS.

SLOVENES, *see* YUGOSLAVS.

SOMALIS, *see* NEGRO AFRICANS.

SOUTH AFRICANS. The total population of
the Union of South Africa is about ten millions.
Of these, just less than seven millions are native
Africans, whose history and way of life are discussed in separate articles. Of the remainder,
two and a quarter millions are of European
descent, three-quarters of a million are coloured
people, and a quarter of a million are Indians.

The first Europeans came to settle in South
Africa in 1652, before which date the country
was occupied by BUSHMEN, HOTTENTOTS (qq.v.),
and Bantu-speaking Africans (*see* NEGRO
AFRICANS). The Portuguese made a landing
there as early as 1487, and the Dutch later established a port of call for their trading ships going
to and from the East. They settled down on the
slopes of Table Mountain, where they established
Cape Town and gradually extended their territory. During the next 150 years, there was steady
but slow immigration from Holland, Germany,
and France, and the population—almost entirely
farmers—moved slowly along the southern coastal
strip to about where Port Elizabeth now stands.

As a result of the Napoleonic wars England
gained control of the Cape in 1806, and in 1820
British settlers began to arrive. In 1836 the
gradual expansion eastwards of the colony was
suddenly speeded up, and many of the Dutch-
speaking farmers, under the leadership of Piet
Retief, Hendrik Potgieter, and others, moved
inland across the mountains on to the great
plateau or highveld to establish their own republics of Natalia, the Transvaal, and the
Orange Free State—a movement known as the
'Great Trek' and one of the great events in South
African history.

This European expansion led to a series of
wars against the Bantu, who tried to defend their
country. The white man, using horses and fire-
arms and initiating what later became known as
the Commando system, was eventually victorious
in these wars. The greatest of the Bantu military
powers, the ZULU (q.v.) under Dingaan, and the
Matabele under Moselikatse, were defeated in
1837–8 by the Dutch *Voortrekkers* (pioneers).
Both peoples rose again, to be again defeated,
this time by the British. In 1879 the Zulu power
was finally broken, and the Matabele were
beaten by the followers of Cecil Rhodes in

Rhodesia in 1893. **A** third great Bantu group,
the Xosa, almost destroyed themselves in 1856
by following the teachings of a local prophet,
who told them to wait for a 'great west wind' to
blow the white man into the sea, when they
would be able to get the white man's crops and
cattle. When the west wind failed to blow, more
than half of the Xosa died of starvation, since
they had eaten all their own cattle and had not
grown any crops.

The Europeans, having conquered the Bantu,
began to fight among themselves for possession
of the country. After the discovery of diamonds
in 1870 at Kimberley and of gold in 1886 at
Johannesburg, there was continual friction between the Boers (or Dutch-speaking farmers),
who had opened up the country under such
leaders as Brand and Paul Kruger, and the
British Government, who, inspired by Cecil
Rhodes, were in turn anxious to control the rich
minerals. This friction resulted in two wars, the
second of which was the Anglo-Boer war of
1899–1902, in which the small Boer Republics
of the Transvaal and the Orange Free State,
under their leaders, Steyn, De Wet, Botha, and
Smuts, fought bravely but in vain for their independence. So, by the Treaty of Vereeniging in
1902, the whole country came under British
rule. In 1910 the two ex-republics were united
with Natal and the Cape Colony to form the
Dominion of the Union of South Africa in the
British Commonwealth of Nations.

Up till fifty years ago South Africa was almost
entirely a farming country. Now, the development of gold, coal, and iron has made it a country
in which mining, industries, and farming are
almost equally important.

The white people are, like those of Canada or
Australia, mainly of northern European stock
and chiefly descended from Dutch, British, or
French immigrants. About 40% of the people
speak English in their homes; the rest speak
Afrikaans, a language derived from Dutch, and
very much like it, but simpler and easy to learn.
It is now a written language as well as a spoken
one; many newspapers and periodicals are
printed in it, and it has a rapidly growing literature. It developed in a farming community and
has farming idioms, many of which refer to oxen
and the ox-wagon—the South African equivalent of the American 'covered wagon'. Afrikaans
and English are the two official languages of the
country.

GROOT CONSTANTIA, AN OLD DUTCH FARM HOUSE IN THE CAPE COLONY. *South African Railways*

The Afrikaans-speaking people are very friendly and sociable, and are famed for their hospitality; they love visiting each other to discuss everything under the sun, but especially politics. They have inherited a love for the open-air life and, now that they cannot hunt wild animals as freely as they used to, have taken to sports—rugby, athletics, and swimming being their favourites. The famous South African rugby teams, the Springboks, take their name from the antelopes which used to be common. The climate of the great inland plateau, where there are more than 300 fine days in a year, gives them plenty of chances to become expert at these games.

They were formerly almost entirely farm-dwellers (hence the name Boers or farmers); but are now to be found with their English-speaking fellow-citizens in almost equal numbers in the gold- and coal-mines, in industries, on the railways, in business and the professions, and in Parliament. Since 1910 the Union has had three Prime Ministers, and all three have been Afrikaans-speaking—Generals Botha, Hertzog, and Smuts.

There is not much difference between the English and the Afrikaans-speaking South Africans. The difference in language has in the past helped to keep the two sections apart, but, as more and more people learn the second—that is, not their own—language, so they make friends among people of the other section, and differences disappear. The position is not quite the same as in Canada, because there the French Canadians are mostly found in one province, while in South Africa, although Natal is largely English-speaking and the Free State largely Afrikaans-speaking, the two races are fairly evenly distributed throughout the country.

About two-thirds of the Afrikaans-speaking people are in favour of establishing an independent republic in South Africa, and this is one of the most hotly discussed subjects in the country. Another subject on which opinion is much divided is the correct attitude the white man should take towards the Bantu. One very widely held opinion is that the Bantu should be given separate areas in which to live—a policy of segregation. Others, but not so many of them, want the Bantu to have much better opportunities of working in industry under better conditions. There is already a large amount of segregation: almost every European town has a native town (or 'location') where the native Africans live. These locations correspond

A GOLD MINE NEAR JOHANNESBURG

This is the greatest gold-producing area in the world
Rand Daily Mail

roughly to the slum areas of English towns, though they are perhaps less overcrowded. On the whole the white man has not yet decided quite what he wants with regard to the native.

In the south-western corner of the country, the area of which Cape Town is the chief city, live about three-quarters of a million Coloured People, who are descended partly from Malay slaves (originally brought to South Africa by the Dutch), and partly from Hottentots; but who also have a lot of white blood in their veins. They are quite different from the Bantu—they have straight hair and thin lips, while the Bantu have crinkled hair and thick lips. They have no language of their own, and mostly speak a dialect of Afrikaans—rather as the cockneys of London speak a dialect of English. Like the cockneys, too, they have a very racy sense of humour, and love quick repartee and practical jokes of all kinds. They are very good builders, printers, craftsmen, and farm-workers, and are largely responsible for the working of the big wine farms in their area, although they very seldom own the farms. Their standard of education is about midway between that of the Europeans, which is fairly high, and that of the Bantu, which is very low.

In Durban and on the Natal coast live about a quarter of a million Indians, the descendants of Indians who first came to Natal about ninety years ago to work on the sugar plantations, but who to-day are landowners, shopkeepers, waiters, tradesmen, and labourers throughout Natal. They are fairly well educated, and form a very live and active group in their own area. Many Natalians are beginning to be afraid of the growing economic power of the Indians, and laws are being passed to segregate them into areas, as the Bantu are segregated.

The Europeans have a high standard of education and literacy: there is compulsory and free schooling up to the age of 16, and it is reasonably easy for even a poor boy or girl to go to one of the many universities or colleges. There are three Medical Schools, three Engineering Schools, and numbers of other colleges including technical and agricultural colleges. At some of these natives are allowed to attend classes, but most of them are for European students only. There is only one university college for non-Europeans who, however, take the same degree examinations as Europeans.

Among the Europeans there is very little class-distinction or snobbishness. In a small town the doctor and the butcher, the teacher and the jailer, the bank manager and the shop assistant will all belong to the same golf or tennis club, and their children will attend the same school and play in the same football teams. The great majority of people, English or Afrikaans speaking, belong to one of the Protestant churches, and this is another factor which tends to bring the people together. Intermarriage between the two races has also helped to remove social as well as racial distinctions.

Instead of class distinction there is colour distinction, or the colour bar as it is called; you will practically never find white and black people belonging to the same sports club, going to the same school, or attending the same cinemas. There are separate buses and railway coaches for natives and Europeans almost everywhere, although this is not so in Cape Town. This policy of social segregation is supported by almost all Europeans of both races; marriages between white and black, for example, are very strongly disapproved of and very seldom take place.

Throughout the country (except in the areas where only natives may live, called Native Reserves) the white man is the owner of land, factories, and houses, while the black man (or woman) does the digging, washing of dishes, and fetching and carrying generally. Most European households have a native or coloured domestic servant. As education spreads among the Bantu, so more of them become artisans, lawyers, doctors, teachers, and so on, and more and more white people are therefore learning to do 'navvy work', or what is called in South Africa 'kaffir work'. This change-over is, however, going on very slowly, and for a long time to come the white people will do the skilled work and the natives the unskilled work.

See also Vol. III: SOUTH AFRICA.
See also Vol. V: KRUGER; RHODES; SMUTS.

SOUTH AMERICANS, *see* ARGENTINES; BOLIVIANS; BRAZILIANS; CHILEANS; COLOMBIA, PEOPLES OF; ECUADOR, PEOPLES OF; PARAGUAYANS; PERUVIANS; URUGUAYANS.

SOVIET CENTRAL ASIAN PEOPLES. 1. These peoples live in a large area which geographers have called the heartland of Eurasia. It stretches from the Caspian Sea in the west to the Chinese province of Sinkiang in the east: to the north lie European Russia and Siberia, and to the south lie Persia and Afghanistan, and beyond that India. Since time immemorial, various peoples and cultures have met, clashed, and mixed there. Conquerors have come and gone—the Greeks under Alexander the Great (329 B.C.), the Arabs (7th century), the Mongols (13th and 15th centuries), and the Tsarist Russians (19th century). Across this region lie the earliest trade routes between the East and the West.

The peoples of this area are for the most part Mongolian by race and speak TURKIC LANGUAGES (q.v. Vol. IV). Their religion they owe to the Arab invaders: in particular, the more settled people are fanatical Moslems of the Sunnite Sect (*see* ISLAM), and their women are subjected to very severe restrictions. The nomad people, however, are much less fanatical.

The main part of the population is still rural, being either settled agricultural people living near the oases, river valleys, and at the foot of mountains, or nomadic cattle-, horse-, and sheep-breeding people who wander over the steppes in search of fertile pasture lands. When the herds of the nomads and, consequently, the need for new pastures increases, the two groups clash. Since the arrival of the Russians in the 19th century, nomadic life has weakened, for the colonizers of Tsarist Russia seized the more fertile lands, and pushed the nomads into the barren parts where life was precarious.

The five principal peoples of Soviet Central Asia, known until recently as Russian Turkistan, are the Kazakhs of Kazakhskaya (camp or country of the Kazakhs), the Kirgiz of Kirgiskaya, the Tadjiks of Tadjikskaya, the Uzbeks of Uzbekiskaya, and the Turkmen of Turkmenskaya.

2. THE KAZAKHS, sometimes called the Kirgiz-Kazakhs, are of Mongol blood and speak primitive Turkish. They were originally nomad stock raisers; but to-day the majority of cattle, sheep, horse, and camel breeders are no longer mainly nomads, although they still live in groups of felt tents called *yurta*. Since wood is scarce they use dried dung for fuel. There are about three million Kazakhs, more than half the total population of the Soviet Socialist Republic of KAZAKHSKAYA (q.v. Vol. III). Their country is enormous but most of it is semi-desert. In the north, however, there are good wheat and rye districts, and round the capital Alma Ata (Father of Apples) are abundant fruit orchards. Towards the end of the Tsarist rule thousands of

SOVIET CENTRAL ASIA

Kazakhs fled to China to escape conscription, and again more fled when the Soviets first introduced collective farming. It is an indication of their love of independence that Kazakhskaya was the last Soviet Socialist Republic to be formed—as late as 1936.

3. THE KIRGIZ. South of Kazakhskaya lie the better-watered highlands of KIRGISKAYA or Kirgiz Soviet Socialist Republic (q.v. Vol. III), bordering with Sinkiang, and believed by many scientists to have been the birthplace of the human race. The Kirgiz and Kazakhs have

KIRGHIZ HORSEMEN
Roy. Geog. Soc.

much in common in language, customs, and mode of life. They are often distinguished as the Kara-Kirgiz (Black Kirgiz) or Mountain Kirgiz. As nomad people they cherish freedom, and travel for hundreds of miles in search of new pastures. They are chiefly sheep and cattle breeders, their livestock playing an important part in the economy of the Soviet Union. Their food is produced by their cattle and horses: mares give each about nine quarts of milk daily, and from the fermented mare's milk the acid and alcoholic drink *kumiss* is made. The Kirgiz are fond of poetry and unwritten folk-lore: indeed, it is only recently that the Kirgiz language has had a written form. Kirgiz women, like Kazakh women of the nomadic or semi-nomadic people, enjoyed a good deal of freedom even before Soviet times. They are not veiled, and occupy a fairly important position in the general life of the community. The Kirgiz S.S.R., formed in 1924, has about one and a half million inhabitants to-day.

4. THE TADJIKS. West of Kirgiskaya, also in the desert highlands bordering on Afghanistan, lies the Soviet Socialist Republic of TADJIKSKAYA (q.v. Vol. III), between Turkistan and Persia, formed in 1924 and the smallest of the Central Asian republics. The Tadjiks (Persian *Taj*, crown) have strong ties with their Sunnite Moslem co-religionists in Afghanistan, and are fanatical in religious observances, neither eating meat nor drinking mare's milk. They are not

Mongoloid in race, and could be taken for Europeans were it not for their dark complexion. Their language belongs to the Aryan family, and they are the only Central Asian people who speak a non-Turk language. The Tadjiks were, until the 16th century, the main population of these Central Asian regions; but from that time on, they had to submit to other races, which made them distrustful and timid. They therefore welcomed the Soviet organization, which made them into a separate republic with about one and a half million inhabitants. They are settled and industrious agriculturists, pursuing farming, horticulture, and sheep breeding. Social changes, especially those improving the status of women, were not introduced easily. Women were employed in silk culture, but the money they made was kept by the men. But now that the women sell their own goods directly to their customers, they are more independent economically. The Tadjiks possess a rich folklore. With the spread of education, many theatres have been opened, and one of their favourite plays is Shakespeare's *Othello* produced in their own language.

5. THE UZBEKS. To the north and west of Tadjikskaya in the plains lies the Uzbek S.S.R. (*see* UZBEKISKAYA, Vol. III). It has the largest population of all the Central Asian republics, over five and a quarter millions, of which about

UZBEK WOMEN AND CHILD
Dorien Leigh

76% are Uzbeks. The ancient capital Tashkent is the centre of most of the republic's industries, and is surrounded by very fertile irrigated lands. About 60% of the Soviet supply of cotton, 'white gold', is grown in Uzbekiskaya. The Uzbeks are related to the Kirgiz, but are a very mixed people. Their name means master of himself (*Uz*, self; *Beg*, master). They are passionately fond of their freedom and resisted Soviet control with some violence. The creation of the Uzbek S.S.R. in 1925 caused much difficulty, and many complicated adjustments had to be made with the legally independent vassal states of Bokhara and Khiva, now included in Uzbekiskaya. The work of the Soviets was not made easier by the Uzbeks' passionate adherence to conservative Moslem customs. Women were kept practically as slaves. Even to-day the poorest house is divided into two, and no man outside the family circle is allowed into the women's quarters. Resistance was so strong that the Soviet Government did not risk forbidding women to hide their faces behind veils. Though some of the younger generation have recently abandoned the custom of veiling, there has been violent opposition, and many a girl who dared to break with tradition was murdered by her relatives. Apart from town buildings most houses are built of mud. They are small and dark but are quickly constructed, do not need timber, which is scarce, and are said to withstand earthquakes particularly well. But they are cold in winter, and in summer are infested by all sorts of vermin, including scorpions. The Autonomous S.S.R. of the Kara-Kalpaks has also been included in Uzbekiskaya since 1936. These people are kindred to the Kirgiz-Kazakhs; but they prefer a settled agricultural, cattle-breeding, and fishing life.

6. The Turkmen. Finally, to the south-east of the Caspian and north of Persia and Afghanistan is Turkmenskaya (q.v. Vol. III), which was formed into a Soviet Socialist Republic in 1925. The country is very arid, so that though it is the second largest republic of Central Asia, it contains only about one and a quarter million inhabitants. These are partly Turkmen and partly Russians. The Turkmen (or Turkomen) are closely related to the Kirgiz and Uzbeks. They are divided into numerous tribes, such as the Tekke, the Saryk, the Salyr, the Yomud, and represent a mixture of various types—Turkish in the north and Persian in the south. Persian

A YOUNG TURKMEN WOODSELLER
Roy. Geog. Soc.

blood came into Turkmenskaya through men and women who were kidnapped as slaves in former times. The Turkmen speak different Turkic dialects, they are Moslems but not fanatical, and their womenfolk enjoy a considerable amount of freedom. Before the days of Russian control the Turkmen's main occupation was brigandage, for which their very good physique gave them great advantages. They had no permanent chief, but only temporary leaders for raids. They regarded labour as degrading, and when they were not on one of their 'expeditions', they passed their time drinking tea, loafing, and telling stories. Under Russian influence much has been done to reclaim land by irrigation and to exploit the raw materials—oil, coal, sulphur, and cotton. Rug-weaving and dyeing, for which the Turkman was renowned, have been encouraged and expanded, and Ashkhabad the capital is still the centre of the rug industry.

7. The Bokharan Jews must also be mentioned among the peoples of Central Asia. They are said to be descendants of Israelites brought to these regions about 600–700 B.C. as prisoners of the kings of Assyria and Babylon. Their position among the Moslems has been difficult. Until the Russians took control, they lived under many restrictions: they had to live in separate quarters; they could ride only on donkeys instead of horses and mules; they were forbidden to wear the turban—instead they wore a high fur-trimmed cap; and they might only wear ropes as girdles. Their main occupation was the dyeing of native silk. They speak a dialect called Sart, which differs little from the Uzbek language. The Russians used the name *Sart* generally for all settled natives, to distinguish them from *Kazakh* (wanderer).

Since the peoples of Central Asia ceased opposing the Russian intervention, considerable progress has been made in developing these countries. Railway communications, essential to the development of such vast lands, have been increased; large irrigation schemes have been undertaken; a formerly illiterate population can for the most part read and write. The peoples' national cultures have been encouraged, and they can take an active part in the direction of their affairs; though the final say rests here, as elsewhere in the U.S.S.R., with the Central Government in Moscow. The economic potentialities of Central Asia and its strategic position between West and East will, moreover, tend to increase in the future the importance of these peoples.

See also RUSSIANS; SIBERIAN PEOPLES.

SPANIARDS.

The Spanish people are a very proud people—there is a saying that no man is so arrogant as a Spaniard. They are strong individualists and therefore not easy to unite under one government. Because of the mountainous character of Spain, there is little contact between the different areas, and this has made the people regional-minded rather than national-minded. If you meet a Spaniard, he will tell you that he is an Andalusian, a Galician, a Castilian, or a Catalan, not that he is a Spaniard. The Spaniards have a reputation for cruelty, largely based on two things, the stories of the Spanish Inquisition and bullfighting. Such ideas can easily be exaggerated; but it is undoubtedly true that the Spaniards, especially in the south, have, together with many other peoples of southern Europe, different standards from our own, particularly in the treatment of animals. Roman Catholicism is the national religion of Spain. Castilian Spanish is the official language; but there are many dialects, of which Galician (similar to Portuguese) is the chief. The Basque and Catalan languages are also spoken.

The earliest known inhabitants of Spain be-longed to the Old Stone Age, and they have left traces of their civilization behind—especially in the wonderful drawings in the cave dwellings of Altâmira and the Pyrenees. Later, though still before written history, there were invasions of Celts in the north, and of a small, dark, long-headed people from North Africa, originating possibly from Asia, called Iberians; and it is from these that the modern Spaniard is descended. The whole peninsula came to be known to the Greeks and Romans as Iberia. Phoenician traders settled in south Spain and may have been responsible for the founding of Cadiz. Spain or Hispania, the Roman word, became part of the Roman Empire, and the Romans built roads, bridges, aqueducts, and fine buildings, the most remarkable being perhaps the amphitheatre at Toledo and the lighthouse at Cadiz.

But the greatest influence on Spanish civilization came with the MOORS (q.v.) from North Africa. At the height of their power, in the 10th and 11th centuries, the Moors ruled most of Spain, and they were not finally expelled until 1492. They brought with them new crops, including the orange, and they introduced and controlled systems of irrigation. They set up water tribunals to deal with disputes over this most vital commodity, and these proved so valuable that even to-day at Valencia a tribunal of peasants meets every Thursday outside the great Cathedral to settle grievances over irrigation. The Moors brought into Spain the Mohammedan art of the Arabs and Persians, and they built palaces and mosques, many of the latter being now Catholic churches. The beautiful Alhambra, the palace of the Moorish kings, still stands at Granada, which was the last stronghold of Moorish power. The houses of the south are built in Moorish fashion around a courtyard or *patio*, planted with orange-trees and cooled by splashing fountains. Around the courtyard are cloisters, where the family may sit out of the sun in summer or take exercise in winter. The outside walls are thick and have no windows. Entrance from the street is through heavy grilled doors, because of the need for defence in bygone days.

Probably the greatest period in the history of the Spanish people was during the 15th and 16th centuries, when they led the world as a sea power, and sent out their great explorers and conquerors—men like COLUMBUS, CORTÉS, and

PIZARRO (qq.v. Vol. V), who set out from Spain to build up their Empire in the New World. This Golden Age produced great painters such as VELAZQUEZ, Murillo, and Ribera, while EL GRECO, a Greek by birth, settled in Spain and filled the churches of Toledo with his religious pictures (qq.v. Vol. V). Of the Spanish writers, CERVANTES (q.v. Vol. V) is the greatest, and his romance *Don Quixote* is still read by all who wish to understand the Spanish people.

Modern Spain is comparatively poor and undeveloped, though the country's natural wealth, both agricultural and mineral, is being more and more exploited every year. Many of the people are very poor, though of recent years the development of social services has relieved poverty. Means of education, both for children and adults, are also increasing, but about one-seventh of the adult population still cannot read or write. There is still a shortage of modern roads and railways, and in some parts of Spain much of the local transport is by donkey and mule along rough and dusty tracks. The most go-ahead and vigorous of the Spanish people have been the Catalonians and the Basques of the western Pyrenees. Spain has suffered by her isolation from the rest of Europe, but more contact with other countries is now breaking down this isolation.

Most of the Spanish people live in towns and villages with white-washed houses huddled close together along narrow winding streets. The narrowness of the streets shields the people from the glare of the sun in summer and the cold winds in winter. Many of the towns are still surrounded by their medieval walls, built for defence against brigands and rebels. In the country life is often very hard, and farming methods primitive. Farmers use wooden ploughs drawn by oxen, and the pressing of the grapes for wine is still occasionally done by human feet. In the big cities, such as Barcelona and Madrid, there are modern buildings and a modern way of life. Most people wear European dress; but, occasionally, at a fashionable ball in Madrid, or in some remote country district where old ways die hard, a Spanish lady may wear the black mantilla and adorn her high headdress with the traditional carved Spanish comb.

The national sport, BULLFIGHTING (q.v. Vol. IX), which plays a part in the life of the people difficult for the modern Englishman to understand, is still very popular, and the

A NARROW STREET IN TOLEDO

toreador is a national hero. The Spanish people love music and 'treading the measure' to the rhythm of the castanets. The vine harvests bring local festivals at which the whole community celebrates with dance, feast, and song, while in any Spanish village the gipsy fiddler will always have an audience.

See also Vol. III: SPAIN; Vol. IV: SPANISH AND PORTUGUESE LANGUAGES.

SPARTANS. The people of the city of Sparta in the Peloponnese in ancient Greece. Sparta was a soldier-state. The Spartan citizens, always very restricted in numbers, devoted themselves exclusively to military training. They were forbidden to have anything to do with business and trade, which was carried on by their subject states who paid taxes to them. All the manual work and the cultivation of the soil was done by slaves. The Spartans had very little interest in art and literature—a great contrast to their rivals in Greece, the Athenians. Sparta itself was not a beautiful city with fine buildings like Athens, but consisted of a group of straggling villages looking like a large military camp.

The training of a Spartan youth was very severe. There was no place for the weak and sickly. Delicate babies were not allowed to live. The youth of Sparta lived a communal life under strict discipline until they were thirty years of age. Their training aimed to develop powers of endurance, courage, and strict obedience, and they passed through a series of tests until they were considered fully qualified. Intellectual education played a very small part. Spartan girls, also, were trained in gymnastics, and the same high standards of endurance and courage were expected from them. Women played an important part in the life of the community.

Sparta grew to be a very strong military power, and the main rival to Athens in Greece. As a result of the Peloponnesian Wars she had become, by 404 B.C., the greatest power in Greece. Her rigid military organization and despotic rule, however, were much hated, so that, after some thirty years, her rivals united to overthrow her, and in 371 B.C. she was defeated in battle by the Thebans. The numbers of Spartans began to decline: in 480 B.C. there had been some 8,000 Spartan citizens, by 371 B.C. only 2,000 were left, and by 242 B.C. there were said to be only 700.

The word 'Spartan' is now used to indicate courageous endurance against physical hardship. In most ways the Spartan way of life, and in particular their rivalry with Athens, was very harmful to Greek prosperity; but such examples of their soldiership as that of the heroic defence of the pass of Thermopylae against the Persians in 480 B.C. by King Leonidas and his Spartan army, have won the admiration of later generations.

See also GREEK CIVILIZATION.

SPELLS AND CHARMS.

SPELLS AND CHARMS. In performing MAGIC (q.v.) the words which accompany the actions are very important, and magic is nearly always accompanied by words. These words may be called spells, charms, or incantations. Spells usually mean words having the power to impose a curse, to bewitch, enchant, and work evil by magic. 'Charm' is sometimes used of evil magic, but is usually meant to counteract evil, to cure illness, oppose witchcraft, and bring good fortune. Objects, as well as forms of words, are sometimes spoken of as 'charms'. 'Incantation' may mean the words uttered in a musical fashion for good or evil magic, and is used when a magician chants in an act of creative wonderworking.

To realize the importance of words in magicmaking, we must remember that simple people think of words as very powerful things. A person's name, for instance, may be regarded as a part of him, just as much as his hand or leg. Indeed, sometimes it is thought to be his soul—as if the important part of him were a kind of name-substance. If a sorcerer then wishes to do harm to a person, he tries to learn his name, because he thinks thereby to obtain power over him. Thus the spells of Finnish wizards begin, 'I know thy birth'. For this reason it is a very common practice for names to be kept secret. Sometimes even a man's wife will not know his real and secret name. He has an 'ordinary name' for everyday use.

A curse is supposed to carry harm directly to the victim, and is not simply a way of expressing ill will towards him; many spells are curses, and are accompanied by actions representing the evil which the person wishes to fall on his victim. The witch or sorcerer acts on the belief that words are so full of power that to say what you wish to happen causes it to happen—just as he or she thinks that by acting a calamity to someone, you bring it to pass. Although a magical spell is supposed to have power in itself to cause harm, yet quite often the names of demons or other spirits are brought into it to add to its effectiveness. Thus magical and religious notions become mingled. So also charms for some good purpose become rather like prayers, when the name of some divinity is invoked in them. Sometimes a spell is used by the sorcerer to compel a spirit to do his will. Here are a few examples of spells and charms:

A Hindu sorcerer used to kill a red-headed lizard saying, 'I am killing so-and-so'. An old Russian charm against fleas, bugs, and beetles is as follows: 'Fleas, bugs, beetles, and all such creatures, behold, I come to you as a guest; my body as bones; my blood as pitch; eat moss but not me. My word is sure. Key. Lock. Amen. Amen. Amen.' In these the sorcerer relies on the words of the charm or spell and the magical actions to do their work, without the aid of spirits. The following words from the ancient

Babylonian records are used by a man who believed his enemy had made a figure of him, to bewitch him, a prayer rather than a charm.

> Those who have made images of me, reproducing my features,
> Who have taken away my breath, torn my hairs,
> Who have rent my clothes, have hindered my feet from treading the dust,
> May the fire-god, the strong one, break their charm.

Some of the charms used by the ancient Egyptians against snake-bite were stories about gods, repeated because they were believed to have magical power. A person making magic may simply tell a story, including in it what he wants to happen. In New Guinea a man who wishes his taro plants to grow well says, 'Once upon a time a man laboured in his field and complained he had no taro shoots. Then came two doves flying. They had devoured much taro, and they perched on a tree in the field and during the night vomited up all the taro. Thus the man got so many taro shoots that he was even able to sell some of them to other people.' This native's wish had become a day-dream, and the day-dream had become a charm.

Since words are believed to be charged with power, sorcerers use spells or charms to give objects of one kind or another special magical qualities. When a Russian shopkeeper or merchant was doing badly in business, he used to go to a sorcerer and ask for his help. This man got some honey and said a charm over it: 'As the bees swarm around this honey, so let the purchasers flock to this merchant because of his wares.' To make the charm complete, the merchant smeared himself with the honey. The ancient Egyptians had a spell for curing bad eyesight. The spell was said over honey, mixed with the brain of a turtle, and then the eyes were anointed with this mess.

A natural step from using spoken words in charms was to write them down, and so have them handy all the time to keep off evil influences. Such charms are all the more useful as, in many countries, it is believed that a curse may float about for years, waiting for an opportunity to alight on the unfortunate person. These inscriptions were carried about in lockets, and so come into the class of 'amulets'—objects worn to keep off evil and bring good fortune. A Tibetan charm to counteract cooking smells in the kitchen, which the gods might dislike, consisted of the character for 'cow' wrapped in hedgehog skin. One Egyptian charm had to be written with myrrh and put in the mouth of a dead cat. It ended up '. . . the sacred Ianiee ien aeo eieeieiei'. These meaningless syllables were supposed to convey the secret name of a god, and so bring him under the sorcerer's power. A magician, who published a book on magic in 1606, gave the spells in code. They were deciphered more than a century later, and were found to consist of commands to spirits to appear and do his bidding.

A very famous charm, supposed to cure fevers and dating from the 2nd century A.D., consists of the word Abracadabra written thus:

```
ABRACADABRA   or thus   ABRACADABRA
 ABRACADABR              BRACADABR
 ABRACADAB                RACADAB
 ABRACADA                  ACADA
 ABRACAD                    CAD
 ABRACA                      A
 ABRAC
 ABRA
 ABR
 AB
 A
```

A MEDICINE MAN IN THE BELGIAN CONGO, COMPOUNDING CHARMS
Roy. Geog. Soc.

And another was a Latin palindrome, in which the same words could be read in different directions:

SATOR
AREPO
TENET
OPERA
ROTAS

People will use nonsense in a spell, and think it all the better magic because they do not understand it. There was a belief that a person upon whom a spell had been cast could escape from it by saying it backwards, thereby, as it were, unwinding it. On the other hand, some witches' spells in Europe consisted of prayers said backwards; but the witch-cult in England and especially on the Continent was a form of devil worship rather than sheer magic (*see* WITCHCRAFT).

In Christian countries heathen charms became something between charms and prayers. A Scottish cure for a sprain consisted of tying a black thread with nine knots around the limb and saying:

> The Lord rade
> And the foal slade;
> He lighted
> And he righted,
> Set joint to joint,
> Bone to bone,
> And sinew to sinew.
> Heal, in the Holy Ghost's name!

Originally, this charm, without the Christian references, was used for curing a lame horse, and was connected with the story from Norse mythology of how Baldur's foal was cured by Odin with spells. In later times people, using it to cure human injuries, did not worry about the mention of a foal being out of place in it.

Many Scottish charms are intended to counteract other spells which were supposed to be dangerous. To all magic there is a counter-magic, and so certain charms are believed to neutralize spells. The MAORIS (q.v.) used to say when a curse had been called down on someone:

> Great curse, long curse,
> Great curse, binding curse,
> Come hither, sacred spell!
> Cause the curser to lie low
> In gloomy night.

In the same way that a magician is supposed to have power over a person if he knows his name and birth, so he has power over certain objects believed to be full of magical quality, if he knows

their origin. When Väinämöinen, the hero in the beautiful Finnish epic, *Kalevala*, wounds himself with his axe, and is unable to staunch the bleeding, he goes to an old man who, by repeating the origin of iron and chanting other charms, is able to heal him.

Prayer is quite distinct from spells and charms; although, as we have seen, charms and prayers may be confused together. In prayer, a person humbly seeks blessing, but does not believe he can command or control the divinity to whom he prays.

See also FOLK-LORE; MAGIC.

SPHINX, *see* MYTHOLOGICAL MONSTERS, Section (*b*).

SPIRITS. A spirit is the animating or life-giving principle in man and in nature, which shows itself in growth, movement, reproduction, and other signs of vitality, such as breathing. Breath, in fact, has often been regarded as the essence of life or soul, so that when an organism ceases to breathe, its soul is thought to have gone out of the body, departing with the last gasp. Souls and spirits are very closely connected, and in all probability the idea of the one is derived from the other. A very widespread and probably very primitive idea of man is of a person made up of a body and a life-principle or soul with an independent existence of its own. This, it is supposed, leaves the body when the latter is asleep, and its adventures are recalled in dreams. Sometimes it spends longer times away from its natural abode, and then the body is in a state of trance. Finally, it departs one day for good, and that means the death of the body.

Now when man first began to think of himself as made up of two parts, the one physical, the other spiritual, he seems to have regarded every other living or moving thing in the same way. So he peopled the whole of nature with spiritual beings, good and evil, whom he held to be responsible for everything that happens in the universe, making them behave in much the same way as himself, although they belonged to the other world. They had supernatural powers, and could help or oppose him in all the affairs of his daily life (*see* NATURE WORSHIP).

In course of time, he began to think of gods with dominion over certain departments of nature. He conceived of a god of the woods—a Silvanus, as the ancient Romans called the impish deity who presided over the woodlands, and in his kindlier moments looked after the interests of hunters and farmers. Similarly, he thought of the winds as under the control of a single divinity, such as Aeolus, who in Greek mythology is said to have kept the winds in a leathern bag, and let them out from time to time to lash the sea into fury. Thus, departmental gods of this kind were just part of the general animation of nature, that is, spiritual beings animating the natural objects or forces in which they were believed to dwell.

Besides these spirits and gods belonging to a different order from mankind, there are the souls or GHOSTS (q.v.) of dead men who, after death, live a life of their own, without their bodies, and are always liable to visit their old haunts on earth. Although these are generally invisible, they often appear in human form, and may be seen by a dreamer while he is asleep, looking as they used to when on earth, like the ghost in *Hamlet*: for the primitive mind thinks of the soul as the flimsy image of the body. On the whole, these visitations are regarded with fear and apprehension, because ghosts at best are uncanny, and always liable to bear a grudge against the living. Even to this day, many people are afraid to walk through a churchyard at night, or go into a room where a corpse is lying in its coffin. It is not surprising, therefore, that ghosts are usually regarded as unwelcome visitors; though, when they are thought to be able to foretell the future, they are sometimes deliberately called back to earth, as in the case of Saul's visit to the woman with 'the familiar spirit', the witch at Endor (1 Sam. xxviii. 8 f.).

If more attention is paid to harmful than to helpful spirits, this is because man is always inclined to take the good for granted and to seek chiefly for causes and remedies for his misfortunes. Therefore, he attributed to evil spirits or to black magic the ills of life that beset him—sickness, calamity, and death—and so imagined himself surrounded by a host of demons ready to trip him up at any moment. They are actively at work, he may think, in thunderstorms, avalanches, hurricanes, earthquakes, drought, plague, pestilence, and famine—in fact in any catastrophe. Some of them are devils who have always been evil spirits, citizens of the underworld; others are the disembodied ghosts of persons who have died a sudden or violent death, and hover about in the air or in the dark recesses of the forests to wreck vengeance on luckless

THE DEATH OF ST. GUTHLAC

The soul, escaping from the saint's mouth, is borne to heaven by angels. The Guthlac Roll, 12th-century MS. (B.M. Harley Roll Y. 6., f. 13). *British Mus.*

mortals whom they happen to meet, or who they believe were responsible for their death.

This side of the picture can be easily exaggerated, for, while man is undoubtedly always on the look out against the attacks of unseen powers, and takes special precautions at critical seasons of the year or at crises in his own life, in fact the majority of spirits are thought of as neither good nor evil. It is only when they are neglected, provoked, or offended that these neutral beings become hostile, and, as we are reminded in the pantomime, the spiritual forces of evil are opposed by those whose purpose is to help man and promote his well-being. For instance, in the religion of ancient Rome the homestead was under the care and patronage of the household spirits and gods, such as Vesta, the spirit of the hearth, Janus, the spirit of the door, and the Lares, the spirits of the home and the fields. In China, also, the ancestors looked after their own people, and the spirits guarded the road, the gate, the path, the door, and the kitchen (*see* CHINESE RELIGION).

Moreover, in Rome, not only the house and the fields, but every man was supposed to have his own guardian spirit, or Genius, and every woman her Juno. In Egypt a spiritual helper called the *ka* was assigned first to the Pharaoh and then to everybody, to be his companion and guide all the days of his life, and at death to prepare a place for him in the next world. This

HUTS FOR THE SPIRITS OF THE DEAD
Belgian Congo. *Roy. Geog. Soc.*

same idea recurs in the Christian belief in guardian angels (*see* ANGEL). So we see that spirits are by no means always regarded as harmful and evilly disposed towards human beings and the world. On the contrary, an important part of their work has been supposed to be of a kindly and friendly nature, and only when they are not properly treated do they become vicious.

SPIRITUALISM. The name given to the practice of communicating, or attempting to communicate, with the spirits of the dead. Though the name is modern, the practice is very ancient. Witch-doctors and medicine-men in primitive societies have believed that they could get into touch with departed spirits. A well-known instance is that recorded in 1 Samuel xxviii, where Saul consulted the woman of Endor in order to speak with the dead prophet Samuel. The practice is said to have been forbidden in Israel even in those early days—certainly a passage in Isaiah (viii. 19–20) shows that the great prophets disapproved of it. The Jewish repugnance to Spiritualism was maintained by Christianity. Witches and wizards have always been regarded as being in league with the devil, and in times of fear and unrest they were often hunted out and persecuted (*see* WITCHCRAFT).

The qualities possessed by these ancient communicants with the spirit world were those we now call psychic, and there can be little doubt that they were similar to those possessed by the modern medium. The difference lies in the use

made of them. In 1848 three sisters, Fox by name, living at Hydesville, New York State, heard mysterious rappings in their home. One of them devised a simple code which, the girls asserted, was answered by rappings in such a way as to prove that they were made by an intelligent being. The news of these happenings caused a great sensation; and from them the modern spiritualistic movement had its origin. Hitherto most Christians had believed that spirits were only invoked to do harm, and that they were evil—which explains the fear and hatred felt towards those who invoked them. Now, however, it was proclaimed that the spirits were good, or at least as good as ordinary people on earth. They dwelt, not with the devil in hell, but in lands far better than this world; and they were continually progressing. Any inquirer could find his friends and relations among them, ready and anxious to give proof that they had survived death. It is still the claim of spiritualists that this proof can be supplied to all who seek it. Whether the proof is sufficient is a matter of dispute. A number of eminent men, including Sir William Barrett and Sir Oliver Lodge, have believed that it is; but the majority are sceptical.

The spiritualistic movement has taken two directions, one scientific and the other religious. In England the Society for Psychical Research was founded in 1882. Its investigations include, not only communications with the dead, but such kindred subjects as the seeing of visions and the hearing of voices, telepathy or thought-transference, as well as GHOSTS (q.v.), haunted houses, and uncanny movements of furniture. It seems clear that such things happen; but more than sixty years' investigation has failed to discover any laws by which they can be explained or controlled. That mediums have access, in varying degrees, to knowledge beyond the ordinary is certain; but how that knowledge comes to them is still a mystery. The balance of evidence, however, is in favour of supposing it to proceed from some deep activity of the human mind, rather than from the spirits of the dead.

It has been suggested that there exists a vast reservoir of life, from which all creatures partake, and in which all experience and knowledge is stored. Tiny insects, which are close to this original source and only slightly differentiated from it, gather from it all the knowledge they need for their short earthly existence. As the

scale of life rises, in animals and at last in man, a new power develops—the power of thinking. This comes to its height in human self-consciousness and reason; and for man, reason is the proper and normal guide to knowledge. But the old direct instinctive channels are not entirely closed; and in some persons, perhaps in all persons at some times, flashes of knowledge come through them, either spontaneously, as in visions, or after artificial stimulation, as when the medium goes into a trance. People who are continuously susceptible to these influences from the beyond are called psychic. In some of them the personality appears to split up and form two, three, or occasionally many personalities, with different characters, speech, and knowledge. It is through such people that the messages, which Spiritualists claim to come from the dead, have proceeded.

When Spiritualism is spoken of, it is generally the religious movement which is meant. The impulse to make psychic communications the basis of a new religion comes from the natural longing to know what has become of our loved ones who have died. This longing has been deepened by the two wars through which we have passed. Spiritualist churches arise whereever a few people can gather together and procure a medium. Messages from the departed are confidently given to all who ask for them. The messages are generally very poor in quality, and concerned for the most part with trivial matters. But when inquirers are in distress through bereavement, they are, in general, not too critical in examining any message which brings them comfort.

The late Sir Arthur Conan Doyle became a Spiritualist, and wrote a book entitled *The New Revelation*, in which he claimed that Spiritualism was the true religion which must now supersede all others. In this book, and in the works of Mr. J. A. Findlay (of which *The Psychic Stream* is the most important), the creed of Spiritualists is set forth. They believe in the Fatherhood of God and the brotherhood of man, doctrines taken from Christianity. Some regard Jesus Christ as the Son of God; others proclaim him to be one of a series of high spirits who have temporarily left the other world to help men on earth. All deny the Atonement; for they insist that man rises by his own efforts, and that no one could bear the sins of another. The next world is conceived as a series of spheres or regions, rising one after another until the final heaven, the abode of God, is reached. Through these, the souls after death travel in a continuous progression, though at different rates. The weakness of Spiritualism as a religion is that it is based on an interpretation of psychic happenings which is, to say the least, doubtful. From a Christian point of view, it tends to obscure God by concentrating attention on the spirits of the departed. True Christianity has God for its supreme object, and endeavours to see all things in him.

STOICISM, *see* Asceticism. *See also* Vol. V: Zeno.

STONEHENGE. This great prehistoric monument on Salisbury Plain is one of the most remarkable and puzzling of our British antiquities, for the Bronze Age stone-circles elsewhere in Britain or on the Continent (to which it otherwise seems clearly related) are not constructed in this way—with horizontal lintels carried on uprights of carefully tooled stone.

The main features of Stonehenge are as follows: a not very large ditch and bank cut in the chalk encloses a circular area, about 340 feet across; there is a gap in the ditch on the north-east to which a wide 'avenue', marked out by a double line of small ditches 60 to 70 feet apart, leads from the direction of the river Avon. Nearly in the middle of this avenue, just outside the gap in the enclosing circular ditch, is a large standing stone. The main standing structure of Stonehenge is within the circular area enclosed by the ditch, and is arranged in this way: on the outside, nearest the ditches, there is a circle 100 feet in diameter, of large stone-uprights of grey sandstone, with continuous lintels of large carefully-shaped stones bridging them across on top. Next comes a circle of smallish stones of speckled bluish-green stone; inside this come two 'horseshoe' settings, one formed by five enormous pairs of sandstone (sarsen) uprights with lintels, and the other formed by more of the bluish stones, also arranged in a horseshoe shape set inside the first horseshoe. In the curve of the horseshoe is a flat oblong slab. Many of the stones have now fallen or have been destroyed; but this plan can be seen quite well.

Excavations were carried out to discover the date and the history of the construction of Stonehenge, and they revealed that, almost certainly,

STONEHENGE. *Aerofilms*

Stonehenge was built in two stages. They showed that just inside the circular ditch and bank there had been holes where, at an early stage in the building of the site, the bluish stones had stood in a simple circle. This seems to have been in the early Bronze Age (about 1900 B.C.), and we may compare the circle and avenue with the similar sacred circle at AVEBURY (q.v.), twenty miles away to the north. Then, later in the Bronze Age, a great scheme of rebuilding seems to have taken place, when the present structure was set up with huge sandstone (sarsen) stones from north Wiltshire in the Avebury region. The blue stones, most surprisingly, have been proved to have come from the Presely Mountains in Pembrokeshire some 200 miles away as the crow flies, though it is probable that they were floated round by sea.

In the rebuilding scheme the blue stones seem to have been taken up from their original places and set up inside the outer sarsen ring, as the Blue-Stone Circle and Horseshoe. The remarkable work of tooling and setting up the huge uprights and lintels may have taken place about 1500 B.C., when a very powerful dynasty of Bronze Age chieftains were ruling in Wessex, and burying their dead in the barrows around Stonehenge.

The excavators also found two circles of holes just outside the sarsen ring, which seem to have held wooden posts, and to have been dug some time just before the Roman Conquest (in the 1st century B.C. or a little later). If the Iron Age priesthood, known to Roman writers as the Druids, ever held ceremonies at Stonehenge, these posts may have been their additions to a monument that was by then already ancient.

Stonehenge faces the rising sun, and on midsummer's day the sunrise takes place in a direct line from the centre of the circle over the single standing stone in the avenue (the Hele, or Sun Stone). This presumably implies that the builders of Stonehenge deliberately set the monument, the Hele Stone, in that particular place for that reason; but no other trustworthy deductions can be drawn from the fact.

See also MEGALITHS; RELIGION, PREHISTORIC.

SUDANESE, *see* NEGRO AFRICANS; NUER.

SUMERIANS. Little more than fifty years ago the very existence of the people whom we now call Sumerians was unknown; but excavations have now proved that, earlier than the already well-known Semitic civilizations of the BABYLONIANS and the ASSYRIANS (qq.v.), there had existed for many centuries, in the fertile delta of the Euphrates and the Tigris, in what is now Iraq, a people whose language and culture was quite different from that of the Babylonians and Assyrians. We have now enough knowledge to form a fairly accurate picture of this, the most ancient civilization of Mesopotamia.

The origin of the Sumerians is still an unsolved problem. Their language does not belong to the Semitic family of languages. We can see, from their pictorial representations of themselves on their monuments, that their physical characteristics were quite different from those of other peoples inhabiting Mesopotamia. In their writings they describe themselves as 'the black-headed people', suggesting that they were a dark-skinned race. They were short, sturdy, and with shaven heads and faces, in contrast to the tall and heavily bearded Semites.

It is fairly certain that they came into the Tigris–Euphrates valley from the north-east, probably through Persia—driven to migrate by changes of climate. The recent excavations of ancient Indian cities at the mouth of the Indus have shown resemblances between these civilizations and that of Sumer; but it is impossible at present to be certain whether this is due to trade relations or to a common origin. Some scholars still hold that the Sumerians are racially akin to the early inhabitants of India (*see* INDIAN CIVILIZATIONS).

Wherever they originally came from, we know that, by about 4000 B.C., they were settled in the region which they called Sumer and Akkad, the alluvial plain which stretches from the mouths of the Tigris and Euphrates for about 200 miles in a north-westerly direction. At that time the head of the Persian Gulf extended 150 miles farther inland than it does at present.

Owing to rapid soil erosion no traces of New Stone Age culture have been discovered; so that, unlike the other great river-valley civilization of the EGYPTIANS (q.v.), it is not possible to trace the gradual growth of civilization in the Tigris–Euphrates valley from its earliest beginnings. But it is certain that, when the Sumerians settled in their new home, they already possessed a well-developed civilization. Whether the Sumerians were the earliest settlers in the delta, or whether they found Semites already in possession, is still unknown. On the whole, it is most likely that the Sumerians were the first comers. Their myths seem to picture the early struggle to tame the rivers, and to bring the fertile soil under cultivation. The Sumerian myth of the Flood points to the tradition of occasions when their hard-won gains were almost destroyed by the hostile forces of the rebellious waters.

The period of Sumerian greatness lasted from 4000 B.C. to the fall of the Amorite dynasty about 1800 B.C.—according to the most recent dating. During this long period, there were many changes and a great deal of development. We shall deal with the civilization of the Sumerians under the three main heads—Organization of Society; Religion; and Arts and Crafts.

A. ORGANIZATION OF SOCIETY. What we know about the early social pattern of the Sumerians we have gathered from the various collections of laws which have survived. The famous Code of Hammurabi (described in the article on Babylonian civilization) was drawn up about 1800 B.C., and was based on earlier bodies of Sumerian law and custom, collected and set in order by Hammurabi's orders. But even earlier collections of Sumerian legal decisions have been found, and from these we can tell that the family was the Sumerian social unit, and the father was the head of the family. Landed property was the most important factor in holding the family together, and the need of securing an heir made it sometimes allowable for a Sumerian to have more than one wife. Adoption of children was also a frequent practice. The

PORTRAIT OF KING GUDEA OF LAGASH
Sumerian sculpture 2600 B.C., in the Louvre. *Giraudon*

THE RUINS OF THE PALACE AT KISH, SUMERIA. *Prof. S. Langdon*

wife enjoyed a high degree of independence; she had her own property, and had the right of inheritance to her husband's estate.

There were three main classes in Sumerian society. The highest class, called *amelu*, included all government officials, soldiers of the regular army, and the priests. The second class consisted of freemen, who were merchants, farmers, and craftsmen. In the third class were found the slaves, whether born in the house or captured in battle. Between these different classes important legal distinctions existed. Offences against members of the amelu class were punished much more severely than those against members of the lower orders. It is probable that this caste system was of military origin, since war was a very important factor in Sumerian society, and the Sumerians were far ahead of their neighbours in military technique.

The normal political unit was the small city-state, ruled over by a priest-king who had the title of *iššakku*. In the early days of Sumerian history the country was largely marsh and swamp, in which islands of cultivated land had been created by irrigation ditches, canals, and dams. These settlements developed into city-states. As more and more of the marsh was reclaimed, various cities sought to bring their neighbours under their own control, and so arose the succession of dynasties—Kish, Erech, Ur, Isin, and so forth—each being named after the city which had, at that time, acquired the leadership in Sumer. But even under rulers such as Sargon of Akkad, who brought the whole of Sumer under his sway and became the centre of a series of legends, the cities continued to rule their own inhabitants and the outlying farmers and cattle-breeders. The irrigation system had to be kept in repair, and this required the continual control and oversight of the iššakku and his officials. Documents show how carefully all matters relating to the land and its needs were watched over and regulated by the central authority. All mortgages, sales, and transfers of landed property were registered; a tenant or owner who farmed his land badly, or neglected to keep his section of the irrigation system in repair, might be heavily fined, or even be deprived of his holding and reduced to slavery. In general, the Sumerians had reached, in these very ancient times, when our own country was still inhabited by primitive savages, a quite remarkably complete and efficient social organization.

B. THE RELIGION OF SUMER. From the earliest times of which we have any knowledge, each of

KIRUNA, A MINING TOWN IN NORTH SWEDEN
Most of the houses are built of wood. *New York Times*

Sweden the people are truly **Nordic** in appearance, with heads longer than they are broad, straight long noses, fair hair, and blue eyes. But to the north and south the people are shorter and darker. In the far north live the Lapps (q.v.), a Mongolian people with broad faces and flat noses.

There are a great many forests in Sweden, and so most of the farms and country-houses are made of timber. The walls of the farm-houses are painted with mineral paint to prevent dry-rot, and the windows and gables are outlined with white paint. Grouped about the dwelling-house are cow-sheds, stables, barns, silos, out-houses, and hen-roosts. The hay, in this damp wooded country, is hung out to dry over wire, stretched between poles. Most of the men are dairy farmers and belong to a co-operative, a system which, as in New Zealand, is used for production as well as for distribution. More than half the population work on farms or in the forests.

In the remoter parts of central Sweden you still find old customs and folk-lore; but the national costume is now little seen except in the Nordiska Museet (Nordic Museum) at Stockholm, which also has examples of wood-carving and other rural crafts.

In the towns, also, many of the buildings are made of timber, and Sweden was the pioneer in the construction of prefabricated houses for her rapidly expanding urban population. One-third of the total population live in towns. Sweden's town planning is good, and much of her architecture fine. In the workers' quarters in Stockholm are blocks of houses built in zigzag fashion, so that the windows of one house do not overlook those of another. The whole of Stockholm is built on islands in the midst of the sund and strömmar (bays and channels) of Lake Mälar, and many a Swedish family live on their own islet, using a motor-boat to reach the mainland.

The Swedes are proud of their past, and preserve its records in many excellent local museums and libraries. Their famous men include Linnaeus, the 18th-century botanist; Swedenborg, scientist and philosopher who died in 1772; Strindberg, the 19th-century dramatist; and

NOBEL, the inventor of dynamite and originator of the Nobel Prize (qq.v. Vol. V). They have always been great travellers and explorers; Dr. Sven Hedin journeyed through unknown Central Asia, and Nordenskjöld was first to master the North-East Passage.

In 1813 Henrik Ling founded the Central Gymnastic Institute in Stockholm, and his ideas on physical culture spread throughout the world. Because of their long snow-bound winter, nearly everyone in Sweden can ski, whilst in summer the young men and women spend their holidays camping, swimming, canoeing, and sailing. The Royal Swedish Yacht Club is the largest in the world.

The Swedes maintain that they are the most democratic people in Europe. Although the country has always been a kingdom, the Swedes never forget that, by a law passed in A.D. 900, the people have the right 'to make or break the King'. They enjoy a high standard of living. Every child goes to school, and a high proportion of them hope to win 'the white cap' awarded after the final matriculation examination. Many attend the universities at Lund or Uppsala, whilst evening classes for working people are popular. Only in the forest and tundra of central and northern Sweden is life more primitive.

The Swedes are proud of the way they have conquered their harsh and difficult country, making the most of their farms, forests, and mines. 'We Swedes', writes one of their authors, 'have ourselves made our country, have cultivated the lands and made the roads.' They have much to show the rest of the world in their way of life, their art, social science, and hygiene.

See also Vol. III: SWEDEN; Vol. IV: GERMANIC LANGUAGES.

SWISS. A Swiss postage stamp has on it the word Helvetia instead of Switzerland. Helvetia was the land of the Helvetii, a mountain tribe which invaded the southern part of Gaul, now France, in 58 B.C. They were defeated and driven back to their mountains by Julius Caesar. These Helvetii were the ancestors of the Swiss people. Their position in the middle of Europe involved these early Swiss in many of Europe's wars. Sometimes they were under the power of one powerful neighbour, sometimes under another. In 1291, three of the Cantons, or provinces, of Helvetia—those known as the Forest Cantons—joined together to fight and defeat the Austrian Archduke Rudolph, who

was then their overlord. One of these Forest Cantons was called Schwyz, and from this came the names Switzerland and Swiss. Neighbouring districts joined the Forest Cantons in their struggle against the Austrians and, when in the 15th century independence was won, these districts remained united with the original Cantons, although they kept their own languages, customs, and ways of religious worship. This was the origin of the Swiss form of Federal Government, and is also the reason why four languages—French, German, Italian, and Romansch—are spoken.

Switzerland is a Confederation, or Federal State. Each of its twenty-two cantons or states has its own courts of justice and can make its own laws. Every Swiss may speak his own language, whether it be German, French, or Italian, and may follow his own religion. The Central Government is by a Federal Assembly of about 200 members, with a Federal Council of seven members, that meets in Berne, the capital. The President is elected by the Assembly and holds office for one year. He is the President of the Swiss Federal Council, not the President of Switzerland.

The type of Swiss known best to the foreigner is the peasant and the farmer, who lives in a wooden chalet under the shadow of the Alps, and grazes his cows in fields of wild flowers and, in the winter, goes about his business on skis. In fact, nearly a quarter of the Swiss population of nearly five millions live in the few big towns, where they make, among other things, the silk and artificial silk, the clocks and watches, the chocolate and condensed milk, which are the best-known products of Switzerland. They are a sturdy, hard-working, and practical people. They are also intensely patriotic and united. But they are good mixers, and combine an intense love of their own country with a power of getting on well with people of other countries. Swiss hotel-keepers are found in almost every part of the world: indeed hotel-keeping, especially in the winter-sports resorts, is an important industry in their own country. A Swiss governess or children's maid slips more easily into a household in another country than a stranger from almost any other nation.

Her central position and the fact that she remained neutral in the two great international struggles of this century has made Switzerland a favourite meeting-place for great international gatherings. The International Postal Union

FERDEN, LÖTSCHENTAL, SWITZERLAND

The little wooden houses are huddled together in the mountain villages. *Swiss Federal Railways*

grew from a conference held at Berne. The Red Cross Society grew from a conference at Geneva. The 'red cross' itself, on a white ground, was chosen as the Society's emblem in compliment to the Swiss, whose national flag is the same sort of cross, but in white upon red. The League of Nations, formed after the First World War, had its headquarters in a great Palace of the Nations in Geneva, where the International Labour Organization also has its headquarters.

See also Vol. III: SWITZERLAND.

SYRIANS. These people live in a land which holds such a key position between East and West that few great events of history have by-passed them. SYRIA (q.v. Vol. III) has been part of the empires of the Egyptians, the Assyrians, the Persians, the Romans, the Moslem Arabs, the Turks, and finally the French (administered under a League of Nations Mandate). From about the 16th century B.C., on the coast of Syria, there grew up the great merchant city-states of the PHOENICIANS (q.v.). On the cliff walls north of Beirut there are a series of carvings and inscriptions recording the passage of armies along the coast of Syria in the course of thirty-three centuries. Syria has been involved in many great European wars, from the CRUSADES (q.v.) to the First and Second World Wars. Her people have hardly ever, until recently, been real masters of their own house. They gained legal independence from France in 1941, and now Syria and the Lebanon are independent states. Together they equal about the size of England and Wales, with a joint population of four and a half millions—three and a half million Syrians and one million Lebanese. Many Syrians live abroad, especially in Egypt and America, and they send a good deal of money home, which has been of great value to a poor country.

It is not surprising that a people with such a history should be of a very mixed racial type. Arab blood as a whole predominates; but there is a considerable element descended from the ancient peoples of Syria, and in later times Armenians, Kurds, Turks, Turkmen, and Europeans have mixed with the population. Two-thirds of the people are engaged in agriculture, stock-raising, and horticulture; but the remainder live in towns such as Beirut, Aleppo, and Damascus (which has been called the oldest city in the world). The life of the peasants in the country is precarious and hard, made doubly insecure, until recently, by regular raids of nomadic tribes of BEDOUIN (q.v.). The peasants therefore tend to overcrowd the towns, and this raises economic and social problems, for there are no important industries to absorb them. The standard of living in the overcrowded towns as well as in the country is very low. The dwellings in the country-side are primitive: cottages in the shape of beehives made of mud-brick, others made of wattle, and others partly of stone with flat roofs. The social distinction between the needy majority leading a hand-to-mouth existence and the few rich landowners and commercial magnates is very great.

About half the population of Lebanon is Christian. (The Maronites have existed from the early days of Christianity.) The rest belongs to the various Moslem sects (*see* ISLAM). The Syrians are nearly all Moslems, the majority being of the Sunnite community. About 13% are Christians.

Those Moslems that are not Sunnite belong to the Shi'iah sect (in Lebanon called *Meta wilah*); and these are further split into three separate communities—the Druzes, the Alawis, and the Ismai'ilis—each with a particular form of unorthodox Shi'ism. Each of these groups has from the 9th century developed local traditions and characteristics, and they have not always been purely religious groups, but also secret societies with political aims.

The Druzes broke away from Orthodox Islam and fled from Egypt to Syria in the 11th century. There is now a strongly organized community, some 70,000 in the Lebanon and about 85,000 in Syria. As the result of strife among the different factions of the Druze nobility many Druzes settled in the Jebel Druze district, where they make up almost all the population. They cling tenaciously to their distinctive customs and their own laws, distrusting Christians and other Moslems, resenting government interference, and being altogether a disturbing element in the country. In 1841 there was a civil war between Druzes and Christians, and in 1860 many Christians were massacred. The quarrel was not only over religion, but was largely a conflict between Christian peasants and Druze landlords. Several times expeditions had to be sent against them, and in 1925–6 the French had great difficulty in subduing a Druze revolt.

The Alawis (they call themselves Nasaris) are hardly Moslems at all, their religious liturgy

The Pole is nearly 40 ft. high, cut from a single tree-trunk. It formerly stood in front of the Chief's hut in a village in Queen Charlotte Is., B.C. The figures are totemic animals or mythical figures representing traditional stories of the Chief's ancestors. He sits on the top, wearing his ceremonial hat. Beneath him is a bear holding a frog; lower down is another bear killing a hunter. At the bottom is a raven

By courtesy of the Curator of the Pitt Rivers Museum, Oxford

A NORTH AMERICAN INDIAN TOTEM-POLE

being largely Christian in origin. They differ from the other minorities in possessing no land-owning class, but are almost all peasants (*fella-heen*) and labourers. There are about 274,000 of them, divided into tribes and sects, but not with any strong communal sense. Their rights as a religious minority were respected under the French Government and are guaranteed in the new Syrian constitution.

The Ismai'ili broke off from the Shi'iahs in the 8th century. They are a compact community of about 24,000, living in the Syrian province of Hama: they mix very little with others, and resent outside interference. They owe religious allegiance to-day to the Aga Khan.

Among the Christians the most important are the Maronites, of whom there are about 340,000, the majority living in the Lebanon. Their name comes from a 5th-century bishop, St. Maro. They became Catholics in the 11th century during the Crusades, and are now one of the biggest communities acknowledging the supremacy of the Pope, but retaining their own (Syriac) liturgy and customs. During the 9th century most of them moved into Lebanon in order to seek safety in the mountains. As well as Maronites there are members of the ORTHO-DOX EASTERN CHURCH (q.v.), the Armenian and Assyrian Churches, groups of Jacobites and members of the NESTORIAN CHURCH (q.v.), and some Roman Catholics.

Besides these religious groups there are many racial minorities. The ARMENIANS (q.v.), some 130,000 in all, came into Syria at the end of the 19th century to escape from Turkish persecutions and massacres, and again in 1939, when their region was transferred to Turkey. They are mostly townspeople, craftsmen, and traders. About 4,000 Assyrians fled from Iraq in 1933 and were settled with League of Nations assistance in Jazirah, and have now become an integral part of the Syrian state. There are about 200,000 Kurds, followers of Islam, many of whom have been in Syria for a long time, though some are recent arrivals. The Kurds have a tribal organization, and many of them live a nomad life. They have a strong nationalist movement, aiming at a Kurdish state. There are about 30,000 Turkmen, and 20,000 Circassians who came into Syria from Circassia to escape Russian domination. There is also a very small group called the Yazidis, who follow an ancient secret religion and speak a dialect of

THE SYRIAN PARLIAMENT
Tribal Sheiks listening to the President's speech
Margot Lubinski

their own. All these peoples speak non-Arabic languages.

Apart from these non-Arabic-speaking minorities the main unifying factor of the Syrians and Lebanese, whether Christian or Moslem (including about 30,000 Jews), is the Arab language. Under the French administration a strong sense of nationalism grew up, and the old animosity between Maronites and Moslems has grown less —in fact, in 1946 the President of the Syrian Republic with its Moslem majority was a Christian Arab, while the President of the Lebanon Republic where Christians predominate was a Moslem. At the height of tension with the French the Christians even began to wear the *tarboosh* (the Moslem tasselled skull-cap) as a sign of Arab solidarity.

Nationalist enthusiasm is mainly to be found in the towns. In the country religious feelings are still strong and sometimes bitter, the standard of life is still low, educational progress not very fast, much of the old way of life still persists, the camel and the motor-car are to be seen side by side on the roads, and there is not yet a very stable national and social fabric.

T

TABOO. When Captain Cook during his voyage to the Pacific Ocean visited the Polynesian island of Tonga in 1777 he found that anything that was forbidden was described as *tabu*. When he visited other islands in the area he discovered that this Polynesian word could include a variety of meanings; but in general 'tabu' signified that a thing was forbidden, and the word was applied in all cases where things were not to be touched. But he was chiefly impressed by the fact that the person of a chief, a corpse, a newly born infant were all tabu, because they were regarded as 'dangerous' in a supernatural sense and so must 'not be lightly approached', being 'set apart' or 'marked off' from common use or contacts. Therefore, when these early travellers introduced the word into the English language (spelt as 'taboo'), they used it to refer to persons, places, and events having these 'dangerous' supernatural qualities—such as a warrior or man of blood, a divine king, a dead body, a sanctuary or shrine, a particular day of the week or season of the year, the name of a god or a magic word. All these are said to be 'taboo', because they are 'marked off' or 'set apart' from the ordinary and commonplace by reason of their sacred character, and are only to be approached with safety when proper precautions are taken. So taboo and RITUAL (q.v.) go hand in hand, the one being the complement of the other.

If a man touches a corpse he becomes tainted with the mysterious supernatural powers connected with death, and is himself henceforth a source of danger and defilement to his fellow men until he has undergone a ceremonial cleansing. That is why the Jews, for example, regarded dead bodies as 'unclean' (Num. xix. 11, 13 ff.), and subjected mourners to so many ritual prohibitions, including even the food they ate (Hos. ix. 4). The earliest idea of sin, in fact, is that of a spiritual uncleanness contracted by coming into contact with something that is sacred, and therefore taboo. Thus, for touching the Ark of the Covenant in Israel, Uzzah is said to have been struck dead (2 Sam. vi. 6 f.), and Jonathan only narrowly escaped with his life when he ate honey, after his father, Saul, had placed a taboo on eating during a battle (1 Sam. xiv. 24, 27). The severe penalties suffered by those who broke the rules concerning the observance of the Sabbath as a taboo day are an example of the same principle, as is also the attitude towards Sunday that was adopted after the Reformation in northern Europe.

Taboos may, therefore, surround a great variety of objects and institutions that are regarded as sacred. Some things, such as a corpse or a newly born baby, are felt to be dangerous, because they are in themselves supernatural and awe-inspiring. Others acquire their supernatural qualities in connexion with their social position or special activities—as in the case of a powerful chief, king, or priest, mourners, warriors, manslayers, &c.; or because of their sacred associations—as in the case of the Jewish Sabbath and the Christian Sunday. Finally, a person or thing may be set apart for religious purposes by an act of consecration, as when a sanctuary, shrine, or church is dedicated, a king is anointed and crowned, and a priest is ordained. In all these ways persons, places, and objects are given a 'ritual status' in society, and so are hedged round with taboos, because they are sacred and in close contact with the supernatural order, which may not be carelessly approached.

Now it would be a mistake to dismiss all this as mere primitive superstition of no value. The institution of taboo plays a very important part in establishing law and order, in controlling the food-supply, and in forbidding that which is thought to be, and often actually is, harmful to good social relations between members of a community. For instance, the rules a woman has to observe when she is expecting a baby, and immediately after its birth, often are beneficial in preventing her from doing things that would not be good for her or the baby at such a time. Furthermore, the taboo gives 'the event' a particular importance for all concerned in it, and helps to unite the family in a common centre of interest. The total effect, in short, is to bind individual men, women, and children into an orderly society, in which each has his or her proper place and part to play for the well-being of the group as a whole.

The rules and regulations demand effort, discipline, and obedience, and represent the crude beginnings of a moral sense of right and wrong. The unforgivable sin is to do anything that is likely to bring ill luck on oneself, because ill luck is catching and therefore to be avoided at all costs, like any other contagious plague. The worst crime of all is to fail in the duty of being a good tribesman, and therefore the strictest taboos are those connected with the laws against incest (i.e. marriage between near relatives). These are essential safeguards in a closely knit society where passions are always liable to get out of hand. If human beings are to live together under such conditions in unity, peace, and concord, these vital points have to be protected by adequate controls, such as the institution of taboo affords.

See also RITUAL.

TAMILS, *see* INDIAN PEOPLES; INDIANS, VILLAGE LIFE; CEYLONESE.

TANGANYIKA, PEOPLES OF, *see* EAST AFRICANS.

TAOISM, *see* CHINESE RELIGION.

TARTARS. The word means 'inhabitants of hell', and is the name loosely given to nearly three million inhabitants of Russia, the descendants of the Turkic and Mongolian people of Tartary in Central Asia east of the Caspian, who invaded Europe in the 13th century. The Tartar invaders were led by Batu, grandson of the Mongol Emperor, JENGHIS KHAN (q.v. Vol. V.) The majority of them were Moslems of Turkic origin (*see* TURKIC LANGUAGES, Vol. IV).

The great Mongol empire of Jenghis Khan spread from Persia to China. An army of some half-million well-trained, swift, and hardy horsemen carried everything before them, devastating the land they conquered, and causing unbelievable human suffering and slaughter. Between 1223 and 1245 they overran Russia, Moravia, Silesia, Hungary, and Bulgaria. Fortunately for Europe they could not sustain their power so far from their headquarters in lands which they had so ruthlessly ravaged. They were finally called off on the death of the great Khan Ogatai in his capital at Karakorum, as their leaders had to go back to elect another Khan. Quarrels

TARTAR HORSEMEN
Chinese painting of the Sung Dynasty, 13th century A.D.
British Mus.

broke out among them and the colossal empire fell to pieces.

But the Tartars of the Golden Horde (called so because of the golden colour of the tent of Batu, their leader), who had established themselves in the south-eastern steppes of Russia, broke away from the Mongols, and for 200 years exercised a crushing despotism over Russia—a tyranny which had a serious effect upon the history of that country. It was not until 1380 that a Russian Prince, Dimitri Donskoi, defeated a great Tartar army at the battle of Konlikovo. Although the power of the Golden Horde was not yet broken, belief in their invincibility was gone; they were growing weaker and disunited and, before the end of the century, Russia was freed from their yoke.

The word Tartar is now used to describe a savage or intractable person, and the expression 'to catch a Tartar' means to meet a person who is more than a match for one.

TASMANIANS. Tasmania was first discovered in 1642 by the Dutch navigator Tasman, who called the land after his patron—Van Diemen's Land. It was not called Tasmania until 1853. French and British ships visited the island at various times during the 18th century, but no determined settlement was made till 1803, when a party, consisting largely of convicts, was dispatched from New South Wales.

The British colonizing party found the island inhabited by some 2,000 aboriginal people, following a more primitive way of life than any other known peoples. These dark-skinned aboriginal people were primitive food-gatherers, making only the simplest use of their natural resources. They lived in small wandering bands of less than fifty people. They built the scantiest shelters—merely unroofed wind-breaks of bark and boughs. They used only rudimentary tools —a short heavy stick for clubbing and throwing, a wooden spear with a point burnt and hardened by fire, a pole for prising up roots or dislodging shell-fish, scrapers and cutters of quartz flakes, very rough reed or bark baskets, and rough rafts made of bundles of eucalyptus bark and propelled by poles. They had no bows, no pottery, no boats, and no nets or fishing-lines to catch the plentiful supply of fish round their coasts. They made little attempt to store food. Their speech varied a great deal from group to group: there were four main branches of their language and some two dozen dialects. Since their climate was good, and their country rich in natural resources, their backwardness is to be explained by their long isolation from more advanced peoples.

When the British began to colonize Tasmania, they found the aborigines troublesome and aggressive. They drove them to one part of the island, killed numbers of them, and deported some to other islands. Under this treatment the natives quickly disappeared, and the last pure-blooded Tasmanian died in 1876.

THE CRICKET GROUND, BURNIE, TASMANIA. *Fox Photos*

The colony of Tasmania began as a penal settlement. After transportation to Australia had ceased, Tasmania received an increased number of convicts, not only from Britain but also from India and the colonies. In 1825 Tasmania became separated from New South Wales, and had its own governor. In 1853 transportations of convicts ceased, and three years later a responsible representative government was set up.

In 1901 Tasmania and the five mainland states federated to form the Commonwealth of AUSTRALIA (q.v. Vol. III), recognized since 1931 as a self-governing nation.

TELEPATHY, *see* GHOSTS; SPIRITUALISM.

TEMPLE. A holy place set apart for the worship of a particular god or spirit or of a number of gods. The solemn rites or ceremonies, held in honour of the divine being to whom it is dedicated, are usually performed by special people—priests or priestesses and their assistants—in a consecrated space in front of the inner shrine or chamber where the image of the god is enthroned. The word 'temple' was originally a Latin word meaning an enclosure set apart for divination by augurs; but later it was the name given to the 'house of god', the place where the image is kept, and eventually to any sacred building set apart for religious worship.

At first shrines were no doubt simple structures, as they are among primitive people to-day. In the Old Stone Age some of the earliest sanctuaries of the human race seem to have been in the dark recesses of caves, where paintings and engravings represented animals upon which man depended for his food. As civilization developed, and more labour and materials became available, sanctuaries were built of huge stones. The most elaborate temple of this kind still standing in Europe is STONEHENGE (q.v.) on Salisbury Plain, and similar sanctuaries are to be found in many parts of the world, especially along and near the sea-coasts in Brittany, the Spanish Peninsula, on both sides of the Mediterranean Sea, and in Asia Minor.

As can be seen from the stories of the Patriarchs in the book of Genesis before the time of Moses, the Hebrew places of worship generally consisted of sacred stones, trees, caves, mountains, or wells, regarded as the abodes of the god, where he manifested himself. It was at such a spot that

PART OF THE GREAT TEMPLE OF AMŪN, KARNAK
Ashmolean Museum, Oxford

Jacob is said to have spent the night on his way to his uncle Laban, and had his dream about the ladder reaching from earth to heaven (Gen. xxviii. 10–12).

When the Israelite tribes returned to the desert after their escape from Egypt, the God of Israel was worshipped at the holy mountain called Horeb or Sinai; but, apparently, only their leader Moses was allowed to visit his God there. For the rest of the people a tent was set apart in the camp, surrounded by a space called the 'holy place'. When the Israelites took possession of Palestine they appear to have carried with them a portable shrine, the Ark of the Covenant, which contained a number of sacred objects thought to have been collected in the desert. The sanctuaries already in existence in Palestine consisted of regular enclosures, surrounded by walls and open to the sky. Within the enclosure stood lines of six or eight upright stones, with a grotto or cave for the god on one side, and on the other a space reserved for the worshippers. For a time the Israelites used

THE THESEUM OR TEMPLE OF HEPHAESTOS, ATHENS

these shrines; but in the reign of Solomon a temple was built on the old sacred hill called Sion at Jerusalem. Solomon's temple was built by foreign workmen, and was probably on the plan of temples in Egypt and Phoenicia. It had two stone pillars, known as Jachin and Boaz, standing at the porch, like those at the entrances to temples in Syria and Egypt. The outer court corresponded to the space in Egyptian temples between the entrance and the impressive hall, with its great columns supporting a roof. The hall led by a flight of steps to the inner shrine of the image of the god, with its lamps, pomegranate, date-palm, and bull designs.

But Solomon's temple, which has long since vanished, was a very small affair compared with the enormous temple of the Egyptian god Amon-Re at Karnak. Pharaoh after Pharaoh added more and more columns to this temple, and one of these, the pillar we know as 'Cleopatra's needle', is now to be seen on the Thames Embankment in London. Some of the later kings built new temples in much the same style as those which had been erected on the banks of the Nile, a thousand years earlier. Other kings restored and enlarged these old temples. Thus Egypt became a land of complex sanctuaries and gigantic royal tombs, the remains of many of which have survived to this day.

In Mesopotamia the most conspicuous feature of the Babylonian temples was a mound, shaped like a flat-topped pyramid, rising in seven terraces. This was situated in the centre of the temple-area, and was approached by steps or an upward path, and there was a shrine at the top (cf. Gen. xi). The idea of pyramidal temples was developed by the SUMERIANS (q.v.), who first brought civilization to Mesopotamia. They furnished the sanctuary with a couch and a holy table. In the great Babylonian temples, later on, there was a long outer hall opening into a smaller one—the holy place—where the image stood in an inner shrine which was entered by the priests alone. As the priests also ruled the city there was, adjoining the sanctuary, a large number of buildings used for the training of priests and for carrying on the general administration and economic life of the city. The temple, therefore, became the civic as well as the religious centre of the community (see BABYLONIAN CIVILIZATION).

In Greece temples were smaller than in Egypt or Babylonia, but they were beautifully proportioned in stone and marble. They were rectangular in shape, and surrounded by graceful columns, with an inner shrine for the image of the god, the altar, and the treasury. One of the finest examples of this architecture is the Parthenon, built of marble, and situated on the Acropolis at Athens, where the earliest citadel stood. This is a small building measuring 225 by 100 feet, but with wonderful proportions, and magnificent sculptures representing incidents from the siege of Troy, battles of the gods, and other incidents from the myths and festivals, as well as queer creatures such as centaurs and giants. Within the shrine with its wooden ceiling was a statue, 42 feet high, of the goddess Athena, the patroness of the city. Greek temples, in fact, were primarily houses for the sacred image of a god, to which a large open space called a *temenos* was added. But they were not places where large congregations assembled, and public business was transacted, as in Egypt and Babylonia. So little were they used that they were generally kept locked.

For practical purposes the big centres of worship were the places where the will and commands of the gods could be discovered by means of oracles, such as dreams, casting lots, interpreting signs, &c. (*see* DIVINATION). The chief of these was the Delphic Oracle where, at the shrine of the god Apollo, it was possible to get an answer to almost any inquiry from the priestess who was always in attendance to consult the oracle, very much as in Israel people resorted to the Ark when they wanted to know what their God would have them do. So great was the fame of Delphi that inquirers came to consult Apollo from all over Greece, Asia Minor, and the Roman Empire. There were several other similar centres, at one of which sick folk slept in the sanctuary of Aesculapius, the god of medicine, to receive miraculous cures through dream oracles. As at Lourdes in France to-day, cures were carefully tested, recorded, and published, so that the fame of the shrine attracted patients from distant cities (*see* PILGRIMAGES).

In the religion of Ancient Rome the *templum* was a sacred place without a roof, dedicated to a god, who was consulted by oracles at a tent within the enclosure. Later, when the Romans adopted the gods and worship of the Greeks and Etruscans, they built temples similar to theirs, with a central chamber for the image. Some were oblong in shape, others circular. At first (about 510 B.C.) they were erected on the Capitoline hill at Rome in the Etruscan style, in honour of Jupiter, Minerva, and Juno. Since the gods were thought to have human needs, every new god who was introduced into the capital had to be given a proper home.

See also GOD; PRIEST; RITUAL.

TEUTONIC, *see* GERMANS.

TEUTONIC KNIGHTS, *see* KNIGHTS, ORDERS OF.

THAI, *see* SIAMESE.

THEISM is the belief in God as existing apart from the world, of which He is the Creator and Sustainer. Such a God can be called The Uncaused Cause of the Universe. God would still exist if there were no world; without God the world would not exist. This belief is, for convenience' sake, labelled Theism, to distinguish it from another form of belief which says that God *is* the universe (*see* PANTHEISM). But children sometimes ask very naturally: 'What did God do before He made the world?' The theist probably believes that there never was a time when God was not actively engaged in creating,

because it is of the very nature of God, so he says, to wish to express Himself. To ask further: 'What did God make the world out of?' is also natural; but it is harder to answer this question simply, because the theist would say that the world is the expression of the thought of God, and being, as a great astronomer has said, 'made of mind-stuff', it cannot be thought of as 'taking up space'. The world is really only a series of events or happenings in space and time. All these events, even the most durable, like mountains, have a beginning and an end. They are themselves only, as it were, patterns made by electric discharges. So, perhaps, it is only the way in which our senses perceive them which makes them, as we say, 'take up room'. We find it easy to think of the floor as solid, the water in our glasses as liquid, and the air we breathe as gas. But these may only be convenient ways of talking, and the real world, as it is known to God's mind, may be quite different. The theist, however, believes (while the pantheist probably does not) that what we call the succession of events one after another is real, and is as much created by God as the events themselves, even though His mind may be able to know the whole series of events all at once.

See also GOD.

THEOSOPHY. This word comes from two Greek words, and means 'wisdom of God', or rather 'wisdom about God'. It is a comparatively new name for a movement which is spoken of in the New Testament. To understand its meaning, it is best to contrast it with 'theology', or 'the doctrine or teaching about God'. Theology, also a Greek word, generally refers to Christian teaching, though it is possible to speak also of 'Moslem theology' and 'Hindu theology'. What has come to be called theosophy differs from theology in several important respects. First, it is never either entirely Christian, entirely Moslem, or entirely Hindu, but claims to combine the truth from all these religions into one system. Second, and this is most important, it claims that the highest truth about Deity is discovered by an inner circle of skilled persons, sometimes known as 'adepts', who practise spiritual exercises in order to get into a state of consciousness in which they see things which are beyond the power of reason to find out. Reason does not enter into the scheme at all. Now theology, on the other hand, admits and welcomes the use of reason in dealing with its data. Although it is certainly true that the Hebrew prophets and Jesus Christ claimed to deliver revelation, i.e. truth about God which was given to their consciousness direct and was not reasoned out, yet from the first reason was applied to such revelation.

The teaching of theosophy dates back to the beginning of the Christian era, when it was known as *gnosis*, a Greek word meaning knowledge of spiritual mysteries. It was always opposed by Christians. Gnostics attempted to make Christianity part of a larger scheme in which Christ was not the central figure; they believed in an inner circle of people possessed of secret knowledge; and they held that only ideas mattered, and that the facts of history had no bearing upon our knowledge of God. Christians disapprove of all these doctrines; but Indian thinkers, past and present, are in sympathy with the last (*see* HINDUISM). Gnosticism faded in the West, though it never quite died out, and after the Reformation in Europe there was some revival.

Then, in the 19th century, a Russian lady called Helena Blavatsky appeared in America, saying that she had come from Tibet, where she had learned secret wisdom from a fellowship of adepts called 'the Great White Lodge'. This fellowship was a sort of universal brotherhood of all religions, based on secret teachings derived not from reason or from Christian revelation, but from the use of spiritual exercises which enable the users to delve into deep mysteries. In 1875 Mme Blavatsky and a retired American colonel, Henry S. Olcott, founded the Theosophical Society, with branches in India, Europe, and America. Colonel Olcott remained president of the Theosophical Society till his death in 1907, when he was succeeded by Mrs. Annie Besant.

The genuineness of Mme Blavatsky's claims and the details of her alleged visit to Tibet are open to grave question, and in other respects it seems likely that she was fraudulent. Mrs. Besant had a hard task to place Theosophy on a more respectable basis, though even she accepted some of Mme Blavatsky's teachings. A more striking figure in later years has been Count Hermann von Keyserling, an Esthonian philosopher, who visited Adyar, the Theosophist centre near Madras, in 1915, and, after a long journey through the east, returned to Germany and set up a 'School of Wisdom' at Darmstadt.

Theosophy to-day is a strange mixture of Christian and non-Christian ideas. It accepts the Hindu doctrines connected with reincarnation, and practises spiritual exercises which are rather like the Hindu *yoga*. It is entirely unscientific and is not guided by reason. It makes a great deal of the secret significance of numbers and letters, and puts forth extravagant claims to the understanding of Bible texts. In spite of its sympathy with Hinduism, orthodox Hindus tend to ignore it, and though it claims to encourage the study of comparative religion it does so in a manner which does not advance that subject.

In 1917 there were reported to be 1,074 branches of the Theosophical Society, distributed over nineteen countries; but the actual total of professing members was small, only 28,673. It is unlikely that there has been any great increase since that date.

THESEUS, *see* GREEK HEROES.

TIBETANS. The Tibetans belong to the great Mongoloid family of mankind; in race they are closely related to the Mongols of Mongolia, and also to the Chinese and the Burmese. They have a language akin to Burmese, but they use a script of their own, rather like that of SANSKRIT (q.v. Vol. IV), which developed in the 7th century A.D. when a vehicle was needed for translating the scriptures of the newly imported Buddhism.

Living as they do in an intensely rigorous climate, and shut in behind mountain barriers, they are physically very hardy, and have preserved their traditional ways of life almost untouched by modernism and the civilization of the West. The bulk of the people, except for the priests, are illiterate; but they are, as a rule, intelligent, friendly, and hospitable. Climate and geography, on the one hand, and their religion, 'lamaism', on the other, determine their way of life.

Because of its dryness and altitude the country can support very few people, and the difficulty of getting a living, as well as the scarcity of women, may account for the system of marriage (polyandry, as it is called) by which, instead of a man having several wives, the woman has several husbands. Then, too, the climate and soil affect the occupation of the people. The great central and northern highlands are too cold for crops or even for trees to grow; so the people are all herdsmen and continually on the move. The herdsmen live in tents—long, low

PROCESSION OF MONKS APPROACHING THE GREAT LAMASERY AT LHASA

constructions of black felt, moored securely against the fierce, ever-present winds. They eat meat, butter, and cheese, and drink great quantities of tea flavoured with rancid butter—a man will commonly drink up to fifty cups of tea in a day. In the more sheltered and better-watered valleys and plains, where the plateau falls away towards India on the south and China on the east, cultivation is possible, and there are villages and towns, fields of barley, and orchards of apricots, peaches, and pears.

Women in Tibet enjoy more freedom and a greater voice in affairs than in most oriental countries. Tibetan children have a hard, but by no means a dreary life, for the Tibetans as a race are a fun-loving, merry people, fond of sports, open-air games, singing, and dancing, and especially of theatrical entertainments, which are performed by troupes of actors travelling through the country. They possess a rich FOLK-LORE (q.v.) which is spread among the people by professional storytellers, many of whom can neither read nor write. On the other side of the picture, the Tibetans are excessively addicted to gambling and drink.

In their everyday habits and customs the people are united by a common religion, lamaism, which enters deeply into their lives, so that the wandering yak-herdsman and the farmer settled in a village have much the same pattern of beliefs. Lamaism is an offshoot of Indian BUDDHISM (q.v.), mixed with primitive Tibetan magical superstitions. In its early form it survives to-day among the section of lamas or priests known as the 'Red Hats'. In the 14th century there came a great reformation or purification, brought about by the 'Luther of Tibet', whose name was Tsong-ka-pa, or 'the man from the Land of Onions'. The lamas who follow his teaching are known as the 'Yellow Hats', and are a much stricter sect than the 'Reds'. The modern Tibetan is ruled by the priesthood, from the Grand Lama reigning in Lhasa to the million or so lamas (they number about one-fifth of the whole population) scattered in lamaseries or monasteries all over the country. As was true of some Christian monasteries in the Middle Ages, very many of the monasteries are filled with ignorant, greedy monks who prey on the superstition of the masses. But some of the monasteries are true centres of piety, learning, and the arts, and many lamas are like the one in Rudyard Kipling's *Kim*. By the sternest austerity and mortification of the flesh they develop great spiritual and mystical powers.

Besides the priests, there is a class of wealthy and powerful nobles. Some are descendants of the kings who ruled in Tibet before the days of lama government. Others spring from the near relations of each successive Grand Lama. When the Dalai Lama dies, his soul passes, according to Tibetan belief, into the body of a new-born boy, who may be the son of the highest or lowest in the land. The fortunate child—who can be recognized by certain bodily marks—then has to be found, and a royal baby-hunt ensues, supervised by the abbots of the principal monasteries. On the last occasion, just before the outbreak of the Second World War, the search lasted for nearly three years before the child was discovered and duly installed on the pontifical throne at Lhasa.

Tibet is perhaps the only important country where priest government still survives. At the head is the Dalai Lama, living in his majestic seven-storied palace of Po-ta-la, just outside Lhasa. The secular governing powers, however, are relegated by him to a Regent, also a priest, who rules with the help of a grand council of four. Tibet has always kept herself aloof from the outside world, allowing foreigners to enter the country only by special permit. China has

TIBETAN WOMAN WEAVING A RUG
Roy. Geog. Soc.

for a long time claimed a general suzerainty over Tibet. Indeed, until the Chinese Revolution of 1912 she kept a permanent garrison at Lhasa. For a time the Governments of Great Britain, India, Russia, and China agreed not to intervene in Tibetan affairs; but since 1950 the Chinese People's Government have ranked Tibet among China's 'Outer Dominions'.

See also Vol. III: TIBET; Vol. IV: CHINESE AND ALLIED LANGUAGES.

TITANS, *see* MYTHOLOGICAL MONSTERS, Section (*a*).

TOTEMISM. The name comes from the word *ototeman*, which, in the dialect of the Ojibwa tribe of North America, means 'his brother-sister-kin'. This curious phrase suggests that totemism has something to do with people living together in social groups, in a very close relationship with one another.

In many parts of the primitive world—among native tribes in North America, Australia, and Africa, in the Melanesian islands of the Pacific Ocean, and in the hills and jungles of India and Ceylon—the people believe that a social group of common descent depends for its origin and identity on an intimate and exclusive relation that exists between all its members and a certain animal or plant, or occasionally an inanimate object, which is regarded as the supernatural ancestor or ally, i.e. the totem. All who belong to the particular clan or group call themselves by the name of the totem, and adopt it as their badge or hereditary mark—very much as boy scouts call themselves Peewits, Wolf-cubs, Foxes, and so on. Indeed, it was upon totemism that Baden Powell based this feature in the organization of his great movement, as a sort of brotherhood of youth; though he gave the primitive custom a very different meaning and purpose.

So close is thought to be the relationship between those who belong to a totemic clan that the members of the group generally regard themselves as blood relations, through their common relationship with the 'elder brother', the totem. For this reason they are often forbidden to marry each other, and have to seek a partner outside their own clan—a practice that is known as 'exogamy', or 'marrying-out'. But in some cases it is quite the opposite: a tribe is divided into groups which have to marry within particular sections of the community. But, however the organization is arranged, totemism is a system of grouping people together through descent from a common supernatural ancestor connected with some aspect of nature. On this social side it deals largely with marriage rules and relationship grouping. In its other aspect (i.e. on the religious side) it is mainly concerned with the food-supply and other human needs, through ceremonies believed to maintain order and well-being in both society and the universe. The species of animals or plants called totems are often those that are used for food, or at any rate are edible; but so great is the 'reverence' for them that members of the clan which is associated with a particular totem are often forbidden to eat it, except, perhaps, very sparingly once a year as a kind of sacramental meal. Such a rite is, in fact, the native equivalent of a 'communion service' (*see* SACRAMENT), since, by eating the sacred species solemnly in this manner, they believe they are strengthened and renewed, because they receive its life.

Some native tribes of Australia carry out rites and ceremonies, especially connected with the totems and their ancestors, at certain spots, to stir up the vitality of the species and make it become abundant. These ceremonies, in fact, reproduce what the people believe that the ancestors of the tribe did at the dawn of creation when, as the Australian Aborigines believed, they gave each group its country, its laws and customs, duties, and responsibilities. But the members of the clan do not perform their rites of increase to benefit themselves, since they are not allowed to eat their totem freely when, as a result of their endeavours, it becomes plentiful. They do, however, get the advantage of the 'increase' rites of neighbouring clans. Therefore, totemism represents a form of collective effort, carried out by the people in a ceremonial manner for the benefit of the community as a whole— and this involves co-operation, foresight, the team spirit, and leadership. This makes for solidarity between local groups, just as the system of kinship and marriage rules prevents jealousy and strife, by forbidding courtship, marriage, and inbreeding among people who live at close quarters.

Some psychologists have suggested that the practice of exogamy, or 'marrying out', began by a jealous father expelling his sons when they grew up, in order to keep their sisters for himself as wives. According to this theory, totemism arose when the brothers, having joined forces

AUSTRALIAN ABORIGINES IN CEREMONIAL DRESS WITH THEIR TOTEM POLE. *Australian Information Bureau*

and killed their father, were struck with remorse at their foul deed, and showed their sorrow by treating with great respect the animal (now become the totem) which represented their slain father, and refusing to marry the women they had tried to secure by their crime. But this theory is not very likely, for there is no evidence that anything of this kind ever really happened in the past in any human community; and certainly it does not occur in primitive society to-day.

Totemism is also connected with the worship of ancestors, especially in Africa, and with ideas about the transference of souls from one body to another. In exercising control over growth in nature and the rainfall, it linked man's environment with the laws and organization governing society. It is hardly likely that a set of beliefs with so many different elements has a single origin; but in its many forms it has played an important part in bringing together the order of nature and of society into a single system, in which the individual and the group each has its proper function for the well-being of mankind as a whole.

See also ANCESTOR WORSHIP; TABOO.

TRITONS, *see* MYTHOLOGICAL MONSTERS, Section (*b*).

THE SACK OF TROY
Painting from an Attic vase, 5th century B.C. Furtwängler-Reichhold, *Griechische Vasenmalerei* (Bruckmann)

TROJANS. Inhabitants of ancient Troy (Ilium), which was situated in the north-west corner of Asia Minor (Turkey). Troy started as a little Late Stone Age village of sun-baked bricks, situated on a hill-top on the Trojan Plain. It was probably founded by traders about 3000 B.C. By 2500 B.C. it had developed into a wealthy, fortified, commercial town, prospering, most likely, on trade in tin brought from eastern Europe by the Danube. It was many times conquered and destroyed, but always recovered its prosperity. Altogether, nine successive cities were built on the hill, each upon the ruins of its predecessor, over a stretch of some 3,000 years.

About 1500 B.C., when the Trojans were at the height of their power, the sixth city of Troy was a splendid rival to Knossos, the Minoan (Cretan) city across the Aegean Sea. It is not likely, however, that the Trojans ever reached anything like the brilliance of the MINOAN CIVILIZATION (q.v.): indeed, it is not certain that they even possessed the art of writing. This city of Troy was the city which the Greeks laid in ruins about 1200 B.C., the heroic tales of which have survived in Homer's epic poem, the *Iliad*.

The Trojan wars with Greece on 'the ringing plains of windy Troy', and the legends of the famous Helen of Troy have been favourite subjects for literature ever since. Stories of the Greek Achilles and Agamemnon and the Trojan Hector and Aeneas, as well as the story of the wooden horse of Troy, are familiar to most people. According to one medieval legend a group of the remnants of the Trojan race made their way to Britain, which they found uninhabited 'except for a few giants'. There they are said to have founded New Troy, which later became London.

All remains of the nine cities of Troy had, in the course of hundreds of years, become buried under a great mound, on which the Turks cultivated cornfields. In 1870 a German, called Schliemann, began to excavate this mound. In course of time, he and his successors dug through the remains of all nine cities, one above another, until they reached the original bare hill-top.

TUAREG. A nomadic camel-owning people, who inhabit a wide area of the central Sahara Desert in North Africa. They are tall, slender people with reddish-yellow skins, dark eyes long wavy black hair, and fine features. They consist of a number of groups of tribes who speak the same language, the most important groups being the people of Ahaggar, the people of Azjer, the people of Air, and the Ifogas of the south-west. Each of these groups has a chief, chosen by the heads of the several tribes.

Their dress consists of cotton clothing dyed with indigo, and the men wear veils which they never take off, even while sleeping. No man would allow himself to be seen without his veil. The veil consists of a long cloth which is wound round the head to form a hood, and then over the mouth and nose, leaving only a narrow slit in front of the eyes.

The Tuareg are divided into three classes, the nobles, who wear a black veil, the 'vassal' class, who wear a white veil, and the slave class. The chiefs of the noble class act as the war leaders, and rule the 'vassal' class. The slaves are owned by both nobles and vassals. A person's status follows that of his mother. If a man, therefore, from the noble class marries a woman of the vassal class, the children will belong to the vassal class.

Though the Tuareg are Moslems by religion, the status of women is much higher than among other Moslem peoples (*see* ISLAM). The men generally have only one wife, and women are allowed a great deal of liberty. They do not wear a veil and are allowed to eat with the men. They can take part in public life, and often know how to read and write. The women of the noble class do no manual work.

The Tuareg have a type of writing which differs from the Arabic script common to the other peoples of North Africa; and they possess a literature, folk-lore, and poetry.

They have some sheep and goats: but camels are the most important possession of the Tuareg.

TUAREG IN NORTHERN NIGERIA. *Margot Lubinski*

The respect paid to a man depends largely on the number of camels he possesses. Camels provide milk for food; camel hair is woven to make tents; the skins are made into bags for water, into footwear, and saddles; transport on long desert journeys is by camel.

In former days the Tuareg often used to carry out raids on their own people and on settled peoples, their main object being to capture livestock and, above all, camels. They did not take life unnecessarily, nor did they make slaves of each other, though they used to steal the slaves of outsiders. They also used to attack caravans crossing the Sahara, unless the traders paid for protection. Their weapons consisted of fine swords, which were greatly prized and handed down from one generation to another, spears, daggers, and large shields of hide.

The main food of the Tuareg consists of milk, and millet porridge seasoned with salt. The millet and salt they often obtain by barter from neighbouring tribes. They have no festivals, such as initiation ceremonies; but marriage feasts are often long and elaborate. They have few arts and crafts: they do not weave or spin, though they make articles of leather, and mats.

See also SAHARA, PEOPLES OF.

TUMULI, *see* BARROWS AND CAIRNS.

TURKS. Turkic-speaking peoples inhabit not only Turkey, but territories which extend eastward from the Aegean Sea in an unbroken line for some 4,000 miles right into outer China. They stretch into Russia, east of the Caspian, northwards as far as, and beyond, the Trans-Siberian railway, and southwards to the mountains of northern Persia, Afghanistan, and Tibet. There are about thirty-eight million Turks in the world to-day, about eighteen millions of whom live in Soviet Russia—more than in Turkey itself. A few millions inhabit northern Persia, Afghanistan, the Balkan states, and Cyprus.

It is assumed among historians that the Turks are a Mongolian people, or at least that they possess a common ancestry with the MONGOLS (q.v.). The Turks of Anatolia and Azerbaijan, by mixing with the local peoples whom they conquered, have lost their Mongolian characteristics; but the Turkmen east of the Caspian possess unmistakably the flat Mongolian features (see SOVIET CENTRAL ASIAN PEOPLES).

The dialects of Turkic, spoken by the numerous peoples which inhabit the so-called 'Turkish lands', are basically the same. They consist of three main divisions: Osmanli, the language of Turkey; Azeri, that of Russian and Persian Azerbaijan; and Turki, that of the Turkmen, east of

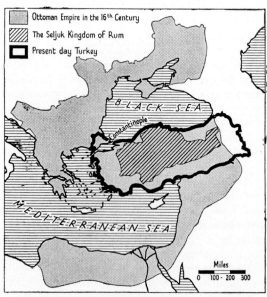

Ottoman Empire in the 16th Century

The Seljuk Kingdom of Rum

Present day Turkey

TURKEY TO-DAY AND UNDER THE OTTOMAN AND SELJUK EMPERORS

the Caspian (see TURKIC LANGUAGES, Vol. IV). The main difference between them to-day is the degree to which they have borrowed words and constructions from neighbouring languages—Persian, Arabic, and (more recently) European. In Turkey the Latin script is now used; in the

eastern regions either the Russian (Cyrillic) or the Arabic script (see ALPHABET, Vol. IV).

Chinese historians record that before A.D. 600 Turkish tribes, migrating westward, had reached the shores of the Caspian Sea and settled there. In the 8th century they came under the power of the great ARAB (q.v.) empire, and were converted to ISLAM (q.v.). After 300 years they overthrew their Arab conquerors and, under the leadership of the important Seljuk clan, they successfully invaded the Eastern Roman Empire, with its headquarters at Constantinople. In Asia Minor they established the kingdom or Sultanate of Rum, and the Seljuk Sultans of Rum were great builders and famous patrons of the arts.

In the 13th century the Mongol conqueror GENGHIS KHAN (q.v. Vol. V), at the head of a powerful army of Mongolians and Turks, swept right across Asia, overwhelmed the Seljuks, and actually reached the Bosphorus. Among the Turks who opposed the invasion was a small tribe, soon to become famous under the name of the Osmanly or Ottoman Turks after their first Sultan, Osman I (1288–1326). By the middle of the 14th century the Ottomans had established themselves as the dominant Turkish power in western Asia. One by one the strongholds of the Eastern Roman or Byzantine Empire fell into their hands until, in 1453, Constantinople itself was captured by the Sultan Mohammed II, and the BYZANTINE EMPIRE (q.v.) came to an end.

For the next hundred years the Ottoman Empire continued to spread. The Sultan's armies, particularly the famous corps of Janissaries, appeared to be almost invincible. They overran a large part of eastern and southern Europe, and for a time threatened the whole continent. During the reign of SULEYMAN THE MAGNIFICENT (q.v. Vol. V) (1520–66) the empire reached the height of its power. It included the territories now known as Anatolia; all the Arab states; Egypt and North Africa; Bulgaria, Roumania, and Yugoslavia; Hungary and a part of Poland; Greece and all the Aegean Islands; the Crimea and the Sea of Azov; Georgia and Russian Azerbaijan.

The Ottoman Empire was built up by military power, and ruled by autocratic monarchs, most of whom were ignorant and contemptuous of the peoples whom they conquered. Some of the sultans, especially in the latter years of the Ottoman Empire, were dissolute rulers, and used their autocratic powers in ways harmful to their country. By the end of the 17th century the decline of the Ottoman Empire had begun, and during the long period of decline, Turkey's most powerful and relentless enemy was Tsarist Russia. For 300 years the two empires were intermittently at war; and it was largely fear and distrust of Russia which prompted the Turkish leaders to throw in their lot with Germany in 1914. The defeat of Germany and her allies at the end of the First World War in 1918 brought about the final collapse of the Turkish Empire. Indeed, had she not produced at this critical moment a leader of outstanding ability, she would probably have ceased to exist as a sovereign independent state.

That leader, Kemal Atatürk, Turkey's soldier-statesman, became the founder of the new Turkish Republic. He accepted the loss of the non-Turkish provinces, but, by a series of brilliant military operations and astute political moves, succeeded in liberating the Turkish homelands, Thrace and Anatolia, from the Greek invaders and the occupying forces of the Allies.

Having freed his country, he proceeded to introduce a series of sweeping reforms. He overthrew the Sultanate, and established a Republic with himself as President. He set about to modernize the schools, to improve the position of women, and to introduce a Western system of law, abolishing the old laws of the Koran, the sacred book of Islam. He brought about the adoption of the Western calendar and the Latin alphabet in Turkey, and he took in hand and developed the railway system and methods of irrigation, farming, industry, and banking. Among other things he abolished the red fez, or Turkish cap—a matter of some psychological importance, for the fez, more than anything else, distinguishes the Turk in appearance from the European.

Atatürk could hardly have carried through all these reforms in the Turkey of that time by democratic means. To get his way he bullied, threatened, and cajoled the National Assembly (or Government), and had his more prominent opponents tried for treason and hanged or driven into exile. At the time of his death in 1938 the Republic was, in fact, a dictatorship. Nevertheless, no name in the long and picturesque history of Turkey is more revered by his countrymen than that of Kemal Atatürk (see MUSTAFA KEMAL, Vol. V), for no Turk can ever forget that he

PEASANT WOMEN IN THEIR NATIONAL COSTUMES
Turkish Embassy

saved his country from disaster. His reforms, which aroused such bitter controversy, have long since been accepted as the foundations of the new Turkey.

Atatürk was succeeded by a wise and cautious statesman, Ismet Inönü, who gradually evolved in Turkey a 'Western' form of democracy. He led his country safely through the crucial period of the Second World War, and although Turkey failed to carry out the terms of her alliance with Britain (1939), which should have brought her into the war against Germany, her neutrality in all likelihood served our cause better, for she was ill-equipped with the engines of modern war. Turkey's foreign policy is now concerned with the protection of the Straits which connect the Black Sea with the Mediterranean, and she looks to Britain, as she has done in the past, to help her.

Modern Turkey has no problem of overpopulation—her average population is only fifty-four to the square mile. The changes brought about by the Republic are at present more obvious in the towns than in the country. Life in the towns has been revolutionized by the emancipation of women and the almost complete disappearance of polygamy (more than one wife), together with the introduction of a free,

A VILLAGE SCHOOL IN TURKEY. *Margot Lubinski*

compulsory, and secular system of education for both sexes, with increasingly good opportunities for higher education. Nationalist enthusiasm is replacing the former enthusiasm for the glory of the Empire and of Islam.

In the country, however, where some four-fifths of the people live, life is changing only very gradually. Except for the big cotton farms in the south, the farms are mostly small peasant holdings. The standard of living is primitive and poor. A village consists of low huts of stone or dried mud surrounding an open space. Water comes from the village well, but sanitation does not exist. The most revolutionary thing in the village is the little whitewashed school-house, appearing now in more and more villages, where the travelling schoolmaster spends perhaps two days a week teaching adults, as well as children, to read and write in the new Latin script. The village market is held in the open space. The women in their drab clothes and black shawls sell fruit, nuts, and vegetables, while the

men sit under trees and smoke and drink coffee. In the eastern regions, on the borders of Iraq and Persia, life is still nomadic and pastoral, the whole village moving into the hills in summer and back to the valleys in winter. The Kurds, a racial minority in Turkey of some million people, mostly live this kind of life. They are an unsettled and fanatically Moslem people who resent the Republic, because it has broken up the undisputed authority of Islam. The Government, however, does not oppose freedom of worship in any way.

The Republic is doing a great deal to spread better methods of agriculture. One method is to send N.C.O.s from the army to be trained at Agricultural Institutes, from which they return to their home villages to show, by example, the new methods. This, as well as constant local instruction and demonstration, is beginning to have its effect.

See also ISLAM.
See also Vol. III: TURKEY.

U

UGANDA, PEOPLES OF, *see* EAST AFRICANS.

ULYSSES, *see* GREEK HEROES (Odysseus).

UNICORN. Belief in the fabulous animal, the unicorn, grew up in the days when little was known about the animals of the world, apart from the common European animals. A Greek writer called Ctesias was the first to tell of it. He said that in India there lived a kind of white ass which had a red, white, and black horn on its forehead; and that drinking cups made of this horn prevented poisoning. Roman writers, who got most of their information about animals from the Greeks, also mention various one-horned animals. Possibly Ctesias saw carvings in stone of animals represented from the side, and thought they had only one horn, or he may have been given some vague information about the Indian rhinoceros.

When the Old Testament was translated into Greek and Latin and later into English, the word for 'wild ox' was translated 'unicorn' (Deut. xxxiii. 17). So a set of new ideas became connected with the fabulous animal. A Roman writer, Aelian, who wrote in Greek, had recorded that it was marvellously gentle to the female; and from this the notion arose that the usually ferocious animal would follow a maiden and put its head on her lap. In 61 B.C. a rhinoceros was brought to Rome, and eventually the ideas about the unicorn became attached to this beast. Writing about it centuries later MARCO POLO (q.v. Vol. V), the traveller to the Mongol court, said very truthfully, 'They are not of that description of animals which suffer themselves to be taken by maidens, but are quite of a contrary nature'. By Shakespeare's time some people were doubtful if the fabulous animals existed: for instance, in *The Tempest* (Act III, Sc. iii. 22) Sebastian, astonished by Prospero's magic, says, 'Now I will believe that there are

unicorns.' However, even in 1801 an article was written arguing that unicorns existed.

The belief that the unicorn's horn prevents poisoning persisted in France until as recently as 1789, where articles, supposed to be made of the horn, were used for testing the king's food for poison. Some, at least, of these cups and utensils were made of rhinoceros horn. In China rhinoceros horn is still supposed to have various marvellous properties.

The idea that the lion and unicorn are rivals is not very old. It is mentioned in Spenser's *Faerie Queene* (ii. 15). The unicorn appeared on gold coins of King James III of Scotland and, later, the two were incorporated in the Scottish

THE UNICORN
Marginal drawing rom the Ormsby Psalter. English *c.* 1290 (MS. Douce 366). *Bodleian Lib.*

Royal Arms. At the Union the unicorn took its place on the left-hand side of the British Royal Arms, with the lion facing it.

See also FABULOUS CREATURES.

UNITARIAN. This religious sect has no set form of belief. It arose in the latter part of the 18th century, when some people, both in England and America, felt that they must attempt to make Christianity less mysterious and more reasonable. Priestley, the discoverer of oxygen, was the leader in England. Here, most Unitarians came over from Presbyterianism, and smaller numbers from the Baptists and Congregationalists.

Unitarians accept Jesus, not as divine, but as the man who taught the Fatherhood of God; and so they say that we should accept his teaching, worship as he did, and live according to the standards he set up. The name Unitarian is to be contrasted with Trinitarian, that is, one who believes in God the Father, Son, and Holy Spirit.

Since Unitarians hold that our Lord is not divine and neither is the Spirit a person, they are left with a simpler statement that God is One Person.

This reducing of traditional Christianity is not perhaps the sort of belief which people accept readily. Unitarians have now about 340 churches in the British Isles and a larger following in America; but they have long been a waning denomination.

See also CHRISTIAN CHURCH; CHURCH OF ENGLAND.

UR, *see* SUMERIAN CIVILIZATION.

URUGUAYANS. The full name of Uruguay in South America is the eastern Republic of the Uruguay river. This describes not only its position, but also one of the most important factors in its history: for Uruguay came into existence as a buffer-state between Argentina on the west and Brazil on the north. The original name of the country was the Banda Oriental, or the Eastern Bank, and its people still like to refer to themselves as *Orientales*.

In the colonial period, when South America was divided between the Portuguese Empire (which afterwards became Brazil) and the Spanish Empire, the Eastern Bank lay as a wedge of no-man's-land between them on the south, just as the Guianas did on the north. It was colonized by both nations; but at length the Spaniards prevailed over the Portuguese, and the Eastern Bank became part of the Spanish Viceroyalty of the Rio de la Plata (*see* ARGENTINES).

When the independence movement began in South America during the Napoleonic Wars, the struggle over the Eastern Bank broke out afresh. While the colonists of Buenos Aires were fighting for their independence against Spain, the colonists of the Eastern Bank were fighting for their independence against Buenos Aires. At the same time the Portuguese invaded the country from Brazil and tried to annex it. For nearly twenty years Uruguay was a battleground, until, in 1828, Argentina and Brazil signed a treaty recognizing it as a free and independent state.

But still Uruguay did not know peace. It suffered partly from Argentine aggressions and partly from civil wars; and during these troubles

GARIBALDI (q.v. Vol. V) and his famous Italian legion of 'Red-Shirts' fought for the freedom of Uruguay before returning to Europe to win the freedom of their own country. From 1830 to 1903, there were only three of Uruguay's presidents who were not either assassinated or forced out of office or involved in revolution.

Since 1903, however, Uruguay has become one of the most prosperous and progressive of the South American states and, indeed, of the world. Like Argentina, it has attracted many settlers from abroad, the majority being Italians and Spaniards. The population is wholly of European descent, the Indians having all died out, and Spanish is the language of the country.

Uruguay has made outstanding progress in political and social reforms. Its educational system, its free medical services, its old-age pensions, its poor relief, its laws protecting the welfare of children and regulating the wages and hours of work of the workers and farmers, are among the most advanced of any country in the world. The great statesman who began this policy of social welfare was Batlle y Ordonez, who was president in 1903–7 and 1911–15. His object was 'the easing of human suffering', and his motto was: 'Modern industry must not be allowed to destroy human beings.' He also inspired a new constitution which, he hoped, would make it impossible for future presidents to become dictators.

The capital of Uruguay is Montevideo, a fine city on the Rio de la Plata nearly opposite Buenos Aires, and one of the great ports of the world. There is a story that, when in 1519 a fleet sailed up the Rio de la Plata under the command of the great Portuguese navigator MAGELLAN (q.v. Vol. V), he exclaimed in Portuguese 'Monte vide eu!' ('I see a mountain!'); and this gave the name to the shore where the capital was afterwards to stand.

Although Uruguay is one of the most progressive and socialistic countries in the world, it is still a pastoral and not an industrial nation. The typical Uruguayan is not the worker in the city, but the *gaucho* or cowboy, rounding up the cattle on the pampas, picturesquely dressed in loose trousers with tight cuffs at the ankles, a soft hat, and a long wool *poncho* or blanket.

See also Vol. III: URUGUAY.

V

VALHALLA, *see* HEAVEN.

VANDALS. These were a people of Germanic origin, racially allied to the GOTHS (q.v.), and were first heard of at the end of the 1st century A.D., in what is now eastern Germany. They worked their way westwards and, at the beginning of the 5th century, had reached Spain, where a large portion of them settled in Andalusia. A few years later, upon the invitation of a Roman governor who was in disgrace in Italy, they crossed to North Africa under their great leader Gaiseric. He soon fell out with the governor, and completed his domination over North Africa by the capture of Carthage in A.D. 439. After this, the Vandals built a powerful fleet, and became, in spite of the Romans, the leading sea-power in the Mediterranean for nearly thirty years. In 455 they invaded Italy and captured Rome. They took from it all that they wanted and retired again to their rich lands in North Africa.

Towards the end of the 5th and in the 6th century they became demoralized by the easy living in Africa, and were finally overthrown by Belisarius, a great Roman general in the reign of the Emperor Justinian. After this they disappeared from history. The fact, however, that they had got possession of the richest Roman corn-bearing provinces in North Africa had made it necessary for the Romans to concentrate on fighting the Vandals in the south, at a time when they needed all their energies to withstand the barbarian invaders in the north. In consequence the Romans had to withdraw their garrison from Britain, and in course of time from France also.

We remember the Vandals to-day because of the word 'vandalism', which means a wanton destruction of beautiful or sacred things. In fact the Vandals were probably no more guilty of vandalism than other of the invading bar-barians of the Middle Ages; but no doubt the epithet grew because of the persecution of Christians carried out by Gaiseric and his son.

VATICAN, *see* ROMAN CATHOLIC CHURCH.

VEDDA (of Ceylon). A small dark-skinned folk living in the forests and jungles of Ceylon. They were the earliest arrivals of the present inhabitants of Ceylon, and were there long before the Sinhalese and Tamils, who drove them from the best lands as early as the 6th century B.C. They are slender, with small heads, deep-set dark eyes, and long black wavy hair, generally worn loose. Many of the Vedda have been in contact with their Sinhalese neighbours and have learnt to keep cattle, grow vegetables and grain, and have adopted from them social and religious customs and language. But there are some tribes, the so-called 'Wild Vedda', who still follow a very primitive way of life, depending for food on wild game, such as elk, deer, pig, as well as birds, fish, lizards, &c., and on roots, wild fruits, and the honey of wild bees which is their favourite food.

The country is rocky and full of caves and overhanging rock ledges, which make good dwelling-places. Though the Vedda know how to build huts, they are cave-dwellers by preference. They will sleep on the bare rock, though they prefer to use skins to lie on. There is always a fire smouldering nearby. The children wear no clothes while they are little. Then the boys follow the simple fashion of their fathers—a strip of cloth (bartered from a pedlar in exchange for honey and wax) tucked fore and aft into a string round the waist. The girls and women wear very little more. The cloth is used not only for clothing—it is useful also for making fire with two bits of wood, for a piece can be torn off to act as tinder.

The women dig up roots, while the boys go with their fathers shooting wild game with bows and arrows and collecting honey. The wild bees build their nests under the overhanging rock ledges: the boys use a ladder made of canes tied together, which they let down over the edge of the rock ledge, and down which they climb till they are level with the nest. They smoke out the bees with burning bunches of green leaves, break off the comb with a wooden fork or an arrow, and drop it into a deerskin bag. The comb is eaten, grubs and all; but much of it is drained to store up honey to exchange for the few things they get by trade—cotton for clothes,

A VEDDA FAMILY AT THE MOUTH OF THEIR CAVE. *British Mus.*

and steel or iron for axe- and arrow-heads. The pedlars never come near the Vedda caves, but shout from some quarter of a mile away until a Vedda appears, bringing pots or gourds of honey or dried flesh, to exchange for trade goods.

The Vedda are cheerful, merry people, easily amused, often bursting into song or dance. Women are well treated as the equals of men: each man has only one wife and guards her jealously. They take care of their children, seldom rebuke and usually spoil them. The children's only education is imitation of their elders, and they marry at an early age. The proper marriage for a boy is to marry his 'cross-cousin', that is, his father's sister's daughter. The boy calls at her house with a present of honey and dried flesh for her father. If his proposals are welcome, the girl gives him a waist string of her own making, and ties it round his waist. That is the marriage ceremony, and they are

henceforth man and wife. The husband will never part with this waist string and, if it wears out, his wife must make him another. Religious customs consist mainly in offerings to the spirits of ancestors, and prayers and dances to ensure their good will (*see* ANCESTOR WORSHIP).

See also CEYLONESE.
See also Vol. III: CEYLON.

VENEZUELANS. Venezuela means 'little Venice', the name given by the Spaniards to the first Indian village they discovered on the shores of this South American country. The Caribbean coast was the first part of the American mainland sighted by Columbus in 1498, and it became known as 'the Spanish Main', i.e. mainland. It lay in the centre of the vast Spanish Empire, and here English pirates preyed upon Spanish galleons as they plied to and fro across the Atlantic. The Orinoco Valley was the scene,

A FRUIT VENDOR IN CARACAS, VENEZUELA. *Paul Popper*

moreover, of the strange Indian legend of *El Dorado*, the Gilded King, whose supposed wealth lured Sir Walter Raleigh on his hapless expeditions in 1595 and 1617.

Venezuela was the first part of the Spanish Empire to revolt against Spain. It declared its independence in 1811, and became the centre from which the great SIMON BOLIVAR (q.v. Vol. V) (1783–1830), the leader of the South American independence movement, liberated the northern half of the continent. Bolivar was himself a native of Caracas, the capital of Venezuela, and his body was brought back to be buried there after he had died in exile. Having freed Venezuela and Colombia, he marched south-west across the Andes to Peru, where he met San Martin coming north-west across the Andes from Argentina. These two marches are among the great epics of military history and accomplished the liberation of a continent.

The history of independent Venezuela has been stormy and uncertain, like that of other South American states. It has had many revolutions and many dictators. The full name of the republic to-day is the United States of Venezuela; it consists of twenty states and has a constitution copied from the United States of America. The population consists of a few Spanish whites and a few Indian tribes, but is mostly of mixed Indian and European blood; there is also an admixture of African blood, which comes from descendants of the negro slaves brought over from West Africa.

See also AMERICAN INDIANS, CENTRAL AND SOUTH. See also Vol. III: VENEZUELA.

VENUS, *see* GODS OF GREECE AND ROME (Aphrodite).

VIKINGS, *see* DANES; NORWEGIANS; SWEDES.

W

WALDENSIAN. A member of a small Christian community who call themselves Vaudois, in the mountains of Piedmont in the Alps. In 1170 a merchant of Lyons in south France, called Peter Waldo, felt a call to leave his commercial life and accept a life of poverty and the work of simple preaching of the Gospel. It was a call like that which came to FRANCIS OF ASSISI (q.v. Vol. V) forty years later. Unfortunately, instead of recognizing this man and his followers —'the Poor Men of Lyons'—as an orthodox Order, the Church persecuted them as heretics. They seem to have had no wish to break from the Church, only to protest (as they had good cause) against the worldliness and laxity of many churchmen. Persecution scattered them over many parts of Europe. Some of these simple societies survived in the seclusion of the French and Italian Alps until the period of the Reformation. Then they threw in their lot with the Reformed Church, i.e. the CALVINIST (q.v.). They form now the Reformed Church of Italy, with a membership of about 30,000, not only in the Alpine valleys, but in many towns and villages outside. They have a ministry with a four years' theological training, a few schools, hospitals, orphanages, and they do a little missionary work in Africa.

See also CHRISTIAN CHURCH.

WALLOONS, *see* BELGIANS.

WELSH. The Welsh have remained a distinctly individual people, although their population is only some 2,593,000, and they are closely associated with a powerful neighbour. They differ from the English in appearance, language, and temperament, and have preserved these differences throughout the centuries. The reason for this is to be found in their origin and history.

The Welsh are the descendants of early Celtic settlers in Britain. These Celtic people were small and long skulled, with dark hair and brown eyes. The modern Welshman has these physical characteristics, and his language, too, is Celtic. The Welshman is vivacious and hot-tempered, emotional and sensitive, and easily moved to laughter or despair. Like all Celts, he loves music, especially singing, and the sound of words. Wales has produced many famous musicians and orators. From the earliest times the Welsh have resented English domination of their country. They used to resist the English with armed force on all possible occasions; but now the spirit of resistance is redirected in fostering their national culture.

The Roman, Saxon, and Norman invasions of England drove the Welsh into the western mountainous region which is now their home. They were never conquered, and they conducted very effective guerrilla warfare from hill-fortresses against the invaders. The Romans stationed a considerable part of their military power on the Welsh border in forts, such as those at Carleon and Chester. Later, the Saxons built a wall, called Offa's Dyke, to mark the boundary between Wales and England, and to prevent raids from the hills. William I established a number of barons on what were called the March estates bordering Wales, so that they

CONWAY CASTLE, NORTH WALES
British Council

should hold the Welsh in check and protect the border. Edward I built castles round the coast, as at Carnarvon and Harlech, and, by a successful trick, got the Welsh to accept his son as Prince of Wales.

Under the leadership of Owen Glendower, a national hero whose deeds are celebrated in Welsh poetry, the Welsh made a last unsuccessful bid for independence in 1405. Under the Tudor kings, themselves descended from the Welsh royal line, there was peace; and by the Act of Union in 1536 Wales was joined politically to England.

The Welsh now foster all the cultural aspects of their nationality by preserving their language, literature, and history. Almost all Welshmen can speak English, which they speak with a distinctive accent and turn of phrase; but Welsh is taught in all schools, and is kept alive by use in conversation every day throughout Wales. The National Eisteddfod, a gathering of bards, meets each year and keeps alive the traditional songs and poetry. The universal love of music is expressed in singing; there are many excellent choirs, especially in the industrial regions, and choral and dramatic societies flourish all over the country, even in small villages.

The religion of the Welsh to-day is Nonconformist, for the most part METHODIST (q.v.). Their emotional temperament, easily moved by oratory, made them susceptible to the 19th century religious revivalists. Their chapels are generally small and often rather bare; but they nearly always have an excellent choir, so that the beauty and fervour of the singing make up for the bareness of the building.

Most of the Welsh living in the region of the South Wales coalfield, and in the smaller industrial region of Flint and Denbigh in the north, are employed in mining and heavy industry. These districts have been hard hit by economic depressions and unemployment, which may be the reason for the vigorous political nationalist movement.

Most of the interior of the country is mountainous with poor soil, suitable for little else than sheep-farming. The whitewashed farm-houses are clean and well managed; but living is hard, and many people have left the land to migrate to the south, in search of employment in industry. In the north-west slate quarries employ a few people, and the magnificent country of Snowdonia has encouraged a tourist trade.

A SOUTH WALES COAL-MINE.
British Council

The Welsh are a poor and thrifty race, living in a country from which it is often hard to get a good living. But despite all their difficulties they never tire of singing the praises of their native land.

See also BRITISH PEOPLES; CELTIC CIVILIZATION.
See also Vol. III: WALES; Vol. IV: WELSH LANGUAGE.

WESLEYAN, *see* METHODIST.

WEST INDIANS. These are the peoples who inhabit the islands of the Caribbean Sea—Cuba, Jamaica, Hispaniola, Puerto Rico, the Bahamas and Barbados, Trinidad, and many others. The people also of the British, French, and Dutch Guianas on the South American mainland are often included.

When Christopher Columbus and his successors landed in the Bahamas in 1492 and, later, in other islands of the Caribbean, they found most of them inhabited by branches, some peaceable, some hostile, of that race to which we now apply the general inclusive term 'Amerindian'. The Spaniards called the natives whom they found in the Bahamas, Lucayans; they regarded them as idle and worthless people, fit only to be used as beasts of burden, and sent most of them to labour in the mines of Hispaniola, where they soon perished. Spanish colonizers of the 16th and 17th century were often very brutal in their methods of colonization.

Elsewhere the discoverers found the gentle Arawaks, or the fierce and truculent Caribs who have given their name to the Caribbean Sea. Some of the early travellers who have written about the Carib race, especially that entertaining French Missionary Père Labat, have remarked on the peculiarity that the Carib men spoke one language and their women another. The explanation of this strange fact lies in the fact that the warlike Caribs often took to wife captured Arawak women, who continued among themselves to speak their own tongue.

The Arawaks have long since disappeared completely from the West Indian islands, while only in one corner of Dominica and in one part of Trinidad are there any pure Caribs left; although a few survived in St. Vincent sufficiently long to be exterminated in the last great eruption of the Soufrière volcano in 1902. The remnants of the pure Caribs in Dominica and Trinidad do not amount to more than 100 to 200 in all, and only in the mainland colonies of British Honduras and Guiana are there any considerable sections of Amerindians.

Thus, these West Indian colonies of the Spaniards and their successors—the British, the French, the Dutch, the Danes, and others—with their great natural riches, were depopulated, except for the handful of European occupiers, and therefore lacked the labour necessary to convert them into immensely profitable tropical plantations. In order to solve this labour problem negro slaves were brought in from West Africa, and the overwhelming majority of the West Indian population of to-day is descended from these African slaves. For about two centuries the slave ships brought these unfortunate people from the West African coasts to the islands of the Caribbean and the adjoining mainland, where they worked the sugar-cane fields and other plantations of their white, and later also coloured owners. Some of them had already been living in a state of serfdom under native chiefs, while others suffered slavery for the first time. They multiplied in these fertile, well-watered countries, and also interbred with the Europeans; and soon there grew up a large West Indian-born population of African and part-African descent. But, assembled as the slaves had been from over a vast area of West Africa with its great mixture of race, customs, and languages, and forcibly removed from their original environment and their tribal mode of life, their descendants rapidly lost nearly everything African, except their physical characteristics. They speak the language of the territories in which they live: English in the British colonies and American possessions; French, ranging according to their social and financial status from Parisian to a very corrupt patois, in the French possessions and the Republic of Haiti; Spanish in Cuba, San Domingo, and Puerto Rico. The French patois is also the language of the peasantry of the British islands of Dominica and St. Lucia; while the people of Curaçao speak a curious jargon called *papiamento*, composed of Spanish, Portuguese, Dutch, English, and Amerindian words.

In the former Spanish possessions of Cuba and Puerto Rico pure-blooded Spaniards form the majority of the population; but elsewhere those of unmixed European descent are very much in the minority, forming in many islands less than 1% of the total, though in the British colony, Barbados, it is about 5%. Some of the British West Indian islands have a long and honourable tradition of self-governing institutions. The Barbados House of Assembly, dating from 1629, is, after the British House of Commons and the House of Assembly of Bermuda, the oldest legislative body in the entire British Empire.

Britain was not the pioneer of the slave-trade, which was started by the Portuguese and the Spaniards, and she led the way in its abolition. The Society for the Suppression of the Slave Trade was founded in London in 1787, in 1807 the slave-trade was forbidden in the British Empire, and in 1833 slavery was abolished and all the slaves freed in the British colonies—a step which other nations followed by degrees. The labour problems which followed the freeing of the slaves were mainly solved by bringing over great numbers of Indians from India to work in the cane-fields of British Guiana and Trinidad, and to a lesser degree of Jamaica. The 'East Indian' community descended from these labourers now forms the greatest individual racial unit of British Guiana, and about one-third of the population of Trinidad. During the 19th century small groups also of Portuguese, Chinese, and Syrians came to the West Indies.

In the course of their history the West Indies have produced more than one impressive figure

WEST INDIAN FAMILY, PORT OF SPAIN. *Canadian Pacific Railway*

of African descent among their people, and these have generally been connected, either by birth or otherwise, with the independent state of Haiti. The Haitian ex-slave, Toussaint l'Ouverture (q.v. Vol. V), who freed his country from the dominion of Napoleon, and Henri Christophe, born a slave in one of the British West Indian islands, who ruled Haiti as king with outstanding vigour and efficiency from 1811 to 1820, are perhaps the greatest negroes who have ever lived. That prolific and versatile story-teller, Alexandre Dumas (q.v. Vol. V), was of West Indian Creole descent in one sense of that term, for his paternal grandmother was a Haitian negress. In the West Indies the term 'Creole' by no means necessarily implies the admixture of coloured blood: it is applied equally correctly to persons of pure European descent born in the West Indies. In fact, the Empress Josephine, the repudiated first wife of Napoleon I, whose gentle and pathetic memory is still affectionately cherished in her birthplace, Martinique, was a Creole.

See also American Indians, Central and South; Vol. III: West Indies; Vol. IV: American-Indian Languages.

WITCHCRAFT. This takes many different forms in various parts of the world; but it always involves the belief in Magic (q.v.). The kinds of people who practise witchcraft, and the circumstances in which they use it, may also vary a great deal. Witchcraft may be good or evil, though we usually think of it as evil. It may be performed by single individuals or by groups of people organized for the purpose. A variety of names are given to different kinds of magic-makers. They may be called magicians or sorcerers, and writers about African peoples often speak of witch-doctors. The term 'shaman' is used by the Eskimoes, Siberian tribes, and North

American Indians for a particular type of sorcerer who goes into a kind of fit or trance, and is believed to be possessed by a spirit, when he is performing magic. In the British Isles workers of magic are commonly called witches, and for us, because of our FAIRY-TALES (q.v.) and FOLK-LORE (q.v.), the word signifies women who work evil magic: men witches are called magicians or wizards. But writers dealing with African customs sometimes use witch instead of witch-doctor when referring to men. In England in times past, and to this day in Scotland, we hear of 'black' and 'white' witches who may be either men or women, but usually women. Black magic is evil, but white magic is good and has the power to counteract evil magic. Here we shall deal particularly with the witches of the British Isles and the continent of Europe.

The witch of our fairy-tales is a sinister old woman who practises magic arts, using SPELLS (q.v.) and incantations to cause people harm.

A WITCH AND HER FAMILIARS
Drawing from the Fairfax MSS., 1621. *British Mus.*

She dances round a cauldron in which she brews enchanted broth, made of various kinds of horrible ingredients:

> Fillet of a fenny snake,
> In the cauldron boil and bake;
> Eye of newt and toe of frog,
> Wool of bat and tongue of dog,
>
> .   .   .   .
>
> And now about the cauldron sing,
> Like elves and fairies in a ring.
>   *Macbeth*, Act IV, Sc. i.

She flies about at night on a broomstick, wearing the traditional 17th-century hat, and can change herself and sometimes other people into animal form. This is a fairly accurate picture of a witch such as our forefathers believed in.

The great difference between ELVES or FAIRIES (qq.v.) and witches is that, while fairies belong to a kind of no-man's-land, half-human, half-supernatural, witches were thought to be real people possessed by the devil or given over to his service. In the past many people were tortured and executed on the charge of being witches, and as recently as 1722 a woman, accused of being a witch, was executed in Scotland.

It was from shortly before the middle of the 15th century to the end of the 17th century that the fear of witches was greatest in European countries, and they were hunted down most unmercifully. People giving evidence at the trials of these women said that they anointed their bodies with some substance which enabled them to fly through the air; that they had animal 'familiars', such as cats and hares, into whose shape they could transform themselves; and that at the witches' 'Sabbaths' groups of thirteen gathered in 'covens' to dance in a ring at night, and worship a horned god who was the devil. Frightened people who were sometimes not quite sane would admit doing just what they were accused of doing, so it is difficult to know the truth in these matters; but there is no doubt that, until recently, in many parts of Europe, very ancient magical practices were carried out in the belief that they would make the crops and herds prosper. It is possible that people who carried on this kind of fertility magic in the Middle Ages were called witches by persons who were afraid of them.

Most witch-doctors and sorcerers, in addition to their activities in doing particular people harm or good, concern themselves with making rain or otherwise altering the weather. One of the indications that, in days gone by, witches in Europe were connected with a fertility ritual is that they were widely believed to be able to raise storms. One of their methods was to throw a cat into the sea, after performing magical rites. Another was to float a small dish in a larger dish full of water: by upsetting the small dish, they were supposed to be able to sink a ship. Once, some witches left such a dish on the ground while they went out across the sea. A duck got into it and splashed about. When they returned they complained about the terrible storm which had beset them on the way. Like all magic-makers, witches believed that, by doing something resembling in some way what they wanted to happen, they could cause it to happen, even at a great distance.

One of the main ideas acted upon by witches in their evil magic was that practices, generally regarded as doing good and bringing blessing, could be made to bring harm by being done the wrong way round. So they used to dance in circles from right to left, instead of, as the sun goes, from left to right; and they also made prayers into spells by saying them backwards. In good ritual images are made as a help to worship; in witchcraft they are made in order to be pierced or destroyed, so that the persons they represent may suffer.

To counteract witchcraft people sometimes try to make the same kind of witchcraft against it. Thus we have a record from Babylonia of a man who said:

The sorceress and witch
Sit in the shadow of the house-wall,
They sit there working magic against me,
And making figures of me.

. . . . .

I will annul thy sorcery and turn back thy charms
in thy mouth.

Another Babylonian recorded this:

A witch hath bewitched me,
A sorceress hath cast her spell upon me,

. . . . .

I have made a figure of the man or woman who
hath bewitched me.

Evidently he pierced or melted the image to

TWO WITCHES DISCOVERED
Woodcut from Matthew Hopkins, *Discoverie of Witches*, 1647

revenge himself on the witch or sorceress. Almost down to our times we hear of people in out-of-the-way places in the British Isles making figures of wax or clay in order to bring harm to other people.

The belief in witches is strongest where people are not educated enough to understand how disasters come about. Such people, if they are suddenly taken ill, for example, at once imagine that someone has bewitched them. If the weather is not suitable for the crops, they believe certain people know how to change it. As people learn the principles of health, and realize that disease is due to such things as germs and bad living conditions, and that the weather depends on atmospheric conditions beyond man's control, the belief in witchcraft tends to die out. Nobody need regret this, as it was responsible for a great deal of cruelty.

See also FOLK-LORE; MAGIC; SPELLS AND CHARMS.

X Y

XOSA, *see* SOUTH AFRICANS.

YAKUTS, *see* SIBERIAN PEOPLES.

YOGA, *see* HINDUISM, section 1.

YUGOSLAVS. This name means Southern Slavs, and it is used for the three branches of the same Slav family—the Serbs, Croats, and Slovenes—which inhabit Yugoslavia. They invaded the Balkans in the 7th century, pressing on till they reached the eastern shore of the Adriatic. Gradually they gave up their wandering life and settled down to cultivate the soil. After much

YUGOSLAV SWORD-DANCE
Paul Popper

quarrelling among themselves and many wars with their neighbours they were united under one great Emperor, who ruled practically the whole of the Balkans in the middle of the 14th century. This Emperor established his capital at Skoplje in the south of modern Macedonia, and this city became a centre of art, learning, and commerce. Soon after his death, however, the country fell victim to the Turkish armies, and in the course of a few years practically the whole of Serbia, Bosnia, and Hercegovina came under Turkish rule. Croatia in the north became part of the Kingdom of Hungary, while Slovenia in the north-west was a province of the Austrian Empire. The Republic of Venice seized most of the eastern shore of the Adriatic in order to protect her shipping, and built or developed the beautiful cities of the Adriatic—Split, Dubrovnik, Zara, and others. For over 400 years the Serbs struggled against their Turkish overlords and clung to the Orthodox Church. Most of the inhabitants of Bosnia and Hercegovina became Moslems; and the Croats and Slovenes were Roman Catholics.

In the beginning of the 19th century the Serbs were at last successful in driving out the Turks; and after the First World War and the collapse of the Austro-Hungarian Empire, the Serbs, Croats, and Slovenes were again, after many centuries, united into the one kingdom of Yugoslavia.

More than 500 years of separation, however, under rulers with widely differing cultures, had made the three main peoples of Yugoslavia so different in outlook and way of life that the problem of welding them together into a united country has not been easy.

The religious divisions were very marked—48% belonged to the Orthodox Church, 37% to the Roman Catholic Church, 11% were Moslems, and in some places there was a large number of Jews. Most Yugoslavs speak 'Serbo-Croat', the Slovenes a slightly different language. The west of the country used the Latin alphabet, the Serbians used the Cyrillic alphabet, and, as a result, they could not read each other's books and newspapers. Each cherished their old traditions: the Serbs prided themselves on their great fighting qualities, the Croats on their culture and commercial abilities, while the Slovenes are a more easy-going people than either of the other two. The Second World War and the bitter struggle against the common enemies, Germany

MARKET WOMEN AT DUBROVNIK. *Paul Popper*

and Italy, did much to bring about a sense of national unity.

The majority of the Yugoslavs are peasants, each family cultivating its own land, the women working as hard if not harder than the men. Along the coast agriculture and fishing are combined, and the women provide the crews for the heavy sailing craft which carry the fruit and vegetables from the islands to the mainland. Before the Second World War conditions of life varied greatly in different parts of the country; in the rich agricultural districts there were substantial farm-houses, and the small towns were becoming prosperous; but in the mountains life was still hard and primitive, and a bad harvest might spell starvation in the spring. Both men and women in the villages used to wear beautiful local costumes, while folk-songs and dances flourished all over the country. Some of the dances were extremely elaborate—for instance, the medieval sword-dance on the island of Korčula. This sword-dance has been performed for centuries by men of the same families, who learn it as small boys. It is partly a dance, and partly a play acted in mime, not entirely different from our mumming plays.

See also Vol. III: YUGOSLAVIA; Vol. IV: RUSSIAN LANGUAGES.

Z

ZENANA. This word is more correctly spelt 'Zanana', and is in origin allied to the Persian word for woman, i.e. *zan*, plural *zanan*. It means the portion of the house in a high-caste Hindu family reserved for the women. The life of the zenana, owing to child-marriage and the unhappy status of widows, and also to the absence of education for women, has had in the past many special dangers and problems. These are gradually being dealt with, as the result of the influence of Western ideas. The zenana system sprang up because of the effect of Moslem teaching on Hindu society. It does not exist among Hindus in south India; but in the north it is considered a sign of respectability, and prevails only among the 'upper classes'.

See also CASTE; HINDUISM; INDIAN PEOPLES.

ZEUS, *see* GODS OF GREECE AND ROME.

ZIONIST, *see* JEWS.

ZODIAC, *see* ASTROLOGY. *See also* Vol. III: CONSTELLATIONS.

ZOROASTRIAN. Zarathustra, who is perhaps better known under the Greek form of his name, 'Zoroaster', was a Persian prophet, who was born about 600 or more years before Christ. Very little is known of his actual history. He seems to have been of priestly rank, was married, and had a daughter. We possess five poems, called *Gathas*, which are almost certainly genuine compositions of his. From these poems we deduce that he came into public life at a time when there was tension between the Persians and some wandering invaders from central Asia, probably Mongols, who were raiding Persia and carrying off cattle. Zarathustra, like Moses, seems to have begun as a champion of his oppressed fellow countrymen; but after a time he showed that his greatest interest was in urging them to be more faithful to one true and holy God (whom he calls Ahura Mazda), and to give up polytheism, or the worship of many gods. The Persian king, Darius, recognized Zarathustra's reforming movement, and ordered the old religion to be given up. His successor, Xerxes, not only suppressed the old religion, but tried to force Zarathustra's faith upon his subjects. This attempt did not succeed and, after some sixty years, much of the earlier polytheism returned, and a system was established under the name of Zarathustra, which contained some of the very features which he had most opposed. Zarathustra claimed that he was trying to bring the Persians back to a still older and purer faith from which they had fallen away. It is rather doubtful, however, whether such a faith had really ever existed.

From then onwards the religion of Persia continued to be Zoroastrian in name right up to A.D. 700 when, as a result of the great Arab conquests, ISLAM (q.v.) entered in. Before this date there were efforts to convert the country to Christianity. Another Persian reformer, Mani, about A.D. 252, also tried to make a new religion out of a mixture of Christianity and old oriental science; but he was flayed alive by order of the Persian king. During the 3rd century A.D. the Persian Empire was becoming a formidable rival to the Roman Empire. The Persian rulers tried to identify the religion of Zoroaster with patriotism; and as they meant to overthrow the Roman Empire, so they meant to establish Zoroastrianism as the supreme religion on earth. They persecuted most of the Christians who looked to Rome for protection; but they protected NESTORIAN Christians (q.v.), since they had broken away from the main Church and therefore were dissociated from Rome. Finally, when the Moslem Arabs conquered Persia in the 7th century A.D., most of the inhabitants of Persia became Moslems, though some of the followers of Zoroastrianism migrated to India, and formed there the community now called PARSEES (q.v.). Parsee is only a modification of the word Persian. The modern Persian Church is the result of 19th-century Christian missionary activity (*see* PERSIANS).

The teaching of Zarathustra himself and the beliefs of Zoroastrians are not entirely the same. It is not safe to suppose that any great teacher taught exactly the same doctrine all his life, because the thought of a great teacher develops. Zarathustra probably began by believing in a number of gods. It seems, however, that by the end of his life he had become a convinced and ardent monotheist, and believed in the goodness and holiness of one God—a God engaged in a continual struggle against evil. Man's life, he said, ought properly to be spent in serving the good God loyally and in sharing his struggle. Zarathustra did not deny the existence of other superhuman beings; but he came to think of them as lower than Ahura Mazda himself, and as merely of the rank of angels. He taught the doctrine of a last judgement, and of heaven and hell, and he may have believed in some kind of heavenly redeemer. Later generations added some stories about him which remind us of many in the Gospels—such as that he was virgin-born, that attempts were made to kill him when a child, and that he was tempted in the wilderness by Angra Mainyu, the Lord of Evil. How much of this was copied from Christianity, and also how much Zarathustra's own teaching influenced the Jews at an earlier date during their captivity in Babylon, we cannot be sure. Certainly, after the conquest of Babylon by the Persian king, Cyrus, the Jews came into contact with the Persians.

After Zarathustra, when Persian religion recovered some of its old features, a tribe called the Magi made itself indispensable as a priesthood. Indeed these Magi seem to have become a sort of sacred caste, not unlike that of the Brahmins in India. They started the custom of exposing the dead to vultures. This derived from the belief that death was caused by a malignant spirit, who must be prevented from harming the living by a very quick disposal of the body of the dead person. The quickest way of destroying the body was either by fire or by letting carrion birds devour it. Fire being sacred, and therefore not to be used for this purpose, the dead body was exposed to vultures. This practice still exists among the Parsees in India, where it is attended with much ceremony (*see* PARSEES). The Magi also practised the interpretation of dreams and the pseudo-science of ASTROLOGY (q.v.); and it is said that they sacrificed a wolf periodically to the powers of evil.

Whatever Zarathustra may himself have thought and taught, these later Magi and their disciples thought of the world as almost exactly like a great game of chess, in which there was, so to speak, a black king (or Lord of Evil) who was about equal in power to the white king (or Lord of Good). This is what is called Dualism. Yet it is doubtful whether anyone was ever a complete Dualist; even the Magians taught that Good would in the end win, and they have also calculated the date of this future victory, which is said to be A.D. 2398.

See also PERSIAN CIVILIZATION.

ZULU. This African negro tribe is made up of southern Bantu people who live chiefly in Zululand, the coastal region of South Africa, south and east of the Drakenberg mountains in north Natal. They are generally strong, well-built people, with fine figures and upright bearing.

Formerly Zululand was divided among a number of small tribes; but these were conquered and united by a chief named Chaka in the early 19th century. He organized a fighting force, which was a terror to the surrounding country for a number of years, and whose outrages finally led to the Zulu wars. In 1879 the Zulu army was routed by the British forces, and the military power of the Zulus came to an end.

The traditional interests of the Zulu lie in cattle and fighting. Cattle are the means by which a man can gather and display his wealth. Fines in the courts are payable by means of cattle, and marriages are arranged by handing over cattle to the family of the bride. Many religious and magical beliefs are associated with them, and men spend much of their lives just looking at their cattle, admiring them and talking about them. The Zulus live in *kraals*—homesteads with cattle pens in the middle of a ring of huts. These huts are round, dome-shaped structures built of saplings stuck into the ground.

Marriages, as among most East African peoples, are arranged through payment of *lobola*, that is, cattle paid to the father of the bride either by the bridegroom himself, or more often contributed by his father or near relations—for it is rare for a young man to have enough cattle of his own. The cattle are not kept by the bride's father, but are shared out among close relatives.

In a Zulu family the children help their parents in their everyday activities. The boys help in looking after the goats of the kraal and in driving away birds from the growing crops. Girls nurse younger children, fetch firewood and water, grind corn, sweep out the huts, and help in cooking. Girls play with small clay and wooden dolls, boys with models of oxen. The boys also have friendly fights with other boys,

A ZULU KRAAL IN NATAL. *South African Railways*

and learn how to throw stones to kill wild animals or birds, and to shoot with bows and arrows.

Formerly, when the boys grew up, they were formed into regiments as warriors of the king. They lived apart in military kraals, and were not allowed to marry until the king gave his permission. They acted as police, messengers, or as a labour corps, and helped to look after the king's cattle. A regiment (or *impi*) numbered 800–1,000 men and had its own war-cry and regimental songs. Their older weapon was the long spear (the assegai), but Shaka used to make his men use the short stabbing-spear, because it forced them to come to grips with the enemy at close quarters. The warriors also had knob-kerries (short sticks with knobbed heads) and shields of strong hide. The different regiments had shields of different colours. Much of this military life survives to-day in ceremonial.

While the young men were undergoing their military service, the care of the cattle remained in the hands of the older men and the boys; and the women looked after the fields. Cultivation is simple, but as they have no means of fertilizing the soil they often have to start new farms. The chief food of the Zulus is milk drunk sour, millet and maize, and vegetables such as pumpkins, peas, and beans.

The chiefs still hold very important positions in Zululand. A chief succeeds to his position by hereditary right, either as the eldest son of the chief's principal wife, or as his nearest male relative. They have larger huts than the rest of the tribe; but there is not much difference in dress and food. The Zulu king still controls all the chiefs, and has to be approached with very great ceremony. He represents the nation at the annual festivals and in the war rites, and also in relation to their ancestral spirits, who are believed to watch over the whole of Zululand. He is in charge of all the magic that affects the nation—magic for rain-making and success in war (*see* MAGIC). He also decides important law cases, and hears appeals from the chiefs' courts. He has a council of chiefs and close relatives to advise him. The king receives from the people many gifts of cattle, beer, and grain; but, in return, he is expected to look after his regiments and to help his people in time of famine.

The chief religion of the Zulus is ANCESTOR WORSHIP (q.v.)—a man worships his own ancestors in the male line, and at feasts and beer-drinking a small libation is always poured out for the ancestors. They also believe in a power which shows itself in rain, thunder, and lightning (*see* NATURE WORSHIP).

See also NEGRO AFRICANS; EAST AFRICANS.